OCT - 8 2015

OCP Java SE 7 Programmer II
Certification Guide

D0851064

OCP Java SE 7 Programmer II Certification Guide

PREPARE FOR THE 1ZO-804 EXAM

MALA GUPTA

MANNING
SHELTER ISLAND

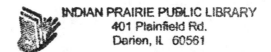

For online information and ordering of this and other Manning books, please visit
www.manning.com. The publisher offers discounts on this book when ordered in quantity.
For more information, please contact

  Special Sales Department
  Manning Publications Co.
  20 Baldwin Road
  PO Box 761
  Shelter Island, NY 11964
  Email: orders@manning.com

Ⅿ Manning Publications Co.   Development editor: Cynthia Kane
   20 Baldwin Road   Technical editor: George Zurowski
   PO Box 761   Copyeditor: Jodie Allen
   Shelter Island, NY 11964   Proofreader: Alyson Brener
                              Technical proofreaders: Roel De Nijs, Jean-François Morin
                                           Typesetter: Dennis Dalinnik
                                      Cover designer: Marija Tudor

ISBN: 9781617291487
Printed in the United States of America
1 2 3 4 5 6 7 8 9 10 – MAL – 20 19 18 17 16 15

To Dheeraj, my pillar of strength

brief contents

contents

11 Concurrency   679

12 Localization   719

13 *Full mock exam*

Available online only at www.manning.com/gupta2

preface

The OCP Java SE Programmer II certification is designed to tell would-be employers that you really know your basic and advanced Java stuff. It certifies that you understand and can work with design patterns and advanced Java concepts like concurrency, multithreading, localization, string processing, and JDBC. The exam preparation helps you to understand the finer details of the Java language and its implementation and usage, which is crucial to writing quality code.

Cracking this exam is not an easy task. Thorough preparation is crucial if you want to pass the exam the first time with a score that you can be proud of. You need to know Java inside and out, and you need to understand the certification process so that you're ready for the challenging questions you'll face on the exam.

This book is a comprehensive guide to the 1Z0-804 exam. You'll explore a wide range of important Java topics as you systematically learn how to pass the certification exam. Each chapter starts with a list of the exam objectives covered in that chapter. Throughout the book you'll find sample questions and exercises designed to reinforce key concepts and prepare you for what you'll see on the real exam, along with numerous tips, notes, and visual aids.

Unlike many other exam guides, this book provides multiple ways to digest important techniques and concepts, including comic conversations, analogies, pictorial representations, flowcharts, UML diagrams, and, naturally, lots of well-commented code.

The book also gives insight into typical exam question mistakes and guides you in avoiding traps and pitfalls. It provides

- Complete coverage of exam topics, all mapped to chapter and section numbers
- Hands-on coding exercises, including particularly challenging ones that throw in a twist
- Instruction on what's happening behind the scenes using the actual code from the Java API source
- Everything you need to master both the concepts and the exam

This book is written for developers with a working knowledge of Java. My hope is that the book will deepen your knowledge, prepare you well for the exam, and that you will pass it with flying colors!

acknowledgments

First and foremost, I thank Dheeraj. He helped me to get started with this book, and his guidance, encouragement, and love enabled me to get over the goal line.

My sincere gratitude to Marjan Bace, publisher at Manning, for giving me the opportunity to author this book.

An extremely talented individual, Cynthia Kane, my development editor at Manning, was a pleasure to work with. She not only helped me improve the organization of the chapters, she also pulled me up whenever the task of completing the book became overwhelming for me.

The contributions of Roel De Nijs, technical proofreader on this book, are unparalleled. His feedback helped me to improve all sections and chapters. Jean-François Morin, technical proofreader for a few chapters, also helped me to improve the book just before it went into production.

Gregor Zurowski, my technical editor, provided great insight and helped iron out technical glitches as the book was being written.

Apart from applying her magic to sentence and language constructions, Jodie Allen, my copyeditor, was very supportive and patient in applying changes across all chapters.

I'd also like to thank Ozren Harlovic, review editor, for managing the review process and meticulously funneling the feedback to me to make this book better.

Mary Piergies, Alyson Brener, and Kevin Sullivan were awesome in their expertise at turning all text, code, and images into publishable form. I am also grateful to Candace Gillhoolley and Ana Radic for managing the promotion of this book.

Next, I'd like to thank all the MEAP readers for trusting me by buying the book while it was being written. I thank them for their patience, suggestions, corrections, and encouragement.

Technical reviewers helped in validating the chapters' contents at various stages of their development. The reviewers' detailed and helpful feedback helped me to improve the book throughout the writing process: Alexander Schwartz, Ashutosh Sharma, Bill Weiland, Colin Hastie, Dylan Scott, Jamie Atkinson, Kevin Vig, Kyle Smith, Manish Verma, Mikael Strand, Mikalai Zaikin, Robin Coe, Simon Joseph Aquilina, Steve Etherington, and Witold Bolt. Special shout-out to Mikalai for his detailed feedback— it helped me to improve the contents enormously.

I thank my former colleagues Harry Mantheakis, Paul Rosenthal, and Selvan Rajan, whose names I have used in coding examples throughout the book. I have always looked up to them.

Finally, I thank my parents and my daughters, Shreya and Pavni. This book would have been not been possible without their unconditional support, love, and encouragement.

about this book

This book is written for developers with a working knowledge of Java who want to earn the OCP Java SE 7 Programmer II certification (exam 1Z0-804). It uses powerful tools and features to make reaching your goal of certification a quick, smooth, and enjoyable experience. This section will explain the features used in the book and tell you how to use the book to get the most out of it as you prepare for the certification exam. More information on the exam and on how the book is organized is available in the Introduction.

Start your preparation with the chapter-based exam objective map

I strongly recommend a structured approach to preparing for this exam. To help you with this task, I've developed a chapter-based exam objective map, as shown in figure 1. The full version is in the Introduction (table 2).

	Exam objective as per Oracle's website	Covered in chapter/section
1	**Java Class Design**	**Chapter 1**
1.1	Use access modifiers: private, protected, and public	Section 1.1
1.2	Override methods	Section 1.3
1.3	Overload constructors and methods	Section 1.2

Figure 1 The Introduction to this book provides a list of all exam objectives and the corresponding chapter and section numbers where they are covered.

The map in the Introduction shows the complete exam objective list mapped to the relevant chapter and section numbers. You can jump to the relevant section number to work on a particular exam topic.

Chapter-based objectives

Each chapter starts with a list of the exam objectives covered in that chapter, as shown in figure 2. This list is followed by a quick comparison of the major concepts and topics covered in the chapter with real-world objects and scenarios.

Exam objectives covered in this chapter	What you need to know
[3.1] Write code that declares, implements, and/or extends interfaces	The need for interfaces. How to declare, implement, and extend interfaces. Implications of implicit modifiers that are added to an interface and its members.
[3.2] Choose between interface inheritance and class inheritance	The differences and similarities between implementing inheritance by using interfaces and by using abstract or concrete classes. Factors that favor using interface inheritance over class inheritance, and vice versa.

Figure 2   An example of the list of exam objectives and brief explanations at the beginning of each chapter

Section-based objectives

Each main section in a chapter starts by identifying the exam objective(s) that it covers. Each listed exam topic starts with the exam objective and its subobjective number.

In figure 3, the number 4.2 refers to section 4.2 in chapter 4 (the complete list of chapters and sections can be found in the contents). The 4.1 preceding the exam objective refers to the objective's numbering in the list of exam objectives on Oracle's website (the complete numbered list of exam objectives is given in table 2 in the Introduction).

4.2   Creating generic entities

[4.1]   Create a generic class

On the exam, you'll be tested on how to create generic classes, interfaces, and methods—within generic and nongeneric classes or interfaces.

Figure 3   An example of the beginning of a section, identifying the exam objective that it covers

Exam tips

Each chapter provides multiple *exam tips* to re-emphasize the points that are the most confusing, overlooked, or frequently answered incorrectly by candidates and that therefore require special attention for the exam. Figure 4 shows an example.

 EXAM TIP   A *type argument* must be passed to the *type parameter* of a base class. You can do so while extending the base class or while instantiating the derived class.

Figure 4   Example of an exam tip; they occur multiple times in a chapter

Notes

All chapters also include multiple notes, which draw your attention to points that should be noted while you're preparing for the exam. Figure 5 shows an example.

 NOTE   Though the exam might not include explicit questions on the contents of a class file after type erasure, it will help you to understand generics better and answer all questions on generics.

Figure 5   Example note

Sidebars

Sidebars contain information that may not be directly relevant to the exam but that is related to it. Figure 6 shows an example.

Using instanceof versus getClass in method equals()

Using `instanceof` versus `getClass` is a common subject of debate about proper use and object orientation in general (including performance aspects, design patterns, and so on). Though important, this discussion is beyond the scope of this book. If you're interested in further details, refer to Josh Bloch's book *Effective Java*.

Figure 6   Example sidebar

Images

I've used a lot of images in the chapters for an immersive learning experience. I believe that a simple image can help you understand a concept quickly, and a little humor can help you to retain information longer.

Simple images are used to draw your attention to a particular line of code (as shown in figure 7).

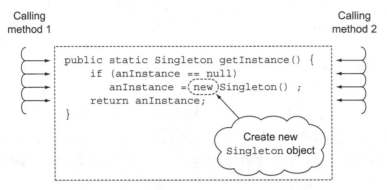

Figure 7 An example image that draws your attention to a particular line of code

As shown in figure 8, I've used pictorial representation to aid better understanding of how Java concepts work.

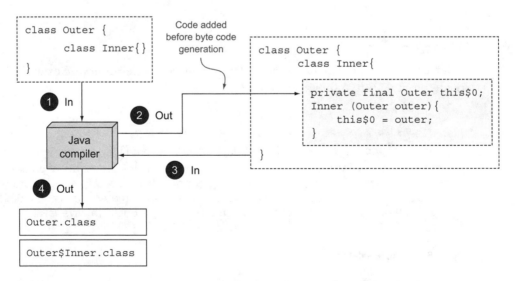

Figure 8 An example of pictorial representation of how the compiler handles data in an array

To reinforce important points and help you retain them longer, a little humor has been added using comic strips (as in figure 9).

Figure 9 An example of a little humor to help you remember that the `finally` block always executes

I've also used images to group and represent information for quick reference. Figure 10 shows an example of a rather raw form of the UML diagram that you may draw on an erasable board while taking your exam to represent an IS-A relationship between classes and interfaces. I strongly recommend that you try to create a few of your own figures like these.

An image can also add more meaning to a sequence of steps explained in the text. For example, figure 11 seems to bring the process of adding and removing items to an ArrayList to life by showing placement of the existing items at each step. Again, try a few of your own. It'll be fun!

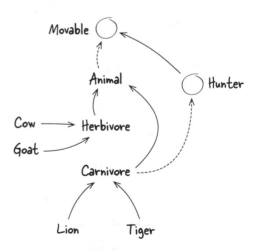

Figure 10 An example of grouping and representing information for quick reference

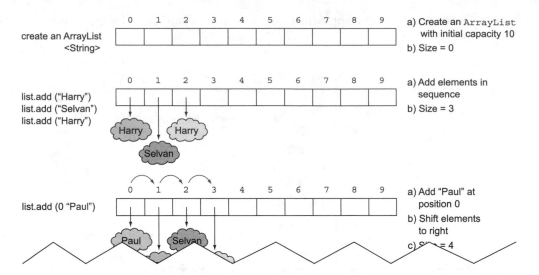

Figure 11   An example image showing how existing elements are placed when items are added to or removed from an `ArrayList`

The exam requires that you know multiple methods from collection classes, File I/O, NIO.2, concurrency, and others. The number of these methods can be overwhelming, but grouping these methods according to their functionality can make this task a lot more manageable. Figure 12 shows an example of an image that groups methods of the Queue class used to work with Deque as FIFO.

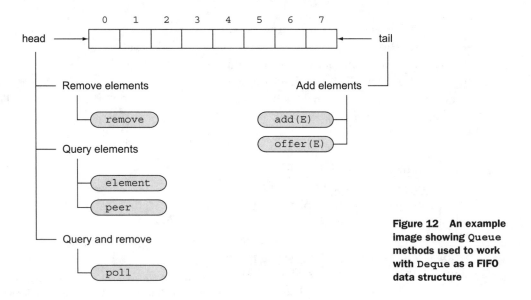

Figure 12   An example image showing Queue methods used to work with Deque as a FIFO data structure

String processing expressions can be hard to comprehend. Figure 13 is an example of an image that can help you understand the strings that match a regular expression.

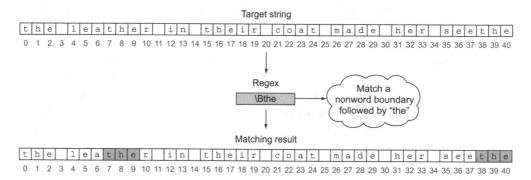

Figure 13 Example of image showing the strings that match a regex pattern

In multithreading, the same code can be executed by multiple threads. Such code can be difficult to comprehend. Figure 14 is an example of an image that clearly shows how the variable values of book:Book might be modified by multiple threads.

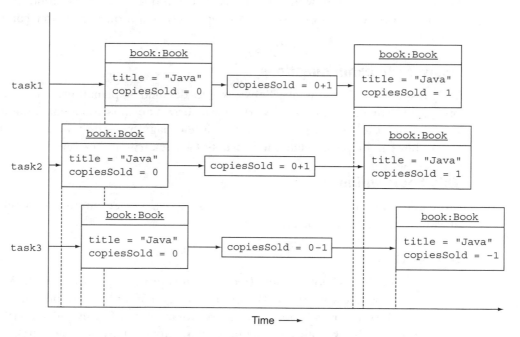

Figure 14 An example of how interleaving threads can lead to incorrect results

Twist in the Tale exercises

Each chapter includes a few Twist in the Tale exercises. For these exercises, I've tried to use modified code from the examples already covered in a chapter, and the "Twist in the Tale" title refers to modified or tweaked code. These exercises highlight how even small code modifications can change the behavior of your code. They should encourage you to carefully examine all of the code on the exam.

My main reason for including these exercises is that on the real exam you may be asked to answer more than one question that seems exactly the same as another. But upon closer inspection, you'll realize that these questions differ slightly, and that these differences change the behavior of the code and the correct answer option.

The answers to all of the Twist in the Tale exercises are given in the appendix.

Review notes

When you're ready to take your exam, don't forget to reread the review notes a day before or on the morning of the exam. These notes contain important points from each chapter as a quick refresher.

Exam questions

Each chapter concludes with a set of sample exam questions. These follow the same pattern as the real exam questions. Attempt these exam questions after completing a chapter.

Answers to exam questions

The answers to all exam questions provide detailed explanations, including why options are correct or incorrect. Mark your incorrect answers and identify the sections that you need to reread. If possible, draw a few diagrams—you'll be amazed at how much they can help you retain the concepts. Give it a try—it'll be fun!

This book online

More information and a bonus chapter consisting of a mock exam can be found online at www.manning.com/gupta2.

Author Online

The purchase of this book includes free access to a private web forum run by Manning Publications, where you can make comments, ask technical questions, and receive help from the author and from other users. To access the forum and subscribe to it, point your web browser to www.manning.com/gupta2. This page provides information on how to get on the forum once you are registered, what kind of help is available, and the rules of conduct on the forum.

Manning's commitment to our readers is to provide a venue where a meaningful dialogue between individual readers and between readers and the author can take place. It is not a commitment to any specific amount of participation on the part of the author, whose contribution to the forum remains voluntary (and unpaid). We suggest you try asking the author some challenging questions lest her interest stray!

The Author Online forum and the archives of previous discussions will be accessible from the publisher's website as long as the book is in print.

About the author

Mala Gupta is passionate about making people employable by bridging the gap between their existing and required skills. In her quest to fulfill this mission, she is authoring books to help IT professionals and students on industry-recognized Oracle Java certifications.

Mala has a master's degree in computer applications along with multiple other certifications from Oracle. With over a decade and a half of experience working in IT as a developer, architect, trainer, and mentor, she has worked with international training and software services organizations on various Java projects. She is experienced in mentoring teams on technical and process skills.

She is the founder and lead mentor of a portal (www.ejavaguru.com) that has offered Java courses for Oracle certification since 2006.

Mala is a firm believer in creativity as an essential life skill. To popularize the importance of creativity, innovation, and design in life, she started "KaagZevar" (www.facebook.com/KaagZevar)—a platform to nurture design and creativity in life.

About the cover illustration

The figure on the cover this book is captioned "The habit of a French merchant in 1700." The illustration is taken from Thomas Jefferys' *A Collection of the Dresses of Different Nations, Ancient and Modern* (four volumes), London, published between 1757 and 1772. The title page states that these are hand-colored copperplate engravings, heightened with gum arabic. Thomas Jefferys (1719–1771) was called "geographer to King George III." An English cartographer who was the leading map supplier of his day, Jefferys engraved and printed maps for government and other official bodies and produced a wide range of commercial maps and atlases, especially of North America. His work as a mapmaker sparked an interest in local dress customs of the lands he surveyed and mapped, which are brilliantly displayed in this four-volume collection.

Fascination with faraway lands and travel for pleasure were relatively new phenomena in the late eighteenth century, and collections such as this one were popular, introducing both the tourist as well as the armchair traveler to the inhabitants of other countries. The diversity of the drawings in Jefferys' volumes speaks vividly of the uniqueness and individuality of the world's nations some 200 years ago. Dress codes have changed since then, and the diversity by region and country, so rich at the time, has faded away. It is now hard to tell the inhabitants of one continent apart from another. Perhaps, trying to view it optimistically, we have traded cultural and visual diversity for a more varied personal life. Or a more varied and interesting intellectual and technical life.

At a time when it is hard to tell one computer book from another, Manning celebrates the inventiveness and initiative of the computer business with book covers based on the rich diversity of regional life of two centuries ago, brought back to life by Jefferys' pictures.

Introduction

This introduction covers

- Introduction to the Oracle Certified Professional (OCP) Java SE 7 Programmer II certification (exam number 1Z0-804)
- Importance of OCP Java SE 7 Programmer II certification
- Detailed exam objectives, mapped to book chapters
- FAQ on exam preparation and on taking the exam
- Introduction to the testing engine used for the exam

This book is intended specifically for individuals who wish to earn the Oracle Certified Professional (OCP) Java SE 7 Programmer II certification (exam number 1Z0-804). It assumes that you have practical experience of working with Java. If you are completely new to Java or to object-oriented languages, I suggest that you start your journey with an entry-level book and then come back to this one.

Disclaimer

The information in this chapter is sourced from Oracle.com, public websites, and user forums. Input has been taken from real people who have earned Java certification, including the author. All efforts have been made to maintain the accuracy of the content, but the details of the exam—including its objectives, pricing, pass score, total number of questions, and maximum duration—are subject to change per Oracle's policies. The author and publisher of the book shall not be held responsible for any loss or damage accrued due to any information contained in this book or due to any direct or indirect use of this information.

Introduction to OCP Java SE 7 Programmer II certification (1Z0-804)

The Oracle Certified Professional Java SE 7 Programmer II certification exam (1Z0-804) covers intermediate and advanced concepts of Java programming, such as the importance of threads, concurrency, localization, JDBC, String processing, and design patterns.

This exam is the second of the two steps in earning the title of OCP Java SE 7 Programmer. The first step is to earn the OCA Java SE 7 Programmer I certification (1Z0-803).

 NOTE   Though you can write the exams 1Z0-803 and 1Z0-804 in any order to earn the title of OCP Java SE 7 Programmer, it is highly recommended that you write exam 1Z0-803 before exam 1Z0-804. Exam 1Z0-803 covers basics of Java and exam 1Z0-804 covers advanced Java topics.

This exam certifies that an individual possesses strong practical skills in intermediate and advanced Java programming language concepts. Table 1 lists the details of this exam.

Table 1   Details for OCP Java SE 7 Programmer II exam (1Z0-804)

Exam number	1Z0-804
Java version	Based on Java version 7
Number of questions	90
Passing score	65%
Time duration	150 minutes
Pricing	US $245
Type of questions	Multiple-choice

The importance of the OCP Java SE 7 Programmer II certification

Real, on-the-job projects need you to understand and work with multiple basic and advanced concepts. Apart from covering the finer details of basic Java-like class design, it covers advanced Java topics like threading, concurrency, localization, File I/O, string processing, exception handling, assertions, collections API, and design patterns. This certification establishes your expertise with these topics, increasing your prospects for better projects, jobs, remuneration, responsibilities, and designations.

The OCP Java SE 7 Programmer II exam (1Z0-804) is an entry-level exam in your Java certification roadmap, as shown in figure 1. This exam is a prerequisite for most of the other Professional and Expert Oracle certifications in Java. The dashed lines and arrows in the figure depict the prerequisites for certifications.

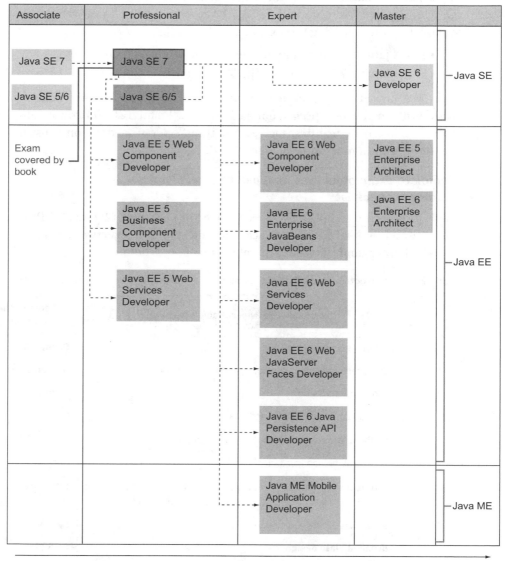

Increasing difficulty level

Figure 1   The OCP Java SE 7 Programmer II certification (1Z0-804) is an entry-level certification in the Java certification roadmap. It's a prerequisite for writing most of the other Professional and Expert certifications in Java.

As shown in figure 1, the Java certification tracks are offered under the categories Associate, Professional, Expert, and Master.

Comparing the OCA Java SE 7 Programmer I (1Z0-803) and OCP Java SE 7 Programmer II (1Z0-804) exams

The confusion about these two exams is due to the similarity in their names, but these are separate exams. Starting with Java 7, Oracle has raised the bar to earn the title of Oracle Certified Professional Java SE 7 Programmer, which now requires successfully completing the following two exams:

- OCA Java SE 7 Programmer I (exam number: 1Z0-803)
- OCP Java SE 7 Programmer II (exam number: 1Z0-804)

The OCA Java SE 7 Programmer certification is designed for individuals who possess basic skills in the Java programming language. Exam 1Z0-803 covers comparatively basic Java language features, such as data types, operators, decision constructs, arrays, methods, inheritance, and exception handling.

Complete exam objectives, mapped to book chapters, and readiness checklist

Table 2 shows the complete list of exam objectives for the OCP Java SE 7 Programmer II exam, which was taken from Oracle's website. All the objectives are mapped to the book's chapters and the section numbers that cover them.

Table 2   Exam objectives and subobjectives mapped to chapter and section numbers

	Exam objective as per Oracle's website	Covered in chapter/section
1	**Java class design**	**Chapter 1**
1.1	Use access modifiers: private, protected, and public	Section 1.1
1.2	Override methods	Section 1.3
1.3	Overload constructors and methods	Section 1.2
1.4	Use the `instanceof` operator and casting	Section 1.5
1.5	Use virtual method invocation	Section 1.3
1.6	Override the `hashCode`, `equals`, and `toString` methods from the `Object` class to improve the functionality of your class	Section 1.4
1.7	Use package and import statements	Section 1.6
2	**Advanced class design**	**Chapter 2**
2.1	Identify when and how to apply abstract classes	Section 2.1
2.2	Construct abstract Java classes and subclasses	Section 2.1
2.3	Use the static and final keywords	Section 2.2

Table 2   Exam objectives and subobjectives mapped to chapter and section numbers

	Exam objective as per Oracle's website	Covered in chapter/ section
2.4	Create top-level and nested classes	Section 2.4
2.5	Use enumerated types	Section 2.3
3	**Object-oriented design principles**	**Chapter 3**
3.1	Write code that declares, implements, and/or extends interfaces	Section 3.1
3.2	Choose between interface inheritance and class inheritance	Section 3.2
3.3	Apply cohesion, low-coupling, IS-A, and HAS-A principles	Sections 3.3, 3.4
3.4	Apply object composition principles (including HAS-A relationships)	Section 3.5
3.5	Design a class using the Singleton design pattern	Section 3.7
3.6	Write code to implement the Data Access Object (DAO) pattern	Section 3.9
3.7	Design and create objects using a Factory pattern	Section 3.8
4	**Generics and collections**	**Chapter 4**
4.1	Create a generic class	Section 4.2
4.2	Use the diamond for type inference	Section 4.3
4.3	Analyze the interoperability of collections that use raw types and generic types	Section 4.4
4.4	Use wrapper classes, autoboxing, and unboxing	Sections 4.11, 4.12
4.5	Create and use `List`, `Set`, and `Deque` implementations	Section 4.7
4.6	Create and use `Map` implementations	Section 4.8
4.7	Use `java.util.Comparator` and `java.lang.Comparable`	Section 4.9
4.8	Sort and search arrays and lists	Section 4.10
5	**String processing**	**Chapter 5**
5.1	Search, parse, and build strings (including `Scanner`, `StringTokenizer`, `StringBuilder`, `String`, and `Formatter`)	Section 5.1
5.2	Search, parse, and replace strings by using regular expressions, using expression patterns for matching limited to: . (dot), * (star), + (plus), ?, \d, \D, \s, \S, \w, \W, \b, \B, [], ()	Sections 5.1, 5.2
5.3	Format strings using the formatting parameters: %b, %c, %d, %f, and %s in format strings	Section 5.3
6	**Exceptions and assertions**	**Chapter 6**
6.1	Use `throw` and `throws` statements	Section 6.1
6.2	Use the `try` statement with multi-`catch` and `finally` clauses	Section 6.4

Table 2 Exam objectives and subobjectives mapped to chapter and section numbers *(continued)*

	Exam objective as per Oracle's website	Covered in chapter/ section
6.3	Develop code that uses `try`-with-resources statements	Section 6.5
6.4	Create custom exceptions	Section 6.2
6.5	Test invariants by using assertions	Section 6.6
7	**Java I/O fundamentals**	**Chapter 7**
7.1	Read and write data from the console	Section 7.5
7.2	Use streams to read from and write to files by using classes in the `java.io` package including `BufferedReader`, `BufferedWriter`, `File`, `FileReader`, `FileWriter`, `DataInputStream`, `DataOutputStream`, `ObjectOutputStream`, `ObjectInputStream`, and `PrintWriter`	Sections 7.2, 7.3, 7.4
8	**Java file I/O (NIO.2)**	**Chapter 8**
8.1	Operate on file and directory paths with the `Path` class	Section 8.1
8.2	Check, delete, copy, or move a file or directory with the `Files` class	Section 8.2
8.3	Read and change file and directory attributes, focusing on the `BasicFileAttributes`, `DosFileAttributes`, and `PosixFileAttributes` interfaces	Section 8.3
8.4	Recursively access a directory tree using the `DirectoryStream` and `FileVisitor` interfaces	Section 8.4
8.5	Find a file with the `PathMatcher` interface	Section 8.5
8.6	Watch a directory for changes with the `WatchService` interface	Section 8.6
9	**Building database applications with JDBC**	**Chapter 9**
9.1	Describe the interfaces that make up the core of the JDBC API (including `Driver`, `Connection`, `Statement`, and `ResultSet`) and their relationships to provider implementations	Section 9.2
9.2	Identify the components required to connect to a database using the `DriverManager` class (including the JDBC URL)	Section 9.3
9.3	Submit queries and read results from the database (including creating statements, returning result sets, iterating through the results, and properly closing result sets, statements, and connections)	Section 9.4
9.4	Use JDBC transactions (including disabling auto-commit mode, committing and rolling back transactions, and setting and rolling back to savepoints)	Section 9.5
9.5	Construct and use `RowSet` objects using the `RowSetProvider` class and the `RowSetFactory` interface	Section 9.6

Table 2 Exam objectives and subobjectives mapped to chapter and section numbers

	Exam objective as per Oracle's website	Covered in chapter/section
9.6	Create and use `PreparedStatement` and `CallableStatement` objects	Section 9.7
10	**Threads**	**Chapter 10**
10.1	Create and use the `Thread` class and the `Runnable` interface	Section 10.1
10.2	Manage and control thread lifecycle	Section 10.2
10.3	Synchronize thread access to shared data	Section 10.3
10.4	Identify code that may not execute correctly in a multi-threaded environment	Section 10.4
11	**Concurrency**	**Chapter 11**
11.1	Use collections from the `java.util.concurrent` package with a focus on the advantages over and differences from the traditional `java.util` collections	Section 11.1
11.2	Use `Lock`, `ReadWriteLock`, and `ReentrantLock` classes in the `java.util.concurrent.locks` package to support lock-free, thread-safe programming on single variables	Section 11.2
11.3	Use `Executor`, `ExecutorService`, `Executors`, `Callable`, and `Future` to execute tasks using thread pools	Section 11.3
11.4	Use the parallel fork/join framework	Section 11.4
12	**Localization**	**Chapter 12**
12.1	Read and set the locale by using the `Locale` object	Section 12.2
12.2	Build a resource bundle for each locale	Section 12.2
12.3	Call a resource bundle from an application	Section 12.2
12.4	Format dates, numbers, and currency values for localization with the `NumberFormat` and `DateFormat` classes (including number format patterns)	Section 12.3
12.5	Describe the advantages of localizing an application	Section 12.1
12.6	Define a locale using language and country codes	Section 12.1

FAQ

You might be anxious when you start your exam preparation or even think about getting certified. This section can help calm your nerves by answering frequently asked questions on exam preparation and on writing the exam.

FAQ on exam preparation

This sections answers frequently asked questions on how to prepare for the exam, including the best approach, study material, preparation duration, and how to test self-readiness.

WILL THE EXAM DETAILS EVER CHANGE FOR THE OCP JAVA SE 7 PROGRAMMER II EXAM?

Oracle can change the exam details for a certification even after the certification is made live. The changes can be made to any of its details, like exam objectives, pricing, exam duration, exam questions, and others. In the past, Oracle has made similar changes to certification exams. Such changes may not be major, but it is always advisable to check Oracle's website for the latest exam information when you start your exam preparation.

WHAT IS THE BEST WAY TO PREPARE FOR THIS EXAM?

Generally, candidates use a combination of resources, such as books, online study materials, articles on the exam, free and paid mock exams, and training to prepare for the exam. Different combinations work best for different people, and there is no one perfect formula for preparation. Select the method—training or self-study—that works best for you. Combine it with a lot of code practice and mock exams.

HOW DO I KNOW WHEN I AM READY FOR THE EXAM?

You can be sure about your exam readiness by *consistently* getting a good score on the mock exams. Generally, a score of 80% and above on approximately 7 mock exams (the more the better) attempted consecutively will assure you of a similar score on the real exam.

HOW MANY MOCK TESTS SHOULD I ATTEMPT BEFORE THE REAL EXAM?

Ideally, you should attempt at least five complete mock exams before you attempt the real exam. The more the better!

I HAVE TWO–FOURS YEARS' EXPERIENCE WORKING WITH JAVA. DO I STILL NEED TO PREPARE FOR THIS CERTIFICATION?

There is a difference between the practical knowledge of having worked with Java and the knowledge required to pass this certification exam. The authors of the Java certification exams employ multiple tricks to test your knowledge. Hence, you need a structured preparation and approach to succeed on the certification exam.

WHAT IS THE IDEAL TIME REQUIRED TO PREPARE FOR THE EXAM?

The preparation time frame mainly depends on your experience with Java and the amount of time that you can spend to prepare yourself. On average, you will require approximately 200 hours of study over two or three months to prepare for this exam. Again, the number of study hours required depends on individual learning curves and backgrounds.

It's important to be consistent with your exam preparation. You cannot study for a month and then restart after, say, a gap of a month or more.

DO I NEED TO COMPLETE ANY TRAINING FROM ORACLE?

Though Oracle requires candidates to complete specific Oracle training programs for a few of its certification courses, it isn't mandatory to complete any training from Oracle for this certification.

DOES THIS EXAM INCLUDE ANY UNSCORED QUESTIONS?

A few of the questions that you write on any Oracle exam may be marked unscored. Oracle's policy states that while writing an exam, you won't be informed whether a question will be scored. You may be surprised to learn that as many as 10 out of the 90 questions on the OCP Java SE 7 Programmer II exam may be unscored. Even if you answer a few questions incorrectly, you stand a chance of scoring 100%.

Oracle regularly updates its question bank for all its certification exams. These unscored questions may be used for research and to evaluate new questions that can be added to an exam.

CAN I START MY EXAM PREPARATION WITH THE MOCK EXAMS?

If you are quite comfortable with the advanced Java language features, then yes, you can start your exam preparation with the mock exams. This will also help you to understand the types of questions to expect on the real certification exam. But if you have little or no experience working with advanced Java concepts, I don't advise you to start with the mock exams. The exam authors often use a lot of tricks to evaluate a candidate on the real certification exam. Starting your exam preparation with mock exams will only leave you confused about the Java concepts.

SHOULD I REALLY BOTHER GETTING CERTIFIED?

Yes, you should, for the simple reason that employers bother about the certification of employees. Organizations prefer a certified Java developer over a noncertified Java developer with similar IT skills and experience. The certification can also get you a higher paycheck than uncertified peers with comparable skills.

FAQ on taking the exam

This section contains a list of frequently asked questions related to exam registration, the exam coupon, do's and don'ts while taking the exam, and exam retakes.

WHERE AND HOW DO I WRITE THIS EXAM?

You can write this exam at an Oracle Testing Center or Pearson VUE Authorized Testing Center. To sit for the exam, you must register and purchase an exam voucher. The following options are available:

- Register for the exam and pay Pearson VUE directly.
- Purchase an exam voucher from Oracle and register at Pearson VUE to take the exam.
- Register at an Oracle Testing Center.

Look for the nearest testing centers in your area, register yourself, and schedule an exam date and time. Most of the popular computer training institutes also have a testing center on their premises. You can locate a Pearson VUE testing site at www.pearsonvue.com/oracle/, which contains detailed information on locating testing centers and scheduling or rescheduling an exam. At the time of registration, you'll need to provide the following details along with your name, address, and contact numbers:

- Exam title and number (OCP Java SE 7 Programmer II, 1Z0-804)
- Any discount code that should be applied during registration
- Oracle Testing ID/Candidate ID, if you have written any other Oracle/Sun certification exam(s)
- Your OPN Company ID (If your employer is in the Oracle Partner Network, you can find out the company ID and use any available discounts on the exam fee.)

How long is the exam coupon valid for?
Each exam coupon is printed with an expiration date. Beware of any discounted coupons that come with an assurance that they can be used past the expiration date.

Can I refer to notes or books while writing this exam?
You can't refer to any books or notes while writing this exam. You are not allowed to carry any blank paper for rough work or even your mobile phone inside the testing cubicle.

What is the purpose of marking a question while writing the exam?
By marking a question, you can manage your time efficiently. Don't spend a lot of time on a single question. You can mark a difficult question to defer answering it while writing your exam. You have an option to review answers to the marked questions at the end of the exam. Also, navigating from one question to another using Back and Next buttons is usually time-consuming. If you are unsure of an answer, mark it and review it at the end.

Can I write down the exam questions and bring them back with me?
No. The exam centers no longer provide sheets of paper for the rough work that you may need to do while taking the exam. The testing center will provide you with either erasable or nonerasable boards. If you're provided with a nonerasable board, you may request another one if you need it.

Oracle is quite particular about certification candidates distributing or circulating the memorized questions in any form. If Oracle finds out that this is happening, it may cancel a candidate's certificate, bar that candidate forever from writing any Oracle certification, inform the employer, or take legal action.

What happens if I complete the exam before or after the total time?
If you complete the exam before the total exam time has elapsed, review your answers and click the Submit or finish button.

If you have not clicked the Submit button and you use up all the exam time, the exam engine will no longer allow you to modify any of the exam answers and will present the screen with the Submit button.

WILL I RECEIVE MY SCORE IMMEDIATELY AFTER THE EXAM?

No, you won't. When you click the Submit exam button, the screen will inform you that your exam results will be available in an hour. Usually Oracle sends you an email when the results can be accessed online. Even if you don't receive an email from Oracle, you could log in and check your result. The result includes your score on each exam objective. The certificate itself will arrive via mail within six to eight weeks.

WHAT HAPPENS IF I FAIL? CAN I RETAKE THE EXAM?

It's not the end of the world. Don't worry if you fail. You can retake the exam after 14 days (and the world will not know it's a retake).

However, you cannot retake a passed exam to improve your score. Also, you cannot retake a beta exam.

The testing engine used in the exam

The UI of the testing engine used for the certification exam is quite simple. (You could even call it primitive, compared to today's web, desktop, and smartphone applications.)

Before you can start the exam, you will be required to accept the terms and conditions of the Oracle Certification Candidate Agreement. Your computer screen will display all these conditions and give you an option to accept the conditions. You can proceed with writing the exam only if you accept these conditions.

Here are the features of the testing engine used by Oracle:

- *The engine UI is divided into three sections*. The UI of the testing engine is divided into the following three segments:
  - *Static upper section*—Displays question number, time remaining, and a checkbox to mark a question for review.
  - *Scrollable middle section*—Displays the question text and the answer options.
  - *Static bottom section*—Displays buttons to display the previous question, display the next question, end the exam, and review marked questions.
- *Each question is displayed on a separate screen*. The exam engine displays one question on the screen at a time. It does not display multiple questions on a single screen, like a scrollable web page. All effort is made to display the complete question and answer options without scrolling, or with little scrolling.
- *Code exhibit button*. Many questions include code. Such questions, together with their answers, may require significant scrolling to be viewed. As this can be quite inconvenient, such questions include a Code Exhibit button that displays the code in a separate window.
- *Mark questions to be reviewed*. The question screen displays a check box with the text "Mark for review" at the top-left corner. A question can be marked using this option. The marked questions can be reviewed at the end of the exam.
- *Buttons to display previous and next questions*. The test includes buttons to display previous and next questions within the bottom section of the testing engine.

- *Buttons to end the exam and review marked questions*. The engine displays buttons to end the exam and to review the marked questions in the bottom section of the testing engine.
- *Remaining time*. The engine displays the time remaining for the exam at the top right of the screen.
- *Question number*. Each question displays its serial number.
- *Correct number of answer options*. Each question displays the correct number of options that should be selected from multiple options.

On behalf of all at Manning Publications, I wish you good luck and hope that you score very well on your exam.

Java class design 1

Exam objectives covered in this chapter	What you need to know
[1.1] Use access modifiers: private, protected, and public	How to use appropriate access modifiers to design classes How to limit accessibility of classes, interfaces, enums, methods, and variables by using the appropriate access modifiers The correct combination of access modifiers and the entities (classes, interfaces, enums, methods, and variables) to which they can be applied The implications of modifying the access modifier of a Java entity
[1.2] Override methods	The conditions and requirements that make a subclass override a base class method How to differentiate among overloaded, overridden, and hidden methods
[1.3] Overload constructors and methods	The need and right rules to overload constructors and methods
[1.4] Use the `instanceof` operator and casting	Understand the right use of the `instanceof` operator, and implicit and explicit object casting and their implications Compilation errors and runtime exceptions associated with the use of the `instanceof` operator and casting
[1.5] Use virtual method invocation	The methods that can and can't be invoked virtually

Exam objectives covered in this chapter	What you need to know
[1.6] Override methods from the `Object` class to improve the functionality of your class	The need to override methods from class `Object`—differentiate correct, incorrect, appropriate, and inappropriate overriding
[1.7] Use package and import statements	How to package classes and use `package`, `import`, and `static import` statements

Classes and interfaces are building blocks of an application. Efficient and effective class design makes a significant impact on the overall application design. Imagine if, while designing your classes, you didn't consider effective packaging, correct overloaded or overridden methods, or access protection—you might lose on extensibility, flexibility, and usability of your classes. For example, if you didn't override methods `hashCode()` and `equals()` correctly in your classes, your *seemingly* "equal" objects might *not* be considered equal by collection classes like `HashSet` or `HashMap`. Or, say, imagine if you didn't use the right access modifiers to protect your classes and their members, they could be subject to unwanted manipulation by other classes from the same or different packages. The creation of overloaded methods is another domain, which is an important class design decision. It eases instance creation and use of methods.

Class design decisions require an insight into understanding correct and appropriate implementation practices. When armed with adequate information you'll be able to select the best practices and approach to designing your classes. The topics covered in this chapter will help you design better classes by taking you through multiple examples. This chapter covers

- Access modifiers
- Method overloading
- Method overriding
- Virtual method invocation
- Use of the `instanceof` operator and casting
- Override methods from class `Object` to improve the functionality of your class
- How to create packages and use classes from other packages

Let's get started with how to control access to your classes and their members, using access modifiers.

1.1 Java access modifiers

 [1.1]   Use access modifiers: private, protected, and public

When you design applications and create classes, you need to answer multiple questions:

- How do I restrict other classes from accessing certain members of a class?
- How do I prevent classes from modifying the state of objects of a class, both within the same and separate packages?

Java access modifiers answer all these questions. Access modifiers control the accessibility of a class or an interface, including its members (methods and variables), by other classes and interfaces within the same or separate packages. By using the appropriate access modifiers, you can limit access to your class or interface, and its members.

Access modifiers can be applied to classes, interfaces, and their members (instance and class variables and methods). Local variables and method parameters can't be defined using access modifiers. An attempt to do so will prevent the code from compiling.

In this section, we'll cover all of the access modifiers—public, protected, and private—as well as *default* access, which is the result when you don't use an access modifier. You'll also discover the effects of changing the access levels of existing types on other code.

> **NOTE**   Access modifiers are also covered in the OCA Java SE 7 Programmer I exam (1Z0-803). If you've written this exam recently, then perhaps you might like to skip sections 1.1.1–1.1.4.

To understand all of these access modifiers, we'll use the same set of classes: Book, CourseBook, Librarian, StoryBook, and House. Figure 1.1 depicts these classes using UML notation.

Classes Book, CourseBook, and Librarian are defined in the package library. Classes StoryBook and House are defined in the package building. Classes StoryBook and CourseBook (defined in separate packages) extend class Book. Using these classes,

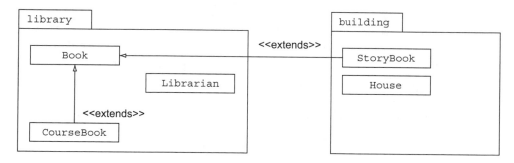

Figure 1.1   A set of classes and their relationships to help understand access modifiers

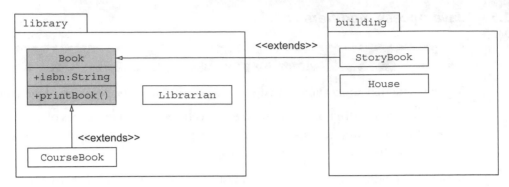

Figure 1.2   Understanding the `public` access modifier

you'll see how the accessibility of a class and its members varies with different access modifiers, from unrelated to derived classes, across packages.

As we cover each of the access modifiers, we'll add a set of instance variables and a method to class `Book` with the relevant access modifier.

1.1.1   *Public access modifier*

This is the least restrictive access modifier. Classes and interfaces defined using the `public` access modifier are accessible across all packages, from derived to unrelated classes.

To understand the `public` access modifier, let's define class `Book` as a public class and add a public instance variable (`isbn`) and a public method (`printBook()`) to it. Figure 1.2 shows the UML notation.

Examine the following definition of class `Book`:

```
package library;                          public
public class Book {                       class Book
    public String isbn;                        public
    public void printBook() {}                 variable
}                                               isbn
                                          public method
                                          printBook()
```

The `public` access modifier is said to be the least restrictive, so let's try to access the public class `Book` and its public members from class `House`. We'll use class `House` because `House` and `Book` are defined in separate packages and they're unrelated. Class `House` doesn't enjoy any advantages of being defined in the same package or being a derived class.

Here's the code for class `House`:

```
package building;
import library.Book;
public class House {
```

```
                    public House() {
Book is        ┌─►      Book book = new Book();
accessible     │        String value = book.isbn;
to House       │        book.printBook();
               │    }
               │
               }
```

Book is accessible to House

isbn is accessible to House

printBook() is accessible to House

In the preceding example, class `Book` and its public members—instance variable `isbn` and method `printBook()`—are accessible to class `House`. They're also accessible to the other classes: `StoryBook`, `Librarian`, and `CourseBook`. Figure 1.3 shows the classes that can access a public class and its members.

1.1.2 Protected access modifier

The members of a class defined using the `protected` access modifier are accessible to

- Classes and interfaces defined in the same package
- All derived classes, even if they're defined in separate packages

 EXAM TIP Members of an interface are implicitly public. If you define interface members as protected, the interface won't compile.

Let's add a protected instance variable `author` and method `modifyTemplate()` to class `Book`. Figure 1.4 shows the class representation.

	Same package	Separate package
Derived classes	✓	✓
Unrelated classes	✓	✓

Figure 1.3 Classes that can access a public class and its members

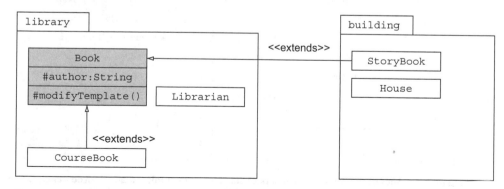

Figure 1.4 Understanding the `protected` access modifier

Here's the code for class Book (I've deliberately left out its public members because they aren't required in this section):

```
package library;
public class Book {
    protected String author;
    protected void modifyTemplate(){}
}
```

                                                    protected
                                                    variable author

                                                    protected method
                                                    modifyTemplate()

Figure 1.5 illustrates how classes from the same and separate packages, derived classes, and unrelated classes access class Book and its protected members.

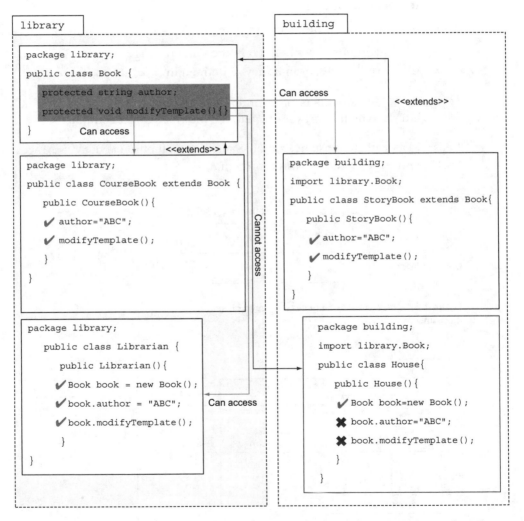

Figure 1.5 Access of protected members of class Book in unrelated and derived classes, from the same and separate packages

Class House fails compilation for trying to access method modifyTemplate()and variable author, as follows:

```
House.java:8: modifyTemplate()has protected access in library.Book
        book.modifyTemplate();
               ^
```

A derived class inherits the protected members of its base class, irrespective of the packages in which they are defined.

Notice that the derived classes CourseBook and StoryBook inherit class Book's protected member variable author and method modifyTemplate(). If class StoryBook tries to instantiate Book using a reference variable and then tries to access its protected variable author and method modifyTemplate(), it won't compile:

```
package building;
import library.Book;
class StoryBook extends Book {
    StoryBook () {
        Book book = new Book();
        String v = book.author;
        book.modifyTemplate();
    }
}
```

Book and StoryBook defined in separate packages

Protected members of Book aren't accessible in StoryBook if accessed using an instance of Book.

 EXAM TIP A concise but not too simple way of stating the previous rule is this: A derived class can inherit and access protected members of its base class, regardless of the package in which it's defined. A derived class in a separate package can't access protected members of its base class using reference variables.

Figure 1.6 shows the classes that can access protected members of a class or an interface.

1.1.3 Default access (package access)

The members of a class defined without using any explicit access modifier are defined with *package accessibility* (also called *default accessibility*). The members with package access are *only* accessible to classes and interfaces defined in the same package. The default access is also referred to as *package-private*. Think of a package as your home, classes as rooms, and things in rooms as variables with default access. These things

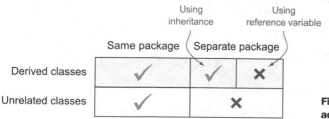

Figure 1.6 Classes that can access protected members

aren't limited to one room—they can be accessed across all the rooms in your home. But they're still private to your home—you wouldn't want them to be accessed outside your home. Similarly, when you define a package, you might want to make accessible members of classes to all the other classes across the same package.

 NOTE While the package-private access is as valid as the other access levels, in real projects, it often appears as the result of inexperienced developers forgetting to specify the access modifier of Java components.

Let's define an instance variable `issueCount` and a method `issueHistory()` with default access in class `Book`. Figure 1.7 shows the class representation with these new members.

Here's the code for class `Book` (I've deliberately left out its public and protected members because they aren't required in this section):

```
package library;              public class
public class Book {           Book              issueCount with
    int issueCount;                             default access
    void issueHistory () {}    issueHistory() with
}                              default access
```

You can see how classes from the same package and separate packages, derived classes, and unrelated classes access class `Book` and its members (instance variable `issueCount` and method `issueHistory()`) in figure 1.8.

Because classes `CourseBook` and `Librarian` are defined in the same package as class `Book`, they can access the members `issueCount` and `issueHistory()`. Because classes `House` and `StoryBook` aren't defined in the same package as class `Book`, they can't access the members `issueCount` and `issueHistory()`. Class `StoryBook` fails compilation with the following error message:

```
StoryBook.java:6: issueHistory () is not public in library.Book; cannot be
    accessed from outside package
        book.issueHistory ();
        ^
```

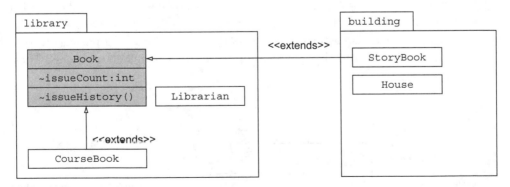

Figure 1.7 Understanding class representations for the default access

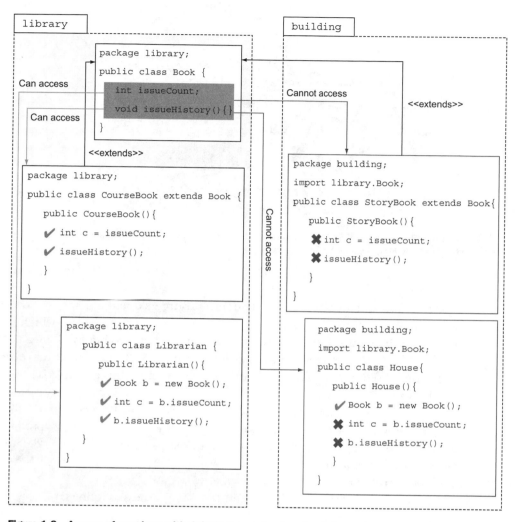

Figure 1.8 **Access of members with default access to class** `Book` **in unrelated and derived classes from the same and separate packages**

Class `House` is unaware of the existence of `issueHistory()`—it fails compilation with the following error message:

```
House.java:9: cannot find symbol
symbol   : method issueHistory ()
location: class building.House
       issueHistory ();
```

DEFINING A CLASS BOOK WITH DEFAULT ACCESS

What happens if you define a class with default access? What will happen to the accessibility of its members if the class itself has default (package) accessibility?

Can be accessed
only by inhabitants
of the island

Far-away island
inaccessble by
air and water

**Figure 1.9   This Superfast Burgers cannot be accessed from outside the island because
the island is inaccessible by air and water.**

Consider this situation: Assume that Superfast Burgers opens a new outlet on a beautiful island and offers free meals to people from all over the world, which obviously includes inhabitants of the island. But the island is inaccessible by all means (air and water). Would the existence of this particular Superfast Burger outlet make any sense to people who don't inhabit the island? An illustration of this example is shown in figure 1.9.

The island is like a package in Java, and the Superfast Burger outlet is like a class defined with default access. In the same way that the Superfast Burger outlet can't be accessed from outside the island on which it exists, a class defined with default (package) access is visible and accessible only within the package in which it's defined. It can't be accessed from outside its package.

Let's redefine class `Book` with default (package) access as follows:

```
package library;
class Book {                              Book now has
    //.. class members                    default access
}
```

The behavior of class `Book` remains the same for classes `CourseBook` and `Librarian`, which are defined in the same package. But class `Book` can't be accessed by classes `House` and `StoryBook`, which reside in a separate package.

Let's start with class `House`. Examine the following code:

```
package building;
import library.Book;                      Book isn't
public class House {}                      accessible in House
```

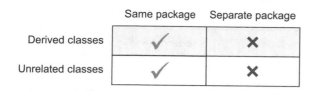

	Same package	Separate package
Derived classes	✓	✗
Unrelated classes	✓	✗

Figure 1.10 Classes that can access members with default (package) access

Class House fails compilation with the following error message:

```
House.java:2: library.Book is not public in library; cannot be accessed from
    outside package
import library.Book;
```

Here's the code of class StoryBook:

```
package building;
import library.Book;
class StoryBook extends Book {}
```

Book isn't accessible in StoryBook

StoryBook cannot extend Book

Figure 1.10 shows which classes can access members of a class or an interface with default (package) access.

Because a lot of programmers are confused about which members are made accessible by using the protected access modifier and no modifier (default), the following exam tip offers a simple and interesting rule to help you remember their differences.

 EXAM TIP Default access can be compared to package-private (accessible only within a package) and protected access can be compared to package-private + *kids* (kids refers to derived classes). Kids can access protected members only by inheritance and not by reference (accessing members by using the dot operator on an object).

1.1.4 *The private access modifier*

The private access modifier is the most restrictive access modifier. The members of a class defined using the private access modifier are accessible only to them. For example, the internal organs of your body (heart, lungs, etc.) are private to your body. No one else can access them. It doesn't matter whether the class or interface in question is from another package or has extended the class—private members *aren't* accessible outside the class in which they're defined.

 EXAM TIP Members of an interface are implicitly public. If you define interface members as private, the interface won't compile.

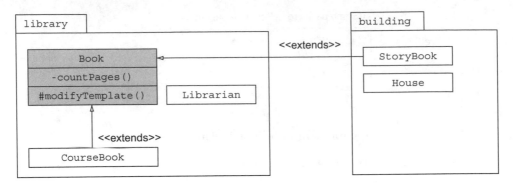

Figure 1.11   Understanding the `private` access modifier

Let's see the private members in action by adding a private method `countPages()` to class `Book`. Figure 1.11 depicts the class representation using UML.

Examine the following definition of class `Book`:

```
package library;
class Book {
    private void countPages () {}        ◁——  Private method
    protected void modifyTemplate(){
        countPages ();               ◁——  Only Book can access
    }                                       its own private
}                                           method countPages()
```

None of the classes defined in any of the packages (whether derived or not) can access the private method `countPages()`. But let's try to access it from class `Course-Book`. I chose class `CourseBook` because both of these classes are defined in the same package, and class `CourseBook` extends class `Book`. Here's the code of `CourseBook`:

```
package library;
class CourseBook extends Book {       ◁——  CourseBook
    CourseBook () {                          extends Book
        countPages ();              ◁——  CourseBook cannot
    }                                       access private method
}                                           countPages()
```

Because class `CourseBook` tries to access private members of class `Book`, it will not compile. Similarly, if any of the other classes (`StoryBook`, `Librarian`, or `House`) try to access private method `countPages()` of class `Book`, it will not compile. Figure 1.12 shows the classes that can access the private members of a class.

 NOTE   For your real projects, it *is* possible to access private members of a class outside them, using *Java Reflection*. But Java Reflection isn't on the exam. So don't consider it when answering questions on the accessibility of private members.

	Same package	Separate package
Derived classes	✗	✗
Unrelated classes	✗	✗

Figure 1.12   No classes can access private members of another class.

1.1.5   Access modifiers and Java entities

Can every access modifier be applied to all the Java entities? The simple answer is *no*. Table 1.1 lists the Java entities and the access modifiers that can be used with them.

Table 1.1   Java entities and the access modifiers that can be applied to them

Entity name	`public`	`protected`	`private`
Top-level class, interface, enum	✓	✗	✗
Nested class, interface, enum	✓	✓	✓
Class variables and methods	✓	✓	✓
Instance variables and methods	✓	✓	✓
Method parameters and local variables	✗	✗	✗

What happens if you try to code the combinations for an X above? None of these combinations will compile. Here's the code:

```
protected class MyTopLevelClass {}
private class MyTopLevelClass {}
protected interface TopLevelInterface {}
protected enum TopLevelEnum {}
```
Won't compile—top-level class, interface, and enums can't be defined with protected and private access.

```
void myMethod(private int param) {}
void myMethod(int param) {
    public int localVariable = 10;
}
```
Won't compile—method parameters and local variables can't be defined using any explicit access modifiers.

Watch out for these combinations on the exam. It's simple to insert these small and invalid combinations in any code snippet and still make you believe that you're being tested on a rather complex topic like threads or concurrency.

 EXAM TIP   Watch out for invalid combinations of a Java entity and an access modifier. Such code won't compile.

Project status: code by Harry fails compilation

Harry   Paul

Figure 1.13   A change in the access modifier of a member of a class can break the code of other classes.

1.1.6   *Effects of changing access modifiers for existing entities*

Shreya, a programmer, changed the access modifier of a member in her class, Book, and see what Harry (another programmer) had to go through the next morning (figure 1.13).

Let's analyze what happened. Why did Harry's code break when Shreya changed her own code? As shown in figure 1.14, Harry's class StoryBook extends class Book created by Shreya. Before the modifications, Harry's class StoryBook accessed the protected member author from its parent class Book. But when Shreya modified the access modifier of the member author from protected to default access, it could no longer be accessed by class StoryBook because they reside in separate packages. So, even though Harry didn't change his code, it didn't compile.

You can change the access modifier of a member in two ways:

- Accessibility is decreased—for example, a public member is made private
- Accessibility is increased—for example, a private member is made public

WHEN ACCESSIBILITY OF AN ENTITY IS DECREASED (MORE RESTRICTIVE)
As shown in figure 1.14, when an entity is made more restrictive, there are chances that other code that uses that entity *might* break.

> **Impact of decreasing accessibility in real-life projects**
> Decreasing the accessibility of entities can affect the overall application in a big way. This is especially important for designing APIs and maintaining software. Many Java developers make the mistake of carelessly decreasing the accessibility of methods or fields, which can result in access issues with other components in a system.

WHEN ACCESSIBILITY OF AN ENTITY IS INCREASED (LESS RESTRICTIVE)
There are no issues when an entity is made less restrictive, say, when access of an entity is changed from default to protected or public. With increased access, an

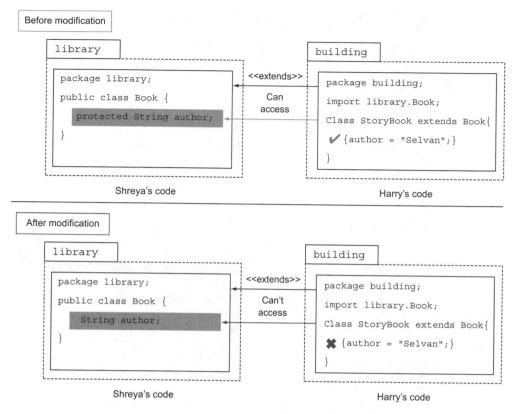

Figure 1.14   Code before and after modification showing why Harry's code failed to compile, even though he didn't change a bit of it.

entity may become visible to other classes, interfaces, and enums to which it wasn't visible earlier.

Apart from being an important exam topic, you're sure to encounter issues related to access modifiers at your workplace in real projects. Let's see whether you can spot a similar issue in the first "Twist in the Tale" exercise.

About the "Twist in the Tale" exercises

For these exercises, I've tried to use modified code from the examples already covered in the chapter. The "Twist in the Tale" title refers to modified or tweaked code. These exercises will help you understand how even small code modifications can change the behavior of your code. They should also encourage you to carefully examine all of the code on the exam. The reason for these exercises is that on the exam, you may be asked more than one question that seems to require the same answer. But on closer inspection, you'll realize that the questions differ slightly, and this will change the behavior of the code and the correct answer option. All answers to "Twist in the Tale" exercises are in the appendix.

Here are the classes written by Shreya and Harry (residing in separate source code files) that work without any issues:

```
package library;              // Class written by Shreya
public class Book {
    protected String author;
}

package building;             // Class written by Harry
import library.Book;
class StoryBook extends Book {
    { author = "Selvan"; }
}
```

On Friday evening, Shreya modified her code and checked it in to the organization's version control system. Do you think Harry would be able to run his code without any errors when he checks out the modified code on Monday morning, and why? Here's the modified code:

```
package library;              // Class written by Shreya
class Book {
    protected String author;
}

package building;             // Class written by Harry
import library.Book;
class StoryBook extends Book {
    { author = "Selvan"; }
}
```

In the next section, we'll cover the need and semantics of defining overloaded methods. You can compare overloaded methods with any action that you might specify with multiple, different, or additional details. Let's get started with understanding the need of defining overloaded methods.

1.2 *Overloaded methods and constructors*

 [1.3] Overload constructors and methods

Overloaded methods are methods with the same name but different method parameter lists. In this section, you'll learn how to create and use overloaded methods.

Imagine that you're delivering a lecture and need to instruct the audience to take notes using paper, a Smartphone, or a laptop—whichever is available to them for the day. One way to do this is to give the audience a list of instructions like

- Take notes using paper.
- Take notes using Smartphones.
- Take notes using laptops.

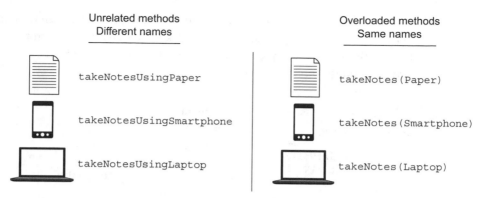

Figure 1.15 Real-life examples of overloaded methods

Another method is to instruct them to "take notes" and then provide them with the paper, a Smartphone, or a laptop they're supposed to use. Apart from the simplicity of the latter method, it also gives you the flexibility to add other media on which to take notes (such as one's hand, some cloth, or the wall) without needing to remember the list of all the instructions.

This second approach—providing one set of instructions (with the same name) but a different set of input values—can be compared to overloaded methods in Java, as shown in figure 1.15.

The implementation of the example shown in figure 1.15 in code is as follows:

```
class Paper {}
class Smartphone {}
class Laptop {}

class Lecture {
    void takeNotes(Paper paper) {}           Overloaded
    void takeNotes(Smartphone phone) {}      method—
    void takeNotes(Laptop laptop) {}         takeNotes()
}
```

Overloaded methods are usually referred to as methods that are defined in the same class, with the same name, but with a different method argument list. A derived class can also overload the methods inherited from its base class as follows:

```
class Paper {}
class Smartphone {}
class Laptop {}

class Lecture {
    void takeNotes(Paper paper) {}
    void takeNotes(Smartphone phone) {}
    void takeNotes(Laptop laptop) {}
}
class Canvas {}
class FineArtLecture extends Lecture {
    void takeNotes(Canvas canvas) {}
}
```

takeNotes() in FineArtLecture overloads takeNotes() from Lecture by specifying a different parameter list.

Overloaded methods make it easier to add methods with similar functionality that work with a different set of input values. Let's work with an example from the Java API classes that we all use frequently: `System.out.println()`. Method `println()` accepts multiple types of method parameters:

```
int intVal = 10;
boolean boolVal = false;
String name = "eJava";

System.out.println(intVal);
System.out.println(boolVal);
System.out.println(name);
```

> Prints an int value
>
> Prints a boolean value
>
> Prints a string value

When you use method `println()`, you know that whatever you pass to it as a method argument will be printed to the console. Wouldn't it be crazy to use methods like `printlnInt()`, `printlnBool()`, and `printlnString()` for the same functionality? I think so, too.

Let's examine in detail the method parameters passed to overloaded methods, their return types, and their access and nonaccess modifiers.

 NOTE   The exam will test you on how you can define correct overloaded methods, which overloaded methods get invoked when you use a set of arguments, and also whether a compiler is unable to resolve the call.

1.2.1   *Argument list*

Overloaded methods accept different lists of arguments. The argument lists can differ in terms of

- The change in the number of parameters that are accepted
- The change in the type of the method parameters that are accepted
- The change in the positions of the parameters that are accepted (based on parameter type, not variable names)

Let's work with some examples to verify these points.

CHANGE IN THE NUMBER OF METHOD PARAMETERS

Overloaded methods that define a different number of method parameters are the simplest among all the method types. Let's work with an example of an overloaded method, `calcAverage()`, which accepts a different count of method parameters:

```
class Result {
    double calcAverage(int marks1, int marks2) {
        return (marks1 + marks2)/2;
    }
    double calcAverage(int marks1, int marks2, int marks3) {
        return (marks1 + marks2 + marks3)/3;
    }
}
```

> Two method arguments
>
> Three method arguments

CHANGE IN THE TYPE OF METHOD PARAMETERS

In the following example, the difference is in the argument list—due to the change in the type of parameters it accepts—to calculate the average of integer and decimal numbers:

```
class Result {
    double calcAverage(int marks1, double marks2) {          ⊲─┐  Arguments—
        return (marks1 + marks2)/2;                              int and double
    }
    double calcAverage(double marks1, double marks2) {       ⊲─┐ Arguments—
        return (marks1 + marks2)/2;                              double and
    }                                                            double
}
```

When you define overloaded methods with object references as parameters, their classes might or might not share an inheritance relationship. When the classes don't share an inheritance relationship, there isn't any confusion with the version of the method that will be called:

```
class Employee {}
class Engineer extends Employee {}
class CEO extends Employee {}
class Travel {
    static String bookTicket(Engineer val) {      ⊲─┐  Engineer and CEO
        return "economy class";                         aren't in the same
    }                                                    inheritance tree
    static String bookTicket(CEO val) {           ⊲─┘
        return "business class";
    }
}
```

For the preceding code, if you call method bookTicket() by passing it a CEO object, it will call the method that accepts a parameter of type CEO—no confusion here. Now, what happens if you define overloaded methods that accept object references of classes which share an inheritance relationship? For example (modifications in code are in **bold**)

```
class Employee {}
class CEO extends Employee {}
class Travel {
    static String bookTicket(Employee val) {      ⊲─┐  Method
        return "economy class";                         parameters—CEO
    }                                                    extends Employee
    static String bookTicket(CEO val) {           ⊲─┘
        return "business class";
    }
}
```

Which of these methods do you think would be called if you pass a CEO object to method bookTicket()? Can a CEO object be assigned to both CEO and Employee?

```
class TravelAgent {
    public static void main(String... args) {                          Prints
        System.out.println(Travel.bookTicket(new CEO()));   ◁—         "business
    }                                                                   class"
}
```

The preceding code calls overloaded method bookTicket() that accepts a CEO, because without any explicit reference variable, new CEO() is referred to using a CEO variable. Now, try to determine the output of the following code:

```
class TravelAgent {
    public static void main(String... args) {
        Employee emp = new CEO();                                      Prints
        System.out.println(Travel.bookTicket(emp));    ◁—              "economy
    }                                                                   class"
}
```

The preceding code prints "economy class" and not "business class" because the type of the reference variable emp is Employee. The overloaded methods are bound at compile time and not runtime. To resolve the call to the overloaded methods, the compiler considers the type of variable that's used to refer to an object.

 EXAM TIP Calls to the overloaded methods are resolved during compilation.

Using the preceding Employee and CEO example, figure 1.16 shows a fun way to remember calls to the overloaded methods are resolved during compilation.

Figure 1.16 Overloaded methods are resolved during compilation.

For the overloaded method `bookTicket()` that defines the method parameter of either `Engineer` or `CEO`, watch out for exam questions that try to call it using a reference variable of `Employee`:

```
class Employee {}
class Engineer extends Employee {}
class CEO extends Employee {}
class Travel {
    static String bookTicket(Engineer val) {          Accepts
        return "economy class";                       Engineer
    }
    static String bookTicket(CEO val) {          Accepts CEO
        return "business class";
    }
    public static void main(String args[]) {          Won't compile—Travel
        Employee emp = new CEO();                      doesn't define method
        System.out.println(bookTicket(emp));           that accepts Employee
    }
}
```

CHANGE IN THE POSITIONS OF METHOD PARAMETERS

The methods are correctly overloaded if they only change the positions of the parameters that are passed to them, as follows:

```
double calcAverage(double marks1, int marks2) {          Arguments—
    return (marks1 + marks2)/2;                           double and int
}
double calcAverage(int marks1, double marks2) {          Arguments—
    return (marks1 + marks2)/2;                           int and double
}
```

Although you might argue that the arguments being accepted are the same, with only a difference in their positions, the Java compiler treats them as different argument lists. Therefore, the previous code is a valid example of overloaded methods. But an issue arises when you try to execute this method using values that can be passed to both versions of the overloaded method. In this case, the code in method `main()` will fail to compile:

```
class MyClass {                                               ❶ Method
    static double calcAverage(double marks1, int marks2) {      parameters—
        return(marks1 + marks2)/2;                              double and int
    }
    static double calcAverage(int marks1, double marks2) {    ❷ Method
        return(marks1 + marks2)/2;                              parameters—
    }                                                           int and double
    public static void main(String[] args) {              ❸ Compiler can't determine
        calcAverage(2, 3);                                   overloaded calcAverage()
    }                                                        that should be called
}
```

In the previous code, ❶ defines the `calcAverage()` method, which accepts two method parameters: a `double` and an `int`. The code at ❷ defines overloaded method calcAverage(), which accepts two method parameters: first an int and then a double. Because an int literal value can be passed to a variable of type double, literal values 2 and 3 can be passed to both overloaded methods, declared at ❶ and ❷. Because this *method call* is dubious, the code at ❸ fails to compile, with the following message:

```
MyClass.java:10: error: reference to calcAverage is ambiguous, both method
calcAverage(double,int) in MyClass and method calcAverage(int,double) in
MyClass match
            calcAverage(2, 3);
        ^

1 error
```

 EXAM TIP For primitive method arguments, if a *call* to an overloaded method is dubious, the code won't compile.

Here's an interesting question: Would an overloaded method with the following signature solve this specific problem?

```
static double calcAverage(int marks1, int marks2)
```

Yes, it will. Because the type of literal integer value is int, the compiler will be able to resolve the call calcAverage(2, 3) to calcAverage(int marks1, int marks2) and compile successfully.

1.2.2 *When methods can't be defined as overloaded methods*

The overloaded methods give you the flexibility of defining methods with the same name that can be passed a different set of arguments. But it doesn't make sense to define overloaded methods with a difference in only their return types or access or nonaccess modifiers.

RETURN TYPE

Methods can't be defined as overloaded methods if they only differ in their return types, as follows:

```
class Result {
    double calcAverage(int marks1, int marks2) {        ◁──┐ Return type of
        return (marks1 + marks2)/2;                          calcAverage() is double
    }
    int calcAverage(int marks1, int marks2) {           ◁──┐ Return type of
        return (marks1 + marks2)/2;                          calcAverage() is int
    }
}
```

The methods defined in the preceding code aren't correctly overloaded methods—they won't compile.

 EXAM TIP When the Java compiler differentiates methods, it doesn't consider their return types. So you can't define overloaded methods with the same parameter list and different return types.

ACCESS MODIFIER

Methods can't be defined as overloaded methods if they only differ in their access modifiers, as follows:

```
class Result {
    public double calcAverage(int marks1, int marks2) {        ⟵┐  Access—public
        return (marks1 + marks2)/2;
    }
    protected double calcAverage(int marks1, int marks2) {     ⟵┐  Access—protected
        return (marks1 + marks2)/2;
    }
}
```

NONACCESS MODIFIER

Methods can't be defined as overloaded methods if they only differ in their nonaccess modifiers, as follows:

```
class Result {
    public synchronized double calcAverage(int marks1, int marks2) {   ⟵┐  Nonaccess
        return (marks1 + marks2)/2;                                         modifier—
    }                                                                       synchronized
    public final double calcAverage(int marks1, int marks2) {          ⟵┐  Nonaccess
        return (marks1 + marks2)/2;                                         modifier—
    }                                                                       final
}
```

Let's revisit the rules for defining overloaded methods.

Rules to remember for defining overloaded methods

Here's a quick list of rules to remember for the exam for defining and using overloaded methods:

- A class can overload its own methods and methods inherited from its base class.
- Overloaded methods must be defined with the same name.
- Overloaded methods must be defined with different parameter lists.
- Overloaded methods might define a different return type or access or nonaccess modifier, but they can't be defined with only a change in their return types or access or nonaccess modifiers.

In the next section, we'll create overloaded versions of special methods, called *constructors*, which are used to create objects of a class.

1.2.3 Overloaded constructors

While creating instances of a class, you might need to assign default values to some of its variables and assign explicit values to the rest. You can do so by overloading the constructors. *Overloaded constructors* follow the same rules as discussed in the previous section on overloaded methods:

- Overloaded constructors must be defined using a different argument list.
- Overloaded constructors can't be defined by a mere change in their access modifiers.

 EXAM TIP   Watch out for exam questions that use nonaccess modifiers with constructors.

Using nonaccess modifiers with constructors is illegal—the code won't compile. Here's an example of class `Employee`, which defines four overloaded constructors:

```
class Employee {
    String name;
    int age;                                    ❶ No-argument
    Employee() {                                   constructor
        name = "John";
        age = 25;                               ❷ Constructor with one
    }                                              String argument
    Employee(String newName) {
        name = newName;
        age = 25;                               ❸ Constructor with
    }                                              two arguments—
    Employee(int newAge, String newName) {         int and String
        name = newName;
        age = newAge;                           ❹ Constructor with
    }                                              two arguments—
    Employee(String newName, int newAge) {         String and int
        name = newName;
        age = newAge;
    }
}
```

In the previous code, the code at ❶ defines a constructor that doesn't accept any arguments, and the code at ❷ defines another constructor that accepts a single argument. Note the constructors defined at ❸ and ❹. Both of these accept two arguments, `String` and `int`. But the placement of these two arguments is different in ❸ and ❹, which is acceptable and valid for overloaded constructors and methods.

INVOKING AN OVERLOADED CONSTRUCTOR FROM ANOTHER CONSTRUCTOR

It's common to define multiple constructors in a class. Unlike overloaded methods, which can be invoked using the name of a method, overloaded constructors are invoked by using the keyword `this`—an implicit reference, accessible to an object, to refer to itself. For instance

```
class Employee {
    String name;                                ❶ No-argument
    int age;                                       constructor
    Employee() {
        this(null, 0);                          ❷ Invokes constructor that
    }                                              accepts two arguments
```

```
    Employee(String newName, int newAge) {
        name = newName;                        ❸ Constructor
        age = newAge;                            that accepts
    }                                            two arguments
}
```

The code at ❶ defines a no-argument constructor. At ❷, this constructor calls the overloaded constructor by passing to it values null and 0. ❸ defines an overloaded constructor that accepts two arguments.

Because a constructor is defined using the name of its class, it's a common mistake to try to invoke a constructor from another constructor using the class's name:

```
class Employee {
    String name;
    int age;
    Employee() {
        Employee(null, 0);        ◁─  Won't compile—you can't
    }                                 invoke a constructor within a
    Employee(String newName, int newAge) {   class by using the class's name.
        name = newName;
        age = newAge;
    }
}
```

Also, when you invoke an overloaded constructor using the keyword this, it must be the first statement in your constructor:

```
class Employee {
    String name;
    int age;
    Employee() {
        System.out.println("No-argument constructor");  ◁─  Won't compile—call to
        this(null, 0);                                        overloaded constructor
    }                                                         must be first statement
    Employee(String newName, int newAge) {                    in constructor.
        name = newName;
        age = newAge;
    }
}
```

That's not all: you can't call a constructor from any other method in your class. None of the other methods of class Employee can invoke its constructor.

Rules to remember for defining overloaded constructors

Here's a quick list of rules to remember for the exam for defining and using overloaded constructors:

- Overloaded constructors must be defined using different argument lists.
- Overloaded constructors can't be defined by just a change in the access modifiers.
- Overloaded constructors can be defined using different access modifiers.

(continued)
- A constructor can call another overloaded constructor by using the keyword `this`.
- A constructor can't invoke a constructor by using its class's name.
- If present, the call to another constructor must be the first statement in a constructor.

INSTANCE INITIALIZERS

Apart from constructors, you can also define an *instance initializer* to initialize the instance variables of your class. An instance initializer is a code block defined within a class, using a pair of { }. You can define multiple instance initializers in your class. *Each* instance initializer is invoked when an instance is created, in the order they're defined in a class. They're invoked before a class constructor is invoked.

Why do you think you need an instance initializer if you can initialize your instances using constructors? Multiple reasons exist:

- For a big class, it makes sense to place the variable initialization just after its declaration.
- *All* the initializers are invoked, irrespective of the constructor that's used to instantiate an object.
- Initializers can be used to initialize variables of anonymous classes that can't define constructors. (You'll work with anonymous classes in the next chapter.)

Here's a simple example:

```java
class Pencil {
    public Pencil() {
        System.out.println("Pencil:constructor");
    }
    public Pencil(String a) {
        System.out.println("Pencil:constructor2");
    }
    {
        System.out.println("Pencil:init1");      ◁──  Added to both
    }                                                  overloaded
    {                                                  constructors
        System.out.println("Pencil:init2");      ◁──
    }
    public static void main(String[] args) {
        new Pencil();
        new Pencil("aValue");
    }
}
```

The output of the preceding code is

```
Pencil:init1
Pencil:init2
Pencil:constructor
```

```
Pencil:init1
Pencil:init2
Pencil:constructor2
```

The next "Twist in the Tale" exercise hides an important concept within its code, which you can get to know only if you try to compile and execute the modified code.

Let's modify the definition of class `Employee` used in the section on overloaded constructors as follows:

```
class Employee {
    String name;
    int age;
    Employee() {
        this("Shreya", 10);
    }
    Employee (String newName, int newAge) {
        this();
        name = newName;
        age = newAge;
    }
    void print(){
        print(age);
    }
    void print(int age) {
        print();
    }
}
```

What is the output of this modified code, and why?

The instance initializer blocks are executed after an implicit or explicit call to the parent class's constructor:

```
class Instrument {
    Instrument() {
        System.out.println("Instrument:constructor");
    }
}
class Pencil extends Instrument {
    public Pencil() {
        System.out.println("Pencil:constructor");
    }
    {
        System.out.println("Pencil:instance initializer");
    }
    public static void main(String[] args) {
        new Pencil();
    }
}
```

Figure 1.17   The order of execution of constructors and instance initializers in parent and child classes

The output of the preceding code is

```
Instrument:constructor
Pencil:instance initializer
Pencil:constructor
```

Figure 1.17 shows a fun way of remembering the order of execution of a parent class constructor, instance initializers, and a class constructor. Paul, our programmer, was having a very hard time remembering the order of execution of all these code blocks. He literally had to stand upside down to get the order right.

 EXAM TIP   If a parent or child class defines static initializer block(s), they execute before all parent and child class constructors and instance initializers—first for the parent and then for the child class.

Now that you've seen how to create the overloaded variants of methods and constructors, let's dive deep into method overriding. These two concepts, overloading and overriding, seem to be confusing for a lot of programmers. Let's get started by clearing the cobwebs.

1.3   *Method overriding and virtual method invocation*

[1.2]   Override methods

[1.5]   Use virtual method invocation

Do you celebrate a festival or an event in exactly the same manner as celebrated by your parents? Or have you modified it? Perhaps you celebrate the same festivals and events, but in your *own* unique manner. In a similar manner, classes can inherit behavior from other classes. But they can redefine the behavior that they inherit—this is also referred to as *method overriding*.

Method overriding is an object-oriented programming (OOP) language feature that enables a derived class to define a specific implementation of an existing base class method to extend its own behavior. A derived class can *override* an instance method defined in a base class by defining an instance method with the same method signature/method name and number and types of method parameters. Overridden methods are also synonymous with *polymorphic methods*. The *static* methods of a base can't be overridden, but they can be *hidden* by defining methods with the same signature in the derived class.

A method that can be overridden by a derived class is called a *virtual method*. But beware: Java has always shied away from using the term *virtual methods* and you will not find a mention of this term in Java's vocabulary. This term is used in other OO languages like C and C++. *Virtual method invocation* is the invocation of the correct overridden method, which is based on the type of the object referred to by an object reference and not by the object reference itself. It's determined at runtime, not at compilation time.

The exam will question you on the need for overridden methods; the correct syntax of overridden methods; the differences between overloaded, overridden, and hidden methods; common mistakes while overriding methods; and virtual method invocation. Let's get started with the need for overridden methods.

 NOTE   A base class method is referred to as the *overridden method* and the derived class method is referred to as the *overriding method*.

1.3.1 *Need of overridden methods*

In the same way we inherit our parents' behaviors but redefine some of the inherited behavior to suit our own needs, a derived class can inherit the behavior and properties of its base class but still be different in its own manner—by defining new variables and methods. A derived class can also choose to define a different course of action for its base class method by overriding it. Here's an example of class Book, which defines a method issueBook() that accepts days as a method parameter:

```
class Book {
    void issueBook(int days) {
        if (days > 0)
            System.out.println("Book issued");
        else
            System.out.println("Cannot issue for 0 or less days");
    }
}
```

Following is another class, CourseBook, which inherits class Book. This class needs to override method issueBook() because a CourseBook can't be issued if it's only for reference. Also, a `CourseBook` can't be issued for 14 or more days. Let's see how this is accomplished by overriding method `issueBook()`:

```java
class CourseBook extends Book {
    boolean onlyForReference;
    CourseBook(boolean val) {
        onlyForReference = val;
    }
    @Override                                          Annotation—
    void issueBook(int days) {                     ❶  @Override
        if (onlyForReference)
            System.out.println("Reference book");      Overrides issueBook()
        else                                       ❷  in base class Book
            if (days < 14)
                super.issueBook(days);                 Calls issueBook()
            else                                   ❸  defined in Book
                System.out.println("days >= 14");
    }
}
```

The code at ❶ uses the annotation `@Override`, which notifies the compiler that this method overrides a base class method. Though optional, this annotation can come in very handy if you try to override a method incorrectly. The code at ❷ defines method `issueBook()` with the same name and method parameters as defined in class `Book`. The code at ❸ calls method `issueBook()` defined in class `Book`; however, it isn't mandatory to do so. It depends on whether the derived class wants to execute the same code as defined by the base class.

 NOTE Whenever you intend to override methods in a derived class, use the annotation `@Override`. It will warn you if a method can't be overridden or if you're actually overloading a method rather than overriding it.

The following example can be used to test the preceding code:

```java
class BookExample  {
    public static void main(String[] args) {       Prints "Reference
        Book b = new CourseBook(true);             book"
        b.issueBook(100);
        b = new CourseBook(false);                 Prints "days
        b.issueBook(100);                          >= 14"
        b = new Book();
        b.issueBook(100);        Prints "Book      b now refers to
    }                            issued"           a Book instance
}
```

Figure 1.18 represents the compilation and execution process of class `BookExample`, as Step 1 and Step 2:

- Step 1: The compile time uses the reference type for the method check.
- Step 2: The runtime uses the instance type for the method invocation.

Now let's move on to how to correctly override a base class method in a derived class.

Step 1

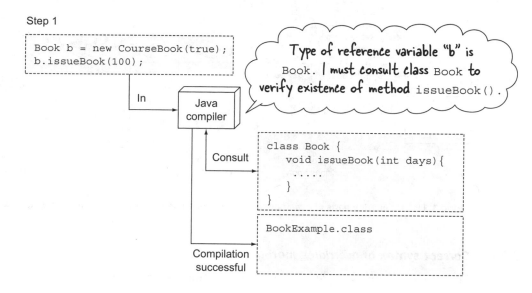

Step 2

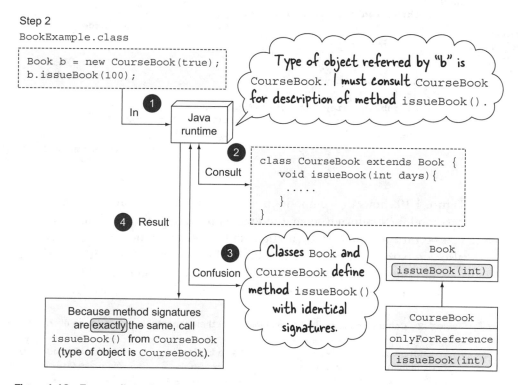

Figure 1.18 To compile `b.issueBook()`, the compiler refers only to the definition of class `Book`. To execute `b.issueBook()`, the Java Runtime Environment (JRE) uses the actual method implementation of `issueBook()` from class `CourseBook`.

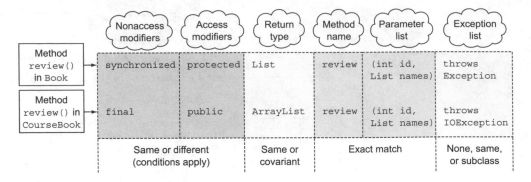

Figure 1.19   Comparing parts of a method declaration for a base class method and overriding method

1.3.2   *Correct syntax of overriding methods*

Let's start with an example of overridden method review(), as follows:

```
class Book {
    synchronized protected List review(int id,
                                        List names) throws Exception {
        return null;
    }
}
class CourseBook extends Book {
    @Override
    final public ArrayList review(int id,
                                   List names) throws IOException {
        return null;
    }
}
```

Method review() in base class Book

CourseBook extends Book

Overridden method review() in derived class CourseBook

Figure 1.19 shows the components of a method declaration: access modifiers, nonaccess modifiers, return type, method name, parameter list, and a list of exceptions that can be thrown (method declaration isn't the same as method signature). The figure also compares the review method defined in base class Book with overriding method review() defined in class CourseBook with respect to these identified parts.

Table 1.2 compares the method components shown in figure 1.19.

Table 1.2   Comparison of method components and their acceptable values for an overriding method

Method component	Value in class Book	Value in class CourseBook	Overriding method review() in class CourseBook
Access modifier	protected	public	Define same access or less restrictive access than method review() in the base class.

Table 1.2 Comparison of method components and their acceptable values for an overriding method

Method component	Value in class Book	Value in class CourseBook	Overriding method `review()` in class CourseBook
Nonaccess modifier	`synchronized`	`final`	Overriding method can use any nonaccess modifier for an overridden method. A nonabstract method can also be overridden to an abstract method. But a final method in the base class cannot be overridden. A static method cannot be overridden to be nonstatic.
Return type	`List`	`ArrayList`	Define the same or a subtype of the return type used in the base class method (covariant return types).
Method name	`review`	`review`	Exact match.
Parameter list	`(int id, List names)`	`(int id, List names)`	Exact match.
Exceptions thrown	`throws Exception`	`throws IOException`	Throw none, same, or a subclass of the exception thrown by the base class method.

EXAM TIP The rule listed in table 1.2 on exceptions in overriding methods only applies to checked exceptions. An overriding method can throw any unchecked exception (`RuntimeException` or `Error`) even if the overridden method doesn't. The unchecked exceptions aren't part of the method signature and aren't checked by the compiler.

Chapter 6 includes a detailed explanation on overridden and overriding methods that throw exceptions. Let's walk through a couple of invalid combinations that are important and very likely to be on the exam.

NOTE Though a best practice, I've deliberately not preceded the definition of the overriding methods with the annotation `@Override` because you might not see it on the exam.

ACCESS MODIFIERS

A derived class can assign the same or more access but not a weaker access to the overriding method in the derived class:

```
class Book {
    protected void review(int id, List names) {}
}
class CourseBook extends Book {
    void review(int id, List names) {}
}
```

Won't compile; overriding methods in derived classes can't use a weaker access.

NONACCESS MODIFIERS

A derived class can't override a base class method marked `final`:

```
class Book {
    final void review(int id, List names) {}
}
class CourseBook extends Book {
    void review(int id, List names) {}
}
```

Won't compile; final
methods can't be
overridden.

ARGUMENT LIST AND COVARIANT RETURN TYPES

When the overriding method returns a subclass of the return type of the overridden method, it's known as a *covariant return type*. To override a method, the parameter list of the methods in the base and derived classes must be *exactly* the same. It you try to use covariant types in the argument list, you'll end up overloading the methods and not overriding them. For example

```
class Book {
    void review(int id, List names) throws Exception {
        System.out.println("Base:review");
    }
}
class CourseBook extends Book {
    void review(int id, ArrayList names) throws IOException {
        System.out.println("Derived:review");
    }
}
```

❶ Argument list—
int and List

Argument
list—int and
ArrayList

At ❶ method `review()` in base class `Book` accepts an object of type `List`. Method `review()` in derived class `CourseBook` accepts a subtype `ArrayList` (`ArrayList` implements `List`). These methods aren't overridden—they're overloaded:

```
class Verify {
    public static void main(String[] args)throws Exception {
        Book book = new CourseBook();
        book.review(1, null);
    }
}
```

Calls review in
Book; prints
"Base:review"

Reference variable
of type Book used
to refer to object
❶ CourseBook.

The code at ❶ uses a reference variable of type `Book` to refer to an object of type `CourseBook`. The compilation process assigns execution of method `review()` from base class `Book` to the reference variable `book`. Because method `review()` in class `CourseBook` *doesn't* override the review method in class `Book`, the JRE doesn't have any confusion regarding whether to call method `review()` from class `Book` or from class `CourseBook`. It moves forward with calling `review()` from `Book`.

 EXAM TIP It's the reference variable type that dictates which overloaded method will be chosen. This choice is made at compilation time.

EXCEPTIONS THROWN

An overriding method must either declare to throw no exception, the same exception, or a subtype of the exception declared to be thrown by the base class method, or else it will fail to compile. This rule, however, doesn't apply to error classes or runtime exceptions. For example

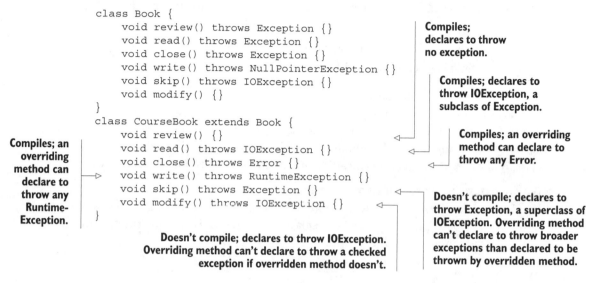

```
class Book {
    void review() throws Exception {}
    void read() throws Exception {}
    void close() throws Exception {}
    void write() throws NullPointerException {}
    void skip() throws IOException {}
    void modify() {}
}
class CourseBook extends Book {
    void review() {}
    void read() throws IOException {}
    void close() throws Error {}
    void write() throws RuntimeException {}
    void skip() throws Exception {}
    void modify() throws IOException {}
}
```

Compiles; declares to throw no exception.

Compiles; declares to throw IOException, a subclass of Exception.

Compiles; an overriding method can declare to throw any Error.

Compiles; an overriding method can declare to throw any Runtime-Exception.

Doesn't compile; declares to throw Exception, a superclass of IOException. Overriding method can't declare to throw broader exceptions than declared to be thrown by overridden method.

Doesn't compile; declares to throw IOException. Overriding method can't declare to throw a checked exception if overridden method doesn't.

 EXAM TIP   An overriding method can declare to throw *any* `RuntimeException` or `Error`, even if the overridden method doesn't.

To remember this preceding point, let's compare exceptions with monsters. Figure 1.20 shows a fun way to remember the exceptions (monsters) that can be on the list of an

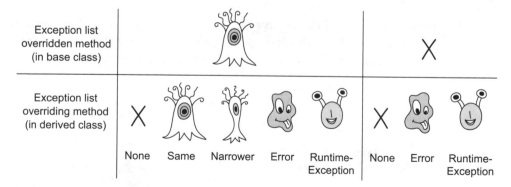

Figure 1.20   Comparing exceptions to monsters. When an overridden method declares to throw a checked exception (monster), the overriding method can declare to throw none, the same, or a narrower checked exception. An overriding method can declare to throw any `Error` or `RuntimeException`.

overriding method, when the overridden method doesn't declare to throw a checked exception and when it declares to throw a checked exception.

1.3.3 *Can you override all methods from the base class or invoke them virtually?*

The simple answer is no. You can override only the following methods from the base class:

- Methods accessible to a derived class
- Nonstatic base class methods

METHODS ACCESSIBLE TO A BASE CLASS
The accessibility of a method in a derived class depends on its access modifier. For example, a private method defined in a base class isn't available to any of its derived classes. Also, a method with default access in a base class isn't available to a derived class in another package. A class can't override the methods that it can't access.

ONLY NONSTATIC METHODS CAN BE OVERRIDDEN
If a derived class defines a static method with the same name and signature as the one defined in its base class, it *hides* its base class method and *doesn't* override it. You can't override static methods. For example

```
class Book {
    static void printName() {              Static method
        System.out.println("Book");        in base class
    }
}
class CourseBook extends Book {
    static void printName() {              Static method
        System.out.println("CourseBook");  in derived class
    }
}
```

Method `printName()` in class `CourseBook` hides `printName()` in class `Book`. It doesn't override it. Because the static methods are bound at compile time, the method `print-Name()` that's called depends on the type of the reference variable:

```
class BookExampleStaticMethod  {
    public static void main(String[] args) {
        Book base = new Book();                    Prints
        base.printName();                          "Book"

        Book derived = new CourseBook();
        derived.printName();                       Prints
    }                                              "Book"
}
```

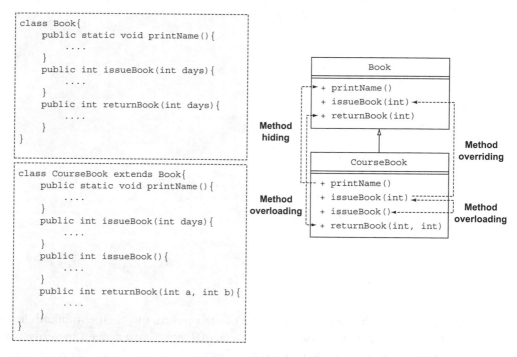

Figure 1.21 Identifying method overriding, method overloading, and method hiding in a base and derived class

1.3.4 Identifying method overriding, overloading, and hiding

It's easy to get confused with method overriding, overloading, and hiding. Figure 1.21 identifies these methods in classes `Book` and `CourseBook`. On the left are the class definitions, and on the right their UML representations.

 EXAM TIP When a class extends another class, it can overload, override, or hide its base class methods. A class can't override or hide its own methods—it can only overload its own methods.

Let's check out the correct code for defining a static or nonstatic method in a derived class that overrides or hides a static or nonstatic method in a base class using the next "Twist in the Tale" exercise.

Twist in the Tale 1.3

Let's modify the code of classes `Book` and `CourseBook` and define multiple combinations of static and nonstatic method `print()` in both these classes as follows:

```
a   class Book{
        static void print(){}
    }
```

```
         class CourseBook extends Book{
             static void print(){}
         }
    b    class Book{
             static void print(){}
         }
         class CourseBook extends Book{
             void print(){}
         }
    c    class Book{
             void print(){}
         }
         class CourseBook extends Book{
             static void print(){}
         }
    d    class Book{
             void print(){}
         }
         class CourseBook extends Book{
             void print(){}
         }
```

Your task is to first tag them with one of the options and then compile them on your system to see if they're correct. On the actual exam, you'll need to verify (without a compiler) if a code snippet compiles or not:

- Overridden print() method
- Hidden print() method
- Compilation error

1.3.5   Can you override base class constructors or invoke them virtually?

The simple answer is no. Constructors aren't inherited by a derived class. Because only inherited methods can be overridden, constructors cannot be overridden by a derived class. If you attempt an exam question that queries you on overriding a base class constructor, you know that it's trying to trick you.

 EXAM TIP Constructors can't be overridden because a base class constructor isn't inherited by a derived class.

Now that you know why and how to override methods in your own classes, let's see in the next section why it's important to override the methods of class java.lang.Object.

1.4 Overriding methods of class Object

[1.6]   Override methods from the Object class to improve the functionality of your class

All the classes in java—classes from the Java API, user-defined classes, or classes from any other API—extend class java.lang.Object, either implicitly or explicitly. Because this section talks about overriding the methods from class Object, let's take a look at its nonfinal and final methods in figure 1.22.

You might write a Java class to be used in your small in-house project or a commercial project, or it could be a part of a library that may be released to be used by other programmers. As you have less control over who uses your class and how it's used, the importance of correctly overriding methods from class Object rises. It's important to override the nonfinal Object class methods so that these classes can be used efficiently by other users. Apart from being able to be used as desired, incorrect overriding of these methods can also result in increased debug time.

Because the final methods can't be overridden, I'll discuss the nonfinal methods of class Object in this section. These methods—clone(), equals(), hashCode(), toString(), and finalize()—define a contract, a set of rules on how to override these methods, specified by the Java API documentation.

1.4.1 Overriding method toString()

Method toString() is called when you try to print out the value of a reference variable or use a reference variable in a concatenation operator. The default implementation of method toString() returns the name of the class, followed by @ and the hash

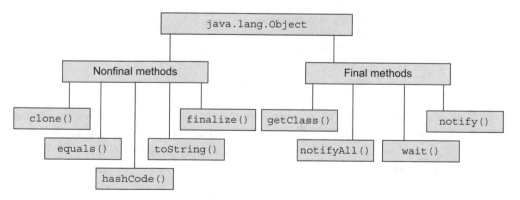

Figure 1.22   Categorization of final and nonfinal methods of class java.lang.Object

code of the object it represents. Following is the code of method toString(), as defined in class Object in the Java API:

**toString() as
defined in
java.lang.Object**

```
public String toString() {
    return getClass().getName() + "@" + Integer.toHexString(hashCode());
}
```

Following is an example of class Book, which doesn't override method toString(). In this case, a request to print the reference variable of this class will call method toString() defined in class Object:

```
class Book {
    String title;
}
class PrintBook {
    public static void main(String[] args) {
        Book b = new Book();
        System.out.println(b);          ←⎯| Prints a value similar
    }                                       to Book@45a877
}
```

Let's override method toString() in class Book. The contract of method toString() specifies that it should return a *concise* but *informative* textual representation of the object that it represents. This is usually accomplished by using the value of the instance variables of an object:

```
class Book {
    String title;
    @Override                             ⎯| toString() uses title
    public String toString() {     ←⎯|    to represent Book
        return title;
    }
}
class Test {
    public static void main(String[] args) {
        Book b = new Book();
        b.title = "Java Certification";   ⎯| Prints book title,
        System.out.println(b);     ←⎯|    "Java Certification"
    }
}
```

If a class defines a lot of instance variables, method toString() *might* include only the important ones—that is, the ones that provide its concise description. In the following example, class Book defines multiple instance variables and uses a few of them in method toString():

```
class Book {
    String title;           ⎯| Instance
    String isbn;               variables to
    String[] author;          store a Book's
    java.util.Date publishDate;  ↓ state
```

```
                    double price;
                    int version;                          Instance variables
                    String publisher;                     to store a Book's
                    boolean eBookReady;                   state
                    @Override
                    public String toString() {
                        return title + ", ISBN:"+isbn + ", Lead Author:"+author[0];
                    }
                }
                class Test {
                    public static void main(String[] args) {
                        Book b = new Book();
                        b.title = "Java Smart Apps";
                        b.author = new String[]{"Paul", "Larry"};    Prints "Java Smart
                        b.isbn = "9810-9643-987";                    Apps, ISBN:9810-9643-
                        System.out.println(b);                       987, Lead Author:Paul"
                    }
                }
```

In the left margin:

toString uses title, isbn, and the first element of array author to describe a Book.

You have overridden method `toString()` inappropriately if it returns any text that's specific to a particular class, for example, the name of a class or a value of a static variable:

```
class Book {
    String title;
    static int bookCopies = 1000;
    @Override
    public String toString() {
        return title + ", Copies:" + bookCopies;      ❶ Overridden
    }                                                     toString() uses static
}                                                         variable of Book.
class CourseBook extends Book {
    static int bookCopies = 99999;                    Static variable
}                                                     bookCopies also
class BookOverrideToString {                       ❷ defined in CourseBook
    public static void main(String[] args) {
        CourseBook b = new CourseBook();
        b.title = "Java Smart Apps";
        System.out.println(b);                        Prints "Java Smart
    }                                                ❸ Apps, Copies:1000"
}
```

In this code, ❶ shows inappropriate overriding of method `toString()` because it uses a static variable. The code at ❷ defines a static variable `bookCopies` in class Course-Book. Because static members are bound at compile time, method `toString()` will refer to the variable `bookCopies` defined in class `Book`, even if the object it refers to is of the type `CourseBook`. ❸ prints the value of the `static` variable defined in class `Book`.

Overriding methods of class `Object` is an important concept. Let it sink in. The next "Twist in the Tale" exercise will ensure that you get the hang of correct overriding of method `toString()`, before moving on to the next section.

Twist in the Tale 1.4

Which of the following classes—Book1, Book2, Book3, or Book4—shows an appropriate overridden method toString()?

```java
class Book1 {
    String title;
    int copies = 1000;
    public String toString() {
        return "Class Book, Title: " + title;
    }
}
class Book2 {
    String title;
    int copies = 1000;
    public String toString() {
        return ""+copies * 11;
    }
}
class Book3 {
    String title;
    int copies = 1000;
    public String toString() {
        return title;
    }
}
class Book4 {
    String title;
    int copies = 1000;
    public String toString() {
        return getClass().getName() + ":" + title;
    }
}
```

1.4.2   Overriding method equals()

Method equals() is used to determine whether two objects of a class should be considered equal or not. Figure 1.23 shows a conversation between two objects, wondering whether they're equal or not.

Figure 1.23 Applying a twist on Shakespeare's quote: "Equal or not equal, that is the question." Method equals() returns a boolean value that determines whether two objects should be considered equal or not.

The default implementation of method `equals()` in class `Object` compares the object references and returns `true` if both reference variables refer to the same object, or `false` otherwise. In essence, it only returns `true` if an object is compared to itself. Following is the default implementation of method `equals()` in class `java.lang.Object`:

```
public boolean equals(Object obj) {
    return (this == obj);
}
```

The exam will question you on the following points:

- The need to override method `equals()`
- Overriding method `equals()` correctly
- Overriding method `equals()` incorrectly

THE NEED TO OVERRIDE METHOD EQUALS()

You need to override method `equals()` for objects that you wish to *equate logically*, which normally depends on the state of an object (that is, the value of its instance variables). The goal of overriding method `equals()` is to check for *equality* of the objects, not to check for the *same* variable references. For two objects of the same class, say, `object1` and `object2`, `equals()` checks whether `object1` is *logically* equal to `object2`, but `object1` isn't necessarily pointing to the *exact same object* as `object2`.

For example, class `String` overrides method `equals()` to check whether two `String` objects define the exact same sequence of characters:

```
String name1 = "Harry";
String name2 = new String ("Harry");         |  Prints
System.out.println(name1.equals(name2));    ◁─┘  "true"
```

In the preceding code, `name1` and `name2` refer to separate `String` objects but define the exact same sequence of characters—`"Harry"`. So `name1.equals(name2)` returns `true`.

AN EXAMPLE

You might need to find out whether the same undergraduate course is or is not offered by multiple universities. In an application, you can represent a university using a class, say, `University`, and each course being offered using a class, say, `Course`. Assuming that each university offers a list of courses, you can override method `equals()` in class `Course` to determine if two `Course` objects can be considered equal, as follows:

```
class Course {
    String title;
    int duration;
    public boolean equals(Object o) {
        if (o != null && o instanceof Course) {
            Course c = (Course)o;
            return (title.equals(c.title) && duration==c.duration);
        }
        else
            return false;
    }
}
```

RULES FOR OVERRIDING METHOD EQUALS()

Method equals() defines an elaborate contract (set of rules), as follows (straight from the Java API documentation):

1 It's *reflexive*—For any non-null reference value x, x.equals(x) should return true. This rule states that an object should be equal to itself, which is reasonable.

2 It's *symmetric*—For any non-null reference values x and y, x.equals(y) should return true if and only if y.equals(x) returns true. This rule states that two objects should be comparable to each other in the same way.

3 It's *transitive*—For any non-null reference values x, y, and z, if x.equals(y) returns true and y.equals(z) returns true, then x.equals(z) should return true. This rule states that while comparing objects, you shouldn't selectively compare the values based on the type of an object.

4 It's *consistent*—For any non-null reference values x and y, multiple invocations of x.equals(y) consistently return true or consistently return false, provided no information used in equals comparisons on the objects is modified. This rule states that method equals() should rely on the value of instance variables that can be accessed from the memory and shouldn't try to rely on values like the IP address of a system, which may be assigned a separate value upon reconnection to a network.

5 For any non-null reference value x, x.equals(null) should return false. This rule states that a non-null object can never be equal to null.

Quite a lot of rules to remember! Let's use an interesting way to remember all these rules, by comparing equals() to *love*. So when you see "x.equals(x)," read it as "x.loves(x)." Read "if x.equals(y) returns true, y.equals(x) must return true" as "if x loves y, y loves x." All these rules are shown in figure 1.24. They'll make more sense when you cover them using these examples.

CORRECT AND INCORRECT OVERRIDING OF METHOD EQUALS()

To override method toString() correctly, follow the method overriding rules defined in section 1.3. Note that the type of parameter passed to equals() is Object. Watch out for exam questions that *seem to* override equals(), passing it to a parameter type of the class in which it's defined. In the following example, class Course doesn't *override* method equals(), it *overloads* it:

```
class Course {
    String title;
    Course(String title) {
        this.title = title;
    }
    public boolean equals(Course o) {          ⟵  Course doesn't override
        return title.equals(o.title);               toString(), it overloads it.
    }
    public static void main(String args[]) {
        Object c1 = new Course("eJava");
        Object c2 = new Course("eJava");
        System.out.println(c1.equals(c2));     ⟵  Prints
    }                                               "false"
}
```

Figure 1.24   A fun way to remember all the rules of the `equals()` **contract by comparing** `equals()` **with** *love*.

EXAM TIP   Use `Object` as the parameter type to `equals()`. Using any other type will *overload* `equals()`.

APPROPRIATE AND INAPPROPRIATE OVERRIDING OF METHOD EQUALS()

If you don't follow the contract of method `equals()` while overriding it in your classes, you'll be overriding it inappropriately. An inappropriately overridden method `equals()` doesn't mean compilation failure.

 EXAM TIP   An inappropriately overridden method `equals()` doesn't mean compilation failure.

In the following code, class `Course` doesn't comply with the symmetric and reflexive rules while overriding method `equals()`. Class `University` shows how these rules aren't adhered to:

```
class Course {
    String title;
    Course(String title) {
        this.title = title;
    }
    public boolean equals(Object o) {        Compares title of
        return (title.equals(o));            course with object
    }                                         passed to equals
}
class University {
    public static void main(String[] args) {          ❶ Shows violation of
        Course c1 = new Course("level1");               symmetric rule—
        String s1 = "level1";                           c1.equals(s1) prints
        System.out.println(c1.equals(s1));              "true" but s1.equals(c1)
        System.out.println(s1.equals(c1));              prints "false"

        System.out.println(c1.equals(c1));      Shows violation of reflexive rule—
    }                                         ❷ c1.equals(c1) prints "false"
}
```

The code at ❶ prints `true` for `c1.equals(s1)` and `false` for `s1.equals(c1)`, which is a clear violation of `equals()`'s symmetric contract, which states that for any non-null reference values x and y, `x.equals(y)` should print `true` if and only if `y.equals(x)` returns true. The `Course` object will not evaluate to `true` in `String`'s method `equals()` because `equals()` in `String` first verifies if the object being compared to it is a `String` object *before* checking to see if their character sequence is the same. At ❷, `c1.equals(c1)` prints `false`, violating the reflexive rule that states that an object should be equal to itself.

Let's work with another example, where class `JavaCourse` violates the *transitive* rule while overriding method `equals()`. Class `JavaCourse` extends class `Course` and defines method `equals()`, which compares its object to both an object of `Course` and `JavaCourse`. Method `equals()` compares the common attributes, if the object being compared is that of the base class `Course`. It also compares all the attributes, if the object being compared is of class `JavaCourse`:

```
class Course {
    String title;
    Course(String title) {
        this.title = title;
    }
    public boolean equals(Object o) {
        if (o instanceof Course) {
            Course c = (Course)o;
            return (title.equals(c.title));
        }
        else
            return false;
    }
}
class JavaCourse extends Course {
    int duration = 0;
    JavaCourse(String title, int duration) {
        super(title);
        this.duration = duration;
    }
    public boolean equals(Object o) {
        if (o instanceof JavaCourse) {
            return (super.equals(o) &&
                    ((JavaCourse)o).duration == duration);
        }
        else if(o instanceof Course) {
            return (super.equals(o));
        }
        else
            return false;
    }
}
```

In the following code for class `University2`, `c1` is equal to `c2` and `c2` is equal to `c3` because these comparisons only check the course `title`. But `c1` isn't equal to `c3` because the course durations aren't the same. Therefore, the overridden method `equals()` in class `JavaCourse` fails the *transitive* rule:

```
class University2 {
    public static void main(String[] args) {
        Course c1 = new JavaCourse("level1", 2);
        Course c2 = new Course("level1");
        Course c3 = new JavaCourse("level1", 12);

        System.out.println(c1.equals(c2));
        System.out.println(c2.equals(c3));
        System.out.println(c1.equals(c3));
    }
}
```

Inappropriate overriding of method `equals()` can result in bizarre behavior. Use of `equals()` by collection classes is explained in detail in chapter 4.

Figure 1.25   Methods `hashCode()` and `equals()` don't call each other.

1.4.3   *Overriding method hashCode()*

First, method `hashCode()` isn't called by method `equals()` or vice versa. The contract of methods `equals()` and `hashCode()` mentions that both these methods should be overridden if one of them is overridden. This makes a lot of programmers believe that perhaps these methods are called by each other, which isn't the case. Figure 1.25 shows a fun way to remember that methods `equals()` and `hashCode()` deny being in a relationship and calling each other.

THE NEED TO OVERRIDE METHOD HASHCODE()

Method `hashCode()` returns a hash-code value for an object, which is used to efficiently store and retrieve values in collection classes that use hashing algorithms, such as `HashMap`. Hashing algorithms identify the *buckets* in which they would store the objects and from which they would retrieve them. A well-written method `hashCode()` ensures that objects are evenly distributed in these buckets. Objects with the same hash-code values are stored in the same bucket. To retrieve an object, its bucket is identified using its hash-code value. If the bucket contains multiple objects, method `equals()` is used to find the target object.

To understand how this works, let's create a class called `MyNumber`, which contains a primitive `long` as its field. It returns a sum of all the individual digits of its field as its method `hashCode()`, as follows:

```
class MyNumber {
    long number;
    MyNumber(long number) {this.number = number;}
    public int hashCode() {
        int sum = 0;
        long num = number;
        do {
            sum += num % 10; num /= 10;
        }
        while( num != 0 );
        return sum;
    }
}
```

Let's assume you add the following keys and values in a HashMap:

```
Map<MyNumber, String> map = new HashMap<>();
MyNumber num1 = new MyNumber(1200);
MyNumber num2 = new MyNumber(2500);
MyNumber num3 = new MyNumber(57123);
map.put(num1, "John");
map.put(num2, "Mary");
map.put(num3, "Sam");
```

Hash-code value 3

Hash-code value 7

Hash-code value 18

With the preceding keys, each bucket contains only one entry. When you request the HashMap to retrieve a value, it would find the corresponding bucket using the key's hash-code value and then it retrieves the value. Now let's add another key-value pair:

```
MyNumber num4 = new MyNumber(57123);
map.put(num4, "Kim");
```

Hash-code value 18

Now the bucket with the hash-code value 18 has two String values. In this case, Hash-Map would use the hashCode() value to identify the bucket and then call method equals() to find the correct object. This explains why distinct hash-code values for distinct values are preferred.

 NOTE Chapter 4 explains in detail how the hashing algorithms in collection classes use methods hashCode() and equals().

OVERRIDING METHOD HASHCODE() CORRECTLY

Here's the signature of method hashCode() as defined in class Object:

```
public native int hashCode();
```

To correctly override method hashCode(), you must follow the rules already discussed in section 1.3. Watch out for exam questions that use the incorrect case for hash-Code()—the correct name uses uppercase C. Figure 1.26 shows a fun way to remember this simple, but important, exam point.

hashCode()

Figure 1.26 The correct case of hashCode() includes a capital C.

if `x.equals(y)==true`

`x.hashCode()==`
`y.hashCode()`
must be `true`

if `x.equals(y)==false`

`x.hashCode()` and
`y.hashCode()` can be
same or different

Figure 1.27 Comparing `equals()` with being in love and `hashCode()` with an address. If two objects are equal, they *must* return the same `hashCode()`. But if two objects return the same `hashCode()`, they *might not* be equal.

To override method `hashCode()` correctly, you must also abide by its contract, as mentioned in the Java documentation. For the exam, the following rules are important:

1 If two objects are equal according to method `equals(Object)`, then calling method `hashCode()` on each of the two objects must produce the same integer result.

2 It's not required that if two objects are unequal according to method `equals (java.lang.Object)`, that calling method `hashCode()` on each of the two objects must produce distinct integer results.

Let's use a fun analogy to remember these rules, as shown in figure 1.27. Let's compare method `equals()` to being in love and method `hashCode()` to a physical address. When two objects are in love with each other, they *must* reside at the same address (this is what they think *before* they marry). Later, if they fall out of love, they might or might not continue to reside at the same address.

Figure 1.27 will make more sense as you work with the code examples in this section. Let's revisit the previous example, including `equals()` and verifying the rules:

```
class MyNumber {
    long number;
    MyNumber(long number) {this.number = number;}
```

```
public int hashCode() {
    int sum = 0;
    long num = number;
    do {
        sum += num % 10; num /= 10;
    }
    while( num != 0 );
    return sum;
}
public boolean equals(Object o) {
    if (o != null && o instanceof MyNumber)
        return (number == ((MyNumber)o).number);
    else
        return false;
}
public static void main(String args[]) {
    MyNumber n1 = new MyNumber(9);
    MyNumber n2 = new MyNumber(18);
    MyNumber n3 = new MyNumber(18);
    System.out.println
        (n1.equals(n2)+":"+n1.hashCode()+":"+n2.hashCode());    ⊲──┘    Prints
                                                                        "false:9:9"
    System.out.println
        (n2.equals(n3)+":"+n2.hashCode()+":"+n3.hashCode());    ⊲──┐
}                                                                   Prints
}                                                                   "true:9:9"
```

The preceding code abides by both the rules of the hashCode() contract, when n2.equals(n3) returns true, n2.hashCode() and n3.hashCode() return the same value. But when n1.equals(n2) returns false, n1.hashCode() and n2.hashCode() might not return distinct values.

Let's modify the preceding code, so that hashCode() returns distinct values when equals() returns false:

```
class MyNumber {
    long number;
    MyNumber(long number) {this.number = number;}
    public int hashCode() {
        return (int)number;
    }
    public boolean equals(Object o) {
        if (o != null && o instanceof MyNumber)
            return (number == ((MyNumber)o).number);
        else
            return false;
    }
    public static void main(String args[]) {
        MyNumber n1 = new MyNumber(9);
        MyNumber n2 = new MyNumber(18);
        MyNumber n3 = new MyNumber(18);
        System.out.println                                              Prints
            (n1.equals(n2)+":"+n1.hashCode()+":"+n2.hashCode());  ⊲──┘   "false:9:18"
        System.out.println
            (n2.equals(n3)+":"+n2.hashCode()+":"+n3.hashCode());  ⊲──┐
    }                                                                   Prints
}                                                                       "true:18:18"
```

NOTE   Using a system-dependent value (like a memory address) is *allowed* in hashCode(). But objects of such classes can't be used as keys in distributed systems because *equal* objects (across systems) will return different hash-code values.

OVERRIDING METHOD HASHCODE() INAPPROPRIATELY

Inappropriate overriding isn't the same as incorrect overriding—the former won't fail compilation but can have issues with object retrieval. On the exam, watch out for questions that will show code for hashCode(), equals(), or both, and query what happens when the class instances are used as keys in collection classes, like HashMap. In this section, you'll work with examples that override hashCode() correctly—syntactically, but not appropriately.

In the previous section you learned why it's important for method hashCode() that two objects return the same value, if they're equal as per method equals(). Failing this condition, an object value will never be able to be retrieved from a HashMap. Let's see what happens when class MyNumber doesn't return the same hashCode() values for its *equal* objects:

```
class MyNumber {
    int primary, secondary;
    MyNumber(int primary, int secondary) {
        this.primary = primary;
        this.secondary = secondary;
    }
    public int hashCode() {                                    ❶ Doesn't print
        return secondary;                                          same hashCode()
    }                                                              value for equal
    public boolean equals(Object o) {                              objects
        if (o != null && o instanceof MyNumber)
            return (primary == ((MyNumber)o).primary);
        else
            return false;
    }
    public static void main(String args[]) {
        Map<MyNumber, String> map = new HashMap<>();           ❷ Prints "true"—
        MyNumber num1 = new MyNumber(2500, 100);                   objects num1
        MyNumber num2 = new MyNumber(2500, 200);                   and num2 are
        System.out.println(num1.equals(num2));                     considered equal.
        map.put(num1, "Shreya");
        System.out.println(map.get(num2));      ❸  Prints
    }                                               "null"
}
```

In the preceding code, even though the code at ❷ prints true, confirming that objects num1 and num2 are considered equal by equals(), the code at ❸ prints null. The reason for this? The hashCode() in MyNumber doesn't return the same values for its equal objects. In method hashCode(), the code at ❶ uses secondary to calculate its value, which isn't used by equals().

Another rule of method hashCode() is that when it's invoked on the same object more than once during the execution of a Java application, hashCode() *must* consistently return the same integer, provided no information used in the equals() comparisons on the object is modified. This integer doesn't need to remain consistent from one execution of an application to another execution of the same application.

Let's see what happens when hashCode() doesn't return the same integer value when it's invoked on the same instance during the execution of a Java application:

```java
class MyNumber {
    int number;
    MyNumber(int number) {this.number = number;}
    public int hashCode() {
        return ((int)(Math.random() * 100));
    }
    public boolean equals(Object o) {
        if (o != null && o instanceof MyNumber)
            return (number == ((MyNumber)o).number);
        else
            return false;
    }
    public static void main(String args[]) {
        Map<MyNumber, String> map = new HashMap<>();
        MyNumber num1 = new MyNumber(2500);
        map.put(num1, "Shreya");
        System.out.println(map.get(num1));
    }
}
```

> Prints random hash-code values on each invocation

> Prints "null" (most probably)

In the preceding code, when you add key-value num1, "Shreya" to HashMap, you most likely won't be able to retrieve Shreya using the same key, num1. This is because each call to num1.hashCode() might return a different value (the chances of returning the same hashCode() values aren't ruled out, but are very low).

INEFFICIENT OVERRIDING OF HASHCODE()

In real projects, always strive for generating distinct values in hashCode(). Distinct hashCode() values and faster object access are directly related in collection objects that use hashing functions to retrieve and store values. Here's an example of inefficient overriding of method hashCode():

```java
class MyNumber {
    long number;
    MyNumber(long number) {this.number = number;}
    public int hashCode() {
        return 1654;
    }
}
```

In the preceding code, method hashCode() returns the same hash-code value for all the objects of MyNumber. This essentially stores all the values in the same bucket, if objects of the above class are used as keys in class `HashMap` (or in similar classes that use hashing), and reduces it to a linked list, drastically reducing its efficiency.

 EXAM TIP   Read the questions on method `hashCode()` carefully. You might be questioned on incorrect, inappropriate, or inefficient overriding of `hashCode()`.

EFFECTS OF USING MUTABLE OBJECTS AS KEYS

Java recommends using immutable objects as keys for collection classes that use the hashing algorithm. What if you don't? The exam might query you on this important question.

Revisiting the example used in the previous section, what happens if the value of the field `number` is changed during the course of the application? In this case, you'll never be able to retrieve the corresponding value in the `HashMap`, because the `HashMap` will not be able to look for the right bucket:

```java
class MyNumber {
    int number;
    MyNumber(int number) {this.number = number;}
    public int hashCode() {
        return number;
    }
    public boolean equals(Object o) {
        if (o != null && o instanceof MyNumber)
            return (number == ((MyNumber)o).number);
        else
            return false;
    }
    public static void main(String args[]) {
        Map<MyNumber, String> map = new HashMap<>();
        MyNumber num1 = new MyNumber(2500);
        map.put(num1, "Shreya");
        num1.number = 100;
        System.out.println(map.get(num1));
    }
}
```

Add value Shreya to HashMap using key num1.

Modify field number of key num1, which is used by equals() and hashCode().

Prints "null"—can't locate object with modified key.

In the preceding code, the field used to determine the hash code of an object is modified in `main()`. With the modified key, `HashMap` won't be able to retrieve its corresponding object.

In the next section, you'll cover when, why, and how you can cast an instance to another type and use the `instanceof` operator.

1.5   *Casting and the instanceof operator*

[1.4]   Use the instanceof operator and casting

Imagine that you enroll yourself for flying classes, where you expect to be trained by an experienced pilot. Even though your trainer might also be a swimming champion, you need not know about it. You need not care about the characteristics and behavior that's not related to flying. Now think of a situation when you do care about the swimming skills of your instructor. Imagine that when you're attending the flying classes, your friend enquires whether your flying instructor also conducts swimming classes and, if yes, whether she would be willing to assist your friend. In this case, a *need* arises to enquire about the swimming skills (additional *existing* skills) of your flying instructor.

Similarly, in Java, you can refer to an object of a derived class using a reference variable of its base class or implemented interface. But you might need to access the members of the derived class, which aren't defined in its base class or the implemented interface. Here's when *casting* can help. Casting shows how an object of a type can be used as an object of another type, either implicitly or explicitly. The instanceof operator is used to logically test whether an object is a valid type of a class or an interface.

1.5.1 *Implicit and explicit casting*

Let's start with the definitions of the interface Printable and classes ShoppingItem and Book to show implicit and explicit casting. Class Book extends class ShoppingItem and implements the interface Printable as follows:

```
public interface Printable {
    void print();
}
public class ShoppingItem {
    public void description() {
        System.out.println("Shopping Item");
    }
}
public class Book extends ShoppingItem implements Printable {
    public void description() {
        System.out.println("Book");
    }
    public void print() {
        System.out.println("Printing book");
    }
}
```

Figure 1.28 shows the inheritance relationship between these classes.

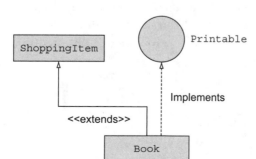

Figure 1.28 Relationship between classes ShoppingItem **and** Book **and the interface** Printable

Now let's create variables of type `Printable` and `ShoppingItem` and assign to them objects of the type `Book`:

```
class Shopping {
    public static void main(String args[]) {
        Book book = new Book();                    ❶ Implicit
        Printable printable = book;            ◁─┘   casting
        printable.print();

        ShoppingItem shoppingItem = book;      ◁─┐
        shoppingItem.description();             ❷ Acceptable
    }
}
```

The code at ❶ shows how an object of type `book` is *implicitly* referred to, or casted to, type `Printable`. The code at ❷ shows how an object of type `book` is *implicitly* referred to, or casted to, type `ShoppingItem`. Objects of subclasses can be implicitly casted to their base classes or the interfaces that they implement.

As shown in the preceding code block for the class `Book`, you can see that `Book` defines a method `description()`. Let's try to access it using the `printable` variable:

```
class Shopping {
    public static void main(String args[]) {     ❶ Won't compile—can't
        Printable printable = new Book();            access method
        printable.description();              ◁─    description() in Printable.
    }
}
```

The code at ❶ fails to compile with the following message:

```
Shopping.java:4: error: cannot find symbol
        printable.description();
                  ^
  symbol:   method description()
  location: variable printable of type Printable
1 error
```

Because the type of the reference variable `printable` is `Printable`, the compiler refers to the definition of the interface `Printable` when you call method `description()` on `printable`. Figure 1.29 shows what happens behind the scenes.

But you know that the actual object is of type `Book`. Is there a way to treat the reference variable `printable` as a `Book`? Yes, there is! You need to inform the compiler you know what you're doing by using an explicit cast, as follows (see also figure 1.30):

```
class Shopping {
    public static void main(String args[]) {
        Printable printable = new Book();
        ((Book)printable).description();
    }
}
```

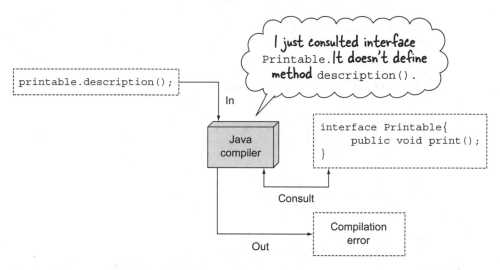

Figure 1.29 The Java compiler doesn't compile code if you try to access `description()`, defined in class `Book`, by using a variable of the interface `Printable`.

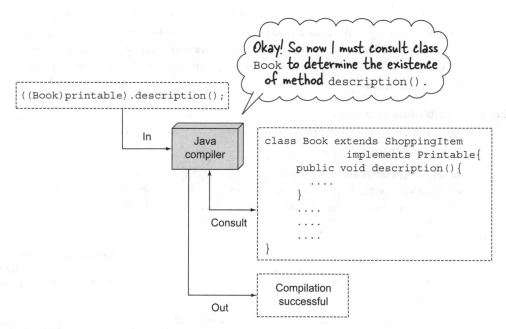

Figure 1.30 Explicit casting can be used to access `description()` defined in class `Book` by using a variable of the interface `Printable`.

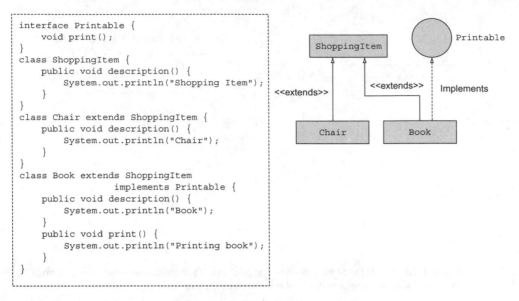

```
interface Printable {
    void print();
}
class ShoppingItem {
    public void description() {
        System.out.println("Shopping Item");
    }
}
class Chair extends ShoppingItem {
    public void description() {
        System.out.println("Chair");
    }
}
class Book extends ShoppingItem
                implements Printable {
    public void description() {
        System.out.println("Book");
    }
    public void print() {
        System.out.println("Printing book");
    }
}
```

Figure 1.31   Set of classes and interfaces, with their UML representation

In the preceding code, (Book) is placed just before the name of the variable, printable, to cast it to Book. Note how a pair of parentheses surrounds (Book)printable. Casting in this line of code is another method of telling the compiler that you know that the actual object being referred to is Book, even though you're using a reference variable of type Printable.

1.5.2   *Combinations of casting*

To work with a combination of casting, let's work with a set of classes and interfaces, as shown in figure 1.31.

ASSIGNMENTS WITH IMPLICIT CASTING

Implicit upcasting is allowed. You can assign a reference variable of a derived class to a reference variable of its own type, its base classes, and the interfaces that it implements as follows:

```
public class UpcastWithImplicitCasting {
    public static void main(String[] arguments) {
        Book book = new Book();

        Chair chair = book;
        ShoppingItem shoppingItem = book;
        Printable printable = book;
        Object object = book;

        Chair chair2 = new Chair();
        Printable printable2 = chair;
    }
}
```

Won't compile—both Book and Chair extend ShoppingItem, but don't belong to a single line of inheritance.

Okay—a book is a ShoppingItem.

Okay—a book is Printable.

Okay—a book is an Object.

Won't compile—Chair doesn't implement Printable.

Implicit downcasting isn't allowed. You can't assign reference variables of a base class to reference variables of its derived classes or to the interfaces that it doesn't implement. For example

Won't compile—a ShoppingItem isn't necessarily a book.

Won't compile—a ShoppingItem isn't Printable.

Won't compile—a ShoppingItem isn't necessarily a chair.

```
public class DowncastWithImplicitCasting {
    public static void main(String[] arguments) {
        ShoppingItem shoppingItem3 = new ShoppingItem();

        Book book3 = shoppingItem3;
        Chair chair3 = shoppingItem3;
        Printable printable3 = shoppingItem3;

        Object object3 = shoppingItem3;
    }
}
```

Okay—a chair is an Object.

 EXAM TIP In the absence of explicit casting, you'll never get `ClassCast-Exception`—a `RuntimeException`.

ASSIGNMENT WITH EXPLICIT CASTING

Both implicit and explicit upcasting are allowed. So, for the exam, let's focus on explicit downcasting.

Java recommends programming to an interface, which implies using reference variables of a base class or implementing interfaces to refer to the actual objects. But you might need to cast an object referred by a base class to its specific type. You can downcast an object to a type that falls in its inheritance tree using explicit casting. For a nonfinal class, you can explicitly cast its object to any interface type, even if the class doesn't implement the interface. Let's see what happens when you accept a method parameter of type `ShoppingItem` and try to cast it explicitly to other types:

```
public class DowncastWithExplicitCasting {
    static void downCast(ShoppingItem item) {
        Book book = (Book)item;
        Chair chair = (Chair)item;
        Printable printable = (Printable)item;
    }
    public static void main(String args[]) {
        ShoppingItem item = new ShoppingItem();
        downCast(item);
    }
}
```

❶ Compiles with casting—will throw ClassCastException; can't downcast instance of parent object to subclass type.

❷ Compiles with casting—will throw ClassCastException; ShoppingItem doesn't implement Printable.

The code at ❶ and ❷ compiles with an explicit cast. But its individual lines will fail at runtime. At runtime, Java can determine the exact type of the object being casted. It throws a `ClassCastException` if you're trying to cast types that aren't allowed.

 NOTE For the exam, you need to be very clear whether an explicit cast will result in a compilation error or a runtime exception (`ClassCastException`).

Does the preceding code make you wonder why an explicit cast from a ShoppingItem instance to Printable is permitted, even though ShoppingItem doesn't implement Printable? It's to allow subclasses of ShoppingItem to implement Printable and use the reference variable of type Printable to refer to its instances. So what happens if you try to cast a final class's instance to an interface it doesn't implement? The code won't compile:

```
interface Printable {}
final class Engineer {}
class Factory {
    public static void main(String[] args) {
        Engineer engineer = new Engineer();
        Printable printable = (Printable)engineer;
    }
}
```

Won't compile—can't cast final class Engineer's instance to Printable.

 EXAM TIP   Class String is defined as a final class. Watch out for questions that explicitly cast String objects to interfaces they don't implement. They won't compile.

What about casting null to a type? You can explicitly cast null to any type without a compilation error or runtime exception (ClassCastException):

```
static void castNull() {
    Book book = (Book)null;
    Chair chair = (Chair)null;
    Printable printable = (Printable)null;
}
```

 EXAM TIP   You can explicitly cast null to any type. It won't generate a compilation error or throw a ClassCastException.

ACCESS OF MEMBERS WITH EXPLICIT CASTING

You can access methods and variables of explicitly casted variables in single or multiple lines of code:

```
public class AccesMembersWithExplicitCasting {
    static void accessMember(ShoppingItem item) {
        Book book = (Book)item;
        book.description();

        ((Book)item).description();
    }
}
```

❶ **Cast a reference variable and access its method in multiple steps.**

❷ **Cast objects and call their members in a single step.**

Here the code at ❶ casts a reference item to Book in one line and then accesses its method description(). At ❷, note how the object referred by item is casted-enclosed within () to call its member method description(). The inclusion in () is due to the fact that the dot operator has precedence over the casting parentheses.

EXAM TIP If you cast an instance to a class outside its inheritance tree, you'll get a compiler error. If you cast an instance to a class within its inheritance tree, but the types don't match at runtime, the code will throw a ClassCastException.

Points to remember for casting

- An instance can be implicitly casted to its superclasses or interfaces that it implements.
- An instance of a nonfinal class can be explicitly casted to any interface at compile time.
- Classes in the same inheritance tree can be casted to each other using explicit casting at compile time.
- Objects of classes that don't form part of the same inheritance tree cannot be casted.
- Casting to an interface is successful at runtime if the class implements the interface.
- Casting to a derived class type is successful at runtime if the casted object is actually a type of the derived class to which it's casted.

In the previous examples, you learned how mismatching of objects and explicit casting can throw a ClassCastException. In the next section, you'll see how you can prevent this by using the instanceof operator to safely cast objects to a type.

1.5.3 Using the instanceof operator

The instanceof operator is used to logically test whether an object is a valid type of a class or an interface. You should proceed with explicit casting only if this operator returns true, or you risk running into a ClassCastException at runtime. For example, consider equals(), which defines a method parameter of type Object. When you override equals() to determine the equality of objects of your class, you might need to query the state of the accepted argument before you move forward with an explicit cast:

```
class Course {
    String title;
    Course(String t) {title = t;}
    public boolean equals(Object obj) {
        if (obj instanceof Course) {
            Course c = (Course)obj;
            return (title.equals(c.title));
        }
        else
            return false;
    }
}
```

❶ Use instanceof to verify if obj is an instance of Course.

❷ Explicitly cast obj to Course.

The code at ❶ ensures that the type of the accepted method parameter—that is, obj—is Course, before it moves forward with the explicit casting of obj to Course ❷.

In the absence of this check, the code at ❷ would execute for all non-null method parameters, which can result in a `ClassCastException` if the object passed to `equals()` isn't of type `Course`.

 EXAM TIP The operator `instanceof` returns `false` if the reference variable being compared to is `null`.

In the previous example, the type of method parameter to `equals()` is `Object`, which is the parent class of all classes. But if the `instanceof` operator uses inconvertible types, the code won't compile. In the following example, the `instanceof` operator uses a reference variable of type `Course` to test whether the object that it refers to can be an *instance of* class `Student`. Because `Course` and `Student` are unrelated, class `Test` won't compile:

```
class Course {}
class Student {}
public class TestInstanceof {
    public static void main(String[] args) {
        Course c = new Course();
        Student s = new Student();
        System.out.println(c instanceof Student);
    }
}
```

Won't compile—can't use `instanceof` to compare inconvertible types.

 EXAM TIP The `instanceof` operator *never* throws a runtime exception; it returns either `true` or `false`. If the `instanceof` operator uses inconvertible types, the code won't compile.

The `instanceof` operator is preceded by a value (literal value or a variable name) and is followed by a class, interface, or enum name. It's acceptable to use the literal value `null` with the `instanceof` operator:

```
class Course {
    public static void main(String[] args) {
        System.out.println(null instanceof Course);
    }
}
```

Prints "false"—null can't be an instance of any class.

 EXAM TIP The literal value `null` isn't an instance of any class. So `<referenceVariable> instanceof <ClassName>` will return `false` whenever the `<referenceVariable>` is null.

Using instanceof versus getClass in method equals()

Using `instanceof` versus `getClass` is a common subject of debate about proper use and object orientation in general (including performance aspects, design patterns, and so on). Though important, this discussion is beyond the scope of this book. If you're interested in further details, refer to Josh Bloch's book *Effective Java*.

Interviewer   `instanceof`

Figure 1.32 **Remember that o in `instanceof` is lowercase.**

Note that o in `instanceof` is lowercase; take a look at figure 1.32 for a fun way of remembering this.

Next we'll move forward with defining the Java classes and interfaces in named packages. This is a common requirement in real Java applications. So let's get started.

1.6 Packages

[1.7]   Use package and import statements

In this section, you'll learn what Java packages are and how to create them. You'll use the `import` statement, which enables you to use simple names for classes and interfaces defined in separate packages.

1.6.1 The need for packages

You can use packages to group together a related set of enums, classes, and interfaces. Packages also provide namespace management. You can create separate packages to define classes for separate projects, such as Android games and online healthcare systems. Further, you can create subpackages within these packages, such as separate subpackages for GUIs, database access, networking, and so on.

 NOTE   In real-life projects, you'll never work with a package-less class or interface. Almost all organizations that develop software have strict package-naming rules, which are often documented.

If you don't include an explicit `package` statement in a class or an interface, it's part of a *default* package.

1.6.2   *Defining classes in a package using the package statement*

You can define classes and interfaces in a package by using the package statement as the first statement in your class or interface (only comments can precede the package statement). Here's an example:

```
package certification;
class ExamQuestion {
    //..code
}
```

The class in the previous code defines a class ExamQuestion in the certification package. You can define an interface, MultipleChoice, in a similar manner:

```
package certification;
interface MultipleChoice {
    //..code
}
```

Figure 1.33 shows the UML representation of the certification package, with class ExamQuestion and interface MultipleChoice.

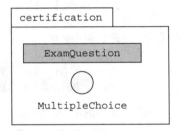

The name of the package in the previous examples is certification. You may use such names for small projects that contain only a few classes and interfaces, but it's common for organizations to use subpackages to define *all* their classes. For example, if folks at Oracle define a class to store exam questions for a Java Associate exam, they might use the package name com.oracle.javacert.associate. For subpackages, the package statement includes the complete package name. Figure 1.34 shows its UML representation along with the corresponding class definition.

Figure 1.33   A UML representation of the certification package, class ExamQuestion, and interface MultipleChoice

 NOTE   A fully qualified name for a class or interface is formed by prefixing its name with its package name (separated by a period). The fully qualified name of the ExamQuestion class is certification.ExamQuestion in figure 1.33 and com.oracle.javacert.associate.ExamQuestion in figure 1.34.

```
package com.oracle.javacert.associate;
class ExamQuestion {
    // variables and methods
}
```

Figure 1.34   A subpackage and its corresponding class definition

Rules to remember about packages

Here are a few important rules about packages:

- Per Java naming conventions, package names should all be in lowercase.
- The package and subpackage names are separated using a dot (.).
- Package names follow the rules defined for valid identifiers in Java.
- For packaged classes and interfaces, the `package` statement is the first statement in a Java source file (a .java file). The exception is that comments can appear before or after a `package` statement.
- There can be a maximum of one `package` statement per Java source code file (.java file).
- All the classes and interfaces defined in a Java source code file will be defined in the same package. There's no way to define them in different packages.

DIRECTORY STRUCTURE AND PACKAGE HIERARCHY

The hierarchy of the classes defined in packages should match the hierarchy of the directories in which these classes and interfaces are defined in the code. For example, class `ExamQuestion` in the `certification` package should be defined in a directory with the name certification. The name of the certification directory and its location are governed by the rules shown in figure 1.35.

Figure 1.35 Matching directory structure and package hierarchy

For the package example shown in figure 1.35, note that there isn't any constraint on the location of the base directory in which the directory structure is defined. Examine figure 1.36.

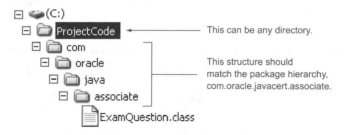

Figure 1.36 There's no constraint on the location of the base directory to define directories corresponding to package hierarchy.

To enable the JRE to find your classes, interfaces, and enums defined in packages, add the base directory that contains your Java code to the class path.

For example, to enable the JRE to locate the `certification.ExamQuestion` class from the previous examples, add the directory C:\MyCode to the class path. To enable the JRE to locate class `com.oracle.javacert.associate.ExamQuestion`, add the directory C:\ProjectCode to the class path.

You don't need to bother setting the class path if you're working with an integrated development environment (IDE). But I strongly encourage you to learn how to work with a simple text editor and how to set a class path. This can be particularly helpful with your projects at work. I've also witnessed many interviewers querying candidates on the need for class paths.

1.6.3 *Using simple names with import statements*

The `import` statement enables you to use *simple names* instead of using *fully qualified names* for classes and interfaces defined in separate packages. Let's work with an example, in which classes `LivingRoom` and `Kitchen` are defined in the package `home` and classes `Cubicle` and `ConferenceHall` are defined in the package `office`. Class `Cubicle` uses (is associated to) class `LivingRoom` in the package `home`, as shown in figure 1.37.

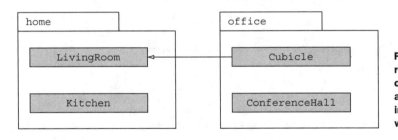

Figure 1.37 A UML representation of classes LivingRoom and Cubicle, defined in separate packages, with their associations

Class `Cubicle` can refer to class `LivingRoom` without using an `import` statement:

```
package office;
class Cubicle {
    home.LivingRoom livingRoom;      ◁──  For no import statement, use fully qualified
}                                          name to refer to LivingRoom from package home
```

Class `Cubicle` can use the simple name for class `LivingRoom` by using the `import` statement:

```
package office;
import home.LivingRoom;              ◁──  Import
                                          statement
class Cubicle {
    LivingRoom livingRoom;           ◁──  No need to use fully qualified
}                                          name of LivingRoom
```

NOTE The import statement doesn't embed the contents of the imported class in your class, which means that importing more classes doesn't increase the size of your own class. It lets you use the simple name for a class or interface defined in a separate package.

1.6.4 *Using packages without using the import statement*

Classes in the java.lang package are automatically imported in all the Java classes, interfaces, and enums. To use simple names for classes, interfaces, and enums from other packages, you should use the import statement. It's possible to use a class or interface from a package without using the import statement by using its fully qualified name:

```
                                          ┌─ Missing import
                                          │  statement
                                        ◄─┘
class AnnualExam {
    certification.ExamQuestion eq;        Define a variable of ExamQuestion
}                                         by using its fully qualified name.
```

But using a fully qualified class name can clutter your code if you use multiple variables of interfaces and classes defined in other packages. *Don't* use this approach in real projects.

For the exam, it's important to note that you can't use the import statement to use multiple classes or interfaces with the same names from different packages. For example, the Java API defines class Date in two commonly used packages: java.util and java.sql. To define variables of these classes in a class, use their fully qualified names with the variable declaration:

```
                              ┌─ Missing import
                              │  statement
                            ◄─┘
class AnnualExam {                            ◄─┐  Variable of type
    java.util.Date date1;                      │  java.util.Date
    java.sql.Date date2;      ◄─┐ Variable of type
}                               │ java.sql.Date
                                  
```

An attempt to use an import statement to import both these classes in the same class will not compile:

```
import java.util.Date;     Code to import classes with same name
import java.sql.Date;      from different packages won't compile
class AnnualExam { }
```

In the preceding code, you want to use a shortcut (Date) but your shortcut refers to either java.util.Date or java.sql.Date. So the Java compiler has no way of knowing which is which (both have Date as their simple name), therefore the compiler error.

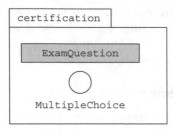

Figure 1.38   A UML representation of the `certification` **package**

1.6.5   *Importing a single member versus all members of a package*

You can import either a single member or all members (classes and interfaces) of a package using the `import` statement. First, revisit the UML notation of the `certification` package, as shown in figure 1.38.

Examine the following code for class `AnnualExam`:

```
import certification.ExamQuestion;          Imports only
class AnnualExam {                          ExamQuestion
    ExamQuestion eq;                Compiles
    MultipleChoice mc;              okay
}                     Will not
                      compile
```

By using the wildcard character, an asterisk (`*`), you can import all of the public members, classes, and interfaces of a package. Compare the previous class definition with the following definition of class `AnnualExam`:

```
import certification.*;         Imports all classes and
class AnnualExam {              interfaces from certification
    ExamQuestion eq;                 Compiles
    MultipleChoice mc;              okay
}                     Also compiles
                      okay
```

When you work with an IDE, it may automatically add `import` statements for classes and interfaces that you reference in your code.

1.6.6   *The import statement doesn't import the whole package tree*

You can't import classes from a subpackage by using an asterisk in the `import` statement. For example, the UML notation in figure 1.39 depicts the package `com.oracle` `.javacert` with class `Schedule` and two subpackages, `associate` and `webdeveloper`. The `associate` package contains class `ExamQuestion`, and the `webdeveloper` package contains class `MarkSheet`.

The following `import` statement will import only the `Schedule` class; it won't import classes `ExamQuestion` and `MarkSheet`:

```
import com.oracle.javacert.*;          Imports
                                       Schedule only
```

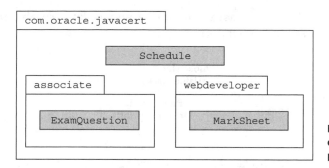

Figure 1.39 A UML representation of the `com.oracle.javacert` package and its subpackages

Similarly, the following `import` statement will import all the classes from the `associate` and `webdeveloper` packages:

```
import com.oracle.javacert.associate.*;
import com.oracle.javacert.webdeveloper.*;
```

Imports ExamQuestion only

Imports MarkSheet only

1.6.7   *Importing classes from the default package*

What happens if you don't include a `package` statement in your class or interface? In this case, they become part of a *default, no-name* package. This default package is automatically imported in the Java classes and interfaces defined within the *same* directory on your system.

For example, classes `Person` and `Office`, which aren't defined in an explicit package, can use each other if they're defined in the same directory:

```
class Person {
    // code
}
class Office {
    Person p;
}
```

Not defined in an explicit package

Person accessible in Office

 EXAM TIP   Members of a named package can't access classes and interfaces defined in the *default* package.

1.6.8   *Static imports*

You can import an individual static member of a class or an interface, or all its static members, by using the `import static` statement. Though accessible using an instance, the static members are usually accessed by prefixing their name with the class or interface names. By using `static import`, you can drop the prefix and just use the name of the static variable or method.

In the following code, class ExamQuestion defines a public static variable named marks and a public static method named print():

```
package certification;
public class ExamQuestion {
    static public int marks;          ← Public static
    public static void print() {        variable marks
        System.out.println(100);      ← Public static
    }                                    method print()
}
```

Variable marks can be accessed in class AnnualExam using the import static statement. The order of the keywords import and static can't be reversed:

```
package university;
import static certification.ExamQuestion.marks;  ← Correct statement is
class AnnualExam {                                  import static, not
    AnnualExam() {            ← Access variable marks  static import
        marks = 20;             without prefixing it
    }                           with its class name
}
```

 EXAM TIP   This feature is called *static imports*, but syntax is import static.

To use all public and static members of class ExamQuestion in class AnnualExam without importing each of them individually, you can use an asterisk with the import static statement:

```
package university;
import static certification.ExamQuestion.*;  ← Imports all static
class AnnualExam {                              members of
    AnnualExam() {                              ExamQuestion
        marks = 20;   ← Uses marks and print() without
        print();        prefixing them with their class names
    }
}
```

Because variable marks and method print() are public, they're accessible to class AnnualExam. By using import static you don't have to prefix them with their class name. But if they were defined using any other access modifier, they wouldn't be accessible in AnnualExam because both these classes are defined in separate packages and AnnualExam doesn't inherit ExamQuestion.

1.7   Summary

This chapter covers the basic building blocks of the Java class design, starting with access modifiers, and then overloading and overriding methods, creating packages, and using classes from other packages.

As a Java programmer, you should understand the role of access modifiers in designing your classes. We covered how access modifiers enable a class to control who can access it, to what extent, and how.

Efficient design and implementation of an application also depends on correct and appropriate overloaded and overridden methods. You witnessed multiple examples on the need for overloading and overriding methods, including the correct ingredients. We also covered why all the methods of a base class can't be overridden.

A discussion of the nonfinal methods of class `java.lang.Object`, which is the parent class of all the Java classes, showed you why and how to override its methods. The methods of class `Object` are called by various other classes and JRE, which makes it crucial for a developer to override the relevant methods from class `Object` before shipping them off to be used by other people.

You also learned how you can use casting to refer to specific behavior of derived class objects when they're referred to their base class references. The `instanceof` operator is used to logically test whether an object is a valid type of a class or an interface.

In the final section, we worked with `package` and `import` statements. It's important to group your classes, interfaces, enums, and other Java entities depending on their functionality. In real programming projects, you'd always work with classes organized in packages.

REVIEW NOTES

This section lists the main points covered in this chapter.

Java access modifiers

- The access modifiers control the accessibility of your class and its members outside the class and package.
- Access modifiers defined by Java are `public`, `protected`, and `private`. In the absence of an explicit access modifier, a member is defined with the *default* access level.
- The `public` access modifier is the least restrictive access modifier.
- Classes and interfaces defined using the `public` access modifier are accessible to related and unrelated classes outside the package in which they're defined.
- The members of a class defined using the `protected` access modifier are accessible to classes and interfaces defined in the same package and to all derived classes, even if they're defined in separate packages.
- The members of a class defined without using an explicit access modifier are defined with package accessibility (also called default accessibility).
- The members with package access are accessible only to classes and interfaces defined in the same package.
- A class defined using default access can't be accessed outside its package.
- The private members of a class are only accessible to itself.
- The `private` access modifier is the most restrictive access modifier.
- A top-level class, interface, or enum can only be defined using the `public` or default access. They can't be defined using `protected` or `private` access.

- Method parameters and local variables can never be defined using an explicit access modifier. They don't have access control–only scope. Either they're in scope or out of scope.
- If accessibility of an existing Java entity or its member is decreased, it can break others' code.

Overloaded methods and constructors

- Overloaded methods are methods with the same name but different method parameter lists.
- A class can overload its own methods and inherited methods from its base class.
- Overloaded methods accept different lists of arguments.
- The argument lists of overloaded methods can differ in terms of change in the number, type, or position of parameters that they accept.
- Overloaded methods are bound at compile time. Unlike overridden methods they're not bound at runtime.
- A call to correctly overloaded methods can also fail compilation if the compiler is unable to resolve the call to an overloaded method.
- Overloaded methods might define a different return type or access or nonaccess modifier, but they can't be defined with only a change in their return types or access or nonaccess modifiers.
- Overloaded constructors must be defined using different argument lists.
- Overloaded constructors can't be defined by just a change in the access modifiers.
- Overloaded constructors can be defined using different access modifiers.
- A constructor can call another overloaded constructor by using the keyword this.
- A constructor can't invoke another constructor by using its class's name.
- If present, the call to another constructor must be the first statement in a constructor.

Method overriding and virtual method invocation

- Method overriding is an OOP language feature that enables a derived class to define a specific implementation of an existing base class method to extend its own behavior.
- A derived class can override an instance method defined in a base class by defining an instance method with the same method signature.
- Whenever you intend to override methods in a derived class, use the annotation @Override. It will warn you if a method can't be overridden or if you're actually overloading a method rather than overriding it.
- Overridden methods can define the same or covariant return types.
- A derived class can't override a base class method to make it less accessible.
- Overriding methods must define exactly the same method parameters; the use of a subclass or parent class results in overloading methods.

- Static methods can't be overridden. They're not polymorphic and they're bound at compile time.
- In a derived class, a static method with the same signature as that of a static method in its base class hides the base class method.
- A derived class can't override the base class methods that aren't accessible to it, such as private methods.
- Constructors cannot be overridden because a base class constructor isn't inherited by a derived class.
- A method that can be overridden by a derived class is called a virtual method.
- Virtual method invocation is invocation of the correct method–determined using the object type and not its reference.

Java packages

- You can use packages to group together a related set of classes and interfaces.
- The package and subpackage names are separated using a period.
- Classes and interfaces in the same package can access each other.
- An import statement allows the use of simple names for classes and interfaces defined in other packages.
- You can't use the import statement to access multiple classes or interfaces with the same names from different packages.
- You can import either a single member or all members (classes and interfaces) of a package using the import statement.
- You can't import classes from a subpackage by using the wildcard character, an asterisk (*), in the import statement.
- A class from the default package can't be used in any named package, regardless of whether it's defined within the same directory or not.
- You can import an individual static member of a class or all its static members by using an import static statement.
- An import statement can't be placed before a package statement in a class. Any attempt to do so will cause the compilation of the class to fail.
- The members of the default package are accessible only to classes or interfaces defined in the same directory on your system.

SAMPLE EXAM QUESTIONS

Q 1-1. Which of the following points should you incorporate in your application design?

- a Create related classes in a single package.
- b Don't make derived classes overload methods from their base class.
- c Expose the functionality of your classes using public methods.
- d Create private methods to work as helper methods for the public methods.

Q 1-2. What is the output of the following code?

```java
class Wood {
    public Wood() {
        System.out.println("Wood");
    }
    {
        System.out.println("Wood:init");
    }
}
class Teak extends Wood {
    {
        System.out.println("Teak:init");
    }
    public Teak() {
        System.out.println("Teak");
    }
    public static void main(String args[]) {
        new Teak();
    }
}
```

   a Wood:init
       Wood
       Teak:init
       Teak

   b Wood
       Wood:init
       Teak:init
       Teak

   c Wood:init
       Teak:init
       Wood
       Teak

   d Wood
       Wood:init
       Teak
       Teak:init

Q 1-3. Examine the following code and select the answer options that are correct individually.

```java
class Machine {
    void start() throws Exception { System.out.println("start machine"); }
}
class Laptop {
    void start() { System.out.println("Start Laptop"); }
    void start(int ms) { System.out.println("Start Laptop:"+ms); }
}
```

   a Class Laptop overloads method start().
   b Class Laptop overrides method start().
   c Class Machine overrides method start().

d Class `Machine` won't compile.

e Class `Laptop` won't compile.

Q 1-4. Given that classes `Class1` and `Class2` exist in separate packages and source code files, examine the code and select the correct options.

```
package pack1;
public class Class1 {
    protected String name = "Base";
}

package pack2;
import pack1.*;
class Class2 extends Class1{
    Class2() {
        Class1 cls1 = new Class1();     //line 1
        name = "Derived";               //line 2
        System.out.println(cls1.name);  //line 3
    }
}
```

a `Class2` can extend `Class1` but it can't access the name variable on line 2.

b `Class2` can't access the name variable on line 3.

c `Class2` can't access `Class1` on line 1.

d `Class2` won't compile.

e Line 3 will print `Base`.

f Line 3 will print `Derived`.

Q 1-5. Select the correct option.

a The declaration of private variables to store the state of an object is encouraged.

b The protected members of a class aren't accessible outside the package in which the class is defined.

c The public members of a class that's defined with default access can be accessed outside the package.

d If you change the signature or implementation of a private method, other classes that use this method cease to compile.

Q 1-6. Given the following code

```
interface Scavenger{}
class Bird{}
class Parrot extends Bird{}
class Vulture extends Bird implements Scavenger{}

class BirdSanctuary {
    public static void main(String args[]) {
        Bird bird = new Bird();
        Parrot parrot = new Parrot();
```

```
            Vulture vulture = new Vulture();
            //INSERT CODE HERE
        }
    }
```

In which of the following options will the code, when inserted at //INSERT CODE HERE, throw a ClassCastException?

   a Vulture vulture2 = (Vulture)parrot;

   b Parrot parrot2 = (Parrot)bird;

   c Scavenger sc = (Scavenger)vulture;

   d Scavenger sc2 = (Scavenger)bird;

Q 1-7. Assuming that all of the following classes are defined in separate source code files, select the incorrect statements.

```
package solarfamily;
public class Sun {
    public Sun() {}
}

package stars;
public class Sun {
    public Sun() {}
}

package skyies;
import stars.Sun;          // line1
import solarfamily.Sun;    // line2
class Sky {
    Sun sun = new Sun();   // line 3
}
```

   a Code compilation fails at line 1.

   b Code compilation fails at line 2.

   c Code compilation fails at line 3.

   d The code compiles successfully and class Sky creates an object of class Sun from the stars package.

   e The code compiles successfully and class Sky creates an object of class Sun from the solarfamily package.

Q 1-8. Select the correct options.

```
class Color {
    String name;
    Color(String name) {this.name = name;}
    public String toString() {return name;}
    public boolean equals(Object obj) {
        return (obj.toString().equals(name));
    }
}
```

a Class `Color` overrides method `toString()` correctly.

b Class `Color` overrides method `equals()` correctly.

c Class `Color` fails to compile.

d Class `Color` throws an exception at runtime.

e None of the above.

Q 1-9. Given the following code

```
class Book {
    String isbn;
    Book(String isbn) {this.isbn = isbn;}
    public int hashCode() {
        return 87536;
    }
}
```

Select the correct option.

a Objects of the class `Book` can never be used as keys because the corresponding objects wouldn't be retrievable.

b Method `hashCode()` is inefficient.

c Class `Book` will not compile.

d Though objects of class `Book` are used as keys, they will throw an exception when the corresponding values are retrieved.

Q 1-10. What is the output of the following code?

```
class Wood {
    String wood = "Wood";
    public Wood() {
        wood = "Wood";
    }
    {
        wood = "init:Wood";
    }
}
class Teak extends Wood {
    String teak;
    {
        teak = "init:Teak";
    }
    public Teak() {
        teak = "Teak";
    }
    public static void main(String args[]) {
        Teak teak = new Teak();
        System.out.println(teak.wood);
        System.out.println(teak.teak);
    }
}
```

a init:Wood
    init:Teak

b init:Wood
    Teak

c Wood
    init:Teak

d Wood
    Teak

Q 1-11. Given the following code

```
class Cloth {}
class Shirt extends Cloth implements Resizable{}
class Shorts extends Cloth {}
interface Resizable {}

class Factory {
    public static void main(String sr[]) {
        Shirt s = new Shirt();
        //INSERT CODE HERE
        System.out.println(res);
    }
}
```

Which options will print true?

a boolean res = new Cloth() instanceof Shirt;

b boolean res = new Shirt() instanceof Resizable;

c boolean res = null instanceof Factory;

d Cloth cloth = new Cloth();
    Shirt shirt = new Shirt();
    boolean res = shirt instanceof cloth;

ANSWERS TO SAMPLE EXAM QUESTIONS

A 1-1. a, c, d

[1.1] Use access modifiers: private, protected, and public
[1.3] Overload constructors and methods
[1.7] Use package and import statements

Explanation: Option (a) is correct. A package enables you to create a namespace to group related classes and interfaces together.

Option (b) is incorrect. A base class overloads its base class method, as required. Making derived classes overload their base class methods doesn't make it an incorrect or inefficient design.

Options (c) and (d) are also correct. The functionality of your classes should be exposed using the public methods. The private methods are called within the class in which they're defined. They usually work as helper methods.

A 1-2. a

[1.3] Overload constructors and methods

Explanation: When a class is compiled, the contents of its initializer block are added to its constructor, just before its own contents. For example, here's the decompiled code for class Wood. As you can see, the contents of its initializer block are added to its constructor:

```
class Wood
{
    public Wood()
    {
        System.out.println("Wood:init");
        System.out.println("Wood");
    }
}
```

A 1-3. a

[1.2] Override methods
[1.3] Overload constructors and methods

Explanation: Class Laptop correctly overloads the method start() by defining a different parameter list.

Options (b) and (c) are incorrect because classes Laptop and Machine are unrelated. A derived class can override its base class method.

Method start() qualifies as a valid overridden method in class Laptop, if Laptop extends class Machine. It's acceptable for an overriding method to not throw any checked exception, even if the base class method is throwing a checked exception.

Options (d) and (e) are incorrect because both classes will compile successfully.

A 1-4. b, d

[1.7] Use package and import statements

Explanation: A derived class can access a protected member of its base class, across packages, directly. But if the base and derived classes are in separate packages, then you can't access protected members of the base class by using reference variables of class Base in a derived class. So, Class2 doesn't compile.

Options (e) and (f) are incorrect because Class2 won't compile.

A 1-5. a

[1.1] Use access modifiers: private, protected, and public
[1.7] Use package and import statements

Explanation: Option (b) is incorrect because the protected members of a class are accessible by the derived classes, outside the package in which the class is defined.

Option (c) is incorrect because a class with default access isn't visible outside the package within which it's defined. If the class isn't visible itself, it doesn't matter whether its members are accessible or not.

Option (d) is incorrect because a private method can't be used outside the class in which it's defined.

A 1-6. b, d

[1.4] Use the instanceof operator and casting

Explanation: `ClassCastException` is thrown at runtime. So the options that don't fail to compile are eligible to be considered for the following question: Will they throw a `ClassCastException`?

Option (a) is incorrect because it fails to compile.

Option (b) is correct because classes `Bird` and `Parrot` are in the same hierarchy tree, so an object of base class `Bird` can be explicitly casted to its derived class `Parrot` at compilation. But the JVM can determine the type of the objects at runtime. Because an object of a derived class can't refer to an object of its base class, this line throws a `ClassCastException` at runtime.

Option (c) is incorrect because class `Vulture` implements the interface `Scavenger`, so this code will also execute without the explicit cast.

Option (d) is correct. An instance of a nonfinal class can be casted to any interface type using an explicit cast during the compilation phase. But the exact object types are validated during runtime and a `ClassCastException` is thrown if the object's class doesn't implement that interface. Class `Bird` doesn't implement the interface `Scavenger` and so this code fails during runtime, throwing a `ClassCast-Exception`.

A 1-7. b

[1.7] Use package and import statements

Explanation: Class `Sky` fails with the following error message:

```
Sky.java:3: error: stars.Sun is already defined in a single-type import
import solarfamily.Sun;
       ^
1 error
```

A 1-8. a

[1.2] Override methods

Explanation: Class `Color` overrides method `toString()` correctly, but not method `equals()`. According to the contract of method `equals()`, for any non-null reference values x and y, x.equals(y) should return true if and only if y.equals(x) returns true—this rule states that two objects should be comparable to each other in the same way. Class Color doesn't follow this rule. Here's the proof:

```
class TestColor {
    public static void main(String args[]) {
        Color color = new Color("red");
        String string = "red";

        System.out.println(color.equals(string));   // prints true
        System.out.println(string.equals(color));   // prints false
    }
}
```

A 1-9. b

[1.6] Override the hashCode, equals, and toString methods from the Object class to improve the functionality of your class

Explanation: Method hashCode() returns the same hash code for all the objects of this class. This essentially makes all the values be stored in the same bucket if objects of the preceding classes are used as keys in class HashMap (or similar classes that use hashing), and reduces it to a linked list, drastically reducing its efficiency.

Option (a) in incorrect. Book instances can be used to retrieve corresponding key values but only in limited cases—when you use the same keys (instances) to store and retrieve values. Even though hashCode() will return the same value for different Book instances, equals() will always compare the reference variables and not their values, returning false.

A 1-10. d

[1.3] Overload constructors and methods

Explanation: When a class is compiled, the contents of its initializer block are added to its constructor just before its own contents. For example, here's the decompiled code for class Wood. As you can see, the contents of its initializer block are added to its constructor:

```
class Wood
{
    public Wood()
    {
        wood = "Wood";            // initial initialization
        wood = "init:wood";       // re-assignment by the initializer block
        wood = "Wood";            // re-assignment by the constructor
    }
    String wood;
}
```

A 1-11. b

[1.4] Use the instanceof operator and casting

Explanation: Option (a) prints `false`.

Option (c) prints `false`. It doesn't fail to compile because `null` is a valid literal value that can be used for objects.

Option (d) fails to compile. The `instanceof` operator must be followed by the name of an interface, class, or enum.

Advanced class design

Exam objectives covered in this chapter	What you need to know
[2.1] Identify when and how to apply abstract classes	The design requirements and implications of using abstract classes in your application.
[2.2] Construct abstract Java classes and subclasses	Construction and inheritance with abstract Java classes.
[2.3] Use the static and final keywords	The need for defining static and final members (classes, methods, initializer blocks, and variables). The implications of defining nonstatic/nonfinal members as static/final members, and vice versa.
[2.4] Create top-level and nested classes	The flavors of nested classes—inner, static nested, method local, and anonymous. The design benefits, advantages, and disadvantages of creating inner classes. How each type of nested class is related to its outer class. The access and nonaccess modifiers that can be used with the definition of these classes and their members.
[2.5] Use enumerated types	How to compare enumerated types with regular classes. How to define enums with constructors, variables, and methods. How to define enums within classes, interfaces, and methods. How to override methods of a particular enum constant. Use of variables of enum types—when to use the enum name and when to leave it. Use of enumerated types in switch constructs. The default methods available to all enums.

While designing your application, you might need to answer questions like these:

- How do I ensure that a derived class implements an inherited behavior in its own specific manner?
- When do I prevent my class from being extended or methods from being overridden?
- When do I make objects share the same copy of a variable and when do I provide them with their own separate individual copy?
- When do I create an inner class to perform a set of related tasks and when do I let the top-level class handle it?
- How do I define constants by using enums?

Design decisions require insight into the benefits and pitfalls of multiple approaches. When armed with adequate information, you can select the best practices and approaches to designing your classes and application.

The topics covered in this chapter will help you answer the aforementioned questions. I'll take you through examples and give you multiple choices to help you determine the best option for designing your classes. This chapter covers

- Abstract classes
- Keywords `static` and `final`
- Enumerated types
- Nested and inner classes

 EXAM TIP Take note of the relationship between an exam objective heading and its subobjectives. For example, the topics of using the `static` and `final` keywords, using enumerated types, and creating top-level and nested classes are included within the main objective *advanced class design*. So, apart from using the correct syntax of all of these, the exam will query you on the impact of their use on the design of a class and an application.

Let's start with the first exam objective in this chapter, identifying when and how to apply abstract classes.

2.1   *Abstract classes and their application*

[2.1]   Identify when and how to apply abstract classes

[2.2]   Construct abstract Java classes and subclasses

Imagine you're asked to bring a bouquet of flowers. Because no particular flower is specified, you can choose any flower. How is the term *flower* used here? It communicates a group of properties and behavior, which are applicable to multiple types of flowers. Flowers like tulip, rose, hibiscus, and lotus, though *similar,* are also *unique*. In this example, you can compare the term *flower* to an abstract class: the term captures basic properties and behavior, yet enforces individual flower types to implement *some* of that behavior in a unique manner—all flowers *must* have petals, though of different size, color, or shape.

In this section, we'll focus on how the exam will test you on identifying abstract classes, and understanding their need, construction, use, and application. We'll also cover the dos and don'ts of creating abstract classes. For the exam, it's important to compare the similarities and differences of abstract classes and concrete classes. These differences affect the creation and use of these classes. Let's start by identifying abstract classes.

2.1.1   *Identify abstract classes*

An abstract class *is* an incomplete class or *is considered to be* incomplete. You define it by using the keyword `abstract`. You can't instantiate an abstract class, but you can subclass it to create abstract or concrete derived classes. The choice of defining an abstract class depends on the application context in which the classes are created; it all depends on the details that you need for a class in an application. For example, a class `Animal` might be defined as an abstract class in one application but not in another.

Imagine that you need to create a simple application, GeoAnimals, which helps young children identify a predefined set of common wild animals, while including basic information like the food the animals eat and their habitat. Figure 2.1 shows (a

Figure 2.1   Classes `Lion`, `Tiger`, and `Elephant` identified for creating the application GeoAnimals

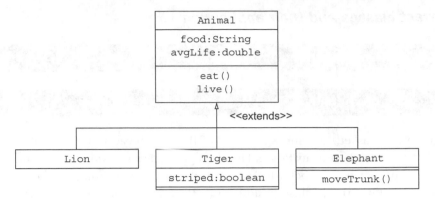

Figure 2.2   **Classes** `Lion`, `Tiger`, **and** `Elephant` **inherit class** `Animal`.

few) classes—Lion, Elephant, and Tiger—that you might identify for this application. I deliberately limited the number of classes to keep the example simple.

As you can see, classes Lion, Tiger, and Elephant have common attributes and behavior. Let's pull out another generic class—say, Animal—and make the rest of the classes extend it. Figure 2.2 shows the new arrangement.

Now the big question: Do you need to define the base class Animal as an abstract class? How can you determine this? You can ask yourself simple questions to answer the big question:

- Should my application be allowed to create instances of the generic class Animal? If no, define class Animal as an abstract class.
- Does class Animal include behavior that's common to all its derived classes, but can't be generalized (*must* it be implemented by the derived classes in their own specific manner)? If yes, define the relevant method as an abstract method and class Animal as an abstract class.

In this sample application, you'd *never* need objects of class Animal because they would always refer to a *specific* type of animal. So class Animal qualifies to be defined as an abstract class. Also, *eating* behavior, though common to all the animals, is unique to every specific animal. So method eat() is a perfect candidate to be defined as an abstract method. Figure 2.3 shows the new arrangement, where class Animal is defined as an abstract class, and method eat() is defined as an abstract method. Now all the derived classes must implement method eat().

Because an abstract class is meant to be extended by other classes, and its abstract methods are meant to be implemented, it's recommended that you document its expected behavior in your real-life projects. This documentation will enable your class to be inherited and used appropriately.

 EXAM TIP   An abstract method doesn't define an implementation. It enforces all the concrete derived classes to implement it.

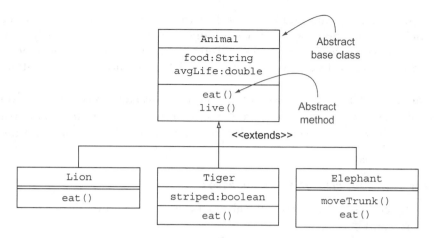

Figure 2.3 **Abstract class `Animal` defines an abstract method `eat()` and is inherited by classes `Lion`, `Tiger`, and `Elephant`.**

Until this point, you've looked at how to identify an abstract class. Does that imply that if you were to define class `Animal` in another application, you'd define it as an abstract class? Not always. For example, an application that counts all living beings, categorized as humans, animals, and plants, might not need to define class `Animal` as an abstract class because the application might not need to create its specific types; it needs only a count of the total animals. If you need to store the *type* of an animal, class `Animal` can define an attribute—say, `species`. This arrangement is shown in figure 2.4.

Another frequently asked question by new programmers or designers is, when is an abstract base class fit to be defined as an interface? Interfaces can be defined only when no implementation of any method is provided. Also, an interface can define only constants, which can't be reassigned another value by the implementing classes. The base class `Animal` discussed previously can't be defined as an interface; it can't define its attributes `food` and `avgLife` as constants. As an example of an interface, the Java package `java.util` contains multiple interfaces, such as `List`. The interface `List` defines multiple methods, which must be implemented by all the implementing classes, such as `ArrayList`.

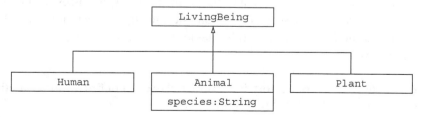

Figure 2.4 **Class `Animal` need not be always defined as an abstract class in *all* applications.**

NOTE   Starting with Java 8, an interface can define a default implementation of its methods, so an implementing class might *not* necessarily override these methods. But this exam is based on Java 7 and I'll continue to refer to an interface as the one that can't define method implementation.

Now that you understand how to identify abstract classes, let's look at how to construct abstract classes and their subclasses, and how to apply them. On the exam, you'll be questioned on correct construction of abstract classes, their subclasses, and their dos and don'ts.

2.1.2   *Construct abstract classes and subclasses*

To keep the code small, let's code the abstract class Animal and only two of its derived classes, Lion and Elephant:

```
abstract class Animal {                          ① Abstract base
    protected String food;                          class Animal
    protected double avgLife;                    ② Properties of
                                                    class Animal
    Animal(String food, double avgLife) {
        this.food = food;                        ③ Constructor
        this.avgLife = avgLife;
    }                                            ④ Abstract
    abstract void eat();                            method eat()

    void live() {
        System.out.println("Natural habitat : forest");   ⑤ Nonabstract
    }                                                         method live()
}
```

At ❶, abstract class Animal is defined by prefixing the class definition with the keyword abstract. The code at ❷ defines attributes to store values for food and average life span: food and avgLife. The code at ❸ defines a constructor for class Animal. You can't instantiate an abstract class, but you can create its constructors, including overloaded constructors. At least one of the Animal constructors must be called by instances of its derived classes. The code at ❹ defines abstract method eat(), which delegates the responsibility of implementing it to the derived classes. You can define class Animal as an abstract class, even if doesn't define any abstract methods. The code at ❺ defines method live(), with an implementation. If required, it can be overridden by the derived classes.

 EXAM TIP   It isn't obligatory for abstract classes to define abstract methods. *Abstract methods* must not define a body.

Following is the definition of derived class `Lion`:

```
class Lion extends Animal{
    Lion(String food, double avgLife) {
        super(food, avgLife);
    }
    void eat() {
        System.out.println("Lion-hunt " + food);
    }
}
```

① Constructor

② Implement method eat()

Class `Lion` extends the base class `Animal`. It defines a constructor at **①**, which accepts a `double` value for average life and a `String` value for food and passes it on to its base class's constructor. At **②**, class `Lion` implements method `eat()`. Let's now define class `Elephant`:

```
class Elephant extends Animal{
    Elephant(String food, double avgLife) {
        super(food, avgLife);
    }

    void eat() {
        System.out.println("Elephant-method eat");
    }

    void moveTrunk() {
        System.out.println("Elephant-method moveTrunk");
    }
}
```

① Constructor

② Implement method eat()

③ New method moveTrunk()

At **①**, class `Elephant` defines a constructor that calls its base class constructor. At **②**, it implements abstract method `eat()` from the base class. At **③**, it defines a new method, `moveTrunk()`.

 EXAM TIP Notice the power of base class constructors to ensure that all derived class constructors pass them a value. The base class `Animal` defines only one constructor that accepts a value for its instance variables `food` and `avgLife`. Because a derived class constructor must call its base class's constructor, classes `Lion` and `Elephant` define a constructor that calls `Animal`'s constructor.

Let's put all these classes to work, in class `GeoAnimals`, as follows:

```
class GeoAnimals{
    Animal[] animals = new Animal[2];

    GeoAnimals() {
        animals[0] = new Lion("Antelope", 20);
        animals[1] = new Elephant("Bananas", 60);
    }
```

① An array of type Animal—base class of Lion and Elephant

② Initialize array animals with separate instances of Lion and Elephant.

```
    void flashcards() {
        for (Animal anAnimal : animals) {
            anAnimal.eat();
            anAnimal.live();
        }
    }

    public static void main(String args[]) {
        GeoAnimals myAnimals = new GeoAnimals();
        myAnimals.flashcards();
    }
}
```

❸ Iterate through objects of array animals, calling methods eat() and live().

❹ Create an instance of GeoAnimals and call method flashcards().

Here's the output of the preceding code (blank lines were added to improve readability):

```
Lion-hunt Antelope
Natural habitat : forest

Elephant-method eat
Natural habitat : forest
```

Let's walk through this code. The code at ❶ declares an array of type Animal. Though you can't create instances of abstract class Animal, an array of Animal can be used to store objects of its derived classes, Lion and Elephant. The code at ❷ initializes animals with instances of classes Lion and Elephant. The code at ❸ iterates through the array animals, calling methods eat() and live() on all its elements. The code at ❹ defines method main() that creates an object of class GeoAnimals, calling method flashcards().

The code in this section walked you through how to create abstract classes and their subclasses, and how to use them. The efficient use of abstract classes lies in their identification in an application. Let's see how well you score on identifying all abstract and concrete classes in an application in the following "Twist in the Tale" exercise.

Twist in the Tale 2.1

The following are names of multiple classes. Your task is to arrange these in an inheritance hierarchy, connecting all base and derived classes. At end of the exercise, all these classes should be connected, with the base class at the top and derived classes below it.

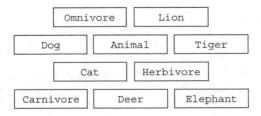

Here's another example that will help you attempt the preceding exercise.

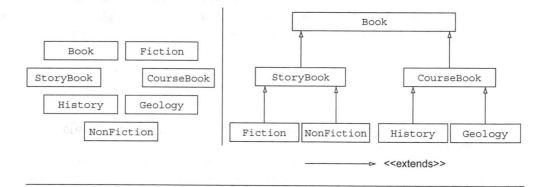

 EXAM TIP   An abstract method can't be defined in a concrete class. It can be defined in an abstract class only.

2.1.3   *Understand the need for abstract classes*

An abstract class represents partial implementation of an object or concept. But why do you need partial implementation? Do abstract classes exist only so other classes can inherit them? These questions are frequently asked by new Java application designers. You might also have to answer these questions on the exam.

You need an abstract class to pull out and group together the common properties and behavior of multiple classes—the same reason you need a nonabstract base class. You define a *base class* as an *abstract class* to prevent creation of its instances. As the creator, you think that it doesn't include enough details to create its own objects. When you define abstract methods in a base class, it *forces* all its nonabstract derived classes to implement the incomplete functionality (abstract methods) in their *own* unique manner.

Because you can't create instances of an abstract class, there's not much sense in creating an abstract base class, which isn't extended by other classes.

 EXAM TIP   Abstract classes make a point loud and clear: they *force* the concrete derived classes to implement a base class's abstract methods, in their own unique manner.

Note that I haven't discussed the need for, advantages of, or disadvantages of creating nonabstract base classes in this section. This section specifically covers base classes that are abstract.

2.1.4   *Follow the dos and don'ts of creating and using abstract classes*

Apart from the points covered in the previous section, the exam will likely include other theoretical and coding questions on the dos and don'ts of creating and implementing abstract classes.

DON'T CREATE AN ABSTRACT CLASS ONLY TO PREVENT CREATION OF ITS OBJECTS

To prevent instantiation of a class by using the operator new, define all its class constructors as private. For example, class java.lang.Math in the Java API doesn't allow creation of its objects by defining its constructor as a private member:

```
package java.lang;
public final class Math{
    private Math() { /*code */}
}
```

DON'T MAKE AN ABSTRACT CLASS IMPLEMENT INTERFACES THAT RESULT IN INVALID METHOD IMPLEMENTATION

When a class implements an interface, the class must implement its methods (unless the class is abstract) to meet the contract. But if the class defines methods with the same name as the one defined in the interface, they should either comply with correct method overriding or overloading rules or else the class won't compile. In the following example, class Animal can't implement interface Live:

```
interface Live{                                    Method eat() that
    boolean eat();              ◄──┘               returns boolean value
}
                                                   Won't compile; method eat() from
                                                   Live and Animal can't coexist.
abstract class Animal implements Live{   ◄──┘
    public abstract void eat();      ◄──┐          Method eat() doesn't
}                                               return any value.
```

Class Animal won't compile because method eat() from interface Live and method eat() defined in class Animal exist as invalid overloaded methods.

DON'T CREATE OBJECTS OF AN ABSTRACT CLASS

Code that creates objects of an abstract class won't compile:

```
abstract class Animal{}
class Forest {                                     Won't compile; can't
    Animal animal = new Animal();   ◄──┘           instantiate abstract classes.
}
```

DON'T DEFINE AN ABSTRACT CLASS AS A FINAL CLASS

A final class can't be extended. On the other hand, abstract classes are created so they can be extended by other classes. Hence, abstract classes can't be defined as final classes.

```
abstract final class Animal {}                  ◄──   Won't compile
```

DON'T FORCE AN ABSTRACT CLASS TO IMPLEMENT ALL METHODS FROM THE INTERFACE(S) IT IMPLEMENTS

An abstract class can implement multiple interfaces. It might not implement *all* the abstract methods from the implemented interface(s), leaving them to be implemented by all its nonabstract derived classes:

```
interface Live{
    void eat();
}
abstract class Animal implements Live{}
```

> Abstract class Animal doesn't implement eat() from interface Live.

DO USE AN OBJECT OF AN ABSTRACT CLASS TO REFER TO OBJECTS OF ITS NONABSTRACT DERIVED CLASSES

An abstract class can't be instantiated. But this doesn't stop you from using a reference variable of an abstract base class to refer to an instance of its nonabstract derived class:

```
abstract class Animal{}
class Deer extends Animal{}
class Forest{
    Animal animal = new Deer();
}
```

> Abstract class variable can refer to instance of its derived class

Comparing an abstract class with a concrete class is obvious, as covered in the next section. This comparison will help you with multiple exam objectives: identifying abstract classes, their construction, and their application.

2.1.5 *Compare abstract classes and concrete classes*

Do you think the constructor of an abstract base class is called in the same manner as that of a concrete base class? Yes, indeed. Table 2.1 answers many more questions like this by comparing abstract and concrete classes.

Table 2.1 Comparing an abstract class with a concrete class

Comparison Category	Abstract class	Concrete class
Create a new type	✓	✓
Use as base class	✓	✓
Extend another class	✓	✓
Implement interfaces	✓	✓
Define attributes and concrete methods	✓	✓
Require at least one constructor to be called by its derived classes	✓	✓
Define abstract methods	✓	✗
Allow object creation	✗	✓

Before moving on to the next section, let's quickly list the points to remember about abstract classes for the exam.

> **Rules to remember for creating abstract classes**
> - An abstract class must be defined by using the keyword `abstract`.
> - An abstract class can extend any other abstract or concrete class and implement other interfaces.
> - An abstract class can define multiple constructors.
> - An abstract class can define instance and static variables.
> - An abstract class can define instance and static methods.
> - An abstract class might not necessarily define an abstract method and can exist without any abstract method.
> - A class can't define an abstract static method.
> - Don't create an abstract class just to prevent creation of its instances.
> - Don't make an abstract class implement interfaces that result in incorrect overloaded or overridden methods.

> **Rules to remember for subclassing an abstract class**
> - A concrete subclass must implement all the abstract methods in its abstract superclass(es).
> - An abstract subclass might not implement all the abstract methods in its abstract superclass(es).
> - A subclass must call at least one constructor from its superclass.

Identification of abstract classes is an important design decision. It changes how other classes might use the abstract class. Similarly, creating classes that can't be extended, creating methods that can't be overridden, or creating class (or static) members are other important design decisions. In the next section, you'll see how you can do so by using the `static` and `final` nonaccess modifiers.

2.2   *Static and final keywords*

 [2.3]   Use the static and final keywords

Defining a class as a final class prevents it from being extended. Similarly, a static variable or method can be accessed without instances of its class; the variable or method is available after its class is loaded into memory. These are a few examples of how the nonaccess modifiers `static` and `final` change the default behavior of a Java entity. For the exam, you need to understand the need for defining static and final members (classes, methods, initializer blocks, and variables) together with their correct definition and use. You also need to know the implications of defining nonstatic/nonfinal members as static/final members, and vice versa.

2.2.1 Static modifier

You can define variables, methods, nested classes, and nested interfaces as static members. They belong to a class and not to instances. They can be accessed soon after their class is loaded into memory. Top-level classes, interfaces, and enums can't be defined as static entities. Watch out for code that declares top-level classes, interfaces, and enums as static members. Such code won't compile. Let's get started with static class variables.

STATIC VARIABLES

Static variables belong to a class and are shared by all its instances. Their value is the same for all instances of their class. A static class variable is created when its class is loaded into memory by the JVM. It can exist and is accessible even if no instances of the class exist. So you can use it to perform operations that span multiple instances of a class. Class Book defines a static class variable bookCount, to count the instances of class Book that are created while your program is running:

```
class Book {
    static int bookCount;          ←──┤  Static variable
    public Book() {                     bookCount
        ++bookCount;           ←──┐  bookCount is incremented
    }                             └─ in constructor
}
class Publisher{
    public static void main(String args[]){
        System.out.println(Book.bookCount);   ←── ❶ Prints "0"
        Book b1 = new Book();
        Book b2 = new Book();
        System.out.println(Book.bookCount);   ←── ❷ Prints "2"
    }
}
```

Assuming that no instances of Book were created earlier, the code at ❶ prints 0. The code at ❷ prints 2 due to creation of two instances of class Book, created on the preceding lines. Each invocation of the construction increments the value of the static class variable bookCount by 1.

 EXAM TIP Unlike instance variables, which are initialized for each instance, static class variables are initialized only once, when they are loaded into memory. The default variable values are false for boolean; '\u0000' for char; 0 for byte; short, int, 0L for long; 0.0F for float; 0.0D for double; and null for objects.

Because the same value of a static class variable is shared across all the instances of a class, if modified, the same modified value is reflected across all instances. In the following code, the value of the static class variable bookCount is accessed and modified using the class name Book and instances b1 and b2 (modifications in bold):

```
class Book {
    static int bookCount;
    public Book() {
        ++bookCount;
    }
}
class Publisher{
    public static void main(String args[]){
        System.out.println(Book.bookCount);
        Book b1 = new Book();
        Book b2 = new Book();
        System.out.println(Book.bookCount);
        b1.bookCount = 10;
        System.out.println(b2.bookCount);
    }
}
```

Prints "0" (access bookCount using class name Book)

Set value of bookCount to 10, using reference variable b1.

Prints "10" (access bookCount using reference variable b2)

 NOTE   For simplicity, I've defined the variable bookCount with default access, which is directly accessed and manipulated outside the class Book. This isn't a recommended approach in real-life projects. Encapsulate your data by defining the class and instance variables as private and make them accessible outside their class through accessor and mutator methods.

On the exam, you're likely to see code that accesses a static class variable by using the name of its class and its instances. Although a static class variable is allowed to be accessed by using instances of a class, it's not a preferred approach; it makes the static class variable seem to belong to an instance, which is incorrect. Always refer to a static class member by using its class name.

 EXAM TIP   You can access a static member by using the name of its class or any of its instances. All these approaches refer to the same static member. The preferred approach is to use a class name; otherwise, a static member *seems* to be tied to an instance, which is incorrect.

A combination of the static and final nonaccess modifiers is used to define *constants* (variables whose value can't change). In the following code, the class Emp defines the constants MIN_AGE and MAX_AGE:

```
class Emp {
    public static final int MIN_AGE = 20;
    static final int MAX_AGE = 70;
}
```

Constant MIN_AGE

Constant MAX_AGE

STATIC METHODS

Static methods don't need instances of a class. They can be called even if no instance of the class exists. You define static methods to access or manipulate static class variables. The static methods can't access nonstatic fields or nonstatic methods. Referring to the example of class Book, which used the static variable bookCount to count all instances of class Book, static methods getBookCount() and incrementBookCount() can be created to access bookCount and manipulate it:

```
class Book {
    private static int bookCount;
    public static int getBookCount(){        Static method to retrieve
        return bookCount;                     value of static variable
    }                                         bookCount

    public void incrementBookCount() {        Static method to
        ++bookCount;                          increment value of static
    }                                         variable bookCount
}
```

You also use static methods to define *utility methods*—methods that *usually* manipulate the method parameters to compute and return an appropriate value:

```
static double average(double num1, double num2, double num3) {
    return(num1+num2+num3)/3;
}
```

A static method might not always define method parameters. For example, the method random in class java.lang.Math doesn't accept any parameters. It returns a pseudo-random number, greater than or equal to 0.0 and less than 1.0.

 EXAM TIP A static method is used to manipulate static class variables or to define utility methods. A utility method may or may not accept method parameters.

WHAT CAN A STATIC METHOD ACCESS?

Neither static class methods nor static class variables can access the nonstatic instance variables and instance methods of a class. But the reverse is true: nonstatic variables and methods can access static variables and methods because the static members of a class exist even if no instances of the class exist. Static members are forbidden from accessing instance methods and variables, which can exist only if an instance of the class is created.

Examine the following code:

```
class MyClass {
    static int x = count();        Compilation
    int count() { return 10; }      error
}
```

This is the compilation error thrown by the previous class:

```
MyClass.java:3: nonstatic method count() cannot be
                          referenced from a static context
    static int x = count();
                       ^
1 error
```

The following code is valid:

```
class MyClass {
    static int x = result();
    static int result() { return 20; }
    int nonStaticResult() { return result(); }
}
```

Static variable referencing a static method

Nonstatic method using a static method

You can use constructors or instance initializer blocks to initialize the instance variables. But how can you initialize the static variables, after they're loaded into memory? *Static initializer blocks* are the answer.

STATIC INITIALIZER BLOCKS

A *static initializer* block is a code block defined using braces and prefixed by the keyword static:

```
static {
    //code to initialize static variables
}
```

Because static variables can't be initialized using the constructors of a class, a static initializer block is used to initialize static variables. This initializer block executes when a class is loaded by the JVM into memory. You can define multiple static initializer blocks in your code, which execute in the order of their appearance. All types of statements are allowed in this block, including declaration, initialization, assignment, and calling of other static variables and methods. In the following example, class AffiliateProgram defines a static variable accountOpenBonus. The variable accountOpenBonus is initialized using a static initializer block:

```
class AffiliateProgram {
    private static int accountOpenBonus;
    static {
        accountOpenBonus = 5;
    }
}
```

Declare static variable

Initialize static variable using a static initializer block

You might argue that you could initialize the static variable accountOpenBonus as follows:

```
class AffiliateProgram {
    private static int accountOpenBonus = 5;
}
```

Declare and initialize a static variable

But what happens if you need to use a calculated value or initialize the value of accountOpenBonus based on the outcome of a condition:

```
class AffiliateProgram {
    private static int accountOpenBonus;
    static {
        if (/* file XYZ exists */)
            accountOpenBonus = 5;
        else
            accountOpenBonus = 15;
    }
}
```

Conditional assignment of variable accountOpenBonus

Again, you might argue that you can move the preceding conditional execution to a static method and use it to initialize variable accountOpenBonus, without using the static initializer block:

```
class AffiliateProgram {
    private static int accountOpenBonus = initAccountOpenBonus();

    private static int initAccountOpenBonus() {
        if (/* file XYZ exists */)
            return 5;
        else
            return 15;
    }
}
```

Conditional assignment of variable accountOpenBonus using static method

What happens if method initAccountOpenBonus() throws a checked exception, say, FileNotFoundException? In this case, you *must* use a static initializer block to assign the returned value from initAccountOpenBonus() to variable accountOpenBonus. As you know, if a method throws a checked exception, its use should either be enclosed within a try block or the method that uses it should declare the exception to be thrown. In this case, neither is possible; the declaration of the variable accountOpen-Bonus can't be enclosed within a try block because this statement doesn't exist within a method or code block. Here's the relevant code:

Won't compile; can't declare and initialize variable using method that throws checked exception

```
import java.io.*;
class AffiliateProgram {
    private static int accountOpenBonus = initAccountOpenBonus();
    private static int initAccountOpenBonus() throws FileNotFoundException
    {
        //relevant code
    }
}
```

And here's the way out:

```
class AffiliateProgram {                                              Static          Static method that
    private static int accountOpenBonus;          ◄──── variable      throws checked
    private static int initAccountOpenBonus()                         exception
                                  throws FileNotFoundException{  ◄──────┘
        //..relevant code
    }
    static {
        try {                                                    ◄──── try block to catch
            accountOpenBonus = initAccountOpenBonus();                 FileNotFoundException
        }                                                             thrown by
        catch (FileNotFoundException e) {                             initAccountOpenBonus()
            //.. relevant code
        }
    }
}
```

static initializer block → static { ... }

Another reason for the existence of a static initializer block is to add values (static or dynamic) to collection objects that have already been initialized. Here's an example:

```
class AddValuesToStaticVariables {                          String array data-
    static private String[] dataStores = new String[5];  ◄─── Stores is initialized.
    static {
        dataStores[0] = "us.ny";                                Add explicit values
        dataStores[1] = "jp.tk";                                to dataStores.
        dataStores[2] = "gr.br";
        //..code that assigns dynamic value to dataStores[]  ◄── Pull values from
    }                                                            the database
}                                                                and add to String
                                                                 array dataStores.
```

The static initializer blocks can be tricky and cumbersome to work with when it comes to debugging them. On the exam, beware of code that defines multiple initializer blocks. If a class defines multiple initializer blocks, they execute in the order of their appearance in a class. Let's examine output of code that defines multiple initializer blocks:

```
class StaticInitBlocks {
    static int staticVar = 10;
    static {
        System.out.println("First");
        ++staticVar;
    }
    static {
        System.out.println("Second");
        ++staticVar;
    }

    static void modifyStaticVar() {
        ++staticVar;
    }
```

```
    public StaticInitBlocks() {
        System.out.println("Constructor:" + staticVar);
    }

    public static void main(String args[]) {
        new StaticInitBlocks();
        modifyStaticVar();
        new StaticInitBlocks();
    }
}
```

Code in a static initializer block executes when a class is loaded in memory by JVM—before creation of its instances. The output of the preceding code is as follows:

```
First
Second
Constructor:12
Constructor:13
```

Can the static and instance initializer blocks access the static or instance variables of a class, like other methods? Let me modify the preceding code and use it for the next "Twist in the Tale" exercise.

Twist in the Tale 2.2

Following is modified code for class DemoMultipleStaticBlocks. Answer the question before you execute it on your system. Which answer correctly shows its output?

```
class DemoMultipleStaticBlocks {
    static {
        ++staticVar;
    }
    static int staticVar ;
    static {
        ++staticVar;
    }
    public DemoMultipleStaticBlocks() {
        System.out.println("Constructor:" + staticVar);
    }
    public static void main(String args[]) {
        new DemoMultipleStaticBlocks();
    }
}
```

   a   Constructor: 2
   b   Constructor: 1
   c   Constructor: 0
   d   Compilation error
   e   Runtime exception

EXAM TIP   On the exam, beware of code that defines multiple initializer blocks. If a class defines multiple initializer blocks, they execute in the order of their appearance in a class.

Watch out for another combination on the exam: initialization of a static class variable and its manipulation in a static block. What do you think is the order of execution in the following code? Will the following example code print 1 or 11?

```
public class AssignManipulateStaticVariable {
    static {
        rate = 10;                          First static initializer
    }                                       block to assign 10 to rate
    static int rate = 0;

    static {
        ++rate;                             Second static initializer block
    }                                       to increment rate by 1
    public AssignManipulateStaticVariable() {
        System.out.println(rate);
    }
    public static void main(String args[]) {
        new AssignManipulateStaticVariable();    ⟵——— Prints "1"
    }
}
```

Declare static variable rate and assign 0 to it.

For the preceding code, the compiler rearranges the code to execute. It declares the static variable age and then picks up the code from all the static initializer blocks and assignment of age and combines them in a single static initializer block, in the order of their occurrence, as follows:

```
static int rate;
static
{
    rate = 10;
    rate = 0;
    ++rate;
}
```

The preceding code explains why `AssignManipulateStaticVariable` prints 1 and not 11.

STATIC CLASSES AND INTERFACES

Let's look at other types of static entities: static classes and interfaces. These are also referred to as *nested classes, static nested classes, static interfaces*, and *static nested interfaces*. You can't prefix the definition of a top-level class or an interface with the keyword `static`. A top-level class or interface is one that isn't defined within another class or interface. The following code fails to compile:

```
static class Person {}
static interface MyInterface {}
```

But you can define a class and an interface as a static member of another class. The following code is valid:

```
class Person {
    static class Address {}          ← Static nested class
    static interface MyInterface {}  ← Static nested interface
}
```

As you know, the static variables and methods of a class are accessible without the existence of any of its objects. Similarly, you can access a static class without an object of its outer class. You'll learn all about the other details of the static classes in section 2.3.2 .

2.2.2 Nonaccess modifier—final

The decision to apply the nonaccess modifier final to a class, interface, variable, or method is an important class design decision. To start, should you define your class as a final class? Yes, if you don't want it to be subclassed. Should you define your method as a final method? Yes, if you don't want any of its subclasses to override it. Do you want to define a variable as a final variable? Yes, if after the variable is initialized, you don't want it to be reassigned another value. Knowing these details will enable you to make the right decisions—when, why, where, and how to apply the nonaccess modifier final and when not to. Apart from testing you on how to use the modifier final in code, the exam will also query you on the implications of its use on the design or behavior of code. Let's start with final variables.

FINAL VARIABLES

The final variables can be initialized only *once*. You can tag all types of variables—static variables, instance variables, local variables, and method parameters—with the nonaccess modifier final. Because of the differences in how these variable types are initialized, they exhibit different behavior. Let's start with defining a static variable as a final variable:

```
class TestFinal {
    static final int staticFinal = 10;
}
```

A final static class variable can be initialized with its declaration, or by using a static initializer block, which is *guaranteed* to execute only once for a class. Because a static method can be called multiple times, it can't define code to initialize a final (static) variable:

```
class TestFinal {
    static final int staticFinal2 = 12345;   ← Static final variable initialized with its declaration

    static final int staticFinal;             ← Static final variable not initialized

    static {                                  ← Static initializer block to initialize static variable
        staticFinal = 1234;
    }
```

```
        static void setStaticFinal(int value) {
            staticFinal = value;
        }
    }
```
Won't compile; static method can execute multiple times and so it can't include initialization of final variable.

Because the constructor of a class executes on creation of every instance of the class, you can't initialize a final static variable in the constructor. The following code won't compile:

```
class FinalStatic {
    static final int finalVar;

    FinalStatic() {
        finalVar = 10;
    }
}
```
Final static variable can't be initialized in constructor of a class

Similarly, though you can initialize a final *instance variable* in the class's constructor or its instance initializer block, you can't initialize it in an instance *method*. Instance methods can execute more than once:

Instance final variable initialized with its declaration

Instance final variable not initialized

```
class InstanceFinalVariables {
    final int finalVar2 = 710;

    final int finalVar;

    InstanceFinalVariables() {
        finalVar = 10;
    }
```
Class's constructor initializes instance final variable

```
    void setValue(int a) {
        finalVar = a;
    }
}
```
Won't compile; a method may execute multiple times and so can't include code to initialize a final variable.

 EXAM TIP   If a static or instance variable is marked `final`, it must be initialized, or the code won't compile.

Interestingly, you can survive code with an uninitialized final local variable, if you don't use it:

```
class MyClass {
    void setValue(int a) {
        final int finalLocalVar1;
        finalLocalVar1 = 20;

        final int finalLocalVar2;
    }
}
```
Final local variable declared and initialized on separate lines

Uninitialized final local variable; compiles successfully

In the preceding code, if you try to use the uninitialized final local variable `final-LocalVar2`, your code won't compile. Modified code is as follows:

```
class MyClass {
    void setValue(int a) {
        final int finalLocalVar1;
        finalLocalVar1 = 20;

        final int finalLocalVar2;

        System.out.println(finalLocalVar2);
    }
}
```

> **Won't compile when you try to use an uninitialized local variable.** ← (points to `System.out.println(finalLocalVar2);`)

Method parameters are initialized when the method is invoked. If a method marks its method parameter(s) as `final`, the method body can't reassign a value to it, as follows:

```
class MyClass {
    void setValue(final int finalMethodParam) {
        finalMethodParam = 10;
    }
}
```

> **Final method parameter** ← (points to `final` in method signature)
> **Won't compile; value can't be assigned to final method parameter.** ← (points to `finalMethodParam = 10;`)

There's a difference between final primitive variables and final object reference variables. The final primitive variables can't change, but the object referred to by final object reference variables can be changed. Only the final reference itself can't be changed:

```
class MyClass {
    void addCondition(final StringBuilder query) {
        query.append("WHERE id > 500");
        query = new StringBuilder("SELECT name FROM emp");
    }
}
```

> **Final method parameter** ← (points to `final StringBuilder query`)
> **Can modify object referred to by final reference variable query.** ← (points to `query.append("WHERE id > 500");`)
> **Won't compile; can't reassign another object to final reference variable query.** ← (points to `query = new StringBuilder("SELECT name FROM emp");`)

CONDITIONAL ASSIGNMENT OF FINAL VARIABLES

What happens when you initialize a final variable within an `if-else` construct, `switch` statement, or `for`, `do-while`, or `while` loop? In this case, code that assigns a value to the final variable *might* not execute. If the Java compiler is doubtful about the initialization of your final variable, the code won't compile. For example, the constructor of `MyClass` assigns a value to its final instance variable `finalVar` by using an `if` statement, as shown in the following code listing.

Listing 2.1   Conditional assignment of final instance variable in class's constructor

```
class MyClass {
    final int finalVar;
    MyClass(double a, double b) {                  ➊ Assigns 20 to
            if (a > b)                                 finalVar if a > b
                    finalVar = 20;        ◁────┘
            else if (b >= a)              ◁──┐  Assigns 30 to finalVar
                    finalVar = 30;           ➋  if b >= a
    }
}
```

Class `MyClass` fails compilation with the following compilation error message:

```
variable finalVar might not have been initialized
```

The code at ➊ assigns a value to `finalVar` if the condition a > b evaluates to `true`. The code at ➋ assigns a value to `finalVar` if condition b >= a evaluates to `true`. The compiler has its doubts about being able to execute (and thus initialize) in all conditions. So, the Java compiler will consider initialization of a final variable complete only if the initialization code will execute in *all* conditions. Adding an `else` branch results in successful code compilation:

```
class MyClass {
    final int finalVar;
    MyClass(double a, double b) {               ➊ Assigns 20 to
        if (a>b)                                   finalVar if a > b
            finalVar = 20;         ◁────┘
        else                       ◁──┐  Assigns 30 to finalVar
            finalVar = 30;            ➋  otherwise
    }
}
```

In the preceding code, ➊ initializes `finalVar` to 30 if the condition a > b evaluates to `true`. Otherwise, it initializes `finalVar` to 30 at ➋. Let's modify the code in listing 2.1 so it uses constant literal values instead of variables, in `if` conditions:

```
class MyClass {
    final int finalVar;
    MyClass(double a, double b) {
        if (1>2)                   ┐  Assigns 10 to
            finalVar = 10;      ◁──┘  finalVar if 1 > 2
        else if (100>10)        ◁──┐  Assigns 20 to finalVar
            finalVar = 20;         ➊  if 100 > 10
    }
}
```

The preceding code compiles successfully, because with the constant values, the compiler can determine that code at ➊ will execute, initializing a value to the final variable for sure.

Let's modify the code again, so it continues to use the variables in the `if` conditions. In listing 2.1, the Java compiler complained that variable `finalVar` might not have been initialized. So let's explicitly assign a value to variable `finalVar`, before the start of the `if` statement, as follows:

```
class MyClass {
    final int finalVar;
    MyClass(double a, double b) {
        finalVar = 100;
        if (a>b)
            finalVar = 20;
        else if (b>=a)
            finalVar = 30;
    }
}
```

❶ Explicit assignment to final variable finalVar

❷ Conditional assignment to final variable finalVar

The code at ❶ initializes `finalVar`, and the code at ❷ tries to assign a value to it, conditionally. Because a final variable can't be reassigned a value, the preceding code fails compilation with the following compilation error message:

```
variable finalVar might already have been assigned
                finalVar = 20;
                ^
```

EXAM TIP On the exam, look out for multiple initializations of a final variable. Code snippets that try to reinitialize a final variable won't compile.

The simplest way to initialize a final variable is to do so with its declaration. If not initialized with its declaration, a static final variable can be initialized in the class's static initializer block. An instance final variable can be initialized in its constructor or the instance initializer block. A local final variable can be assigned a value in the method in which it's defined. A final method parameter can't be reassigned a value within the method.

It's time for you to attempt the next "Twist in the Tale" exercise, which tests you on understanding assignment of a base class's final instance variable from the derived class.

Twist in the Tale 2.3

Let's modify the code used in the preceding examples so class `MyClass` does not initialize its final instance variable `finalVar`. This variable is initialized in its derived class, `MyDerivedClass`, as follows:

```
abstract class MyClass {
    public final int finalVar;
}
class MyDerivedClass extends MyClass {
    MyDerivedClass() {
        super();
        finalVar = 1000;
    }
}
```

Your task is to first think about the possible output of the following code before you compile it on your system:

```
class Test {
    {System.out.println(new MyDerivedClass().finalVar);}
    public static void main(String args[]) {
        new Test();
    }
}
```

FINAL METHODS

The final methods defined in a base class can't be overridden by its derived classes. The final methods are used to prevent a derived class from overriding the implementation of a base class's method. Can you think of any scenario where you'd need this? Picture this: the base class of all the Java classes, `java.lang.Object`, defines multiple final methods—wait, notify, getClass. Methods `wait()` and `notify()` are used in threading and synchronization. If the derived classes were allowed to override these methods, how do you think Java would implement threading and synchronization?

If a derived class tries to override a final method from its base class, it won't compile, as follows:

```
class Base {                          Final method
    final void finalMethod() {}       in base class
}
class Derived extends Base {          Won't compile; final method in
void finalMethod() {}                 base class can't be overridden.
}
```

The preceding code fails to compile, with the following compilation error message:

```
finalMethod() in Derived cannot override finalMethod() in Base
    final void finalMethod() {}
             ^
  overridden method is final
1 error
```

As you know, you can override only what is inherited by a derived class. The following code compiles successfully, even though the derived class *seems* to override a final method from its base class:

```
class Base {                                  Private methods aren't
    private final void finalMethod() {}       inherited by derived classes.
}
class Derived extends Base {                  Compiles
    final void finalMethod() {}               successfully
}
```

The base class's private methods aren't inherited by a derived class. In the previous code, method `finalMethod()` is defined as a private method in class `Base`. So it doesn't matter whether it's marked as a final method. Method `finalMethod()` defined in class `Derived` doesn't override the base class's method `finalMethod()`. Class `Derived` defines a new method, `finalMethod()`.

 EXAM TIP The private methods of a base class aren't inherited by its derived classes. A method using the same signature in the derived class isn't an overridding method, but a new method.

FINAL CLASSES

You can prevent a class from being extended by marking it as a `final` class. But why would you do so? A class marked as a final class can't be derived by any other class. For example, class `String`, which defines an immutable sequence of characters, is defined as a final class. It's a core class, which is used in a lot of Java API classes and user-defined classes. What happens, say, if a developer extends class `String` and modifies its `equals()` method to return a value `true` for all method parameter values passed to it? Because we can't extend the final class `String`, let's create a class `MyString` and override its `equals()` method to return `true` without comparing any values:

```java
class MyString {
    String name;
    MyString (String name) {this.name = name;}
    public boolean equals(Object o) {
            return true;
    }
}
```

Many classes from the Java API, like `HashMap` and `ArrayList`, rely heavily on the correct implementation of `equals()` for searching, deleting, and retrieving objects. Imagine the effect it would have if you try to use objects of class `MyString` in an `ArrayList` and retrieve a matching value:

```java
class UseMyStringInCollectionClasses {
    public static void main(String args[]) {
        ArrayList<MyString> list = new ArrayList<>();
        MyString myStrEast = new MyString("East");
        MyString myStrWest = new MyString("West");
        list.add(myStrEast);
        System.out.println(list.contains(myStrWest));
    }
}
```

Creates ArrayList—list

Add only one element to list—myStrEast

Prints "true"—list can find myStrWest, which was never added to it.

Surprisingly, the preceding code prints `true` even though `list` doesn't contain a matching `MyString` object. This is because method `contains90` in `ArrayList` uses the `equals()` (overridden) method of the objects it holds. If you can't get all of this explanation, don't worry. Collection classes are covered in detail in chapter 4. Imagine the havoc that objects of an extended `String` class can cause, if class `String` wasn't defined as a final class, was allowed to be extended, and its methods overridden.

You can mark a class as a final class by prefixing its definition with the keyword `final`:

```
final class FinalClass {
    //.. this need not be detailed here
}
```
Class is marked final by adding final to its definition.

You can't reverse the position of the keywords `final` and `class`:

```
class final ClassBeforeFinalWontCompile  {}
```
Won't compile; position of keywords class and final can't be interchanged.

The original intent of defining an abstract class was to extend it to create more meaningful and concrete classes. Because a final class can't be extended, you can't define a class both as final and abstract:

```
abstract final class FinalAbstractClassDontExist {}
```
Won't compile; a class can't be defined both as final and abstract.

If you try to extend a final class, your class won't compile:

```
final class Base {}
class Derived extends Base {}
```
Final class

Won't compile; can't extend a final base class.

 EXAM TIP Look out for trick questions on the exam that extend final classes from the Java API, like class `String` and the wrapper classes `Byte`, `Short`, `Integer`, `Long`, `Float`, `Double`, `Boolean`, and `Character`. When you don't look at the source code of the base class and see that it's marked `final`, it's easy to overlook that the classes that extend it won't compile. Though the authors of this exam claim not to include trick questions, they also state that they expect the candidates to know "their stuff."

The enumerated types share some characteristics of the `final` keyword. Enumerated types enable you to define a new type, but with a predefined set of objects. Let's see how in the next section.

2.3 *Enumerated types*

 [2.5] Use enumerated types

Think of the courses offered by a university or maybe even the roles within an organization: each defines a finite and predefined set of objects. These finite and predefined sets of objects can be defined as enumerated types, or *enums*. An enum defines a new custom data type (like interfaces and classes). Users are allowed to use only *existing* enum objects; they can't create new enum objects. *Type safety* was the main reason for introducing enumerated types in Java version 5.0, discussed further in the following section.

2.3.1 Understanding the need for and creating an enum

Let's assume that you have been assigned the task of creating a gaming application that can be played at exactly three levels: beginner, intermediate, and expert. How would you restrict your variable to be assigned only these three values?

You can accomplish this by creating an enum. An enum enables you to create a *type*, which has a *fixed* set of *constants*. Following is an example of the enum Level, which defines three programming levels:

```
enum Level { BEGINNER, INTERMEDIATE, EXPERT }        ◁─┤ The enum values are
                                                         constant values.
```

An enum lets you define a new type, the way classes and interfaces enable you to define your own types. The preceding line of code creates a new type, Level, which defines the constants BEGINNER, INTERMEDIATE, and EXPERT of type Level. (Syntactically, you can use any case for defining these constant values, but following Oracle's recommendation of using uppercase letters for constant values will save you a lot of headaches.) These constants are also static members and are accessible by using the name of the enum in which they're defined.

You can assign a gaming level, defined by the enum Level for a game. Let's define a class, Game, which defines an instance variable, gameLevel, of type Level, as follows:

```
class Game {
    Level gameLevel;        ◁─┤ Variable of
}                              type Level
```

Class GameApp defines a field game of type Game and initializes it as follows:

```
class GameApp {
    Game game = null;

    public void startGame () {
        game = new Game();
        game.gameLevel = Level.BEGINNER;        ◁─┤ Assigns constant
    }                                               BEGINNER
}
```

The class GameApp demonstrates the real benefit of all this enum business. Because the variable gameLevel (defined in class Game) is of type Level, you can assign *only one* of the constants defined in the enum Level—that is, Level.BEGINNER, Level.INTERMEDIATE, or Level.EXPERT.

Let's look into the finer details of enums, as discussed in the next section.

2.3.2   *Adding implicit code to an enum*

When you create an enum, Java adds implicit code and modifiers to its members. These details will help you explain the behavior of enum constants, together with how to access and use them. Let's work with the enum Level created in the previous section (2.3.1) and decompile its Level.class file, using a decompiler (like JD):

```
enum Level { BEGINNER, INTERMEDIATE, EXPERT }
```

A decompiler converts Java byte code (.class) to a Java source file (.java). The newly created Java source file will include any implicit code that was added during the compilation process. Listing 2.2 shows decompiled enum Level (to make the code easier to understand, I've added some comments):

Listing 2.2   Decompiled enum Level

```
final class Level extends Enum                      ← 1 enum is implicitly
{                                                       declared final.
    public static final Level BEGINNER;             ⎫ 2 enum constants are
    public static final Level INTERMEDIATE;         ⎬   implicitly public,
    public static final Level EXPERT;               ⎭   static, and final.

    private static final Level $VALUES[];           ← Array to store
                                                      reference to all
    static                                          3 enum constants
    {
        BEGINNER = new Level("BEGINNER", 0);
        INTERMEDIATE = new Level("INTERMEDIATE", 1);  4 Creation of
        EXPERT = new Level("EXPERT", 2);                enum constants
        $VALUES = (new Level[] {                        occurs in static
            BEGINNER, INTERMEDIATE, EXPERT              initializer block
        });
    }
    public static Level[] values()                  ← Method values return
    {                                                 an array of all enum
        return (Level[])$VALUES.clone();            5 constants.
    }
    public static Level valueOf(String s)           ← Method valueOf() parses a
    {                                                 String value and returns
        return (Level)Enum.valueOf(Level, s);       6 corresponding enum constant
    }
    private Level(String s, int i)                  ← Private
    {                                               7 constructor
        super(s, i);
    }
}
```

In the decompiled code, at **1** you can notice that an enum is implicitly defined as a final entity. At **2** you can notice that all enum constants are implicitly declared as public, final, and static variables. The code at **3** defines an array to store a reference to all enum constants. The variables are declared at ❷ and ❸. They are initialized in a static initializer block at ❹. Method `values()` returns an array of all enum constants at ❺ and `valueOf()` returns an enum constant for a corresponding `String` value at ❻. The code at ❼ defines a private constructor.

If the enum constants are themselves created in a static initializer block, when does a static initializer block in an enum execute? See for yourself in the next "Twist in the Tale" exercise.

Twist in the Tale 2.4

Let's add some code to the enum `Level` so it defines a constructor and a static initializer block. Examine the code and determine the correct options that follow.

```
enum Level {
    BEGINNER;
    static{ System.out.println("static init block"); }
    Level(){
        System.out.println("constructor");
    }
    public static void main(String... args){
        System.out.println(Level.BEGINNER);
    }
}
```

    a constructor
       static init block
       BEGINNER

    b static init block
       constructor
       BEGINNER

    c constructor
       static init block
       beginner

    d static init block
       constructor
       beginner

In listing 2.2 you'll notice that all enum constants of BEGINNER, INTERMEDIATE, and EXPERT are created in the order they were defined and assigned an ordinal: 0, 1, and 2. Are enum constants created in this manner? Let's check it out in the next section.

2.3.3 Extending java.lang.Enum

All enums in Java extend the abstract class `java.lang.Enum`, defined in the Java API. As always, it's interesting to peek at the source code from the Java API, to understand why some pieces of code behave in a particular way. Let's look at the (partial) code of class `java.lang.Enum`, which will help you get the hang of how the enum constants are created, their order, and their default names. Please note that the comments aren't part of the code from class `java.lang.Enum`. These comments have been added to clarify the code for you.

Listing 2.3   Partial code listing of class `java.lang.Enum`

```
public abstract class Enum<E extends Enum<E>>             Name of the
implements Comparable<E>, Serializable {                 enum constant
    private final String name;        ←
    private final int ordinal;        ←                  Position of
                                                         enum constant
    protected Enum(String name, int ordinal) {           Name and position of
        this.name = name;                                enum constant is saved
        this.ordinal = ordinal;                          on its creation
    }

    public String toString() {          Default implementation
        return name;                    of toString() returns
    }                                   name of enum constant

    public final String name() {        Method name() is marked final
        return name;                    and can't be overridden; returns
    }                                   enum constant's name.
    //.. rest of the code
}
```

The class `Enum` defines only one constructor with `String` and `int` parameters to specify its name and ordinal (order). Every enum constant is implicitly assigned an order on its creation. Let's refer back to the example of enum `Level` as defined in listing 2.2. The enum constant values `BEGINNER`, `INTERMEDIATE`, and `EXPERT` are created *within* the enum `Level`, in its static initializer block (refer to code listing 2.1), as follows:

```
public static final level BEGINNER = new Level ("BEGINNER", 0);
public static final level INTERMEDIATE = new Level ("INTERMEDIATE", 1);
public static final level EXPERT = new Level ("EXPERT", 2);
```

 EXAM TIP Watch out for exam questions that use methods like `Collections.sort()` from the Collections API to sort enum constants. The default order of enum constants is their order of definition. The enum constants aren't sorted alphabetically.

Now, examine the following code:

```
public class TestEnum {                                  Prints
    public static void main(String args[]) {             "BEGINNER"
        System.out.println(Level.BEGINNER.name());  ←
        System.out.println(Level.BEGINNER);         ←    Also prints "BEGINNER"
    }                                                    by calling method
}                                                        toString()
```

Note both methods—toString() and name() defined in java.lang.Enum—return the value of the instance variable name (revisit code listing 2.3—class java.lang.Enum defines an instance variable name). Because method name() is a final method, you can't override it. But you can override method toString() to return any description that you want.

 EXAM TIP For an enum constant BEGINNER in enum Level, calling System.out.println(Level.BEGINNER) returns the name of the enum constant—that is, BEGINNER. You can override toString() in an enum to modify this default return value.

Because a class can extend from only one base class, an attempt to make your enum extend any other class will fail. The following code won't compile:

```
class Person {}
enum Level extends Person { BEGINNER, INTERMEDIATE, EXPERT }
```
Won't compile

But you can make your enum implement any number of interfaces. A class can extend only one base class but can implement multiple interfaces. The following code compiles successfully:

```
interface MyInterface {}
enum Level implements MyInterface { BEGINNER, INTERMEDIATE, EXPERT }
```
Will compile

You can't explicitly make a class extend java.lang.Enum:
```
class MyClass extends java.lang.Enum {}
```
Won't compile

 EXAM TIP An enum implicitly extends java.lang.Enum, so it can't extend any other class. But a class can't explicitly extend java.lang.Enum.

2.3.4 *Adding variables, constructors, and methods to your enum*

You can add variables, constructors, and methods to an enum. You can also override the nonfinal methods from the java.lang.Enum class. Following is an example:

```
enum IceCream {
    VANILLA, STRAWBERRY, WALNUT, CHOCOLATE;

    private String color;

    public String getColor() {
        return color;
    }

    public void setColor(String val) {
        color = val;
    }
```

1 enum constants

2 Instance variable in enum IceCream

3 Method getColor()

4 Method setColor()

```
    public String toString() {
            return "MyColor:"+ color;
    }
}
```
← ⑤ **Override method toString()**

The code at ❶ defines a list of enum constants: VANILLA, STRAWBERRY, WALNUT, and CHOCOLATE in enum IceCream. Note that this constant list must be the first in the enum definition and should be followed by a semicolon. A semicolon is optional if you don't add methods and variables to your enum. The code at ❷ defines an instance variable color in enum IceCream. The code at ❸ and ❹ adds methods get-Color() and setColor() to enum IceCream. The code at ❺ overrides the public toString() method inherited from class java.lang.Enum.

 EXAM TIP   The enum constant list must be the first in the enum definition and should be followed by a semicolon. A semicolon is optional if you don't add methods and variables to your enum.

You can call the methods defined in the preceding example, as follows:

```
public class UseIceCream {
    public static void main(String[] args) {                ❶
        IceCream.VANILLA.setColor("white");              ← ❷
        System.out.println(IceCream.VANILLA.getColor()); ← 
        System.out.println(IceCream.VANILLA);            ← ❸
    }
}
```

The output of this code is as follows:

```
white
MyColor:white
```

Are you thinking that the code at ❶ is invalid because enum values are constant values? Note that this code is absolutely valid. VANILLA is a type of enum IceCream, and you can call methods that are available to it. The code at ❷ calls the method get-Color(), and the code at ❸ calls method toString(), which was overridden in enum IceCream.

You can also define constructors in your enum and override methods that apply only to particular enum constants, as follows in listing 2.4 (modifications in bold):

Listing 2.4   enum IceCream with custom constructor and constant specific class body

```
enum IceCream {
    VANILLA("white"),
    STRAWBERRY("pink"),
```

```
WALNUT("brown") {
    public String toString() {
        return "WALNUT is Brown in color";
    }
    public String flavor() {
        return "great!";
    }
},
CHOCOLATE("dark brown");

private String color;
IceCream(String color) {
    this.color = color;
}
public String toString() {
    return "MyColor:" + color;
}
}
```

① Methods defined between { and } are available only to enum constant WALNUT.

This method can't be executed. **②**

③ Constructor that accepts string

The code at **①**, known as a *constant specific class body*, defines overridding methods for a particular enum constant, WALNUT. The code at **③** defines a constructor for enum IceCream, but it can be used only within an enum. A constructor in an enum can be defined only with *default* or private access; public and protected access levels aren't allowed.

EXAM TIP An enum can't define a constructor with public or protected access level.

In the preceding code, it might be strange to note that though you can define a method flavor() at **②**, you can't call it, as follows:

```
public class UseIceCream {
    public static void main(String[] args) {
        System.out.println(IceCream.VANILLA);
        System.out.println(IceCream.WALNUT);
        //System.out.println(IceCream.WALNUT.flavor());
    }
}
```

Prints "MyColor:white"

Prints "WALNUT is Brown in color"

Won't compile

This behavior can be attributed to WALNUT creating an anonymous class and overriding the methods of enum IceCream. But it's still referenced by a variable of type IceCream, which doesn't define the method flavor. If this leaves you guessing about what all this stuff with anonymous classes is, you can go grab a glass of anonymous inner classes in section 2.4.4.

Let's see how class IceCream's constant WALNUT returns a custom value for its toString() method, that it overrides in its constant specific class body. In the following example, class IceCreamParlor uses method values() to access all enum constants and outputs their values:

```
class IceCreamParlor {
    public static void main(String args[]) {
```

```
        for (IceCream ic : IceCream.values())          Method values()
            System.out.println(ic);                     returns an array of
    }                                                    all enum constants.
}
```

The output of the preceding code is

```
MyColor:white
MyColor:pink
WALNUT is Brown in color
MyColor:dark brown
```

In the preceding output, notice how the String representation of WALNUT differs from the other enum constants.

 EXAM TIP   An enum constant can define a constant specific class body and use it to override existing methods or define new variables and methods.

2.3.5   *Where can you define an enum?*

You can define an enum as a top-level enum, or as a member of a class or an interface. Until now, you worked with a top-level enum. The following code shows you how to define an enum as a member of another class or interface:

```
class MyClass {
    enum Level { BEGINNER, INTERMEDIATE, EXPERT }          enum as a member
}                                                           of other class
interface MyInterface {
    enum Level { BEGINNER, INTERMEDIATE, EXPERT }          enum as a member
}                                                           of an interface
```

But you can't define an enum local as a method. For example, the following code won't compile:

```
class MyClass {
    void aMethod() {
        enum Level { BEGINNER, INTERMEDIATE, EXPERT }
    }
}
```

At the end of this section on enums, let's revisit the important rules that you should remember for the exam.

> **Rules to remember about enums**
> - An enum can define a main method. This means that you can define an enum as an executable Java application.
> - The enum constant list must be defined as the first item in an enum, before the declaration or definition of methods and variables.

(continued)

- The enum constant list might not be followed by a semicolon, if the enum doesn't define any methods or variables.
- When an enum constant overrides an enum method, the enum constant creates an anonymous class, which extends the enum.
- An enum constant can define a constant specific class body and use it to override existing methods or define new variables and methods.
- An enum implicitly extends `java.lang.Enum`, so it can't extend any other class. But a class can't explicitly extend `java.lang.Enum`. An enum can implement interface(s).
- An enum can never be instantiated using the keyword `new`.
- You can define multiple constructors in your enums.
- An enum can't define a constructor with `public` or `protected` access level.
- An enum can define an abstract method. Just ensure to override it for all your enum constants.
- The enum method `values()` returns a list of all the enum constants.
- An enum can be defined as a top-level enum, or as a member or another class or interface. It can't be defined local to a method.

When you're consuming a lot of information, missing the small and simple details is easy. Let's check whether you remember and can spot some basic information about enums in the next "Twist in the Tale" exercise.

Twist in the Tale 2.5

Let's modify the code used in enum IceCream in this section. Examine the code and determine the correct options that follow.

```
public enum IceCreamTwist {
    VANILLA("white"),
    STRAWBERRY("pink"),
    WALNUT("brown"),
    CHOCOLATE("dark brown");

    String color;

    IceCreamTwist(String color) {
        this.color = color;
    }
    public static void main(String[] args) {
        System.out.println(VANILLA);            //line1
        System.out.println(CHOCOLATE);          //line2
    }
}
```

   a Compilation error: Can't run an enum as a standalone application.

   b Compilation error at (#1) and (#2): Can't access VANILLA and CHOCOLATE in a static main method.

c No errors. Output is

```
VANILLA
CHOCOLATE
```

d No errors. Output is

```
white
dark brown
```

An enum defines a new type with limitations. Similarly, nested and inner classes define a new type with constraints on their use. Defined within another class, nested and inner classes are characterized with a different set of behavior that sets them apart from the top-level classes. Let's uncover these details in the next section.

2.4   *Static nested and inner classes*

[2.4]   Create top-level and nested classes

A *nested class* is a class defined within another class. Nested classes that are declared as static are referred to as *static nested classes*. Nested classes that aren't declared as static are referred to as *inner classes*. Like a regular top-level class, an inner or static nested class can define variables and methods.

You can also define inner classes within methods and without a name. Figure 2.5 shows the types of inner classes, distinguished by their placement within the top-level class and whether they are defined as and with static members.

Before we dive into a detailed discussion of all the flavors of the inner classes, table 2.2 provides a quick definition of the types of inner classes.

Table 2.2   Flavors of inner classes and their definitions

Type of inner class	Description
Static or static nested class	Is a static member of its enclosing class and can access all the static variables and members of its outer class
Inner or member class	Is an instance member of its enclosing class. It can access all the instance and static members of its outer class, including private members.
Method local inner class	Is defined within a method. Local inner classes are local to a method. They can access all the members of a class, including its private members, but they can be accessed only within the method in which they're defined.
Anonymous inner class	Is a local class without a name

For the exam, you'll need to know why inner classes and static nested classes are important in the design of an application, their advantages and disadvantages, and how to create and use them. Let's start with a discussion of the advantages of inner

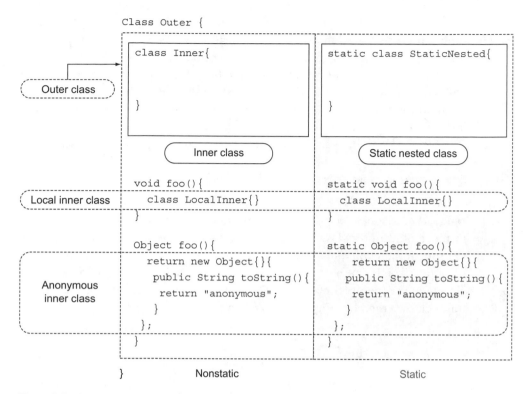

Figure 2.5 An outer class showing all types of inner classes that it can define: inner class, static nested class, local inner class, and anonymous inner class

classes, followed by a detailed discussion of all these classes. At the end of this section, we'll discuss their disadvantages.

2.4.1 Advantages of inner classes

Inner classes offer multiple advantages. To start, they help you objectify the functionality of a class, within it. For example, you might define a class `Tree`, which defines operations to add objects, remove objects, and sort them based on a condition. Instead of defining methods and variables to sort them within the class `Tree`, you could encapsulate sorting functionality within another class `TreeSort`. Because the class `TreeSort` would always work with `Tree` and might not be needed outside the class `Tree`, `TreeSort` can be defined as an inner class within class `Tree`. Another example for using inner classes is as parameter containers. Instead of using long method signatures, inner classes are often used to keep method signatures compact by passing reference parameters of inner classes instead of a long list of individual parameters.

Just as you can organize your top-level classes by using packages, you can further organize your classes by using inner classes. Inner classes might not be accessible to all other classes and packages.

Inner classes also offer a neat way to define callback methods. For example, consider a user-interface-intensive GUI application, which defines multiple controls (buttons, keys, and screen) to accept a user's input. These user controls should register listeners, which are classes that define methods that are called back, when a user control receives an input. Instead of defining a single class to handle all callback methods for multiple user controls, you can use inner classes to define callback methods for individual user controls.

Let's start with the simplest type of inner class: a static nested class.

2.4.2   *Static nested class (also called static inner class)*

A *static nested class* is a static class that's defined (nested) within another class. It's referred to as a nested class and not an inner class because it isn't associated with any instance of its outer class. You'd usually create a static nested class to encapsulate partial functionality of your main class, whose instance can exist without the instance of its outer class. It can be accessed like any other static member of a class, by using the class name of the outer class. A static nested class is initialized when it's loaded with its outer class in memory. Figure 2.6 shows a static nested class.

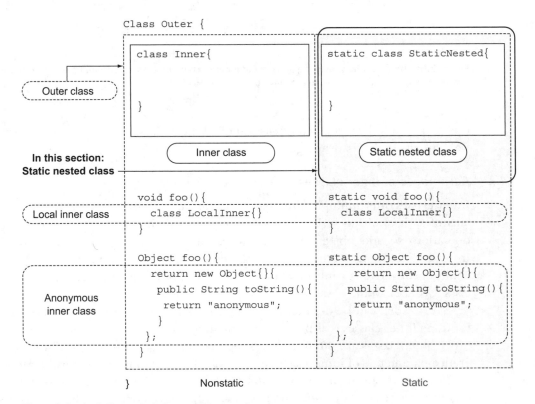

Figure 2.6   A static nested class within an outer class

In the following (simplified) example, class DBConnection defines a static nested class, DBConnectionCache, which creates and stores database connections with default connection values. When requested a database connection, class DBConnection checks if a default connection for the specified database exists. If yes, it returns the default connection; otherwise it creates and returns a new connection.

```
class DBConnection {
    public DBConnection (String username, String pwd, String URL) {
        // code to establish a Database connection
    }
    public DBConnection OracleConnection
                (String username, String pwd, String URL) {
        DBConnection conn = DBConnectionCache.getDefaultOracleConnection();
        if (conn != null) {
            return conn;
        }
        else {
            //establish and return new DBconnection using method parameters
        }
    }
    /*
     * Oversimplified version of a static nested class which uses default
     * values to establish DB connections and store them in a static array
     */
    static class DBConnectionCache {
        static DBConnection connections[];
        static {
            connections = new DBConnection[3];
            connections[0] = new DBConnection
                (/*arguments to establish a connection to an ORACLE DB*/);
            connections[1] = new DBConnection
                (/*arguments to establish a connection to a MySQL DB*/);
        }
        static DBConnection getDefaultOracleConnection() {
            return connections[0];
        }
        static DBConnection getDefaultMySQLConnection() {
            return connections[1];
        }
    }
}
```

 EXAM TIP In the preceding example, access to nested class DBConnection-Cache can be restricted by using an appropriate access modifier with its definition.

In the next section, you'll work with one of the most important points to be tested on the exam—how to instantiate static nested classes.

Let's code class `StaticNested` as shown in figure 2.6:

```
class Outer {
    static int outerStatic = 10;
    int outerInstance = 20;

    static class StaticNested {
        static int innerStatic = 10;
        int innerInstance = 20;
    }
}
```

 NOTE A static nested class isn't usually referred to as an inner class, because it isn't associated with an object of the outer class.

When you create a static nested class, it's compiled as a separate class file. The .class file for a static nested file includes the name of its outer class. On compiling the code shown in the preceding example, the compiler generates two .class files, Outer.class and Outer$StaticNested.class.

As with a regular top-level class, a static nested class is a type and you can instantiate it. Multiple separate instances of a static nested class can be created. Each instance of the static nested class can have a different value for its instance variables. Let's instantiate the `StaticNested` class from the preceding example code:

```
class Outer {
    static int outerStatic = 10;
    int outerInstance = 20;

    static class StaticNested {
        static int innerStatic = 10;
        int innerInstance = 20;
    }
    public static void main(String args[]) {
        StaticNested nested1 = new StaticNested();
        Outer.StaticNested nested2 = new Outer.StaticNested();

        nested1.innerStatic = 99;
        nested1.innerInstance = 999;

        System.out.println(nested1.innerStatic + ":" +
                                      nested1.innerInstance);
        System.out.println(nested2.innerStatic + ":" +
                                      nested2.innerInstance);
    }
}
```

When static nested class is instantiated within its outer class, it doesn't need to be prefixed with its outer class name (though it can).

Modify only the value of innerInstance for nested1.

Modify the value of innerStatic for all instances of StaticNested.

Prints "99:999"

Prints "99:20"

When a static nested class is instantiated outside its outer class, you *must* prefix it with its outer class name:

When static nested class is instantiated outside its outer class, it must be prefixed with its outer class name

```
class AnotherClass {
    Outer.StaticNested nested1 = new Outer.StaticNested();
    StaticNested nested2 = new StaticNested();
}
```

Won't compile

```
StaticNested one = new StaticNested();                    ✓
Outer.StaticNested two = new Outer.StaticNested();        ✓

StaticNested three = new Outer.new StaticNested();        ✗
StaticNested four = new Outer().new StaticNested();       ✗
StaticNested five = Outer.new StaticNested();             ✗
```

Figure 2.7   Correct and incorrect instantiation of a static nested class

For the exam, it's important to remember the syntax of instantiating a static nested class: the count of operator new and its placement. It uses the new operator once, just before the name of the static nested class. Figure 2.7 highlights correct and incorrect instantiation code snippets.

Another point that you must remember when instantiating a static nested class is when to prefix the name of a static nested class with its outer class. Figure 2.8 shows

Figure 2.8   An interesting way to remember that you *must* prefix the name of the static inner class with its outer class when referring to it outside its outer class.

an interesting way to remember that you *must* prefix the name of the static inner class with its outer class when you're referring to it outside its outer class. For the rest of the cases you might, but it isn't mandatory, prefix the name of the static nested class with its outer class. In figure 2.8 when method `Shreya` doesn't prefix `StaticNested` with its outer class, outside the class `Outer`, `StaticNested` doesn't seem to recognize the call.

ACCESSING MEMBERS OF A STATIC NESTED CLASS

To access the static members of a static nested class, you need not create an object of this class. You need an object of a static nested class to access its instance members. Here's an example:

Object of StaticNested class required to access its instance members

```
class Outer1 {
    public static void main(String args[]) {
        System.out.println(new Outer.StaticNested().innerInstance);
        System.out.println(Outer.StaticNested.innerStatic);
    }
}
```

Object of StaticNested class not required to access its static members

 NOTE On the exam, you might be asked whether you can instantiate a static nested class, how to instantiate it, and whether it can define instance or static members, or both.

ACCESS LEVELS OF A STATIC NESTED CLASS

A static nested class can be defined using all access levels: `private`, *default* access, `protected`, and `public`. The accessibility of the static nested class depends on its access modifier. For example, a `private` static nested class can't be accessed outside its outer class. The access of a static nested class also depends on the accessibility of its outer class. If the outer class is defined with the default access, an inner nested class with `public` access won't make it accessible outside the package in which its outer class is defined.

MEMBERS OF OUTER CLASS ACCESSIBLE TO STATIC NESTED CLASS

A static nested class can access only the static members of its outer class. An example follows.

```
class Outer {
    static int outerStatic = 10;
    int outerInstance = 20;

    static class StaticNested {
        static int innerStatic = outerStatic;
        int innerInstance = outerInstance;;
    }
}
```

Can't access instance variables from a static nested class

> **Rules to remember about static nested classes**
> - To create an object of a static nested class, you need to prefix its name with the name of its outer class (necessary only if you're outside the outer class).
> - A static nested class can define both static and nonstatic members.
> - You need not create an object of a static nested class to access its static members. They can be accessed the way static members of a regular class are accessed.
> - You should create an object of a static nested class to access its nonstatic members, by using the operator `new`.
> - A static nested class can be defined using any access modifier.
> - A static nested class can define constructor(s).

2.4.3 *Inner class (also called member class)*

The definition of an *inner class* is enclosed within another class, also referred to as an *outer class*. An inner class is an *instance member* of its outer class. An instance of an *inner class* shares a special bond with its *outer class* and can't exist without its instance. Figure 2.9 illustrates the placement of an inner class within an outer class.

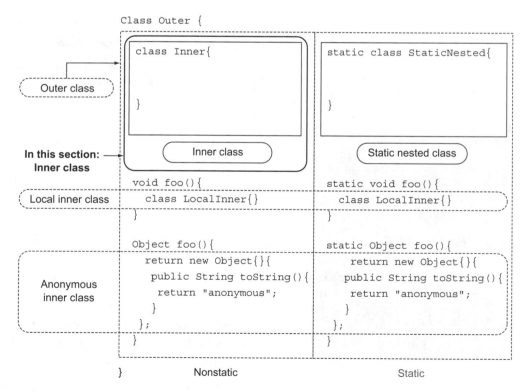

Figure 2.9 Placement of an inner class within an outer class

You'd usually create an inner class to encapsulate partial functionality of your main class such that the existence of the inner class instance isn't possible without its outer class instance. This is in contrast to a nested static class, which can be used without an instance of its outer class.

For example, the following code defines a class Tree and an inner class TreeSort. Tree defines operations to add, remove, and sort objects based on a condition. Instead of defining methods and variables to sort the tree elements within class Tree, it encapsulates sorting functionality within class TreeSort. Class TreeSort would always work with Tree and might not be needed without class Tree:

```
class Node {
    Object value;                        ←──┐  Instances of Node
    Node left, right;                       │  used to store Tree
}                                           │  elements
class Tree {
    Tree() {}
    Node rootNode;
    void addElement(Object value) {
        //.. code //
    }
    void removeElement(Object value) {
        //.. code //
    }
    void sortTree(boolean ascending) {
        new TreeSort(ascending).sort();    ←──┐  Defining sorting code
    }                                         │  in a separate inner
                                              │  class makes class Tree
    class TreeSort{                           │  simpler and cleaner.
        boolean ascendingSortOrder = true;
        TreeSort(boolean order) {
            ascendingSortOrder = order;
        }
        void sort() {
            // outer class's rootNode and sort tree values
            // sorting code can be complex
        }
    }
}
```

Figure 2.10 illustrates the bare-bones *inner class* Inner, defined within another class, Outer, and how the compiler generates separate class files for the outer and inner classes.

Throughout this section, I refer to the concept of outer and inner classes as *outer class* and *inner class*. I refer to names of the outer class and inner class by using code font.

 NOTE You can create an *outer class* and *inner class* using any names. The names of these classes are chosen as Outer and Inner so it's easy for you to recognize them.

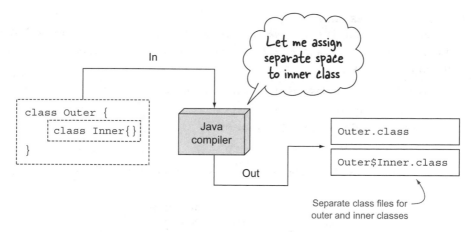

Figure 2.10 **The compiler generates separate class files for an outer class and inner class.** **The name of the inner class is prefixed with the name of the outer class and a $ sign.**

CHARACTERISTICS OF INNER CLASSES

Because an *inner class* is a member of its outer class, an *inner class* can be defined using any of the four access levels: public, protected, *default access,* and private. Like a regular top-level class, an inner class can also define constructors, variables, and methods. But an inner class can't define nonfinal static variables or methods, as shown in figure 2.11.

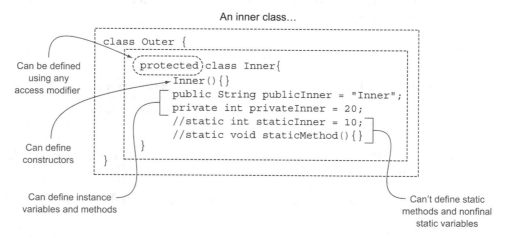

Figure 2.11 **Characteristics of an *inner class*: it can be defined using any access modifier, can define constructors, and can define instance variables and methods. An inner class can define static members variables but not static methods.**

CREATION OF AN INNER CLASS

Whenever you instantiate an *inner class*, remember that an instance of an inner class can't exist without an instance of the *outer class* in which it's defined. Let's look at creating an inner class:

- Within an outer class, as an instance member
- Within a method of an outer class
- Within a static method of an outer class
- Outside the outer class

First, a definition of a bare-bones outer class and inner class follows:

```
class Outer {                          ◄────────┐  Bare-bones
    class Inner {}      ◄──  Bare-bones            outer class
}                           inner class
```

Class `Outer` can instantiate inner class `Inner` as its instance member (additions in bold), as follows:

```
class Outer {
    Inner objectInner = new Inner();   ◄─┐  Creation of object of class
    class Inner {}                         Inner in class Outer, as its
}                                          instance member
```

In the previous code, like all instance variables, `objectInner` can access an instance of its outer class and its members, `Outer`. Similarly, an instance of an inner class created within an *instance* method of an outer class can access the instance of its outer class. So, you can instantiate class `Inner` within an instance method of class `Outer`, as follows (additions in bold):

```
class Outer {
    Inner in = new Inner();
    class Inner {}
    void aMethod () {                      Instantiation of class
        Inner objectInner = new Inner();   Inner in class Outer
    }                                      within its method
}
```

 EXAM TIP You *must* have an outer class instance to create an inner class instance.

Now, let's try to instantiate class `Inner` within a static method of class `Outer` (additions in bold):

```
class Outer {
    class Inner {}
    static void staticMethod() {        ❶ Won't
        Inner in = new Inner();      ◄─    compile
    }
}
```

The code at ❶ doesn't compile because in method staticMethod() there's no outer class instance to tie the inner class instance to, which is required for creation of its *inner class* Inner. But it's possible to instantiate class Outer in the method static-Method(). When you have an Outer instance, you can instantiate Inner:

```
class Outer {
    class Inner {}
    static void staticMethod () {
        Outer outObj = new Outer();
        Inner innerObj = outObj.new Inner();
    }
}
```

❶ **Instance of Outer can be created in method staticMethod()**

❷ **Instance of Inner is created by calling operator new on Outer instance**

The code at ❶ creates outObj, an Outer instance in the static method static-Method(). outObj is used to create an instance of class Inner at ❷ because you need an outer class instance to create an inner class instance. It's interesting to note that the operator new is called on outObj to create the innerObj instance. Have you invoked the operator new on an object earlier? The operator new is always used to instantiate a class. But to instantiate an *inner class* by using an instance of an *outer class*, you should invoke the operator new on the *outer class*'s instance.

Following is another way of creating the instance innerObj, using a single line of code:

```
class Outer {
    class Inner {}
    static void staticMethod () {
        Inner innerObj = new Outer().new Inner();
    }
}
```

❶ **Single line of code creates inner class object in outer class's static method**

The code at ❶ may look bizarre, because it contains two occurrences of the operator new. The first occurrence of this operator is used to create an instance of Outer. The second occurrence is used to create an instance of class Inner.

If another class wants to create an instance of class Inner, it needs an instance of class Outer. If it doesn't have one, it should first create one, just like with method staticMethod() in the previous code snippet:

```
class Foo {
    Inner inner;
    Foo () {
        Outer outer = new Outer();
        inner = outer.new Inner();
    }
}
```

Won't compile

What makes the preceding code fail compilation? Inner isn't a top-level class, so its variable type should include the name of its outer class, Outer, so class Foo can find this class. The following code compiles successfully and creates an Inner instance:

```
class Foo {
    Outer.Inner inner;
    Foo () {
        Outer outer = new Outer();
        inner = outer.new Inner();
    }
}
```

> **Outside its outer class, the type of inner class should include the name of its outer class.**

Similarly, a static method of class Foo can instantiate Inner, as follows:

```
class Foo {
    public static void main(String args[]) {
        Outer outer = new Outer();
        Outer.Inner inner = outer.new Inner();
    }
}
```

 EXAM TIP   The accessibility of an *inner class* outside its *outer class* depends on the access modifier used to define the inner class. For example, an inner class with default access can't be accessed by classes in different packages than the outer class.

WHAT CAN AN INNER CLASS ACCESS?

An inner class is a part of its outer class. Therefore an inner class can access all variables and methods of an outer class, including its private members and the ones that it inherits from its base classes. An inner class can also define members with the same name as its outer class, as shown in figure 2.12.

```
class Outer
    private String privateOuter = "Outer";                    private variable of
    private int sameName = 20;                                class Outer accessible
    class Inner{                                              in class Inner
        String publicInner = privateOuter;
        int sameName = Outer.this.sameName;
    }
}
```

Object of class Outer can be accessed using Outer.this in class Inner

Figure 2.12   An inner class can access all the members of its outer class, including its private members. Outer class members with the same name as inner class members can be accessed using Outer.this, where Outer is the name of the outer class.

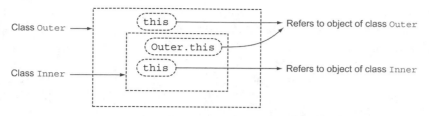

Figure 2.13   An inner class uses `this` to refer to its own object and `<name_of_its_outer_class>.this` to refer to its outer class's object.

An object uses the reference `this` to refer to its own object. An inner class can use the reference `this` to refer to its own object, and the name of its outer class followed by `.this` to refer to the object of its outer class, as shown in figure 2.13.

CAN AN INNER CLASS COEXIST WITH ONLY ITS OUTER CLASS?

Yes, an inner class can exist only with an object of its outer class. When a compiler compiles an inner class, it seems to insert code in the inner class, which defines an instance variable of its outer class, initialized using its constructor, as illustrated in figure 2.14.

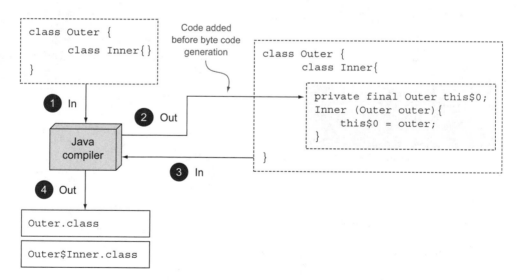

Figure 2.14   Java instantiates an inner class by passing it an outer class instance.

Rules to remember about inner classes

- You can create an object of the inner class within an outer class or outside an outer class.
- When an inner class is created outside its outer class, its type name should include the name of its outer class, followed by a dot (.) and then the name of the inner class.
- To create an inner class with a static method of an outer class, or outside an outer class, call the operator `new` on the object of the outer class to instantiate the inner class.
- An inner class can't define static methods. It can define final static variables but nonfinal static variables aren't allowed.
- Members of the inner class can refer to all variables and methods of the outer class.
- An inner class can be defined with all access modifiers.
- An inner class can define constructors.
- An inner class can define variables and methods with any access level.

It's time to attempt a quick exercise on inner classes in the following "Twist in the Tale" exercise.

Twist in the Tale 2.6

Apart from modifying the code used in an earlier example, I have also modified the class names for this exercise. Your task is to examine the following code and determine the correct answer option.

```java
class Flower {
    String color = "red";
    Petal[] petals;
    private class Petal {
        public Petal() {System.out.println(color);}
        String color = "purple";                 // line 1
        static final int count = 3;              // line 2
    }
    Flower() {
        petals = new Petal[2];                   // line 3
    }
    public static void main(String args[]) {
        new Flower();
    }
}
```

a Code prints red twice.

b Code prints purple twice.

c Code prints red three times.

d Code prints purple three times.

e Code prints nothing.

f Code fails compilation due to code at (#1).

g Code fails compilation due to code at (#2).

h Code fails compilation due to code at (#3).

Anonymous classes are another type of inner class. As their title suggests, they don't have a name. In the next section, you'll see why we need unnamed inner classes, and when and how they are created.

2.4.4 *Anonymous inner classes*

As the name implies, an *anonymous inner class* isn't defined using an *explicit* name. An anonymous inner class is created when you combine instance creation with inheriting a class or implementing an interface. Anonymous classes come in handy when you wish to override methods for only a particular instance. They save you from defining new classes. The anonymous class might override none, few, or all methods of the inherited class. It must implement all methods of an implemented interface. The newly created object can be assigned to any type of variable—static variable, instance variable, local variable, method parameter, or returned from a method. Let's start with an example of an anonymous inner class that extends a class.

ANONYMOUS INNER CLASS THAT EXTENDS A CLASS

Let's start with a class Pen:

```
class Pen{
    public void write() {
        System.out.println("Pen-write");
    }
}
```

This is how a class, say, Lecture, would *usually* instantiate Pen:

```
class Lecture {
    Pen pen = new Pen();
}
```

Let's replace this *usual* object instantiation by overriding method write, *while* instantiating Pen. To override method write() for this particular instance, we insert a class definition between () and ; (() and ; are in bold):

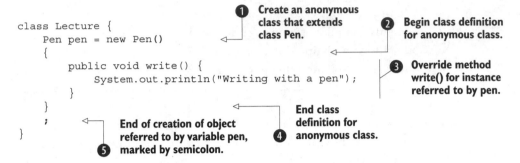

The preceding code creates an anonymous class, which extends class Pen. The object reference pen refers to an object of this anonymous class.

The code at ❶ creates an object. Note that this line of code isn't followed by a semicolon. Instead, it's followed by an opening brace at ❷, which starts the definition of the anonymous class that extends Pen. The code at ❸ overrides method write() from the *base class* Pen. The closing brace at ❹ marks the end of the definition of the anonymous class. The code at ❺ defines the semicolon, which is used to mark the end of object creation, which started at ❶. I've deliberately placed the semicolon on a separate line so you can clearly identify the start and end of the anonymous class. It's usual to place this semicolon after the closing brace, used to mark the end of the anonymous class.

You can create an anonymous class even if you don't override any methods of class Pen:

```
class Lecture {
    static Pen pen = new Pen(){};      ◄─── Create an anonymous class, which extends
                                             Pen but doesn't override its methods.

    public static void main(String args[]) {
        System.out.println(new Pen());    ◄─── Prints a value similar to Pen@1034bb5;
        System.out.println(pen);               new Pen() returns an object of Pen.
    }                                     ◄─── Prints a value similar to Lecture$1@15f5897;
}                                              pen refers to an instance of anonymous class
                                               that extends Pen.
```

Similarly, you can pass an anonymous class instance to a method parameter. Now let's see an example of method notes() in class Lecture, which accepts a method parameter of type Pen:

```
class Pen{
    public void write() {
        System.out.println("Pen-write");
    }
}
```

```
class Lecture {
    public void notes(Pen pen) {
        pen.write();
    }
}
```

> ◁─┐ **Method notes() accepts parameter of type Pen.**

Here's how another class—say, `Student`–calls `notes()` from class `Lecture`, subclassing `Pen`, and passing the object to it:

```
class Student {
    void attendLecture() {
        Lecture lecture = new Lecture();
        lecture.notes(new Pen() {
            public void write() {
                System.out.println("Okay! I am writing");
            }
        }
        );
    }
}
```

> │ **Call notes() by passing it newly baked object of anonymous subclass of Pen.** ◁─┘

The preceding code can seem to be more complex than the previous example. To understand it better, let's build this code, line by line. In class `Student`, you call `notes()` on object reference `lecture`:

```
class Student {
    void attendLecture() {
        Lecture lecture = new Lecture();
        lecture.notes(/* need to pass Pen object */);
    }
}
```

In the next step, I'll replace the comment in the preceding code with `new Pen() {}`, so I'm ready to subclass `Pen` (additions in bold):

```
class Student {
    void attendLecture() {
        Lecture lecture = new Lecture();
        lecture.notes(new Pen(){});
    }
}
```

I'll insert the definition of overridden method `write()` within the curly brace `{}` of the `Pen` anonymous inner class declaration, included in the method parameter to `notes()` (additions in bold):

```
class Student {
    void attendLecture() {
        Lecture lecture = new Lecture();
        lecture.notes(new Pen(){public void write() {
                System.out.println("Okay! I am writing");
            }});
    }
}
```

Let's indent the code, to improve the readability:

```
class Student {
    void attendLecture() {
        Lecture lecture = new Lecture();
        lecture.notes(new Pen(){
            public void write() {
                System.out.println("Okay! I am writing");
            }
        });
    }
}
```

You can use an anonymous inner class to return a value from a method:

```
class Outer{
    Object foo() {
        return new Object() {
            public String toString() {
                return "anonymous";
            }
        };
    }
}
```

Create an anonymous class that subclasses class Object.

Override method toString() from class Object.

ANONYMOUS INNER CLASS THAT IMPLEMENTS AN INTERFACE

Until now, you should have read that you can't instantiate interfaces; you can't use the keyword new with an interface. Think again. Examine the following code, in which the class BirdSanctuary instantiates the interface Flyable by using the keyword new:

```
interface Flyable{
    void fly();
}
class BirdSanctuary {
    Flyable bird = new Flyable(){
        public void fly() {
            System.out.println("Flying high in the sky");
        }
    };
}
```

Use new to instantiate interface.

Don't worry; you've been reading correctly that you can't use the operator new with an interface. The catch in the preceding code is that bird refers to an object of an anonymous inner class, which implements the interface Flyable.

The anonymous class used to instantiate an interface in the preceding code saved you from creating a class beforehand, which implemented the interface Flyable.

 EXAM TIP   An anonymous inner class can extend at most one class or implement one interface. Unlike other classes, an anonymous class can neither implement multiple interfaces, nor extend a class and implement an interface together.

HOW TO ACCESS ADDITIONAL MEMBERS IN ANONYMOUS CLASSES

By using an anonymous class, you can override the methods from its base class or implement the methods of an interface. You can also define new methods and variables in an anonymous class (in bold):

```java
interface Flyable{
    void fly();
}

class BirdSanctuary {
    Flyable bird = new Flyable(){
        public void fly() {
            System.out.println("Flying high in the sky");
        }
        public void hungry(){
            System.out.println("eat");
        }
    };

}
```

You can't call the additional member, method hungry(), using the reference variable bird. Why? The type of the reference variable bird is Flyable. So the variable bird can access only the members defined in interface Flyable. The variable bird can't access additional methods and variables that are defined in anonymous classes that implement it.

ANONYMOUS CLASS DEFINED WITHIN A METHOD

When an anonymous inner class is defined within a method, it can access only the final variables of the method in which it's defined. This is to prevent reassignment of the variable values by the inner class. Examine the following example.

```java
class Pizza{
    Object margarita() {
        String ingredient = "Cheese";
        return new Pizza() {
            public String toString() {            ❶ Won't
                System.out.println(ingredient);      compile
                return "margarita";
            }
        };
    }
}
```

The code at ❶ will compile if ingredient is modified to be defined as a final local variable.

The last type of inner class on this exam is a method local inner class, which can be created within methods and code blocks like initializer blocks, conditional constructs, or loops. I'll discuss these in the next section.

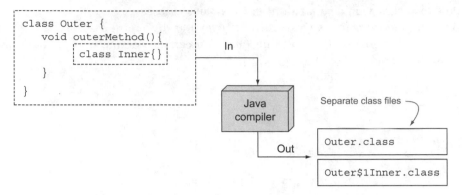

Figure 2.15   Compiler generates separate class files for an outer class and method local inner class. The name of the method local inner class is prefixed with the name `Outer` **class, a $ sign, and an integer.**

2.4.5   *Method local inner classes*

The *method local inner classes* are defined within static or instance methods of a class. Though these classes can also be defined within code blocks, they are typically created within methods. So their discussion will be limited to their creation in methods. Figure 2.15 shows the definition of a bare-bones method local inner class, `Inner`, defined within method `outerMethod()` of class `Outer`. The Java compiler generates separate class files for the classes `Outer` and `Inner`. Because a class can define method local inner classes with the same name in separate methods, the Java compiler adds a number to the name of the compiled file for the local inner classes.

A class can define multiple method local inner classes, with the same class name, in separate methods, as follows:

```
class Outer {
    void outerMethod () {          Class Inner defined in
        class Inner { }            method outerMethod()
    }
    static void outerMethod2 () {  Class Inner defined in
        class Inner { }            method outerMethod2()
    }
}
```

For the preceding code, the Java compiler will generate three class files: `Outer.class`, `Outer$1Inner.class`, and `Outer$2Inner.class`.

CHARACTERISTICS OF METHOD LOCAL INNER CLASSES

Recall that none of the variables within a method can be defined using any *explicit* modifier (`public`, `protected`, `private`). Similarly, method local inner classes can't be defined using any explicit access modifier. But a method local inner class can define its own constructors, variables, and methods by using any of the four access levels:

```
class Outer {
    private int privateOuter = 10;        Can't be defined using an
    void outerMethod () {                 explicit access modifier
        class Inner {              ◄─┘
            protected Inner() {}          Can define its constructs, variables,
            public int publicInner = 100; and methods using any access level
            int privateInner = privateOuter;   ◄─┐
        }                                 Can access all members,
    }                                     including private members,
}                                         of its outer class
```

But a method local inner class can't define static variables or static methods.

CREATION OF A LOCAL INNER CLASS

A *method local inner class* can be created only within the method in which it's defined. Also, its object creation can't appear before the declaration of the *local inner class*, as shown in the following code:

```
class Outer {
    void outerMethod () {              Won't
        //Inner in1 = new Inner();  ◄─┘ compile
        class Inner {}
        Inner in2 = new Inner();   ◄─┐ Will
    }                                  compile
}
```

WHAT CAN A METHOD LOCAL INNER CLASS ACCESS?

A method local inner class can access all variables and methods of its *outer class*, including its private members and the ones that it inherits from its base classes. A method local inner class can also define members with the same name as its outer class. In this case, the members of the outer class can be referred to by using the name of the outer class followed by the implicit reference this. Class Inner can access members of class Outer by using Outer.this, as shown in the following code:

```
class Outer {
    private int privateOuter = 10;
    void outerMethod () {                    Local inner class can
        class Inner {                        access all members
            protected Inner() {}             of its outer class,
            public int publicInner = 100;    including private
            int privateInner = Outer.this.privateOuter;  ◄─┘ members.
        }
    }
}
```

2.4.6 *Disadvantages of inner classes*

Using inner classes is an advanced concept, and it can be difficult for inexperienced programmers to identify, implement, and maintain them.

On translation to byte code, inner classes can be accessed by classes in the same package. Because inner classes can access the private members of their outer class, they could break the designed encapsulation. You need to be careful when you create the inner and static nested classes.

2.5   *Summary*

This chapter covers abstract classes, static and final keywords, enumerated types, and nested and inner classes. The choice of identifying abstract classes isn't straightforward. This chapter showed you simple examples so you're well aware of their need, importance, advantages, and shortcomings.

Application of the static and final nonaccess modifiers are important design decisions. You should know about the Java entities that can use these modifiers, together with how they change the default behavior of the entities. Incorrect design decisions can make an application inefficient and difficult to extend or maintain.

This chapter covered enums that are used to create a new type with a finite and predefined set of objects. The definition of an enum can be as simple as including only the name of enum constants, or as complex as including variables, constructors, and methods. The exam is sure to test you on the finer details of enums, all covered in this chapter.

Static nested classes, inner classes, anonymous inner classes, and method local inner classes were also covered. An inner class shares an intimate relation with its outer class. Inner classes help you objectify the functionality of a class. Identification of an inner class is also an important design decision. It can help you further organize your code and allow limited access to your inner classes. But an overdose of the inner and nested classes can make your application difficult to work with and manage.

REVIEW NOTES

This section lists the main points covered in this chapter.

Abstract classes

- An *abstract class* is defined by using the keyword abstract. It defines variables to store the state of an object. It may define abstract and nonabstract methods.
- An abstract class must not necessarily define abstract methods. But if it defines even one abstract method, it must be marked as an abstract class.
- An abstract class can't be instantiated.
- An abstract method doesn't have any implementation. It represents a behavior that's required by all derived classes of an abstract class. Because the base class doesn't have enough details to implement an abstract method, the derived classes are left to implement it in their own specific manner.
- An abstract class can't be instantiated.
- An abstract class *forces* all its nonabstract-derived classes to implement the incomplete functionality in their own unique manner.

- A base class should be defined as an abstract class so it can implement the available details but still prevent itself from being instantiated.
- An abstract class can be extended by both abstract and concrete classes. If an abstract class is extended by another abstract class, the derived abstract class *might* not implement the abstract methods of its base class.
- If an abstract class is extended by a concrete class, the derived class *must* implement all the abstract methods of its base class, or it won't compile.
- A derived class must call its superclass's constructor (implicitly or explicitly), irrespective of whether the superclass or derived class is an abstract class or concrete class.
- An abstract class can't define abstract static methods. Because static methods belong to a class and not to an object, they aren't inherited. A method that can't be inherited can't be implemented. Hence this combination is invalid.
- Efficient use of an abstract class lies in the identification of an abstract class in your application design so you can define common code for your objects and leave the ones that are more specific, by defining them as abstract. You can enforce the derived classes to implement these abstract methods.

Nonaccess modifier—static

- Static members (fields and methods) are common to all instances of a class, and aren't unique to any instance of a class.
- Static members exist independently of any instances of a class, and may be accessed even when no instances of the class have been created.
- Static members are also known as *class fields* or *class methods* because they are said to belong to their class, and not to any instance of that class.
- A static variable and method can be accessed using the name of an object reference variable or the name of a class.
- A static method and variable can't access nonstatic variables and methods of a class. But the reverse works: nonstatic variables and methods can access static variables and methods.
- Static classes and interfaces are a type of nested classes and interfaces.
- You can't prefix the definition of a top-level class or an interface with the keyword `static`. A top-level class or interface is one that isn't defined within another class or interface.

Nonaccess modifier—final

- You can't reinitialize a final variable defined in any scope—class, instance, local, or method parameter.
- An instance final variable can be initialized either with its declaration in the initializer block or in the class's constructor.

- A static final variable can be initialized either with its declaration or in the class's static initializer block.
- You can't initialize a final instance variable in an instance method because it can't be guaranteed to execute only once. Such a method won't compile.
- You can't initialize a final static variable in a static method because it can't be guaranteed to execute only once. Such a method won't compile.
- If you don't initialize a final local variable in a method, the compiler won't complain, as long as you don't use it.
- If you try to access the value of a final local variable before assigning a value to it, the code won't compile.
- The Java compiler considers initialization of a final variable complete *only* if the initialization code will execute in *all* conditions. If the Java compiler can't be sure of execution of code that assigns a value to your final variable, it will complain (code won't compile) that you haven't initialized a final variable. If an `if` construct uses constant values, the Java compiler can predetermine whether the `then` or `else` blocks will execute. In this case, it can predetermine whether these blocks of code will execute to initialize a final variable.
- A final instance variable defined in a base class can't be initialized in the derived class. If you try to do so, your code won't compile.
- Final methods defined in a base class can't be overridden by its derived classes.
- Final methods are used to prevent a derived class from overriding the implementation of a base class's method.
- Private final methods in a base class aren't inherited by derived classes. A method defined using the same method signature in a derived class isn't an overridden method, but a new method.
- A final class can't be extended by any other class.
- A class is defined as final so that it can't be extended by any other class. This prevents objects of derived classes from being passed on to reference variables of their base classes.
- An interface can't be defined as final because an interface is abstract, by default. A Java entity can't be defined both as final and abstract.

Enumerated types

- Enumerated types are also called *enums*.
- An enum enables you to create a *type*, which has a *fixed* set of *constants*.
- An enum can never be instantiated using the keyword `new`.
- Unlike a class, which is defined using the keyword `class`, an enumerated type is defined using the keyword `enum`, and can define multiple variables and methods.
- If you define a variable of an enum type, it can be assigned constant values only from that enum.
- All enums extend the abstract class `java.lang.Enum`, defined in the Java API.

- Because a class can extend from only one base class, an attempt to make your enum extend any other class will fail its compilation.
- The enum constants are implicit static members.
- An enum can implement any interface, but its constants should implement the relevant interface methods.
- An enum can define an abstract method. Just ensure that you override it for all your enum constants.
- You can add instance variables, class variables, instance methods, and class methods to your enums.
- An enum can't use instance variables in the overridden methods for a particular enum constant.
- You can override nonfinal methods from class `java.lang.Enum`, for individual (or all) enum constants.
- Your enums can also define constructors, which can be called from within the enum.
- You can define multiple constructors in your enums.
- Enum constants can define new methods, but these methods can't be called on the enum constant.
- You can define an enum as a top-level enum or within another class or interface.
- You can't define an enum local to a method.
- An enum can define a main method.

Static nested classes

- This class isn't associated with any object of its outer class. Nested within its outer class, it's accessed like any other static member of a class—by using the class name of the outer class.
- A static nested class is accessible outside the class in which it's defined by using names of both the outer class and inner class.
- You can define both static and nonstatic members in a static nested class.
- A static nested class can define constructors.
- To access the static members of a static nested class, you need not create an object of this class. You need an object to access the instance members of this class.
- The accessibility of the nested static class depends on its access modifier. For example, a private static nested class can't be accessed outside its class.
- A static nested class can access only the static members of its outer class. Similarly, the outer class can access only the static members of its nested inner class. An attempt to access instance members on either side will fail compilation unless it's accessed through an instance of the outer or static nested class.
- All access levels can be used with this class—`public`, `protected`, *default*, and `private`.

Inner classes

- An inner class is an *instance member* of its outer class.
- An object of an *inner class* shares a special bond with its *outer class* and can't exist without its instance.
- An inner class can be defined using any of the four access levels—public, protected, *default*, and private.
- Members of an inner class can refer to all variables and methods of an outer class.
- An inner class can define constructors.
- An inner class can define variables and methods with any access.
- An inner class can't define static methods and nonfinal static variables.
- You can create an object of an inner class within an outer class or outside an outer class.
- Outside the outer class an inner class is instantiated using

```
Outer.Inner inner = new Outer().new Inner();
```

Anonymous inner classes

- An anonymous inner class is created when you combine object instance creation with inheriting a class or implementing an interface.
- An anonymous inner class might override none, few, or all methods of the inherited class.
- An anonymous inner class must implement all methods of the implemented interface.
- An instance of an anonymous class can be assigned to any type of variable (static variable, instance variable, or local variable) or method parameter, or be returned from a method.
- The following line creates an anonymous inner class that extends Object and assigns it to a reference variable of type Object:

```
Object obj = new Object(){};
```

- The following line calls a method, say aMethod(), passing to it an instance of an anonymous class that implements Runnable:

```
aMethod(new Runnable() {
    public void run() {}
});
```

- When an anonymous inner class is defined within a method, it can access only the final variables of the method in which it's defined. This is to prevent reassignment of the variable values by the inner class.
- Though you can define variables and methods in an anonymous inner class, they can't be accessed using the reference variable of the base class or interface, which is used to refer to the anonymous class instance.

Method local inner classes

- Method local inner classes are defined within a static or instance method of a class.
- A class can define multiple method local inner classes, with the same class name, but in separate methods.
- Method local inner classes can't be defined using any explicit access modifier.
- A method local inner class can define its own constructors, variables, and methods by using any of the four access levels—public, protected, *default*, and private.
- A method local inner class can be created only within the method in which it's defined. Also, its object creation can't appear before its declaration.
- A method local inner class can access all variables and methods of its *outer class*, including its private members and the ones that it inherits from its base classes. It can only access the final local variables of the method in which it's defined.
- A method local inner class can define members with the same name as its outer class. In this case, the members of the outer class can be referred to by using Outer.this.

SAMPLE EXAM QUESTIONS

Q 2-1. Select the correct statement(s) based on the following code:

```
enum Keywords {
    ASSERT(1.4),                             // line1
    DO, IF, WHILE;                           // line2
    double version = 1.0;                    // line3

    Keywords() {                             // constructor 1
        this.version = 1.0;                  // constructor 1
    }                                        // constructor 1

    Keywords(double version) {               // constructor 2
        this.version = version;              // constructor 2
    }                                        // constructor 2

    public static void main(String args[]) {
        Keywords[] keywords = Keywords.values();
        for (Keywords val:keywords) System.out.println(val);
    }
}
```

- **a** The enum keywords won't compile due to code at (#1).
- **b** The enum keywords won't compile due to code at either (#2) or (#3).
- **c** If you swap the complete code at (#1) and (#2) with code at (#3), enum keywords will compile successfully.
- **d** The enum keywords will fail to compile due to the declaration of multiple constructors.
- **e** None of the above

Q 2-2. Consider the following definition of class `Foo`:

```
abstract class Foo {
    abstract void run();
}
```

Which of the classes correctly subclass `Foo`? (Choose all that apply.)

a ```
       class Me extends Foo {
           void run() {/* ... */}
       }
       ```
**b**  ```
       abstract class You extends Foo {
           void run() {/* ... */}
       }
       ```
c ```
       interface Run {
           void run();
       }
       class Her extends Foo implements Run {
           void run() {/* ... */}
       }
       ```
**d**  ```
       abstract class His extends Foo {
           String run() {/* ... */}
       }
       ```

Q 2-3. Which lines of code, when inserted at `//INSERT CODE HERE`, will print the following:

```
BASKETBALL:CRICKET:TENNIS:SWIMMING:
```

```
enum Sports {
    TENNIS, CRICKET, BASKETBALL, SWIMMING;
    public static void main(String args[]) {
    // INSERT CODE HERE
    }
}
```

a `for (Sports val:Sports.values()) System.out.print(val+":");`

b `for (Sports val:Sports.orderedValues()) System.out.print(val+":");`

c `for (Sports val:Sports.naturalValues()) System.out.print(val+":");`

d `for (Sports val:Sports.ascendingValues()) System.out.print(val+":");`

e None of the above

Q 2-4. Given that classes `Outer` and `Test` are defined in separate packages and source code files, which code options, when inserted independently at `//INSERT CODE HERE`, will instantiate class `Inner` in class `Test`? (Choose all that apply.)

```
// Source code-Outer.java
package ejava.ocp;
public class Outer {
    public static class Inner{}
}
```

```
// Source code-Test.java
package ejava.exams;
import static ejava.ocp.Outer.Inner;
class Test {
    //INSERT CODE HERE
}
```

    a `Inner inner = new Inner();`

    b `Outer.Inner inner = new Outer.Inner();`

    c `Outer.Inner inner = new Inner();`

    d `Outer.Inner inner = Outer.new Inner();`

Q 2-5. Given the following definition of classes `Outer` and `Inner`, select options that can be inserted individually at `//INSERT CODE HERE`. (Choose all that apply.)

```
class Outer {
    void aMethod() {
        class Inner {
            // INSERT CODE HERE
        }
    }
}
```

    a `protected Inner() {}`

    b `final static String name = "eJava";`

    c `static int ctr = 10;`

    d `private final void Inner() {}`

    e `Outer outer = new Outer();`

    f `Inner inner = new Inner();`

    g `static void print() {}`

    h `static final void print() {}`

Q 2-6. Given the following definition of enum `Size`, select the commented line number(s) in class `MyClass`, where you can insert the enum definition individually. (Choose all that apply.)

```
enum Size {SMALL, MEDIUM, LARGE}
class MyClass {
    // line1
    void aMethod() {
        //line2
    }
    class Inner {
        //line3
    }
    static class StaticNested{
        //line4
    }
}
```

a The code at (#1)

b The code at (#2)

c The code at (#3)

d The code at (#4)

Q 2-7. Given the following code, which option, when inserted at /*INSERT CODE HERE*/, will instantiate an anonymous class referred to by the variable floatable?

```
interface Floatable {
    void floating();
}
class AdventureCamp {
    Floatable floatable = /*INSERT CODE HERE*/
}
```

a new Floatable();

b new Floatable(){};

c new Floatable() { public void floating() {}};

d new Floatable() public void floating() {};

e new Floatable(public void floating()) {}};

f new Floatable() { void floating() {}};

g None of the above

Q 2-8. What is the output of the following code? (Choose all that apply.)

```
interface Admissible {}                         // line1
class University {
    static void admit(Admissible adm) {
        System.out.println("admission complete");
    }
    public static void main(String args[]) {
        admit(new Admissible(){});              // line2
    }
}
```

a The class prints admission complete.

b The class doesn't display any output.

c The class fails to compile.

d University will print admission complete if code at (#2) is changed to the following:

```
admit(new Admissible());
```

e Class University instantiates an anonymous inner class.

f If Admissible is defined as a class, as follows, the result of the preceding code will remain the same:

```
class Admissible {}
```

Q 2-9. Which of the following statements are correct? (Choose all that apply.)

   a An abstract class must define variables to store the state of its object.

   b An abstract class might define concrete methods.

   c An abstract class might not define abstract methods.

   d An abstract class constructor might be called by its derived class.

   e An abstract class can extend another nonabstract class.

   f An abstract class can't define static final abstract methods.

Q 2-10. Which of the classes, when inserted at `//INSERT CODE HERE`, will create an instance of class `Inner`? (Choose all that apply.)

```
class Outer {
    class Inner {}
}
class Test {
    //INSERT CODE HERE
}
```

   a `Outer.Inner inner = new Outer.Inner();`

   b `Outer.Inner inner = Outer().new Inner();`

   c `Outer.Inner inner = Outer.new Inner();`

   d `Outer.Inner inner = new Outer().new Inner();`

   e `Outer.Inner inner = new Inner();`

   f `Outer outer = new Outer();`
      `Inner inner = new Outer.Inner();`

   g `Outer outer = new Outer();`
      `Outer.Inner inner = outer.new Inner();`

   h `Outer outer = new Outer();`
      `Inner inner = new outer.Inner();`

Q 2-11. Select the incorrect options. (Choose all that apply.).

   a An anonymous inner class always extends a class, implicitly or explicitly.

   b An anonymous inner class might not always implement an interface.

   c An anonymous inner class is a direct subclass of class `java.lang.Object`.

   d You can make an anonymous inner class do both—explicitly extend a user-defined class and an interface.

   e An anonymous inner class can implement multiple user-defined interfaces.

Q 2-12. Select the correct options for the classes `Satellite` and `Moon`:

```
abstract class Satellite{
    static {
        ctr = (int)Math.random();                // line1
    }
```

```
        static final int ctr;                    // line2
}
class Moon extends Satellite{
    public static void main(String args[]) {
        System.out.println(Moon.ctr);            // line3
    }
}
```

    a Code at only (#1) fails compilation.

    b Code at either (#1) or (#2) fails compilation.

    c Code at (#3) fails compilation.

    d Code compiles and executes successfully.

Q 2-13. What is the output of the following code?

```
enum BasicColor {
    RED;
    static {
        System.out.println("Static init");
    }
    {
        System.out.println("Init block");
    }
    BasicColor(){
        System.out.println("Constructor");
    }
    public static void main(String args[]) {
        BasicColor red = BasicColor.RED;
    }
}
```

    a Init block
        Constructor
        Static init

    b Static init
        Init block
        Constructor

    c Static init
        Constructor
        Init block

    d Constructor
        Init block
        Static init

Q 2-14. What is the output of the following code?

```
enum Browser {
    FIREFOX("firefox"),
    IE("ie"){public String toString() {return "Internet Browser";}},
    NETSCAPE("netscape");
    Browser(String name){}
```

```
public static void main(String args[]) {
    for (Browser browser:Browser.values())
        System.out.println(browser);
}
}
```

a FIREFOX
   Internet Browser
   NETSCAPE

b FIREFOX
   INTERNET BROWSER
   NETSCAPE

c FIREFOX
   IE
   NETSCAPE

d firefox
   ie
   netscape

Q 2-15. What is the output of the following code?

```
class Base {
    static {
        System.out.print("STATIC:");
    }
    {
        System.out.print("INIT:");
    }
}
class MyClass extends Base {
    static {
        System.out.print("static-der:");
    }
    {
        System.out.print("init-der:");
    }
    public static void main(String args[]) {
        new MyClass();
    }
}
```

a STATIC:INIT:static-der:init-der:

b INIT:STATIC:init-der:static-der:

c STATIC:static-der:INIT:init-der:

d static-der:init-der:STATIC:INIT:

Q 2-16. Select the correct statements. (Choose all that apply.).

a An abstract class can't define static final variables.

b The abstract methods defined in an abstract base class must be implemented by all its derived classes.

c   An abstract class enforces all its concrete derived classes to implement its abstract behavior.

d   An abstract class might not define static methods.

e   The initialization of the final variables defined in an abstract base class can be deferred to its derived classes.

ANSWERS TO SAMPLE EXAM QUESTIONS

A 2-1. e

[2.3] Use the static and final keywords
[2.5] Use enumerated types

Explanation: The code compiles successfully. An enum can define and use multiple constructors. The declaration of enum constants must follow the opening brace of the enum declaration. It can't follow the definition of variables or methods.

A 2-2. a, b

[2.1] Identify when and how to apply abstract classes
[2.2] Construct abstract Java classes and subclasses

Explanation: When a class extends another class or implements an interface, the methods in the derived class must be either valid overloaded or valid overridden methods.

Option (c) is incorrect. The concrete class `Her` extends `Foo` and implements `Run`. To compile `Her`, it must implement `run()` with `public` access so that it implements `run()` with default access in class `Foo` and `run()` with `public` access in interface `Run`:

```
class Her extends Foo implements Run {
    public void run() {}
}
```

Because class `Her` in option (c) defines `run()` with default access, it fails to implement public `run()` from interface `Run` and fails compilation.

Option (d) is incorrect. Method `run()` defined in class `His` and method `run()` defined in class `Foo` don't form either valid overloaded or overridden methods.

A 2-3. e

[2.5] Use enumerated types

Explanation: Option (a) is incorrect. The code in this option will print the natural order of the definition of the enum (the order in which they were defined):

```
TENNIS:CRICKET:BASKETBALL:SWIMMING:
```

Options (b), (c), and (d) define nonexistent enum methods. Code in these options won't compile.

A 2-4. a

[2.4] Create top-level and nested classes
[2.5] Use enumerated types

Explanation: Due to the following static `import` statement, only the nested static class `Inner` is visible in class `Test`:

```
import static ejava.ocp.Outer.Inner;
```

Class `Outer` isn't visible in class `Test`. Options (b) and (c) will instantiate class `Inner` if the following `import` statement is included in class `Test`:

```
import ejava.ocp.Outer;
```

A 2-5. a, b, d, e, f

[2.4] Create top-level and nested classes

Explanation: You can define final static variables in a method local inner class, but you can't define non-final static variables, static methods, or static final methods. You can define constructors with any access modifier in a local inner class.

A 2-6. a, d

[2.4] Create top-level and nested classes
[2.5] Use enumerated types

Explanation: You can't define an enum within a method or a nonstatic inner class.

A 2-7. c

[2.4] Create top-level and nested classes

Explanation: To instantiate an anonymous class that can be referred to by the variable `floatable` of type `Floatable`, the anonymous class must implement the interface, implementing all its methods.

Because interface `Floatable` defines method `floating()` (methods defined in an interface are implicitly public and abstract), it must be implemented by the anonymous class. Only option (c) correctly implements method `floating()`. Following is its correctly indented code, which should be more clear:

```
new Floatable() {
    public void floating() {
    }
};
```

Option (b) doesn't implement `floating()`. Option (a) tries to instantiate the interface `Floatable`, which isn't allowed. Option (f) looks okay, but isn't because it makes the method `floating()` more restrictive by not defining it as public.

A 2-8. a, e, f

[2.4] Create top-level and nested classes

Explanation: Options (b) and (c) are incorrect because the class compiles successfully and prints a value.

Option (d) is incorrect because it tries to instantiate the interface `Admissible` and not an instance of the anonymous inner class that implements `Admissible`.

Option (e) is correct because code at (#2) instantiates an anonymous inner class, which implements the interface `Admissible`. Because the interface `Admissible` doesn't define any methods, code at (#2) doesn't need to implement any methods.

Option (f) is correct. If `Admissible` is defined as a class, the anonymous inner class at (#2) will subclass it. Because `Admissible` doesn't define any abstract methods, there aren't any added complexities.

A 2-9. b, c, e, f

[2.1] Identify when and how to apply abstract classes

Explanation: Note the use of can, must, and might or might not in these options. Note that this isn't a test on English grammar or vocabulary. The meaning of an exam question will completely change depending on whether it uses "can" (feasible), "must" (mandatory), or "might" (optional) in a question.

Option (a) is incorrect because it isn't mandatory for an abstract class to define instance variables.

Option (d) is incorrect because the constructor of all base classes—concrete or abstract—must be called by their derived classes.

Option (f) is a correct statement. The combination of `final` and `abstract` modifiers is incorrect. An abstract method is meant to be overridden in the derived classes, whereas a final method can't be overridden.

A 2-10. d, g

[2.4] Create top-level and nested classes

Explanation: An inner class is a member of its outer class and can't exist without its instance. To create an instance of an inner class outside either the outer or inner class, you must do the following:

- If using a reference variable, use type `Outer.Inner`.
- Access an instance of the `Outer` class.
- Create an instance of the `Inner` class.

To create instances of both the `Outer` and `Inner` classes on a single line, you must use the operator `new` with both the `Outer` class and `Inner` class, as follows:

```
new Outer().new Inner();
```

If you already have access to an instance of `Outer` class, say, `outer`, call `new Inner()` by using `outer`:

```
outer.new Inner();
```

A 2-11. c, d, e

[2.4] Create top-level and nested classes

Explanation: Note that you have to select incorrect statements in this question. This can be confusing, because most of the time on the exam, you're asked to select correct options.

Option (a) is a correct statement. If an anonymous inner class extends a class, it subclasses it explicitly. When it implements an interface, it implicitly extends class `java.lang.Object`. If an anonymous inner class doesn't subclass a class implicitly, it implicitly extends `java.lang.Object`.

Option (b) is a correct statement. An anonymous inner class might not always implement an interface.

Option (c) is an incorrect statement. An anonymous inner class isn't *always* a direct subclass of class `java.lang.Object`, if it extends any other class explicitly.

Option (d) is an incorrect statement. You can't make an anonymous inner class extend both a class and an interface explicitly. I deliberately used the words *user-defined classes* and *user-defined interfaces* so you wouldn't assume that an anonymous class implicitly subclasses a class from a Java API.

Option (e) is an incorrect statement. You can't make an anonymous class implement multiple interfaces explicitly.

A 2-12. d

[2.2] Construct abstract Java classes and subclasses
[2.3] Use the static and final keywords

Explanation: No compilation or runtime issues exist with this code. A static initializer block can access and initialize a static variable; it can be placed before the static variable declaration. A static variable defined in a base class is accessible to its derived class. Even though class `Moon` doesn't define the static variable `ctr`, it can access the static variable `ctr` defined in its base class `Satellite`.

A 2-13. a

[2.3] Use the static and final keywords
[2.5] Use enumerated types

Explanation: The creation of enum constants happens in a static initializer block, before the execution of the rest of the code defined in the `static` block. Here's the decompiled code for enum `BasicColor`, which shows how enum constants are initialized in the static block. To initialize an enum constant, its constructor is called. Note that the contents of the default constructor and instance initializer blocks are added to the new constructor implicitly defined during the compilation process:

```java
final class BasicColor extends Enum
{
    public static BasicColor[] values()
    {
        return (BasicColor[])$VALUES.clone();
    }

    public static BasicColor valueOf(String s)
    {
        return (BasicColor)Enum.valueOf(BasicColor, s);
    }

    private BasicColor(String s, int i)
    {
        super(s, i);
        System.out.println("Init block");
        System.out.println("Constructor");
    }

    public static void main(String args[])
    {
        BasicColor basiccolor = RED;
    }

    public static final BasicColor RED;
    private static final BasicColor $VALUES[];

    static
    {
        RED = new BasicColor("RED", 0);
        $VALUES = (new BasicColor[] {
            RED
        });
        System.out.println("Static init");
    }
}
```

 NOTE   If you try to compile the preceding code it won't compile because classes can't directly extend java.lang.Enum. I've included this code just to show you how the Java compiler modifies code of an enum and adds additional code to it. It explains why an enum constructor executes before its static block.

A 2-14. a

[2.5] Use enumerated types

Explanation: An enum extends class java.lang.Enum, which extends class java.lang .Object. Each enum constant inherits method toString() defined in class java .lang.Enum. Class java.lang.Enum overrides method toString() to return the enum constant's name.

An enum constant can override any of the methods that are inherited by it. The enum `Browser` defines a constructor that accepts a `String` method parameter, but it doesn't use it. All enum constants, except enum constant `IE`, print the name of the constant itself.

A 2-15. c

[2.3] Use the static and final keywords

Explanation: When you instantiate a derived class, the derived class instantiates its base class. The static initializers execute when a class is loaded in memory. So the order of execution of static and instance initializer blocks is as follows:

- 1) Base class static initializer block
- 2) Derived class static initializer block
- 3) Base class instance initializer block
- 4) Derived class instance initializer block

A 2-16. c, d

[2.1] Identify when and how to apply abstract classes
[2.3] Use the static and final keywords

Explanation: Option (a) is incorrect. An abstract class can define static final variables.

Option (b) is incorrect. The abstract methods defined in an abstract base class must be implemented by all its concrete derived classes. Abstract derived classes might not implement the abstract methods from their abstract base class.

Option (e) is incorrect. The initialization of a final variable defined in an abstract base class must complete in the class itself—with its initialization, in its initializer block, or in its constructor. It can't be deferred to its derived class.

Object-oriented design principles

Exam objectives covered in this chapter	What you need to know
[3.1] Write code that declares, implements, and/or extends interfaces	The need for interfaces. How to declare, implement, and extend interfaces. Implications of implicit modifiers that are added to an interface and its members.
[3.2] Choose between interface inheritance and class inheritance	The differences and similarities between implementing inheritance by using interfaces and by using abstract or concrete classes. Factors that favor using interface inheritance over class inheritance, and vice versa.
[3.3] Apply cohesion, low-coupling, IS-A, and HAS-A principles	Given a set of IS-A and HAS-A relationships, how to implement them in code. Given code snippets, how to correctly identify the relationships (IS-A or HAS-A) implemented by them. How to identify and promote low coupling and high cohesion.
[3.4] Apply object composition principles (including HAS-A relationships)	Given that an object can be composed of multiple other objects, how to determine the types of compositions— and implement them in code.
[3.5] Design a class using the Singleton design pattern	How to implement the Singleton design pattern. The need for the existence of exactly one copy of a class.
[3.6] Write code to implement the DAO pattern	The usability of the DAO pattern. How this pattern enables separation of data access code in an application.
[3.7] Design and create objects using a Factory pattern	The need for, use of, and benefits of a Factory for creating objects. How this pattern is used in the existing Java API classes.

Have you ever tried to find out the secret(s) behind the most successful people? Almost all agree to follow a set of lifelong principles. So, articles like "Three Common Habits of the Most Successful People" might include points similar to these:

- Never hit the snooze button when the alarm goes off in the morning, so you aren't delaying your actions.
- First things first: prioritize your work.
- Follow your passion and do what you love, because you'll be working almost all your life.

These are the principles that successful people follow (though perhaps in a different manner) to achieve the greatest height of success.

Similarly, *object-oriented design (OOD) principles* enable you to create better application designs, which are manageable and extensible. For example, as a programmer or designer, you know that application requirements typically change. Implementing these modified needs requires changes in the existing code, which usually introduces bugs. Chances are that if the application design implements OOD principles, the modification task will require comparatively less effort. Again, as an example, if your application's design uses the design principles of low coupling and high cohesion, chances are low that changes in a class will affect another class.

Design patterns (for example, the Singleton pattern) also help you design better applications. Unlike inheritance, a design pattern is an example of experience reuse and not code reuse. Building sloping roofs in areas that receive a lot of snowfall can be compared to using a design pattern. A sloping roof was identified as a solution to avoid accumulation of snow on rooftops after multiple people faced issues with flat roofs. Just as a sloping roof is applicable specifically to areas receiving snowfall, a design pattern resolves a *specific* design issue.

Obviously, we can see that the object-oriented design principles are important, but what specifically do you need to know for the exam? Well, the exam will test you on what object-oriented design principles are and how to apply them in your applications. You'll likely find questions on the creation of and preferred use of classes and interfaces to design your application, and how to relate and use Java objects together. In addition, you'll need to know how to make the best use of design patterns in your application. Yes, this is a lot, but I promise to walk you through each piece so you're prepared. This chapter covers

- Interfaces—their declaration, implementation, and application
- Choosing between class inheritance and interface inheritance
- Relationships between Java objects
- Application of object composition principles
- Implementation of IS-A and HAS-A relationships between objects
- Singleton design pattern
- Data Access Object (DAO) design pattern
- Factory design pattern

Interfaces are one of the most powerful concepts in Java. Believe me, not many designers completely understand how to use them *effectively* in their design. To be a good application designer, you *must* know how to do so. Let's start with a quick example: in how many ways can you refer to your father? Apart from being your father, he could also be referred to as a friend, guide, husband, swimmer, orator, teacher, manager, and much more. How can you achieve the same in Java, to refer to the same object by using multiple types? In the next section, you'll learn about the need for using interfaces, followed by declaring, implementing, and extending them. Let's get started.

3.1   *Interfaces*

 [3.1]   Write code that declares, implements, and/or extends interfaces

Before we deep-dive into working with interfaces, note that the term *interface* has multiple meanings. First, an interface is a type created by using the keyword `interface`. For example, the following code creates the interface `Movable`:

```
interface Moveable {
    void move();
}
```

An interface in its second meaning is more general. It's how two systems can interact with each other (like your television and the remote control). It's how classes can interact with each other, using their public methods. For class `Person`, its interface (public methods) refers to its methods `eat()` and `work()`:

```
class Person {
    public void eat() {}
    public void work() {}
}
```

Figure 3.1 represents an interface as a type and as a group of public methods of a class.

Note that this exam objective refers to an *interface* as a type, which is created using the keyword `interface`.

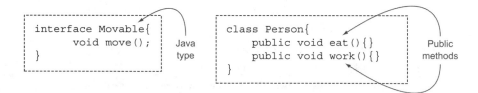

Figure 3.1   The term *interface* has two meanings: a type created using the keyword `interface` and a group of public methods of a class.

3.1.1 *Understanding interfaces*

We all, quite often, use interfaces in our lives. For example, when you refer to some-one as a *runner*, do you care whether that person is also an orator, a parent, or an entrepreneur? You care only that the person is able to *run*. The term *runner* enables you to refer to unrelated individuals, by opening a small window to each person and accessing behavior that's applicable to *only* that person's capacity as a runner. Some-one can be referred to as a runner only if that person supports characteristics relevant to running, though the specific behavior can depend on the person.

In the preceding example, you can compare the term *runner* to a Java interface, which defines the required behavior *run*. An interface can define a set of behaviors (methods) and constants. It delegates the implementation of the behavior to the classes that implement it. Interfaces are used to refer to multiple related or unrelated objects that share the same set of behavior. Figure 3.2 compares the interface *runner* with a small *window* to an object, which is concerned only about the running capabili-ties of that object.

Similarly, when you design your application by using interfaces, you can use similar windows (also referred to as *specifications* or *contracts*) to specify the behavior that you need from an object, without caring about the specific type of objects. Separating the required behavior from its implementation has many benefits. As an application designer, you can use interfaces to *establish* the behavior that's required from objects, promoting flexibility in the design (new classes that implement an interface can be created and used later). Interfaces make an application manageable, extensible, and less prone to propagation of errors due to changes to existing types.

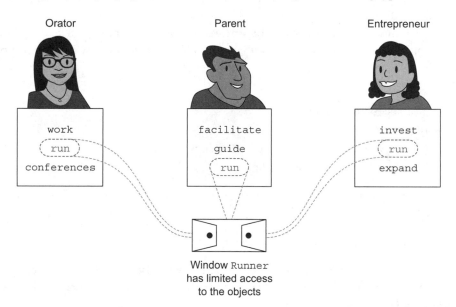

Figure 3.2 You can compare an interface with a window that can connect multiple objects but has limited access to them.

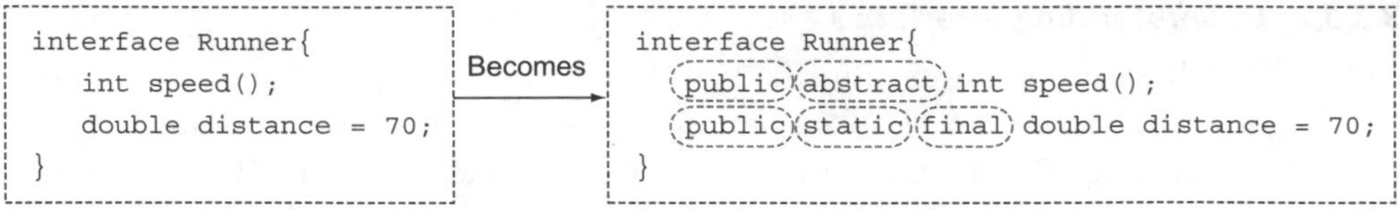

```
interface Runner{                         interface Runner{
    int speed();             Becomes          (public)(abstract) int speed();
    double distance = 70;                      (public)(static)(final) double distance = 70;
}                                         }
```

Figure 3.3   All the methods of an interface are implicitly public and abstract. Its variables are implicitly public, static, and final.

3.1.2   *Declaring interfaces*

You can define methods and constants in an interface. Declaring an interface is simple, but don't let this simplicity take you for a ride. For the exam, it's important to understand the implicit modifiers that are added to the members of an interface. All methods of an interface are implicitly public and abstract, and its variables are implicitly public, static, and final. Let's start with the interface `Runner` that defines a method `speed()` and a variable `distance`. Figure 3.3 shows how implicit modifiers are added to the members of interface `Runner` during the compilation process.

Why do you think these implicit modifiers are added to the interface members? Because an interface is used to define a contract, it doesn't make sense to limit access to its members—and so they are implicitly public. An interface can't be instantiated, and so the value of its variables should be defined and accessible in a static context, which makes them implicitly static. Because an interface is a contract, its implementations shouldn't be able to change it, so the interface variables are implicitly final. Interface methods are implicitly abstract so that it's mandatory for the classes to implement them.

The exam will also test you on the various components of an interface declaration, including access and nonaccess modifiers. Here's the complete list of the components of an interface declaration:

- Access modifiers
- Nonaccess modifiers
- Interface name
- All extended interfaces, if the interface is extending any interfaces
- Interface body (variables and methods), included within a pair of curly braces { }

To include all the possible components, let's modify the declaration of the interface `Runner`:

```
public strictfp interface Runner extends Athlete, Walker {}
```

The components of the interface `Runner` are shown in figure 3.4. To declare any interface, you *must* include the keyword `interface`; the name of the interface; and its body, marked by {}.

public	strictfp	interface	Runner	extends	Athlete, Walker	{ }
Access modifier	Nonaccess modifier	Keyword	Interface name	Keyword	Name of interfaces extended by interface `Runner`	Curly braces
Optional	Optional	(Compulsory)	(Compulsory)	Optional	Optional	(Compulsory)

Figure 3.4 Components of an interface declaration

The optional and compulsory components of an interface can be summarized as listed in table 3.1.

Table 3.1 Optional and compulsory components of an interface declaration

Compulsory	Optional
Keyword `interface`	Access modifier
Name of the interface	Nonaccess modifier
Interface body, marked by the opening and closing curly braces { }	Keyword `extends`, together with the name of the base interface(s). (Unlike a class, an interface can extend multiple interfaces.)

 EXAM TIP The declaration of an interface can't include a class name. An interface can never extend any class.

Can you define a top-level, *protected* interface? No, you can't. For the exam, you must know the answer to such questions about the correct values for each component that can be used with an interface declaration. Let's dive into these nuances.

VALID ACCESS MODIFIERS FOR AN INTERFACE

You can declare a *top-level interface* (the one that isn't declared within any other class or interface), with only the following access levels:

- `public`
- No modifier (default access)

If you try to declare your top-level interfaces by using the other access modifiers (`protected` or `private`), your interface will fail to compile. The following definitions of the interface `MyInterface` won't compile:

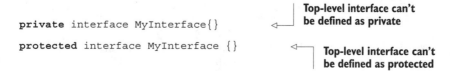

```
private interface MyInterface{}
```
Top-level interface can't be defined as private

```
protected interface MyInterface {}
```
Top-level interface can't be defined as protected

EXAM TIP   All the top-level Java types (classes, enums, and interfaces) can be declared using only two access levels: `public` and default. Inner or nested types can be declared using any access level.

VALID ACCESS MODIFIERS FOR MEMBERS OF AN INTERFACE

All members of an interface—variables, methods, inner interfaces, and inner classes (yes, an interface can define a class within it!)—are public by default. Interfaces support only the `public` access modifier. Using other access modifiers results in compilation errors.

```
interface MyInterface {                    ❶ Won't
    private int number = 10;        ◄────     compile
    protected void aMethod();            ◄────        Won't
    interface interface2{}                   ◄────    compile      interface2 is
    public interface interface4{}    ◄────                         implicitly prefixed
}                                                                  with public.
                                               Interface member can
                                               be prefixed with public
```

The code at ❶ fails compilation with the following error message:

```
illegal combination of modifiers: public and private
    private int number = 10;
```

SPECIAL CHARACTERISTICS OF METHODS AND VARIABLES OF AN INTERFACE

Methods in interfaces are public and abstract by default. The following methods defined individually in an interface are equivalent:

```
int getMembers();
public abstract int getMembers();
```

Variables defined in interfaces are public, static, and final by default. The following variables defined individually in an interface are equivalent:

```
int maxMembers = 100;
public static final int maxMembers = 100;
```

Because the interface variables are implicitly final, you can define only *constants* in an interface. Ensure that you initialize these constants, or your code won't compile:

```
interface MyInterface {              Won't compile; variables
    int number;               ◄────  within interface must be
}                                     initialized.
```

VALID NONACCESS MODIFIERS FOR AN INTERFACE

You can declare a top-level interface with only the following nonaccess modifiers:

- `abstract`
- `strictfp`

 NOTE   The `strictfp` keyword guarantees that results of all floating-point calculations are identical on all platforms.

If you try to declare your top-level interfaces by using the other nonaccess modifiers (`final`, `static`, `transient`, `synchronized`, or `volatile`), the interface will fail to compile. All of the following interface declarations fail to compile:

```
final interface MyInterface {}
static interface MyInterface {}
transient interface MyInterface {}
synchronized interface MyInterface {}
volatile interface MyInterface {}
```

Won't compile; invalid nonaccess modifiers used with interface declaration

A nested interface can be defined using the nonaccess modifier `static` (any other nonaccess modifier isn't allowed):

```
class Outer {
    static interface MyInterface1 {}
}
```

Nested interface

With good coverage of interface declaration, let's start making classes implement interfaces.

3.1.3 *Implementing interfaces*

You can compare implementing an interface to signing a contract. When a concrete class declares its implementation of an interface, it agrees to implement all its abstract methods. A class can implement multiple interfaces. For example, class `Home` implements `Livable` and `GuestHouse`:

```
interface Livable {
    void live();
}
interface GuestHouse {
    void welcome();
}
class Home implements Livable, GuestHouse {
    public void live() {}
    public void welcome() {}
}
```

abstract method live()

abstract method welcome()

Class uses keyword implements to implement interface

If you don't implement all the methods defined in the implemented interfaces, a class can't compile as a concrete class. Let's modify the code of class `Home`, as follows:

```
class Home implements Livable, GuestHouse {
    public void welcome() {}
}
```

The compiler says it all:

```
House.java:7: error: Home is not abstract and does not override
abstract method live() in Livable
class Home implements Livable, GuestHouse {
^
1 error
```

So a class can choose not to implement all the methods from the implemented interface(s) and still compile successfully, but only if it's defined as an abstract class, as follows:

```
abstract class Home implements Livable, GuestHouse {    ⟵  Abstract class doesn't have to
    public void welcome() {}                                implement all methods from
}                                                           implemented interfaces
```

 EXAM TIP   A *concrete* class must implement all the methods from the interfaces that it implements. An *abstract* class can choose not to implement all the methods from the interfaces that it implements.

DEFINING AND ACCESSING VARIABLES WITH THE SAME NAME

A class can define an instance or a static variable with the same name as the variable defined in the interface that it implements. In the following class, the interface `Livable` defines variables `status` and `ratings`. Class `Home` implements `Livable` and defines instance variable `status` and static variable `ratings`, with a default access level:

```
interface Livable {
    boolean status = true;              public
    int ratings = 10;                   variables
}
class Home implements Livable {
    boolean status;                     Variables with
    static int ratings = 7;             default access
    Home() {
        System.out.println(status);            Prints
        System.out.println(Livable.status);    "true"

        System.out.println(ratings);           Prints "7"
        System.out.println(Livable.ratings);   Prints "11"
    }
}
```

Prints "false" (points to first println(status))

 EXAM TIP   A class can define an instance or a static variable with the same name as the variable defined in the interface that it implements. These variables can be defined using any access level.

FOLLOWING METHOD OVERRIDING RULES FOR IMPLEMENTING INTERFACE METHODS

The methods in an interface are public, by default. So, trying to assign weaker access to the implemented method in a class won't allow it to compile:

```
interface Livable {                     public
    void live();                        method
}
class Home implements Livable {         Won't compile;
    void live() {}                      method implemented
}                                       using weaker access
```

The compilation error message says it all:

```
House.java:8: error: live() in Home cannot implement live() in Livable
    void live() {}
         ^
  attempting to assign weaker access privileges; was public
1 error
```

 EXAM TIP Because interface methods are implicitly public, the implementing class must implement them as public methods, or else the class will fail to compile.

IMPLEMENTING MULTIPLE INTERFACES THAT DEFINE METHODS WITH THE SAME NAME

Methods in the interfaces don't define any implementation; they come without any baggage. But what happens if a class implements multiple interfaces that define methods with the same name? Let's add a method live() to interface GuestHouse (modifications in bold):

```
interface Livable {                    Interface Livable
    void live();                       defines method live().
}
interface GuestHouse {                 Interface GuestHouse also
    void welcome();                    defines method live().
    void live();
}
```

Class Home implements two interfaces, Livable and GuestHouse, both of which define method live():

```
class Home implements Livable, GuestHouse {
    public void live() {               Method live() in
        System.out.println("live");    Home has only one
    }                                  implementation.
    public void welcome() {
        System.out.println("welcome");
    }
}
```

Both the Java compiler and Java Runtime Environment are good with the preceding code. Because the signature of method live() is the same in both interfaces, Livable and GuestHouse, class Home needs to define only one implementation for method live() to fulfill both contracts (interface implementations).

OVERLAPPING METHOD IMPLEMENTATIONS WITH THEIR OVERLOAD VERSIONS

A class can try to implement multiple interfaces that define methods with the same name. But in doing so, you can have a not-so-pleasant cocktail of overlapping method implementations and their overloaded versions. We have two scenarios here:

- Correctly overloaded methods
- Invalid overloaded methods

Overloaded methods are defined by using the same name but a different parameter list. For example, when implemented in class Home, method live() defined in the interface Livable overloads method live() defined in the interface GuestHouse. Class Home must implement both these methods:

```
interface Livable {
    void live();                        ◁─┐  live() doesn't accept any
}                                          │  method parameters.
interface GuestHouse {
    void live(int days);                  ◁──┐  live() accepts a
}                                            │  method parameter.
class Home implements Livable, GuestHouse {
    public void live() {                 ◁─┐  Correctly overloaded
        System.out.println("live");        │  method live() from Livable
    }
    public void live(int days) {          ◁─┐  Correctly overloaded
        System.out.println("live for " + days);  │  method live() from
    }                                            │  GuestHouse
}
```

You can't define overloaded methods by changing only the return type of methods. What happens if method live() in the interfaces Livable and GuestHouse returns different types? In this case, class Home needs to implement both versions of method live(), which can't be qualified as overloaded methods. So class Home doesn't compile in this case:

```
interface Livable {               │  live() returns
    String live();               ◁─┘  String.
}
interface GuestHouse {            │  live() returns
    void live();                ◁─┘  nothing—void.
}                                              ┌  Class Home
class Home implements Livable, GuestHouse {  ◁─┘  won't compile.
    public String live() {       ◁─┐  When implemented in class Home,
        return null;               │  both versions of live() qualify as
    }                              │  incorrectly overloaded methods.
    public void live() {         ◁─┘
        System.out.println("live" );
    }
}
```

Here's the compiler error for class Home:

```
Home.java:11: error: method live() is already defined in class Home
    public void live() {
           ^
Home.java:7: error: Home is not abstract and does not override abstract
 method live() in GuestHouse
class Home implements Livable, GuestHouse {
 ^
```

```
Home.java:8: error: live() in Home cannot implement live() in GuestHouse
    public String live() {
                  ^
   return type String is not compatible with void
3 errors
```

 EXAM TIP A class can implement methods with the same name from multiple interfaces. But these must qualify as correctly overloaded methods.

3.1.4 Extending interfaces

An interface can inherit multiple interfaces. Because all the members of an interface are implicitly `public`, a derived interface inherits all the methods of its super interface(s). An interface uses the keyword `extends` to inherit an interface, as shown in the following example:

```
interface GuestHouse {
    void welcome();
}
interface PayingGuestHouse extends GuestHouse {
    void paidBreakfast();
}
interface StudentPGHouse extends PayingGuestHouse {
    void laundry();
}
interface ChildFriendly {
    void toys();
}
interface FamilyPGHouse extends ChildFriendly, PayingGuestHouse {
    void kitchen();
}
```

The preceding code is shown in figure 3.5 as a UML diagram.

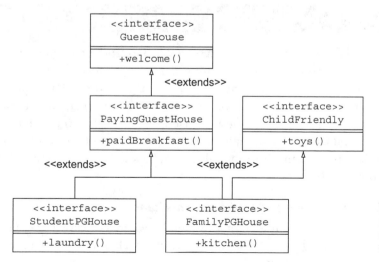

Figure 3.5 UML relationships between interfaces that extend other interfaces

By extending interfaces, you can combine methods of multiple interfaces. In the previous example, the interface `FamilyPGHouse` combines the methods of the interfaces `ChildFriendly`, `PayingGuestHouse`, and `GuestHouse`.

When a class implements an interface, it should implement all the methods defined in the interface and its base interfaces, unless it's declared as abstract. If, for example, a class implements the interface `PayingGuestHouse`, that class must implement method `paidBreakfast()` defined in the interface `PayingGuestHouse`, and method `welcome()` defined in the interface `GuestHouse`. Let's work with a concrete example of a class implementing interfaces in the next section.

Rules to remember about interfaces

- An interface is abstract by definition.
- An interface can define only public, abstract methods and public, static, final variables.
- An interface uses the keyword `extends` to inherit other interfaces.
- A class can *implement* multiple interfaces. An interface can *extend* multiple interfaces.
- An interface can define inner interfaces and (surprisingly) inner classes too.
- If a class doesn't implement all the methods of the interface that it implements, the class *must* be defined as an abstract class.
- A class uses the keyword `implements` to implement an interface.
- If a class implements multiple interfaces that define methods with the same name, the interface methods must either qualify as correctly overloaded or overridden methods, or else the class won't compile.

3.2   *Class inheritance versus interface inheritance*

 [3.2]   Choose between interface inheritance and class inheritance

A class can implement interface(s) and a class can also extend a class and override its methods. So the big question is, while designing classes and interfaces in your application, how do you implement inheritance to reuse existing code? Would you prefer that your class inherit another (abstract or concrete) class or implement an interface? There is no straight answer to this question. Depending on the requirements, you might need to extend a class or implement an interface, because each offers a different set of benefits. To make this informed decision, let's focus on the similarities and differences in both approaches.

3.2.1   *Comparing class inheritance and interface inheritance*

An interface doesn't include implementation details, whereas a class does. This basic distinction has introduced differences in inheriting a class and implementing an interface. These differences are listed in table 3.2.

Table 3.2   Differences between class inheritance and interface inheritance

	Class inheritance	Interface inheritance
Instantiation of derived class	Instantiation of a derived class instantiates its base class.	Interfaces can't be instantiated.
How many?	A class can extend only one base class.	A class can implement multiple interfaces.
Reusing implementation details	A class can reuse the implementation details of its base class.	An interface doesn't include implementation details.
Modification to base class implementation details	With the modified base class, a derived class might cease to offer the functionality it was originally created for; it may also fail to compile.	Interfaces don't include implementation details.

Now for the similarities between class and interface inheritance. In both cases, you can refer to a derived class or implementing class by using a variable of the base class or implemented interface.

3.2.2   *Preferring class inheritance over interface inheritance*

Class inheritance scores better when you want to reuse the implementation already defined in a base class. It also scores better when you want to add new behavior to an existing base class. Let's examine both of these in detail.

REUSING THE IMPLEMENTATION FROM THE BASE CLASS

When we create any class, we extend and reuse class `java.lang.Object`. The class `Object` defines code to take care of all the threading and object-locking issues, together with providing default implementation for methods like `toString()`, `hashCode()`, and `equals()`. Method `toString()` returns a textual description (`String`) of an instance. Methods like `hashCode()` and `equals()` enable objects to be stored and retrieved efficiently in hash-based collection classes like `HashMap`. What do you think would happen if class `java.lang.Object` was defined as an interface? In this case, you'd need to implement all these methods for every class that you created.

But it's not useful to replicate this type of boilerplate code across many implementation classes. So class inheritance comes in handy here.

ADDING NEW BEHAVIOR IN ALL DERIVED CLASSES

Imagine you created a set of entities (`Lion`, `Elephant`), identified their common behavior, and moved the common behavior to their common base class (`Animal`). Because you control the definition of all these classes, you might add new behavior to your base class and make it available to all the derived classes. Examine the following definition of the abstract class `Animal` and nonabstract class `Lion`, which extends class `Animal`:

```
public abstract class Animal {
    public abstract void move();
    public abstract void live();
}
```

```
public class Lion extends Animal {
    public void move(){/*...*/}
    public void live(){/*...*/}
}
```

Let's add another method to `Animal` (modifications in bold):

```
public abstract class Animal {
    public abstract void move();
    public abstract void live();                  ┌── Addition of new
    public void eat() {/*...*/}         ◁─────────┘   method eat
}
public class Lion extends Animal {
    public void move(){/*...*/}
    public void live(){/*...*/}
}
```

The addition of public method `eat()` in class `Animal` makes it available to all subclasses of `Lion`, implicitly. But adding or modifying behavior in a base class is not always a bed of roses, as you'll see in the next section.

3.2.3 *Preferring interface inheritance over class inheritance*

You may prefer interface inheritance over class inheritance when you need to define multiple contracts for classes.

IMPLEMENTING MULTIPLE INTERFACES

Imagine you need to use a class that can be executed in a separate `thread` *and* can be attached as an `ActionListener` to a GUI component. You can achieve this by making your class implement multiple interfaces that support these functionalities—interfaces `Runnable` and `ActionListener`:

```
class MyClass implements Runnable, ActionListener {
    //..code to implement methods from interface
    //..Runnable and ActionListener
}
```

Interface implementation has one major advantage: a class can implement multiple interfaces, to support multiple functionality. For the preceding example, you can pass instances of class `MyClass` to all methods that define parameters of type `Runnable` or `ActionListener`.

DEFINING A NEW CONTRACT FOR EXISTING CLASSES TO ABIDE BY

Starting with Java version 7, a new language feature has been added to the exception handling: auto-closing resources by using a `try-with-resources` statement. The intent is to define a `try` statement that can use streams that can be *auto-closed*, releasing any system resources associated with them. This prevents Java objects from using resources that are no longer required. These unused and unclosed resources can lead to resource leakage. Though a `try` statement provides a `finally` clause that can be used by programmers to close streams, at times it isn't being used to do so. So to manage resources automatically, Java designers introduced the `try-with-resources` statement. The objects that can be used with this statement need to define a `close` method, so this method can be called to automatically close and release used resources. To apply this constraint, Java designers at Oracle started by defining interface `java.lang.AutoCloseable`, as follows:

```
package java.lang;
public interface AutoCloseable {
    void close() throws Exception;
}
```

The `try-with-resources` statement can declare only objects that implement the interface `java.lang.AutoCloseable`. Prior to Java 7 (starting with Java 5), many input and output streams from the Java IO API implemented the interface `java.io.Closeable`:

```
public abstract class Reader implements Readable, Closeable {
public abstract class Writer implements Appendable, Closeable, Flushable {
public abstract class InputStream implements Closeable {
public abstract class OutputStream implements Closeable, Flushable {
```

To accommodate the use of class instances mentioned in the preceding code, the existing interface `java.io.Closeable` was tricked (read: modified) into extending `java.lang.AutoCloseable`:

```
package java.io;
import java.io.IOException;
   public interface Closeable extends AutoCloseable {
     public void close() throws IOException;
}
```

Also, any user-defined class that implements the interface `java.lang.AutoCloseable` or any of its subinterfaces can be used with a `try-with-resources` statement. Here's a quick example of using a `try-with-resources` statement:

```
void openFile(String filename) throws Exception {
    try (FileInputStream fis = new FileInputStream(new File(filename))) {   ⟵
            /* ... */
    }
}
```

> Object of FileInputStream can be declared in
> try-with-resources because FileInputStream
> implements Closeable (which extends AutoCloseable).

As you'll see in chapter 6, a `try` block in `try-with-resources` can exist without any companion `catch` or `finally` block.

Interface inheritance added new behavior to classes like `Reader` and `Writer` without breaking their existing code. Inheritance of the interface `AutoCloseable` by `Closeable` defines multiple contracts for instances of these classes. They can now be assigned to a reference variable of type `AutoCloseable`, enabling them to be used with a `try-with-resources` statement.

Several other classes and interfaces implement or extend `AutoCloseable`, among the main Java Database Connectivity (JDBC) interfaces (`Connection`, `Statement`, `ResultSet`) and several Java Sound API interfaces.

FRAGILE DERIVED CLASSES

Adding to or modifying a base class can affect its derived classes. Adding new methods to a base class can result in breaking the code of a derived class. Consider this initial arrangement, which works well:

```
public abstract class Animal {
    void move(){}
}
class Lion extends Animal {
    void live(){}
}
```

Now consider a modified arrangement: a new method live() is added to base class Animal. Because live() clashes (because of an incorrectly overridden method) with the existing method live() in its derived class Lion, Lion will no longer compile:

```
public abstract class Animal {
    void move(){}
    String live(){
        return "live";
    }
}
class Lion extends Animal {
    void live(){}
}
```

New method added to Animal

live() in Lion neither overloads nor overrides live() in Animal.

 EXAM TIP   Class inheritance isn't always a good choice because derived classes are fragile. If any changes are made to a base class, a derived class might break. Extending classes that are from another package or are poorly documented aren't good candidates for base classes.

If a base class chooses to modify the implementation details of its methods, the derived classes might not be able to offer the functionality they were supposed to, or they might respond differently. Consider this initial arrangement:

```
public abstract class Animal {
    String currentPosition;
    public void move(String newPosition){
        currentPosition = newPosition;
    }
}
class Lion extends Animal {
    void changePosition(String newPosition) {
        super.move(newPosition);
        System.out.println("New Position:" + newPosition);
    }
}
class Test{
    public static void main(String args[]) {
        new Lion().changePosition("Forest");
    }
}
```

Prints "New Position:Forest" once

Imagine that `Animal` adds another line of code to method `move()`. Let's see how it changes the code output of class `Test` (modification in bold):

```
public abstract class Animal {
    String currentPosition;
    public void move(String newPosition){
        currentPosition = newPosition;
        System.out.println("New Position:" + newPosition);
    }
}
class Lion extends Animal {
    void changePosition(String newPosition) {
        super.move(newPosition);
        System.out.println("New Position:" + newPosition);
    }

    public static void main(String args[]) {
        new Lion().changePosition("Forest");
    }
}
```

> Implementation details modified; new code line added

> Prints "New Position:Forest" twice

 EXAM TIP   There isn't any clear winner when it comes to selecting the better option from class inheritance and interface inheritance. Analyze the given conditions or situations carefully to answer questions on this topic.

Imagine the thought process required to modify the core Java classes when its new version is planned or executed. As you witnessed in the preceding example, changes to a base class can break the code of its derived classes.

In the next "Twist in the Tale" exercise, let's try to figure out how an already-defined class implements the interface `AutoCloseable`, or any of its subinterfaces, so it can be used with a `try-with-resources` statement.

Twist in the Tale 3.1

As shown in the preceding examples, a try-with-resources statement can declare resources (objects) that implement the interface `java.lang.AutoCloseable` or any of its subinterfaces. A programmer has defined a class `MyLaptop` as follows, and wants to use it with a try-with-resources statement. Which option will enable the programmer to achieve this goal?

```
class MyLaptop {
    public int open()    {
        /* some code */
        return 0;
    }
    public void charge() {
        /* some code */
    }
```

```
    public int close()    {
        /* some code */
        return 1;
    }
}
```

    a Make class `MyLaptop` implement interface `java.lang.AutoCloseable`.

    b Make class `MyLaptop` implement interface `java.io.Closeable`, which extends interface `java.lang.AutoCloseable`.

    c Create a new interface `MyCloseable` that extends `java.lang.AutoCloseable`, and make class `MyLaptop` implement it.

    d Class `MyLaptop` can't implement interface `java.lang.AutoCloseable` or any of its subinterfaces because of the definition of its method `close()`.

In the next section, you'll work with how to identify and implement IS-A and HAS-A principles in code.

3.3 *IS-A and HAS-A relationships in code*

 [3.3] Apply cohesion, low-coupling, IS-A, and HAS-A principles

You'll be amazed at how easily you can identify and implement IS-A and HAS-A relationships between classes and objects, if you remember one simple rule—follow the literal meaning of these terms:

- *IS-A*—This relationship is implemented when
  - A class extends another class (derived class IS-A base class)
  - An interface extends another interface (derived interface IS-A base interface)
  - A class implements an interface (class IS-A implemented interface)
- *HAS-A*—This relationship is implemented by defining an instance variable. If a class—say, `MyClass`—defines an instance variable of another class—say, `Your-Class`—`MyClass` HAS-A `YourClass`. If `MyClass` defines an instance variable of an interface—say, `YourInterface`—`YourClass` HAS-A `YourInterface`.

 EXAM TIP Representing IS-A and HAS-A relationships by using (quick) UML diagrams can help you on the exam. Though you may not see UML diagrams on the exam, creating quick UML diagrams on an erasable board (or something similar) provided to you during the exam will help you answer these questions.

The exam will test whether you can identify and implement these relationships in your code, so let's start with an example of an IS-A relationship.

3.3.1 *Identifying and implementing an IS-A relationship*

An *IS-A relationship* is implemented by extending classes or interfaces and implementing interfaces. Traverse the inheritance tree *up* the hierarchy to identify this relationship. A derived class IS-A *type* of its base class and its implemented interfaces. A derived interface IS-A type of its base interface. The reverse isn't true; a base class or interface *isn't a* type of its derived class or interface.

IDENTIFYING AN IS-A RELATIONSHIP

Here's a simple but long example for you to read and comprehend:

```
interface Movable {}
interface Hunter extends Movable {}

class Animal implements Movable {}
class Herbivore extends Animal {}
class Carnivore extends Animal implements Hunter {}

class Cow extends Herbivore {}
class Goat extends Herbivore {}

class Lion extends Carnivore {}
class Tiger extends Carnivore {}
```

Which of the following options do you think are correct?

- Cow IS-A `Hunter`.
- Tiger IS-A `Herbivore`.
- Cow IS-A `Movable`.
- Animal IS-A `Herbivore`.

To answer this question, refer to the preceding code, and you'll notice that the interface `Hunter` is implemented only by class `Carnivore`. Class `Cow` doesn't extend class `Carnivore`. So, Cow IS-A `Hunter` is incorrect.

Similarly, you can refer to the preceding code to answer all the other options. Option 2 is incorrect because class `Tiger` doesn't extend class `Herbivore`. Option 3 is correct because the interface `Movable` is implemented by class `Animal`, which is the base class of `Herbivore`, extended by class `Cow`.

Option 4 is incorrect because you can't traverse the hierarchy tree *down* to determine an IS-A relationship. Evaluate it like this: An `Herbivore` IS-A type of `Animal` with some additions or modifications because an `Herbivore` can modify (override) methods of class `Animal` and add new ones. But `Animal` IS-NOT-A `Herbivore`. Animal *can also be* a `Carnivore`.

Phew! So we had to refer to the code multiple times to answer each option. How about representing the relationships between these classes and interfaces by using UML notation, as shown in figure 3.6?

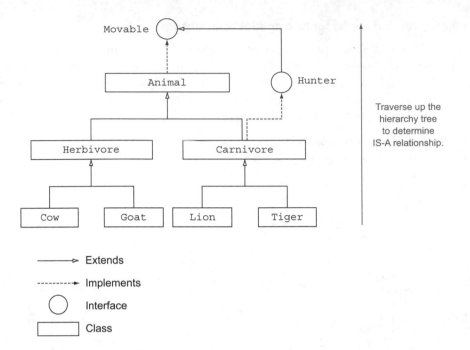

Traverse up the
hierarchy tree
to determine
IS-A relationship.

Figure 3.6   A UML representation can help answer questions about IS-A relationships between classes and interfaces.

If you can traverse up, from a derived class or interface to a base class or interface, following the connecting arrows (lined or dashed), the derived entity shares an IS-A relationship with the base entity. If you think that the preceding figure seems to depict a rather polished form of a class-and-interface relationship, look at figure 3.7, which shows the same relationship in a rather raw form.

I understand that you may not have the time or patience to draw neat diagrams during the exam because of time constraints or space available to you on an erasable board. The main point to remember is to use correct connecting lines to connect two types. Use an arrow to show an IS-A relationship and a line to show a HAS-A relationship.

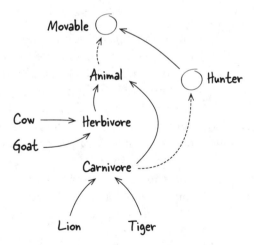

Figure 3.7   A rather raw form of the UML diagram that you may draw on an erasable board while taking your exam to represent an IS-A relationship between classes and interfaces

When I attempted this exam, I drew similar not-so-good-looking diagrams. Believe me, they helped me answer questions quickly, without referring to the code again and again. Also, the questions on the exam may not use names that indicate an obvious relationship between classes and interfaces. The next "Twist in the Tale" exercise will ensure that you get the hang of this point.

Twist in the Tale 3.2

Using the following code

```
interface InterH {}
interface SameY extends InterH {}

class JamD implements InterH {}
class SunP extends JamD {}
class BreaU extends JamD implements SameY {}
```

your task is to identify which of the following statements are true:

- **a** SunP IS-A InterH.
- **b** JamD IS-A SameY.
- **c** InterH IS-A InterH.
- **d** SameY IS-A JamD.

First attempt the exercise without drawing a UML diagram, and then by drawing and using a UML diagram. Do you think using the UML diagram helps you answer the questions more quickly?

 EXAM TIP The key to finding the types that participate in an IS-A relationship is to find your way, up the hierarchy tree, in the direction of the arrows. This technique will not only help you with the exam, but also take you a long way in your professional career.

IMPLEMENTING AN IS-A RELATIONSHIP

You can implement an IS-A relationship by extending classes or interfaces, or by implementing interfaces. Here is a quick set of rules for implementing inheritance between classes and interfaces in code:

- A class inherits another class by using the keyword extends.
- A class implements an interface by using the keyword implements.
- An interface inherits another interface by using the keyword extends.

How will you implement the following relationship in code?

```
Herbivore IS-A Animal
```

Because you don't know whether either `Herbivore` or `Animal` refers to a class or an interface, you have the following possibilities:

- `Herbivore` and `Animal` are classes. `Herbivore` extends `Animal`.
- `Herbivore` and `Animal` are interfaces. `Herbivore` extends `Animal`.
- `Herbivore` is a class, and `Animal` is an interface. `Herbivore` implements `Animal`.

Figure 3.8 shows these three possible implementations.

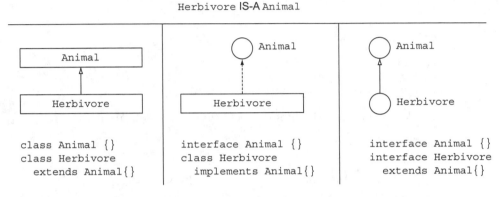

```
Herbivore IS-A Animal
```

```
class Animal {}              interface Animal {}            interface Animal {}
class Herbivore              class Herbivore               interface Herbivore
   extends Animal{}             implements Animal{}           extends Animal{}
```

Figure 3.8   How to implement an IS-A relationship, if you don't know whether the relationship is between classes, interfaces, or both

Now, let's add another relationship to the previous one. How would you implement the following relationship and rules in code?

- Herbivore IS-A Animal.
- Carnivore IS-A Animal.
- Animal can define only abstract methods and constants.

The third rule makes it clear that `Animal` is an interface. But you still don't know whether `Herbivore` and `Carnivore` are classes or interfaces. So you can have the following possibilities:

- `Herbivore` and `Carnivore` are interfaces that extend the interface `Animal`.
- `Herbivore` and `Carnivore` are classes that implement the interface `Animal`.
- `Herbivore` is a class that implements the interface `Animal`. `Carnivore` is an interface that extends the interface `Animal`.
- `Herbivore` is an interface that extends the interface `Animal`. `Carnivore` is a class that implements the interface `Animal`.

These relationships can be implemented as shown in figure 3.9.

The exam may specify a similar set of rules and ask you to choose the code that you think correctly implements the specified conditions. Let's work through another set

Herbivore IS-A Animal
Carnivore IS-A Animal
Animal can only define abstract methods and constants

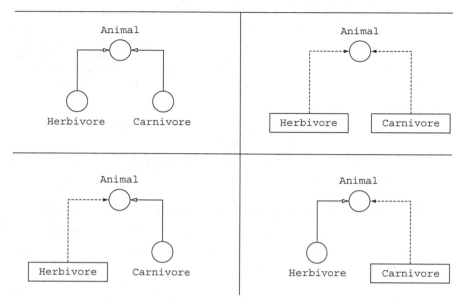

Figure 3.9   How to implement an IS-A relationship between three entities, one of which is an interface

of rules and implement the relationships in code. How would you implement the following relationships and rules in code?

1 Abc IS-A Xyz.
2 Abc defines methods and instance variables.
3 Xyz can declare only abstract methods.
4 Xyz IS-A Lmn.

Rule 2 states that Abc is a class, because an interface can't define instance variables. Rule 3 states that Xyz is an interface, because a class can declare both abstract and nonabstract methods. When you go up the hierarchy tree of an interface, you can find only another interface. In other words, Lmn is also an interface. The preceding rules evaluate to the following:

- Abc is a class.
- Xyz and Lmn are interfaces.
- Abc implements Xyz.
- Xyz extends Lmn.

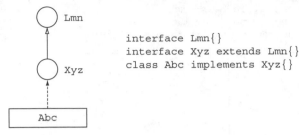

```
interface Lmn{}
interface Xyz extends Lmn{}
class Abc implements Xyz{}
```

Figure 3.10   Implementing a set of rules and an IS-A relationship between three entities: two interfaces, and a class

After the evaluation, these rules seem simple to implement. Figure 3.10 shows the relationships in UML notation and in code.

When a class defines an instance variable of another class, they share a HAS-A relationship, covered in the next section.

3.3.2   *Identifying and implementing a HAS-A relationship*

As compared to an IS-A relationship, a *HAS-A relationship* is easy to identify and implement. I hope this statement relieves you! Consider this definition of the bare-bones class Engine:

```
class Engine {}
```

Which of the following classes (Statistics, Car, PartsFactory, TestCar) do you think shares a HAS-A relationship with class Engine?

```
class Statistics {
    static Engine engine;          ◁── Statistics defines class
}                                       variable of type Engine.
class Car {
    Engine engine;                 ◁── Car defines instance
}                                       variable of type Engine.
class PartsFactory {
    Object createEngine() {
        Engine engine = new Engine();   ◁── PartsFactory defines
        //.. code                           local variable of
        return engine;                      type Engine.
    }
}
class TestCar {
    boolean testEngine(Engine engine) {   ◁── TestCar defines
        //.. code                             method parameter
    }                                         of type Engine.
}
```

Of all the preceding classes—Statistics, Car, PartsFactory, and TestCar—only Car shares a HAS-A relationship with the class Engine because Car defines an instance variable of type Engine. Note that it doesn't matter whether the instance variable engine in class Car is initialized with an object. The HAS-A relationship is shared by the classes.

EXAM TIP   Classes and interfaces can share a HAS-A relationship with each other. If a class or interface—say, `Type1`—defines an instance variable of a class or interface—say, `Type2`, `Type1` HAS-A `Type2` is correct. The reverse isn't correct. Also, the HAS-A relationship is shared by classes, and so the relationship isn't affected, whether the instance variable is initialized or not.

The exam doesn't stop at the IS-A and HAS-A relationships. Let's see how *high cohesion* and *low coupling* can improve your application design.

3.4   *Cohesion and low coupling*

      [3.3]   Apply cohesion, low-coupling, IS-A, and HAS-A principles

Focused teams and team members are known to deliver better results. On the other hand, highly dependent departments, teams, or team members might perform poorly. The same principles can be applied to application design. Focused classes and modules (cohesion) that aren't highly dependent (or coupled) on other classes or modules are generally easy to work with, reusable, and maintainable. Let's start with the design principle cohesion, which supports creation of focused modules and classes.

3.4.1   *Cohesion*

Cohesion refers to how focused a class or a module is. *High cohesion* refers to a well-focused class or module, whereas *low cohesion* refers to a class or module that doesn't have a well-defined responsibility. Such modules or classes might perform multiple actions, which could have been assigned to separate classes.

Imagine a book editor who is supposed to edit book content, manage the book-printing process, and reach out to new authors for new book ideas. Let's define this editor by using a class, say, `Editor`:

```
class Editor{
    public void editBooks() {}
    public void manageBookPrinting() {}
    public void reachOutToNewAuthors() {}
}
```
Low cohesion; Editor is performing diverse set of unrelated tasks

Because this editor is managing multiple tasks over a period of time, managing all these processes might become difficult. Also, working with multiple responsibilities can prevent the editor from specializing in *all* these processes. Let's limit the tasks to the book-editing process:

```
class Editor{
    public void useEditTools() {}
    public void editFirstDraft() {}
    public void clearEditingDoubts() {}
}
```
High cohesion; Editor is performing multiple but related tasks.

The preceding example creates a highly cohesive class, `Editor`. Highly cohesive classes are easy to use. In the preceding example, class `Editor` provides a one-stop solution for all editing tasks. Highly cohesive classes are also easy to maintain and reuse; whenever you need to add or modify any editing-related process, you know which class you need to refer to: class `Editor`.

 EXAM TIP   Well-designed applications aim for highly cohesive classes and modules.

Classes and modules also perform better if they are least affected by the changes made to other classes or modules. Let's work with this aspect in detail in the next section on coupling.

3.4.2   *Coupling*

Coupling refers to how much a class or module knows about other classes or modules. If a class—say, `Editor`—interacts with another class—say, `Author`—by using its interface (public methods), then classes `Editor` and `Author` are *loosely coupled*. But if class `Editor` can access and manipulate `Author` by using its nonpublic members, these classes are *tightly coupled*.

Let's code the class `Author`:

```
class Author {
    String name;
    String skypeID;
    public String getSkypeID() {
        return skypeID;
    }
}
```

 NOTE   The terms *low coupling* and *loose coupling* refer to the same concept. They are often used interchangeably.

The modified class `Editor` is tightly coupled with class `Author`. The method `clearEditingDoubts` in class `Editor` accesses the nonpublic member `skypeId` of class `Author`:

```
class Editor{
    public void clearEditingDoubts(Author author) {
        setUpCall(author.skypeID);
        converse(author);
    }
    void setUpCall(String skypeID) { /* */}
    void converse(Author author) {/* */}
}
```
Tight coupling; nonpublic variable skypeID is referred to outside its class Author.

What happens, say, if a programmer changes the name of the variable `skypeID` in class `Author` to `skypeName`? The code of class `Editor` won't compile. As long as the public interface of a class remains the same, it's free to change its implementation details. In this case, the name of instance variable `skypeID` forms part of `Author`'s implementation details. One suggested solution is to use the public method `getSkypeID()` in class `Editor` (changes in bold):

```
class Author {
    String name;
    String skypeName;
    public String getSkypeID() {
        return skypeName;
    }
}
class Editor{
    public void clearEditingDoubts(Author author) {
        setUpCall(author.getSkypeID());
        converse(author);
    }
    void setUpCall(String skypeID) { /* */}
    void converse(Author author) {/* */}
}
```

Change in instance variable name won't affect classes that access this method

Loose coupling; public method getSkypeID() accesses Author's skypeName.

Interfaces also promote loose coupling across classes and modules. Assume that the entity `Author` is defined as an interface, which can be implemented by specialized authors such as `TechnicalAuthor`. Here's the new arrangement:

```
interface Author {
    String getSkypeID();
}
class TechnicalAuthor implements Author{
    String name;
    String skypeName;
    public String getSkypeID() {
        return skypeName;
    }
}
class Editor{
    public void clearEditingDoubts(Author author) {
        setUpCall(author.getSkypeID());
        converse(author);
    }
    void setUpCall(String skypeID) { /* */}
    void converse(Author author) {/* */}
}
```

❶ **interface Author**

❷ **Class TechnicalAuthor implements Author.**

❸ **Loose coupling; method clearEditingDoubts() uses interface to access concrete implementations**

The code at ❶ defines the entity `Author` as an interface. At ❷, class `TechnicalAuthor` implements `Author`. At ❸, the type of parameter passed to method `clearEditing-Doubts()` is the interface `Author`. So method `clearEditingDoubts()` is guaranteed to access only public members of instances of `Author`. Also, because method `clear-EditingDoubts()` can be passed objects of classes that implement `Author`, it can also accept instances of classes that are created later, such as `FictionWriter`, which implement `Author`.

EXAM TIP   Well-designed applications aim for loosely coupled classes and modules.

The tips for creating well-designed applications don't end here. The next section covers object composition principles.

3.5   *Object composition principles*

 [3.4]   Apply object composition principles (including HAS-A relationships)

How can you *use* the existing functionality of a class? Inexperienced programmers or newcomers to the Java programming language and OOP often answer this question by saying, "inheritance." They shouldn't be completely blamed for this incorrect answer. Many books, articles, and programmers overemphasize inheritance—which is correct in a way, because inheritance is an important concept. But this might leave a lot of newcomers with the wrong impression that inheriting a class is the best way to use another class. Most of the time, you can use another class by *composing* your own class with an object of another class. Let's start with a quick example:

```
class Engine { /* code */ }
class Wheel { /* code */ }
class Car {
    Engine engine;                          Car is composed of
    Wheel[] wheels = new Wheel[5];          Engine and Wheel.
}
```

 EXAM TIP   Object composition enables you to use the existing functionality of classes without extending them. The approach is simple: create and use objects of other classes in your own class.

Look around for examples of classes defined by your peers, in books or articles, or in the Java API. You'll be amazed to notice that composition is *the* way to use a class, when you want to use the functionality of any other class. You should inherit a class only when you think that the derived class is a type of its base class. For example, it's correct to say that `RacingCar` is a type of `Car`. But it's incorrect to say that `Engine` is a type of `Car`.

There's another reason to favor object composition over inheritance: a base class is *fragile* (refer to the subsection "Fragile Derived Classes" in section 3.2.3 for an example). A change to a base class can have major effects on all its derived classes. For example, changing the method signature of a public method in a base class can lead to broken code of all its derived classes. A change in the nonpublic variables or methods of a base class can affect its derived classes, *if* the variables or methods are used by the derived classes.

The remaining sections cover the design patterns on the exam. Before you dive into the details of the design patterns, let's look at what they are and why we need them.

3.6   Introduction to design patterns

People who live in regions that experience snowfall build sloping roofs so that snow and ice don't accumulate on the rooftops. This "pattern" of designing sloping roofs was identified after multiple persons faced *similar* difficulties and found *similar* solutions. Now this is an established practice. Being ignorant about the design pattern of building a sloping roof can cause you a lot of rework later. Similarly, in the computing domain, multiple design patterns have been documented by observing recurring programming, behavioral, or implementation issues.

3.6.1   What is a design pattern?

A *design pattern* identifies a specific problem and suggests a solution to it. It's neither ready-made code that you can drop in your projects nor a framework to use. For example, you *might* document the *sloping-roof* design pattern as

- *Design pattern name:* Sloping roof
- *Problem:* Accumulation of snow and ice on rooftops
- *Suggested solution:* Build sloping roofs for all houses, offices, and buildings in areas that receive snowfall during any time of the year. This enables snow or ice from rooftops to slide and fall to the ground.

Notice the design pattern doesn't include actual materials or tools to build a house.

 NOTE   No formal format of documentation of a design pattern exists. You can document it the way you like.

3.6.2   Why do you need a design pattern?

Design patterns offer *experience reuse* and not *code reuse*. Design patterns help you reuse the *experience* of application designers and developers in terms of the guidelines that you can follow to implement commonly occurring programming scenarios. By using design patterns for known issues in your application, you'll benefit from the experience of others and be less likely to reinvent the wheel.

 NOTE   The Singleton and Factory design patterns are creational patterns initially described in the Gang of Four (GoF) book *Design Patterns: Elements of Reusable Object-Oriented Software* by Gamma et al. (Addison-Wesley, 1995). DAO is an integration-tier core J2EE pattern; see *Core J2EE Patterns: Best Practices and Design Strategies,* Second Edition, by Deepak Alur, John Crupi, and Dan Malks (Prentice Hall, 2003).

In the next section, we'll cover the first design pattern that is covered on this exam: the Singleton design pattern.

3.7 Singleton pattern

 [3.5] Design a class using the Singleton design pattern

Singleton is a creational design pattern that ensures that a class is instantiated only once. The class also provides a global point of access to it.

So under what conditions would you want to have only one object of a class? Wouldn't the object feel lonely because there's only one of its kind?

3.7.1 Why do you need this pattern?

Imagine the issues that can be caused by multiple browser caches or multiple thread pools. In these scenarios, you might need only one object of a class to encapsulate all operations for managing a pool of resources, and to also serve as a global point of reference. Other common examples include a single instance of Device Manager to manage all the devices on your system, and a single instance of a print spooler to manage all the printing jobs.

3.7.2 Implementing the Singleton pattern

Implementation of the `Singleton` class involves a single class. But don't let this simplicity dismiss the finer details that you should get right. Let's move on to the basics of implementing the Singleton pattern:

1 Define a private constructor for the class that implements the Singleton pattern. To prevent any other class from creating an object of this class, mark the constructor of this class as a `private` member:

```
class Singleton {
    private Singleton() {
        System.out.println("Private Constructor");
    }
}
```

Now, no class can execute `new Singleton()` to create an instance of this class. But if no other class can create objects of this class, how will they use it? The class that implements the Singleton pattern creates and manages its sole instance by defining a static variable to store this instance.

2 Define a private static variable to refer to the *only* instance of the `Singleton` class. A static variable ensures that the class stores and accesses the same instance. In the following code, the variable `anInstance` is a class variable:

```
class Singleton {
    private static Singleton anInstance = null;
    private Singleton() {
        System.out.println("Private Constructor");
    }
}
```

A well-encapsulated class should enable access to its members by using well-defined interfaces. So let's create a method to access the private variable `anInstance`.

3 Define a public static method to *access* the only instance of the `Singleton` class. Before you access the variable `anInstance`, you should create it. The creation and return of this variable is usually defined as follows (additions to previous code in bold):

```
class Singleton {
    private static Singleton anInstance = null;
    public static Singleton getInstance() {
        if (anInstance == null)
            anInstance = new Singleton();
        return anInstance;
    }
    private Singleton() {
        System.out.println("Private Constructor");
    }
}
```

If anInstance hasn't been initialized

Initialize anInstance

Return anInstance

A class can request an object of class `Singleton` by calling the static method `getInstance()`:

```
class UseSingleton {
    public static void main(String args[]) {
        Singleton singleton1 = Singleton.getInstance();
        Singleton singleton2 = Singleton.getInstance();
        System.out.println(singleton1 == singleton2);
    }
}
```

New instance of class Singleton created and returned when accessed first time

Previously created instance returned for subsequent calls to method getInstance()

Prints "true"

The output of this code confirms that an object of class `Singleton` is created only once:

```
Private Constructor
true
```

These steps ensure that only one object of class `Singleton` ever exists. But what happens if multiple classes request an object of class `Singleton` at exactly the same time? This *may* lead to the creation of more than one object of class `Singleton`. Don't worry; we have ways to fix this one too, as discussed in the next section.

3.7.3 *Ensuring creation of only one object in the Singleton pattern*

Though the previous code *seems* to guarantee that only one instance of `Singleton` will be created, concurrent access of method `getInstance()` may result in creation of multiple instances. This can be a problem in multithreaded environments, such as application servers and servlet engines. Before you fix the issue of concurrent creation of an object in a Singleton pattern, you need to ensure that you understand the finer details of this issue. So let's get started.

UNDERSTANDING THE PROBLEM OF CONCURRENT ACCESS

Imagine that two objects request class `Singleton` to return its instance at *exactly the same time*, by calling method `getInstance()`:

```
class Singleton {
    private static Singleton anInstance = null;
    public static Singleton getInstance() {
        if (anInstance == null)
            anInstance = new Singleton();
        return anInstance;
    }
    private Singleton() {
        System.out.println("Private Constructor");
    }
}
```

Because each call will discover that the variable `anInstance` hasn't been initialized, each method call will create a new object and assign it to the variable `anInstance`. Method `getInstance()` may also return separate objects for each call. This is shown in figure 3.11.

If you think that it doesn't make a difference if you create multiple objects of a class that implements the Singleton pattern, think again. The definition of the previously defined class `Singleton` is oversimplified. Real classes that implement the Singleton pattern define much more meaningful code in their constructors—for example, initializing their own resources, starting threads, or creating database or network connections. Obviously, a class won't like to do all these again, when it's not supposed to.

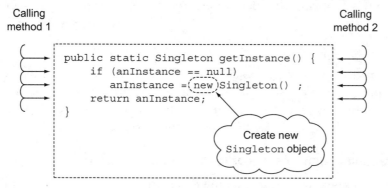

Figure 3.11   Multiple concurrent calls to method `getInstance()` can create multiple objects of class `Singleton`.

FIXING CONCURRENT CREATION: EAGER INITIALIZATION

There are multiple ways to ensure that an object of a class that implements the Singleton pattern is initialized only once. To begin with, *eager initialization* will enable you to initialize the static variable as soon as the class is loaded:

Eager initialization; anInstance is ❶ initialized as soon as class loaded

```java
class Singleton {
    private static final Singleton anInstance = new Singleton();    ◁──
    public static Singleton getInstance() {
        return anInstance;                              ◁── Simply returns
    }                                               ❷ anInstance
    private Singleton() {
        System.out.println("Private Constructor");
    }
}
```

The code at ❶ executes when the class is loaded by the Java class loaders. So an object of class `Singleton` is created before any class requests it. When any other object requests an object of class `Singleton`, using method `getInstance()`, the code at ❷ simply returns the Singleton instance `anInstance`. The preceding code ensures that multiple objects of class `Singleton` aren't created.

FIXING CONCURRENT CREATION: SYNCHRONIZED LAZY INITIALIZATION

Though this seems to be the perfect solution, eager initialization creates an object of class `Singleton`, even if it's never used. Don't worry; every problem has a solution. Let's not employ eager initialization and synchronize method `getInstance()`:

```java
class Singleton {
    private static Singleton anInstance;            ◁── No eager
                                                        initialization
    synchronized public static Singleton getInstance() {    ◁── Method
        if (anInstance == null)                              getInstance()
            anInstance = new Singleton();                    defined as
        return anInstance;                                   synchronized
    }                                                   ❶ method
    private Singleton() {
        System.out.println("Private Constructor");
    }
}
```

Method `getInstance()` is defined as a synchronized method at ❶. This means that multiple threads or objects can't execute this method concurrently. So this again saves us from multiple-object creation of a class implementing the Singleton pattern. If you're thinking that this is the last way to fix multiple-object creation issues for a `Singleton` class, take a deep breath, my friend, because there's more to it.

On the exam, you might also see a variation of the previously defined synchronized method `getInstance()`. Because synchronized methods don't allow concurrent execution, your application may feel a performance hit if a lot of classes in your application call method `getInstance()`. Java can rescue you this time, by synchronizing method `getInstance()` partially (if you're new to threading and concurrency and can't understand the following code, don't worry. Just refer to chapters 10 and 11 on threading and concurrency):

```
public static Singleton getInstance() {
    if (anInstance == null) {
        synchronized (Singleton.class) {
            if (anInstance == null)
                anInstance = new Singleton();
        }
    }
    return anInstance;
}
```

Don't synchronize complete method

Synchronize code block that creates new object

After the thread acquires a lock on `Singleton.class` and enters the synchronized block, the code checks whether `anInstance` is `null` (again), before creating a new object. This is to ensure that after the lock is acquired, the condition hasn't changed and `anInstance` is still `null`.

 EXAM TIP   On the exam, all of these approaches (eager initialization, synchronization of the complete method `getInstance()`, and partial synchronization of method `getInstance()`) may be presented, and you may be questioned about the right approach for implementing the Singleton pattern. All these approaches are good. Beware of modified code that tries to synchronize a partial `getInstance()` method, which doesn't synchronize the code that creates an object of `Singleton`.

USING ENUMS
By using enums, you can implement the Singleton pattern in a thread-safe manner. Here's a simple implementation:

```
public enum Singleton {
    INSTANCE;

    public void initCache(){
        //..code
    }
}
```

Because enum instances can't be created by any other class, the enum `Singleton` will ensure the existence of only *one* of its instances, `Singleton.INSTANCE`.

 NOTE   Even though using a single-element enum is the best way to implement the Singleton pattern, you must know all the previously discussed approaches to answer questions on this topic on the exam.

After making yourself aware of the multiple rules that you need to follow to apply the Singleton pattern, test yourself on it with the next "Twist in the Tale" exercise.

> **Twist in the Tale 3.3**
>
> Does the class in the following code apply the Singleton pattern correctly?
>
> ```
> class Singleton {
>     private Singleton anInstance;
>     synchronized public Singleton getInstance() {
>         if (anInstance == null)
>             anInstance = new Singleton();
>         return anInstance;
>     }
> }
> ```

 NOTE The Singleton pattern is also referred to as an anti-pattern. It has been overused by developers and designers, who make a lot of assumptions about the applications that use it. It also makes testing difficult.

Even before the Singleton pattern was officially recognized and used, *single-object instances with global access* have been implemented using static variables. But this has its own set of disadvantages.

3.7.4 *Comparing Singleton with global data*

Programmers have been creating and using single instances of a class by defining them as static variables for quite a long time. Some of them do that even now. But doing so requires the following serious considerations:

- *Possibility of creating multiple objects of the same type*—Using a static variable doesn't stop you (or any other user) from creating another object of the class and referring to it by another name. Limiting creation of only one object is the responsibility of the application developer and isn't included as part of the class design in this case. This, as you know, can introduce issues when multiple (unwanted) objects are created.
- *Eager initialization*—Static variables are usually initialized before any class uses them. This risks allocation of resources and other processing that may never have been required or used (for example, initializing resources of the class used as a global variable) and other tasks that it may define in its constructor (for example, starting threads, or creating database or network connections).
- *Pollution of namespace*—Using multiple static variables within an application is sure to pollute the namespace, which is, again, not a preferred approach.

The API of a language, product, or service can be huge, and it isn't possible for users to know about all its classes. It makes a lot of sense to be able to create and use objects of a class by specifying a set of requirements. The Factory pattern makes this feasible. Apart from hiding the implementation details of object creation, it enables developers to extend an API and users to use the newer classes.

3.8   *Factory pattern*

[3.7]   Design and create objects using a factory pattern

Imagine you need to open files, say, Hello.doc and Hello.xml, programmatically using your Java application. To do so, you'd need instances of classes, say, `WordProcessor` and `TextEditor`, that can open these files. One of the obvious approaches is to use the operator `new` to create an instance of `WordProcessor` and `TextEditor` to open files. But this would result in tight coupling between the application that opens files and the classes that are used to open the files. What happens if you need to use another class, say, `QuickProcessor`, to open .doc files in the future?

In this section, you'll work with how to use the Factory pattern to prevent tight coupling between classes. This pattern also eliminates direct constructor calls in favor of invoking a method. One of the most frequently used design patterns, multiple Factory patterns exist:

- Simple Factory or Static Factory pattern
- Factory Method pattern
- Abstract Factory pattern

On the exam, most of the questions on the Factory pattern refer to the Simple Factory pattern.

3.8.1   *Simple Factory pattern (or Static Factory pattern)*

This pattern creates and returns objects of classes that extend a common parent class or implement a common interface. The objects are created without exposing the instantiation logic to the client. The calling class is decoupled from knowing the exact name of the instantiated class.

Figure 3.12 shows the UML class diagram for classes used in the sample code to exhibit the Simple Factory pattern.

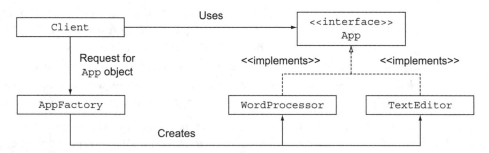

Figure 3.12   UML class diagram for interfaces and classes implementing the Simple Factory pattern

In the following sample code, class `Client` is decoupled from knowing the exact subclass, either `WordProcessor` or `TextEditor`, that it needs to open a file. It calls `AppFactory`'s method `getAppInstance()`, passing it the file extension, which returns an appropriate `App` object. It gives you the flexibility of modifying class `AppFactory` without impacting class `Client`. You might want to modify method `getAppInstance()` to return another `App` instance, say, `XMLEditor`, to open a .txt file. For instance

```java
interface App {
    void open(String filename);
}
class WordProcessor implements App {
    public void open(String filename) {
        System.out.println("Launch WordProcessor using " + filename);
    }
}
class TextEditor implements App {
    public void open(String filename) {
        System.out.println("Launch TextEditor using " + filename);
    }
}
class AppFactory {
    public static App getAppInstance(String fileExtn) {
        App appln = null;
        if (fileExtn.equals(".doc")) {
            appln = new WordProcessor();
        }
        else if (fileExtn.equals(".txt") ||
            fileExtn.equals(".xml")) {
            appln = new TextEditor();
        }
        return appln;
    }
}
class Client{
    public static void main(String args[]) {
        App app = AppFactory.getAppInstance(".doc");
        app.open("Hello.doc");
        App app2 = AppFactory.getAppInstance(".xml");
        app2.open("Hello.xml");
    }
}
```

Interface App implemented by classes WordProessor and TextEditor

Implements Simple Factory pattern by returning App object according to parameter value

Client is decoupled from classes TextEditor and WordProcessor; it calls AppFactory.getAppInstance() to get App object.

 NOTE Because method `getAppInstance()` in class `AppFactory` is a static method, this pattern is also referred to as the Static Factory pattern or Factory Class pattern.

Method `getAppInstance()` is manageable with just a few comparisons (`if-else`) statements. What happens if method `getAppInstance()` is supposed to return `App` instances for a wide variety of file extensions? Because it can become unmanageable, let's work with a variation of the Simple Factory pattern—that is, the Factory Method pattern.

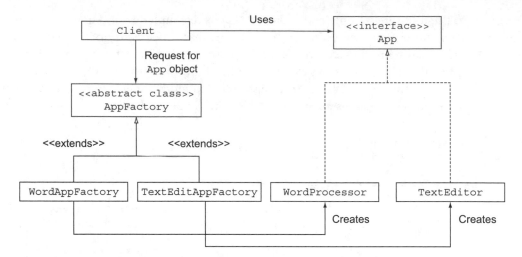

Figure 3.13   UML class diagram for interfaces and classes implementing the Factory Method pattern

3.8.2   *Factory Method pattern*

The intent of the Factory Method pattern is to define an interface for creating an object but let subclasses decide which class to instantiate. The Factory Method pattern lets a class defer instantiation to its subclasses.

Figure 3.13 shows the UML class diagram for classes used in the sample code to exhibit the Factory Method pattern.

In the following example code, to get the required App object, class Client uses one of the subclasses of abstract class AppFactory and calls its method getAppInstance(). Method getAppInstance() calls method getApp(), which is a factory method defined as an abstract method in class AppFactory. It is implemented by its concrete factory classes, WordAppFactory and TextEditAppFactory. The subclasses WordAppFactory and TextEditAppFactory implement getApp() to return a specific App object. It allows Client to use WordProcessor and TextEditor, but decouples it from knowing their names. This arrangement promotes flexibility to change the App object returned from concrete factory classes (WordAppFactory and TextEditAppFactory):

```
interface App {                                                    ◁─┐
    void open(String filename);                                      │  Interface App
}                                                                    │  implemented
class WordProcessor implements App {                               ◁─┤  by classes
    public void open(String filename) {                              │  Word-
        System.out.println("Launch WordProcessor using " + filename);│  Processor and
    }                                                                │  TextEditor
}                                                                    │
class TextEditor implements App {                                  ◁─┘
    public void open(String filename) {
        System.out.println("Launch TextEditor using " + filename);
    }
}
```

```
abstract class AppFactory {                    ◁──  Abstract
    public App getAppInstance() {                    Factory class
        App appln = getApp();
        return appln;
    }                                               Factory
    public abstract App getApp();            ◁──    Method
}
class WordAppFactory extends AppFactory {
    public App getApp() {                      ◁──
        return new WordProcessor();                  Implement Factory
    }                                                Method to return a
}                                                    specific App object.
class TextEditAppFactory extends AppFactory {
    public App getApp() {                      ◁──
        return new TextEditor();
    }
}                                                    Client class uses variable
class Client {                                       of Abstract Factory
    public static void main(String args[]) {         pattern to refer to a
        AppFactory factory = new WordAppFactory();  ◁── concrete factory object
        App app = factory.getAppInstance();        ◁──
        app.open("Hello.doc");                          Because factory refers to
                                                        WordAppFactory object,
        app = new TextEditAppFactory().getAppInstance();  call to getAppInstance()
        app.open("Hello.xml");                          returns WordProcessor
    }                                                   object
}
```

Concrete Factory classes

Now, what happens if you were required to create *families* of related classes, such as applications that can open rich format files for editing in Windows and Mac systems? Because these systems might use separate applications for similar purposes, let's modify the example used in the previous section to use the Abstract Factory pattern.

3.8.3 *Abstract Factory pattern*

The Abstract Factory pattern is used to create a family of related products (in contrast, the Factory Method pattern creates one type of object). This pattern also defines an interface for creating objects, but it lets subclasses decide which class to instantiate.

Figure 3.14 shows the UML class diagram for classes used in the sample code to exhibit the Abstract Factory pattern.

In the following example code, to get the required App and Font objects, class Client uses one of the subclasses of abstract class AppFactory and calls its methods getAppInstance() or getFontInstance(). The Concrete Factory pattern classes WordAppFactory and TextEditAppFactory return an appropriate concrete object for the interfaces App and Font. This pattern also allows Client to use WordProcessor, TextEditor, RichFont, and RegularFont, but decouples it from knowing their names. This arrangement also promotes flexibility to change the App or Font object

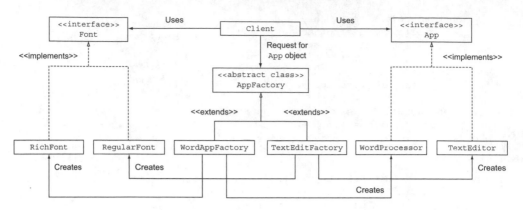

Figure 3.14 UML class diagram for interfaces and classes implementing the Abstract Factory pattern

returned from Concrete Factory pattern classes (`WordAppFactory` and `TextEdit-AppFactory`).

```
interface App { /* code */ }
class WordProcessor implements App { /* code */ }
class TextEditor implements App { /* code */ }
```
interface App implemented by classes WordProcessor and TextEditor

```
interface Font { /* code */ }
class RichFont implements Font { /* code */ }
class RegularFont implements Font { /* code */ }
```
interface Font implemented by classes RichFont and RegularFont

```
abstract class AppFactory {
    protected abstract App getApp();
    protected abstract Font getFont();

    public App getAppInstance() {
        App appln = getApp();
        return appln;
    }
    public Font getFontInstance() {
        Font font = getFont();
        return font;
    }
}
```
Abstract Factory class

```
class WordAppFactory extends AppFactory {
    protected App getApp() {
        return new WordProcessor();
    }
    protected Font getFont() {
        return new RichFont();
    }
}

class TextEditAppFactory extends AppFactory {
    protected App getApp() {
        return new TextEditor();
    }
```
Concrete Factory classes

```
        protected Font getFont() {
            return new RegularFont();
        }
}

class ClientAbstractFactoryMethod {
    public static void main(String args[]) {
        AppFactory factory1 = new WordAppFactory();
        App app1 = factory1.getAppInstance();
        Font font1 = factory1.getFontInstance();
        System.out.println(app1 + ":" + font1);

        AppFactory factory2 = new TextEditAppFactory();
        App app2 = factory2.getAppInstance();
        Font font2 = factory2.getFontInstance();
        System.out.println(app2 + ":" + font2);
    }
}
```

Concrete Factory class used to create objects of App and Font

 NOTE The sample code used in the sections on Factory Method and Abstract Factory patterns can use `App` or `Font` as an interface or abstract or concrete class.

In the next section, you'll learn the terms and phrases that the exam uses to test you on the benefits of using the Factory pattern.

3.8.4 *Benefits of the Factory pattern*

The exam won't ask you to select the benefit of a specific Factory pattern—that is, Simple Factory, Factory Method, or Abstract Factory. Here are the benefits that apply to all Factory patterns:

- Prefer method invocation over direct constructor calls
- Prevent tight coupling between a class implementation and your application
- Promote creation of cohesive classes
- Promote programming to an interface
- Promote flexibility. Object instantiation logic can be changed without affecting the clients that use objects. They also allow addition of new concrete classes.

Here's a list of what doesn't apply or isn't related to the Factory pattern:

- It doesn't eliminate the need of overloading constructors in class implementations.
- It doesn't encourage the use of any particular access modifier. It isn't compulsory to define private members to use this pattern.
- It won't slow your application.
- It isn't related to how to monitor objects for change.

The exam will question you on the classes from the Java API that use this pattern. Let's cover them in the next section.

3.8.5   *Using the Factory pattern from the Java API*

You'll find this important design pattern in multiple classes in the Java API.
Some of these classes are listed in table 3.3.

Table 3.3   Classes and methods from the Java API that use the Factory pattern

Class	Method	Description
java.util.Calendar	getInstance()	Gets a calendar using the default time zone and locale.
java.util.Arrays	asList()	Returns a fixed-size list backed by the specified array.
java.util.ResourceBundle	getBundle()	Overloaded versions of this method return a resource bundle using the specified base name, target locale, class loader, and control.
java.sql.DriverManager	getConnection()	Establishes and returns a connection to the given database URL.
java.sql.DriverManager	getDriver()	Attempts to locate and return a driver that understands the given URL.
java.sql.Connection	createStatement()	Overloaded version of this method creates a statement object for sending SQL statements to the database and generates ResultSet objects with the given type, concurrency, and holdability.
java.sql.Statement	executeQuery()	Executes the given SQL statement, which returns a single ResultSet object.
java.text.NumberFormat	getInstance() getNumberFormat()	Returns a general-purpose number format for the current default locale.
java.text.NumberFormat	getCurrencyInstance()	Returns a currency format for the current default locale.

Table 3.3 Classes and methods from the Java API that use the Factory pattern

Class	Method	Description
`java.text.NumberFormat`	`getIntegerInstance()`	Returns an integer format for the current default locale.
`java.util.concurrent.Executors`	`newFixedThreadPool()` `newCachedThreadPool()` `newSingleThreadExecutor()`	Creates a thread pool.

 NOTE Refer to chapter 12 for detailed coverage of the Factory method `getInstance()` defined in class `NumberFormat`.

Almost all applications need to store data to a persistent medium in one form or another. Data persistence can range from using simple text files to full-fledged database management systems. In the next section, we'll cover how the Data Access Object (DAO) pattern enables you to separate code that communicates with the data source from the classes that use the data.

3.9   DAO pattern

 [3.6] Write code to implement the DAO pattern

Imagine your employee application needs to read its data from and write to multiple sources like flat files, relational databases, XML, or JSON. Add to this the differences in accessing the data for different vendor implementations. How would your application manage to work with data stored in a different format, with different data management systems, offering separate features, using separate APIs? This section shows you how the DAO pattern helps in a similar situation.

3.9.1   What is the DAO pattern?

The DAO pattern abstracts and encapsulates all access to a data store (flat files, relational databases, XML, JSON, or any other data source). It manages the connection with the data source to access and store the data. It shields a client from knowing how to retrieve or store data and lets it specify what data to retrieve and store. So it makes the client code flexible to work with multiple data sources.

 EXAM TIP The DAO pattern decouples classes that define business or presentation logic from the data persistence details.

3.9.2   Implementing the DAO pattern

Identify the data that you need to store to or retrieve from a data store (say, `Emp`). Define an interface, a DAO, say, `EmpDAO`, to expose the data's CRUD operations. The

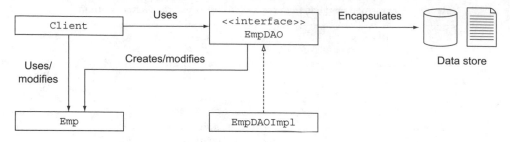

Figure 3.15   UML class diagram of classes and interfaces implementing the DAO pattern

implementation details are hidden from clients and defined in a class (say, `EmpDAO-Impl`). If the implementation details to access data in the data source change, it doesn't affect a client. This pattern allows an application to adapt to different data stores or its version without affecting a client. Figure 3.15 shows the UML class diagram of classes implementing the DAO pattern.

In the following sample code, class `Emp` encapsulates the employee data that can be read from and stored to multiple types of data stores. The interface `EmpDAO` exposes the operations that can be performed with `Emp` objects in a data store. Class `EmpDAOImpl` implements `EmpDAO`, connecting to a data store and retrieving `Emp` from it and updating it in the data store. Note how class `Client` is decoupled from the data storage and retrieval details. Class `Client` works with `EmpDAO` and not with its specific implementation.

```
class Emp {
    int id;
    String name;
    int age;
    String address;
}
interface EmpDAO {
    public int create(Emp e);
    public Emp get(int id);
    public boolean delete(Emp e);
    public boolean update(Emp e);
    public Collection<Emp> getAll();
}
class EmpDAOImpl implements EmpDAO {
    public int create(Emp e) {
    /* connect to datastore, insert data for employee e */
    }
    public Emp get(int id) {
    /* connect to datastore, retrieve and return data for employee-id id */
    }
    public boolean delete(Emp e) {
    /* connect to datastore and delete data for employee-id e.id */
    }
```

```
        public boolean update(Emp e) {
        /* connect to datastore and update employee data */
        }
        public Collection<Emp> getAll() {
        /* connect to datastore, retrieve emp data, return as Collection */
        }
}
class Client {
        public static void main(String args[]) {
            Emp emp = new Emp();
            emp.id = 10; emp.name = "Harry";
            emp.age = 39; emp.address = "UK";

            EmpDAO dao = new EmpDAOImpl();
            dao.create(emp);
            emp.name = "Harry M"; emp.age = 40;
            dao.update(emp);

            Emp emp2 = dao.get(11);
            if (emp2 != null) dao.delete(emp2);
        }
}
```

Annotations:
- **Create Emp object.** → `Emp emp = new Emp();`
- **Initialize emp object.** → `emp.id = 10; emp.name = "Harry"; emp.age = 39; emp.address = "UK";`
- **Create instance of EmpDAO.** → `EmpDAO dao = new EmpDAOImpl();`
- **Insert emp data in data store using method create().** → `dao.create(emp);`
- **Update emp object in data store.** → `dao.update(emp);`
- **Modify existing values of emp object.** → `emp.name = "Harry M"; emp.age = 40;`
- **Retrieve object from data store.** → `Emp emp2 = dao.get(11);`
- **Delete data corresponding to retrieved data from data store.** → `if (emp2 != null) dao.delete(emp2);`

 EXAM TIP   The CRUD operations form the basis of the DAO pattern.

The preceding example uses only one implementation of the DAO interface. How would an application manage working with multiple DAO implementations? You can use the Factory pattern—that is, Simple Factory, Factory Method, or Abstract Factory—with the DAO pattern to work with multiple DAO implementations, as shown in the next section.

 EXAM TIP   The exam might ask you whether it's common to use the Factory pattern with the DAO pattern. The answer is yes (as shown in the next section). But it isn't mandatory to use the Factory pattern with the DAO pattern (as shown in this section).

3.9.3   *Using the Simple Factory pattern with the DAO pattern*

You can use a Factory pattern to work with multiple DAO pattern implementations. The following example uses the Simple Factory pattern. Method `getInstance()` in class `DAOFactory` returns an instance of the `EmpDAO` implementation, which can be used by a client class (`Client`). I haven't repeated the class details deliberately for `Emp` and `EmpDAO` to keep the code short. They're the same as used in the example in the preceding section. The code for classes `EmpDAOOracleImpl` and `EmpDAOMySQL-Impl` can be assumed to be the same as the code for class `EmpDAOImpl` used in the preceding example.

```
class Emp { /* code */ }
interface EmpDAO { /* code */ }
```

```
class EmpDAOOracleImpl implements EmpDAO { /* code */ }
class EmpDAOMySQLImpl implements EmpDAO { /* code */ }

abstract class DAOFactory {
    public static int ORACLE = 1;
    public static int MYSQL = 2;
    public static EmpDAO getEmpDAOInstance(int DBtype) {
        if (DBtype == ORACLE)
            return new EmpDAOOracleImpl();
        else if (DBtype == MYSQL)
            return new EmpDAOMySQLImpl();
        else
            return null;
    }
}
class Client {
    public static void main(String args[]) {
        EmpDAO empDAO = DAOFactory.getEmpDAOInstance(DAOFactory.ORACLE);
        Emp emp = new Emp();
        emp.id = 10; emp.name = "Harry";
        emp.age = 39; emp.address = "UK";
        empDAO.create(emp);
    }
}
```

DAOFactory uses Simple Factory pattern.

EmpDAO implementation for Oracle Database

EmpDAO implementation for MySQL Database

Static Factory pattern to return implementation of EmpDAO

Get EmpDAO implementation for Oracle DB.

Insert emp data in data store.

 NOTE   To keep the code simple, this and the next section use DAO implementation classes for only two different data stores, Oracle and MySQL.

In the next section, you'll see how you can decouple data storage and retrieval for multiple type of objects (`Emp`, `Dept`) from multiple data stores (Oracle, MySQL) using the Factory Method or Abstract Factory patterns with the DAO pattern.

3.9.4   *Using the Factory Method or Abstract Factory pattern with the DAO pattern*

In the following example, class `Client` needs to store and retrieve objects of `Emp` and `Dept` to and from a data store. To decouple `Client` from the persistence details, the interfaces `EmpDAO` and `DeptDAO` define all data store operations with `Emp` and `Dept` objects.

The example code defines implementation classes for Oracle and MySQL data stores. Classes `EmpDAOOracleImpl` and `DeptDAOOracleImpl` define implementation details for an Oracle data store and classes `EmpDAOMySQLImpl` and `DeptDAOMySQLImpl` define implementation details for a MySQL data store. The abstract class `DAOFactory` defines abstract methods `getEmpDAO()` and `getDeptDAO()`, which are implemented by its subclasses `OracleDAOFactory` and `MySQLDAOFactory`.

To store `Emp` and `Dept` objects to an Oracle database, class `Client` can use `Oracle-DAOFactory`, and to store them to a MySQL database, class `Client` can use `MySQLDAO-Factory`:

```
class Emp { /* code */ }
class Dept { /* code */ }
```

Data objects to persist

```
interface EmpDAO { /* code */ }
interface DeptDAO { /* code */ }                        DAO pattern

class EmpDAOOracleImpl implements EmpDAO { /* code */ }       DAO pattern
class DeptDAOOracleImpl implements DeptDAO { /* code */ }     implementation for
                                                             Oracle database

class EmpDAOMySQLImpl implements EmpDAO { /* code */ }        DAO pattern
class DeptDAOMySQLImpl implements DeptDAO { /* code */ }      implementation for
                                                             MySQL database
abstract class DAOFactory {
    protected abstract EmpDAO getEmpDAO();
    protected abstract DeptDAO getDeptDAO();               Abstract Factory
    public EmpDAO getEmpDAOInstance() {                    pattern class
        return getEmpDAO();
    }
    public DeptDAO getDeptDAOInstance() {
        return getDeptDAO();
    }
}

class OracleDAOFactory extends DAOFactory {
    protected EmpDAO getEmpDAO() {                         Factory to return
        return new EmpDAOOracleImpl();                     Oracle DAO
    }                                                      implementations
    protected DeptDAO getDeptDAO() {
        return new DeptDAOOracleImpl();
    }
}
class MySQLDAOFactory extends DAOFactory {
    protected EmpDAO getEmpDAO() {                         Factory to return
        return new EmpDAOMySQLImpl();                      MySQL DAO
    }                                                      implementations
    protected DeptDAO getDeptDAO() {
        return new DeptDAOMySQLImpl();
    }
}

class Client {                                             Create
    public static void main(String args[]) {              OracleDAOFactory.
        DAOFactory factory = new OracleDAOFactory();
        EmpDAO empDAO = factory.getEmpDAOInstance();       Access EmpDAO and
        DeptDAO deptDAO = factory.getDeptDAOInstance();    DeptDAO implementations.

        Emp emp = new Emp();
        empDAO.create(emp);                    Insert emp data
                                               in database.
        Dept dept = new Dept();
        deptDAO.update(dept);                  Update dept data
    }                                          in database.
}
```

In the next section, you'll see what terms and phrases the exam might use to test you on the benefits of using the DAO pattern.

3.9.5   *Benefits of the DAO pattern*

The benefits of the DAO pattern are

- It abstracts and encapsulates all access to a data source. It manages the connection to the data source to obtain and store data.
- It promotes programming to an interface. It completely hides the data access implementation from its clients.
- It decouples the business logic layer and persistence layer. It makes the code independent of any changes to a data source or its vendor (for example, plaintext, XML, LDAP, MySQL, Oracle, or DB2).
- It promotes flexibility. Because the interfaces accessible to client classes don't change, new implementation classes can be added.
- The DAO pattern might also include Factory pattern classes.
- It prevents tight coupling between client classes and DAO implementation classes. It promotes the creation of cohesive classes.

Design patterns help you to reuse the experience of other programmers to create robust application designs. When you work with real-life projects, identify recurrent issues across projects and their probable solutions. You never know, you might identify and pen your own design patterns. Good luck to you!

3.10   *Summary*

In this chapter, you covered interfaces and how to use them in class design. Given the task of designing an application, API, or framework, you need to define multiple interfaces and abstract classes. But the choice of using abstract classes and interfaces isn't straightforward.

An interface can define only constants and abstract methods. The methods of an interface are implicitly abstract and can't define any implementation details. The interfaces are used to define a *contract*, which all the classes should adhere to. Interfaces only specify the behavior that should be supported by their implementing classes; the implementation details are left for the classes.

You can subclass an abstract class to create concrete classes only if you implement all of the class's abstract methods. Similarly, a concrete class should implement all the methods of an interface.

For the exam, you also need to know when to use interface inheritance and when to use class inheritance. Class inheritance helps you reuse implementation details provided in the base classes, so the derived classes don't have to write all the code themselves. Class inheritance also scores better when you want to add new behavior to an existing base class. You may prefer interface inheritance over class inheritance when you need to define multiple contracts for classes. Interface implementation has one major advantage of allowing a class to implement multiple interfaces, so an object of the class can be assigned to variables of multiple interface types.

Java objects share multiple relationships with other objects. IS-A and HAS-A are two important relationships shared by Java objects. The IS-A relationship is implemented using inheritance. You can implement the IS-A relationship by extending classes, extending interfaces, and implementing interfaces. When a class has an instance variable of a certain type, the class HAS-A <certain-type>.

Both inheritance and composition enable you to reuse the functionality of a class, but with a difference. Most often, newcomers to programming or OOP aren't sure whether to use inheritance or composition, to use another object. So they inherit a class when they want to use it in another class. You should use inheritance when the extended class is a specialized type of the base class. You should use composition when you simply want to use the functionality being offered by a class in another class.

Design patterns help you reuse the experience of other application designers and developers, in terms of the guidelines and suggested solutions for implementing an application's commonly occurring logic. A design pattern enables you to reuse experience and not code. We discussed all three design patterns that are on the exam: Singleton, DAO, and Factory method.

Singleton is a class design pattern that ensures that a class is instantiated only once. The class also provides a global point of access to it. This pattern is usually applied to only one class. Common examples include a single instance of Device Manager to manage all the devices on your system, or a single instance of print spooler to manage all printing jobs. To apply the Singleton pattern, you should mark the constructor of a class as `private` so that no other class can call it. Make the class itself create the sole instance, referred by a static variable. You can define a static method to access this sole instance.

The Factory pattern prevents tight coupling between the classes it uses from their concrete class implementation. It also eliminates direct constructor calls in favor of invoking a method. Multiple variations of this pattern exist: Simple Factory, Factory Method, and Abstract Factory.

The Simple Factory pattern creates and returns objects of classes that extend a common parent class or implement a common interface. The objects are created without exposing the instantiation logic to the client. The calling class is decoupled from knowing the exact name of the instantiated class. The intent of the Factory Method pattern is to define an interface for creating an object but let subclasses decide which class to instantiate. The Factory Method pattern lets a class defer instantiation to its subclasses. The Abstract Factory pattern is used to create a family of related products (in contrast, the Factory Method pattern creates one type of object). This pattern also defines an interface for creating objects, but it lets subclasses decide which class to instantiate.

You learned what the DAO pattern is and how to implement it in code. This pattern encapsulates all access to the persistent store to access and manipulate the data. The DAO pattern also manages the connection to the data store to retrieve and store the data. Usually, a DAO class accesses and manipulates a separate data object. An application usually defines a separate DAO for separate data objects that should be persisted. You need this design pattern so you can decouple data access code from the business logic. This eases the transition from using various data storage formats and vendors and creates more cohesive classes. The DAO pattern is frequently used with the Factory pattern.

REVIEW NOTES

This section lists the main points covered in this chapter.

Interfaces

- An interface is an example of separating the behavior that an object should support from its implementation. An interface is used to define behavior by defining a group of abstract methods.
- All members (variables and methods) of an interface are implicitly public.
- You declare an interface using the keyword `interface`. An interface can define only public, final, static variables and public, abstract methods.
- The methods of an interface are implicitly abstract and public.
- The variables of an interface are implicitly public, static, and final.
- You can declare a top-level interface only with public and default access. Valid nonaccess modifiers that can be applied to an interface are `abstract` and `strictfp`.
- An interface that's defined within another interface can be defined with any access modifier.
- An interface can't extend a class.
- An interface can extend multiple interfaces. It can't implement another interface.
- An interface can define inner interfaces and (surprisingly) inner classes too.
- Because all the members of an interface are implicitly public, a derived interface inherits all the methods of its base interface.
- You can compare interface implementation to the signing of a contract. When a concrete class declares an implementation of an interface, it agrees to and must implement all its abstract methods.
- If you don't implement all the methods defined in the implemented interfaces, a class can't compile as a concrete class. A concrete class must implement all the methods from the interfaces that it implements. An abstract class might not implement all the methods from the interfaces that it implements.
- A class can define an instance or a static variable with the same name as the variable defined in the interface that it implements. These variables can be defined using any access level.
- Because the methods in an interface are implicitly public, if you try to assign a weaker access to the implemented method in a class, it won't compile.

- A class can inherit methods with the same name from multiple interfaces. There are no compilation issues if these methods have exactly the same method signature or if these methods can coexist in the implemented class as overloaded methods. The class won't compile if these methods coexist as incorrectly overloaded or overridden methods.

Class inheritance versus interface inheritance

- Class inheritance scores better when you want to reuse the implementation already defined in a base class. It also scores better when you want to add new behavior to an existing base class.
- You can add new behavior to an abstract or nonabstract base class, and you may not break all the classes that subclass it.
- You may prefer interface inheritance over class inheritance when you need to define multiple contracts for classes.
- Interface implementation has one major advantage of allowing a class to implement multiple interfaces, so an object of the class can be assigned to variables of multiple interface types.

IS-A and HAS-A relationships in code

- An IS-A relationship is implemented using inheritance.
- You can traverse the inheritance tree *up* the hierarchy to identify an IS-A relationship. A derived class IS-A *type* of its base class and its implemented interfaces. A derived interface IS-A type of its base interface. A base class or interface *is not a* type of its derived class or interface.
- The key to finding the entities that participate in an IS-A relationship is to find your way, up the hierarchy tree, in the direction of the arrows. This technique not only will help you with the exam, but also will take you a long way in your professional career.
- You can implement an IS-A relationship by extending classes, extending interfaces, or implementing interfaces.
- A HAS-A relationship is implemented using association.
- The relationship `MyClass` HAS-A `YourClass` is implemented by defining an instance variable of type `YourClass` in `MyClass`. Defining an instance variable of type `MyClass` in `YourClass` will implement the relationship `YourClass` HAS-A `MyClass`.

Cohesion and low coupling

- Cohesion refers to how focused a class or a module is.
- High cohesion refers to a well-focused class or module, whereas low cohesion refers to a class or module that doesn't have a well-defined responsibility.
- Well-designed applications aim for highly cohesive classes and modules.

- Coupling refers to how much a class or module knows about other classes or modules.
- Loosely coupled classes interact with each other by using their interface (public methods).
- Low coupling and loose coupling refer to the same concept and are often used interchangeably.
- Well-designed applications aim for loosely coupled classes and modules.

Object composition principles

- Newcomers to programming often extend a class when they want to use a class in another class. They use inheritance in place of composition.
- You should extend a class (inheritance) when you want the objects of the derived classes to reuse the interface of their base class.
- You should define an object of another class (composition) when you want to use the functionality offered by the class.

Singleton pattern

- Singleton is a creational design pattern that ensures that a class is instantiated only once. The class also provides a global point of access to it.
- It is used in scenarios when you might need only one object of a class.
- Implementation of the Singleton pattern involves a single class.
- A class that implements the Singleton pattern must define its constructor as `private`.
- A Singleton class uses a static private reference variable to refer to its sole instance.
- A Singleton class defines a static method to access its sole instance.
- To avoid threading issues with the creation of the sole instance of the Singleton class, you might use either of the following to create its sole instance:
  - Eager initialization—instantiate the object with its declaration
  - Synchronized lazy initialization—create the instance using a synchronized method or code block
- You can also use enums to implement the Singleton pattern because enum instances can't be created by any other class.
- On the exam, all of these approaches (eager initialization, synchronization of the complete method `getInstance()`, and partial synchronization of method `getInstance()`) may be presented, and you may be questioned about the right approach for implementing the Singleton pattern. All these approaches are good. Beware of modified code that tries to synchronize a partial method `getInstance()`, which doesn't synchronize the code that creates an object of `Singleton`.

Factory pattern

- One of the most frequently used design patterns, multiple flavors of this pattern exist: Simple Factory, Factory Method, and Abstract Factory.
- The Simple Factory pattern creates and returns objects of classes that extend a common parent class or implement a common interface. The objects are created without exposing the instantiation logic to the client. The calling class is decoupled from knowing the exact name of the instantiated class.
- The intent of the Factory Method pattern is to define an interface for creating an object but let subclasses decide which class to instantiate. The Factory Method pattern lets a class defer instantiation to its subclasses.
- The Abstract Factory pattern is used to create a family of related products (in contrast, the Factory Method pattern creates one type of object). This pattern also defines an interface for creating objects but it lets subclasses decide which class to instantiate.
- The benefits of the Factory pattern are
  - Prefers method invocation over direct constructor calls
  - Prevents tight coupling between a class implementation and your application
  - Promotes creation of cohesive classes
  - Promotes programming to an interface
  - Promotes flexibility. Object instantiation logic can be changed without affecting the clients that use objects. It also allows the addition of new concrete classes.
- The following don't apply to the Factory pattern:
  - It doesn't eliminate the need of overloading constructors in class implementations.
  - It doesn't encourage the use of any particular access modifier. It isn't compulsory to define private members to use this pattern.
  - It won't slow your application.
  - It isn't related to how to monitor objects for change.
- The Java API uses the Factory pattern in many of its classes, including
  - `Calendar.getInstance()`
  - `Arrays.asList()`
  - `ResourceBundle.getBundle()`
  - `DriverManager.getConnectionEstablish()`, `DriverManager.getDriver()`
  - `Connection.createStatement()`
  - `Statement.executeQuery()`
  - `NumberFormat.getInstance()`, `NumberFormat.getNumberFormat()`, `NumberFormat.getCurrencyInstance()`, `NumberFormat.getIntegerInstance()`
  - `Executors.newFixedThreadPool()`, `Executors.newCachedThreadPool()`, `Executors.newSingleThreadExecutor()`

DAO pattern

- The DAO pattern encapsulates all communication with a persistent store to access and manipulate the stored data.
- The DAO pattern also manages the connection to the data store to retrieve and store the data.
- An application usually defines separate DAO classes for each type of data object that should be persisted.
- The CRUD operations form the basis of the DAO pattern.
- The DAO pattern removes the direct dependency between an application and the data persistence implementation.
- The DAO pattern is frequently used with the Factory pattern.

SAMPLE EXAM QUESTIONS

Q 3-1. What is the output? Choose the best answer.

```
interface Online {
    String course = "OCP";
    int duration = 2;
}
class EJavaGuru implements Online {
    String course = "OCA";
    public static void main(String args[]) {
        EJavaGuru ejg = new EJavaGuru();
        System.out.print(ejg.course);              // n1
        System.out.print(EJavaGuru.duration);      // n2
    }
}
```

- a Compilation fails at line n1.
- b Compilation fails at line n2.
- c Compilations fails at both lines n1 and n2.
- d Code prints "OCA2".
- e Code prints "OCP2".
- f Code throws a runtime exception.

Q 3-2. In the next Java version, designers are planning to create a new switch statement. This statement should be able to accept an object of type SwitchArgument and be able to call method defaultValue() on it. Which of the following options describe feasible (workable) options?

- a Define class SwitchArgument and make class java.lang.Object extend class SwitchArgument.
- b Define method defaultValue in class java.lang.Object.
- c Define interface SwitchArgument with no methods. The classes that need to be used in this switch statement can implement interface SwitchArgument.

d Define interface `SwitchArgument` with method `defaultValue()`. The classes that need to be used in this `switch` statement can implement interface `Switch-Argument`.

Q 3-3. Given the following code, select the correct options:

```
class AbX {}
class Sunny extends AbX {}
interface Moon {}
class Sun implements Moon {
    Sunny AbX;
}
```

- **a** Sunny IS-A Moon.
- **b** Sunny HAS-A AbX.
- **c** Sun HAS-A AbX.
- **d** Sun HAS-A Sunny.
- **e** AbX HAS-A Moon.
- **f** Sun IS-A Abx.
- **g** Sunny IS-A Abx.

Q 3-4. Given the following statements, chose the options that are correct individually:

- ABCD can't define instance variables.
- XYZ can only define public methods.
- ABCD can extend XYZ.
- XYZ can't implement ABCD.
- LMN can define instance variables.
- LMN can't extend ABCD.

- **a** ABCD is a class.
- **b** ABCD is an interface.
- **c** XYZ is a class.
- **d** XYZ is an interface.
- **e** LMN is a class.
- **f** LMN is an interface.

Q 3-5. Which of the following options are correct?

- **a** If you add a method to your interface, you'll break all the classes that implement it.
- **b** If you add a nonabstract method to a base abstract class, its subclasses might not always succeed to compile.

   c When you work with an interface type, you decouple from its implementation.

   d Code that works with a reference variable of an abstract base class works with any object of its subclasses.

Q 3-6. Given the following statements, choose the corresponding code implementation:

- Apple HAS-A Ball.
- Ball IS-A Cone.
- Cone HAS-A Apple.
- Dot IS-A Ball.

   a
```
class Apple { String Ball; }
class Cone { String Apple; }
class Ball extends Cone {}
class Dot extends Ball {}
```

   b
```
class Apple {Ball Ball;}
class Cone {Apple Apple;}
class Ball extends Cone {}
class Dot extends Ball {}
```

   c
```
class Apple {Ball aVar;}
class Cone {Apple age;}
class Ball extends Cone {}
class Dot extends Ball {}
```

   d
```
class Apple {Ball var;}
interface Cone {Apple a;}
interface Ball implements Cone {}
interface Dot implements Ball {}
```

Q 3-7. What is true about interfaces? (Choose all that apply.)

   a They force an implementing class to provide its own specific functionality.

   b An object of a class implementing an interface can be referred to by its own type.

   c An interface can define constructors to initialize its final variables.

   d An interface can define a static initializer block to initialize its variables.

Q 3-8. Select all incorrect statements.

   a An abstract class may define abstract methods.

   b An abstract class forces all its concrete derived classes to implement all its abstract methods.

   c An abstract class does provide enough details for its objects to be created.

   d An abstract class is used to group the common behaviors of a set of similar objects, but which itself may be incomplete.

   e An abstract class may not be used to create a new type.

   f You can create an instance of an abstract class.

Q 3-9. Assuming that the names of the classes used in the following code represent the actual objects, select the correct options.

```
class Ray {}
class Satellite {}
class Sun { Ray rays; }
class Moon extends Satellite {}
class Earth {}
class SolarSystem {
    Earth a;
    Moon b;
}
```

   a Sun is associated with Ray.

   b Moon is composed of Satellite.

   c SolarSystem is composed of Earth and Moon.

   d SolarSystem is associated with Earth.

   e SolarSystem is associated with Moon.

   f Ray is composed of Sun.

Q 3-10. Given the following code, which options correctly declare, implement, and extend these interfaces?

```
interface Coverable {}
interface Package {}
interface Ship extends Coverable, Package {}
```

   a `class Book implements Ship {}`

   b `class Container implements Coverable {}`
       `class Bottle extends Container{}`

   c `interface Voyage implements Ship {}`
       `class Fan implements Voyage {}`

   d `interface Delivery extends Ship{}`
       `interface Payment extends Package, Delivery{}`
       `class Product extends Payment {}`

Q 3-11. Which of the following code options implements the Singleton pattern correctly?

   a
```
class King {
    private static King king = null;
    private King() {}
    public static King getInstance() {
        king = new King();
        return king;
    }
}
```

```
b  class King {
       private static King king = new King();
       public static King getInstance() {
           return king;
       }
   }

c  class King {
       private static King king = new King();
       private King() {}
       private static King getInstance() {
           return king;
       }
   }

d  class King {
       private static King king;
       public static King getInstance() {
           if (king == null)
               king = new King();
           return king;
       }
   }
```

e None of the above

Q 3-12. Given the following definition of class King, which option, when replacing //INSERT CODE HERE//, implements the Singleton pattern correctly? (Choose all that apply.)

```
class King {
    private static String name;
    private static King king = new King();
    // INSERT CODE HERE //
    public static King getInstance() {
            return king;
    }
}
```

a private King() {}

b private King() {
       name = null;
   }

c private King() {
       name = new String("King");
   }

d private King() {
       if (name != null)
           name = new String("King");
   }

e None of the above

Q 3-13. Given the following definition of class King, which option, when replacing //INSERT CODE HERE//, implements the Singleton pattern correctly with no concurrent creation of objects of class King? (Choose all that apply.)

```
class Jungle {}
class King {
    private static King king = null;
    private King() {}
    //INSERT CODE HERE//
}
```

```
a  public static synchronized King getInstance() {
       if (king == null)
               king = new King();
       return king;
   }
```

```
b  public static King getInstance() {
       if (king == null) {
               synchronized (Jungle.class){
                       king = new King();
               }
       }
       return king;
   }
```

```
c  public static King getInstance() {
       synchronized (Jungle.class){
               if (king == null) {
                       king = new King();
               }
       }
       return king;
   }
```

```
d  synchronized static public King getInstance() {
       synchronized (Jungle.class){
               if (king == null) {
                       king = new King();
               }
       }
       return king;
   }
```

Q 3-14. Given the following statements, select all options that are correct individually:

- Class Queen implements the Singleton pattern.
- Class King implements the Singleton pattern.
- Class Prince doesn't implement the Singleton pattern.
- Class Princess doesn't implement the Singleton pattern.

a Only class Queen can create an object of class King.
b Either class King or class Queen can create an object of class King.

    c Only class `King` can create its object.

    d Both classes `King` and `Queen` can create objects of `Prince` and `Princess`.

    e All classes (`King`, `Queen`, and `Princess`) can create objects of `Prince`.

Q 3-15. Given the definition of class `Person` as follows, which options do you think are correct implementations of a class that implements the DAO pattern for class `Person` (there are no compilation issues with this code)?

```
class Person {
    int id;
    String name;
    int age;
}
```

    a
```
class PersonDAO {
    class DAO {
        Person person;
    }
}
```

    b
```
class PersonDAO {
    Person findPerson(int id) { /* code */ }
    Person seekPerson(int id) { /* code */ }
}
```

    c
```
class PersonDAO {
    static Person findPerson(int id) { /* code */ }
    static int create(Person p) { /* code */ }
    static int update(Person p) { /* code */ }
    static int delete(Person p) { /* code */ }
}
```

    d
```
class PersonDAO {
    Person findPerson(int id) { /* code */ }
    int create(Person p) { /* code */ }
    int update(Person p) { /* code */ }
    int delete(Person p) { /* code */ }
}
```

Q 3-16. Select the correct statements:

    a The DAO pattern helps decouple code that inserts data in persistence storage from code that deletes data in persistence storage.

    b The DAO pattern helps encapsulate persistence data logic.

    c The DAO eases migration of persistent data from one vendor to another.

    d The DAO promotes low coupling and high cohesion.

Q 3-17. Given the following definition of class `Person`, which of its methods would you need to move to another class, say, `PersonDAO`, to implement the DAO pattern?

```
class Person {
    int id;
    String name;
    int age;
    int getId() {return id;}
    void setId(int id) {this.id = id;}
    String getName() {return name;}
    void setName(String name) {this.name = name;}
    int getAge() {return age;}
    void setAge(int age) {this.age = age;}
    void find() { /* code to find Person with this id in DB */ }
    void insert() { /* code to insert Person with its details in DB */ }
    void modify() { /* code to update Person with this id in DB*/ }
    void remove() { /* code to remove Person with this id in DB */ }
}
```

- **a** Methods `getId()`, `setId()`, `find()`, `insert()`, `modify()`, `remove()`
- **b** Methods `find()`, `insert()`, `modify()`, `remove()`
- **c** Methods `getId()`, `setId()`, `getName()`, `setName()`, `getAge()`, `setAge()`
- **d** Methods `getId()`, `setId()`

Q 3-18. Given

```
class Animal {}
class Herbivore extends Animal {}
class Carnivore extends Animal {}
class Cow extends Herbivore {}
class Tiger extends Carnivore {}
class Client{
    public void createAnimal(String eatingHabits) {
        Animal foo = null;
        if (eatingHabits.equals("grass"))
            foo = new Cow();
        else if (eatingHabits.equals("deer"))
            foo = new Tiger();
    }
}
```

What are the benefits of moving creation of `Animal` instances from class `Client` to a separate class, say, `Animals`?

- **a** To enable class `Client` to use `Animal` instances without the need to know its instance creation logic
- **b** To promote extensibility—specific `Animal` classes can be added later, which might be returned by class `Animals`
- **c** To implement the Singleton pattern
- **d** To implement DAO
- **e** To enable low coupling and high cohesion

Q 3-19. Given

```
interface Animal {}
class Cat implements Animal {}
class Tiger implements Animal {}
class Factory {
    static Animal getInstance(String type) {
        if (type.equals("Tiger"))
            return new Tiger();
        else if (type.equals("Cat"))
            return new Cat();
        else
            return getAnimal();
    }
    private static Animal getAnimal() {
        return new Cat();
    }
}
```

Select code that initializes an `Animal` reference using a `Factory`:

- **a** `Animal animal = Factory.getInstance();`
- **b** `Animal animal = Factory.getAnimal();`
- **c** `Animal animal = Factory.getInstance("Animal");`
- **d** `Animal animal = Factory.getAnimal("Tiger");`
- **e** `Animal animal = new Factory().getInstance("Cat");`

Q 3-20. Which of the following use the Factory pattern? (Choose all that apply.)

- **a** `Object.equals();`
- **b** `Calendar.getInstance()`
- **c** `DriverManager.getDriver();`
- **d** `Object.wait();`
- **e** `NumberFormat.getDateInstance();`

ANSWERS TO SAMPLE EXAM QUESTIONS

A 3-1. d

[3.1] Write code that declares, implements, and/or extends interfaces

Explanation: Class `EJavaGuru` defines an instance variable `course`. Interface `Online` also defines a variable with the same name—`course` (which is implicitly static). Class `EJavaGuru` implements `Online`. Using `EJavaGuru`'s `instanceName.course` will refer to its instance variable. Using `Online.course` will refer to the variable `course` from `Online`. Using `EJavaGuru.course` will result in a compilation error. Code on line n1 compiles successfully and prints `OCA`.

Because the variables defined in an interface are implicitly static and final, the variable `duration` can be accessed as `EJavaGuru.duration`. Code on line n2 compiles successfully and prints 2.

However, a class can't define static and instance variables with the same name. The following class won't compile:

```
class EJavaGuru {
    String course;
    static String course;
}
```

A 3-2. d

[3.2] Choose between interface inheritance and class inheritance

Explanation: Option (a) is incorrect. `java.lang.Object` is the base class of all classes in Java. Making class `java.lang.Object` extend another class can be extremely risky. Adding a method with a particular signature can break code of some other class, if it has defined a method with the same name (`defaultValue()`) but a different signature that isn't compatible, forming invalid overloaded methods.

Option (b) is incorrect. Because the requirement expects an object of Switch-Argument, adding just method `defaultValue()` to class `java.lang.Object` won't serve the purpose. To define a new type, we need to define `SwitchArgument` as either a class or an interface.

Option (c) is incorrect. The requirement mentions that the object of Switch-Argument, passed to a switch statement, should define method `defaultValue()`. Defining this method in interface `SwitchArgument` ensures that all classes that implement interface `SwitchArgument` define method `defaultValue()`.

Option (d) is correct. Creation of type `SwitchArgument` as an interface with method `defaultValue()` provides a convenient option for all existing classes that want to be passed as an argument to the switch statement. When the classes implement the interface `SwitchArgument`, they'll be responsible for implementing method `defaultValue()`.

A 3-3. d, g

[3.3] Apply cohesion, low-coupling, IS-A, and HAS-A principles

Explanation Option (a) is incorrect. Classes Sunny and Moon are unrelated.

Option (b) is incorrect. Class Sunny extends class AbX; it doesn't define a variable of type AbX. The correct relationship here would be Sunny IS-A AbX.

Option (c) is incorrect. Class Sun defines a variable of type Sunny. So the correct relation would be Sun HAS-A Sunny. The IS-A and HAS-A relationships don't reflect the names of the variables.

Option (d) is correct. Class Sun defines a variable of type Sunny, so the relationship Sun HAS-A Sunny is correct.

In option (e), class AbX doesn't define any variable of type Moon, so this relationship is incorrect.

In option (f), class Sun doesn't extend class AbX, so this relationship is incorrect.

In option (g), class Sunny extends class AbX, so this relationship is correct.

A 3-4. b, d, e

[2.1] Identify when and how to apply abstract classes
[2.2] Construct abstract Java classes and subclasses
[3.1] Write code that declares, implements, and/or extends interfaces

Explanation: Option (a) is incorrect. As specified, ABCD can't define an instance variable, but a class can define instance variables.

Option (b) is correct. All the variables defined in an interface are implicitly public, final, and static. The static variables can't exist as instance variables.

Option (c) is incorrect. XYZ can't exist as a class. As specified, XYZ can define only public methods, whereas a class can define nonpublic methods.

Option (d) is correct. XYZ can exist as an interface because all the methods in an interface are implicitly public. All methods in a class aren't implicitly public.

Option (e) is correct, and (f) is incorrect. LMN is a class because it can define instance methods and can't extend ABCD, an interface.

A 3-5. a, b, c, d

[2.1] Identify when and how to apply abstract classes
[2.2] Construct abstract Java classes and subclasses
[3.1] Write code that declares, implements, and/or extends interfaces

Explanation: Option (a) is correct. If you add a method to your interface, all the classes that implement the interface will fall short on the definition of the newly added method and will no longer compile.

Option (b) is correct. If you add a nonabstract method to your base class, you *can* break its subclasses. If a subclass method has the same name as the newly added method in the base class, which doesn't qualify as a valid overloaded or overriding method, the subclass won't compile.

Option (c) is correct. When you work with an interface type, you're free to work with any object that implements the interface.

Option (d) is correct. Objects of all subclasses can be assigned to a reference variable of its abstract or nonabstract base class. So code that works with the abstract base class will work with objects of any of its subclasses.

A 3-6. b, c

[3.3] Apply cohesion, low-coupling, IS-A, and HAS-A principles

Explanation: An IS-A or a HAS-A relationship is defined between the types of the variables, and not their names.

Option (a) is incorrect. Class Apple HAS-A String and not Ball.

Option (b) is correct. Class Apple defines a variable Ball of type Ball. So Apple HAS-A Ball. It's acceptable to define a variable with the name of its class. Class Cone defines a variable Apple of type Apple. So it satisfies the relationship Cone HAS-A Apple. Class Ball extends class Cone, so it satisfies Ball IS-A Cone. Class Dot extends class Ball. So it satisfies Dot IS-A Ball.

Option (c) is also correct. Class Apple defines a variable aVar of type Ball. So Apple HAS-A Ball. Class Cone defines a variable age of type Apple. So it satisfies the relationship Cone HAS-A Apple. Class Ball extends class Cone, so it satisfies Ball IS-A Cone. Class Dot extends class Ball. So it satisfies Dot IS-A Ball.

Option (d) is incorrect. An interface can't implement another interface. It can only extend it.

A 3-7. a, b

[3.1] Write code that declares, implements, and/or extends interfaces

Explanation: Options (c) and (d) are incorrect. An interface can neither define a constructor nor a static initializer block.

A 3-8. c, e, f

[2.1] Identify when and how to apply abstract classes

Explanation: Option (c) is an incorrect statement, because objects of an abstract class can't be created, even if the class doesn't define any abstract method.

Option (e) is an incorrect statement. An abstract class defines a new type. This type can be used to define variables in multiple scopes (instance variables, static variables, method parameters, and local variables).

Option (f) is an incorrect statement, because you can't create an object of an abstract class.

A 3-9. a, c, d, e

[3.4] Apply object composition principles (including HAS-A relationships)

Explanation: Option (a) is correct. Sun gives out rays, so Sun is associated with Ray. Option (b) is incorrect. Moon is a type of Satellite. Composition is a whole-part relationship; if the enclosing object goes out of scope, the part also goes out of scope.

Option (c) is correct. If `SolarSystem` goes out of scope, all the objects that it's composed of, including `Earth` and `Moon`, will go out of scope.

Options (d) and (e) are correct. Composition is a special type of association, and objects in this relationship are associated with each other.

Option (f) is incorrect. `Ray` isn't composed of `Sun`. It's the other way around: `Sun` is composed of `Ray`. If `Sun` goes out of scope, `Ray` also goes out of scope (is no longer visible).

A 3-10. a, b

[3.1] Write code that declares, implements, and/or extends interfaces

Explanation: Option (c) is incorrect, because an interface (`Voyage`) can't implement another interface (`Ship`).

Option (d) is incorrect, because a class (`Product`) can't extend an interface (`Payment`).

A 3-11. e

[3.5] Design a class using the Singleton design pattern

Explanation: Option (a) is incorrect. It creates a new object of class `King`, whenever method `getInstance()` is called. On the contrary, the Singleton pattern creates only one instance of a class.

Option (b) is incorrect. A Singleton should define a `private` constructor so that no other class can create its objects. The class defined in this option doesn't define any constructor. In the absence of a constructor, the Java compiler creates a default constructor for a class with the access modifier as that of the class itself. Because the class in this option is defined with default or package access, a constructor with default access will be created for it by the Java compiler. Because other classes can use its constructor to create new objects of this class, it doesn't qualify as a Singleton.

Option (c) is incorrect. There is no way to access an object of class `King` outside the class itself. Variable `king` is a static private variable, so it can't be accessed directly. The constructor of the class is marked `private`, so it can't be used to create objects of this class. Method `getInstance()` is also private, so no other class can call it.

Option (d) is incorrect. Though the variable `king` is private, and method `get-Instance` creates and returns an object of class `King`, the catch here is that this class doesn't define a constructor. As mentioned in the explanation of option (b), in the absence of a constructor, the Java compiler creates a default constructor. Because other classes can use its constructor to create new objects of this class, it doesn't qualify as a Singleton.

A 3-12. a, b, c, d

[3.5] Design a class using the Singleton design pattern

Explanation: All the options are trying to confuse you with the correct implementation of method `getInstance()` of a class that uses the Singleton pattern with its constructor. A class that implements the Singleton pattern should have a private constructor, so no other class can create its objects. The implementation of the constructor isn't detailed by the Singleton pattern. The class may choose to include or exclude whatever it feels is good for it.

A 3-13. a, c, d

[3.5] Design a class using the Singleton design pattern

Explanation: In option (a), the complete method `getInstance()` is synchronized, which ensures that only one `Thread` executes this method and creates an instance of class `King` (assigning it to the static variable `king`), if it's `null`.

Option (b) is incorrect. Method `getInstance()` synchronizes only the code `king = new King();`. So multiple methods can still execute method `getInstance()` concurrently and query whether the variable `king` is `null`. If, say, two threads find it `null`, they both will execute the following code (though not at the same time):

```
king = new King();
```

When the second `Thread` executes the preceding code, it creates and assigns another object of class `King` to variable `king`. This method fails to prevent multiple creations of objects of class `King`.

Option (c) is correct. Method `getInstance()` synchronizes the part of the method that creates an object of class `King`. When the control is within the `synchronized` block, the code checks again to confirm that variable `king` is still `null`. If true, it creates an object of class `King` and assigns it to the variable `king`.

Option (d) is correct. It defines the same code as option (c), but with a difference: this option applies the `synchronized` keyword to the method also. Though synchronizing the code block and the complete method isn't required, it isn't incorrect to do so. Because this method prevents creation of multiple objects of class `King`, it qualifies as a correct implementation of method `getInstance()`.

A 3-14. c, d, e

[3.5] Design a class using the Singleton design pattern

Explanation: Options (a) and (b) are incorrect and (c) is correct. Only a class that implements the Singleton pattern can create its object, because its constructor is marked `private`. No other class can. Only class `King` can create its own object by calling its constructor from its other method.

Options (d) and (e) are correct. If a class doesn't implement the Singleton pattern, we can assume that creation of its multiple objects is allowed. So another class can also create its objects.

A 3-15. c, d

[3.6] Write code to implement the DAO pattern

Explanation: Options (a) and (b) are incorrect. A class that implements the DAO pattern should define methods for CRUD operations (create, retrieve, update, and delete). Options (a) and (b) don't define all these methods.

Options (c) and (d) are correct. Both these options define methods for CRUD operations. You can implement these methods as static or nonstatic.

A 3-16. b, c, d

[3.6] Write code to implement the DAO pattern

Explanation: Option (a) is incorrect. The DAO pattern helps separate and decouple application logic from persistence storage logic. It isn't used to decouple different data manipulation operations.

A 3-17. b

[3.6] Write code to implement the DAO pattern

Explanation: To implement the DAO pattern, you should move the methods that interact with the persistent data storage to a separate class. In class Person, the getter and setter methods are for assigning and retrieving object fields. They don't work with data in persistence storage. The rest of the methods (find(), insert(), modify(), and remove()) work with persistent data and should be moved to another class to implement the DAO pattern. The DAO pattern doesn't specify any rules for conventions on naming these methods and the type that they return.

A 3-18. a, b, e

[3.7] Design and create objects using a Factory pattern

Explanation: Here's one of the ways you can move Animal instance creation logic to class Animals:

```
class Amimals{
    public static Animal createAnimal(String eatingHabits) {
        Animal foo = null;
        if (eatingHabits.equals("grass"))
            foo = new Cow();
```

```
            else if (eatingHabits.equals("deer"))
                foo = new Tiger();
            return foo;
        }
    }
```

Option (a) is correct. Moving method `createAnimal()` to a separate class frees class `Client` from knowing the logic of creating `Animal` instances. It can call `Animals.createAnimal()`, passing it a `String` value to get an appropriate `Animal` instance.

Option (b) is correct. Method `createAnimal()` in class `Animals` can be modified to include instantiation of other specific `Animal` instances without modifying its API.

Options (c) and (d) are incorrect. The stated modification is neither related to data persistence nor to creating just one instance of a class.

Option (e) is correct. With the modification, class `Client` doesn't need to know about the specific implementations of class `Animal`. Class `Client` can concentrate on using `Animal` instances rather than knowing how to create them.

A 3-19. c, e

[3.7] Design and create objects using a Factory pattern

Explanation: Class `Factory` doesn't expose the object creation logic of `Animal` objects and uses the Factory pattern to create and return its instances.

Option (a) won't compile. Though you might dismiss it as a trivial or tricky option, note that it's easy to find similar options on the exam.

Options (b) and (d) won't compile because `getAnimal()` is a private method and it doesn't define the method parameters.

Option (e) is correct. A static method can be accessed using both the class name and an instance.

A 3-20. b, c, e

[3.7] Design and create objects using a Factory pattern

Explanation: Methods `equals()` and `wait()` in class `Object` don't use the Factory pattern.

Generics and collections

Exam objectives covered in this chapter	What you need to know
[4.1] Create a generic class	How to define generic classes, interfaces, and methods with single and multiple type parameters How to define generic methods with a generic or regular class
[4.2] Use the diamond for type inference	How to drop the type from the angle brackets to instantiate generic classes How to use wildcards to create and instantiate generic classes
[4.3] Analyze the interoperability of collections that use raw types and generic types	What happens when you lose type safety by using variables of raw types and objects of generic types How to determine and differentiate scenarios that would generate compilation errors and warnings
[4.4] Use wrapper classes, autoboxing, and unboxing	How and when values are boxed and unboxed when used with wrapper classes
[4.5] Create and use `List`, `Set`, and `Deque` implementations	How to create objects of the `List` interface (`ArrayList`, `LinkedList`), objects of the `Deque` interface (`ArrayDeque`, `LinkedList`), and objects of the `Set` interface (`HashSet`, `LinkedHashSet`, and `TreeSet`) How each implementing class stores data, manipulates it, searches it, and iterates over it How the `List`, `Set`, and `Deque` implementations use methods `hashCode()`, `equals()`, `compare()`, and `compareTo()` Given a set of requirements, how to choose the best interface or its implementing class

Exam objectives covered in this chapter	What you need to know
[4.6] Create and use Map implementations	How to instantiate Map objects: HashMap, LinkedHashMap, and TreeMap How Map implementations use methods hashCode(), equals(), compare(), and compareTo()
[4.7] Use java.util.Comparator and java.lang.Comparable	How to define natural and custom ordering of objects of a class
[4.8] Sort and search arrays and lists	How to sort and search arrays and lists using methods from classes Arrays and Collections Importance of using sorted collections for searching values

Imagine you need to collect pencils at your workplace. You request all your fellow workers to drop their pencils in a box at the main entrance of the office. When you open the box the next day, you also find ink pens and marker pens (!), which you didn't ask for. Even though you mentioned pencils, people could add pens to the box because no one stopped them from doing so. Now imagine that you could use a box that wouldn't allow adding any item other than a pencil. Would you prefer it? If you answered yes, you'd prefer to use generics. In Java, *generics* empower you to specify the type of objects that you'd like to work with so that you don't work with other types—knowingly or unknowingly.

Now imagine that you need to sort all the collected pencils according to their color and size. Would you like to do that yourself, or would you prefer a magic box that would accept all the pencils and return them to you in a sorted order? If you chose the magic box, you'd like using the collections framework. The Java collections framework includes multiple interfaces and classes to store and manipulate a collection of objects, including the methods that sort and search them.

This chapter covers

- Creating and using generic types
- Using the diamond for type inference
- Analyzing the interoperability of collections that use raw types and generic types
- Using wrapper classes, autoboxing, and unboxing
- Creating and using List, Set, and Deque implementations
- Creating and using Map implementations
- Working with the java.util.Comparator and java.lang.Comparable interfaces
- Sorting and searching arrays and lists

Let's start with an introduction to generics, in the next warm-up section. Feel free to skip it and move to the next section if you're an experienced generics programmer.

4.1   *Introducing generics: WARM-UP*

Generics enable you to abstract over types. They add type safety to collection classes. Introduced with Java version 5.0, generics enable developers to detect certain bugs during compilation so they can't creep into the runtime code. Debugging an application is a costly affair, in terms of the time and effort required to find a bug and then fix it. The sooner you can detect a bug, the easier it is to fix it. While developing software, it's easier to fix a bug during unit testing than it is to fix the same bug during integration testing or, say, when it shows up months after an application goes live. A bug is easier to fix in the development phase than in the maintenance phase.

4.1.1   *Need for introducing generics*

Before generics were introduced, programmers used to *assume* that a class, interface, or method would work with a *certain* data type. For example, figure 4.1 shows how a programmer would *assume* that the `ArrayList` referred to by `lst` would contain `String` objects. But because `lst` is a collection of objects of type `Object`, it can accept any type of data (other than primitives). An issue can creep in when these different types of objects are treated as `String` types during runtime.

 NOTE   In figures 4.1 and 4.2, `ArrayList-lst` is created with an initial capacity (and not size) of two elements. The size of an `ArrayList` increases as more elements are added to it.

With the introduction of generics, programmers could indicate their intent of using a particular type of data with a class, interface, or method (not enums, because enums can't have generic type parameters). Figure 4.2 shows how you can indicate that an

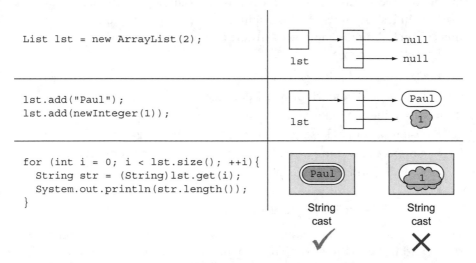

Figure 4.1   **Before generics were added, collection classes like `ArrayList` allowed the addition of any type of data. A programmer's assumption of adding only a particular type of data to a collection was met with a casting exception at runtime.**

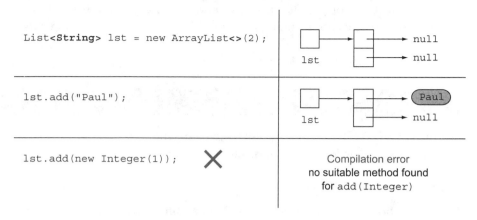

```
List<String> lst = new ArrayList<>(2);
```
```
lst.add("Paul");
```
```
lst.add(new Integer(1));
```

Figure 4.2 Post-generics, you can mark your intent of using a particular data type with a class, method, or interface. If the code doesn't adhere to the restrictions, the code fails to compile.

`ArrayList` referred to by `lst` will accept only objects of type `String`. Code that tries to add an object of any other type won't compile.

As shown in figure 4.2, with generics, the incorrect data type is determined during compilation. This compilation-time safety enables you to identify bugs during development, thus building better code.

 EXAM TIP The basic purpose behind using generics is to enable you to mark your intent of using a class, method, or interface with a particular data type. Generics add compile-time safety to collections.

4.1.2 Benefits and complexities of using generics

Apart from compile-time safety, you also get the following benefits with generics:

- *Removing explicit casts*—Prior to generics, you needed to add casts when you had a list with strings and you wanted to get a string out of the list. With generics this isn't needed anymore.
- *Better code readability*—Without explicit casting, code is less cluttered, which improves readability.
- *Developing generic algorithms*—Just as you need not hard-code values when you work with methods and can accept them as method parameters, generics help you parameterize over data types and develop algorithms that work with multiple data types.

But every new concept or approach has its own set of limitations and complexities, and using generics is no exception. As you work through this chapter, you'll see how adding generics to the collections framework created new complexities. (Coverage is limited to the exam topics.)

In the next section, you'll create your own generic entities. If you haven't already worked with generic entities, it might take a while for all the related concepts to sink in.

4.2   *Creating generic entities*

 [4.1]   Create a generic class

On the exam, you'll be tested on how to create generic classes, interfaces, and methods—within generic and nongeneric classes or interfaces.

4.2.1   *Creating a generic class*

In this section, we'll start with an example of a nongeneric class and then modify it to create a generic class. You'll learn how to use a generic class and how important variable naming conventions are for the type parameters.

A NONGENERIC CLASS
To understand how to create a generic class, let's begin with an example of a *non*generic class, Parcel:

```
class Parcel {
    private Object obj;
    public void set(Object obj) {
        this.obj = obj;
    }
    public Object get() {
        return obj;
    }
}
```

Class ParcelNonGeneric can use class Parcel, calling its method set() to assign an object of class Book. It can retrieve this object by using get() and cast it to class Phone(!). Even though not desired, it's allowed:

```
class Phone{}
class Book{}

class ParcelNonGeneric {
    public static void main(String args[]) {
        Parcel parcel = new Parcel();
        parcel.set(new Book());
        System.out.println((Phone)parcel.get());
    }
}
```

Assign object of Book

Cast object of Book to Phone; code compiles but throws ClassCastException at runtime.

ADDING TYPE SAFETY TO A NONGENERIC CLASS
Let's see how you add *type safety* to class Parcel. Let's define class Parcel as a generic class by adding a *type parameter* to it, so that you can retrieve only the object type that you assign to it, as shown in figure 4.3.

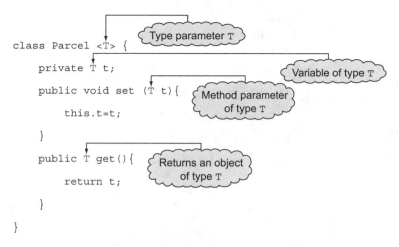

Figure 4.3   How to convert a nongeneric class to a generic class by adding type parameters

As shown in the preceding code, the declaration of generic class `Parcel` includes the type parameter T. After adding the type information, it's read as `Parcel<T>` or `Parcel` of T. The generic class `Parcel<T>` defines a private instance variable of type T, and `get()` and `set()` methods to retrieve and set its value. Methods `get()` and `set()` use the parameter type T as their method parameter and return type.

 EXAM TIP   The first occurrence of T is different from its remaining occurrences because only the first one is surrounded by <>.

USING A GENERIC CLASS
Having seen how to create a generic class, let's see how you can use it. Class `UseGeneric-Parcel` instantiates `Parcel` and calls its methods `get()` and `set()`. Note that you don't need an explicit cast when you use `Book` instance by calling `parcel.get()`:

```
class Book{}
class UseGenericParcel {
    public static void main(String args[]) {
        Parcel<Book> parcel = new Parcel<Book>();
        parcel.set(new Book());
        Book myBook = parcel.get();
    }
}
```

Parameterized type Parcel<Book> indicates Parcel will work with instances of Book.

set() accepts Book instance.

get() returns Book instance; no explicit casts required.

With the generic class `Parcel`, `UseGenericParcel` can use method `set()` to assign an object of type `Book`. But `UseGenericParcel` can't cast the retrieved object to an unrelated class, say, `Phone`. If it tries to do so, the code won't compile (as shown in figure 4.4).

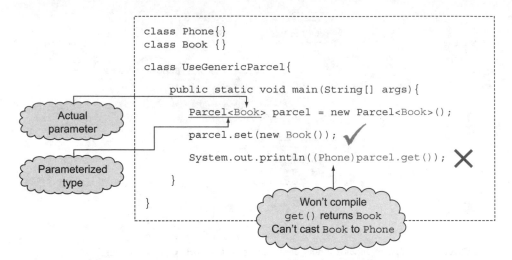

Figure 4.4   A class that uses a generic class uses a parameterized type, replacing the formal parameter with an actual parameter. Also, invalid casts aren't allowed.

 EXAM TIP   A type parameter can be used in the declaration of classes, variables, method parameters, and method return types.

VARIABLE NAMES USED FOR TYPE PARAMETERS

You must follow the variable naming rules for type parameters; for instance, you can't use Java keywords. As per Oracle's naming conventions, you should use uppercase single characters for type parameters. This also sets them apart from other variables and method parameters, which use *camelCase*. Though the constants use uppercase, they aren't *usually* limited to single characters.

Now, what happens if you don't follow the conventions for naming type parameters? Here's an interesting exam question. For the modified definition of class `Parcel` in the following code, do you think method `set()` can be passed `String` objects?

```
class MyClass{}
class Parcel<MyClass>{
    private MyClass t;
    public void set(MyClass t) {
        this.t = t;
    }
}
```

Yes, it can. In the preceding code, `MyClass` is used as a *placeholder* for a type argument that you pass to class `Parcel`—it doesn't refer to class `MyClass`. So you can instantiate `Parcel`, passing it a type argument, say, `String`, and pass a `String` value to its method `set()`. For example

```
class UseParcel {
    public static void main(String args[]) {
        Parcel<String> parcel = new Parcel<>();
```

```
        parcel.set("OCP");
        System.out.println(parcel.get().length());
    }
}
```

GENERIC CLASS EXTENDING ANOTHER GENERIC CLASS

A generic class can be extended by another generic class. In the following example, generic class GenericBookParcel<T> extends generic class Parcel<T>:

```
class Parcel<T> {}
class GenericBookParcel<T> extends Parcel<T> {}    ◁──   Generic
                                                          extended class
```

In all cases, an extended class must be able to pass type arguments to its base class. For the preceding example, the type argument passed to class GenericBookParcel is passed to its base class, Parcel, when you instantiate GenericBookParcel. For example

```
GenericBookParcel<String> parcel = new GenericBookParcel<>();
```

The preceding example passes argument String to GenericBookParcel's type parameter T. But if you define GenericBookParcel in a way that it can't pass an argument to the parameters of its base class, the code won't compile. Do you think the following code will compile?

```
class Parcel<T> {}
class GenericBookParcel<X> extends Parcel<T> {}    ◁──   Won't compile; no way
                                                          to pass argument to T
```

No, it won't. In the preceding code, class GenericBookParcel defines a type parameter X, but doesn't include T in its type parameter list. Because this arrangement prevents GenericBookParcel from passing type arguments to its base class Parcel, it fails to compile.

You can also define new type parameters for a derived class when you extend a generic base class. In the following example, class GenericBookParcel defines two type parameters X and T:

```
class Parcel<T> {}
class GenericBookParcel<X, T> extends Parcel<T> {}    ◁──   Compiles
                                                             successfully
```

Here's another example, in which the derived class passes type arguments to its generic base class in its declaration:

```
class Parcel<T> {}
class GenericBookParcel<X> extends Parcel<Book> {}  //    ◁──   Type argument
                                                                Book passed to
                                                                base class Parcel
```

 EXAM TIP   A *type argument* must be passed to the *type parameter* of a base class. You can do so while extending the base class or while instantiating the derived class.

NONGENERIC CLASS EXTENDING A GENERIC CLASS

You can extend a generic base class to define a nongeneric base class. To do so, the derived class doesn't define any type parameters but passes arguments to all type parameters of its generic base class. For example

```
class Parcel<T>{}
class NonGenericPhoneParcel extends Parcel<Phone> {}
```

In the preceding example, NonGenericPhoneParcel is a nongeneric class that passes argument Phone to its base class Parcel<T>.

Watch out for exam questions that try to pass type arguments to a nongeneric class. For class NonGenericPhoneParcel defined in the preceding example code, the following code won't compile:

```
NonGenericPhoneParcel<String> var = new NonGenericPhoneParcel<>();   ◄──┤ Won't
                                                                        compile
```

 EXAM TIP   You can't pass type arguments to a nongeneric class.

MULTIPLE TYPE PARAMETERS

The example of generic class Parcel used in this section defines one type parameter. A generic class with multiple type parameters takes the following form:

```
class ClassName <T1, T2, …, Tn> { /* code */}
```

In the next section on generic interfaces, you'll also work with multiple type parameters.

4.2.2 *Working with generic interfaces*

A generic interface enables you to abstract over types. In this section, you'll see how to define and implement generic interfaces.

DEFINING A GENERIC INTERFACE

The declaration of a generic interface includes one or more type parameters. Let's look at an example of a generic interface that can accept multiple type parameters: the MyMap interface accepts two type parameters and defines methods put() and get(). You can compare the MyMap interface to a simplified version of the Map interface, defined in the java.util package:

```
                                          MyMap accepts two type
                                          parameters—K and V.
interface MyMap<K, V>{            ◄──
    void put(K key, V value);        ◄──┤   put() accepts a key of type
    V get(K key);                 ◄──┐      K and a value of type V.
}
                                  For a key of type K, get()
                                  returns a value of type V.
```

NONGENERIC CLASS IMPLEMENTING A GENERIC INTERFACE

When a nongeneric class implements a generic interface, the type parameters don't follow the class name. For the implemented interface, the type parameters are replaced by actual types:

```
class MapLegendNonGeneric implements MyMap<String, Integer> {
    public void put(String s, Integer i) {}
    public Integer get(String s) { return null; }
}
```

In the preceding example, `MapLegendNonGeneric` is a nongeneric class which implements generic interface `MyMap` (defined in the previous section).

When implementing a generic interface, take note of the type parameters and how they are used in method declarations (method parameters and return types). The methods of an implementing class must implement or override all the interface methods. In the following example, class `MapLegendNonGeneric` won't compile because it doesn't override the abstract method `get(String)` in `MyMap` (the return type of `get()` is declared to be `String`, not `Integer`):

```
class MapLegendNonGeneric implements MyMap<String, Integer> {
    public void put(String s, Integer i) {}
    public String get(String s) { return null; }    ◁─┐ Won't
}                                                        │ compile
```

 EXAM TIP A nongeneric class can implement a generic interface by replacing its type parameters with actual types.

GENERIC CLASS IMPLEMENTING A GENERIC INTERFACE

Here's an example of declaring a generic class that implements a generic `MyMap` interface. To pass the type parameter information to a class, the type parameters must follow both the name of the class and the interface implemented by the class:

```
interface MyMap<K, V>{
    void put(K key, V value);
    V get(K key);
}
class MapLegendGeneric<K, V> implements MyMap<K, V> {    ◁─┐
    public void put(K key, V value) { }
    public V get(K key) { return null; }
}
```

Type parameters are included right after class and interface names.

You might also choose a combination. In the following examples, the classes define only one parameterized type, `V` or `K`. While implementing the `MyMap` interface, the classes pass actual parameters (`String` or `Integer`) to one of the interface's parameterized types (`K` or `V`):

```
class MapLegendGeneric2<V> implements MyMap<String, V> {
    public void put(String key, V value) {}
    public V get(String key) { return null; }
}
```

```
class MapLegendGeneric3<K> implements MyMap<K, String> {
    public void put(K key, String value) {}
    public String get(K key) { return null; }
}
```

It's important to use a correct combination of type parameters and actual parameters in the method declarations. The following class won't compile because class Map-LegendGeneric<K> doesn't implement method put(K key, String value) from the MyMap interface:

```
class MapLegendGeneric4<K> implements MyMap<K, String> {
    public void put(Object value, K key) {}        ◁─┐ Won't
    public String get(K key) { return null; }         │ compile
}
```

 EXAM TIP   Generic classes and interfaces are collectively referred to as *generic types*.

4.2.3 *Using generic methods*

A generic method defines its own formal type parameters. You can define a generic method in a generic or a nongeneric class.

GENERIC METHODS DEFINED IN A NONGENERIC CLASS OR INTERFACE

A nongeneric class doesn't define type parameters. To define a generic method in a nongeneric class or interface, you must define the type parameters with the method, in its *type parameter section*. A method's type parameter list is placed just after its access and nonaccess modifiers and before its return type. Because a type parameter could be used to define the return type, it should be known *before* the return type is used. An example

```
abstract class Courier {
    public <E> void deliver(E[] array) {          ◁─────   Nongeneric
        for (E item : array) {                 ◁──────     class
            System.out.println("Delivering - " + item);   Generic
        }                                                  method
    }
}
```

 EXAM TIP   For a generic method (defined in a nongeneric class or interface), its type parameter list is placed just after the access and nonaccess modifiers and before its return type.

GENERIC METHODS DEFINED IN A GENERIC CLASS OR INTERFACE

The following example defines a generic interface, and a generic method that defines its own type parameter.

```
                                              ┌─ Generic interface
                                              │  declaration
interface Map<X, Y>{                     ◁────┘
    <T> void mapMaterial(T t);   ◁──   Generic method declaration
}                                      with its own type parameters
```

You can also define a generic constructor in a generic class:

```
class Phone<X> {
    <T> Phone(T t) {
        //..code
    }
}
```

Generic constructor declaration with type parameter T

Generic class declaration with type parameter X

Instantiating `Phone`

```
Phone<Double> c = new Phone<Double>("Android");
```

In the following "Twist in the Tale" exercise, let's see whether you can determine the difference between the presence and absence of angle brackets in a definition of generic entities.

Twist in the Tale 4.1

Consider this definition of the `Map` interface discussed in a previous section:

```
interface MyMap<K, V>{
    void put(K key, V value);
    V get(K key);
}
```

Now modify that definition to the following:

```
interface MyMap<K, V>{
    void put(K key, V value);
    <V> get(K key);
}
```

Do you think these modifications will make any difference to the definition of the `MyMap` interface?

In the next section, let's see how you can limit the parameter types that you can pass to a generic class, interface, or method.

4.2.4 Bounded type parameters

You can limit the type of objects that can be passed as arguments to generic classes, interfaces, and methods by using bounded type parameters.

NEED FOR BOUNDED TYPE PARAMETER

Without a bounded type parameter (and explicit type casting), you can access only the members defined in the superclass of all classes—that is, class `Object`.

In the following example, the generic class `Parcel` won't be able to access method `getWeight()` of class `Gift`:

```
abstract class Gift{
    abstract double getWeight();
}
```

```
class Book extends Gift{
    public double getWeight() {return 3.2;}
}
class Phone extends Gift{
    public double getWeight() { return 1.1; }
}
class Parcel<T>{
    private T t;
    public void set(T t) {
        this.t = t;
    }
    public void shipParcel() {
        if (t.getWeight() > 10)
            System.out.println("Ship by courier ABC");
        else
            System.out.println("Ship by courier XYZ");
    }
}
```

**Won't compile;
type of t is Object.**

To access members of class `Gift` in `Parcel`, you can limit the type of objects that can be passed to class `Parcel` (to `Gift` and its subclasses) by using bounded parameters (discussed next).

DEFINING BOUNDED TYPE PARAMETERS

You can specify the bounds to restrict the set of types that can be used as type arguments to a generic class, interface, or method. It also enables access to the methods (and variables) defined by the bounds.

Let's restrict the type of objects that can be passed to class `Parcel` to `Gift` so that the methods of class `Parcel` can access the methods and variables of class `Gift`. Because the definitions of classes `Gift`, `Book`, and `Phone` are the same as in the preceding section, they aren't repeated in the following code:

```
class Parcel<T extends Gift>{
    private T t;
    public void set(T t) {
        this.t = t;
    }
    public void shipParcel() {
        if (t.getWeight() > 10)
            System.out.println("Ship by courier ABC");
        else
            System.out.println("Ship by courier XYZ");
    }
}
```

**❶ Bounded type
parameter**

**❷ Compiles; type
of t is Gift.**

In the preceding code, the code at ❶ defines a bounded parameter for class `Parcel` with its bounds as class `Gift`. Because the bound of t is `Gift`, its method `getWeight()` can be accessed using t ❷.

The keyword `implements` isn't used to specify the bound as an interface. The following code won't compile:

```
class Parcel<T implements Serializable>{}
```
          Won't compile

EXAM TIP For a bounded type parameter, the bound can be a class, interface, or enum, but not an array or a primitive type. All cases use the keyword `extends` to specify the bound. If the bound is an interface, the `implements` keyword isn't used.

On the exam, you might see a question that tries to instantiate a generic class by passing it a type argument that doesn't comply with its bounded parameter. What do you think happens in this case—a compilation error or a runtime exception? What do you think is the output of the following code, which tries to instantiate class `Parcel` with type parameter `<T extends Gift>`?

```
Parcel<String> p = new Parcel<>();
```

The preceding code will not compile because the type argument `String` isn't within bounds of type variable `T`.

DEFINING MULTIPLE BOUNDS

A type parameter can have multiple bounds. The list of bounds consists of one class and/or multiple interfaces. The following example defines a generic class `Parcel`, the type parameter `T` of which has multiple bounds:

```
interface Wrappable{}
interface Exchangeable{}
class Gift{}
class Parcel <T extends Gift, Exchangeable, Wrappable>{}
```

In this case, the type argument that you pass to the bounded type parameter must be a subtype of all bounds. If you try to pass a type argument that doesn't subtype all the bounds, your code won't compile.

 EXAM TIP For a type parameter with multiple bounds, the type argument must be a subtype of all bounds.

4.2.5 *Using wildcards*

The wildcard `?` represents an unknown type. You can use it to declare the type of a parameter; a local, instance, or static variable; and return value of generic types. But you can't use it as a type argument to invoke a generic method, create a generic class instance, or for a supertype.

NEED TO USE AN UNKNOWN TYPE

Before you understand how to use the wildcard, you must know where and why you need it. Say you're given the following class inheritance tree:

```
class Gift{}
class Book extends Gift{}
class Phone extends Gift{}
```

You can assign an object of class `Book` or `Phone` to a reference variable of type `Gift`:

```
Gift gift = new Book();
gift = new Phone();
```

But the following assignment isn't valid:

```
List<Gift> wishList = new ArrayList<Book>();
```
◁——— **Won't compile**

You can assign an ArrayList to a variable of type List. But the type that you pass to it in the angle brackets must be the same. Though ArrayList<T> implements List<T> for any type T, ArrayList<Book> implements neither ArrayList<Gift> nor List<>. So assignment of ArrayList<Book> to a variable of type List<Gift> isn't allowed with generics.

 EXAM TIP   You can assign an instance of a subclass, say, String, to a variable of its base class, Object. But you can't assign ArrayList<String> to a variable of type List<Object>. Inheritance doesn't apply to the type parameters.

You can use a wildcard to get around this. In the following example, you can assign an ArrayList of *any* type to wishList:

```
List<?> wishList = new ArrayList<Book>();
```
◁——— **? refers to any type**

Because ? refers to an unknown type, wishList is a list of an unknown type. So it's acceptable to *assign* a list of Book objects to it.

ADDING OBJECTS TO COLLECTIONS DEFINED USING A WILDCARD

On the exam, take note of code that tries to add objects to collections that are defined by using the wildcard. Referring to our example, if you try to add or insert a Book instance into the ArrayList referred by the variable wishList, the code won't compile:

```
List<?> wishList = new ArrayList<Book>();
wishList.add(new Book());
```
◁—— **? refers to any type**

◁—— **Won't compile**

Because of the ? you can invoke method add() with literally any object—String, Integer, Book, Phone, and others. But ArrayList<Book> should only have Book instances. Because the compiler can't guarantee it, it forbids adding anything to the list when using a wildcard ?.

ITERATING COLLECTIONS WITH A WILDCARD

You can iterate a collection defined using wildcard ?. Note that the type of the variable used to refer to the list values is Object—the base class of all Java classes. Here's an example of using ? in wrapGift() to iterate a List of *any* type:

```
class Gift{}
class Book extends Gift{
    String title;
    Book(String title) {
        this.title = title;
    }
```
◁——┐ **Class Book extends Gift.**

```
            public String toString() {
                return title;
            }
        }
    }
    class Courier {
        public static void wrapGift(List<?> list) {      ◄
            for (Object item : list) {
                System.out.println("GiftWrap - " + item);
            }
        }
        public static void main(String args[]) {
            List<Book> bookList = new ArrayList<Book>();
            bookList.add(new Book("Oracle"));
            bookList.add(new Book("Java"));
            wrapGift(bookList);

            List<String> stringList = new ArrayList<String>();
            stringList.add("Paul");
            stringList.add("Shreya");
            wrapGift(stringList);
        }
    }
```

wrapGift will accept list of any unknown type

Type of variable item is Object, superclass of all objects.

wrapGift will accept a list of Book objects.

wrapGift will accept a list of String objects.

 EXAM TIP When you use a wildcard to declare your variables or method parameters, you lose the functionality of adding objects to a collection. In this case, using the add method will result in compilation failure.

The wildcard ? accepts objects of *all* unknown types. Let's use bounded wildcards to limit the types of objects that we can use.

4.2.6 *Using bounded wildcards*

To restrict the types that can be used as arguments in a parameterized type, you can use bounded wildcards.

UPPER-BOUNDED WILDCARDS

You can restrict use of arguments to a type and its subtypes by using <? extends Type>, where *Type* refers to a class, interface, or enum.

 EXAM TIP In upper-bounded wildcards, the keyword extends is used for both a class and an interface.

Consider the following classes:

```
class Gift{}
class Book extends Gift{}
class Phone extends Gift{}
```

For a variable that uses the upper-bounded wildcard <? extends Gift>, the following assignments are valid:

Book and Phone extend Gift.
```
List<? extends Gift> myList1 = new ArrayList<Gift>();      ◄
List<? extends Gift> myList2 = new ArrayList<Book>();
List<? extends Gift> myList3 = new ArrayList<Phone>();
```
Though Gift doesn't extend itself, this assignment is valid.

Let's see how you can use the upper-bounded wildcard in method parameters. Let's modify the method `wrapGift()`, used in the previous section, to restrict its type arguments to `Gift` or its subclasses (modifications in bold):

```
public static void wrapGift(List<? extends Gift> list) {
    for (Gift item : list) {
        System.out.println("GiftWrap - " + item);
    }
}
```
◁── **wrapGift() will accept List of Gift or List of classes that extend Gift.**

 EXAM TIP   In the preceding method `wrapGift()`, the loop variable `item` can be of type `Gift` or its subtype, `Object`.

For the preceding method, you can pass to it `List` of `Gift` or objects that extend class `Gift`. If you try to pass it a list of any other object type, it won't compile.

```
List<Book> bookList = new ArrayList<Book>();
bookList.add(new Book("Oracle"));
bookList.add(new Book("Java"));
wrapGift(bookList);
```
◁── **With bounded wildcard <? extends Gift>, wrapGift() will accept List of class Book.**

```
List<String> stringList = new ArrayList<String>();
stringList.add("Paul");
stringList.add("Shreya");
wrapGift(stringList);
```
◁── **Won't compile; with bounded wildcard <? extends Gift>, wrapGift() won't accept List of class String.**

For the exam, you must know the operations that are allowed for variables declared by using upper-bounded wildcards. You can iterate and read values from a collection declared with upper-bounded wildcards. But you can't write any values to the collection. For example, you can't add *any* object to a `List` defined as `List<? extends Gift>` because such a list can refer to a list of either `Gift`, `Book`, or `Phone`. Adding a mismatched object can pollute the list, which isn't allowed.

 EXAM TIP   For collections defined using upper-bounded wildcards, you can't add any objects. You can iterate and read values from such collections.

It's interesting to note that class `String` is a final class that can't be subclassed. If you try to define a class that extends class `String`, it won't compile:

```
class MyClass extends String {}
```
◁── **Won't compile; can't extend final class String.**

But it's acceptable to define an upper-bounded wildcard that extends class `String`. Here's the modified code:

```
public static void wrapGift(List<? extends String> list) {
    for (String item : list) {
        System.out.println("GiftWrap - " + item);
    }
}
```
◁── **Accept objects of class String or objects of classes that extend String.**

EXAM TIP You can use final classes in upper-bounded wildcards. Although `class X extends String` won't compile, `<? extends String>` will compile successfully.

LOWER-BOUNDED WILDCARDS

You can restrict use of type arguments to a type and its base or supertypes by using `<? super Type>`, where *Type* refers to a class, interface, or enum. Consider the following classes:

```
class Gift{}
class Book extends Gift{}
class Phone extends Gift{}
```

For a variable that uses the lower-bounded wildcard `<? super Gift>`, note the following assignments:

Gift extends Object.

```
List<? super Gift> myList1 = new ArrayList<Gift>();      ◀── Though Gift isn't its own superclass, this assignment is valid.
List<? super Gift> myList2 = new ArrayList<Object>();
List<? super Gift> myList3 = new ArrayList<Phone>();     ◀──┤ Won't compile; gift doesn't extend Phone.
List<? super Phone> myList4 = new ArrayList<Gift>();     ◀──
```

Valid; Phone extends Gift.

So, what can you read from and add to collection objects defined using lower-bounded wildcards? Here's an example:

```
List<? super Gift> list = new ArrayList<Gift>();    ◀── List<? super Gift> is assigned ArrayList<Gift>.
list.add(new Gift());
list.add(new Book());                               Can add instances of Gift or its subclasses to List<? super Gift>.
list.add(new Phone());
list.add(new Object());                             ◀── Won't compile
for (Object obj : list) System.out.println(obj);    ◀── Elements are read as instance Object, superclass of Gift.
```

 EXAM TIP In the preceding example, the loop variable `obj` can't be of type `Gift`.

Table 4.1 lists wildcard and bounded wildcard variables, and the types of values that can be read from and written to them.

Table 4.1 Variables and the values that can be read from or added to them

Variable	Read objects of type	Write objects of type
`List<?>`	`Object`	N/A
`List<? extends Gift>`	`Gift`	N/A
`List<? super Gift>`	`Object`	`Gift` and its subclasses

4.2.7 *Type erasure*

When class `UseGenericParcel` instantiates `Parcel`, it uses the parameterized type `Parcel<Book>`, replacing the formal type parameter `T` with the actual parameter `Book`. When you do this, you can *assume* to be using the following definition of class `Parcel`, where all references of `T` are replaced with `Book`:

```
class Parcel<Book>{
    private Book t;
    public void set(Book t) {
        this.t = t;
    }
    public Book get() {
        return t;
    }
}
```

This isn't how a generic class is compiled; this is how it behaves.

Though the preceding code can help to a great extent to show how a generic class behaves, it's incorrect. It might make you think that you have access to multiple versions of compiled code, which is incorrect. In this section, you'll see that type information is erased during the compilation process; this is called *type erasure*.

On compilation, the type information of a generic class or an interface is erased. The compilation process generates one class file for each generic class or interface; separate class files aren't created for parameterized types.

 EXAM TIP When a generic class is compiled, you don't get multiple versions of the compiled class files. A generic class gets compiled into a single class file, erasing the type information during the compilation process.

The compiler erases the type information by replacing all type parameters in generic types with `Object` (for unbounded parameter types) or their bounds (for bounded parameter types). The compiler might insert type casts to preserve type safety and generate bridge methods to preserve polymorphism in extended generic types.

 NOTE Though the exam might not include explicit questions on the contents of a class file after type erasure, it will help you to understand generics better and answer all questions on generics.

ERASURE OF GENERIC TYPE IN CLASSES, INTERFACES, AND METHODS

For a generic class `Parcel`, which uses an unbounded type parameter, say, `T`

```
class Parcel<T>{
    private T t;
    public void set(T t) {
        this.t = t;
    }
    public T get() {
        return t;
    }
}
```

On compilation, the Java compiler replaces all occurrences of T with Object:

```
class Parcel {
    private Object t;
    public void set(Object t) {
        this.t = t;
    }
    public Object get() {
        return t;
    }
}
```

Here's an example of an interface that uses both bounded and unbounded type parameters:

```
interface MyMap<K extends String, V>{
    void put(K key, V value);
    V get(K key);
}
```

For the preceding interface, the Java compiler would replace all occurrences of K with its first bound class, String, and V with Object:

```
interface MyMap {
    void put(String key, Object value);
    Object get(String key);
}
```

Similarly, for generic methods, the unbounded and bounded type parameters are replaced by Object or their first bound class. For the generic method deliver() in class Courier

```
abstract class Courier {
    public <E> void deliver(E[] array) {
        for (E item : array) {
            System.out.println("Delivering - " + item);
        }
    }
}
```

The Java compiler would replace all occurrences of E with Object:

```
abstract class Courier {
    public void deliver(Object[] array) {
        for (Object item : array) {
            System.out.println("Delivering - " + item);
        }
    }
}
```

BRIDGE METHODS

The Java compiler might need to create additional methods, referred to as bridge methods, as part of the type erasure process. In the following example, class `Book-Parcel` extends `Parcel<Book>`:

```
class Book {}
class Parcel<T>{
    private T t;
    public void set(T t) {
        this.t = t;
    }
}
class BookParcel extends Parcel<Book> {
    public void set(Book book) {
        super.set(book);
    }
}
```

For the preceding code, during type erasure, the Java compiler erases and adds a *bridge method* to class `BookParcel`—that is, `set(Object)`. This is to add type safety to class `BookParcel`, ensuring that only `Book` instances can be assigned to its field `t`. Because method `set(Object)` accepts `Object` but casts it to `Book`, it will throw a `ClassCastException` for any other object type:

```
class Parcel {
    private Object t;
    public void set(Object obj) {
        t = obj;
    }
}
class BookParcel extends Parcel {
    public void set(Book book) {
        super.set(book);
    }
    public void set(Object obj) {          Throws ClassCastException
        set((Book)obj);                    for objects others than Book
    }
}
```

4.2.8 *Refreshing the commonly used terms*

Table 4.2 lists the new terms that were introduced with generics, which you are sure to see on the exam.

Table 4.2   Commonly used terms with generics and their meanings

Term	Meaning
Generic types	A generic type is a generic class or a generic interface, having one or more type parameters in its declaration.
Parameterized types	An invocation of a generic type is generally known as a parameterized type. For generic type `List<E>`, `List<String>` is a parameterized type.

Table 4.2 Commonly used terms with generics and their meanings

Term	Meaning
Type parameter	You use type parameters to define generic classes, interfaces, or methods. E in `List<E>` is a type parameter.
Type argument	A type argument specifies the type of objects to be used for a type parameter. For `List<String>`, `String` is a type argument.
Wildcard	A wildcard is represented by a ? (a question mark). It refers to an unknown type.
Bounded wildcard	A wildcard is bounded when it is a base or supertype of a type.
Raw type	The name of a generic class, or a generic class without any type arguments, is a raw type. For `List<E>`, `List` is a raw type.

In the next section, you'll learn how the compiler can determine type arguments if you don't specify them while creating instances of generic types.

4.3   Using type inference

 [4.2]   Use the diamond for type inference

Imagine solving a riddle with multiple constraints in the form of hints. You resolve the constraints to derive the answer. You can compare *type inference* with generating and solving constraints to promote flexibility in a programming language. Here's a simple (nongeneric) example: Java constrains the numeric operands of an addition operator (+) to be at least promoted to the int data type. So when + is used with int and short types, the type of the resultant value can be *inferred* to be an int type. *Type inference* is a Java compiler's capability to determine the argument type passed to an expression or method by examining its declaration and invocation.

With generics, you usually use angle brackets (<>, also referred to as the *diamond*) to specify the type of arguments to instantiate a generic class or invoke a generic method. What happens if you don't specify the type arguments? The Java compiler *might* be able to infer the argument type by examining the declaration of the generic entity and its invocation. But if it can't, it'll throw a warning, an error, or an exception. In this section, you'll see how to answer the exam questions on using the diamond for type inference to instantiate generic classes and invoke generic methods.

 NOTE   By throwing an *unchecked warning*, the compiler states that it can't ensure type safety. The term *unchecked* refers to *operations* that might result in violating type safety. This occurs when the compiler doesn't have enough type information to perform all type checks.

4.3.1   *Using type inference to instantiate a generic class*

When generics were introduced with Java 5, it was mandatory to include the type arguments to instantiate a generic class. Consider the generic class `Parcel`:

```
class Parcel<T>{
    //..code
}
```

The following code instantiates `Parcel`, passing it type argument `String`:

```
Parcel<String> parcel = new Parcel<String>();
```
⊲─┤ **Type arguments included to invoke constructor of generic class Parcel.**

But with Java 7, you can drop the type arguments required to invoke the constructor of a generic class and use an empty set of type arguments, `<>`:

```
Parcel<String> parcel = new Parcel<>();
```
⊲─┤ **With Java 7, empty set of type arguments can invoke constructor of generic class**

In the preceding code, the compiler can infer the type argument passed to `Parcel` as `String`. But an attempt to drop the diamond will result in a compilation warning:

```
Parcel<String> parcel = new Parcel();
```
⊲─┤ **Compilation warning; attempt to assign raw type to generic type**

Imagine another situation. What happens if you attempt to try it the other way around? Do you think the following code is valid?

```
Parcel<> parcel = new Parcel<String>();
```
⊲── **Won't compile**

The preceding code won't compile. Imagine what happens if `Parcel` defines a generic constructor:

```
class Parcel<T>{
    <X> Parcel(X x) {}
    public static void main(String[] args) {
        new Parcel<String>(new StringBuilder("Java"));
    }
}
```
⊲─┤ **Compiler infers type of formal parameter X as StringBuilder.**

In the preceding code, `String` is passed as an explicit type argument to the type parameter `T`. The type of the parameter `X` (specified by the constructor) is inferred by the compiler to be `StringBuilder`, which is passed to `Parcel`'s constructor.

4.3.2 Using type inference to invoke generic methods

A Java compiler can't infer the type parameters by using the diamond in the case of generic methods. It uses the type of the actual arguments passed to the method to infer the type parameters. Let's add the generic method `deliver()` to class `Parcel`:

```
class Parcel<T> {
    public <X> void deliver(X x) {
        System.out.println(x.getClass());
    }
    public static void main(String args[]) {
        Parcel<String> parcel = new Parcel<>();
        parcel.<Integer>deliver(new Integer(10));
        //parcel.<>deliver(new Integer(10));
        parcel.deliver("Hello");
    }
}
```

Type parameter X to generic method deliver()

Outputs type of argument passed to deliver().

Type of parameter X is Integer; determined using Integer object passed to deliver().

Won't compile; can't use < > with generic method.

Type of parameter X is String; inferred using actual argument passed to deliver().

Here's the output of the preceding code:

```
class java.lang.Integer
class java.lang.String
```

The next section covers an important topic: mixing generic and raw types. For the exam, you must know how the code behaves when you mix them: compilation warnings, errors, and runtime exceptions. You should also understand that by mixing them, you risk losing type safety.

4.4 Understanding interoperability of collections using raw types and generic types

 [4.3]   Analyze the interoperability of collections that use raw types and generic types

Before we start with *how* collections that use a raw type operate with generic types, you should know *why* this interoperability was allowed. When generics were introduced with Java 5, there was a *lot* of *existing* Java code, which didn't use generics. Because a new enhancement can't render existing code useless, the existing code that didn't use generics needed to be valid and interoperable, to be made to work with generics. This is also referred to as *migration compatibility*. This, however, introduced multiple complications, including generation of bridge methods and explicit casts.

To recap, when a generic class is used without its type information, it's referred to as its *raw type*. For example, for the generic class `Parcel<T>`, its raw type is `Parcel`.

EXAM TIP   Raw types exist only for generic types. Watch out for exam questions that might mention raw types for nongeneric classes and interfaces.

Let's examine the interoperability of code that mixes the assignment of objects of generic types with reference variables of raw types, and vice versa.

4.4.1   *Mixing reference variables and objects of raw and generic types*

You can assign a parameterized type to its raw type. But the reverse will give a compiler warning. Consider the following generic class:

```
class Parcel<T> {
    private T t;
    public void set(T t) {
        this.t = t;
    }
    public T get() {
        return t;
    }
}
```

The following assignment is allowed:

```
Parcel parcel = new Parcel<Phone>();
```

But you lose the type information for the class Parcel in the preceding code. When you call its method set() (passing it a method parameter of *any* type), you'll get a compiler warning:

```
Parcel parcel = new Parcel<Phone>();
parcel.set("harry");
```

◄— **Because you lose type information when you use variable of raw type, you can pass String object to set(), instead of Phone object**

Here's the detailed warning that the compiler generates when you compile the code using the flag -Xlint:unchecked, which informs you that the raw type Parcel is unable to comprehend type parameter T:

```
warning: [unchecked] unchecked call to set(T) as a member of the raw type
Parcel
        parcel.set(new String("harry"));
                  ^
  where T is a type-variable:
    T extends Object declared in class Parcel
1 warning
```

This happens because the variable parcel of raw type Parcel doesn't have access to generic type information.

On the exam, watch out for code that mixes raw with generic type. For such code, you'll need to determine whether the code compiles with or without any warning, or throws a runtime exception. In the following code (for class Parcel defined in this section), `parcel.set(Phone)` will compile with a warning, but attempt to assign the return value of `parcel.get()` to a variable of type `Phone`:

```
Parcel parcel = new Parcel<Phone>();
parcel.set(new Phone());
Phone phone = parcel.get();
```

Compiles with warning

Won't compile; with reference variable of raw type

 EXAM TIP   When you mix raw with generic types, you might get a compiler warning or error, or a runtime exception.

Let's get our heads around this with a pictorial representation (see figure 4.5). I've deliberately used interface `List` and class `ArrayList` from the collections framework because you might get to see them in similar code on this exam.

Figure 4.5   When you use a reference variable of a raw type, you lose the type information.

Now, let's try to assign a raw type to a parameterized type:

```
Parcel<Phone> parcel = new Parcel();
```

This code generates the following compilation warning:

```
warning: [unchecked] unchecked conversion
        Parcel<Phone> parcel = new Parcel();
                               ^

  required: Parcel<Phone>
  found:    Parcel
```

But it doesn't generate any compiler warning for methods that accept type parameters:

```
Parcel<Phone> parcel = new Parcel();     ◄──┐
parcel.set(new Phone());                 ◄──
//parcel.set(new String());             ◄───
Phone phone = parcel.get();             ◄──
```

Generates compilation warning

No compiler warnings

Compiles successfully

Won't compile if uncommented; reference variable parcel knows it's the parameter types.

Let me modify this preceding code and use a combination of raw and generic types in the next "Twist in the Tale" exercise. If you can answer this question correctly, you'll answer it correctly on the exam too!

Twist in the Tale 4.2

Consider the definition of the following generic type MyMap and class CustomMap that implements it:

```
interface MyMap<K, V>{
    void put(K key, V value);
    V get(K key);
}
class CustomMap<K, V> implements MyMap<K, V> {
    K key;
    V value;
    public void put(K key, V value) {
        this.key = key; this.value = value;
    }
    public V get(K key) {
        return value;
    }
}
```

Which options are true about the following code?

```
class Twist4_2 {
    public static void main(String args[]) {
        CustomMap map = new CustomMap<Integer, String>();  //1
        map.put(new String("1"), "Selvan");                //2
```

```
        String strVal = map.get(new Integer(1));        //3
        System.out.println(strVal);                     //4
    }
}
```

a Class `Twist4_2` will compile successfully if you replace line 1 with the following line:

```
CustomMap<Integer, String> map = new CustomMap();
```

b Code on line 2 will generate a compiler warning.

c Code on line 3 will compile if the type of variable `strVal` is `Object`.

d The code outputs `null` without any modifications.

On the exam, you might see questions on generics that include other classes from the collection framework, like `Stack`. So the next example uses `Stack` (covered in detail later in this chapter).

Let's look at another scenario, where we mix a method that uses parameters of raw types with actual objects that include generic type information:

❶ pushItems() defines parameter of raw type

Instantiates Stack of String objects. **❸**

Pushes String object. **❹**

```
class Interoperability {
    public static void pushItems(Stack stackParam, Object item) {
        stackParam.push(item);
    }
    public static void main(String args[]) {
        Stack<String> stackObj = new Stack<String>();
        stackObj.push("Paul");
        pushItems(stackObj, new Integer(77));
        String value = stackObj.pop();
        System.out.println(value);
    }
}
```

Generates warning: [unchecked] unchecked call to push(E) as member of raw type Stack. **❷**

Calls pushItems(), which pushes Integer to stackObj. **❺**

Throws ClassCastException at runtime. **❻**

The code at **❶** defines method `pushItems()`, with parameter of raw type `Stack`. Whenever you use a raw type, you lose all the type information. So the code at **❷** throws a compilation warning stating that you made an unchecked call to `push(E)`. It's warning you that you might end up adding incorrect data to your `Stack` object. Code in method `main()` instantiates a `Stack` of `String` objects at **❸**. At **❹**, the code pushes a `String` object to `stackObj`. So far, so good. A call to method `pushItems()` **❺** pushes an `Integer` object to `stackObj`. Why is this allowed? Because the method parameter `stackParam` is of a raw type, there is no type information, so the compiler doesn't know that the original object (`stackObj`) only allows strings; therefore, the integer is successfully pushed to the stack allowing only strings (`stackObj`). The code at **❻** throws a `ClassCastException` at runtime because the type of the returned object is `Integer` and not `String`.

That's exactly one of the possible problems when you mix generics with nongenerics code. That's also why you get that compiler warning: to warn you that the compiler can't protect you from doing stupid things, like putting an integer in an only-string stack.

As per polymorphism, you can assign an object of a subclass to reference a variable of its base class. But this subtyping rule doesn't work when you assign a collection-of-a-derived-class object to a reference variable of a collection of a base class. Let's see why in the next section.

4.4.2   Subtyping with generics

Because the class `ArrayList` implements the `List` interface, you can assign an object of `ArrayList` to a reference variable of `List`. Similarly, because class `String` extends class `Object`, you can assign an object of `String` to a reference variable of `Object`.

With generics, you must follow certain subtyping rules. The following line is valid because a generic class is a subtype of its raw type:

```
List list = new ArrayList<String>();
```

But the following isn't valid:

```
List<Object> list = new ArrayList<String>();        <──  Won't compile
```

This assignment isn't allowed. If you declare a reference variable `List<Object> list`, whatever you assign to the `list` must be of generic type `Object`. A subclass of `Object` is not allowed. Figure 4.6 shows the relationship between the interface `List`, class `Array-List`, and classes `Object` and `String`. It also shows the related valid and invalid code.

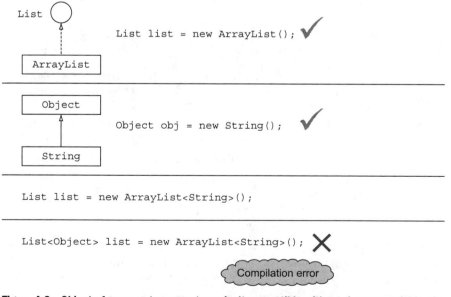

Figure 4.6   Object of `ArrayList<String>` isn't compatible with a reference variable of type `List<Object>`.

Apart from generics, this exam will also test you on the collections framework. It'll include many implementations of the interfaces List, Set, Deque, and Map, together with classes Comparator and Comparable. It'll also test you on how to search and sort arrays and lists. The next warm-up section introduces collections and the collections framework. Experienced developers can skip the introduction section.

4.5   *Introducing the collections framework: WARM-UP*

Imagine that you have to process a list of results submitted by registered users of your website for an opinion poll. You aren't concerned about the order of receiving or processing these results, but you won't accept multiple votes from the same user. Imagine that in another case, you're creating a drawing application that includes an Undo button. You need to keep track of the order in which the drawing commands are selected, so you can undo the last command. Duplicate commands are allowed in a drawing application. Imagine yet another case, when you're looking up a word in a dictionary. The words are ordered alphabetically, but duplicate words don't exist in the dictionary.

These scenarios show examples of needing to *store* and *retrieve* collections of data in various manners. For one collection, you might need to retrieve data in the order in which it was generated. For another collection, you might not allow duplicate values but would prefer data to be sorted on a data item. Figure 4.7 depicts these examples,

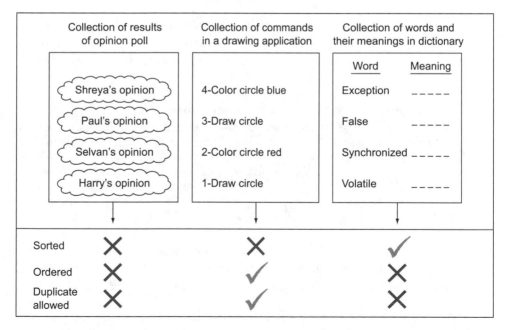

Figure 4.7   Depending on how you need to process a collection of data, you might need a data structure that can sort the collection values, retain the insertion order of the elements, and not allow duplicate elements.

along with a table on their requirements: whether the structure used to store the data needs to be sorted, be ordered, or allow duplicate values.

A *collection* is an object that can group other objects. Each object in a collection is referred to as an *element*. The Java collections framework is architecture for representing and manipulating collections. This framework defines many interfaces to support the need for storing a collection of data in various formats. These collections might need to be ordered, to be sorted, to allow duplicate values, to be immutable, to be of fixed size, and more. The collections framework includes high-performance, high-quality implementations of useful data structures to store a collection of your objects. It includes the following:

- *Interfaces*—Multiple interfaces like List, Set, Deque, and Map model the data structures used for storing, accessing, and manipulating a collection of data.
- *Implementations*—Concrete classes like ArrayList, HashSet, and TreeMap implement the interfaces.
- *Algorithms*—Classes like Collections and Arrays contain utility methods like sort() and search() for sorting and searching List objects or arrays.

 NOTE   Don't confuse the *interface* Collection with the *class* Collections. Collection is the base interface in the collections framework that is extended by most of the other interfaces. Class Collections defines utility methods to operate on or return collections.

Figure 4.8 shows the main interfaces and their implementations in the collections framework (limited to exam coverage). It also shows the classes Collections and Arrays, which define utility methods to sort and search List or array objects.

> ## The importance of the collection framework
> A recruiting manager once asked me why my technical architect places so much emphasis on the ability of a possible recruit to work with data structures and on the recruit's experience with the collections framework. I replied that the collections framework is an *extremely powerful and flexible* framework. A developer who can use its existing classes to store and search data effectively or who can craft out a custom implementation by using the existing framework will be an asset to any organization.

But at the same time, using the collections framework can be overwhelming. The key to optimal use of the collections framework is to get the basics right. So, let's start with the base interface in the Java collections framework: Collection.

 EXAM TIP   All the collection classes are generic; they all define type parameters. Watch out for exam questions that use them without type parameters; these are referred to as raw types.

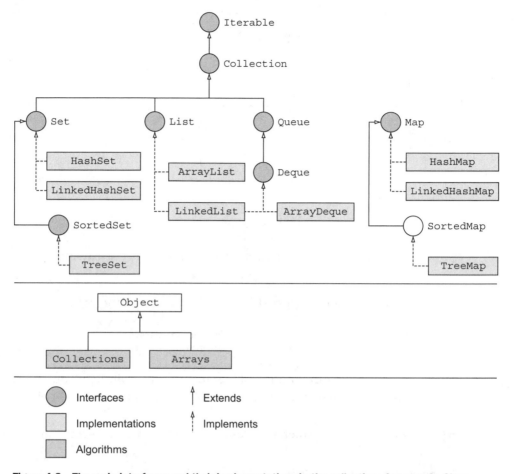

Figure 4.8 The main interfaces and their implementations in the collections framework. Class `Collections`, a utility class that implements various algorithms for searching and sorting, is also a part of the collections framework.

4.6   *Working with the Collection interface*

[4.5]   Create and use List, Set, and Deque implementations

The interface `Collection<E>` represents a group of objects known as its elements. There is no direct implementation of `Collection`; no concrete class implements it. It's extended by more-specific interfaces such as `Set`, `List`, and `Queue`. This collection is used for maximum generality—to work with methods that can accept objects of, say, `Set`, `List`, and `Queue`. Figure 4.9 shows the basic `Collection` interface and its main subinterfaces.

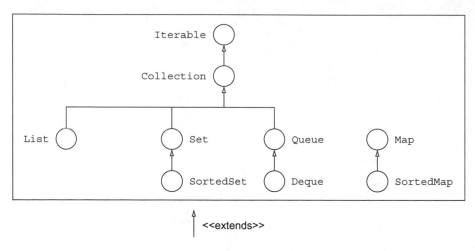

Figure 4.9   **The core** `Collection` **interface and the main interfaces that extend it**

All collection classes are generic. Here's the declaration of the `Collection` interface:

```
public interface Collection<E>
            extends Iterable<E>
```
| **All collection classes are generic.**

A thorough understanding of the `Collection` interface will help you absorb a *lot* of concepts and classes that we cover in the rest of this chapter.

 EXAM TIP   The `Map` interface doesn't extend the core `Collection` interface.

4.6.1   *The core Collection interface*

The `Collection` interface implements the `Iterable` interface, which defines method `iterator()`, enabling all the concrete implementations to access an `Iterator<E>` to iterate over all the collection objects. So for all the implementing classes, you'd be able to access an `Iterator` to iterate over its elements.

When you work with the concrete implementations of the collections framework, you'll notice that almost all the classes provide two constructors: a void (no-argument) constructor and another that accepts a single argument of type `Collection`. The former creates an empty collection, and the latter creates a new collection with the same elements as its argument, dropping any elements that don't fit the new collection being created. As an interface, `Collection` can't enforce this requirement because it can't define a constructor. But the classes that implement this interface implement it.

The methods of the `Collection` interface aren't marked synchronized. The synchronized methods result in a performance drop, even in single-threaded code, and so the creators of the collections framework opted out for them. If you've worked with

> ## Unsupported operations
> When specific concrete classes implement the methods defined from the `Collection` interface, the classes might not need to support all its operations specified. For example, a list that's immutable might not support the `Collection`'s method `add()` that adds elements to itself. In this case, this immutable list can choose to return `false` or throw `UnsupportedOperationException` from method `add()`. All methods of the `Collection` interface that modify itself specify (but don't mandate) that classes that don't support these operations *might* throw `Unsupported-OperationException`.

or read about the `Hashtable` or `Vector` classes, which were introduced before the Java collections framework, you'd notice that the methods of these data structures are synchronized. With the existing collections framework, you can get the same functionality (without synchronization) by using the collection classes `HashMap` and `ArrayList`.

 NOTE The main target of the exam is to prepare you to write efficient, real-world applications. A solid understanding of the collections framework will go a long way for you, both on the exam and in your career.

4.6.2 *Methods of the Collection interface*

Figure 4.10 shows the methods of the `Collection` interface, grouped by their functionality: methods that modify `Collection`, methods that query it, and miscellaneous.

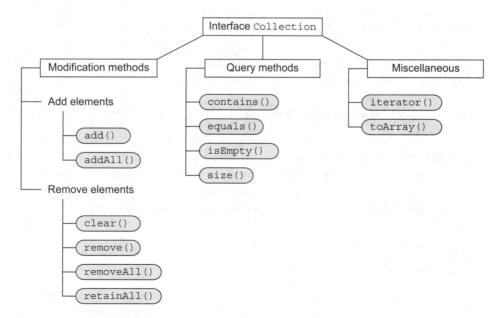

Figure 4.10   Methods defined in the `Collection` interface, grouped by their functionality

Because most of the interfaces implement the Collection interface, most of the implementation classes include methods to add, remove, and query its elements and retrieve an Iterator to retrieve the collection elements. The implementation, though, varies across classes.

As you proceed and work with the implementation of classes in the collection framework, you'll notice that almost all the classes mention that the Iterator returned by method iterator() is *fail-fast*. This implies that if you try to modify the structure of a collection by adding or removing elements from it, *after* the Iterator is created, the Iterator will throw the exception ConcurrentModificationException. But this doesn't happen if you modify the collection by using the Iterator's own add or remove methods. This important behavior prevents collections from returning arbitrary values during concurrent access.

As we move on to the next section to discuss more interfaces (namely, Set, List, and Deque), you'll notice how each of them *might* suggest a different implementation of the methods from the Collection interface, to support the specific data structure that they represent.

4.7   *Creating and using List, Set, and Deque implementations*

[4.5]   Create and use List, Set, and Deque implementations

Each of the interfaces List, Set, and Deque model different data structures. The List interface allows null and duplicate values and retains the order of insertion of objects. Set doesn't allow addition of duplicate objects. Deque is a linear collection that supports the insertion and removal of elements at both its ends.

In the following sections, when you further explore these interfaces and their implementations, you'll notice the similarities in how each implementation is created. Let's explore the List interface and its implementations.

4.7.1   *List interface and its implementations*

The List interface models an ordered collection of objects. It returns the objects to you in the order in which you added them to a List. It allows you to store duplicate elements. Figure 4.11 shows valid example data that you'd typically store in a List.

In a List, you can control the position where you want to store an element. This is the reason that this interface defines overloaded methods to *add, remove,* and *retrieve*

List of shopping items

1. External HDD
2. iPhone5s
3. Wooden frame
4. Black ink

Sequence of pizza orders

1. Deliver XYZ to ABC.
2. Deliver ABX to YYY.
3. Deliver MM to ZZ.
4. Deliver XYZ to ABC.

Figure 4.11   Examples of data elements that you could store in a List

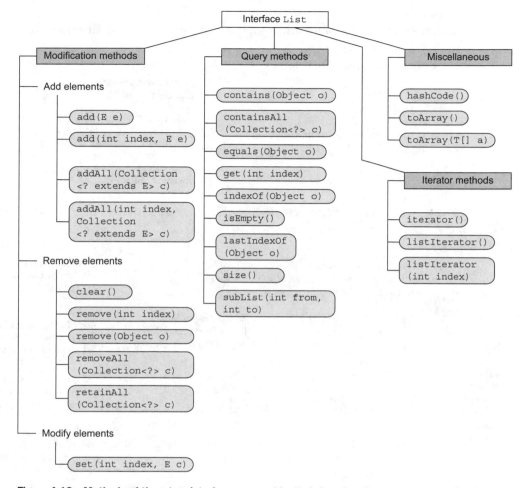

Figure 4.12   Methods of the `List` interface, grouped by their functionality

elements at a particular position. Apart from including the `iterator` method to return an `Iterator`, `List` also includes a method to return a `ListIterator`, to iterate the complete list or a part of it. Figure 4.12 shows the methods of the `List` interface, grouped by their functionality to help you to retain the information better.

In this section, I'll cover only one of the two implementations of interface `List`: `ArrayList` (shown in figure 4.13). Because the other `List` implementation, `LinkedList`, also implements the interface `Deque`, I'll cover it in the next section on `Deque`.

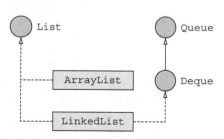

Figure 4.13   The `List` interface and its implementations (on the exam)

ARRAYLIST CLASS

An `ArrayList` is a resizable array implementation of the `List` interface. It's interesting to note that internally, an `ArrayList` uses an array to store its elements. An Array-List defines multiple constructors:

```
ArrayList()
ArrayList(Collection<? extends E> c)
ArrayList(int initialCapacity)
```

Constructs empty list with initial capacity of 10

Constructs list containing elements of specified collection, in the order they're returned by iterator

Constructs empty list with specified initial capacity

Class `ManipulateArrayList` creates an `ArrayList` and manipulates it using methods `add()`, `remove()`, `set()`, and `contains()`:

```
class ManipulateArrayList {
    public static void main(String args[]) {
        ArrayList<String> list = new ArrayList<>();

        list.add("Harry");
        list.add("Selvan");
        list.add("Harry");

        list.add(0, "Paul");

        list.remove("Harry");

        String oldValue = list.set(0, "Shreya");

        list.get(7);

        System.out.println("list contains Harry : " +
                               list.contains("Harry"));

        ListIterator<String> iterator = list.listIterator();
        while (iterator.hasNext())
            System.out.println(iterator.next());
    }
}
```

Creates ArrayList with default initial capacity of 10.

Adds String objects Harry, Selvan, and Harry; duplicate values allowed

Adds String object Paul at first position, shifting existing list elements to right

Uses equals() to find and remove first occurrence of value matching String Harry

Replaces value at position 0 with String Shreya, retrieving replaced value.

Retrieves element at position 7; throws IndexOutOfBoundsException because only three elements remain in list

contains() searches sequentially and uses equals() to find first matching occurrence

List can return multiple iterators, Iterator and ListIterator.

hasNext() returns boolean value indicating whether iterator can access more values

next() accesses and returns next value

It's interesting to note that an `ArrayList` uses the `size` variable to keep track of the number of elements inserted in it. By default, an element is added to the first available position in the array. But if you add an element to an earlier location, the rest of the list elements are shifted to the right. Similarly, if you remove an element that isn't the last element in the list, `ArrayList` shifts the elements to the left. As you add more elements to an `ArrayList` that can't be added to its existing array, it allocates a bigger array and copies its elements to the new array. An `ArrayList` maintains a record of its size, so that you can't add elements at arbitrary locations. Figure 4.14 shows how elements are added, removed, and modified in an `ArrayList`.

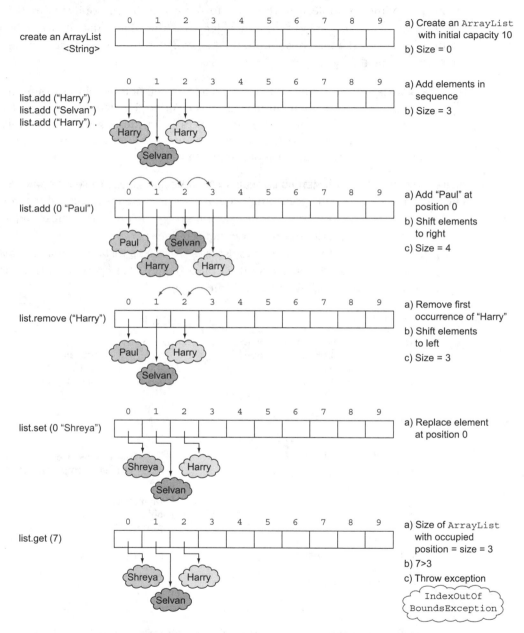

Figure 4.14 An `ArrayList` offers a resizable array. Internally, it uses an array to store its elements. It manipulates this array to add, remove, or modify `ArrayList` elements. The elements of the internal array are moved to the left or right, when elements are removed from or added to it, respectively. If the `ArrayList` exceeds the existing size of the internal array, its elements are copied to a new array with increased size.

What happens when you ask an `ArrayList` to remove an object by using method `remove(Object obj)`? It *sequentially* searches the `ArrayList` to find the target object. Have you ever wondered how the class `ArrayList` determines the equality of objects? In the preceding example, you're trying to remove a `String` object with the value `Harry`. `ArrayList` compares the target object and the object that it stores by using method `equals()`. If a match is found, the `ArrayList` removes the first occurrence of the `String` value `Harry`.

 EXAM TIP   To remove an element, an `ArrayList` first searches through its elements to find an element that can be considered equal to the target element. It does so by calling method `equals()` on the target object and its own objects, one by one. If a matching element is found, `remove(Object)` removes the *first* occurrence of the match found.

IMPORTANCE OF THE EQUALS METHOD IN FINDING AND REMOVING VALUES FROM AN ARRAYLIST

The example code in the preceding section uses `String` instances, which override method `equals()`. Let's work with an example in which the class, whose objects are stored by an `ArrayList`, doesn't override method `equals()`.

In the following example, class `UsingEquals` stores `Emp` instances in an `ArrayList`. Class `UsingEquals` tries to remove an `Emp` object from its `ArrayList` by using method `remove()`. Do you think it'll work? Here's the code:

```
class UsingEquals {
    public static void main(String args[]) {
        ArrayList<Emp> list = new ArrayList<Emp>();        Create an
        list.add(new Emp(121, "Shreya"));                  ArrayList of
        list.add(new Emp(55, "Harry"));                    Emp objects.
        list.add(new Emp(15, "Paul"));
        list.add(new Emp(121, "Shreya"));

        System.out.println(list.size());        ◁──┐  Prints "4"

        Emp emp = new Emp (121, "Shreya");
        list.remove(emp);                        ◁──┐  Tries to remove object
                                                       referred by emp from list
        System.out.println(list.size());        ◁──
    }                                            No match found; no
}                                                objects removed;
class Emp {                                       prints "4".
    int id;
    String name;
    Emp(int id, String name) {
        this.id = id;
        this.name = name;
    }
}
```

In the preceding example, no `Emp` objects were removed from `list`. This is because `Emp` doesn't define method `equals()`, so the default implementation of method `equals()` of class `Object` is used. As you already (should) know, this compares the object references for equality and not the object contents. So method `remove()` fails to find a matching object referred by `emp` in `list`. The answer is to override method `equals()` in class `Emp` (modified code in bold):

```
class Emp {
    int id;
    String name;
    Emp(int id, String name) {
        this.id = id;
        this.name = name;
    }
    public boolean equals(Object obj) {
        if (obj instanceof Emp) {
            Emp emp = (Emp)obj;
            if (emp.id == this.id && emp.name.equals(this.name))
                return true;
        }
        return false;
    }
}
```

> equals() returns true when Emp is compared with another Emp that shares same value for instance variables id and name

With the preceding definition of class `Emp`, class `UsingEquals` will be able to find and remove a matching value for the `Emp` instance referred by `emp`.

 EXAM TIP If you're adding instances of a user-defined class as elements to an `ArrayList`, override its method `equals()` or else its methods `contains()` or `remove()` might not behave as expected.

I've often observed that when people read the collection framework (which is seemingly complicated), they tend to overlook simple concepts. For example, here's one simple concept: reference variables store a reference to the object that they refer to, and they can be reassigned a new object. In the next "Twist in the Tale" exercise, let's see how this concept can be used on the exam to test you on the collection framework.

Twist in the Tale 4.3

What is the output of the following code?

```
import java.util.*;
class RemoveArrayListElements {
    public static void main(String args[]) {
        ArrayList<Integer> list = new ArrayList<>();
        Integer age1 = 20;
        Integer age2 = 20;
        list.add(age1);
        list.add(age2);
        System.out.print(list.size() + ":");
        age1 = 30;
        list.remove(age1);
        System.out.print(list.size());
    }
}
```

a   1:1

b   2:1

c   2:2

d   1:0

e   2:0

 EXAM TIP   The `ArrayList` methods `clear()`, `remove()`, and `removeAll()` offer different functionalities. `clear()` removes all the elements from an `ArrayList`. `remove(Object)` removes the first occurrence of the specified element, and `remove(int)` removes the element at the specified position. `removeAll()` removes from an `ArrayList` all of its elements that are contained in the specified collection.

The other important methods of class `ArrayList` are `get()` and `contains()`.

The other implementation of the `List` interface, `LinkedList`, also implements the `Deque` interface, covered in the next section.

4.7.2   *Deque interface and its implementations*

A *queue* is a linear collection of objects. A `Deque` is a double-ended queue, a queue that supports insertion and deletion of elements at both its ends. Let's revisit the hierarchy of the `Deque` interface, as shown in figure 4.15. The `Deque` interface extends the `Queue` interface.

As a double-ended queue, a `Deque` can work as both a *queue* and a *stack*. A queue is a linear collection of elements, in which the elements are added to one end and are processed (or taken off) from the other end. For example, in a queue of people at a

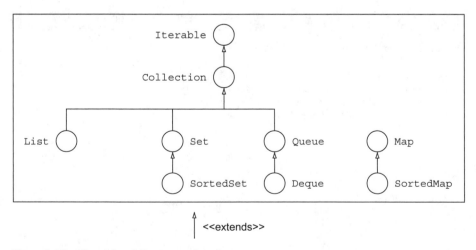

Figure 4.15   Hierarchy of the `Deque` interface

Figure 4.16　**Real-world examples of a queue and a stack**

ticket counter, new persons enter the queue at its *end*. The tickets are issued to the people at its beginning. A queue is also referred to as a first in, first out (FIFO) list.

A *stack* is a linear collection of elements that allows objects to be added and removed at the same end. For example, in a stack of plates, the plates are always added to the top and removed from the top. A stack is also referred to as a last in, first out (LIFO) list data structure. Figure 4.16 shows real-world examples of a queue and a stack.

The Deque interface defines multiple methods to add, remove, and query the existence of elements from both its ends. Because Deque works as both a *queue* and a *stack*, it's easier to get a hang of its methods if you understand the operations and corresponding methods used for queues and stacks. As I mentioned previously, in a queue, elements are typically added to its tail (or end), and taken off from its head (or beginning). Figure 4.17 shows the Queue methods (Deque extends Queue) used to add elements to the end of a queue and remove or query elements from its beginning.

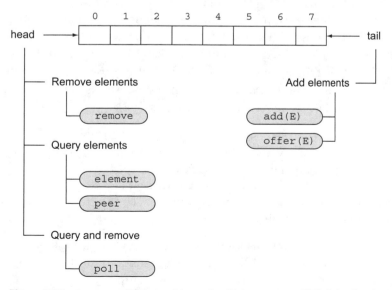

Figure 4.17　Queue **methods used to work with** Deque **as a FIFO data structure**

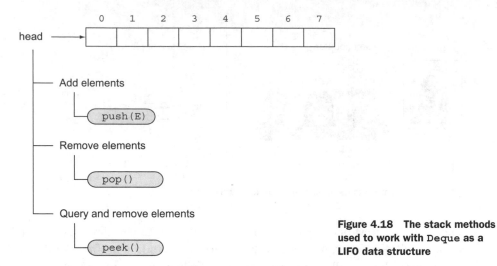

Figure 4.18 The stack methods used to work with `Deque` as a LIFO data structure

Now, let's see how a `Deque` works as a stack. In a stack, elements are added and taken off the same end of the queue: its head. Figure 4.18 shows the stack methods used to add and remove elements from its head, using `Deque` as a LIFO data structure.

For a stack, which allows insertion at only one end, the purpose of method `push()` is implicit: elements are added at (and removed from) the top. Similarly, with `Queue`, which usually enables insertion only at its tail, the purpose of method `add()` or `offer()` seems implicit: to insert elements at the tail of the list. Now, because `Deque` supports a double-linked list, supporting insertion at both its ends, method `add()` or `offer()` could be ambiguous. So `Deque` supports other methods with explicit purposes, including `addFirst()`, `addLast()`, `offerFirst()`, and `offerLast()`. So you can see multiple methods that serve the same purpose. Figure 4.19 shows the `Deque` interface, representing it as a list with a head and tail. Elements of all implementations of `Deque` might not be implemented as a contiguous list. It's just to show the beginning and end of a list. This figure shows the methods that are used to add, delete, and query methods at both ends of `Deque`. The figure also shows other methods that remove and query the `Deque` elements at random positions.

 EXAM TIP The legacy class `Stack` is used to model a LIFO list. The addition, removal, and query operations of a `Stack` are named `push()`, `pop()`, and `peek()`. Though the `Deque` interface isn't related to `Stack`, `Deque` supports a double-ended queue and can be used as a `Stack`. `Deque` also defines the methods `push()`, `pop()`, and `peek()` to add, remove, and query elements at its beginning.

Though the `Deque` implementations aren't required to prohibit the addition of `null` values, it is strongly recommended that they do because certain `Deque` implementations return `null` to signal that the underlying list is empty.

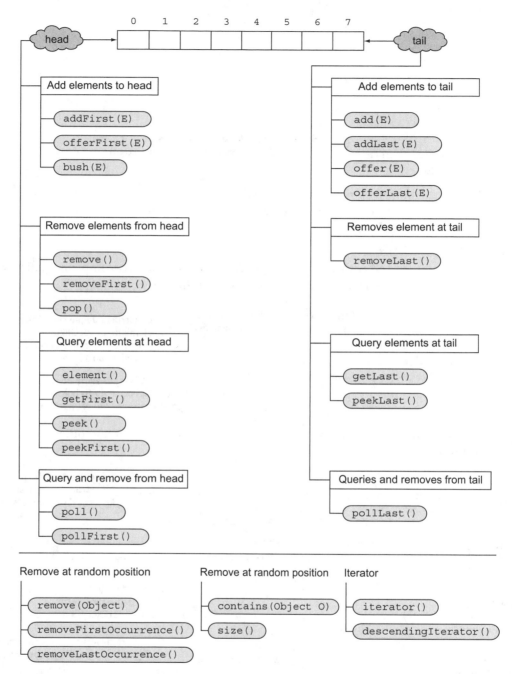

Figure 4.19 Deque methods used to add, remove, and query elements at both its ends. The figure also includes other methods, which operate at random positions.

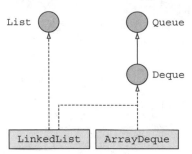

Figure 4.20   The Deque **interface and its implementations (on the exam)**

IMPLEMENTATIONS OF THE DEQUE INTERFACE

This section covers two main Deque implementations: ArrayDeque and LinkedList, as shown in figure 4.20.

CLASS ARRAYDEQUE

Let's get started with class ArrayDeque. It's a resizable array implementation of the Deque interface. Here's a list of constructors of this class:

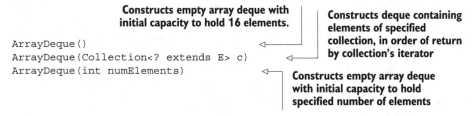

```
ArrayDeque()                           ←    Constructs empty array deque with
                                            initial capacity to hold 16 elements.
ArrayDeque(Collection<? extends E> c)  ←    Constructs deque containing
                                            elements of specified
                                            collection, in order of return
                                            by collection's iterator
ArrayDeque(int numElements)            ←    Constructs empty array deque
                                            with initial capacity to hold
                                            specified number of elements
```

Let's work with an example using the ArrayDeque constructor and other methods from this class:

```java
import java.util.*;
class TestArrayDeque {
    public static void main(String... args) {
        String strArray[] = {"A1", "B2", "C3"};

        ArrayDeque<String> arrDeque = new
                    ArrayDeque<String>(Arrays.asList(strArray));

        arrDeque.push("D4");
        arrDeque.offer("E5");

        //arrDeque.push(null);

        System.out.println(arrDeque.pop());
        System.out.println(arrDeque.remove());

        arrDeque.add("F6");
        System.out.println(arrDeque.peek());

        System.out.println(arrDeque);         #J
    }
}
```

String array → String strArray[] = {"A1", "B2", "C3"};

Creates ArrayDeque from String List; Arrays.asList converts array to List.

push() adds element at Deque beginning → arrDeque.push("D4");

offer() adds element at Deque end → arrDeque.offer("E5");

Can't add null to ArrayDeque; will throw NullPointerException.

pop() returns and removes element at Deque beginning

remove() also returns and removes element at Deque beginning

add() adds an element to end of queue

peek() queries and returns element at beginning of queue

Here's the output of the preceding code:

```
D4
A1
B2
[B2, C3, E5, F6]
```

Whenever `Deque` adds or removes an element, it modifies its pointers to the beginning and end. The take-away from the preceding code is that you need to take note of the methods that add to the beginning or end of the list. You also need to take note of methods like `peek()`, which only queries `Deque`; `remove()`, which removes elements from `Deque`; and `poll()`, which queries and removes an element from `Deque`. Method `poll()` queries and removes, and method `remove()` just removes. Method `poll()` returns `null` when `Deque` is empty and `remove()` throws a runtime exception.

 EXAM TIP All the insertion methods (`add()`, `addFirst()`, `addLast()`, `offer()`, `offerFirst()`, `offerLast()`, and `push()`) throw a `NullPointer-Exception` if you try to insert a `null` element into an `ArrayDeque`.

This is a classic example of how to implement a requirement or a recommendation in a concrete class. The `Deque` interface suggests that the implementing classes shouldn't allow `null` elements because some of its special methods return `null` to indicate that the underlying `Deque` is empty. To implement this suggestion, the methods that add elements to class `ArrayDeque` throw `NullPointerException` when you try to add a `null` element to it.

You can iterate over the elements of `Deque` by using an `Iterator`, returned by methods `iterator()` and `descendingIterator()`.

 NOTE Together with the `Deque`-specific methods discussed in this section, `ArrayDeque` also implements methods inherited from the `Collection` interface, such as `contains()`, `indexOf()`, and others.

CLASS LINKEDLIST

Class `LinkedList` implements both the `List` and `Deque` interfaces. So it's a double-linked list implementation of the `List` and `Deque` interfaces. It implements all `List` and `Deque` operations. Unlike `ArrayDeque`, it permits addition of `null` elements.

Here are the constructors of class `LinkedList`:

```
                                        Constructs     Constructs list containing elements
                                        empty list.    of specified collection, in order of
LinkedList()                    ←──────┘               return by collection's iterator
LinkedList(Collection<? extends E> c)   ←──────┘
```

So what happens when you add elements to or remove elements from a `LinkedList`? Let's work with an example:

```java
import java.util.*;
class TestLinkedList {
```

```
public static void main(String... args) {
    LinkedList<String> list = new LinkedList<String>();

    list.offer("Java");
    list.push("e");
    list.add(1, "Guru");

    System.out.println(list);

    System.out.println(list.remove("e"));

    Iterator<String> it = list.iterator();
    while(it.hasNext()) System.out.println(it.next());
}
}
```

Creates empty LinkedList of String objects.

Uses push() to add String "e" to beginning.

Uses offer() to add String "Java" to end

Uses add(1, "Guru") to insert "Guru" at position 1, adjusting references for adjacent values.

Finds and removes first matching occurrence for String object "e"

Iterates in sequential manner, from first element to last

Figure 4.21 shows how a LinkedList maintains a reference to its first and last elements. It also shows how, in the absence of using an array, each node in a LinkedList maintains a reference to its previous and next element. Whenever you add elements to or remove elements from a LinkedList, it modifies the previous and next references of its adjacent elements. As you can see, because each list element maintains a reference to its previous and next element, this list can be traversed in forward and reverse directions.

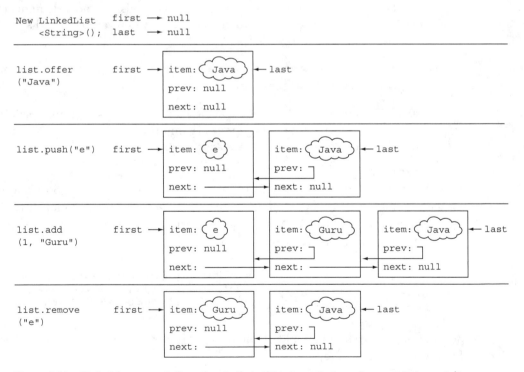

Figure 4.21   Pictorial representation of code that adds elements to and removes elements from a LinkedList

Note the difference in internal manipulation of an `ArrayList` or `ArrayDeque` and a `LinkedList`. A `LinkedList` doesn't move a set of elements when you add a new element to it. It modifies the value of the reference variables `prev` and `next`, for adjacent elements, to keep track of its sequence of elements. This is unlike `ArrayList` or `ArrayDeque`, which copy a set of array elements to the right or left, when elements are added to or removed from it.

On the exam you'll get questions to choose the most appropriate interface or class based on a given scenario. A `LinkedList` is like an `ArrayList` (ordered by index) but the elements are double-linked to each other. So besides the methods from `List`, you get a bunch of other methods to add or remove at the beginning and end of this list. So it's a good choice if you need to implement a queue or a stack. A `LinkedList` is useful when you need fast insertion or deletion, but iteration might be slower than an `ArrayList`.

 EXAM TIP Because a `LinkedList` implements `List`, `Queue`, and `Deque`, it implements methods from all these interfaces.

In the next "Twist in the Tale" exercise, let me modify the preceding code and see whether you can determine how that affects the code output. Let's see whether you still remember the inheritance concepts covered in chapter 3.

Twist in the Tale 4.4

What is the output of the following code?

```java
import java.util.*;
class TestLinkedList {
    public static void main(String... args) {
        List<String> list = new LinkedList<String>();

        list.offer("Java");
        list.push("e");
        list.add(1, "Guru");
        list.remove("e");

        System.out.println(list);
    }
}
```

 a [Guru, Java]
 b [Java, Guru]
 c [e, Guru, Java]
 d Compilation error
 e Runtime exception

Let's explore another important interface, `Set`, and its implementing classes in the following section.

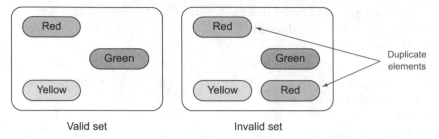

Figure 4.22 **Valid and invalid examples of** Set

4.7.3 *Set interface and its implementations*

The Set interface models the mathematical *Set* abstraction. It's a collection of objects that doesn't contain duplicate elements. Figure 4.22 shows valid and invalid examples of Set.

 EXAM TIP   The Set interface doesn't allow duplicate elements and the elements are returned in no particular order.

To determine the equality of objects, Set uses its method equals(). For two elements, say e1 and e2, if e1.equals(e2) returns true, Set doesn't add both these elements. Set defines methods to add and remove its elements. It also defines methods to query itself for the occurrence of specific objects. Because it indirectly implements the Iterable interface, it includes method iterator() to retrieve an Iterator. It also includes methods to convert it into an array. Figure 4.23 shows the methods of the Set interface, grouped for convenience.

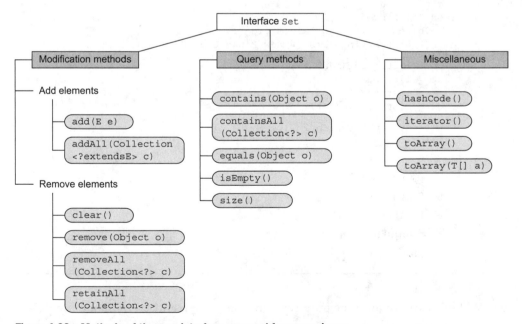

Figure 4.23 **Methods of the** Set **interface, grouped for convenience**

The exam will query you on the use of Set and its methods. For example, it may query on the appropriate scenarios for using Set or its implementation. It might include a question such as this: When you try to add duplicate String values to a Set, does it throw an exception or simply ignore the duplicate value?

The answer to these questions can vary with the implementing classes. For example, one implementation may return false if you add a duplicate String value, but another may throw an exception. Let's look at implementations of the Set interface, how they're related, and the behavior of their methods in the next section.

4.7.4 *Set implementation classes*

For the exam, we'll work on the main Set implementation classes: HashSet, LinkedHashSet, and TreeSet, as shown in figure 4.24.

CLASS HASHSET

Class HashSet implements the Set interface. As required by the Set interface, it doesn't allow duplicate elements. Also, it makes no guarantee to the order of retrieval of its elements. It's implemented using a HashMap. To store and retrieve its elements, a HashSet uses a hashing method, accessing an object's hashCode value to determine the bucket in which it should be stored.

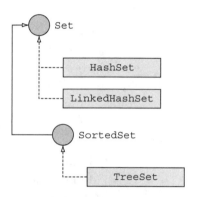

Figure 4.24 The Set interface and its implementations (on the exam)

Before I discuss HashSet further, it's important that you understand the meaning of *buckets* and importance of methods hashCode() and equals(). Let's use a simple example of a hotel—when guests leave the hotel they must leave their room key at reception. There the key is put in one big bucket. So when guests arrive they say their room number and the receptionist has to go through all the keys until he finds the matching one (compare it with method equals()). Then a new system is introduced. Instead of having one big bucket, they have some smaller buckets, each with a label (1–9). From now on they apply the same algorithm each time—when the room key is left at reception, the receptionist adds all numbers of the room and repeats this process until just 1 number is left (e.g. 236 -> 2+3+6=11 -> 1+1=2). The key is put in the bucket with that number (hashCode). When guests arrive and want their key back, they say the room number, the receptionist applies the algorithm (compare it with hashCode()), goes to the corresponding bucket, and searches for the matching room key (method equals()).

Let's see what happens when the class AddElementsToHashCode tries to add unique and duplicate objects to a HashSet:

```
class AddElementsToHashSet {
    public static void main(String args[]) {
        String str1 = new String("Harry");
        String str2 = new String("Shreya");
```

```
          String str3 = new String("Selvan");
          String str4 = new String("Shreya");
                                                          Create new
          HashSet<String> set = new HashSet<>();  ◁──┘  HashSet<String>
Add str1
 to set.  └─▷ set.add(str1);
              set.add(str2);  ◁──┘   Add str2 to set.
Add str3   ┌─▷ set.add(str3);       Duplicate String "Shreya".
 to set.   │    set.add(str4);  ◁──  Not added to set.        Prints Harry, Shreya,
                                                              and Selvan (not
                                                              always in this order).
          for (String e : set) System.out.println(e);  ◁──
      }
  }
```

In the preceding code, the string object `"Shreya"` referred by the variable `str4` isn't added to set. `HashSet` uses the `hashCode()` values of the string objects to determine the appropriate bucket to add them to. A bucket can store multiple objects. Before adding an object, `HashSet` compares its existing elements in the target bucket by using methods `hashCode()` and `equals()` to avoid duplicates being added.

A few important points about working with the preceding example code on `HashSet`:

- Method `hashCode()` doesn't call method `equals()`.
- Method `equals()` doesn't call method `hashCode()`.
- Classes should override their `hashCode()` methods efficiently to enable collection classes like `HashSet` to store them in separate buckets.

To make the concept sink in, here's the next "Twist in the Tale" exercise for you. Let's examine the role of `equals()` and `hashCode()` in storing and retrieving elements in `HashSet`.

Twist in the Tale 4.5

Given the following definition of class `Person`, which options are correct for class `Twist4_5`?

```
class Person {
    String name;
    Person(String name) { this.name = name; }
    public String toString() { return name; }
}
class Twist4_5 {
    public static void main(String args[]) {
        HashSet<Person> set = new HashSet<Person>();
        Person p1 = new Person("Harry");
        Person p2 = new Person("Shreya");
        Person p3 = new Person("Selvan");
        Person p4 = new Person("Shreya");
        set.add(p1);
        set.add(p2);
        set.add(p3);
```

```
        set.add(p4);
        for (Person e : set) System.out.println(e);
    }
}
```

a HashSet adds all fours objects, referred to by variables p1, p2, p3, and p4.

b If class Person overrides method hashCode() as follows, only p1 would be added
   to set:

```
public int hashCode() {
    return 10;
}
```

c If class Person overrides both methods hashCode() and equals() as follows,
   only p1 would be added to set:

```
public boolean equals(Object o) {
    return true;
}
public int hashCode() {
    return 10;
}
```

d If class Person overrides only method equals() as follows, only p1, p2, and p3
   will be added to set:

```
public boolean equals(Object o) {
    if (o instanceof Person) {
        return this.name.equals(((Person)o).name);
    }
    else
        return false;
}
```

The following example shows some of the methods of class HashSet in action:

```
import java.util.*;
class ManipulateHashSet {
    public static void main(String args[]) {
        List<String> list = new ArrayList<String>();      Creates and
        list.add("Shreya");                                populates ArrayList.
        list.add("Selvan");

        HashSet<String> set = new HashSet<String>();       Adds all elements from
        set.add("Harry");                                  list; no duplicate elements.
        set.addAll(list);

        System.out.println(set.contains("Shreya"));        Returns true.
        System.out.println(set.remove("Selvan"));

        for (String e : set) System.out.println(e);        Selvan is removed
    }                                                      from HashSet.
}
```

EXAM TIP   Watch out for questions that add `null` to a `HashSet`. A `HashSet` allows storing of only one `null` element. All subsequent calls to storing `null` values are ignored.

Class `HashSet` uses hashing algorithms to store, remove, and retrieve its elements. So it offers constant time performance for these operations, assuming that the hash function disperses its elements properly among its buckets. Covering writing an efficient hash function is beyond the scope of this book. You can find complete books on this topic. Efficient and faster removal, addition, and retrieval of objects have always been a requirement, and many have completed a doctorate on it.

NOTE   Access the source code of class `String` from the Java API. Examine how it overrides `hashCode()`, using its individual characters to generate its hash code.

CLASS LINKEDHASHSET

A `LinkedHashSet` offers the benefits of a `HashSet` combined with a `LinkedList`. It maintains a double-linked list running through its entries. As with a `LinkedList`, you can retrieve objects from a `LinkedHashSet` in the order of their insertion. Like a `HashSet`, a `LinkedHashSet` uses hashing to store and retrieve its elements quickly. A `LinkedHashSet` permits `null` values. `LinkedHashSet` can be used to create a copy of a `Set` with the same order as that of the original set.

In the following example code, class `UseLinkedHashSet` creates `LinkedHashSet` of `City`. It uses method `add()` to add individual `City` instances and method `addAll()` to add all objects of the specified collection:

```
class City {
    String name;
    City(String name) {
        this.name = name;
    }
    public String toString() {
        return name;
    }
}
class UseLinkedHashSet {
    public static void main(String args[]) {
        Set<City> route = new LinkedHashSet<>();

        route.add(new City("Seattle"));           Objects from LinkedAdd-
        route.add(new City("Copenhagen"));         Set can be retrieved in
        route.add(new City("NewDelhi"));           their insertion order.

        List<City> extendedRoute = new ArrayList<>();    List extends
        extendedRoute.add(new City("Beijing"));          Collection.
        extendedRoute.add(new City("Tokyo"));

        route.addAll(extendedRoute);              addAll() accepts
                                                  Collection object.
        Iterator<City> iter = route.iterator();
        while (iter.hasNext())                    Prints "false" because City
            System.out.println(iter.next());      doesn't override equals().
```

```
        System.out.println(route.contains(new City("Seattle")));
    }
}
```

The output of the preceding code is:

```
Seattle
Copenhagen
NewDelhi
Beijing
Tokyo
false
```

In the preceding code, note that addAll() accepts a Collection object. So you can add elements of an ArrayList to a LinkedHashSet. The order of insertion of objects from extendedRoute to route is determined by the order of objects returned by extendedRoute's iterator (ArrayList objects can be iterated in the order of their insertion). Because you can retrieve objects from a LinkedHashSet in the order of their insertion, iter iterates the City objects in the order of their insertion (as shown in the code output).

 EXAM TIP Watch out for exam questions that create a LinkedHashSet by using a reference variable of type List. A LinkedHashSet implements the Collection and Set interfaces, not List.

The next class on the exam is TreeSet, which uses a *binary tree* behind the scenes.

CLASS TREESET

A TreeSet stores all its unique elements in a sorted order. The elements are ordered either on their natural order (achieved by implementing the Comparable interface) or by passing a Comparator, while instantiating a TreeSet. If you fail to specify either of these, TreeSet will throw a runtime exception when you try to add an object to it.

Unlike the other Set implementations like HashSet and LinkedHashSet, which use equals() to compare objects for equality, a TreeSet uses method compareTo() (for the Comparable interface) or compare() (for the Comparator interface) to compare objects for equality and their order. As discussed in detail in the next sections on the Comparator and Comparable interfaces, the implementation of method compare() or compareTo() should be consistent with method equals() of the object instances, which are added to a TreeSet. If two object instances are *equal* according to their method equals(), but not according to their methods compare() or compareTo(), the Set can exhibit inconsistent behavior.

Constructors of class TreeSet

Constructs new, empty tree set, sorted according to specified comparator	Constructs new, empty tree set, sorted according to natural ordering of its elements	Constructs new tree set containing elements in specified collection, sorted according to natural ordering of elements

```
TreeSet()
TreeSet(Collection<? extends E> c)
TreeSet(Comparator<? super E> comparator)
TreeSet(SortedSet<E> s)
```

Constructs new tree set containing same elements and using same ordering as specified sorted set

Behind the scenes, a TreeSet uses a *Black-Red binary tree*. This tree modifies itself as you add more values to it so it has the least number of levels and the values are distributed as evenly as possible. Let's create a TreeSet, using another collection of objects:

```
class TestTreeSet {
    public static void main(String args[]) {
        String[] myNames = {"Shreya", "Harry", "Paul", "Shreya", "Selvan"};
        TreeSet<String> treeSetNames = new
                      TreeSet<String>(Arrays.asList(myNames));
        Iterator it = treeSetNames.descendingIterator();
        while (it.hasNext())
            System.out.println(it.next());
    }
}
```

TreeSet created using List of String values

descendingIterator() returns TreeSet values in descending order.

Prints "Shreya Selvan Paul Harry".

 EXAM TIP   In the absence of passing a Comparator instance to a TreeSet constructor, the objects that you add to a TreeSet must implement Comparable. In the preceding example, String (which implements Comparable) objects are added to the TreeSet. Watch out for storing objects of wrapper classes, Enum and File in a TreeSet; they all implement Comparable. The natural order of enum constants is the order in which they're declared. StringBuffer and StringBuilder don't implement Comparable.

All the collection classes include constructors to use another collection object to instantiate itself. But depending on how it's implemented, it might not include all the elements from the collection passed to its constructor.

A List allows the addition of duplicate elements, but a Set doesn't. In the preceding example, when you create a TreeSet using a List, which contains duplicate elements, one of the duplicate elements is dropped from the TreeSet. TreeSet also includes iterators to iterate over its values in ascending or descending order.

4.8   *Map and its implementations*

 [4.6]   Create and use Map implementations

Unlike the other interfaces from the collections framework, like List and Set, the Map interface doesn't extend the Collection interface. In this section, you'll work with Map and SortedMap interfaces and their implementations like HashMap, Linked-HashMap, and TreeMap.

4.8.1   *Map interface*

Imagine locking or unlocking the door of your home using a key. This key allows you to restrict access to your home to a key holder. You can compare a Map with a pool of keys, mapped to the values that they can unlock. A key can map to a 0 or a 1 value.

A `Map` doesn't allow the addition of duplicate keys. Items added to a `Map` aren't ordered. The retrieval order of items from a `Map` object isn't guaranteed to be the same as its insertion order. The `Map` interface declares methods to add or delete a key-value pair or query the existence of a key or value. It also defines methods to retrieve the set of keys, values, and key-value pairs.

 EXAM TIP `Map` objects don't allow the addition of duplicate keys.

The addition of a `null` value as a key or value depends on a particular `Map` implementation. For example, `HashMap` and `LinkedHashMap` allow the insertion of `null` as a key, but `TreeMap` doesn't—it throws an exception.

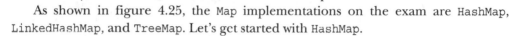

Figure 4.25   The `Map` interface and its implementations (on the exam)

As shown in figure 4.25, the `Map` implementations on the exam are `HashMap`, `LinkedHashMap`, and `TreeMap`. Let's get started with `HashMap`.

4.8.2   HashMap

A `HashMap` is a hash-based `Map` that uses the hash value of its key (returned by `hashCode()`) to store and retrieve keys and their corresponding values. Each key can refer to a 0 or 1 value. The keys of a `HashMap` aren't ordered. The `HashMap` methods aren't synchronized, so they aren't safe to be used in a multithreaded environment.

 EXAM TIP The keys of a `HashMap` aren't ordered. The `HashMap` methods aren't synchronized, so they aren't safe to be used in a multithreaded environment.

CREATING A HASHMAP AND ADDING VALUES TO IT

Let's create a `HashMap` that stores employee names as keys and their salaries as the corresponding values. The following code creates a `HashMap` with a default initial capacity and adds values to it using method `put(Object key, Object value)`:

```
Map<String, Double> salaryMap = new HashMap<>();
salaryMap.put("Paul", 8888.8);
salaryMap.put("Shreya", 99999.9);
salaryMap.put("Selvan", 5555.5);
```

`HashMap` defines another constructor (declaration shown below), which accepts a `Map` object:

```
HashMap(Map<? extends K,? extends V> m)
```

You can use the preceding constructor to create a `HashMap` by passing it another `Map` instance:

```
Map<String, Double> salaryMap = new HashMap<>();
Map<String, Object> copySalaryMap = new HashMap<>(salaryMap);
```

The exam might question you on whether the addition or removal of key-value pairs to and from salaryMap will reflect in copySalaryMap. The following example shows that when you delete a key-value pair from salaryMap, it's *not* removed from copy-SalaryMap:

```
Map<String, Double> salaryMap = new HashMap<>();
salaryMap.put("Paul", 8888.8);
salaryMap.put("Shreya", 99999.9);
Map<String, Object> copySalaryMap = new HashMap(salaryMap);
```
◁── Create copy-SalaryMap using salaryMap.

```
Set<String> keys = copySalaryMap.keySet();
for (String k : keys)
    System.out.println(k);
```
◁── Outputs two key values.

```
salaryMap.remove("Paul");
```
◁── Remove a key-value pair from salaryMap.

```
keys = copySalaryMap.keySet();
for (String k : keys)
    System.out.println(k);
```
◁── Still outputs two key values.

 EXAM TIP You can create a HashMap by passing its constructor another Map object. Additions of new key-value pairs or deletions of existing key-value pairs in the Map object passed to the constructor aren't reflected in the newly created HashMap.

On the exam watch out for the type of the key and value used by the Map object that you pass to the HashMap constructor. The following code won't compile:

```
Map<String, Double> salaryMap = new HashMap<>();
Map<Object, String> copySalaryMap = new HashMap<>(salaryMap);
```
◁── **Won't compile**

Because a HashMap stores objects as its keys and values, it's common to see code that stores another collection object (like an ArrayList) as a value in a Map (on the exam). For example

```
Map<String, List<Double>> salaryMap = new HashMap<>();
```

When working with generics, note how the type parameters are passed to constructors. You can replace the preceding code with the following:

```
Map<String, List<Double>> salaryMap = new HashMap<String, List<Double>>();
```

But the following are invalid instantiations:

```
Map<String, List<Double>> salaryMap = new HashMap<<>, List<>>();
Map<String, List<Double>> salaryMap = new HashMap<String, List<>>();
Map<String, List<Double>> salaryMap =
                    new HashMap<String, ArrayList<Double>>();
```
Won't compile

RETRIEVING KEYS AND VALUES

You can call method get() on a HashMap to retrieve the value for a key. For example

```
enum IceCream {CHOCOLATE, STRAWBERRY, WALNUT};

Map<String, List<IceCream>> iceCreamMap = new HashMap<>();

List<IceCream> iceCreamLst = new ArrayList<>();
iceCreamLst.add(IceCream.WALNUT);
iceCreamLst.add(IceCream.CHOCOLATE);

iceCreamMap.put("Shreya", iceCreamLst);
System.out.println(iceCreamMap.get("Shreya"));
```
⟵┘ **Prints "[WALNUT, CHOCOLATE]"**

On the exam, you might see a code snippet similar to the preceding code, with a difference in type arguments passed to the initialization of HashMap. The following code compiles without any warning:

```
Map<String, List> iceCreamMap = new HashMap<>();
```

Methods containsKey() and containsValue() check for the existence of a key or a value in a Map, returning a boolean value. Methods get() and containsKey() rely on appropriate overriding of key's hashCode() and equals() methods (discussed in detail in the previous section on HashSet). In the following example, class Emp doesn't override these methods. Do you think method get() will work as expected?

```
class Emp {
    String name;
    String name) {
        this.name = name;
    }
}
Map<Emp, Emp> empMgrMap = new HashMap<>();
empMgrMap.put(new Emp("Shreya"), new Emp("Selvan"));
System.out.println(empMgrMap.get(new Emp("Shreya")));
```
⟵┘ **Prints "null"**

The preceding code outputs null.

 EXAM TIP The String class and all the wrapper classes override their hashCode() and equals() methods. So they can be correctly used as keys in a HashMap.

Let's see how overriding methods hashCode() and equals() helps. Here's the modified code, in which class Emp overrides methods hashCode() and equals():

```
class Emp {
    String name;
    Emp(String name) {
        this.name = name;
    }
    public int hashCode() {
        return name.hashCode();
    }
```

```
        public boolean equals(Object o) {
            if (o instanceof Emp)
                return ((Emp)o).name.equals(name);
            else
                return false;
        }
    }
    class Test {
        public static void main(String args[]) {
            Map<Emp, Emp> empMgrMap = new HashMap<>();
            empMgrMap.put(new Emp("Shreya"), new Emp("Selvan"));
            System.out.println(empMgrMap.get(new Emp("Shreya")));
        }
    }
```

> **EXAM TIP** HashMap uses hashing functions to add or retrieve key-value
> pairs. The key must override both methods equals() and hashCode() so
> that it can be added to a HashMap and retrieved from it.

Do you think methods containsKey() and containsValue() will work as expected, if
class Emp overrides only method equals() and not method hashCode()? Here's the
modified code (Emp doesn't override hashCode()):

```
    class Emp {
        String name;
        Emp(String name) {
            this.name = name;
        }
        public boolean equals(Object o) {
            if (o instanceof Emp)
                return ((Emp)o).name.equals(name);
            else
                return false;
        }
    }
    class Test {
        public static void main(String args[]) {
            Map<Emp, Emp> empMgrMap = new HashMap<>();
            empMgrMap.put(new Emp("Shreya"), new Emp("Selvan"));
            System.out.println(empMgrMap.containsKey(new Emp("Shreya")));      Prints "false"
            System.out.println(empMgrMap.containsValue(new Emp("Selvan")));
        }
    }
```

Prints "true"

Class Emp in the preceding example overrides method equals() and not method
hashCode(). Because method containsKey() uses both methods hashCode() and
equals() to determine the equality of keys, the code at ❶ outputs false. Because
method containsValue() uses method equals() and not method hashCode() to
determine the equality of HashMap values, the code at ❷ outputs true.

> **EXAM TIP** When objects of a class that only overrides method equals()
> and not method hashCode() are used as keys in a HashMap, contains-
> Key() will always return false.

ADDING DUPLICATE OR NULL KEYS

What happens if you add a duplicate key to a `HashMap`? Will the method call be ignored or will its new value replace the key's previous value? The latter is true. At the end of execution of the following code, `salaryMap` will store `99999.9` as the value for key `"Paul"`.

```
Map<String, Double> salaryMap = new HashMap<>();
salaryMap.put("Paul", 8888.8);
salaryMap.put("Paul", 99999.9);
```

 EXAM TIP If you add a key-value pair to a `HashMap` such that the key already exists in the `HashMap`, the key's old value will be replaced with the new value.

Do you think you can add a key-value pair to a `HashMap` with `null` as the key? The `HashMap` allows the addition of a maximum of one `null` key. For example

```
Map<String, Double> salaryMap = new HashMap<>();
salaryMap.put(null, 88.8);
salaryMap.put(null, 99.9);
System.out.println(salaryMap.get(null));        Prints
String s = null;                                 "99.9"
salaryMap.put(null, 77.7);                       Prints
System.out.println(salaryMap.get(s));            "77.7"
```

 EXAM TIP You can add a value with `null` as the key in a `HashMap`.

REMOVING HASHMAP ENTRIES

You can use method `remove(key)` or `clear()` to remove one or all key-value pairs of a `Map`. Method `remove()` removes the mapping for the specified key from a `Map` if it is present. It returns the value associated with the key, or `null` if the key doesn't exist in the map. Method `remove()` is simple to work with. For example

```
Map<String, Double> salaryMap = new HashMap<>();
salaryMap.put("Paul", 88.8);                       Removes Paul, 88.8
System.out.println(salaryMap.remove("Paul"));      pair and prints "88.8".
```

 EXAM TIP Method `remove()` can return a `null` value, irrespective of whether the specified key exists in a `HashMap`. It might return `null` if a matching key isn't present in `HashMap`, or if `null` is stored as a value for the specified key.

What happens if you try to remove a key-value pair from a `HashMap` that uses `List` as a key? Here's an example:

```
Map<List, String> flavorNameMap = new HashMap<>();

List<IceCream> iceCreamLst = new ArrayList<>();
iceCreamLst.add(IceCream.WALNUT);
iceCreamLst.add(IceCream.CHOCOLATE);
```

```
flavorNameMap.put(iceCreamLst, "Shreya");

List<IceCream> iceCreamLst2 = new ArrayList<>();
iceCreamLst2.add(IceCream.WALNUT);
iceCreamLst2.add(IceCream.CHOCOLATE);

System.out.println(flavorNameMap.remove(iceCreamLst2));    ◁─┐
```

Matches key referred by iceCreamLst and removes value "Shreya".

Because the size and order of elements in lists `iceCreamLst` and `iceCreamLst2` are the same, they're considered equal by their `equals()` methods. The `ArrayList` also overrides its `hashCode()`, returning the same hash-code values for equal lists. This enables method `remove()` to find the specified list and remove its corresponding values.

 EXAM TIP   For a `HashMap`, methods that query or search a key use the key's methods `hashCode()` and `equals()`.

Method `clear()` doesn't accept any method arguments and returns `void`. At the end of execution of the following code, `salaryMap` wouldn't have any key-value pairs:

```
Map<String, Double> salaryMap = new HashMap<>();
salaryMap.put("Paul", 88.8);
salaryMap.put("Shreya", 88.8);
salaryMap.clear();
```

 EXAM TIP   Method `remove()` removes a maximum of one key-value pair from a `HashMap`. Method `clear()` clears *all* the entries of a `HashMap`. Method `remove()` accepts a method parameter but `clear()` doesn't.

DETERMINING THE SIZE OF HASHMAP

You can use methods `size()` and `isEmpty()` to query a `HashMap`'s size. Method `size()` returns an `int` value representing the count of key-value mappings in a `HashMap`. Method `isEmpty()` returns a boolean value—`true` represents a `HashMap` with no key-value mappings.

COPYING ANOTHER MAP OBJECT

You can use method `putAll()` to copy all the mappings from the specified map to a `HashMap`. What happens if the source and target `HashMap` have the same keys? If the map reference passed to `putAll()` defines keys that already exist in this map, then the values in this map are replaced. For example

```
Map<Integer, String> map = new HashMap<>();
map.put(1, "Shreya");
map.put(11, "Paul");

Map<Integer, String> anotherMap = new HashMap<>();
anotherMap.put(1, "Harry");

anotherMap.putAll(map);    ◁─┤
```

For Integer value 1, anotherMap has value "Shreya".

EXAM TIP   Method putAll() accepts an argument of type Map. It copies all the mappings from the specified map to the map that calls putAll(). For common keys, the values of the map that calls putAll() are replaced with the values of the Map object passed to the putAll() method.

RETRIEVING KEYS, VALUES, AND KEY-VALUE PAIRS

The Map interface defines methods keySet(), values(), and entrySet() to access keys, values, and key-value pairs of a Map. The following example shows these methods in action:

```
enum Color {RED, BLUE, YELLOW};

Map<Color, String> colorMap = new HashMap<>();
colorMap.put(Color.RED, "Passion");
colorMap.put(Color.BLUE, "Stability");
colorMap.put(Color.YELLOW, "Energy");

Collection<String> mood = colorMap.values();
Set<Color> colors = colorMap.keySet();
Set<Map.Entry<Color, String>> colorsMood = colorMap.entrySet();

for (String s : mood)
    System.out.println(s);

for (Color c : colors)
    System.out.println(c);

for (Map.Entry pair : colorsMood)
    System.out.println(pair.getKey() + ":" + pair.getValue());
```

Because the order of iteration of a HashMap might change, the following is one of the probable outputs of the preceding code:

```
Passion
Energy
Stability
RED
YELLOW
BLUE
RED:Passion
YELLOW:Energy
BLUE:Stability
```

 EXAM TIP   Method values() returns a Collection object, method keySet() returns a Set object, and method entrySet() returns a Map.Entry object.

Class HashTable legacy code

Class HashTable wasn't a part of the collections framework initially. It was retrofitted to implement the Map interface in Java 2, making it a member of the Java Collection framework. But it's considered legacy code. It's roughly equivalent to a HashMap, with some differences. The operations of a HashMap aren't synchronized, whereas the operations of a HashTable are synchronized. But if you need to work with a HashMap in a multithreaded environment (which needs synchronized methods), you can use class ConcurrentHashMap (covered in chapter 11).

Unlike a HashMap, a HashTable doesn't allow the addition of null keys or values.

4.8.3   *LinkedHashMap*

The LinkedHashMap IS-A HashMap with a predictable iteration order. Like a Linked-List (covered previously in this chapter), a LinkedHashMap maintains a double-linked list that runs through all its entries. This linked list is used to retrieve the LinkedHashMap elements in the order they were inserted. Like a HashMap, the methods of a LinkedHashMap aren't synchronized.

The following example shows that (unlike a HashMap) a LinkedHashMap would always iterate over its elements in their order of insertion:

```
Map<String, Integer> colorMap = new HashMap<>();
colorMap.put("Red", 1);
colorMap.put("Blue", 2);
colorMap.put("Yellow", 3);
colorMap.put("Purple", 4);
colorMap.put("Orange", 5);

for (Integer i : colorMap.values())          Iteration order of map elements
    System.out.print(i);                     can vary with each execution

System.out.println("");

Map<String, Integer> linkedColorMap = new LinkedHashMap<>();
linkedColorMap.put("Red", 1);
linkedColorMap.put("Blue", 2);
linkedColorMap.put("Yellow", 3);
linkedColorMap.put("Purple", 4);
linkedColorMap.put("Orange", 5);

for (Integer i : linkedColorMap.values())          Prints "12345"
    System.out.print(i);
```

Here's a probable output of the code:

```
21345
12345
```

 NOTE   Methods to add, retrieve, remove, or query the elements of a LinkedHashMap work in a similar manner as discussed in the previous section on HashMap.

4.8.4 TreeMap

A `TreeMap` is sorted according to the natural ordering of its keys or as defined by a `Comparator` passed to its constructor. It implements the `SortedMap` interface. Like `HashMap` and `LinkedHashMap`, the operations of a `TreeMap` aren't synchronized, which makes it unsafe to be used in a multithreaded environment.

 NOTE The `Comparable` and `Comparator` interfaces are discussed in detail in the next section.

Because the key-value pairs of a `TreeMap` are always sorted, querying a `TreeMap` (using methods `containsKey()` and `get()`) is faster in comparison to querying keys of other unsorted implementations of the `Map` interface.

In one of the previous sections, you learned how `HashMap` uses methods `hashCode()` and `equals()` of its key to add, remove, or query it. But `TreeMap` performs all key comparisons by using method `compareTo()` or `compare()` of its keys. Two keys are considered equal by a `TreeMap` if the key's method `compareTo()` or `compare()` considers them equal.

Let's get started by creating some `TreeMap` objects.

CREATING TREEMAP OBJECTS

When you create a `TreeMap` object, you should specify how its keys should be ordered. A key might define its natural ordering by implementing the `Comparable` interface. If it doesn't you should pass a `Comparator` object to specify the key's sort order.

Because this is an important point to note for the exam, I'll cover multiple scenarios here. Let's start with instantiating a `TreeMap`, which uses enum objects as its keys (enums define their natural order by implementing the `Comparable` interface):

```
enum IceCream {STRAWBERRY, CHOCOLATE, WALNUT};

Map<IceCream, String> flavorMap = new TreeMap<>();     ◁──┐  Natural order of enums
flavorMap.put(IceCream.CHOCOLATE, "Paul");                │  is their sequence of
flavorMap.put(IceCream.STRAWBERRY, "Shreya");             │  declaration

for (String s : flavorMap.values())
    System.out.println(s);
```

The output of the preceding code is:

```
Shreya
Paul
```

In the preceding output, note that `IceCream.STRAWBERRY` precedes `IceCream.CHOCOLATE`. The natural order of enum elements is the sequence in which they're defined. The set of *values* that you retrieve from a `TreeMap` is sorted on its *keys* and not on its *values*.

 EXAM TIP The natural order of enum elements is the sequence in which they're defined. The set of *values* that you retrieve from a `TreeMap` is sorted on its *keys* and not on its *values*.

All the wrapper classes and `String` class implement the `Comparable` interface, so you can use their objects as `TreeMap` keys. Let's see what happens when you use objects of a user-defined class, say, `Flavor`, which doesn't define its natural sort order, as keys to `TreeMap`:

```
class Flavor {
    String name;
    Flavor(String name) {
        this.name = name;
    }
}
class CreateTreeMap {
    public static void main(String args[]) {
        Map<Flavor, String> flavorMap = new TreeMap<>();
        flavorMap.put(new Flavor("Chocolate"), "Paul");
    }
}
```

Flavor class doesn't implement Comparable.

TreeMap instantiation doesn't throw an exception.

Throws Class-CastException.

In the preceding code, note that you can instantiate a `TreeMap` by neither passing it a `Comparator` object, nor using keys that implement the `Comparable` interface. But an attempt to add a key-value pair to such a `TreeMap` will throw a runtime exception.

 EXAM TIP You can create a `TreeMap` without passing it a `Comparator` object or without using keys that implement the `Comparable` interface. But adding a key-value pair to such a `TreeMap` will throw a runtime exception, `ClassCastException`.

Now, what happens if the keys used in a `TreeMap` define a natural order and a `Comparator` object is also passed to a `TreeMap` constructor? What happens if the natural order of the keys doesn't match with the order defined by the `Comparator` object? Or, is the natural order of keys ignored if a `Comparator` object is passed to a `TreeMap` object? Let's answer these questions using the next example:

```
class Flavor implements Comparable<Flavor> {
    String name;
    Flavor(String name) {
        this.name = name;
    }
    public int compareTo(Flavor f) {
        return this.name.compareTo(f.name);
    }
}

class MyComparator implements Comparator<Flavor> {
    public int compare(Flavor f1, Flavor f2) {
        return f2.name.compareTo(f1.name);
    }
}

class CreateTreeMap {
    public static void main(String args[]) {
        Map<Flavor,String> flavorMap = new TreeMap<>(new MyComparator());
```

Natural order of Flavor instances is alphabetical order of its names.

MyComparator orders Flavor instances in reverse alphabetical order of its names.

TreeMap creation

```
        flavorMap.put(new Flavor("Chocolate"), "Paul");
        flavorMap.put(new Flavor("Vanilla"), "Selvan");

        for (Flavor flavor : flavorMap.keySet())
            System.out.println(flavor.name);
    }
}
```

The output of the preceding code is:

```
Vanilla
Chocolate
```

The preceding code shows that when you pass a `Comparator` object to a `TreeMap` constructor, the natural order of its keys is ignored.

 EXAM TIP   When you pass a `Comparator` object to a `TreeMap` constructor, the natural order of its keys is ignored.

Class `TreeMap` implements the `SortedMap` interface. Watch out for similar code on the exam that tries to instantiate a `SortedMap`. It won't compile. For example

```
Map<String, String> map = new SortedMap<String, String>();   ⟵——— Won't compile
```

COMPARING KEYS: TREEMAP VERSUS HASHMAP

Unlike a `HashMap`, a `TreeMap` uses method `compare()` or `compareTo()` to determine the equality of its keys. In the following example, a `TreeMap` can access the value associated with a key, even though its key doesn't override its method `equals()` or `hashCode()`:

```
class Flavor implements Comparable<Flavor> {
    String name;
    Flavor(String name) {
        this.name = name;
    }
    public int compareTo(Flavor f) {
        return this.name.compareTo(f.name);
    }
}
class CreateTreeMap {
    public static void main(String args[]) {
        Map<Flavor, String> flavorMap = new TreeMap<>();
        flavorMap.put(new Flavor("Chocolate"), "Paul");
        flavorMap.put(new Flavor("Apple"), "Harry");                    ⎤ Prints
        System.out.println(flavorMap.get(new Flavor("Apple")));  ⟵——⎦ "Harry"
    }
}
```

In this section on `TreeMap`, you learned how user-defined classes can use the `Comparable` and `Comparator` interfaces to define a natural or custom order of objects. The next section covers these interfaces in detail.

4.9   *Using java.util.Comparator and java.lang.Comparable*

 [4.7]   Use java.util.Comparator and java.lang.Comparable

Until now, you have used method `equals()` to compare objects for equality. But when it comes to sorting a collection of objects, you must also compare objects to determine whether an object is less than or greater than another object. To do so, you can use two interfaces: `java.lang.Comparable` and `java.util.Comparator`.

4.9.1   *Comparable interface*

The `Comparable` interface is used to define the *natural order* of the objects of the class that implements it. It is a generic interface (using `T` as type parameter) and defines only one method, `compareTo(T object)`, which compares the object to the object passed to it as a method parameter. It returns a negative integer, zero, or a positive integer if this object is less than, equal to, or greater than the specified object. Here's the definition of the `Comparable` interface:

```
package java.lang;
public interface Comparable<T> {        ⟵┐   Generic
    public int compareTo(T o);               │   interface
}
```

Here's an example of class `Person` that implements the `Comparable` interface:

```
class Person implements Comparable<Person> {
    String name;
    int age;
                                            ┌   Person constructor
    Person (String name, int age) {   ⟵──┘   accepts name and age.
        this.name = name;
        this.age = age;
    }
    public int compareTo(Person person) {    │   Natural order of instances of Person
        return (this.age-person.age);        │   is based on int value of its age
    }
    public String toString() {     │  Overridden toString()
        return name;               │  to return name
    }
}
```

 EXAM TIP   The `Comparable` interface is used to define the *natural order* of the objects of the class that implements it.

Some collection classes, like `TreeSet` and `TreeMap`, store their elements in a sorted order. You can specify the sort order of the elements by making their class implement the `Comparable` interface. Here's an example in which `TreeSet` stores instances of class `Person`, which implements `Comparable`:

```
class TestComparable {
    public static void main(String args[]) {
        TreeSet<Person> set = new TreeSet<>();
```

```
        set.add(new Person("Shreya", 12));
        set.add(new Person("Harry", 40));
        set.add(new Person("Paul", 30));

        Iterator<Person> iterator = set.iterator();
        while(iterator.hasNext()) {
            System.out.println(iterator.next());
        }
    }
}
```

The TreeSet values are returned in ascending order of age of class Person. Here's the output of the preceding code:

```
Shreya
Paul
Harry
```

 EXAM TIP Method compareTo() returns a negative integer, zero, or a positive integer if this object is less than, equal to, or greater than the specified object.

It's important to note that the implementation of method compareTo() should be consistent with the implementation of method equals(). This rule is recommended, but not required.

For any two object instances a and b, if a.compareTo(b) returns a value 0, then a.equals(b) should return true. Let's see what happens if we implement compareTo() in an inconsistent manner in class Person and add its instances to a TreeSet (changes in bold):

```
class Person implements Comparable<Person> {
    String name;
    int age;

    Person (String name, int age) {
        this.name = name;
        this.age = age;
    }
    public int compareTo(Person person) {        │ compareTo
        return 0;                                 │ returns 0.
    }
    public String toString() {
        return name;
    }
}
class TestComparable {
    public static void main(String args[]) {
        TreeSet<Person> set = new TreeSet<>();

        Person p1 = new Person("Shreya", 12);
        Person p2 = new Person("Harry", 40);
        Person p3 = new Person("Paul", 30);
```

```
        set.add(p1);
        set.add(p2);         p2 and p3 aren't added to set because
        set.add(p3);         Set doesn't allow duplicate values.

        Iterator<Person> iterator = set.iterator();
        while(iterator.hasNext()) {                        Prints only one
            System.out.println(iterator.next());    ←──┘  value, Shreya.
        }
    }
}
```

Classes like `TreeSet` and `TreeMap` store their elements in a sorted order. Before `set` adds the second element, `p2`, it compares it to the existing element, `p1`. Because `p1.compareTo(p2)` returns 0, `set` doesn't add the *duplicate element* and returns `false`. The same steps are repeated when `set` tries to add `p3`. At the end, only one element, `p1`, is added to `set`.

> **QUICK EXERCISE**   Modify method `compareTo()` in the preceding example so that `TreeSet` returns the values in descending order of `Person`'s age.

What if you want to sort the elements of class `Person` based on its instance variable, name? Also, can you do this if you can't modify the source code of class `Person`? Yes, it's possible by using the `Comparator` interface, as discussed in the next section.

4.9.2   *Comparator interface*

The `Comparator` interface is used to define the *sort order* of a collection of objects, without requiring them to implement this interface. This interface defines methods `compare()` and `equals()`. You can pass `Comparator` to sort methods like `Arrays.sort` and `Collections.sort`. It's also passed to collection classes like `TreeSet` and `TreeMap` that require ordered elements.

The `Comparator` interface is used to specify the sort order for classes that

- Don't define a natural sort order
- Need to work with an alternate sort order
- Don't allow modification to their source code so that natural ordering can be added to them

 EXAM TIP   Unlike the `Comparable` interface, the class whose objects are being compared need not implement the `Comparator` interface.

Here's the source code for this interface:

```
package java.util;
public interface Comparator<T> {
    int compare(T o1, T o2);
    boolean equals(Object obj);
}
```

Like the `Comparable` interface, method `compare()` in `Comparator` returns a negative integer, zero, or a positive integer if o1 is less than, equal to, or greater than o2. Let's modify the example used in the preceding section to use `Comparator` instead of `Comparable`:

```java
import java.util.*;
class TestComparator {
    public static void main(String args[]) {
        TreeSet<Person> set = new TreeSet<>(
            new Comparator<Person>(){
                public int compare(Person p1, Person p2) {
                    return (p1.age-p2.age);
                }
            }
        );
        set.add(new Person("Shreya", 12));
        set.add( new Person("Harry", 40));
        set.add(new Person("Paul", 30));

        Iterator<Person> iterator = set.iterator();
        while(iterator.hasNext()) {
            System.out.println(iterator.next());
        }
    }
}

class Person {
    String name;
    int age;
    Person (String name, int age) {
        this.name = name;
        this.age = age;
    }
    public String toString() {
        return name;
    }
}
```

Class `TreeSet` is passed an anonymous inner class.

Class `Person` doesn't implement the `Comparator` interface.

The output of the preceding code is:

```
Shreya
Paul
Harry
```

As you noticed, class `Person` no longer needs to implement `Comparable`. Class `TreeSet` accepts `Comparator` to define the sort order of its elements. What happens if class `Person` implements the `Comparable` interface, which sorts it on `name`, and the `Comparator` interface sorts it on `age`? What do you think is the output of the code in the next "Twist in the Tale" exercise?

Twist in the Tale 4.6

What is the output of the following class?

```java
class Twist4_6 {
    public static void main(String args[]) {
        TreeSet<Person> set = new TreeSet<>(new Comparator<Person>(){
            public int compare(Person p1, Person p2) {
                return (p1.age-p2.age);
            }
        });
        Person p1 = new Person("Shreya", 12);
        Person p2 = new Person("Harry", 40);
        Person p3 = new Person("Paul", 30);
        set.add(p1);
        set.add(p2);
        set.add(p3);
        Iterator<Person> iterator = set.iterator();
        while(iterator.hasNext()) {
            System.out.print(iterator.next()+":");
        }
    }
}
class Person implements Comparable<Person>{
    String name;
    int age;
    Person (String name, int age) {
        this.name = name;
        this.age = age;
    }
    public int compareTo(Person person) {
        return name.compareTo(person.name);
    }
    public String toString() { return name; }
}
```

  a   Shreya:Paul:Harry:

  b   Harry:Paul:Shreya:

  c   Paul:Shreya:Harry:

  d   Harry:Shreya:Paul:

Like the `Comparable` interface, the implementation of method `compare()` in `Comparator` should be consistent with the implementation of method `equals()`. For any two object instances a and b, if `compare(a, b)` returns a value 0, then `a.equals(b)` should return `true`.

In the next section, let's see why you need sorted data and how to use `Comparable` and `Comparator` to sort and search arrays and lists.

4.10 Sorting and searching arrays and lists

[4.8] Sort and search arrays and lists

How do you view the list of names in a phone directory or the list of selected candidates for admission to a university? Usually, these lists are sorted on their names or on their registration numbers (for university students). Do you think it's easier and faster to find a particular name or a candidate in a sorted list? Yes, it is.

You might need data in a sorted order for multiple reasons: to display information in an ascending or descending order, or to search for particular data. Searching data is always faster in a sorted list. Searching an unsorted list requires comparing *all* list elements with the target element, resulting in a time- and processing-intensive task. In today's world, when we're overwhelmed with data, fast searching and retrieval of data is crucial.

For the exam, you need to know how to search and sort arrays and `List` by using the existing methods from the collections framework classes, `Arrays` and `Collections` to be specific. The OCP Java SE 7 Programmer II exam won't ask you to create or write your own sorting methods. Let's get started with the sorting methods that are accessible using classes `Arrays` and `Collections`.

4.10.1 Sorting arrays

The class `Arrays` in the collections framework defines multiple methods to sort arrays of primitive data types and objects. You can use these methods to sort either a complete array or a part of it. Table 4.3 lists the sorting methods for arrays of `byte`, `int`, and `Object`. The class `Arrays` defines similar methods for other primitive data types: `char`, `short`, `long`, `float`, and `double`. *Please note that I've deliberately excluded them from this list to keep the table short.*

Table 4.3 Class `Arrays` defines sort methods for arrays of `Object` and all primitive data types (excluding type `boolean`)

Method name	Method description
static void sort(byte[] a)	Sorts the specified array into ascending numerical order
static void sort(byte[] a, int fromIndex, int toIndex)	Sorts the specified range of the array into ascending order
static void sort(int[] a)	Sorts the specified array into ascending numerical order
static void sort(int[] a, int fromIndex, int toIndex)	Sorts the specified range of the array into ascending order
static void sort(Object[] a)	Sorts the specified array of objects into ascending order, according to the natural ordering of its elements

Table 4.3   Class `Arrays` defines sort methods for arrays of `Object` and all primitive data types (excluding type `boolean`) (continued)

Method name	Method description
`static void sort(Object[] a, int fromIndex, int toIndex)`	Sorts the specified range of the specified array of objects into ascending order, according to the natural ordering of its elements
`static <T> void sort(T[] a, Comparator<? super T> c)`	Sorts the specified array of objects according to the order induced by the specified comparator
`static <T> void sort(T[] a, int fromIndex, int toIndex, Comparator<? super T> c)`	Sorts the specified range of the specified array of objects according to the order induced by the specified comparator

 EXAM TIP   All the methods in table 4.3 that sort a partial array accept `fromIndex` and `toIndex` values. The element stored at position `from-Index` is sorted, but the element stored at position `toIndex` isn't.

Let's look at a simple example of sorting an `int` array:

```
class SortArrays {
    public static void main(String args[]) {
        int[] intArray = {20, 14, 4, 10, 5, 3};          int array with
        for (int a:intArray) System.out.print(a + " ");  6 elements
        Arrays.sort(intArray);                           Sorts all elements
        System.out.println();                            of array intArray.
        for (int a:intArray) System.out.print(a + " ");

        System.out.println();
                                                         Reinitializes
        intArray = new int[]{20, 14, 4, 10, 5, 3};       intArray.
        for (int a:intArray) System.out.print(a + " ");
        Arrays.sort(intArray, 1, 5);                     Sorts elements at
        System.out.println();                            positions 1, 2, 3, and 4,
        for (int a:intArray) System.out.print(a + " ");  excluding element at
    }                                                    position 5.
}
```

 EXAM TIP   A quick reminder that the index of an array is 0-based.

The output of the preceding code is as follows:

```
20 14 4 10 5 3
3 4 5 10 14 20
20 14 4 10 5 3
20 4 5 10 14 3
```

When you sort an array of objects using the `sort` method from class `Arrays`, it uses the natural sort order of the instances. If the objects don't specify a natural sort order, an overloaded version of `sort` can be passed a `Comparator`. A lot of classes like `String` and wrapper classes implement `Comparable` and define a natural sort order. The `String` values are sorted in alphabetical or lexicographic order. On the exam you might be queried about the natural sorting order of `String` values, which differ only in the case of their letters. What do you think is the output of the following sorting operation?

```
String[] strArray = {"ocP", "oCP", "OcP", "OCp", "Ocp"};
for (String str:strArray) System.out.print(str + " ");
Arrays.sort(strArray);
System.out.println();
for (String str:strArray) System.out.print(str + " ");
```

Literal String values that differ only in their case

sort() sorts strArray

Prints OCp OcP Ocp oCP ocP

Each character has a corresponding ASCII or Unicode value. The uppercase letters have a lower ASCII value than their lowercase counterparts.

 EXAM TIP Watch out for exam questions that sort string objects starting with a space. A space has a lower ASCII or Unicode value than lowercase or uppercase letters. Let's see how you can use a comparator to sort the objects of a user-defined class:

```
class SortObjects {
    public static void main(String args[]) {
        Person p1 = new Person("Shreya", 32);
        Person p2 = new Person("Harry", 40);
        Person p3 = new Person("Paul", 30);

        Person[] objArray = new Person[]{p1, p2, p3};

        Arrays.sort(objArray,
            new Comparator<Person>(){
                public int compare(Person p1, Person p2) {
                    return (p1.age-p2.age);
                }
            }
        );
        for (Person p:objArray) System.out.print(p + " ");
    }
}
class Person {
    String name;
    int age;
    Person (String name, int age) {
        this.name = name;
        this.age = age;
    }
    public String toString() {
        return name+":"+age;
    }
}
```

sort() is passed array of instances of Person and comparator that defines sort order for Person instances

The preceding code sorts the `Person` instances on the increasing order of their ages, printing this:

```
Paul:30 Shreya:32 Harry:40
```

Imagine what happens if you neither use a `Comparator` nor define a natural ordering for your class. Find out by attempting the next "Twist in the Tale" exercise.

Twist in the Tale 4.7

What is the output of the following class?

```java
import java.util.*;
class Twist4_7 {
    public static void main(String args[]) {
        Person p1 = new Person("Shreya", 32);
        Person p2 = new Person("Harry", 40);
        Person p3 = new Person("Paul", 30);

        Person[] objArray = new Person[]{p1, p2, p3};

        Arrays.sort(objArray);

        for (Person p:objArray) System.out.print(p + " ");
    }
}
class Person {
    String name;
    int age;
    Person (String name, int age) {
        this.name = name;
        this.age = age;
    }
    public int compareTo(Person person) {
        return (this.age-person.age);
    }
    public String toString() {
        return name+":"+age;
    }
}
```

a   Shreya:32 Paul:30 Harry:40

b   Paul:30 Shreya:32 Harry:40

c   Shreya:32 Harry:40 Paul:30

d   Compilation error

e   Runtime exception

4.10.2 *Sorting List using Collections*

Class `Collections` defines two sorting methods to sort objects of `List`:

Sorts specified list into ascending order, according to natural ordering of elements

```
static <T extends Comparable<? super T>> void sort(List<T> list)
static <T> void sort(List<T> list, Comparator<? super T> c)
```

Sorts specified list according to order induced by specified comparator

Here's an example of sorting a list using method `Collections.sort()`:

```java
class SortList {
    public static void main(String args[]) {
        List<Integer> integers = new ArrayList<>();
        integers.add(new Integer(200));
        integers.add(new Integer(87));
        integers.add(new Integer(999));

        for (Integer i : integers) {
            System.out.println(i);
        }

        System.out.println("After calling Collections.sort()");
        Collections.sort(integers);

        for (Integer i : integers) {
            System.out.println(i);
        }
    }
}
```

The output of the preceding code is:

```
200
87
999
After calling Collections.sort()
87
200
999
```

What would happen if we add another item to a list after it was sorted? Will it be sorted too? Let's find out using the next example:

```java
class SortList {
    public static void main(String... args) {
        Star s1 = new Star("Sun", 7777.77);
        Star s2 = new Star("Sirius", 999999.99);
        Star s3 = new Star("Pilatim", 222.22);

        List<Star> list = new ArrayList<>();
        list.add(s1); list.add(s2); list.add(s3);
```

Creates new ArrayList, referred by list.

Adds Star instances to list.

```
        Collections.sort(list);                                          ◁─────┐ ──   Sorts list.
        list.add(new Star("Litmier", 4444.44));          ◁────────────┐
        Collections.reverse(list);                              ◁────────────┘──┐

        for (Star star:list) System.out.println(star);          │
    }                                                                                         Adds another Star
}                                                                                             instance to list;
class Star implements Comparable<Star> {                                        this isn't sorted.
    String name;
    double mass;                                                                       Reverses order of
    Star(String name, double mass) {                                          list; doesn't sort in
        this.name = name;                                                              descending order.
        this.mass = mass;
    }
    public int compareTo(Star other) {
        return (int)(this.mass - other.mass);
    }
    public String toString(){
        return name + ":" + mass;
    }
}
```

Here's the output of the preceding code:

```
Litmier:4444.44
Sirius:999999.99
Sun:7777.77
Pilatim:222.22
```

 EXAM TIP   Once sorted, new elements are added to a list according to the specific algorithm used by the underlying data structure. After you sort elements of an `ArrayList`, the new elements are added to its end.

4.10.3 *Searching arrays and List using collections*

Classes `Arrays` and `Collections` define method `binarySearch()` to search a sorted array or a `List` for a matching value using the binary search algorithm. The list or array *must* be sorted according to the natural order of its elements or as specified by `Comparator`. If you pass this method an unsorted list, the results are undefined. If more than one value matches the target key value to be searched, this method can return any of these values. Method `binarySearch()` returns the index of the search key, if it is contained in the list; otherwise it returns (-(insertion point) - 1). The insertion point is defined as the point at which the key would be inserted into the list: the index of the first element greater than the key, or `list.size()` if all elements in the list are less than the specified key. Note that this guarantees that the return value will be >= 0 if and only if the key is found.

Following is the declaration of the overloaded method `binarySearch()`, which searches the specified array for the specified value using the binary search algorithm:

```
static int binarySearch(byte[] a, byte key)
static int binarySearch(int[] a, int key)
static int binarySearch(Object[] a, Object key)
static <T> int binarySearch(T[] a, T key, Comparator<? super T> c)
```

The preceding list includes the searching methods for the primitive data types byte and int and objects. I've deliberately not included the overloaded methods for the rest of the primitive data types (char, short, long, float, and double) to keep it manageable. For example

```java
public class SortSearch {
    static final Comparator<Integer> INT_COMPARATOR =
                                new Comparator<Integer>() {
        public int compare (Integer n1, Integer n2) {
            return n2.compareTo(n1);
        }
    };

    public static void main(String args[]) {
        ArrayList<Integer> list = new ArrayList<>();
        list.add(9999);
        list.add(10);
        list.add(55);
        list.add(28);

        Collections.sort(list, null);
        System.out.println(Collections.binarySearch(list, 55));

        Collections.sort(list, INT_COMPARATOR);
        System.out.println(Collections.binarySearch(list, 55));
    }
}
```

The output of the preceding code is

```
2
1
```

Here's the list of the overloaded method binarySearch(), which searches a range of the specified array for the specified value by using the binary search algorithm. Again, I've deliberately excluded the overloaded version of these methods for the rest of the primitive data types (char, short, long, float, and double) to keep the list manageable:

```java
static int binarySearch(byte[] a, int fromIndex, int toIndex, byte key)
static int binarySearch(int[] a, int fromIndex, int toIndex, int key)
static int binarySearch(Object[] a, int fromIndex, int toIndex, Object key)
static <T> int binarySearch(T[] a, int fromIndex, int toIndex, T key,
Comparator<? super T> c)
```

Here's the list of methods defined in class Collections to search the specified list for the specified object using the binary search algorithm:

```java
static <T> int binarySearch(List<? extends Comparable<? super T>> list, T key)
static <T> int binarySearch(List<? extends T> list, T key, Comparator<? super
T> c)
```

Similar to method binarySearch(), which accepts List objects, method binary-Search()v that accepts arrays requires the array to be sorted in an ascending order, or else the results are undefined. The output value in the following example is undefined:

```java
import java.util.*;
public class SearchArray {
    public static void main(String[] args) {
        Object[] myArray = new Object[3];
        myArray[0] = "Java";
        myArray[1] = "EJava";
        myArray[2] = "Guru";
        int position = Arrays.binarySearch(myArray, "Java");
        System.out.println(position);
    }
}
```

On the exam you might see a question that stores different object types in an array of type Object[]. What do you think is the output of the following code?

```java
import java.util.*;
public class SearchArray2 {
    public static void main(String[] args) {
        Object[] myArray = new Object[3];
        myArray[0] = "Java";
        myArray[1] = 10;
        myArray[2] = 'z';
        int position = Arrays.binarySearch(myArray, "Java");
        System.out.println(position);
    }
}
```

The preceding code throws a ClassCastException at runtime when it tries to convert Integer value 10 to String.

4.11   *Using wrapper classes*

 [4.4]   Use wrapper classes, autoboxing, and unboxing

Java defines a wrapper class for each of its primitive data types. The wrapper classes are used to *wrap* primitives in an object, so they can be added to a collection object. Wrapper classes help you write cleaner code, which is easy to read. For this exam, you should be able to use these wrapper classes and understand how boxing and unboxing applies to these classes.

4.11.1   *Class hierarchy of wrapper classes*

All the wrapper classes are immutable. They share multiple usage details and methods. Figure 4.26 shows their hierarchy.

All the numeric wrapper classes extend the class java.lang.Number. Classes Boolean and Character directly extend class Object. All the wrapper classes implement the

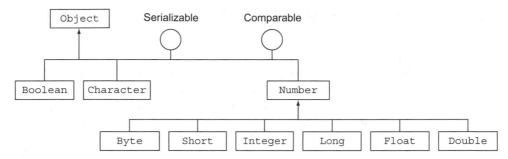

Figure 4.26 Hierarchy of wrapper classes

interfaces `java.io.Serializable` and `java.lang.Comparable`. All these classes can be serialized to a stream, and their objects define a natural sort order.

4.11.2 Creating objects of the wrapper classes

You can create objects of all the wrapper classes in multiple ways:

- *Assignment*—By assigning a primitive to a wrapper class variable
- *Constructor*—By using wrapper class constructors
- *Static methods*—By calling the static method of wrapper classes, like `valueOf()`

For example

```
Boolean bool1 = true;
Character char1 = 'a';
Byte byte1 = 10;
Double double1 = 10.98;
```
Autoboxing

```
Boolean bool2 = new Boolean(true);
Character char2 = new Character('a');
Byte byte2 = new Byte((byte)10);
Double double2 = new Double(10.98);
```
Constructors that accept primitive value

Won't compile
```
//Character char3 = new Character("a");
Boolean bool3 = new Boolean("true");
Byte byte3 = new Byte("10");
Double double3 = new Double("10.98");
```
Constructors that accept String

```
Boolean bool4 = Boolean.valueOf(true);
Boolean bool5 = Boolean.valueOf(true);
Boolean bool6 = Boolean.valueOf("TrUE");
Double double4 = Double.valueOf(10);
```
Using static method valueOf()

You can create objects of the rest of the wrapper classes (`Short`, `Integer`, `Long`, and `Float`) in a similar manner. All the wrapper classes define constructors to create an object using a corresponding primitive value or as a `String`.

Another interesting point to note is that neither of these classes defines a default no-argument constructor. Because wrapper classes are immutable, it doesn't make sense to initialize the wrapper objects with the default primitive values if they can't be modified later.

 EXAM TIP   All wrapper classes (except `Character`) define a constructor that accepts a `String` argument representing the primitive value that needs to be wrapped. Watch out for exam questions that include a call to a no-argument constructor of a wrapper class. None of these classes defines a no-argument constructor.

You can assign a primitive value directly to a reference variable of its wrapper class type—thanks to *autoboxing*. The reverse is *unboxing*, when an object of a primitive wrapper class is converted to its corresponding primitive value. I'll discuss autoboxing and autounboxing in detail in the next section.

4.11.3 *Retrieving primitive values from the wrapper classes*

All wrapper classes define methods of the format *primitive*Value(), where *primitive* refers to the exact primitive data type name. Table 4.4 shows a list of the classes and their methods to retrieve corresponding primitive values.

Table 4.4   Methods to retrieve primitive values from wrapper classes

Boolean	Character	Byte, Short, Integer, Long, Float, Double
`booleanValue()`	`charValue()`	`byteValue()`, `shortValue()`, `intValue()`, `longValue()`, `floatValue()`, `doubleValue()`

It's interesting to note that all numeric wrapper classes define methods to retrieve the value of the primitive value they store, as a `byte`, `short`, `int`, `long`, `float`, and `double`.

4.11.4 *Parsing a string value to a primitive type*

To get a primitive data type value corresponding to a string value, you can use the static utility method parseDataType(), where DataType refers to the type of the return value. Each wrapper class (except `Character`) defines a method, to parse a `String` to the corresponding primitive value, listed as follows:

Table 4.5   Parsing methods defined by wrapper classes

Class name	Method
Boolean	`public static boolean parseBoolean(String s)`
Character	no corresponding parsing method
Byte	`public static byte parseByte(String s)`
Short	`public static short parseShort(String s)`
Integer	`public static int parseInt(String s)`

Table 4.5   Parsing methods defined by wrapper classes

Class name	Method
Long	`public static long parseLong(String s)`
Float	`public static float parseFloat(String s)`
Double	`public static double parseDouble(String s)`

All these parsing methods throw a `NumberFormatException` for invalid values. Here are some examples:

```
Long.parseLong("12.34");
```
← **Throws NumberFormatException:**
12.34 isn't valid long.

```
Byte.parseByte("1234");
```
← **Throws NumberFormatException:**
1234 is out of range for byte.

```
Boolean.parseBoolean("true");
```
← **Returns Boolean true.**

```
Boolean.parseBoolean("TrUe");
```
← **No exceptions; the String**
argument isn't case-sensitive.

4.11.5   Difference between using method valueOf() and constructors of wrapper classes

Method `valueOf()` returns an object of the corresponding wrapper class when it's passed an argument of a primitive type or `String`. Then what is the difference between method `valueOf()` and constructors of these classes, which also accept method arguments of a primitive type and `String`?

Wrapper classes `Character`, `Byte`, `Short`, `Integer`, and `Long` cache objects with values in the range of –128 to 127. These classes define inner static classes that store objects for the primitive values –128 to 127 in an array. If you request an object of any of these classes, from this range, method `valueOf()` returns a reference to a predefined object; otherwise, it creates a new object and returns its reference:

```
Long var1 = Long.valueOf(123);
Long var2 = Long.valueOf("123");
System.out.println(var1 == var2);
```
← **Prints "true"; var1 and var2**
refer to same cached object.

```
Long var3 = Long.valueOf (223);
Long var4 = Long.valueOf (223);
System.out.println (var3 == var4);
```
← **Prints "false"; var3 and var4**
refer to different objects.

4.11.6   Comparing objects of wrapper classes

The wrapper classes correctly implement methods `hashCode()` and `equals()`, so you can use them in collection framework classes as keys in a map. In the following example, you can use `Double` objects as keys in a `HashMap`:

```
public class UseWrapperAsKeysInMap {
    public static void main(String[] args) {
```

```
            Map<Double, String> map = new HashMap<>();
            map.put(6.6, "OCA");
            map.put(7.7, "OCP");                                    Prints "OCA"
            System.out.println(map.get(6.6));          ⟵
            System.out.println(map.get(new Double(7.7)));   ⟵     Prints "OCP"
        }
}
```

 EXAM TIP   Integer literal values are implicitly converted to `Integer` objects and decimal literal values are implicitly converted to `Double` objects.

Let's modify the preceding code and try to retrieve the string value "OCP" using a `Float` object with value 7.7. Do you think objects of `Double` and `Float` with the same values are considered equal?

```
public class UseWrapperAsKeysInMap {
    public static void main(String[] args) {
        Map<Double, String> map = new HashMap<>();
        map.put(6.6, "OCA");
        map.put(7.7, "OCP");                                      Outputs 'OCA'
        System.out.println(map.get(6.6));             ⟵
        System.out.println(map.get(new Float((float)7.7)));  ⟵  Outputs 'null'
    }
}
```

In the preceding code, a `Float` object with a value can't be used to retrieve the value that was added to a `HashMap` using a `Double` instance. Their values don't matter.

 EXAM TIP   The objects of different wrapper classes with the same values are not equal.

All the wrapper classes also implement the `Comparable` interface. You can compare them using method `compareTo()` and use them in collection framework classes that use natural ordering (like `TreeSet`). Method `compareTo()` returns a negative integer, zero, or a positive integer as this object is less than, equal to, or greater than the specified object. What do you think is the output of the following code that adds `Boolean` instances to a `HashSet`?

```
public class UseTreeSetWithWrapperClasses {
    public static void main(String[] args) {
        TreeSet<Boolean> set = new TreeSet<Boolean>();
        set.add(new Boolean(true));
        set.add(new Boolean("FaLSe"));
        set.add(Boolean.valueOf("TrUe"));
        for (Boolean b : set)
            System.out.println(b);
    }
}
```

The output of the preceding code is

```
false
true
```

EXAM TIP　When arranged in natural sort order, `false` precedes `true`.

In the preceding code, you can add `Boolean` instances to a `HashSet` because `Boolean` implements the `Comparable` interface. Because `HashSet` ignores the addition of duplicate values, only one `Boolean.false` object is added to `HashSet`. When instances of a class that doesn't implement `Comparable` are added to a `HashSet`, a `ClassCast-Exception` is thrown at runtime.

The next section covers autoboxing and unboxing, used by a compiler to convert primitive values to wrapper objects and vice versa.

4.12　*Autoboxing and unboxing*

 [4.4]　Use wrapper classes, autoboxing, and unboxing

Autoboxing is the automatic conversion of a primitive data type to an object of the corresponding wrapper class (you *box* the primitive value). *Unboxing* is the reverse process (you *unbox* the primitive value), as shown in figure 4.27.

The wrapper classes use autoboxing and unboxing features quite frequently:

```
Double d1 = new Double(12.67);
System.out.println(d1.compareTo(21.68));
```
Prints -1, since
12.67 < 21.68

Compare the use of the preceding method against the following method defined by class `Double`:

```
public int compareTo(Double anotherDouble)
```

Wait—did I just mention that method `compareTo()` defined in the class `Double` accepts an object of class `Double` and not a `double` primitive data type? Then why does the preceding code compile? The answer is autoboxing. Java converted the primitive `double` to an object of class `Double` (by using method `valueOf()`), so it works correctly. The Java compiler converted it to the following at runtime:

```
Double d1 = new Double(12.67D);
System.out.println(d1.compareTo(Double.valueOf(21.68D)));
```

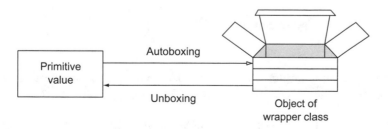

Figure 4.27　Autoboxing and unboxing

Now examine the following code (an example of unboxing with autoboxing):

```
public class Unboxing {
    public static void main (String args[]) {                    List of
        ArrayList<Double> list = new ArrayList<Double>();         Double
        list.add(12.12);                 Autoboxing-Add double
        list.add(11.24);
        Double total = 0;
        for (Double d : list)
            total += d;              Unbox to use operator
    }                                += with total
}
```

In the preceding code, at the end of execution of the for loop, total will be assigned a Double value of 23.36. The arithmetic operators like += can't be used with objects. So why do you think the code compiles? In this example, the Java compiler converted the preceding code to the following at runtime:

```
public class Unbox {
    public static void main(String args[]) {
        ArrayList list = new ArrayList();
        list.add(new Double(12.12D));
        list.add(new Double(87.98D));
        Double total = Double.valueOf(0.0D);
        for(Iterator iterator = list.iterator(); iterator.hasNext();)
        {
            Double d = (Double)iterator.next();
            total += total.doubleValue() + d.doubleValue();
        }
    }
}
```

In the previous section, I mentioned that wrapper classes are immutable. So, what happens when you *add* a value to the variable total, a Double object? In this case, the variable total refers to a *new* Double object.

 EXAM TIP Wrapper classes are immutable. Adding a primitive value to a wrapper class variable doesn't modify the value of the object it refers to. The wrapper class variable is assigned a new object.

Here's another interesting question. What happens if you pass null as an argument to the following method?

```
public int increment(Integer obj) {
    return ++i;
}
```

Because the Java compiler would call obj.intValue() to get obj's int value, passing null to method increment() will throw a NullPointerException.

 EXAM TIP Unboxing a wrapper reference variable, which refers to null, will throw a NullPointerException.

With the preceding exam tip, you've completed the coverage of generics and collections topics for the exam. With an understanding of all the related nuances under your belt, you'll be able to write better code in real projects. Good luck to you.

4.13 Summary

We started this chapter with a warm-up section on generics, including the need for their introduction and the benefits and complexities of using them. The chapter covered the creation of generic classes, interfaces, and methods. It included how to define and use single and multiple type parameters. You can use bounded type parameters to limit the type of objects that can be passed as arguments to generic classes, interfaces, and methods. We also covered the wildcard ? to declare a type of a variable or a return type of a method. Bounded wildcards enable you to restrict the types that can be used as arguments in a parameterized type. You learned how type erasure removes the type information during the compilation process so that you get only one class file for each generic class on the interface on compilation. Type erasure also creates bridge methods.

By using type inference, a compiler can determine type arguments if you don't specify them while creating instances of generic types. But if it can't, it'll throw a warning, an error, or an exception. Mixing of raw and generic types was allowed to use code that existed before generics were introduced. If not used correctly, you might get a compiler warning or error, or a runtime exception, when you mix raw with generic types. With generics, you must follow certain subtyping rules. A generic class is a subtype of its raw type. An object of `ArrayList<String>` isn't compatible with a reference variable of type `List<Object>`.

You also worked with the collections framework, an architecture for representing and manipulating collections. You worked with the main interfaces, their implementations, and the algorithms used to manipulate collection objects. The `Collection` interface is extended by the `List`, `Deque`, and `Set` interfaces (but not by the `Map` interface). The `Collection` interface defines methods to manipulate and query its elements.

The `List` interface models an ordered collection of objects. It returns the objects to you in the order in which you added them to a `List`. It allows you to store duplicate elements. The `List` implementations on the exam are `ArrayList` and `LinkedList`.

A `Queue` is a linear collection of objects. A `Deque` is a double-ended queue, a queue that supports the insertion and deletion of elements at both its ends. The `Deque` implementations on the exam are `LinkedList` and `ArrayDeque`.

The `Set` interface models the mathematical `Set` abstraction. It's a collection of objects that doesn't contain duplicate elements. Set implementations on the exam are `HashSet`, `LinkedHashSet`, and `TreeSet`.

A `Map` stores a pool of key-value pairs. It doesn't allow the addition of duplicate keys. Items added to a `Map` aren't ordered. The retrieval order of items from a `Map` object isn't guaranteed to be the same as its insertion order. `Map` implementations on the exam are `HashMap`, `LinkedHashMap`, and `TreeMap`.

Class `HashTable` wasn't a part of the collections framework initially. It was retrofitted to implement the `Map` interface in Java 2, making it a member of the Java Collection framework. But it's considered legacy code. It's roughly equivalent to a `HashMap`, with some differences. The operations of a `HashMap` aren't synchronized, whereas the operations of a `HashTable` are synchronized.

The `Comparable` interface is used to define the natural order of objects. The `Comparator` interface is used to define the custom order for objects when you don't want to use their natural order, can't define or redefine their natural order, or need a custom order. These interfaces are used by multiple interfaces and classes to sort objects like `TreeSet`, `TreeMap`, `Collections.sort()`, and `Arrays.sort()`. Classes `Arrays` and `Collections` define methods to sort and search arrays and lists.

The wrapper classes are used to wrap primitive types so that they can be used with collection classes. Autoboxing is the automatic conversion of a primitive data type to an object of the corresponding wrapper class (you box the primitive value). Unboxing is the reverse process.

REVIEW NOTES

This section lists the main points covered in this chapter.

Creating generic entities

- You define a generic class, interface, or method by adding one or more type parameters to it.
- A class that uses a generic class uses a parameterized type, replacing the formal parameter with an actual parameter. Also, invalid casts aren't allowed.
- Java's naming conventions limit the use of single uppercase letters for type parameters. Though not recommended, using any valid identifier name for type parameters is acceptable code.
- A generic class can be extended by another generic or nongeneric class.
- An extended class must be able to pass type arguments to its generic base class. If it doesn't, the code won't compile.
- When a nongeneric class extends a generic class, the derived class doesn't define any type parameters but passes arguments to all type parameters of its generic base class.
- A generic interface is defined by including one or more type parameters in its declaration.
- When a nongeneric class implements a generic interface, the type parameters follow the interface name.
- When a generic class implements a generic interface, the type parameters follow both the class and the interface name.
- A generic method defines its own formal type parameters. You can define a generic method in a generic or a nongeneric class.

- To define a generic method in a nongeneric class or interface, you must define the type parameters with the method in its type parameter section.

- A method's type parameter list is placed just after its access and nonaccess modifiers and before its return type. Because a type parameter could be used to define the return type, it should be known before the return type is used.

- You can define a generic method in a generic class or interface, defining its own type parameters.

- You can also define a generic constructor in a generic class.

- You can specify the bounds to restrict the set of types that can be used as type arguments to a generic class, interface, or method. It also enables access to the methods (and variables) defined by the bounds.

- For a bounded type parameter, the bound can be a class, an interface, or an enum, but not an array or a primitive type. All cases use the keyword `extends` to specify the bound. If the bound is an interface, the `implements` keyword isn't used.

- A type parameter can have multiple bounds. The list of bounds consists of one class or multiple interfaces.

- For a type parameter with multiple bounds, the type argument must be a subtype of all bounds.

- The wildcard ? represents an unknown type. You can use it to declare the type of a parameter; a local, instance, or static variable; and a return value of generic types. But you can't use it as a type argument to invoke a generic method, create a generic class instance, or for a supertype.

- You can assign an instance of a subclass, say, `String`, to a variable of its base class, `Object`. But you can't assign `ArrayList<String>` to a variable of type `List<Object>`. Inheritance doesn't apply to type parameters.

- When you use a wildcard to declare your variables or method parameters, you lose the functionality of adding objects to a collection.

- To restrict the types that can be used as arguments in a parameterized type, you can use bounded wildcards.

- In upper-bounded wildcards, the keyword `extends` is used for both a class and an interface.

- For collections defined using upper-bounded wildcards, you can't add any objects. You can iterate and read values from such collections.

- You can use final classes in upper-bounded wildcards. Although `class X extends String` won't compile, `<? extends String>` will compile successfully.

- You can restrict the use of type arguments to a type and its supertypes or base types by using `<? super Type>`, where `Type` refers to a class, interface, or enum.

- Type information is erased during the compilation process; this is called type erasure.

- When a generic class is compiled, you don't get multiple versions of the compiled class files.

- The compiler erases the type information by replacing all type parameters in generic types with `Object` (for unbounded parameter types) or their bounds (for bounded parameter types).
- The Java compiler might need to create additional methods, referred to as bridge methods, as part of the type erasure process.

Using type inference

- If you don't specify the type of type arguments to instantiate a generic class or invoke a generic method, the Java compiler might be able to infer the argument type by examining the declaration of the generic entity and its invocation. If the type can't be inferred, you might get a compilation warning, an error, or an exception.
- By throwing an unchecked warning, the compiler states that it can't ensure type safety. The term *unchecked* refers to operations that might result in violating type safety. This occurs when the compiler doesn't have enough type information to perform all type checks.
- Starting with Java 7, you can drop the type arguments required to invoke the constructor of a generic class and use a diamond—that is, `<>`. But an attempt to drop the diamond will result in a compilation warning.
- A Java compiler can't infer the type parameters by using the diamond in the case of generic methods. It uses the type of the actual arguments passed to the method to infer the type parameters.

Understanding interoperability of collections using raw types and generic types

- Raw types exist only for generic types.
- You can assign a parameterized type to its raw type, but the reverse will give a compiler warning.
- When you assign a parameterized type to its raw type, you lose the type information.
- When you mix raw types with generic types, you might get a compiler warning or error or a runtime exception.
- You can assign an object of a subclass to reference a variable of its base class. But this subtyping rule doesn't work when you assign a collection-of-a-derived-class object to a reference variable of a collection of a base class.
- If you declare a reference variable `List<Object>` to a list, whatever you assign to the list must be of generic type `Object`. A subclass of `Object` isn't allowed.

Working with the Collection interface

- The `Collection<E>` interface represents a group of objects known as its elements.
- There's no direct implementation of `Collection`; no concrete class implements it. It's extended by more specific interfaces such as `Set`, `List`, and `Queue`.

- This collection is used for maximum generality—to work with methods that can accept objects of, say, Set, List, and Queue.
- All collection classes are generic.
- The Map interface doesn't extend the core Collection interface.
- The Collection interface implements the Iterable interface, which defines method iterator(), enabling all the concrete implementations to access an Iterator<E> to iterate over all the collection objects.
- The methods of the Collection interface aren't marked as synchronized.

Creating and using List, Set, and Deque implementations

- The List interface models an ordered collection of objects. It returns the objects to you in the order in which you added them. It allows you to store duplicate elements.
- In a List you can control the position where you want to store an element. This is the reason that this interface defines overloaded methods to add, remove, and retrieve elements at a particular position.
- Method listIterator() of List can be used to iterate the complete list or a part of it.
- An ArrayList is a resizable array implementation of the List interface.
- An ArrayList uses the size variable to keep track of the number of elements inserted in it. By default, an element is added to the first available position in the array. But if you add an element to an earlier location, the rest of the list elements are shifted to the right.
- If you remove an element that isn't the last element in the list, ArrayList shifts the elements to the left.
- An ArrayList maintains a record of its size so that you can't add elements at arbitrary locations.
- ArrayList's method remove() sequentially searches the ArrayList to find the target object, using method equals() to compare its elements with the target object.
- If a matching element is found, remove(Object) removes the first occurrence of the match found.
- If you're adding instances of a user-defined class as elements to an ArrayList, override its method equals() or else its method contains() or remove() might not behave as expected.
- The ArrayList methods clear(), remove(), and removeAll() offer different functionalities. clear() removes all the elements from an ArrayList. remove (Object) removes the first occurrence of the specified element, and remove(int) removes the element at the specified position. removeAll() removes from an ArrayList all of its elements that are contained in the specified collection.
- A Deque is a double-ended queue, a queue that supports the insertion and deletion of elements at both its ends.

- As a double-ended queue, a `Deque` can work as both a queue and a stack.
- The `Deque` interface defines multiple methods to add, remove, and query the existence of elements from both its ends.
- Methods `addFirst()`, `addLast()`, `offerFirst()`, and `offerLast()` add and remove elements from the top and tail.
- `Deque` also defines methods `push()`, `pop()`, and `peek()` to add, remove, and query elements at its beginning.
- `ArrayDeque` and `LinkedList` implement the `Deque` interface.
- `ArrayDeque` is a resizable array implementation of the `Deque` interface.
- `Deque`'s method `peek()` only queries elements, it doesn't remove them.
- `Deque`'s method `remove()` just removes an element.
- `Deque`'s method `poll()` returns `null` when `Deque` is empty and `remove()` throws a runtime exception.
- All the insertion methods (`add()`, `addFirst()`, `addLast()`, `offer()`, `offerFirst()`, `offerLast()`, and `push()`) throw a `NullPointerException` if you try to insert a `null` element into an `ArrayDeque`.
- You can iterate over the elements of `Deque` by using an `Iterator`, returned by methods `iterator()` and `descendingIterator()`.
- Class `LinkedList` implements both the `List` and `Deque` interfaces. So it's a double-linked list implementation of the `List` and `Deque` interfaces.
- Unlike `ArrayDeque`, `LinkedList` permits addition of `null` elements.
- A `LinkedList` is like an `ArrayList` (ordered by index) but the elements are double-linked to each other. So besides the methods from `List`, you get a bunch of other methods to add or remove at the beginning and end of this list. So it's a good choice if you need to implement a queue or a stack. A `LinkedList` is useful when you need fast insertion or deletion, but iteration might be slower than an `ArrayList`.
- Because a `LinkedList` implements `List`, `Queue`, and `Deque`, it implements methods from all these interfaces.
- The `Set` interface models the mathematical `Set` abstraction.
- The `Set` interface doesn't allow duplicate elements and the elements are returned in no particular order.
- To determine the equality of objects, `Set` uses their method `equals()`. For two elements, say e1 and e2, if `e1.equals(e2)` returns `true`, `Set` doesn't add both these elements.
- `Set` defines methods to add and remove its elements. It also defines methods to query itself for the occurrence of specific objects.
- Class `HashSet` implements the `Set` interface. It doesn't allow the addition of duplicate elements and makes no guarantee to the order of retrieval of its elements.
- `HashSet` is implemented using a `HashMap`.

- To store and retrieve its elements, a `HashSet` uses a hashing method, accessing an object's `hashCode()` value to determine the bucket in which it should be stored.
- Method `hashCode()` doesn't call method `equals()`.
- Method `equals()` doesn't call method `hashCode()`.
- Classes should override their `hashCode()` methods efficiently to enable collection classes like `HashSet` to store them in separate buckets.
- A `HashSet` allows storing of only one `null` element. All subsequent calls to storing `null` values are ignored.
- Class `HashSet` uses hashing algorithms to store, remove, and retrieve its elements. So it offers constant time performance for these operations, assuming that the hash function disperses its elements properly among its buckets.
- A `LinkedHashSet` offers the benefits of a `HashSet` combined with a `LinkedList`. It maintains a double-linked list running through its entries.
- As with a `LinkedList`, you can retrieve objects from a `LinkedHashSet` in the order of their insertion.
- Like a `HashSet`, a `LinkedHashSet` uses hashing to store and retrieve its elements quickly.
- A `LinkedHashSet` permits `null` values.
- `LinkedHashSet` can be used to create a copy of a `Set` with the same order as that of the original set.
- `LinkedHashSet`'s method `addAll()` accepts a `Collection` object. So you can add elements of an `ArrayList` to a `LinkedHashSet`. The order of insertion of objects from `ArrayList` to `LinkedHashSet` is determined by the order of objects returned by `ArrayList`'s iterator (`ArrayList` objects can be iterated in the order of their insertion).
- A `TreeSet` stores all its unique elements in a sorted order. The elements are ordered either on their natural order (achieved by implementing the `Comparable` interface) or by passing a `Comparator` while instantiating a `TreeSet`. If you fail to specify either of these, `TreeSet` will throw a runtime exception when you try to add an object to it.
- Unlike the other `Set` implementations like `HashSet` and `LinkedHashSet`, which use `equals()` to compare objects for equality, a `TreeSet` uses method `compareTo()` (for the `Comparable` interface) or `compare()` (for the `Comparator` interface) to compare objects for equality and their order.
- If two object instances are equal according to their method `equals()`, but not according to their method `compare()` or `compareTo()`, a `Set` can exhibit inconsistent behavior.
- Classes `Enum` and `File` implement the `Comparable` interface. The natural order of enum constants is the order in which they're declared. Classes `StringBuffer` and `StringBuilder` don't implement the `Comparable` interface.

Map and its implementations

- Unlike the other interfaces from the collections framework, like `List` and `Set`, the `Map` interface doesn't extend the `Collection` interface.

- A `Map` defines key-values pairs, where a key can map to a 0 or 1 value.

- `Map` objects don't allow the addition of duplicate keys.

- The addition of a `null` value as a key or value depends on a particular `Map` implementation. A `HashMap` and `LinkedHashMap` allow insertion of `null` as a key, but `TreeMap` doesn't—it throws an exception.

- A `HashMap` is a hash-based `Map` that uses the hash value of its key (returned by `hashCode()`) to store and retrieve keys and their corresponding values. Each key can refer to a 0 or 1 value. The keys of a `HashMap` aren't ordered. The Hash-Map methods aren't synchronized, so they aren't safe to be used in a multi-threaded environment.

- You can create a `HashMap` by passing its constructor another `Map` object. Additions of new key-value pairs or deletions of existing key-value pairs in the `Map` object passed to the constructor aren't reflected in the newly created `HashMap`.

- Because a `HashMap` stores objects as its keys and values, it's common to see code that stores another collection object (like an `ArrayList`) as a value in a `Map`.

- You can call method `get()` on a `HashMap` to retrieve the value for a key.

- Methods `containsKey()` and `containsValue()` check for the existence of a key or a value in a `HashMap`, returning a `boolean` value. Methods `get()` and `containsKey()` rely on appropriate overriding of a key's methods `hashCode()` and `equals()`.

- Class `String` and all the wrapper classes override their methods `hashCode()` and `equals()`, so they can be correctly used as keys in a `HashMap`.

- `HashMap` uses hashing functions to add or retrieve key-value pairs. The key must override both methods `equals()` and `hashCode()` so that it can be added to a `HashMap` and retrieved from it.

- When objects of a class that only overrides method `equals()` (and not method `hashCode()`) are used as keys in a `HashMap`, `containsKey()` will always return `false`.

- If you add a key-value pair to a `HashMap` such that the key already exists in the `HashMap`, the key's old value will be replaced with the new value.

- You can add a value with `null` as the key in a `HashMap`.

- You can use method `remove(key)` or `clear()` to remove one or all key-value pairs of a `HashMap`.

- Method `remove()` can return a `null` value, irrespective of whether the specified key exists in a `HashMap`. It might return `null` if matching a key isn't present in `HashMap`, or if `null` is stored as a value for the specified key.

- For a `HashMap`, methods that query or search a key use the key's methods `hashCode()` and `equals()`.

- Method remove() removes a maximum of one key-value pair from a HashMap. Method clear() clears all the entries of a HashMap. Method remove() accepts a method parameter but clear() doesn't.
- You can use methods size() and isEmpty() to query a HashMap's size.
- You can use method putAll() to copy all the mappings from the specified map to a HashMap.
- Method putAll() accepts an argument of type Map. It copies all the mappings from the specified map to the map that calls putAll(). For common keys, the values of map that call putAll() are replaced with the values of the Map object passed to putAll().
- The Map interface defines methods keySet(), values(), and entrySet() to access keys, values, and key-value pairs of a HashMap.
- Method values() returns a Collection object, method keySet() returns a Set object, and method entrySet() returns a Map.Entry object.
- Class HashTable wasn't a part of the collections framework initially. It was retrofitted to implement the Map interface in Java 2, making it a member of the Java Collection framework. But it's considered legacy code. It's roughly equivalent to a HashMap with some differences. The operations of a HashMap aren't synchronized, whereas the operations of a HashTable are synchronized.
- The LinkedHashMap IS-A HashMap with a predictable iteration order. Like a LinkedList, a LinkedHashMap maintains a double-linked list, which runs through all its entries.
- A LinkedHashMap will always iterate over its elements in their order of insertion.
- A TreeMap is sorted according to the natural ordering of its keys or as defined by a Comparator passed to its constructor.
- TreeMap implements the SortedMap interface. Like HashMap and LinkedHashMap, the operations of a TreeMap aren't synchronized, which makes it unsafe to be used in a multithreaded environment.
- The TreeMap performs all key comparisons by using method compareTo() or compare(). Two keys are considered equal by a TreeMap if the key's method compareTo() or compare() considers them equal.
- When you create a TreeMap object, you should specify how its keys should be ordered. A key might define its natural ordering by implementing the Comparable interface. If it doesn't you should pass a Comparator object to specify the key's sort order.
- The set of values that you retrieve from a TreeMap is sorted on its keys and not on its values.
- You can create a TreeMap without passing it a Comparator object or without using keys that implement a Comparable interface. But adding key-value pairs to such a TreeMap will throw a runtime exception, ClassCastException.

- When you pass a `Comparator` object to `TreeMap` constructor, the natural order of its keys is ignored.
- Because a `TreeMap` uses method `compare()` or `compareTo()` to determine the equality of its keys, it can access the value associated with a key, even though its key doesn't override its method `equals()` or `hashCode()`.

Using java.util.Comparator and java.lang.Comparable

- The `Comparable` interface is used to define the natural order of the objects of the class that implements it.
- `Comparable` is a generic interface (using `T` as type parameter) and defines only one method, `compareTo(T object)`, which compares the object to the object passed to it as a method parameter.
- Method `compareTo()` returns a negative integer, zero, or a positive integer if this object is less than, equal to, or greater than the specified object.
- The `Comparator` interface is used to define the sort order of a collection of objects, without requiring them to implement this interface.
- The `Comparator` interface defines methods `compare()` and `equals()`.
- You can pass `Comparator` to sort methods like `Arrays.sort()` and `Collections.sort()`.
- A `Comparator` object is also passed to collection classes like `TreeSet` and `TreeMap` that require ordered elements.
- The `Comparator` interface is used to specify the sort order for classes that
  - Don't define a natural sort order
  - Need to work with an alternate sort order
  - Don't allow modification to their source code so that natural ordering can be added to them

Sorting and searching arrays and lists

- Class `Arrays` in the collections framework defines multiple methods to sort complete or partial arrays of primitive data types and objects.
- When method `Arrays.sort()` accepts `fromIndex` and `toIndex` values to sort a partial array, the element stored at position `fromIndex` is sorted, but the element stored at position `toIndex` isn't.
- A space has a lower ASCII or Unicode value than lowercase or uppercase letters. When arranged in an ascending order, a `String` value that starts with a space is placed before the `String` values that don't start with a space.
- Class `Collections` defines method `sort()` to sort objects of `List`.
- Classes `Arrays` and `Collections` define method `binarySearch()` to search a sorted array or a `List` for a matching value using the binary search algorithm. The array or `List` must be sorted according to the natural order of its elements or as specified by `Comparator`. If you pass this method an unsorted list, the

results are undefined. If more than one value matches the target key value to be searched, this method can return any of these values.

- Method binarySearch() returns the index of the search key if it's contained in the list; otherwise it returns (-(insertion point) - 1). The insertion point is defined as the point at which the key would be inserted into the list: the index of the first element greater than the key, or list.size() if all elements in the list are less than the specified key. Note that this guarantees that the return value will be >= 0 if and only if the key is found.

Using wrapper classes

- All the wrapper classes are immutable.
- All the wrapper classes implement the Comparable interface. All these classes define their natural order.
- You can create objects of all the wrapper classes in multiple ways:
  - *Assignment*—By assigning a primitive to a wrapper class variable
  - *Constructor*—By using wrapper class constructors
  - *Static methods*—By calling the static method of wrapper classes, like valueOf()
- All wrapper classes (except Character) define a constructor that accepts a String argument representing the primitive value that needs to be wrapped. Watch out for exam questions that include a call to a no-argument constructor of a wrapper class. None of these classes defines a no-argument constructor.
- To get a primitive data-type value corresponding to a string value, you can use the static utility method parseDataType(), where DataType refers to the type of the return value.
- Wrapper classes Character, Byte, Short, Integer, and Long cache objects with values in the range of –128 to 127. These classes define inner static classes that store objects for the primitive values –128 to 127 in an array. If you request an object of any of these classes, from this range, method valueOf() returns a reference to a predefined object; otherwise, it creates a new object and returns its reference.
- Integer literal values are implicitly converted to Integer objects and decimal literal values are implicitly converted to Double objects.
- The objects of different wrapper classes with the same values aren't equal.
- When arranged in natural sort order, false precedes true.

Autoboxing and Unboxing

- Autoboxing is the automatic conversion of a primitive data type to an object of the corresponding wrapper class (you box the primitive value). Unboxing is the reverse process (you unbox the primitive value).
- Wrapper classes are immutable. Adding a primitive value to a wrapper class variable doesn't modify the value of the object it refers to. The wrapper class variable is assigned a new object.

- Unboxing a wrapper reference variable, which refers to null, will throw a Null-PointerException.

SAMPLE EXAM QUESTIONS

Q 4-1. Which of the following options creates a generic class that can be passed multiple generic types? (Choose all that apply.)

```
a  class EJavaMap<A , B> {}

b  class EJavaMap<A a, B b> {}

c  class EJavaMap<Aa extends String, Bb extends Object> {
       void add(Aa a) {}
       void add(Bb a) {}
   }

d  class EJavaMap<Aa, Bb> {
       void add(Aa a, Bb b) {}
   }
```

Q 4-2. Which of the following statements are true about generic classes, interfaces, and methods?

- a If you define a generic class, you must define its corresponding raw class explicitly.
- b On compilation, type information is erased from a generic class.
- c A generic method can be defined within a generic class or a regular class.
- d Generic interfaces might not accept multiple generic type parameters.

Q 4-3. Which of the following options when inserted at //INSERT CODE HERE would compile successfully without any warning? (Choose all that apply.)

```
class Box<T> {
    T t;
    Box(T t) {
        this.t = t;
    }
    T getValue() {
        return t;
    }
}
class Test {
    public static void main(String args[]) {
    //INSERT CODE HERE
    }
}
```

- a Box box = new Box("abcd");
- b Box<String> box = new Box<>("String");
- c Box<String> box = new Box<String>("Object");
- d Box<Object> box = new Box<String>("String");

Q 4-4. Consider this pre-generics implementation of method concat() in class MyString:

```
class MyString {
    public static String concat(List list) {              //1
        String result = new String();                     //2
        for (Iterator iter = list.iterator(); iter.hasNext(); ) {  //3
            String value = (String)iter.next();            //4
            result += value;                               //5
        }
        return result;
    }
}
```

Which three of the following changes together will allow method concat() to be used with generics without generating unchecked warnings?

   a Replace line 1 with public static String concat(List<String> list) {.

   b Replace line 1 with public static String concat(List<Integer> list) {.

   c Remove code on line 3.

   d Remove code on line 4.

   e Change code on line 3 to for (String value : list) {.

   f Change code on line 3 to for (String value : list.listIterator()) {.

Q 4-5. What happens when you try to compile and execute the following class with Java 7? (Choose all that apply.)

```
class EJava {
    public static void main(String args[]) {
        ArrayList list = new ArrayList();
        list.add("ABCD");
        list.add(1);
        list.add(new Thread());

        for (Object obj:list) System.out.println(obj);
    }
}
```

   a Class EJava fails to compile with Java 7.

   b Class EJava compiles with a compilation warning when compiled with Java 7.

   c Class EJava iterates though all the objects of the list and prints their values as returned by their method toString().

   d Class EJava prints the first list value and throws a ClassCastException while trying to print the second list element.

Q 4-6. What is the output of the following code?

```
import java.util.*;
public class MyHashSet {
    public static void main (String [] args) {
        Set<Phone> set = new TreeSet<>();
        set.add(new Phone("Harry"));
```

```
            set.add(new Phone("Paul"));
            set.add(new Phone("Harry"));
            set.add(new Phone("Paul"));

            Iterator <Phone> iterator = set.iterator ();

            while (iterator.hasNext()) {
                Phone ph = iterator.next();
                switch (ph.toString()){
                    case "Harry": System.out.print("?Harry? ");
                             break;
                    case "Paul": System.out.print("<Paul> ");
                             break;
                }
            }
            System.out.print("Set size=" + set.size());
        }
    }
    class Phone{
        String manufacturer;
        Phone(String value) {
            manufacturer = value;
        }
        public String toString() {
            return manufacturer;
        }
    }
```

a   <Paul> ?Harry? ?Harry? <Paul> Set size=4

b   <Paul> ?Harry? <Paul> ?Harry? Set size=4

c   ?Harry? ?Harry? <Paul> <Paul> Set size=4

d   <Paul> ?Harry? Set size=2

e   ?Harry? <Paul> Set size=2

f   Compilation error

g   Runtime exception

h   The output is unpredictable.

Q 4-7. Given the following code, which code options when inserted at //INSERT CODE
HERE will sort the keys in props?

```
class EMap {
    public static void main(String... args) {
        HashMap props = new HashMap();
        props.put("Harry", "Manth");
        props.put("Paul", "Rosen");
        props.put("Alm", "Bld");
        Set keySet = props.keySet();
        //INSERT CODE HERE
    }
}
```

a   `Arrays.sort(keySet);`

b   `Collections.sort(keySet);`

c   `Collection.sort(keySet);`

d   `Collections.arrange(keySet);`

e   `keySet = new TreeSet(keySet);`

f   `keySet = new SortedSet(keySet);`

Q 4-8. Which code option(s) when inserted at `//INSERT CODE HERE` will make class EJava print Harry?

```
class EJava {
    public static void main(String args[]) {
        String myArray[] = {"Harry", "Shreya",
                                    "Selvan", "Paul"};
        //INSERT CODE HERE
        System.out.println(myArrayList.get(0));
    }
}
```

a   `List <?> myArrayList = new LinkedList<?>(Arrays.asList(myArray));`

b   `List <?> myArrayList = new LinkedList<>(Arrays.asList(myArray));`

c   `List <? extends String> myArrayList = new LinkedList<>(Arrays.asList`
    `(myArray));`

d   `List myArrayList = new LinkedList(Arrays.asList(myArray));`

e   `List myArrayList = new LinkedList<String>(Arrays.asList(myArray));`

Q 4-9. Which statements are true about method `hashCode()`?

a   Method `hashCode()` is used by classes such as `HashMap` to determine inequality of objects.

b   Method `hashCode()` is used by classes such as `HashSet` to determine equality of objects.

c   Method `hashCode()` is used by class `Collections.sort` to order the elements of a collection.

d   Method `hashCode()` is used by classes like `HashSet`, `TreeSet`, and `HashMap`, which use hashing to group their elements into hash buckets.

e   An efficient `hashCode()` method includes use of a particular algorithm recommended by Java.

Q 4-10. What is the output of the following code? (Choose all that apply.)

```
import java.util.*;
class MyHash {
    public static void main(String args[]) {
        Person p1 = new Person("Shreya");
        Person p2 = new Person("Harry");
```

```
        Person p3 = new Person("Paul");
        Person p4 = new Person("Paul");
        HashSet<Person> set = new HashSet<>();
        set.add(p1);
        set.add(p2);
        set.add(p3);
        set.add(p4);
        System.out.println(set.size());
    }
}
class Person {
    String name;
    Person(String name) {
        this.name = name;
    }
    public int hashCode() {
        return 20;
    }
    public boolean equals(Object obj) {
        return true;
    }
}
```

- a 0
- b 1
- c 2
- d 3
- e 4
- f Compilation error
- g Runtime exception

Q 4-11. Which code option when inserted at //INSERT CODE HERE will enable you to sort instances of class Student using their natural order and add them to a TreeSet?

```
class Student implements Comparator<Student> {
    String id;
    String name;
    //INSERT CODE HERE
}
```

- a public boolean compare(Object obj1, Object obj2) {/* relevant code here */}
- b public int compare(Object obj1, Object obj2) {/* relevant code here */}
- c public boolean compareTo(Student s1, Student s2) {/* relevant code here */}
- d public boolean compare(Object obj1) {/* relevant code here */}
- e public int compare(Student obj1) {/* relevant code here */}
- f None of the above

Q 4-12. Select true statements about method `hashCode()`.

- **a** Classes `HashSet` and `HashMap` use method `hashCode()` to store and retrieve their values.
- **b** Class `TreeSet` can use method `hashCode()` to store and retrieve its elements.
- **c** Method `hashCode()` is used to test for object equality and inequality for a class.
- **d** If `hashCode()` for two objects of the same class returns the same value, the objects are considered equal.
- **e** For a class, method `hashCode()` can be used to test for object inequality.

ANSWERS TO SAMPLE EXAM QUESTIONS

A 4-1. a, c, d

[4.1] Create a generic class

Explanation: Though Java recommends using single letters like `T` or `V` to specify the type, using the letters `A` and `B` is correct in option (a) as per the syntax.

Option (b) is incorrect because it uses invalid syntax to specify the type parameters to a class. To specify multiple type parameters in a class declaration, you need to specify a placeholder for only the type—not its variables.

Option (c) and (d) are correct. It's acceptable to define the type parameters as a subtype of an existing Java class. Though not recommended, it's acceptable to use type parameters with more than one letter: `Aa` and `Bb`.

A 4-2. b, c

[4.1] Create a generic class

Explanation: Option (a) is incorrect. A raw type doesn't include the generic information. For the generic type `List<T>`, its raw type is `List`. You don't need to define a raw type explicitly for any generic class or interface. You can access the raw type of all the generic types.

Option (d) is incorrect. Like generic classes, generic interfaces can define any number of generic type parameters.

A 4-3. b, c

[4.2] Use the diamond for type inference
[4.3] Analyze the interoperability of collections that use raw types and generic types

Explanation: Option (a) generates a compilation warning, because it uses generic code without its type information.

Options (b) and (c) are correct. The type that you use for declaring a variable of class `Box` is `String`, as in `Box<String> box`. Class `Box` defines only one constructor that accepts an object of its type parameter. Even though you can just use the angle brackets and drop the type parameter `String` from it, you must pass a `String` object to the constructor of class `Box` or a subclass. The following code also compiles without warning (and I pass an instance of a subclass of the generic type parameter into the constructor):

```
Box<Object> box3 = new Box<Object>("Object");
```

Option (d) fails to compile. Even though class `String` subclasses class `Object`, the reference variable box of type `Box<Object>` can't refer to objects of `Box<String>`.

A 4-4. a, d, e

[4.3] Analyze the interoperability of collections that use raw types and generic types

Explanation: The options (a), (d), and (e), when implemented together, will allow method `concat()` to be used with generics without generating any warnings.

   Option (b) is incorrect. Replacing line 1 with `public static String concat (List<Integer> list) {` would generate a `ClassCastException` at runtime, if a list other than a list of integer objects is passed to method `concat()`.

   Option (c) is incorrect because a `for` loop is required to iterate through the list objects.

   Options (d) and (e) are correct. With generics, you can use an advanced `for` loop to iterate through list elements. Because the object type is already specified (as `String`), the advanced `for` loop returns `String` objects, which don't require an explicit cast.

   Option (f) is incorrect and won't compile.

A 4-5. b, c

[4.3] Analyze the interoperability of collections that use raw types and generic types

Explanation: The code executes, printing all the values of the objects added to the `List`. Method `toString()` is implicitly called when you try to print the value of an object.

   Using a raw type of interface is allowed post-introduction of generics. This is allowed for backward compatibility with nongenerics code.

   But all uses of the add methods with `List`'s raw type will compile with the following compilation warning:

```
warning: [unchecked] unchecked call to add(E) as a member of the raw type
    ArrayList
        list.add("ABCD");
             ^
  where E is a type-variable:
    E extends Object declared in class ArrayList
```

A 4-6. g

[4.5] Create and use List, Set, and Deque implementations

Explanation: The code fails at runtime with the following message because class Phone doesn't implement the java.lang.Comparable interface:

```
Exception in thread "main" java.lang.ClassCastException: Phone
can't be cast to java.lang.Comparable.
```

This exception is thrown when the code tries to add a value to set. A TreeSet should be able to sort its elements either by using their natural order or by using a Comparator object passed to TreeSet's constructor. A class defines its natural sort order by implementing the Comparable interface. Class Phone doesn't define its natural order. Also, while instantiating set, no Comparator object is passed to TreeSet's constructor.

You can instantiate a TreeSet that neither uses elements with a natural sort order nor is passed a Comparator object. But such a TreeSet will throw a runtime exception when you try to add an element to it.

A 4-7. e

[4.6] Create and use Map implementations

Explanation: Option (a) is incorrect because method sort() of class Arrays sorts only arrays, not HashMap.

Option (b) is incorrect. Method sort() of class Collections sorts List objects, not HashMap.

Option (c) is incorrect because Collection isn't defined in the Java API.

Option (d) is incorrect because method arrange() isn't defined in class Collections.

Option (f) is incorrect because SortedSet is an interface, which can't be instantiated.

A 4-8. b, c, d, e

[4.2] Use the diamond for type inference
[4.3] Analyze the interoperability of collections that use raw types and generic types
[4.5] Create and use List, Set, and Deque implementations

Explanation: Option (a) is incorrect. This code won't compile. When Java runtime instantiates a LinkedList object, it must know the type of objects that it stores—either implicitly or explicitly. But, in this option, the type of the LinkedList object is neither stated explicitly nor can it be inferred.

Option (b) is correct. The wildcard ? is used to refer to any type of object. Here you're creating a reference variable myArrayList, which is a List of any type. This reference variable is initialized with LinkedList object, whose type is inferred by the argument passed to the constructor of LinkedList.

Option (c) is correct. This option uses the bounded wildcard `<? extends String>`, restricting the unknown type to be either class `String` or any of its subclasses. Even though `String` is a final class, `? extends String` is acceptable code.

Option (d) generates a compiler warning because it uses raw types.

Option (e) doesn't generate a compiler warning because the object creation uses generics.

A 4-9. a

[4.5] Create and use List, Set, and Deque implementations

Explanation: Option (b) is incorrect. Method `equals()` is used to determine the equality of objects.

Option (c) is incorrect. Class `Collections` defines two overloaded versions of method `sort()`. Both accept a `List` object, with or without a `Comparator` object. Method `sort()` sorts a `List` passed to it into ascending order, according to the natural ordering of its elements, or by using the order specified by a `Comparator` object.

Option (d) is incorrect. Though `HashSet` and `HashMap` use `hashCode()` for hashing, `TreeSet` doesn't.

Option (e) is incorrect. Java doesn't recommend any particular algorithm for writing an efficient `hashCode()` method. But Java does recommend writing an efficient algorithm.

A 4-10. b

[4.5] Create and use List, Set, and Deque implementations

Explanation: Method `HashSet()` uses method `hashCode()` to determine an appropriate bucket for its element. If it adds a new element to a bucket that already contains an element, `HashSet` calls `equals` on the elements to determine whether they're equal. `HashSet` doesn't allow duplicate elements. When it adds a `Person` object, the same `hashCode` value makes it land in the same bucket. Calling the `equals()` method returns `true`, signaling that an attempt is being made to add a duplicate object, which isn't allowed by `HashSet`.

A 4-11. f

[4.5] Create and use List, Set, and Deque implementations
[4.7] Use java.util.Comparator and java.lang.Comparable

Explanation: Instances of a class are sorted using its *natural order*, if the class implements the `Comparable` interface and not `Comparator`.

The `Comparator` interface is used to define how to compare two objects for sorting (less than, equal to, or greater than). Unlike the `Comparable` interface, the `Comparator` interface need not be implemented by the class whose objects are to be sorted. The Comparator interface can be used to define an order for objects if the objects don't define their natural order. It can also be used to define a custom order for objects. You can use a Comparator object to define an order for objects, the natural order of which you can't define or modify. When you pass a Comparator object to the instantiation of a collection class like TreeMap, the TreeMap uses the order as defined by the Comparator object, ignoring the natural order of its keys.

For example, the following class defines a custom (descending) order for String objects:

```
class DescendingStrings implements Comparator<String> {
    public int compare(String s1, String s2) {
        return s2.name.compareTo(s1.name);
    }
}
```

A 4-12. a, e

[4.5] Create and use List, Set, and Deque implementations
[4.6] Create and use Map implementations

Explanation: In option (a), classes HashSet and HashMap use hashing to store and retrieve their values. Hashing uses the hashCode value to determine the bucket in which the values should be stored.

Option (b) is incorrect. TreeSet ignores the hashCode values. A TreeSet stores its elements based on its key's natural ordering or the ordering defined by a Comparator.

Options (c) and (d) are incorrect, and (e) is correct. The hashCode value is used to test for object inequality. If two objects return different hashCode values, they can never be equal. But if your objects return the same hashCode values, they can be unequal (if their equals() returns false).

String processing 5

Exam objectives covered in this chapter	What you need to know
[5.1] Search, parse, and build strings (including `Scanner`, `String-Tokenizer`, `StringBuilder`, `String`, and `Formatter`)	The methods that can be used to parse and build strings, from classes `Scanner`, `StringTokenizer`, `StringBuilder`, and `Formatter`.
[5.2] Search, parse, and replace strings by using regular expressions, using expression patterns for matching limited to . (dot), * (star), + (plus), ?, \d, \D, \s, \S, \w, \W, \b, \B, [], ()	What regular expressions (regex) are and how they're used to search, parse, and replace strings. Understand the use of the relevant API classes in the `java.util.regex` package.
[5.3] Format strings using the formatting parameters %b, %c, %d, %f, and %s in format strings	The purpose of formatting parameters to format strings and other data types. How to determine code output when invalid combination of format parameters and data types is used.

Imagine that after completing a 500-page draft of your novel, you want to change the name of your main character from *Beri* to *Bery*. This should be simple, right? You can use your word processor's Find/Replace option and be well on your way. From a text file, you pull out a list of email addresses of all the publishers to whom you wish to submit your manuscript. But before using these addresses, you want to run a quick check to ensure that they're valid—that they include an @ sign and a dot (.), followed by a domain name. This should also be simple. You can use your email client to check them. Now, imagine your novel becomes a best seller, and your publisher wants to translate it into multiple languages. Wow! Assuming that your novel includes numbers and decimal numbers, the publisher would also need to reformat these numbers based on the language that your text is translated into. Various languages might use different separators in decimal numbers. Though not a straightforward task, it's feasible.

Finding and replacing text, validating it, and formatting numbers in different ways are all examples of common requirements. Java applications might need to perform similar common data manipulation and formatting tasks. To accomplish this, Java includes flexible and powerful classes and methods to search, parse, replace, and format data. This chapter covers

- How classes from the Java API (`String`, `StringBuilder`, `Scanner`, `String-Tokenizer`, `Formatter`) can help you search, parse, build, and replace strings
- Regular expressions and what you can do with them
- How to format strings by using format specifiers

Even though you might be familiar with working with the Java programming language, it's possible that you didn't get an opportunity to work with regular expressions (regex) in Java (or in any other programming language). Now available to be used with most programming languages, either integrated or as an external library, regex is a powerful and flexible language to describe data and search matching data. But this chapter's coverage of regex is limited to the exam topics.

Let's start with the basic differences between searching text for exact matches and searching for regex patterns.

5.1 Regular expressions

[5.2] Search, parse, and replace strings by using regular expressions, using expression patterns for matching limited to . (dot), * (star), + (plus), ?, \d, \D, \s, \S, \w, \W, \b, \B, [], ().

As opposed to exact matches, you can use regex to search for data that matches a *pattern*. Let's imagine that in addition to changing the name of your main character in your novel, you want to change all references of *sun* to *moon*. Though the solution might seem as simple as using Find/Replace, how would you go about it if in some places in the novel, *sun* is misspelled as *sin*, *son*, or *sbn*?

Figure 5.1 compares searching for a fixed literal value (`sun`) with finding a *regex pattern* (`s.n`) against a target string value: `sun soon son`.

As shown in figure 5.1, the literal search string `sun` finds one match, starting at position 0, in the target string `sun soon son`. Unlike the unmatched values, I've highlighted the matching value with a dark background. On the other hand, the regex pattern `s.n` (the dot is a *metacharacter* that can match any character) finds two

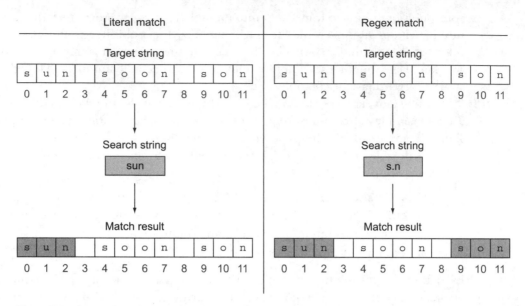

Figure 5.1   Comparing the matching of literal values with finding regex patterns

matches: sun and son, starting at positions 0 and 9 in the target search string sun soon son.

Similarly, you can use regex to find text that matches a pattern and to perform operations such as these:

- *Check method arguments*—Determine whether a string value starts with Sh and ends with either y or a. Determine whether author@manning is a valid email address.
- *Validate user input*—Verify whether 765-981-abc is a correct phone number.
- *Search usernames in a text file*—Find the ones that are exactly 10 characters long, starting with a letter *A* and followed by 4 digits and 5 letters.

All of these are common examples of needing regular expressions to *describe* your target data and find it in a stream (a string, a file, a network connection).

 NOTE   After you've found your target data, you can manipulate it any way you like: replace it, print it to a file, alert a user about invalid data, and so forth.

As I move on with this chapter, I'll show you how to use metacharacters, character classes, and quantifiers in regex. You'll see how to use them in code to search for matching data and manipulate it.

Before I take a plunge into this topic, let me reiterate that *regular expressions* is a relatively big topic, and this book limits its coverage to the exam topics. Though I can't guarantee that you'll start writing amazing regex after reading this chapter, you'll definitely be comfortable using them, and of course, ready to answer the relevant exam questions.

Let's see what a regular expression is and how to evolve one.

5.1.1 *What is a regular expression?*

The example in the previous section showed you that exact matches might not be able to find all your matching data. In such cases, you need to define *patterns* of data (for example, s.n) that can match your target data. You can define these patterns by using regular expressions. Regular expressions come with a syntax (which we'll cover in the next few pages). With that syntax you can create a pattern to describe target search data.

What's the difference between describing data and specifying it? When you *describe* data, you detail out its attributes or characteristics. When you *specify* data, you state the exact data. In the example shown in figure 5.1, the regex s.n describes the data as follows:

- The first character must be *s*.
- Allow any character at the second position.
- The third character must be *n*.

 NOTE *Regular expressions* is also referred to as a language because it has its own syntax. Regex refers to both the language and the data patterns that it defines.

Let's work with some examples so that this definition makes more sense. First up, character classes.

5.1.2 *Character classes*

Character classes aren't classes defined in the Java API. The term refers to a set of characters that you can enclose within square brackets ([]). When used in a regex pattern, Java looks for exactly *one* of the specified *characters* (not words).

Referring to our example of the novel, imagine that you want to search for all occurrences of the phrase *organized an event*. But *organized* is also written as *organised* (in the United Kingdom). Instead of searching your manuscript twice—first for *organized* and then for *organised*—you can use the character class [sz] in the search string organi[sz]ed. [sz] would match either *s* or *z* so you can find both *organized* and *organised*.

Let's work with another example, one you might see on the exam. Figure 5.2 shows how character class [fdn] is used to find an exact match of *f, d,* or *n*. With a target string *I am fine to dine at nine*, the regex [fdn]ine matches the words *fine, dine,* and *nine,* at positions 5, 13, and 21.

Let's see how you can use Java classes Pattern and Matcher (covered in detail later in the chapter) from the java.util.regex package to work with searching the text shown in the preceding example.

Target string

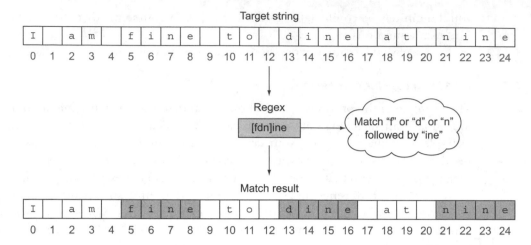

Figure 5.2   Character class [fdn] matches exactly one occurrence of *f*, *d*, or *n*.

Listing 5.1   Simple code to work with regex using `Pattern` and `Matcher`

```
import java.util.regex.*;
class UseRegex{
    public static void main(String[] args) {
        String targetString = "I am fine to dine at nine";
        String regex = "[fdn]ine";

        Pattern pattern = Pattern.compile(regex);
        Matcher matcher = pattern.matcher(targetString);
        while (matcher.find()) {
            System.out.println(matcher.group() + " starts at " +
                               matcher.start() + ", ends at " +
                               matcher.end());
        }
    }
}
```

1 Target string to be searched

2 Regex pattern

3 Instantiate Pattern using factory method compile().

4 Matcher created from pattern specifying target string

5 while matches found

6 Prints matching text, start and end position.

 NOTE   Building a string by using the concatenation operators (+ and +=) isn't a recommended practice. Later in this chapter, you'll see how to use formatting classes and parameters such as %s and %d to include and format variable values in `String` literal values.

Here's the output of the preceding code:

```
fine starts at 5, ends at 9
dine starts at 13, ends at 17
nine starts at 21, ends at 25
```

The code at **1** defines the target string to be searched. The code at **2** defines the regex pattern. The code at **3**, class `Pattern`, a compiled representation of a regex, is instantiated. Because this class doesn't define any public constructor, you must instantiate it by using its factory method `compile()`. Method `compile()` compiles a regular expression into a `Pattern` object. At ❹, class `Matcher` is instantiated by calling method `matcher()` on the `Pattern` instance. `Matcher` will match the given input against this pattern. Class `Matcher` is an engine that performs match operations on a character sequence by interpreting a regex pattern. It also doesn't define a public constructor.

Method `find()` of class `Matcher` returns `true` as long as it can find more matches of a regex in a target string. At ❺, the `while` loop executes for all matches found. The code at ❻ uses methods `group()`, `start()`, and `end()` to extract the matched string, its start position in the target string, and its end position in the target string.

Compare the values returned by `matcher.start()` and `matcher.end()` in the output shown for the preceding example and in figure 5.2. The substring *fine* occupies positions 5, 6, 7, and 8 in the target string *I am fine to dine at nine*. But `matcher.end()` returns the value 9. Beware of this on the exam. It can be combined in a tricky manner with other methods like `String`'s method `substring()`.

 EXAM TIP If a matched string occupies index positions 1, 2, and 3 in a target string, method `end()` of class `Matcher` returns the value 4 for the corresponding call on `end()`. You can expect trick questions on this returned value on the exam.

Table 5.1 list examples of simple character classes that you can use to create regex patterns and find them in target data.

Table 5.1   Examples of regex patterns that use simple character classes

Class type	Regex pattern	Description
Simple	`[agfd]`	Match exactly one from a, g, f, or d
Range	`[a-f0-7]`	Match exactly one from the range a to f (both inclusive) or 0 to 7 (both inclusive)
Negation	`[^123k-m]`	Match exactly one character that is not 1, 2, or 3 or from the range k to m (both inclusive)

 EXAM TIP If the Java Runtime engine determines that a pattern is invalid, it throws the runtime exception `PatternSyntaxException`. On the exam, when you see a question on the possible output of a string processing code, examine the regex pattern for invalid values.

5.1.3 *Predefined character classes*

Java's regex engine supports predefined character classes for your convenience. Table 5.2 lists the predefined classes included on this exam. You can test these regex using the class `UseRegex` included in listing 5.1.

 NOTE   To use a regex pattern that includes a backslash (\), you must *escape* the \ in the pattern by preceding it with another \. The character literal \ has a special meaning; it's used as an escape character. To use it as a literal, it must be escaped.

Table 5.2 Predefined character classes on this exam

Character class	Description
.	Any character (may or may not match line terminators)
\d	A digit: `[0-9]`
\D	A nondigit: `[^0-9]`
\s	A whitespace character: [space, `\t` (tab), `\n` (new line), `\x0B` (end of line), `\f` (form feed), `\r` (carriage)]
\S	A nonwhitespace character: `[^\s]`
\w	A word character: `[a-zA-Z_0-9]`
\W	A nonword character: `[^\w]`

The dot (`.`) is a metacharacter that matches *any* character. Metacharacters are special characters, which have special meanings. The search regex pattern `1.3` is not used to find *1.3* in the target string. It'll find the digit 1 followed by *any* character, followed by the digit 3. For example, it'll also find all of these: 123, 1M3, 193, 1)3, 1.3, 1,3, and 1+3.

Table 5.3 lists example target strings, regex patterns, and the result of finding a regex pattern in the target string. Figure 5.3, a pictorial representation of table 5.3, shows a target string, the regex pattern that is applied to the target string, and the results. The regex pattern that could be matched in the target string is highlighted

Table 5.3 Examples of target strings, regex patterns that use predefined character classes, and their matching results.

Target string	Regex	Match found	Start and end positions of match found
A5C7M%	\d	Yes	5 starts at 1, ends at 2 7 starts at 3, ends at 4
A5C7M%	\D	Yes	A starts at 0, ends at 1 C starts at 2, ends at 3 M starts at 4, ends at 5 % starts at 5, ends at 6

Table 5.3 **Examples of target strings, regex patterns that use predefined character classes, and their matching results.**

Target string	Regex	Match found	Start and end positions of match found
A B 890	\s	Yes	(First space) starts at 1, ends at 2 (Second space) starts at 3, ends at 4 (Third space) starts at 4, ends at 5
A B $890	\S	Yes	A starts at 0, ends at 1 B starts at 2, ends at 3 $ starts at 4, ends at 5 8 starts at 5, ends at 6 9 starts at 6, ends at 7 0 starts at 7, ends at 8
A b$9;	\w	Yes	A starts at 0, ends at 1 b starts at 2, ends at 3 9 starts at 4, ends at 5
A b$9;	\W	Yes	(Space) starts at 1, ends at 2 $ starts at 3, ends at 4 ; starts at 5, ends at 6

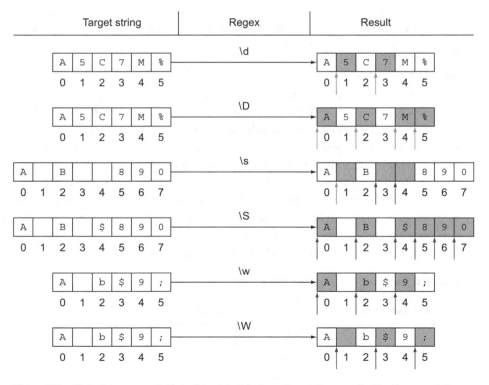

Figure 5.3 **Pictorial representation of target strings, regex pattern applied to them, and the matches found, including matching positions**

with a colored background. The starting position numbers of the matched string are marked with an up arrow.

Let's code an example that uses a predefined character class and replace all the matching occurrences with a literal string:

```
class UsePredefinedCharacterClass{
    public static void main(String[] args) {
        String targetString = "A b$9;";
        String regex = "\\W";

        Pattern pattern = Pattern.compile(regex);
        Matcher matcher = pattern.matcher(targetString);
        String replacedStr = matcher.replaceAll("[]");

        System.out.println(replacedStr);
    }
}
```

Target search string — Instantiates Pattern and compiles regex pattern.

Regex to be searched

Creates a matcher that will match given input against this pattern.

Replaces all matches found with literal [].

Prints A[]b[]9[].

The preceding code uses the illustration in figure 5.3. It uses Matcher's replaceAll() to replace all matching regex patterns in the target string with a string literal.

 EXAM TIP   Because String objects are immutable, calling replaceAll() won't change the contents of String referred to by the variable target-String in the preceding code example. replaceAll() creates and returns a new String object with the replaced values. Watch out for questions based on it on the exam.

5.1.4   *Matching boundaries*

Say you want to find all occurrences of the word *the* in your book. To do that, you'd need to search for the text *the*. Well, the same is true when you want to match *the*, which can be part of another word, for example, *their, leather,* or *seethe*. So you need a way to limit your searches to the start or end of a word. *Matching boundaries* can help you with this. You can match boundaries including the start of a line, a word, a nonword, or the end of a line by using regex patterns. Table 5.4 lists the boundary constructs that you're likely to see on the exam. Even though the boundary constructs ^ (beginning of line) and $ (end of line) aren't explicitly included in the exam objectives, you might see them in answer options that are incorrect. To ward off any confusion, I've included them in this section. These constructs also might be helpful in your projects at work.

Table 5.4   Boundary constructs on this exam

Boundary construct	Description
\b	A word boundary
\B	A nonword boundary
^	Beginning of a line
$	End of a line

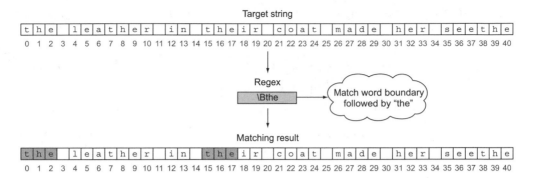

Figure 5.4 Matching regex pattern `\Bthe` against the string value `the leather in their coat made her seethe`. `\B` is a word boundary. When placed before the text *the*, it limits searches to finding words that *start* with *the*.

Let's see what happens when you match the regex pattern `\bthe` against the literal string value `the leather in their code made her seethe`, as shown in figure 5.4.

As shown in figure 5.4, `\bthe` matches words that start with *the*, including *the* and *their*. The first match is found at position 0, and the second match is found at position 15, in *their*. What if you want to find words that include *the* but don't start with *the*?

Let's modify the regex pattern `\bthe` used in the preceding example to `\Bthe`; instead of matching words that start with *the*, you'll match words that don't start with *the*. Figure 5.5 shows the matching values.

The regex pattern `\Bthe` matches all occurrences of *the* that aren't at the beginning of a word. For the match found at position 7 in the word *leather*, it doesn't matter whether *the* is followed by any other character or a word boundary. What do you think will be the output of matching the regex patterns `^the` and `the$` against the literal string value `the leather in their coat made her seethe`? Try it out using a simple code snippet.

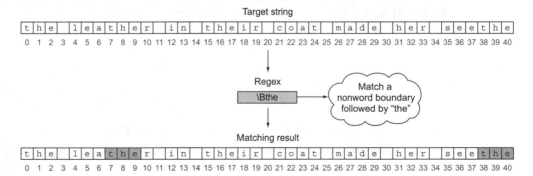

Figure 5.5 Matching regex pattern `\Bthe` against the string value `the leather in their coat made her seethe`. `\B` is a nonword boundary. When placed before the text *the*, it limits its searches to finding words that *don't start* with *the*.

It's time to test your skills in determining matching values for a regex pattern, in the first "Twist in the Tale" exercise.

Twist in the Tale 5.1

Consider the following string literal value:

```
String targetString = "The leather in their coat made her seethe";
```

Which of these options correctly defines a regex pattern for searching the literal string for *the* at either the beginning or end of a word, but not in its middle?

- a   `String regex = "\\Bthe\\B";`
- b   `String regex = "\\bthe\\B";`
- c   `String regex = "\\Bthe\\b";`
- d   `String regex = "\\bthe|the\\b";`

It's interesting to note that none of these regex options is invalid, and each produces output. Can you also determine the matched *the* for all these options?

5.1.5   *Quantifiers*

Imagine you want to search for the word *colour* or *color* in your book. A layman would search the book text first for *colour* and then again for *color*. A smart searching tool could search for both strings using a single search string by using quantifiers in the search string. You can specify the number of occurrences of a pattern to match in a target value by using quantifiers. The coverage of quantifiers is limited to greedy quantifiers on this exam. You could also use possessive or reluctant quantifiers. But because they aren't on the exam, I won't cover them any further. Table 5.5 describes the greedy quantifiers.

Table 5.5   Greedy quantifiers

Quantifier (Greedy)	Description
X?	Matching X, once or not at all
X*	Matching X, zero or more times
X+	Matching X, one or more times

The greedy quantifiers are so named because they make the matcher read the complete input string before starting to get the first match. If the matcher can't match the entire input string, it backs off the input string by one character and attempts again. If repeats this until a match is found or until no more characters are left. At the end, depending on whether you asked it to match zero, one, or more occurrences, it'll try to match the pattern against zero, one, or more characters from the input string.

USING ? TO MATCH ZERO OR ONE OCCURRENCE

- In all the preceding examples, we tried to search for exactly one occurrence of a particular digit or character. What if you want to match zero or one occurrence of a letter? For example, *color* in the United States is spelled *colour* in the United Kingdom. How will you match all occurrences of *colour* or *color* in a text file? The metacharacter ? can help: *Search string*—I am colour in UK and color in US

- *Regex*—`colou?r`

- Searches for *colour* or *color*

- In the preceding example, you apply ? to a single letter. You can also apply ? to a group of characters. How would you search for occurrences of *August* and *Aug* in a text? To do so, you can *group* the required characters by using parentheses and place ? right after them: *Search string*—It can be written as August or Aug

- *Regex*—`Aug(ust)?`

- Searches for *August* or *Aug*

- Imagine you need to search for the words *ball, mall, fall,* and *all* by using a regular expression in the target text: *Search string*—A ball can fall in a mall with all

- *Regex*—`[bmf]?all`

- Searches for *ball, mall, fall,* or *all*

In this example, because ? is applied to the character class `[bmf]`, it can be used to search for a single occurrence of either *b, m, f,* or none of these. Note that `[bmf]` without ? wouldn't match the text *all*.

In the sections to follow, I'll cover working with a combination of ?, square brackets, and curly brackets. The set of combinations and permutations that can be used with a language feature makes it interesting, and at the same time overwhelming! The key to conquer such features is to understand a simpler concept before moving on to the next level.

ZERO LENGTH MATCHES WITH ?

Let's try to match the regex `d?` against the target string `bday`. Following are the target strings and the corresponding code with its output:

- *Search string*—bday

- *Regex*—`d?`

- Searches for zero or one occurrence of letter *d*

Following is the relevant code:

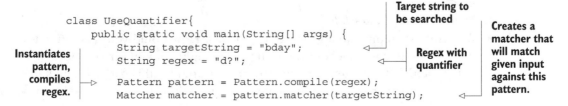

```
class UseQuantifier{
    public static void main(String[] args) {
        String targetString = "bday";
        String regex = "d?";

        Pattern pattern = Pattern.compile(regex);
        Matcher matcher = pattern.matcher(targetString);
```

```
    while (matcher.find()) {
        System.out.printf("Found :%s: starts at %d, ends at %d",
                          matcher.group(),
                          matcher.start(),
                          matcher.end());
        System.out.println();
    }
  }
}
```

 NOTE   You can use the preceding code (class `UseQuantifier`) to match a regex pattern against a string value, listing the start and end positions of the matches found.

Here's the output of this code:

```
Found :: starts at 0, ends at 0
Found :d: starts at 1, ends at 2
Found :: starts at 2, ends at 2
Found :: starts at 3, ends at 3
Found :: starts at 4, ends at 4
```

Does this output make you wonder why five matches are found? Remember that ? will match zero or one occurrence of the letter *d*. The regex engine found zero matches, with length 0, at positions 0, 2, 3, and 4. It found one match (with length 1) at position 1. Figure 5.6 illustrates the found matches.

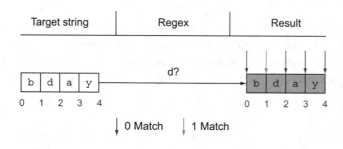

Figure 5.6   Matching regex pattern d? against the string value bday

USING * TO MATCH ZERO OR MORE OCCURRENCES

- You can use the metacharacter * to match zero or more occurrences of a regex. The regex `fo*d` will match all occurrences of words in which *o* occurs zero or more times: *Search string*—food, fod, fooodder, fd
- *Regex*—`fo*d`
- Matches *food, fod, foood, fd*
- You can also apply * to a group of characters. How would you search for text that starts with a letter, ends with a letter, and might contain zero or more digits in between? Let's create the regex pattern to search for this pattern. The letters could be either in lowercase or uppercase. You know that \d or [0-9] can be

used to match any digit and that [A-Za-z] can be used to match any letter in lowercase or uppercase. Because the digit can appear zero or more times, we evolve the regex as follows: *Search string*—b234a A6Z abc

- *Regex*— [A-Za-z] \d* [A-Za-z]
- Searches for text starting and ending with a letter and containing zero or more digits in between

The regex [A-Za-z] \d* [A-Za-z] matches b234a, A6Z, and ab in the preceding search string. It matches ab because \d* asked it to look for zero or more occurrences of digits. Because ab has zero digits between *a* and *b*, it's matched. It won't match bc because b was already consumed for matching ab.

- Now, what if you need to modify the preceding example, to limit the digits that appear between the letters to a range of 1 to 5? This is simple: just replace \d* with [1-5]. Examine the following: *Search string*—b234a A6Z abc
- *Regex*— [A-Za-z] [1-5] * [A-Za-z]
- Searches for text starting and ending with a letter, and containing zero or more digits in the range 1–5 in between

The preceding regex [A-Za-z] [1-5] * [A-Za-z] matches only b234a and ab in the target string b234a A6Z abc. It doesn't match A6Z because 6 isn't in the range 1–5.

Zero Length Matches with *

Since * matches zero or more occurrences of a pattern, it also occurs in zero length matches, that is, a match wherein the specified pattern can't be found. Revisit the previous subsection, "Zero length matches with ?". If you replace the pattern d? with d*, the code will output the same result because * also matches zero occurrences of a pattern, like the metacharacter ?.

Using + to match one or more occurrences

- You can use the metacharacter + to match one or more occurrences of a regex. For example, the regex fo+d will match all occurrences of words, where *o* occurs one or more times: *Search string*—food, fod, fooodder, fd
- *Regex*—fo+d
- Matches *food, fod, foood*

You can also apply + to a group of characters. How would you search for text that starts with a letter and ends with a letter and may contain one or more digits in between? We know that \d can be used to match any digit and that [A-Za-z] can be used to match any letter in lowercase or uppercase. Because the digit can appear one or more times, you can evolve the regex as follows:

- *Search string*—b234a A6Z abc
- *Regex*— [A-Za-z] \d+ [A-Za-z]
- Searches for text starting and ending with a letter and containing one or more digits in between
- Matches b234a A6Z

The regex matches b234a and A6Z in the preceding search string. It doesn't match ab because \d+ asks it to look for one or more digits. Because ab has zero digits between a and b, it isn't matched!

Now, what if we need to modify the preceding example to limit the digits that appear between the letters in the range of 1 to 5? This is simple: just replace \d+ with [1-5]+. Examine the following:

- *Search string*—b234a A6Z abc
- *Regex*—[A-Za-z][1-5]+[A-Za-z]
- Searches for text starting and ending with a letter and containing one or more digits in the range of 1–5 in between
- Matches b234a

This regex matches only b234a in the search string. It doesn't match A6Z because 6 isn't in the range 1–5. It doesn't match ab because it doesn't have a digit in the range of 1–5 between the letters *a* and *b*. Since + looks for one or more occurrences of a pattern, it *doesn't* qualify for zero length matches.

 NOTE   For this exam, you should know how to use the ?, *, and + metacharacters in regex. Metacharacters have a different meaning for the regex engine.

If you don't remember how many instances *, +, and ? match, table 5.6 lists a silly but simple set of questions and answers that might help you remember.

Table 5.6   Questions and answers to help remember the number of matches for *, +, and ?

Metacharacter	Occurrence	Funny question	Silly answer to funny question
*	0 or many	How many *stars* can you see?	0 in a cloudy sky, many in a clear sky
?	0 or 1	What can be the answer to one of the most important *questions*: Do you love me?	Yes (1) or no (0)
+	1 or more	How many spouses can you *add* in your life?	1 or more

5.1.6   *Java's regex support*

Java incorporated regex support by defining the java.util.regex package in version 1.4. Regex in Java supports Unicode as it matches against CharSequence objects. This package defines classes for matching character sequences against the patterns specified by regular expressions. For this, you particularly need the Matcher and Pattern classes.

I've used these classes in the coding examples in the previous sections. Class Pattern is a compiled representation of a regular expression. It doesn't define a public constructor. You can instantiate this class by using its factory method `compile()`. Here's an example:

```
Pattern pattern = Pattern.compile("a*b");
```

After you create a `Pattern` object, you must instantiate a `Matcher` object, which can be used to find matching patterns in a target string. Class `Matcher` is referred to as an engine that scans a target `CharSequence` for a matching regex pattern. Class `Matcher` doesn't define a public constructor. You can create and access a `Matcher` object by calling the instance method `matcher()` on an object of class `Pattern`:

```
Matcher m = p.matcher("aaaaab");
```

After you have access to the `Matcher` object, you can do the following:

- Match a complete input sequence against a pattern.
- Match the input sequence starting at the beginning.
- Find multiple occurrences of the matching pattern.
- Retrieve information about the matching groups.

 NOTE Class `Matcher` is an engine that interprets a `Pattern` and matches it against a character sequence.

With the addition of the `java.util.regex` package, Java also added methods, like `matches()`, to existing classes, like `String`, which matched string values with the given regular expression. However, behind the scenes, `String.matches()` calls method `matches()` defined in class `Pattern`. At times, such methods might also manipulate the values themselves, *before* using classes `Pattern`/ `Matcher`, to support regex.

In the next section, I'll continue working with more examples of creating and using regex patterns, using classes `String`, `StringBuilder`, `Scanner`, and `StringTokenizer`. Class `String` defines multiple methods to search and replace string values based on exact and regex patterns. But class `StringBuilder` doesn't support search or replace methods based on regex. You'll see how you can use `Scanner` and `String-Tokenizer` to parse and tokenize streams (such as text in a file) by using exact text or regex patterns.

 NOTE The use of `StringTokenizer` is discouraged in new code. This legacy class is retained for backward compatibility. Use classes from the `java.util.regex` package or `String.split()` to get the functionality of `StringTokenizer`.

5.2   *Searching, parsing, and building strings*

When did you last search the internet for your favorite music, the latest news, or stock prices? Most people do that every day, every hour. Apart from searching the internet, people also search printed hardcopies. Searching text, and tokenizing and parsing it, are important and integral tasks to complete a lot of other tasks. Java includes multiple classes like `Scanner`, `StringTokenizer`, `StringBuilder`, `String`, and `Formatter` to accomplish searching, parsing, and building strings. Let's get started with how to search for exact matches and regex patterns.

> [5.1]   Search, parse, and build strings (including Scanner, StringTokenizer, StringBuilder, String, and Formatter)

> [5.2]   Search, parse, and replace strings by using regular expressions, using expression patterns for matching limited to . (dot), * (star), + (plus), ?, \d, \D, \s, \S, \w, \W, \b, \B, [], ()

5.2.1   *Searching strings*

Class `String` defines multiple methods to search strings for exact matches of a single character or string. These methods allow searching from the beginning of a string, or starting or ending at a specified position.

METHODS INDEXOF() AND LASTINDEXOF()

Both methods `indexOf()` and `lastIndexOf()` find a matching character or string in a string and return the matching position. Method `indexOf()` returns the *first* matching position of a character or string, starting from the specified position of the string, or from its beginning. Method `lastIndexOf()` returns the *last* matching position of a character in the entire string, or its subset (position 0 to the specified position). Figure 5.7 shows a pictorial representation of a string, use of these methods, and the positions of the matches found.

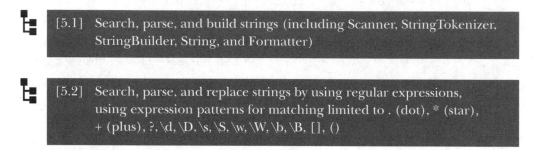

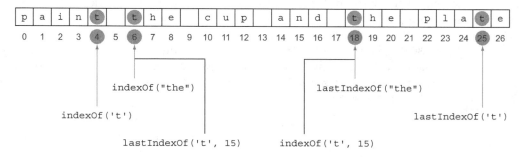

Figure 5.7   Showing use of methods `indexOf()` and `lastIndexOf()`

Here's the code that implements the methods shown in figure 5.7:

```
String sentence = "paint the cup and the plate";
System.out.println(sentence.indexOf('t'));            ⟵  Prints "4"
System.out.println(sentence.lastIndexOf('t', 15));    ⟵  Prints "6"

System.out.println(sentence.indexOf("the"));          ⟵  Prints "6"
System.out.println(sentence.indexOf('t', 15));        ⟵  Prints "18"

System.out.println(sentence.lastIndexOf("the"));      ⟵  Prints "18"
System.out.println(sentence.lastIndexOf('t'));        ⟵  Prints "25"
```

Both methods `indexOf()` and `lastIndexOf()` differ in the manner in which they search a target string: `indexOf()` searches in increasing position numbers, and `lastIndexOf()` searches backward. Due to this difference, `indexOf('a', -100)` will search the complete string, but `lastIndexOf('a', -100)` won't. In a similar manner, because `lastIndexOf()` searches backward, `lastIndexOf('a', 100)` will search this string, but `indexOf('a', 0)` or `indexOf('a', -100)` won't. This is shown in figure 5.8.

Here's the code that implements the methods shown in figure 5.8:

```
String sentence = "paint the cup and the plate";

System.out.println(sentence.indexOf('a'));            Search
System.out.println(sentence.indexOf('a', 0));         forward
System.out.println(sentence.indexOf('a', -100));
System.out.println(sentence.indexOf('a', 100));

System.out.println(sentence.lastIndexOf('a'));
System.out.println(sentence.lastIndexOf('a', 0));     Search
System.out.println(sentence.lastIndexOf('a', 100));   backward
System.out.println(sentence.lastIndexOf('a', -100));
```

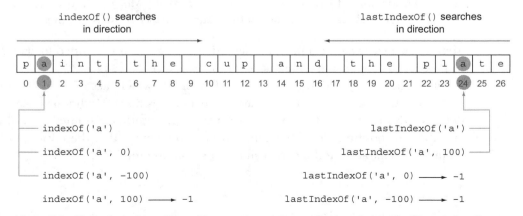

Figure 5.8 Methods `indexOf()` and `lastIndexOf()` search a target string in different directions.

EXAM TIP   Methods indexOf() and lastIndexOf() don't throw a compilation error or runtime exception if the search position is negative or greater than the length of the string. If no match is found, they return -1.

METHOD CONTAINS()

Method contains() searches for exact matches in a string and returns true if a match is found, false otherwise. Because contains() accepts a method parameter of type CharSequence, you can pass to it both a String or a StringBuilder object:

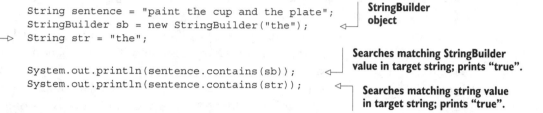

```
String sentence = "paint the cup and the plate";
StringBuilder sb = new StringBuilder("the");
String str = "the";

System.out.println(sentence.contains(sb));
System.out.println(sentence.contains(str));
```

String object

StringBuilder object

Searches matching StringBuilder value in target string; prints "true".

Searches matching string value in target string; prints "true".

METHODS SUBSEQUENCE() AND SUBSTRING()

Both methods subSequence() (uppercase *S*) and substring() (no uppercase letter) return a substring of the string. Here's the signature of these methods:

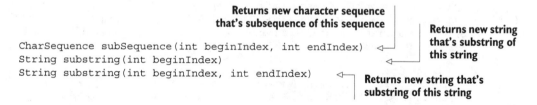

Returns new character sequence that's subsequence of this sequence

Returns new string that's substring of this string

```
CharSequence subSequence(int beginIndex, int endIndex)
String substring(int beginIndex)
String substring(int beginIndex, int endIndex)
```

Returns new string that's substring of this string

 EXAM TIP   To remember the return types of methods subSequence() and substring() on the exam, just remember that the names of these methods can be used to determine their return type. Method subSequence() returns CharSequence, and method substring() returns String.

Method subSequence() simply calls method substring(); it was added to class String in Java 1.4 to support implementation of the interface CharSequence by class String. Method substring() defines overloaded versions, which accept one or two int method parameters to specify the start or the end positions. Method subSequence() defines only one variant: the one that accepts two int method parameters for the start and the end position. For the exam, you must remember that these methods don't include the character at the end position, as shown in figure 5.9.

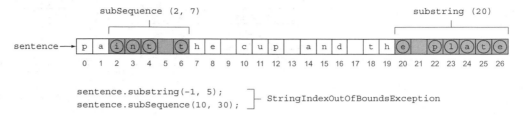

sentence.substring(-1, 5);
sentence.subSequence(10, 30); ⎤— StringIndexOutOfBoundsException

Figure 5.9 Methods `subSequence()` and `substring()` don't include the character at the last position in their return value.

 EXAM TIP Methods `subSequence()` and `substring()` don't include the character at the end position in the result string. Also, unlike methods `indexOf()` and `lastIndexOf()`, they throw the runtime exception `String-IndexOutOfBoundsException` for invalid start and end positions. The subtraction value from `endIndex – beginIndex` is the number of chars these methods will return.

METHOD SPLIT()

Method `split(String regex)` and method `split(String regex, int limit)` in class `String` search for a matching regex pattern and split a string into an array of string values. Figure 5.10 shows how the string `paint-the-cup-cop-and-cap` is split with the regex pattern `c.p`. As discussed in the previous section on regex, the dot in regex `c.p`, will match exactly one character.

 NOTE *Tokenizing* is the process of splitting a string, based on a separator, into tokens. A separator can be a character, text, or a regex. For example, if string `1234;J Perry;94.75` is split using a semicolon as the separator, the tokens that you'll get are `1234`, `J Perry`, and `94.75`.

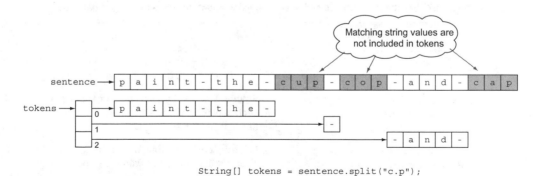

String[] tokens = sentence.split("c.p");

Figure 5.10 The `String` array returned by `split()` doesn't contain the values that it matches to split the target string.

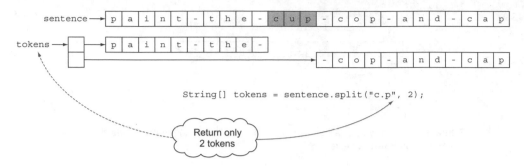

Figure 5.11   You can limit the maximum number of tokens returned by `split()`.

You can limit the maximum number of tokens that you want to retrieve by using `split(String regex, int limit)`. Figure 5.11 shows how the target string `paint-the-cup-cop-and-cap` is split with `split("c.p", 2)`. Because the total number of tokens is limited to two, the regex pattern `c.p` is matched only once. The remaining string after the first match is stored as the second array value.

If `limit` is nonpositive, then the regex pattern will be applied as many times as possible and the array `tokens` can have any length. If `limit` is passed 0, the regex pattern will be applied as many times as possible, but `tokens` won't include trailing empty strings.

5.2.2   *Replacing strings*

Finding and replacing characters or text is a common requirement. You can use multiple methods to find and replace text or regex by using class `String`. As mentioned previously, the methods that accept the interface `CharSequence` as a parameter can accept arguments of all the implementing classes: `String`, `StringBuffer`, and `StringBuilder`. Table 5.7 lists the replacing methods defined in class `String`.

Table 5.7   Methods to replace string values, using exact matches and regex patterns

Method	Description
`replace(char old, char new)`	Returns a new string resulting from finding and replacing *all* occurrences of `old` character with `new` character
`replace(CharSequence old, CharSequence new)`	Returns a new string resulting from finding and replacing each substring of this string that matches the `old` target sequence with the specified `new` replacement sequence
`replaceAll(String regex, String replacement)`	Replaces each substring of this string that matches the given regular expression with the given replacement
`replaceFirst(String regex, String replacement)`	Replaces the first substring of this string that matches the given regular expression with the given replacement

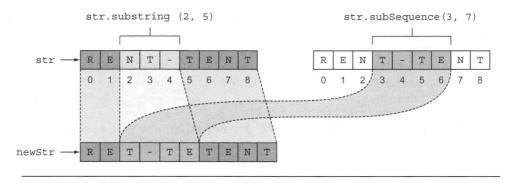

```
newStr = str.replace(str.substring(2, 5), str.subSequence(3, 7));
```

Figure 5.12 An example of using `replace()` to create a new string (`newStr`) that replaces a substring of `str` with another substring of `str`

METHOD REPLACE()

On the exam, you're likely to see chained method invocation with `String` methods. What happens when method `replace()` tries to replace a substring of a string with another substring of the same string? Also, what happens if these string values that are searched and replaced overlap? Here's an example:

```
String str = "RENT-TENT";
String newString = str.replace(
                    str.substring(2, 5),
                    str.subSequence(str.indexOf("T"),
                                    str.lastIndexOf('N')));
System.out.println(newString);
```

Figure 5.12 helps explain this code. To make the code simpler to show and understand, I've replaced `str.indexOf("T")` and `str.lastIndexOf('N')` with their return values—that is, 3 and 7—which are passed as arguments to `str.subSequence()`.

As shown in figure 5.12, method `replace()` creates and returns a new string, `newStr`, by replacing the occurrence of the characters it finds at positions 2, 3, and 4 of `str`, with the characters it finds at positions 3, 4, 5, and 6 of `str`. The length of the replacement string can be greater than, equal to, or smaller than the substring that it replaces.

METHOD REPLACEALL()

This method searches for matching regex patterns in a string and replaces them with the specified string value. An example follows:

```
String str = "cat cup copp";
String newString = str.replaceAll("c.p\\B", "()");
System.out.println(newString);
```

◁— Target string to be searched

◁— Finds regex pattern c.p\B and replaces it with ().

◁— Prints "cat cup ()p".

If no match in the target string is found, replaceAll() returns the contents of the original string.

 EXAM TIP Unlike replace(), replaceAll() doesn't accept method parameters of type CharSequence. Watch out for the passing of objects of class StringBuilder to replaceAll().

The combination of the overloaded methods replace(), replaceAll(), and replace-First() can be confusing on the exam. Take note of the method parameters that can be passed to each of these methods. Let's attempt our next "Twist in the Tale" exercise, which should help you get a better grasp of all these string replacement methods and regex patterns.

Twist in the Tale 5.2

I've modified the code used in a previous example for this exercise. Execute this code on your system and select the correct answer.

```
class ReplaceString2 {
    public static void main(String[] args) {
        String str = "cat cup copp";
        String newString = str.replaceAll("c.p\\b", "()");    //line4
        System.out.println(newString);
    }
}
```

a The code outputs cat () copp.

b The code outputs cat cup ()p.

c The code outputs cat cup copp.

d If code marked with comment line 4 is replaced with the following code, it'll output cat () copp:

```
String newString = str.replaceFirst("c.p\\b", "()");
```

e If code marked with comment line 4 is replaced with the following code, it'll output cat () ()p:

```
String newString = str.replace("c.p", "()");
```

f If code marked with comment line 4 is replaced with the following code, it'll output cat cup copp:

```
String newString = str.replace(new StringBuilder("cat"), "()");
```

OTHER METHODS

For this exam, you must also know about other commonly used `String` methods that you can use to compare string values, match a substring, and determine whether a string starts or ends with a literal value, as listed in table 5.8.

Table 5.8 Methods for comparing string values

Method	Description
endsWith(String suffix)	Returns `true` if this string ends with the specified `suffix`
startsWith(String prefix)	Returns `true` if this string starts with the specified `prefix`
startsWith(String prefix, int offset)	Returns `true` if the substring of this string beginning at the specified index starts with the specified `prefix`
compareTo(String anotherStr)	Compares this string with `anotherStr` lexicographically. Returns a negative, zero, or positive value depending on whether this string is less than, equal to, or greater than `anotherStr`.
compareToIgnoreCase(String anotherStr)	Compares this string with `anotherStr` lexicographically, ignoring case differences. Returns a negative, zero, or positive value depending on whether this string is less than, equal to, or greater than `anotherStr`.
equals(Object object)	Returns `true` if the object being compared defines the same sequence of characters
equalsIgnoreCase(String anotherStr)	Compares this `String` to `anotherStr`, ignoring case considerations

You need to be careful with `String` class methods that accept integer values as index positions to start or end their searches. Here's an example of the values returned by the overloaded method `startsWith()`, when you pass negative, zero, or positive values to it:

```
String str = "Start startup, time to start";
System.out.println(str.startsWith("Start"));         Prints
System.out.println(str.startsWith("Start", 0));      "true"

System.out.println(str.startsWith("Start", -1));     Prints
System.out.println(str.startsWith("Start", 1));      "false"
```

When comparing letters, is a greater than, smaller than, or equal to A? When comparing letters lexicographically, note that a letter in lowercase is greater than its uppercase. The following example outputs a positive value:

```
                                                     Outputs positive
                                                     number
String a = "a";
String b = "A";
System.out.println(a.compareTo(b));                  Outputs negative
System.out.println(b.compareTo(a));                  number
```

EXAM TIP   Lexicographically, a lowercase letter is greater than its equivalent uppercase letter. Method `compareTo()` returns a negative number (not necessarily −1) if the `String` object on which it's called is lexicographically smaller than the one it's compared to.

Don't let the simplicity of these methods take you for a ride. When chained, they can become difficult to answer. What do you think is the output of the following code?

```
String str = "Start startup, time to start";
System.out.println(str.substring(0,1).compareTo(str.substring(6,7)));
```

Execute the preceding code on your system and find out the answer yourself.

The next section covers how to parse and tokenize `String` by using class `Scanner`.

5.2.3   *Parsing and tokenizing strings with Scanner and StringTokenizer*

Parsing is the process of analyzing a string to find tokens or items. For example, you can parse the text `9187` to find the integer value `9187`. As you know, the same number can be stored as text or as an integer value.

SCANNER CLASS

Class `Scanner` can be used to parse and tokenize streams. (Streams are covered in chapter 7.) `Scanner` is a simple text scanner, which can parse primitive types and strings. `Scanner` tokenizes its input string by using a pattern, which can be a character, a string literal, or a regex. You can then use the resulting tokens, converting them to different data types. Here's a quick look at the constructors relevant for this exam:

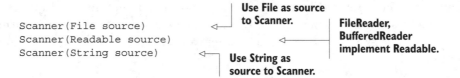

```
Scanner(File source)
Scanner(Readable source)
Scanner(String source)
```

Use File as source to Scanner.

FileReader, BufferedReader implement Readable.

Use String as source to Scanner.

Now that you know the sources available to `Scanner`, let's work with an example of tokenizing a `String` with the default delimiter:

```
Scanner scanner = new Scanner("The \tnew \nProgrammer exam");
while (scanner.hasNext())
    System.out.println (scanner.next());
```

String contains spaces, tab (\t), and newline character (\n).

Here's the output of this code:

```
The
new
Programmer
exam
```

If no delimiter is specified, a pattern that matches whitespace is used by default for a `Scanner` object. You can specify the required regex by calling its method `use-Delimiter()` as follows:

```
Scanner scanner = new Scanner("The1new22Programmer exam6");   ◁── Target string
scanner.useDelimiter("[\\d]+");                                    with letters
                            ◁── Uses regex [\d]+              and digits
while (scanner.hasNext())        to tokenize text.
    System.out.println(scanner.next());   ◁──
                                    Finds and returns
                                    next token
```

The output of this code is as follows:

```
The
new
Programmer exam
```

What if you want to do the reverse in this example: print out the numbers 1, 22, and 6 and leave the characters? You just change the regex to be used as a delimiter, as follows:

```
scanner.useDelimiter("[\\sA-Za-z]+");   ◁── Reads regex [\sA-Za-z]+ as a match for 1 or
                                             more occurrences of whitespace, character,
                                             or letter in uppercase or lowercase.
```

Method `next()` defined in class `Scanner` returns an object of type `String`. This class defines multiple `nextXXX()` methods, where XXX refers to a primitive data type. Instead of returning a string value, these methods return the value as the corresponding primitive type.

```
Scanner scanner = new Scanner ("Shreya,20,true");   | Retrieves next
scanner.useDelimiter(",");                           | string value
System.out.println(scanner.next());   ◁──                   Retrieves
System.out.println(scanner.nextInt());   ◁──                next int value
System.out.println(scanner.nextBoolean());   ◁──
                                    Retrieves next
                                    Boolean value
```

The following example parses the target string by using the regex `[\\sA-Za-z]+`, which is for one or more occurrences of a whitespace or a letter. The tokenized numbers are retrieved using `nextInt()`:

```
                                    Target string contains combination
                                    of words, numbers, spaces
Scanner scanner = new Scanner ("1 2 4 The new 55 Programmer 44 exam");   ◁──
scanner.useDelimiter("[\\sA-Za-z]+");   ◁── Delimiter is any combination
int total = 0;                               of whitespace/letters.
while (scanner.hasNextInt())
    total = total + scanner.nextInt();   ◁── nextInt returns
System.out.println(total);                    int value.
```

The output of this code is 106 (1 + 2 + 4 + 55 + 44). For the exam, make note of the multiple hasNext(), hasNextXxx(), next(), and nextXxx() methods. Methods has-Next() and hasNextXxx() only return true or false but don't advance. Only methods next() and nextXxx() advance in the input. So you'll have to be careful or you'll end up with a program which runs eternally, like this one:

```
Scanner scanner = new Scanner ("1 2 4 The new 55 Programmer 44 exam");
scanner.useDelimiter("[\\s]+");
int total = 0;
while (scanner.hasNext())
    if (scanner.hasNextInt())
        total = total + scanner.nextInt();
System.out.println(total);
```

Class Scanner also defines method findInLine(), which tries to match the specified pattern with no regard to delimiters in the input. Here's an example:

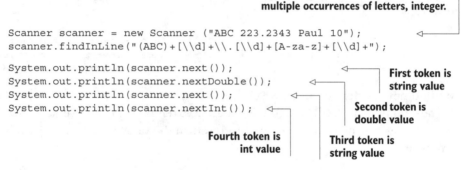

Target string contains ABC, double value, multiple occurrences of letters, integer.

Find regex that matches text.

```
Scanner scanner = new Scanner ("ABC 223.2343 Paul 10");
scanner.findInLine("(ABC)+[\\d]+\\.[\\d]+[A-za-z]+[\\d]+");

System.out.println(scanner.next());
System.out.println(scanner.nextDouble());
System.out.println(scanner.next());
System.out.println(scanner.nextInt());
```

First token is string value

Second token is double value

Third token is string value

Fourth token is int value

The output of this code is as follows:

```
ABC
223.2343
Paul
10
```

 NOTE   The decimal values (float and double) are Locale-specific (Locale is covered in chapter 12). For decimal numbers, a Locale might use a decimal comma or a decimal point.

What happens when there's a mismatch in the next token and the method used to retrieve the data? Does it lead to a compilation error or a runtime exception? Let's uncover an important concept in our next "Twist in the Tale" exercise.

Twist in the Tale 5.3

The following code contains a mismatch in the type of token retrieved (a can be stored as a character or string) and the method (nextInt) used to retrieve this data. What's the output of the following code?

```
import java.util.*;
public class MyScan {
    public static void main(String[] args) {
        String in = "1 a 10 . 100 1000";
        Scanner s = new Scanner(in);
        int accum = 0;
        for(int x = 0; x < 4; x++) {
            accum += s.nextInt();
        }
        System.out.println(accum);
    }
}
```

- a   The code prints 1111.
- b   The code doesn't compile.
- c   The code throws java.util.InputMismatchException.
- d   The code throws java.util.MismatchException.
- e   The code throws java.util.ParsingException.

STRINGTOKENIZER CLASS

You can use the StringTokenizer class to break a string into tokens. To separate the tokens you can specify the delimiter to be used either at the time of instantiating StringTokenizer or on a per-token basis. In the absence of an explicit delimiter, a whitespace is used.

```
StringTokenizer st = new StringTokenizer("start your startup");
while (st.hasMoreTokens()) {
    System.out.println(st.nextToken());
}
```

The preceding code uses a whitespace as a delimiter and outputs:

```
start
your
startup
```

Methods hasMoreTokens() and hasMoreElements() in class StringTokenizer return a boolean value indicating whether more tokens are available or not. Methods next-Token() and nextElement() return the next token. The return type of method nextToken() is String and of method nextElement() is Object.

If the delimiter used to instantiate StringTokenizer is null, the constructor doesn't throw an exception. But trying to access the resultant tokens or invoking any other method on the StringTokenizer instance results in a NullPointerException:

```
StringTokenizer st = new StringTokenizer("start your startup", null);
System.out.println(st.hasMoreElements());     ◁───┐
```
Throws NullPointerException because delimiter is null.

NOTE StringTokenizer is a legacy class that's retained for compatibility reasons. Oracle recommends use of method split() of class String or classes from a regex package to get the same functionality.

Apart from searching, parsing, and manipulating strings, formatting strings is another frequently used feature. Let's format some string values.

5.3 *Formatting strings*

[5.3]   Format strings using the formatting parameters %b, %c, %d, %f, and %s in format strings

How often do you use the operator + to concatenate a String value with the value of another variable (for example, "name:"+emp+"age:"+age)? Do you find this expression cumbersome to use? This section discusses formatting classes, methods, and parameters that can replace the + operator for concatenating String and other variable values. You can also write the formatted text to OutputStream, File, or StringBuilder. Let's start with identifying the classes that you can use to format strings.

5.3.1 *Formatting classes*

Class java.util.Formatter and I/O classes like PrintStream and PrintWriter define methods to format strings (coverage of formatting classes is limited to exam topics).

You can use class Formatter to write formatted strings to a file, stream, or StringBuilder objects. Class Formatter is an interpreter for printf-style format strings. This class provides support for layout justification and alignment; common formats for numeric, string, and date/time data; and locale-specific output. This type of formatted printing is heavily inspired by C's printf.

On the exam you'll be queried on how to write formatted strings to the standard output. You can use class System to access the standard input, standard output, and error output streams. The standard output in class System is made accessible using a static variable, out, which is of type PrintStream (remember using System.out.println()). Class PrintStream defines methods to output formatting strings.

5.3.2 *Formatting methods*

Class Formatter defines the overloaded method format() to write a formatted string to its destination using the default or specified Locale (covered in chapter 12), format string, and arguments:

```
format(String format, Object... args)
format(Locale l,String format, Object... args)
```

To output formatted strings to the standard output, you can use class `PrintStream` and its overloaded methods `format()` and `printf()`, which use the default or specified `Locale`, format strings, and arguments:

```
format(String format, Object... args)
format(Locale l,String format, Object... args)
printf(String format, Object... args)
printf(Locale l, String format, Object... args)
```

Behind the scenes, method `printf()` simply calls method `format()`. Also the number of method arguments that these methods accept is the same. So you really need to work with one method to format the strings.

 EXAM TIP `System.out.println()` can't write formatted strings to the standard output; `System.out.format()` and `System.out.printf()` can.

Here's a quick example to write a formatted string to the standard output and to a file:

```
import java.util.Formatter;
import java.io.File;
class FormattedStrings {
    public static void main(String args[]) throws Exception {
        String name = "Shreya";

        Formatter formatter = new Formatter(new File("data.txt"));   ←── Destination is
                                                                          file data.txt.
        formatter.format("My name is %s", name);     ←── Format
        formatter.flush();                               parameter %s.

        System.out.printf("My name is %s", name);    ←── Destination is
    }                                                     standard output.
}
```

In the preceding code, `%s` is replaced with the value of variable name. In the next section, let's see how to define format strings, the formatting parameters (on the exam), and their elements.

 NOTE Because class `Locale` and Java I/O classes are covered in chapters 12 and 7, I won't include other examples about these classes here.

5.3.3 Defining format strings

To use methods `format()` and `printf()`, you need to define a format string that defines *how* to format text and an object argument list that defines *what* to format. You can define a combination of fixed text and one or more embedded format specifiers, to be passed to formatting methods. The format specifier takes the following form:

```
%[argument_index$] [flags] [width] [.precision] conversion_char
```

Table 5.9 describes the format specifier elements.

Table 5.9 Format specifier elements and their purposes

Format specifier element	Optional/ required	What it means
argument_index	Optional	Decimal integer indicating the position of the argument in the argument list. The first argument is referenced by 1$, the second by 2$, and so forth.
flags	Optional	Set of characters that modify the output format. The set of valid flags depends on the conversion.
width	Optional	A non-negative decimal integer indicating the minimum number of characters to be written to the output.
precision	Optional	A non-negative decimal integer usually used to restrict the number of characters. The specific behavior depends on the conversion.
conversion_char	Required	A character indicating how the argument should be formatted. The set of valid conversions for a given argument depends on the argument's data type.

 NOTE The conversion characters on the exam are %b, %c, %d, %f ,and %s.

How to work with format specification

The general syntax is as follows:

```
%[arg_index$][flags][width][.precision]conversion_char
```

- Compulsory element—A format specification must start with a % sign and end with a conversion character.
- Optional elements—arg-index, flags, width, and .precision are all optional.
- Anything before a % and after the conversion character is printed as it is. For example, printf("xxx%1$dyyy%2$dzzz", 10, 20) outputs xxx10yyy20zzz.
- You need to remember the following flags:
  - - Left-justify this argument; must specify width as well.
  - + Include a sign (+ or -) with this argument. Applicable only if conversion character is d or f (for numbers).
  - 0 Pad this argument with zeros. Applicable only if conversion character is d or f (for numbers). Must specify width as well.
  - , Use locale-specific grouping separators (for example, the comma in 123,456). Applicable only if conversion character is d or f (for numbers).
  - (Enclose negative numbers in parentheses. Applicable only if conversion character is d or f (for numbers).

Let's get started with how to use the formatting parameter %b.

5.3.4   *Formatting parameter %b*

If the target argument arg is null, then %b prints the result as false. If arg is boolean or Boolean, the result is the String returned by String.valueOf(). Otherwise, the result is true.

```
String name = "Shreya";
Integer age = null;
boolean isShort = false;
```

%b prints "true" for non-null values.

%b prints "false" for null values.

%b evaluates and outputs boolean value

```
System.out.format("Name %b, age %b, isShort %b", name, age, isShort);
```

The preceding code formats the text as follows:

```
Name true, age false, isShort false
```

Now, what happens if there's a mismatch in the number of arguments passed to method format() and the number of times %b appears in the format string? If the number of arguments exceeds the required count, the *extra* variables are quietly ignored by the compiler and JVM. In the following example, the extra variables in the first line are ignored and it outputs Name true. But for the second line because the number of required arguments falls short, the JVM throws java.util.MissingFormat-ArgumentException at runtime:

```
System.out.format("Name %b", name, age, isShort);
System.out.printf("Name %b, age %b", name);
```

Ignores extra variables

Throws runtime exception

EXAM TIP   If the count of formatting parameters is more than the arguments passed to methods format() or printf(), then java.util.Missing-FormatArgumentException is thrown at runtime.

This format specifier accepts primitive and reference variables and, hence, you can pass any type of argument to this format specifier. Examine the following examples, which use different combinations of *flags, width,* and *precision*:

Flag left-justifies the text true.

```
System.out.format("\nName defined %10b.", name);
System.out.format("\nName defined %.1b.", name);
System.out.format("\nName defined %-10b.", name);
```

Minimum width specified as 10 adds 6 spaces before result true.

Precision 1 truncates length of result to t.

Here's the output of the preceding code:

```
Name defined       true.
Name defined t.
Name defined true       .
```

EXAM TIP   You can pass any type of primitive variable or object reference to %b.

5.3.5   *Formatting parameter %c*

%c outputs the result as a Unicode character. Examine the following examples:

Prints
"{"

```
System.out.printf("\nChar %c", new Character('\u007b'));
```
Prints "(Om)" in Devanagari script.

```
System.out.printf("\nChar %c", '\u6124');
```
Throws runtime exception if target can't be converted to Unicode character.

```
System.out.printf("\nChar %c", new Boolean(true));
```

```
System.out.printf("\nChar %c", .'\affff');
```
Values with invalid Unicode values (\affff) won't compile.

If the target can't be converted to a Unicode character, a runtime exception is thrown:

```
Exception in thread "main" java.util.IllegalFormatConversionException: c !=
java.lang.Boolean
```

> **EXAM TIP**   You can pass only literals and variables that can be converted to a Unicode character (char, byte, short, int, Character, Byte, Short, and Integer) to the %c specifier. Passing variables of type boolean, long, float, Boolean, Long, Float, or any other class will throw Illegal-FormatConversionException.

5.3.6   *Formatting parameters %d and %f*

Did you ever notice that the amount displayed in your bank statements is formatted in a particular manner—say, for example, a maximum width of 20 digits, with exactly 2 digits after the decimal point, and grouped according to the locale-specific information? Let's see how you can do this by formatting a float or double value, using the format specifier %f. In the following examples, I've used square brackets in the results displayed ([]) to help you determine how the numbers are formatted with padding and left justification:

Prints "[12.123450]".

Outputs value with width 10, zero padded; prints "[012.123450]".

```
System.out.printf("[%f]", 12.12345);
System.out.printf("[%010f]", 12.12345);
System.out.printf("[%-10f]", 12.12345);
System.out.printf("[%10.2f]", 12.98765);
System.out.printf("[%,f]", 123456789.12345);
```

Value with width 10, left-justified; prints "[12.123450]".

Value with width 10, exactly 2 digits after decimal point; prints "[12.99]".

**Locale-specific grouping using ',';
prints "[123,456,789.123450]".**

> **NOTE**   Because the formatting of the numbers is specific to your default locale, you might not see the same output as mentioned in the preceding code.

Though you can assign an int literal to a float or double variable (float f = 10 or long d = 10), you can't use int variables or literal values with %f. The following code will throw an IllegalFormatConversionException runtime exception:

```
System.out.printf("[%,f]", 12345);
```

 EXAM TIP By default, %f prints six digits after the decimal. It also rounds off the last digit. You can pass literal values or variables of type float, double, Float, and Double to the format specifier %f.

You can format the integers as follows:

Prints "[12345]".

```
System.out.printf("[%d]", 12345);
System.out.printf("[%010d]", 12345);
System.out.printf("%(,d", -123456789);
System.out.printf("[%-10.2d]", 12345);
```

Outputs value with width 10, zero padded; prints "[0000012345]".

Negative numbers enclosed within parentheses; prints "(-123,456,789)".

Throws java.util.IllegalFormatPrecisionException at runtime; can't specify precision with integers.

 EXAM TIP You can pass literal values or variables of type byte, short, int, long, Byte, Short, Integer, or Long to the %d format specifier. The code throws runtime exceptions for all other types of values.

Also, the flags +, 0, (, and , (comma) can be specified only with the numeric specifiers %d and %f. If you try to use them with any other format specifier (%b, %s, or %c), you'll get a runtime exception.

5.3.7 *Formatting parameter %s*

%s is a general-purpose format specifier that can be applied to both primitive variables and object references. For primitive variables, the value will be displayed; for object references, method toString() of the object is called:

```
String name = "Harry";
Integer age = null;
String[] skills = {"Java", "Android"};
System.out.format("Name is %s, age is %s, skills are %s", name,
age,skills);
```

In the preceding code, format() sends the following to the standard output (the exact integer value following @ will vary on your system):

```
Name is Harry, age is null, skills are [Ljava.lang.String;@1d9dc39
```

 EXAM TIP You can pass any type of primitive variable or object reference to the format specifier %s.

It's interesting to note how you can specify the `argument_index` to change the arguments used at a particular location. Let's specify the argument index in the preceding example to swap the variables `name` and `age`:

```
age = 40;
System.out.format("Name is %2$s, age is %1$s", name, age);
```

The output of the code is as follows:

```
Name is 40, age is Harry
```

 EXAM TIP You can specify that the `argument_index` change the arguments used at a particular location.

5.4   Summary

String processing is a relatively big topic, so we started this chapter with an outline of what to expect on the exam. The exam covers searching, parsing, replacing, and formatting strings. It also covers formatting primitive data types and object references. We covered the classes that you need to know and their respective methods to work with this functionality. Classes `String` and `StringBuilder` are used to work with strings, to modify, search, and replace their values. Class `Scanner` is used to tokenize data and manipulate it.

When you search data, you can look for either exact matches or a pattern of data. A regular expression (or regex) is a powerful language that can be used to define data patterns to be searched for. I limited discussion of regex to the patterns included on the exam. I covered Java's regex support with the `java.util.regex` package. At the end of the chapter, you learned how to control and define the format of your data (primitive values and objects) by using class `Formatter` and its utility methods, in a locale-specific or custom format.

REVIEW NOTES

This section lists the main points covered in this chapter.

Regular expressions

- Regular expressions, or regex, are used to define patterns of data to be found in a stream.
- A regex has a syntax, which can be defined by using regular and special characters.
- As opposed to exact matches, you can use regex to search for data that matches a pattern.
- Character classes aren't classes defined in the Java API. The term refers to a set of characters that you can enclose within square brackets `[]`.
- Java supports predefined and custom character classes.

- You create a custom character class by enclosing a set of characters within square brackets []:
  - [fdn] can be used to find an exact match of f, d, or n.
  - [^fdn] can be used to find a character that doesn't match either f, d, or n.
  - [a-cA-c] can be used to find an exact match of either a, b, c, A, B, or C.
- You can use these predefined character classes as follows:
  - A dot matches any character (and may or may not match line terminators).
  - \d matches any digit: [0-9].
  - \D matches a nondigit: [^0-9].
  - \s matches a whitespace character: [(space), \t (tab), \n (new line), \x0B (end of line), \f (form feed), \r (carriage)]
  - \S matches a non-whitespace character: [^\s].
  - \w matches a word character: [a-zA-Z_0-9].
  - \W matches a nonword character: [^\w].
- To use a regex pattern in Java code that includes a backslash, you must escape the \ by preceding it with another \. The character literal \ has a special meaning; it's used as an escape character. To use it as a literal, it must be escaped.
- For the exam, you'll need to know these boundary matchers:
  - \b indicates a word boundary.
  - \B indicates a nonword boundary.
  - ^ indicates the beginning of a line.
  - $ indicates the end of a line.
- You can specify the number of occurrences of a pattern to match in a target value by using quantifiers.
- The coverage of quantifiers on this exam is limited to the following greedy quantifiers:
  - X? matches X, once or not at all.
  - X* matches X, zero or more times.
  - X+ matches X, one or more times.
  - X{min,max} matches X, within the specified range.
- Regex in Java supports Unicode, as it matches against the CharSequence objects.
- Class Pattern is a compiled representation of a regular expression. It doesn't define a public constructor. You can instantiate this class by using its factory method compile().
- Class Matcher is referred to as an engine that scans a target CharSequence for a matching regex pattern. Class Matcher doesn't define a public constructor. You can create and access a Matcher object by calling the instance method matcher() on an object of class Pattern.
- When you have access to the Matcher object, you can match a complete input sequence against a pattern, match the input sequence starting at the beginning,

find multiple occurrences of the matching pattern, or retrieve information about the matching groups.

Search, parse, and build strings

You can search strings for exact matches of characters or strings, at the beginning of a string, or starting at a specified position, using `String` class's overloaded methods `indexOf` (note the capital O).

- Method `indexOf()` returns the first matching position of a character or string, starting from the specified position of this string, or from its beginning.
- Method `lastIndexOf()` returns the last matching position of a character in the entire string, or its subset (position 0 to the specified position).
- Methods `indexOf()` and `lastIndexOf()` differ in the manner that they search a target string—`indexOf()` searches in increasing position numbers and `lastIndexOf()` searches backward. Due to this difference, `indexOf('a', -100)` will search the complete string, but `lastindexOf('a', -100)` won't. In a similar manner, because `lastIndexOf()` searches backwards, `lastIndexOf('a', 100)` will search the string, but `indexOf('a', 0)` or `indexOf('a', -100)` won't.
- Methods `indexOf()` and `lastIndexOf()` don't throw a compilation error or runtime exception if the search position is negative or greater than the length of this string. If no match is found, they return –1.
- Method `contains()` searches for an exact match in this string. Because `contains()` accepts a method parameter of interface `CharSequence`, you can pass to it both a `String` and a `StringBuilder` object.
- Methods `subSequence` (uppercase *S*) and `substring` (no uppercase letter) accept `int` parameters and return a substring of the target string.
- Method `substring()` defines overloaded versions, which accept one or two `int` method parameters to specify the start and end positions.
- Method `subSequence()` defines only one variant, the one that accepts two `int` method parameters for the start and end positions.
- Methods `subSequence()` and `substring()` don't include the character at the end position in the result `String`. Also, unlike methods `indexOf()` and `lastIndexOf()`, they throw the runtime exception `StringIndexOutOfBoundsException` for invalid start and end positions.
- The name of methods `subSequence()` and `substring()` can be used to determine their return type. `subSequence()` returns `CharSequence` and `substring()` returns `String`.
- Methods `split(String regex)` and `split(String regex, int limit)` in class `String` search for a matching regex pattern and split a `String` into an array of string values.
- The `String` array returned by `split()` doesn't contain the values that it matches to split the target string.

- You can limit the maximum number of tokens that you want to retrieve by using `split(String regex, int limit)`.
- `replace(char oldChar, char newChar)` returns a new `String` resulting from finding and replacing all occurrences of the `old` character with the `new` character.
- `replace(CharSequence oldVal, CharSequence newVal)` returns a new `String` resulting from finding and replacing each substring of the string that matches the `old` target sequence with the specified `new` replacement sequence.
- `replaceAll(String regex, String replacement)` replaces each substring of the string that matches the given regular expression with the given replacement.
- `replaceFirst(String regex, String replacement)` replaces the first substring of the string that matches the given regular expression with the given replacement.
- Unlike `replace()`, `replaceAll()` doesn't accept method parameters of type `CharSequence`. Watch out for the passing of objects of class `StringBuilder` to `replaceAll()`.
- The combination of the `replace`, `replaceAll`, and `replaceFirst` overloaded methods can be confusing on the exam. Take note of the method parameters that can be passed to each of these methods.
- `Scanner` can be used to parse and tokenize strings.
  - If no delimiter is specified, a pattern that matches whitespace is used by default for a `Scanner` object.
  - You can specify a custom delimiter by calling its method `useDelimiter()` with a regex.
  - Method `next()` returns an object of type `String`.
  - `Scanner` also defines multiple `nextXXX` methods, where XXX refers to a primitive data type. These methods return the value as the corresponding primitive type.
  - Methods `hasNext()` and `hasNextXxx()` only return `true` or `false` but don't advance. Only methods `next()` and `nextXxx()` advance in the input.
  - Method `findInLine()` matches the specified pattern with no regard to delimiters in the input.

Formatting strings

- Class `java.util.Formatter` is an interpreter for `printf`-style format strings.
- A formatter provides support for layout justification and alignment; common formats for numeric, string, and date/time data; and locale-specific output.
- `Formatter`'s `format()` is used to format data.
- To use `format()`, you need to define a format string that defines how to format text and an object argument list that defines what to format.
- You can define a combination of fixed text and one or more embedded format specifiers, to be passed to the method's `format()` first argument.

- The format specifier takes the following form:

  `%[argument_index$] [flags] [width] [.precision]conversion`

- A format specification must start with a `%` sign and end with a conversion character:
  - `b` for `boolean`
  - `c` for `char`
  - `d` for `int`, `byte`, `short`, and `long`
  - `f` for `float` and `double`
  - `s` for `String`

- If the number of arguments exceeds the required count, the extra variables are quietly ignored by the compiler and JVM. But if the number of required arguments falls short, the JVM throws a runtime exception.

- The `-` indicates to left-justify this argument; you must specify width as well. Number flags (only applicable for numbers, conversion chars `d` and `f`) are as follows:
  - The `+` indicates to include a sign (`+` or `-`) with this argument.
  - `0` indicates to pad this argument with zeros. Must specify width as well.
  - `,` indicates to use locale-specific grouping separators (for example, the comma in 123,456).
  - `(` is used to enclose negative numbers in parentheses.

- The flags `+`, `0`, `(`, and `,` can be specified only with the numeric specifiers `%d` and `%f`. If you try to use them with any other format specifier (`%b`, `%s`, or `%c`), you'll get a runtime exception.

- Format specifier `%b`
  - You can pass any type of primitive variable or object reference to specifier `%b`.
  - If the target argument `arg` is `null`, then `%b` outputs the result as `false`. If `arg` is `boolean` or `Boolean`, the result is the `String` returned by `String.valueOf()`. Otherwise, the result is `true`.

- Format specifier `%c`
  - `%c` outputs the result as a Unicode character.
  - You can pass only literals and variables that can be converted to a Unicode character (`char`, `byte`, `short`, `int`, `Character`, `Byte`, `Short`, and `Integer`) to the `%c` specifier. Passing variables of type `boolean`, `long`, `float`, `Boolean`, `Long`, `Float`, or any other class will throw `IllegalFormatConversionException`.

- Format specifier `%f`
  - You can format decimal numbers (`float`, `Float`, `double`, and `Double`) by using the format specifier `%f`.
  - By default, `%f` prints six digits after the decimal. It also rounds off the last digit.

- Format specifier `%d`
  - You can format integers (`byte`, `short`, `int`, `long`, `Byte`, `Short`, `Integer`, `Long`) by using the format specifier `%d`.
  - If you pass literal values or variables of type `float`, `double`, `Float`, or `Double` to the format specifier `%d`, the code will throw a runtime exception.

- Format specifier %s
  - %s outputs the value for a primitive variable. For reference variables, it calls toString() on objects that are not null and outputs null for null values.
  - You can pass any type of primitive variable or object reference to specifier %s.

SAMPLE EXAM QUESTIONS

Q 5-1. What is the output of the following code?

```
class Format1 {
    public static void main(String... args) {
        double num1 = 7.12345678;
        int num2 = (int)8.12345678;
        System.out.printf("num1=%f, num2=%2d, %b", num1, num2, num2);
    }
}
```

a   num1=7.123456, num2= 8, true

b   num1=7.123456, num2=8, true

c   num1=7.123457, num2= 8, true

d   num1=7.123457, num2=8 , true

e   num1=7.1234, num2=8, false

f   num1=7.1234, num2=8.1234, true

g   Compilation error

h   Runtime exception

Q 5-2. Given the following command line

```
java Regex1 \d\d 761cars8 5dogs-total846
```

what is the output of the following code?

```
class Regex1 {
    public static void main(String[] args) {
        Pattern pattern = Pattern.compile(args[0]);
        Matcher matcher = pattern.matcher(args[1]);
        boolean found = false;
        while(found = matcher.find()) {
            System.out.println(matcher.group());
        }
    }
}
```

a   76
    61

b   76

   c 76
      61
      84
      46

   d 76
      84

   e No output

Q 5-3. Given the following variables, which options will throw exceptions at runtime?

```
String eJava = "Guru";
Integer start = 100;
boolean win = true;
Float duration = new Float(-1099.9999);
```

   a `System.out.format("%d", eJava);`

   b `System.out.printf("%s", start);`

   c `System.out.printf("[%-12b]", win);`

   d `System.out.format("%s12", eJava);`

   e `System.out.format("%d", duration);`

   f `System.out.format("[%+,-(20f]", duration);`

Q 5-4. What is the output of the following code?

```
Scanner scanner = new Scanner("ThemeXtheirXcarpet77");
scanner.useDelimiter("t.*e");
while (scanner.hasNext())
    System.out.println (scanner.next());
```

   a ThemeX
      the
      t77

   b ThemeX
      t77

   c The
      the

   d t77

   e Compilation error

   f Runtime exception

Q 5-5. Which options will output the following code?

```
Hello true 123456
```

   a `System.out.print("%s %b %d", new StringBuilder("Hello"), "false",`
      `123456);`

```
b   System.out.printf("%s %b %d", new String("Hello"), "false", 123456);
c   System.out.format("%s %b %d", new StringBuilder("Hello"), "false",
    123456);
d   System.out.println("%s %b %d", new StringBuilder("Hello"), "false",
    123456.70);
e   System.out.printf("%s %b %d", new StringTokenizer("Hello"), "false",
    123456);
f   System.out.format("%s %b %d", ("Hello"), "FALSE", new Integer(123456));
```

Q 5-6. What is the output of the following code?

```
class StringCompare {
    public static void main(String[] args) {
        String mgr1 = "Paul & Harry's new office";
        StringBuilder emp = new StringBuilder("Harry");
        System.out.println(mgr1.contains(emp));
    }
}
```

  a   true

  b   false

  c   Compilation error

  d   Runtime exception

 NOTE   This question includes reading from a file that's covered in chapter 7. In the exam it's usual to see questions that are based on multiple exam topics.

Q 5-7. Given that the content of the file data.txt is

```
Harry;8765,Per[fect
```

which options are correct for the following code?

```
public class StrToken {
    public static void main(String[] args) throws Exception {
        BufferedReader br = new BufferedReader(new FileReader("data.txt"));
        String line;
        StringTokenizer st;
        while ((line = br.readLine()) != null) {
            st = new StringTokenizer(line, "[,;]");          //line1
            while (st.hasMoreElements())
            System.out.println(st.nextElement());
        }
        br.close();
    }
}
```

a The code prints

```
Harry
8765
Per
fect
```

b The code prints

```
Harry
8765
Per[fect
```

c The code prints

```
Harry;8765
Per[fect
```

d If the code on line //line1 is changed to the following, it'll output the same results:

```
st = new StringTokenizer(line, "[,;$]");          //line1
```

e Code fails to compile.

f Code throws a runtime exception.

Q 5-8. What is the output of the following code?

```
String eJava = "e Java Guru";
if(eJava.matches("u.u")){
    String[] tokens = eJava.split("\\Bu");
    for (String token : tokens) System.out.println(token);
}
else {
    System.out.println(eJava.replace(
                        eJava.subSequence(3, 4), eJava.substring(11)));
}
```

a e Java G

  r

b e Java Guru

c e Jv Guru

d e Juvu Guru

e `java.lang.StringIndexOutOfBoundsException: String index out of range: 11`

f Code fails to compile.

Q 5-9. Which option, when used as a format specifier, will format the decimal literal value 14562975.6543 to use at least the locale-specific grouping separator and include a sign with it (+ or -)? (Choose all that apply.)

a `%+,3f`

b `%,+20f`

```
c   %+,f
d   %,+f
e   %()f
f   %-,f
g   %0.+f
```

Q 5-10. Given the following string, which code options use the correct regex to replace the first letter of all words with *A*, leave the remaining string unchanged, and print the replaced string value?

```
String target = "amita, matinda,shreya,mike, and anthony are arrogant";
```

a   `System.out.println(target.subSequence("[\\b]\\w", "A"));`

b   `System.out.println(target.replace("\\b\\w", "A"));`

c   `System.out.println(target.replaceAll("\\s\\b\\w", "A"));`

d   `System.out.println(target.replace("\\s\\b\\w", "A"));`

e   `System.out.println(target.modify("\\b\\w", "A"));`

f   `System.out.println(target.replaceAll("\\b\\w", "A"));`

g   None of the above

ANSWERS TO SAMPLE EXAM QUESTIONS

A 5-1. c

[5.3] Format strings using the formatting parameters: %b, %c, %d, %f, and %s in format strings

Explanation: By default, `%f` prints out six digits after the decimal number. It also rounds off the last digit. So num1=`%f` outputs 7.123457 and not 7.123456.

Because the double literal 8.12345678 is explicitly casted to an int value, num2 contains the integer part of the double literal 8.12345678, that is, 8. `%2d` sets the total width of the output to 2 digits, padded with spaces and right-aligned by default. It outputs a space preceding the digit 8.

For all non-Boolean primitive values, `%b` outputs true.

A 5-2. b

[5.2] Search, parse, and replace strings by using regular expressions, using expression patterns for matching limited to: . (dot), * (star), + (plus), ?, \d, \D, \s, \S, \w, \W, \b, \B, [], ()

Explanation: The last argument (5dogs-total846) is ignored when you use the following command line because a space precedes it.

```
java -ea Regex1 \d\d 761cars8 5dogs-total846
```

When you pass the regex by using the command-line arguments, you don't need to escape the backslashes. It's required only for literal string values.

\d\d will match two adjacent digits in the literal 761cars8—that is, 76. It won't match 61 because the digit 6 was already consumed in finding 76. By default, Java's regex engine won't use characters that have already been consumed.

A 5-3. a, e

[5.3] Format strings using the formatting parameters: %b, %c, %d, %f, and %s in format strings

Explanation: You'll get runtime exceptions if you use either of the following for a format specifier:

- An invalid data type
- An invalid combination of flags

Options (a) and (e) throw runtime exceptions because they use the format specifier %d, which must be used only with integer literal values or variables, and not with String or decimal numbers.

Option (b) won't throw any exception because you can pass any type of primitive variable or object reference to the format specifier %s. Also, this option doesn't use any format flag that's invalid to be used with %s.

Option (c) won't throw any exceptions. You can specify the alignment and width element -12 with %b.

Option (d) won't throw any exceptions. The value 12 that follows %s is not part of the width element, but a literal value following %s, so it's a completely valid format string.

A 5-4. b

[5.1] Search, parse, and build strings (including Scanner, StringTokenizer, String-Builder, String, and Formatter)
[5.2] Search, parse, and replace strings by using regular expressions, using expression patterns for matching limited to: . (dot), * (star), + (plus), ?, \d, \D, \s, \S, \w, \W, \b, \B, [], ().

Explanation: The code compiles successfully and throws no exceptions at runtime. So options (e) and (f) are incorrect.

In the regex t.*e, the metacharacter . matches any character, and * is a greedy quantifier. t.*e searches for the letter *t* and scans all the remaining letters to find the last occurrence of the letter *e*. The string theirXcarpe matches this regex pattern. So theirXcarpe is used as a delimiter to the tokenizer ThemeXtheirXcarpet77. Text preceding and following this delimiter is returned as tokens.

A 5-5. b, c, f

[5.3] Format strings using the formatting parameters: %b, %c, %d, %f, and %s in format strings.

Explanation: Options (a) and (d) won't compile. The type of the variable `out` in class `System` is `PrintStream`. `PrintStream`'s methods `print()` and `println()` accept just one method parameter. They're overloaded to accept parameters of all the primitive types and object references. But, they don't accept format strings and arguments.

Option (b) is correct. The format specifier `%b` returns the value `true` for non-null values for object references other than `Boolean` or `boolean`.

Option (c) is correct. The format specifier `%s` calls method `toString()` on an object reference to get its `String` representation. Method `toString()` of class `String-Builder` creates and returns a new `String` by using the sequence stored by the `StringBuilder`. So printing a `StringBuilder` doesn't print a value similar to `String-Builder@135d`.

Option (e) is incorrect. `%s` calls `StringTokenizer`'s method `toString()` to access its `String` representation. This option outputs a value similar to this:

```
java.util.StringTokenizer@750159 true 123456
```

Option (f) is correct. Methods `printf()` and `format()` provide exactly the same functionality. Behind the scenes, `printf()` calls `format()`.

A 5-6. a

[5.1] Search, parse, and build strings (including Scanner, StringTokenizer, String-Builder, String, and Formatter)

Explanation: Method `contains()` accepts a method parameter of type `CharSequence`, and so an object of class `StringBuilder` is acceptable (class `StringBuilder` implements the interface `CharSequence`). Method `contains()` returns `true`, if the specified `String` equivalent can be found in the `String` object on which this method is called.

A 5-7. a, d

[5.1] Search, parse, and build strings (including Scanner, StringTokenizer, String-Builder, String, and Formatter)
[5.2] Search, parse, and replace strings by using regular expressions, using expression patterns for matching limited to: . (dot), * (star), + (plus), ?, \d, \D, \s, \S, \w, \W, \b, \B, [], ().

Explanation: On the exam, you're likely to see questions based on multiple exam objectives, just as this question covers file handling and string processing.

Class `StringTokenizer` doesn't accept the delimiter as a regex pattern. When `[,;]` is passed as a delimiter to class `StringTokenizer`, the occurrence of either of these characters acts as a delimiter. So the line read from file data.txt is delimited using `,` `;` and `[`.

Because the text in file data.txt doesn't include `$`, changing the delimiter text from `[,;]` to `[,;$]` won't affect the output.

A 5-8. c

[5.1] Search, parse, and build strings (including Scanner, StringTokenizer, String-Builder, String, and Formatter)
[5.2] Search, parse, and replace strings by using regular expressions, using expression patterns for matching limited to: . (dot), * (star), + (plus), ?, \d, \D, \s, \S, \w, \W, \b, \B, [], ().

Explanation: Method `matches()` doesn't look for a matching subsequence. It matches the complete string value against the given regex pattern. Because the regex pattern `u.u` matches a subsequence and not the entire string value `e Java Guru`, it returns `false`.

The length of string `eJava` is 11, so `eJava.substring(11)` doesn't throw `StringIndexOutOfBoundsException`. It returns an empty string, which replaces string `"a` in string value `e Java Guru`, resulting in `e Jv Guru`.

A 5-9. a, b, c, d

[5.3] Format strings using the formatting parameters: %b, %c, %d, %f, and %s in format strings.

Explanation: You must use the following for the required format:

- `%f`
- Flag + to include a sign
- Flag , to use locale-specific grouping

Options (a), (b), (c), and (d) use the correct format specifier, `%f`. The flags + and , can appear in any order. It's acceptable to specify the width of the numeric literal.

If the total width specified with the format specifier is less than the width of the argument passed to it, it's ignored. If the width specified after the decimal is less than the number of digits stored by the value to be formatted, it's rounded off.

Options (e), (f), and (g) are incorrect. They either include an invalid combination of flags or don't include the required flags.

A 5-10. f

[5.1] Search, parse, and build strings (including Scanner, StringTokenizer, String-Builder, String, and Formatter)
[5.2] Search, parse, and replace strings by using regular expressions, using expression patterns for matching limited to: . (dot), * (star), + (plus), ?, \d, \D, \s, \S, \w, \W, \b, \B, [], ().

Explanation: Option (a) is incorrect because it doesn't compile. You can only pass integer values as parameters, not strings. Method subSequence() doesn't replace string values. It extracts and returns a matching subsequence of a string.

Options (b) and (d) are incorrect because replace() doesn't accept a regex pattern. It replaces exact matches of a string value.

Option (c) is incorrect—not all strings have a space in front of the first letter, so the replace() option isn't performed on every word in the string. \\s will also match and replace the spaces (or whitespace, but not a combination of both).

Option (e) is incorrect because modify() doesn't exist.

Option (f) is correct. replaceAll() can be passed a regex and its replacement. All matching regex values in the string are replaced with the specified replacement string. The regex pattern \b\w matches a word boundary (\b) followed by a word character (\w)— that is, a-zA-Z_0-9.

Exceptions and assertions

6

Exam objectives covered in this chapter	What you need to know
[6.1] Use the `throw` statement and `throws` clause	How to define methods that throw exceptions. The difference between the `throw` statement and the `throws` clause. The different combinations of defining overriding methods, when the overridden or overriding methods throw checked exceptions.
[6.2] Use the `try` statement with multi-catch and `finally` clauses	How to use this new language feature with Java 7. How to prevent coding the same set of statements for multiple exception handlers. How to catch multiple and unrelated exceptions in a single `catch` block.
[6.3] Auto-close resources with a `try`-with-resources statement	How to use a `try`-with-resources statement so you never forget to close resources such as file handlers and URL connections. When a `try`-with-resources statement throws exceptions, how to handle them. How to define a `try`–with-resources statement without a `catch` or `finally` block.
[6.4] Create custom exceptions	How to create your own exceptions, including subclasses. How to use them in your code.
[6.5] Test invariants by using assertions	The need for and purpose of assertions. The correct syntax of an `assert` statement. Correct and incorrect usage of assertions for variants and flow control. How to enable and disable assertions.

First let's talk about exception handling. Imagine that the pilot of an airplane has an accident just an hour before the flight's scheduled takeoff. The airline manages the situation by arranging for an alternate pilot, enabling the flight to take off at the scheduled time. What a relief for both the passengers and the airline. This example illustrates how an exceptional condition (a pilot's accident) that was outside the immediate control of the airline can modify the initial flow of an action (the predefined airline flight operation). It demonstrates the need to handle such unexpected conditions appropriately (the arrangement of an alternate pilot). Can you imagine the inconvenience that would be caused to all the passengers if the airline had no alternate plan to arrange for another pilot and recover from this situation?

Similarly, it's important for a Java application to handle unexpected or exceptional conditions so it doesn't fail, exit abruptly, or return invalid values. Java's *exception handling* is a mechanism that lets you do just that. It enables you to build robust applications that can recover from exceptional conditions that may arise during the course of a program, by defining an alternate flow of actions.

Now let's talk about assertions. Whenever you board an international flight, the airline staff checks your visa and stamps your passport. Imagine what would happen if they missed stamping your passport at emigration? Would you be in trouble, at immigration, when you fly back to your own country? As you can see, a failed assumption that all passports were stamped at emigration can cause issues with immigration. For such cases, the airline would examine the existing procedures and formulate new checks so that a similar situation doesn't occur again.

Just as a failed assumption can help an airline identify an existing flaw in its operations, a failed assumption in an application can help identify and fix errors in the application logic during its development. It's difficult to find subtle bugs in the implementation of *application logic* when a programmer uses predefined assumptions (believe me—it happens a lot). You must use assertions to check assumptions in the program logic, variable values, and pre- and postconditions of methods, to avoid bugs or errors. An assertion offers a way of indicating what should always be true.

Exception handling helps you gracefully handle an exceptional condition by defining an alternate flow of action. On the other hand, assertions help you identify and fix potential application logic errors.

Exception handling is covered in both the OCA Java SE 7 Programmer I exam (1Z0-803) and OCP Java SE 7 Programmer II exam (1Z0-804). This chapter covers exception-handling topics that are specific to the latter exam. Assertions are covered only by the second exam. This chapter covers

- The throw statement and throws clause
- The try statement with multi-catch and finally clauses (new in Java 7)
- Auto-closing resources with a try-with-resources statement (new in Java 7)
- Custom exceptions
- Testing invariants by using assertions

This chapter assumes that you're already aware of the basic exception handling covered by the OCA Java SE 7 Programmer I exam. If required, you can refer to *OCA Java SE 7 Programmer I Certification Guide: Prepare for the 1Z0-803 Exam* (Manning, 2013), which covers Java's basic exception handling.

Let's get started with the use of the throw statement and the throws clause.

6.1 *Using the throw statement and the throws clause*

> **[6.1]** Use the throw statement and throws clause

Imagine that you're assigned the task of finding a specific book, and then reading and explaining its contents to a class of students. The required sequence looks like the following:

- Get the specified book.
- Read aloud its contents.
- Explain the contents to a class of students.

But what happens if you can't find the specified book? You can't proceed with the rest of the actions without it, so you need to report back to the person who assigned the task to you. This unexpected event (missing book) prevents you from completing your task. By reporting it, you want the *originator* of this request to take corrective or alternate steps.

Let's code the preceding task as method teachClass(), as shown in figure 6.1, and use it to compare the throw statement and the throws clause. This example code is for demonstration purposes only, because it uses methods locateBook(), readBook(), and explainContents(), which aren't defined.

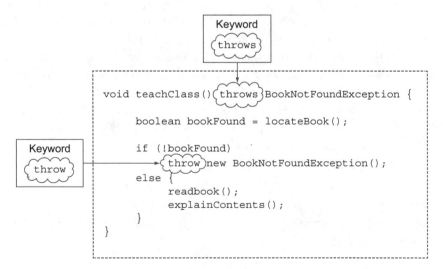

Figure 6.1 Comparing the throw statement and the throws clause

The code in figure 6.1 is simple to follow. On execution of `throw new BookNot-FoundException`, the execution of `teachClass()` halts. The JVM creates an instance of `BookNotFoundException` and sends it off to the caller of `teachClass()` so alternate arrangements can be made.

The `throw` statement is used to *throw* an instance of `BookNotFoundException`. The `throws` statement is used in the declaration of method `teachClass()` to signal that it can throw `BookNotFoundException`.

Why does a method choose to throw an exception as opposed to handling it itself? It's a contract between the *calling* method and the *called* method. Referring to method `teachClass()` shown in figure 6.1, the *caller* of `teachClass` would like to be informed if `teachClass()` is unable to find the specified book. Method `teachClass()` doesn't handle `BookNotFoundException` because its responsibilities don't include how to work around a missing book.

The preceding example helps identify a situation when you'd *want* a method to throw an exception, rather than handling it itself. It shows you how to use and compare the statement `throw` and clause `throws`—to *throw* exceptions and to signal that a method *might* throw an exception. The example also shows that a calling method can define alternate code, when the called method doesn't complete successfully and throws an exception. Apart from testing this logic, the exam will test you on how to create and use methods that throw checked or unchecked (runtime) exceptions and errors, along with several other rules.

Before you move forward with the chapter, it's important to clearly identify all kinds of exception classes as shown in figure 6.2.

Here's a list of different kinds of exceptions:

- *Exception classes*—Refers to `Throwable` class and all its subclasses
- *Error classes*—Refers to `Error` class and all its subclasses
- *Runtime exception classes*—Refers to `RuntimeException` class and all its subclasses
- *Unchecked exception classes*—Refers to runtime exception classes and error classes
- *Checked exceptions classes*—Refers to all exception classes other than the unchecked exception classes. Class `Throwable` and any of its subclasses that aren't a subclass of either `Error` or `RuntimeException` are checked exceptions.

Now let's create a method that throws checked exceptions.

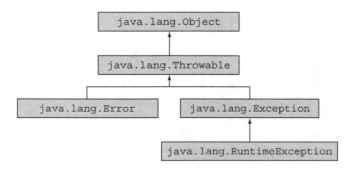

Figure 6.2 Using exception hierarchy to identify all kinds of exception classes

6.1.1 Creating a method that throws a checked exception

Let's create a simple method that doesn't handle the checked exception thrown by it, by using the statement `throw` and clause `throws`. Class `DemoThrowsException` defines method `readFile()`, which includes a `throws` clause in its method declaration. The actual throwing of an exception is accomplished by the `throw` statement:

> **throws statement indicates method can throw FileNotFoundException or one of its subclasses**

```java
import java.io.FileNotFoundException;
class DemoThrowsException {
    public void readFile(String file) throws FileNotFoundException {
        boolean found = findFile(file);
        if (!found)
            throw new FileNotFoundException("Missing file");
        else {
            //code to read file
        }
    }
    boolean findFile(String file) {
        //code to return true if file can be located
    }
}
```

> **If file can't be found, code creates and throws instance of FileNotFound-Exception by using throw statement**

A method can have multiple comma-separated class names of exceptions in its `throws` clause. Including runtime exceptions or errors in the method declaration isn't required. Including them in the documentation is the preferred way to mention them. A method can still throw runtime exceptions or errors without including them in its `throws` clause.

EXAM TIP Syntactically, you don't always need a combination of the `throw` statement and `throws` clause to create a method that throws an exception (checked or unchecked). You can replace the `throw` statement with a method that throws an exception.

6.1.2 Using a method that throws a checked exception

To use a method that throws a *checked exception*, you must do one of the following:

- *Handle the exception*—Enclose the code within a `try` block and *catch* the thrown exception.
- *Declare it to be thrown*—Declare the exception to be thrown by using the `throws` clause.
- *Handle and declare*—Implement both of the preceding options together.

EXAM TIP The rule of either handling or declaring an exception is also referred to as the handle-or-declare rule. To use a method that throws a checked exception, you must either handle the exception or declare it to be thrown. But this rule only applies to the checked exceptions and not to the unchecked exceptions.

In the following example, method useReadFile() *handles* FileNotFoundException (a checked exception) thrown by readFile() by using a try-catch block:

```
class DemoThrowsException {
    public void readFile(String file) throws FileNotFoundException {
        //..code
    }
    void useReadFile(String name) {
        try {
            readFile(name);
        }
        catch (FileNotFoundException e) {
            //code
        }
    }
}
```

useReadFile uses readFile that throws FileNotFoundException

Call to readFile should be enclosed in try block because it throws checked FileNotFoundException

A modified definition of method useReadFile() *declares to throw* a FileNotFound-Exception:

```
class DemoThrowsException {
    public void readFile(String file) throws FileNotFoundException {
        //..code
    }
    void useReadFile(String name) throws FileNotFoundException{
        readFile(name);
    }
}
```

readFile need not be enclosed in try-catch block

useReadFile() declares that it could throw FileNotFound-Exception.

The compiler doesn't complain if you mix the preceding approaches. Method use-ReadFile() can handle FileNotFoundException itself and still declare it to be thrown (highlighted in bold):

```
import java.io.*;
class DemoThrowsException {
    public void readFile(String file) throws FileNotFoundException {
        //..code
    }
    void useReadFile(String name) throws FileNotFoundException{

        try {
            readFile(name);
        }
        catch (FileNotFoundException e) {
            //code
        }
    }
}
```

readFile is enclosed in try-catch block

useReadFile() declares that it could throw FileNotFound-Exception.

So what happens when `FileNotFoundException` is thrown by method `readFile()`? Will its `catch` block handle `FileNotFoundException`, or will `readFile()` throw the exception to its calling method? Let's find out in our first "Twist in the Tale" exercise.

Let's modify some of the code used in the previous examples. Which answer correctly shows the output of class `TwistThrowsException`?

```java
import java.io.*;
class TwistThrowsException {
    public void readFile(String file) throws FileNotFoundException {
        System.out.println("readFile");
        throw new FileNotFoundException();
    }
    void useReadFile(String name) throws FileNotFoundException {
        System.out.println("useReadFile");
        try {
            readFile(name);
        }
        catch (FileNotFoundException e) {
            //code
        }
    }
    public static void main(String args[]) {
        new TwistThrowsException().useReadFile("a");
    }
}
```

   a   `useReadFile`
       `readFile`
       `FileNotFoundException thrown at runtime`

   b   `useReadFile`
       `FileNotFoundException thrown at runtime`

   c   Compilation error

   d   `FileNotFoundException` thrown at runtime

   e   `useReadFile`
       `readFile`

Did you ever happen to debug or fix a piece of code written by someone else? During such a session, have you ever noticed that to avoid coding multiple exception handlers (prior to Java 7), programmers often caught an overly broad exception, which often made its way into the production code? The next tip shows why you must avoid that technique.

Practical issues with catching an overly broad exception

Many times (prior to Java 7), developers took a shorter route to handle all checked exceptions: they defined just one exception handler, `java.lang.Exception`. Here's an example:

```
class MyCustomException extends Exception {}
class MultiCatch {
    void myMethod(Connection con, String fileName) {
        try {
            // code
        }
        catch (Exception e) {
            // code
        }
    }
}
```

Code that might throw MyCustomException, FileNotFoundException, or SQLException

Catch all types of checked and runtime exceptions.

This, of course, has issues, because `java.lang.Exception` is the superclass of all exceptions, including `RuntimeException`. The preceding `catch` block will *silently* catch all types of runtime exceptions also. It might become difficult to debug such code—it might log the same message for different exceptions or might try to handle all types of exceptions in the same way, which might not have been the intent.

6.1.3   *Creating and using a method that throws runtime exceptions or errors*

While creating a method that throws a runtime exception or error, including the exception or error name in the `throws` clause isn't required. A method that throws a runtime exception or error isn't subject to the handle-or-declare rule.

Let's see this concept in action by modifying the preceding example so method `readFile()` throws a `NullPointerException` (a runtime exception) when a null value is passed to it (code changes are shown in bold in this example and throughout the rest of the chapter):

```
import java.io.FileNotFoundException;
class DemoThrowsException {
    public void readFile(String file) throws FileNotFoundException {
        if (file == null)
            throw new NullPointerException();
        boolean found = findFile(file);
        if (!found)
            throw new FileNotFoundException("Missing file");
        else {
            //code to read file
        }
    }
    boolean findFile(String file) {
        //code to return true if file can be located
    }
}
```

throws clause indicates that this method can throw FileNotFoundException

Code throws NullPointerException, but it's not included in throws clause.

The exam might trick you by including the names of runtime exceptions and errors in one method's declaration and leaving them out in another. (You *can* include the name of unchecked exceptions in the throws clause, but you don't have to.) Assuming that the rest of the code remains the same, the following method declaration is correct:

```
public void readFile(String file)
                    throws NullPointerException, FileNotFoundException {
    //rest of the code remains same
}
```

Though not required, including runtime exceptions in throws clause is valid

 EXAM TIP Adding runtime exceptions or errors to a method's declaration isn't required. A method can throw a runtime exception or error irrespective of whether its name is included in its throws clause.

Table 6.1 lists common errors and runtime exceptions. All are covered in detail in *OCA Java SE 7 Programmer I Certification Guide.*

Table 6.1 Common errors and exceptions

Runtime exceptions	Errors
ArrayIndexOutOfBoundsException	ExceptionInInitializerError
IndexOutOfBoundsException	StackOverflowError
ClassCastException	NoClassDefFoundError
IllegalArgumentException	OutOfMemoryError
IllegalStateException	
NullPointerException	
NumberFormatException	

6.1.4 *Points to note while using the throw statement and the throws clause*

Apart from understanding the need for throwing exceptions and using their syntax, you need to know a few rules about throwing exceptions with the throw statement and the throws clause. These rules are presented in this section.

A METHOD CAN THROW A SUBCLASS OF CHECKED EXCEPTION MENTIONED IN ITS THROWS CLAUSE, NOT ITS SUPERCLASS

Because class IOException is a superclass of class FileNotFoundException, method readFile() can't throw an object of class IOException:

throws clause includes FileNotFoundException

```
class DemoThrowsException {
    public void readFile(String file) throws FileNotFoundException {
        boolean found = findFile(file);
```

```
        if (!found)
            throw new IOException("Missing file");    ⊲──┐  Won't compile; can't
        else {                                            throw object of
            //code to read file                           superclass of checked
        }                                                 exception mentioned
    }                                                     in throws clause.
    boolean findFile(String file) {
        //code to return true if file can be located
    }
}
```

Let's modify the definition of method readFile() by declaring it might throw an IOException. Because IOException is a superclass of class FileNotFoundException, readFile() can throw an object of FileNotFoundException:

```
class DemoThrowsException {
    public void readFile(String file) throws IOException {   ⊲──┐  throws clause
        boolean found = findFile(file);                          includes IOException
        if (!found)
            throw new FileNotFoundException("Missing file");  ⊲──┐  Will compile;
        else {                                                     can throw object
            //code to read file                                    of derived class of
        }                                                          checked exception
    }                                                              mentioned in
    boolean findFile(String file) {                                throws clause.
        //code to return true if file can be located
    }
}
```

Note that this rule doesn't apply to errors and runtime exceptions.

 EXAM TIP An overriding method can throw any error or runtime exception, irrespective of whether they're thrown by the overridden method or not.

A METHOD CAN HANDLE THE EXCEPTION AND STILL DECLARE IT TO BE THROWN

This is usually done by methods whose exception handlers might throw the same exception. Method useReadFile() handles the FileNotFoundException and also declares it to be rethrown:

```
class DemoThrowsException {
    public void readFile(String file) throws FileNotFoundException {
        //..code
    }                                                                      useReadFile()
    void useReadFile(String name) throws FileNotFoundException {   ⊲──┐  could throw
        try {                                                             FileNotFound-
            readFile(name);                                               Exception.
        }
        catch (FileNotFoundException e) {            ⊲──┐
            //..code                                       Code is valid;
            throw e;      ⊲──┐  FileNotFoundException      useReadFile()
        }                      instance will be handed over to  handles FileNot-
    }                          method that calls useReadFile()  FoundException
}                                                              from readFile().
```

A METHOD THAT DECLARES A CHECKED EXCEPTION TO BE THROWN MIGHT NOT ACTUALLY THROW IT
Method readFile() includes the name of the checked exception FileNotFound-
Exception in its throws clause, but doesn't throw it:

```
import java.io.FileNotFoundException;
class DemoThrowsException {
    public void readFile(String file) throws FileNotFoundException {
        System.out.println("readFile:" + file);
    }
}
```

Compiles successfully even if readFile() doesn't throw FileNotFoundException.

But do you think you can call readFile() as a method that doesn't throw an exception (without enclosing it within a try-catch block or declaring the exception)? Let's check it out in our next "Twist in the Tale" exercise.

Twist in the Tale 6.2

What is the output of class ThrowsException?

```
import java.io.FileNotFoundException;
class TwistThrowsException {
    public void readFile(String file) throws FileNotFoundException {
        System.out.println("readFile:" + file);
    }
    public static void main(String args[]) {
        System.out.println("main");
        new TwistThrowsException().readFile("Hello.txt");
    }
}
```

  a main
     readFile:Hello.txt

  b main
     readFile:Hello.txt
     FileNotFoundException thrown at runtime

  c Compilation error

  d FileNotFoundException thrown at runtime

YOU CAN RETHROW EXCEPTIONS WITH MORE-INCLUSIVE TYPE CHECKING
Starting with Java 7, the variable type that you use to rethrow an exception can be more generic in the catch block:

```
class GenericVariableTypeToRethrowException {
    public static void main(String args[])
                        throws IOException, SQLException {
        String source = "DBMS";
```

Method declares to throw exceptions IOException and SQLException

```
    try {
        if (source.equals("DBMS"))
            throw new SQLException();
        else
            throw new IOException();
    }
    catch (Exception e) {
        throw e;
    }
}
}
```

Type of variable e in catch block is Exception, more generic than IOException and SQLException

Catch block rethrows caught exception

In the preceding code, the `try` block can throw two types of checked exceptions: `SQLException` or `IOException`. But the type of the variable e in the `catch` block is `Exception`, which is a superclass of `SQLException` and `IOException`. Prior to Java 7, this code would fail to compile because `main()` is trying to throw an object of `Exception` from its `catch` block, when its method declaration states that it can throw an `IOException` or `SQLException`. (For checked exceptions, a method can't throw a superclass of the exception included in its declaration.) With Java 7, the preceding code compiles successfully, because the compiler can determine that the type of the checked exception received by the `catch` block would always be either `IOException` or `SQLException`. So it's okay to throw it, even though the type of the variable e is `Exception`.

Do you think the code will compile successfully if instead of rethrowing the exception in the `catch` block, you create a new object of class `Exception` and throw it? No, it won't. It would be a direct violation of the contract between the declarations of exceptions that method `main()` states to be throwing and what it *actually* throws. The following modified example won't compile:

```
class GenericVariableTypeToRethrowException2 {
    public static void main(String args[])
                        throws IOException, SQLException {
        String source = "DBMS";
        try {
            if (source.equals("DBMS"))
                throw new SQLException();
            else
                throw new IOException();
        }
        catch (Exception e) {
            throw new Exception();
        }
    }
}
```

Method declares to throw IOException and SQLException

Won't compile; catch block creates and throws Exception instance.

 EXAM TIP   With Java 7, you can rethrow exceptions with more inclusive type checking.

A METHOD CAN DECLARE TO THROW ALL TYPES OF EXCEPTIONS, EVEN IF IT DOESN'T

In the following example, class ThrowExceptions defines multiple methods that declare to throw different exception types. Class ThrowExceptions compiles successfully, even though its methods don't include the code that might throw these exceptions:

```
class ThrowExceptions {
    void method1() throws Error {}
    void method2() throws Exception {}
    void method3() throws Throwable {}
    void method4() throws RuntimeException {}
    void method5() throws FileNotFoundException {}
}
```

Though a try block can define a handler for unchecked exceptions not thrown by it, it can't do so for checked exceptions (other than Exception):

```
class HandleExceptions {
    void method6() {
        try {}
        catch (Error e) {}
    }
    void method7() {
        try {}
        catch (Exception e) {}
    }
    void method8() {
        try {}
        catch (Throwable e) {}
    }
    void method9() {
        try {}
        catch (RuntimeException e) {}
    }
    void method10() {
        try {}
        catch (FileNotFoundException e) {}            Won't
    }                                                  compile
}
```

In the preceding code, method6(), method7(), method8(), and method9() compile even though their try blocks don't define code to throw the exception being handled by their catch blocks. But method10() won't compile.

 EXAM TIP   A method can declare to throw any type of exception—checked or unchecked—even if it doesn't. But a try block can't define a catch block for a checked exception (other than Exception) if the try block doesn't throw that checked exception or uses a method that declares to throw that checked exception.

Before moving on to the next section, let's summarize the points to remember for the throw statement and the throws clause.

Rules to remember about the throw statement and the throws clause

- The `throw` statement is used within a method to throw an instance of a checked exception, a runtime exception, or an error.
- The `throws` clause is used with a method's declaration to list the exceptions that a method can throw.
- A method can include multiple comma-separated exception and error class names in its `throws` clause.
- The rule of either handling or declaring a checked exception is also referred to as the handle-or-declare rule.
- To use a method that throws a checked exception, you must either handle the exception or declare it to be thrown.
- The handle-or-declare rule only applies to the checked exceptions and not to the unchecked exceptions.
- Including runtime exceptions or errors in a `throws` clause isn't required.
- Adding unchecked exceptions or errors in the `throws` clause adds no obligations about handling them in a `try-catch` block.
- A method can throw a more specific exception subclass than the one mentioned in its `throws` clause, but not a more generic one (superclass).
- A method can handle a checked or unchecked exception and still declare it to be thrown.
- A method that declares a checked exception to be thrown might not throw it.
- With Java 7, you can rethrow exceptions with more inclusive type checking.
- A method can declare to throw any type of exception—checked or unchecked— even if it doesn't. But a `try` block can't define a `catch` block for a checked exception (other than `Exception`) if the `try` block doesn't throw that checked exception or uses a method that declares to throw that checked exception.

You can throw your own custom exceptions from methods by using the `throw` and `throws` statements, in the same way you work with exception classes from the Java API. Why do you need to create custom exception classes, when you can use exception classes that are already defined in the Java API? Let's discover in the next section.

6.2 *Creating custom exceptions*

 [6.4] Create custom exceptions

Take a look at figure 6.3, which shows just a few of the existing exceptions from the Java API.

What information do you gather when a piece of code throws a `FileNotFound-Exception` or `ArrayIndexOutOfBoundsException`? Without reading the code, you can know that `FileNotFoundException` was probably thrown by code that couldn't locate a specified file. Similarly, `ArrayIndexOutOfBoundsException` will probably be thrown by code that tried to access an array element at an index position out of its bounds.

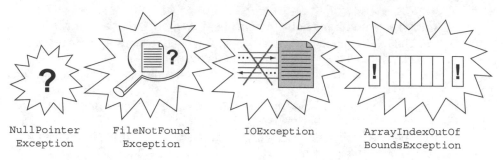

NullPointer   FileNotFound   IOException   ArrayIndexOutOf
Exception   Exception   BoundsException

Figure 6.3   Existing exceptions defined in the Java API

The name of an exception can convey a lot of information to other developers or users, which is one of the main reasons for defining a custom exception. A custom exception can also be used to communicate a more descriptive message. For example, assume that you're developing an API to enable users to connect to your server to access its services. How can you communicate failure of the login process to a user, which can arise from multiple reasons such as a database connectivity issue or inappropriate user access privileges? One of the preferred approaches is to define and use custom exceptions.

Custom exceptions also *help* you restrict the escalation of implementing specific exceptions to higher layers. For example, data access code on your server that accesses persistent data may throw a SQLException. But users connecting to your server should not be returned this exception. You may catch SQLException and throw another checked or unchecked exception (the choice of throwing a checked or unchecked exception is beyond the scope of this book). If you can't find an appropriate existing exception, create one!

6.2.1   *Creating a custom checked exception*

You can subclass java.lang.Exception (or any of its subclasses) to define custom exceptions. To create custom checked exceptions, subclass java.lang.Exception or its subclasses (which aren't subclasses of RuntimeException). Let's revisit the exception classes in figure 6.4.

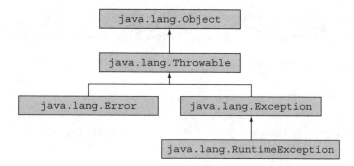

Figure 6.4   Hierarchy of Exception and Error classes

A word of caution here: even though you can extend class `java.lang.Throwable` to create your own exceptions, it isn't recommended. Class `Throwable` is the superclass of classes `java.lang.Error` and `java.lang.Exception`. The exception handler for this class will *catch* all types of errors and exceptions! For example, say an `OutOf-MemoryError` brings the JVM into an unstable state. Catching it as a subclass of `Error` or `Throwable` would be undesirable and potentially dangerous. Obviously, you may not want this behavior.

 EXAM TIP Don't extend class `java.lang.Throwable` to create your own exceptions, even though you can. Class `Throwable` is the superclass of classes `java.lang.Error` and `java.lang.Exception`. The exception handler for this class will *catch* all types of errors and exceptions.

Often organizations prefix the name of a custom exception with their organization, project, or module name. Let's create a custom exception, `LoginException`, which is a checked exception:

```
class LoginException extends Exception {}
```
⊣ **LoginException is a checked exception.**

Let's add constructors to it, a no-argument constructor and one that accepts a description of an exception or problem that occurred, as follows:

```
class LoginException extends Exception{
    public LoginException() {
        super();
    }
    public LoginException(String message) {
        super(message);
    }
}
```
← **No-argument constructor**

← **Constructor that accepts String**

Note that an exception class is like any other class to which you add your own methods and variables. Let's define another class, `UserActivity`, which defines method `login()`. This method creates an instance of `LoginException` and throws it if a user is unable to log in successfully. Note that I've tried to show how (checked) exceptions are thrown in real-world applications. Because the main focus here is to *throw* a checked exception, I haven't implemented method `findInDatabase()`, as it would have been implemented in the real world. It's simply reduced to returning a `false` value. Examine the following code:

Add throws clause to method declaration

```
class UserActivity {
    public void login(String user, String pwd) throws LoginException {
        if (!findInDatabase(user, pwd))
            throw new LoginException("Invalid username or password");
    }
```
← (throws clause)

← **Instantiate LoginException and throw it.**

```
        private boolean findInDatabase(String user, String pwd) {
            // code that returns true if user/ pwd
            // combination found in database
            // false otherwise
            return false;
        }
    }
```

6.2.2 *Creating a custom unchecked exception*

Class `Error`, class `RuntimeException`, and their derived classes are collectively referred to as *unchecked exception classes*.

You can subclass `java.lang.RuntimeException` to create a custom runtime exception. Here is the modified class `LoginException`:

```
class LoginException extends RuntimeException{
    public LoginException() {
            super();
    }
    public LoginException(String message) {
            super(message);
    }
}
```

◁— **Since LoginException extends RuntimeException, now it's an unchecked exception.**

You can throw this exception (now a runtime, or unchecked, exception) in the same manner as mentioned previously in class `UserActivity`. The only change is that (though allowed) now you no longer need to include the `throws` clause in method `login()`'s declaration, as follows:

```
class UserActivity {
    public void login(String username,String pwd) {
    if (!findInDatabase(username, pwd))
        throw new LoginException("Invalid username or password");
    }
    private boolean findInDatabase(String username, String pwd) {
    // code that returns true if username/ pwd
    // combination found in database
    // false otherwise
    return false;
    }
}
```

◁— **No need to define throws clause in method declaration for runtime exception**

To create custom `Error` classes, you can subclass `java.lang.Error` by extending it. But `Error` classes represent serious exceptional conditions, which shouldn't be thrown programmatically.

On the exam, you'll see both custom exceptions and exceptions from the Java API. Though overriding methods that throw exceptions isn't explicitly defined as a separate exam topic, you're likely to be tested on it.

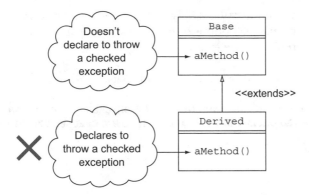

Figure 6.5 If an overridden method doesn't declare to throw any *checked* exception, the overriding method can't declare to throw a *checked* exception.

6.3   *Overriding methods that throw exceptions*

In this section, you'll work through compilation issues that occur with overridden and overriding methods, when either of them declares to throw a checked exception. Multiple combinations exist, as shown in figures 6.5 and 6.6.

 EXAM TIP   With overriding and overridden methods, it's all about which checked exceptions an overridden method and an overriding method declare, not about the checked exceptions both actually throw.

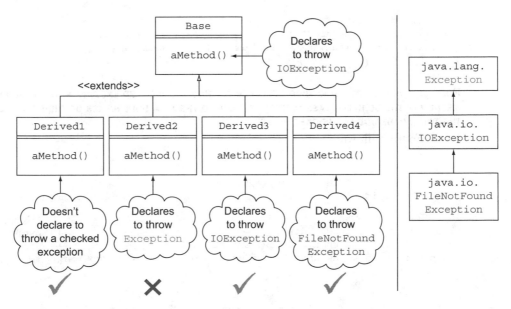

Figure 6.6 If an overridden method declares to throw a *checked* exception, the overriding method can choose to declare to not throw any checked exception, throw the same exception, or throw a more specific exception. The overriding method can't declare to throw a more generic checked exception.

EXAM TIP   Method overriding rules apply *only* to checked exceptions. They don't apply to runtime exceptions or errors. Beware: you're likely to be tested on this difference on the exam.

Let's work with all these combinations by using code snippets.

RULE 1: IF A BASE CLASS METHOD DOESN'T DECLARE TO THROW A CHECKED EXCEPTION, AN OVERRIDING METHOD IN THE DERIVED CLASS CAN'T DECLARE TO THROW A CHECKED EXCEPTION

Examine the following code:

```
class Base {
    public void aMethod() {}
    public void noRuntimeException() {}
}
class Derived extends Base {
    public void aMethod() throws Exception {}          ⟵  This line fails
                                                           to compile.
    public void noRuntimeException() throws RuntimeException {}   ⟵  This line
                                                                      compiles
}                                                                  successfully.
```

RULE 2: IF A BASE CLASS METHOD DECLARES TO THROW A CHECKED EXCEPTION, AN OVERRIDING METHOD IN THE DERIVED CLASS CAN CHOOSE NOT TO DECLARE TO THROW ANY CHECKED EXCEPTION

Examine the following code:

```
class Base {
    public void aMethod() throws IOException {}
    public void withRuntimeException() throws RuntimeException {}
}
class Derived1 extends Base {
    public void aMethod() {}                         Both lines compile
    public void withRuntimeException() {}            successfully.
}
```

RULE 3: IF A BASE CLASS METHOD DECLARES TO THROW A CHECKED EXCEPTION, AN OVERRIDING METHOD IN THE DERIVED CLASS CANNOT DECLARE TO THROW A SUPERCLASS OF THE EXCEPTION THROWN BY THE ONE IN THE BASE CLASS

Examine the following code:

```
class Base {
    public void aMethod() throws IOException {}
    public void withRuntimeException() throws NullPointerException {}
}
class Derived2 extends Base {
    public void aMethod() throws Exception {}          ⟵  This line fails
                                                           to compile.
    public void withRuntimeException() throws RuntimeException{}
}
```

RULE 4: IF A BASE CLASS METHOD DECLARES TO THROW A CHECKED EXCEPTION, AN OVERRIDING METHOD IN THE DERIVED CLASS CAN DECLARE TO THROW THE SAME EXCEPTION

The following code compiles successfully:

```
class Base {
    void aMethod() throws IOException {}
    void methodUncheckedEx() throws Error {}
}
class Derived3 extends Base {
    void aMethod() throws IOException {}
    void methodUncheckedEx() throws NullPointerException {}
}
```

RULE 5: IF A BASE CLASS METHOD DECLARES TO THROW A CHECKED EXCEPTION, AN OVERRIDING METHOD IN THE DERIVED CLASS CAN DECLARE TO THROW A DERIVED CLASS OF THE EXCEPTION THROWN BY THE ONE IN THE BASE CLASS

The following code compiles successfully:

```
class Base {
    void aMethod() throws IOException {}
}
class Derived4 extends Base {
    void aMethod() throws FileNotFoundException {}
}
```

After working with the method overriding rules that include throwing exceptions, let's use the `try` statement with multi-catch and `finally` clauses. Starting with Java 7, the `try` statement can *catch* multiple exceptions in the same handler, as discussed in the next section.

6.4 Using the try statement with multi-catch and finally clauses

> [6.2] Use the try statement with multi-catch and finally clauses

Prior to Java 7, if a `try` block needed to execute the same action for multiple exceptions thrown, it had to define separate handlers for each of them. Starting with Java 7, you can *catch* multiple, unrelated exceptions with one handler, also called a multi-`catch`.

6.4.1 Comparing single-catch handlers and multi-catch handlers

The multi-`catch` comes in handy if you need to execute the same action for handling multiple, unrelated exceptions. I specifically mention unrelated exceptions, because an exception handler for, say, `MyException`, can handle `MyException` and all of its subclasses. You can compare this approach of defining separate exception handlers

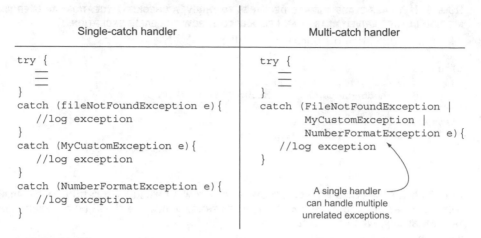

Figure 6.7   Comparing the differences between executing the same action with single-catch and multi-catch exception handlers

(prior to Java 7) with defining only one exception handler to execute the same steps for multiple unrelated exceptions (starting in Java 7) by using figure 6.7.

Now that you know the difference between a multi-catch and single-catch handler, let's dive into the details of defining multi-catch handlers with finally clauses.

6.4.2   *Handling multiple exceptions in the same exception handler*

You should know the basic syntax for creating and using multi-catch blocks, together with the *gotchas* that may be used on the exam. So let's start with the basic syntax of multi-catch blocks.

BASIC SYNTAX OF MULTI-CATCH BLOCK

To *catch* multiple exceptions in a single handler, just separate the different exception types with a vertical bar (|). The following is an example of a try block that defines code that can handle FileNotFoundException and SQLException (or any of their subclasses) using a multi-catch block:

```
Line1>  class MultiCatch {
Line2>      void myMethod(Connection con, String fileName) {
Line3>          try {
Line4>              File file = new File(fileName);
Line5>              FileInputStream fin = new FileInputStream(file);

Line6>              Statement stmt = con.createStatement();
Line7>          }
Line8>          catch (FileNotFoundException | SQLException e) {
Line9>              System.out.println(e.toString());
Line10>         }
Line11>     }
Line12>}
```

Might throw FileNotFound-Exception

Might throw SQLException

Executes if line 5 throws FileNotFoundException or line 6 throws SQLException or any of their subclasses.

In the preceding code, the exception handler will execute if the code throws File-NotFoundException, SQLException, or any of their subclasses.

FINALLY BLOCK CAN FOLLOW MULTI-CATCH BLOCK
A multi-catch block can be followed by a finally block. Here's an example:

```
class MultiCatchWithFinally {
    void myMethod(Connection con, String fileName) {
        try {
            File file = new File(fileName);
            FileInputStream fin = new FileInputStream(file);

            Statement stmt = con.createStatement();
        }
        catch (FileNotFoundException | SQLException e) {
            System.out.println(e.toString());
        }
        finally {
            System.out.println("finally");        ⟵⟍ finally block can follow
        }                                              multi-catch block
    }
}
```

The syntax seems to be simple. So let's look at some of the *gotchas* that you need to be aware of for the exam.

EXCEPTIONS THAT YOU CATCH IN A MULTI-CATCH BLOCK CAN'T SHARE AN INHERITANCE RELATIONSHIP
What happens if you add another line of code in the previous example, which involves reading from FileInputStream, which might throw an IOException? Let's add IOException to the list of exceptions being caught in the multi-catch block:

```
class MultiCatch {
    void myMethod(Connection con, String fileName) {              May throw
        try {                                                     FileNotFound-
            File file = new File(fileName);                       Exception
            FileInputStream fin = new FileInputStream(file); ⟵⟍
            fin.read();
                                                                  May throw
            Statement stmt = con.createStatement();         ⟵⟍  SQLException
        }
        catch (IOException| FileNotFoundException | SQLException e) { ⟵⟍ Fails to
            System.out.println(e.toString());                            compile
        }
    }
}
```

> May throw IOException → `fin.read();`

This code fails compilation with the following error message:

```
MultiCatch.java:13: error: Alternatives in a multi-catch statement cannot
be related by subclassing
            catch (IOException | FileNotFoundException | SQLException e) {
                   ^
  Alternative FileNotFoundException is a subclass of alternative IOException
1 error
```

Looks like the code fails to compile because the IOException is caught before the FileNotFoundException. In regular catch blocks, if you catch a superclass exception before a derived class exception, the code won't compile. So let's swap the order of IOException and FileNotFoundException in the preceding code:

```
class MultiCatch {
    void myMethod(Connection con, String fileName) {
        try {
            File file = new File(fileName);
            FileInputStream fin = new FileInputStream(file);
            fin.read();

            Statement stmt = con.createStatement();
        }
        catch (FileNotFoundException | IOException| SQLException e) {
            System.out.println(e.toString());
        }
    }
}
```

Might throw IOException

Might throw FileNotFound-Exception

Might throw SQLException

Swapping exception types doesn't make a difference; code fails to compile.

The code fails compilation with the following message:

```
Alternatives in a multi-catch statement cannot be related by subclassing
        catch (FileNotFoundException | IOException | SQLException e) {
                                       ^
  Alternative FileNotFoundException is a subclass of alternative IOException
1 error
```

So the takeaway from the previous examples is that you can't use subclasses as alternative types in a multi-catch block. The correct multi-catch block for code that may throw an IOException, FileNotFoundException, and SQLException is as follows:

```
class MultiCatch {
    void myMethod(Connection con, String fileName) {
        try {
            ..
        }
        catch (IOException | SQLException e) {
            System.out.println(e.toString());
        }
    }
}
```

Code that might throw IOException, FileNotFound-Exception, or SQLException

Catch IOException (superclass of FileNotFoundException) and SQLException or any of their subclasses.

Because multi-catch blocks are used to execute the same piece of code, when multiple exceptions are thrown, it makes no sense to use subclasses.

COMBINING MULTI-CATCH AND SINGLE-CATCH BLOCKS

You can combine multi-catch and single-catch blocks, as shown in the following code:

```
class MultiAndSingleCatch {
    void myMethod(Connection con, String fileName) {
```

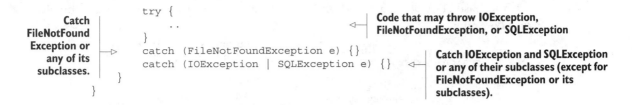

Catch
FileNotFound
Exception or
any of its
subclasses.

```
try {
    ..
}
catch (FileNotFoundException e) {}
catch (IOException | SQLException e) {}
}
}
```

Code that may throw IOException,
FileNotFoundException, or SQLException

Catch IOException and SQLException
or any of their subclasses (except for
FileNotFoundException or its
subclasses).

 EXAM TIP   Watch out for a combination of multi-catch and single-catch exception handlers on the exam. They can get quite tricky.

USING A SINGLE EXCEPTION VARIABLE IN THE MULTI-CATCH BLOCK

It's easy to overlook that even though a multi-catch handler defines multiple exception types, it must use only one variable. Figure 6.8 defines two multi-catch exception handlers. The latter multi-catch block uses multiple variables, which is incorrect and won't compile.

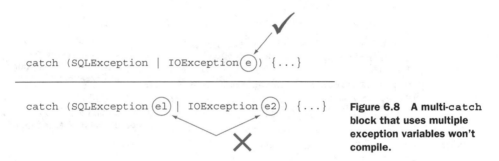

Figure 6.8   A multi-catch block that uses multiple exception variables won't compile.

IN A MULTI-CATCH BLOCK, VARIABLE E IS IMPLICITLY FINAL

In a multi-catch block, the variable that accepts the exception object is implicitly final. A final variable can't be reassigned a value. So if you try to reassign a value to the variable of the multi-catch exception handler, the code won't compile:

```
class MultiCatch {
    void myMethod(Connection con, String fileName) {
        try {
            ..
        }
        catch (IOException| SQLException e) {
            e = new FileNotFoundException();
        }
    }
}
```

Code that may throw
IOException or SQLException

Catch IOException
and SQLException.

Won't compile; can't
reassign value to variable e
because it's implicitly final.

TYPE OF EXCEPTION VARIABLE IN A MULTI-CATCH BLOCK

In a multi-catch block, the type of the reference variable that accepts the exception object is a common base class of all the exception types mentioned in a multi-catch block. In the following code, the type of the reference variable ex is Exception, the common base class of Exception1 and Exception2. This is why calling info() on ex won't compile:

```java
class Exception1 extends IOException{

    public String info() {
        return "I'm Base Exception";
    }
}

class Exception2 extends Exception{

    public String info() {
        return "I'm Derived Exception";
    }
}

class TestVariableTypeInMultiCatch {
    public static void main(String args[]) {
        try {
            int a = 10;

            if (a <= 10)throw new Exception1();
            else throw new Exception2();
        }
        catch (Exception1 | Exception2 ex) {

            System.out.println(ex.info());
        }
    }
}
```

Custom exception Exception1 extends IOException.

Exception1 defines method info.

Custom exception Exception2 extends Exception.

Exception2 defines method info.

Type of variable ex is Exception, common superclass of Exception1 and Exception2.

Won't compile; class Exception doesn't define method info.

Okay, let's modify the code from the previous example so it prints out the value of variable ex, in the next "Twist in the Tale" exercise.

Twist in the Tale 6.3

Which answer correctly shows the output of class TestMultiCatch?

```java
import java.io.*;

class Exception1 extends IOException{}
class Exception2 extends Exception{}

class TestMultiCatch {
    public static void main(String args[]) {
        try {
            int a = 10;
            if (a <= 10)throw new Exception1();
            else throw new Exception2();            // line1
        }
        catch (Exception1 | Exception2 ex) {
            System.out.println(ex);
        }
    }
}
```

    a Value similar to `Exception1@96a34`

    b Value similar to `Exception2@45a86e`

    c `Exception1`

    d `Exception2`

Do you think this code will compile successfully if you comment the code marked with `//line1`?

And what would happen if both custom exceptions used in the preceding example code implement an interface?

```
interface IEx {
    String info();
}
class Exception1 extends IOException implements IEx{         ← Custom exception
    public String info() {                                     Exception1 extends
        return "I'm Base Exception";                           IOException;
    }                                                          implements IEx.
}

class Exception2 extends Exception implements IEx {          ← Custom exception
    public String info() {                                     Exception2 extends
        return "I'm Derived Exception";                        Exception;
    }                                                          implements IEx.
}

class TestVariableTypeInMultiCatch {
    public static void main(String args[]) {
        try {
            int a = 10;

            if (a <= 10)throw new Exception1();               Variable ex is an
            else throw new Exception2();                      intersection type,
        }                                                     with Exception and
        catch (Exception1 | Exception2 ex) {                ← IEx as its bounds.
            System.out.println(ex.info());              ←
        }                                                   Compiles
    }                                                       successfully.
}
```

In the preceding code, variable ex is of *intersection type* with `Exception` and `IEx` as its bounds. You can call methods accessible to class `Exception` and interface `IEx` on the reference variable ex.

    The next section covers another major language enhancement in Java: auto-closing resources by using a `try-with-resources` statement.

6.5   *Auto-closing resources with a try-with-resources statement*

> [6.3]   Auto-close resources with a try-with-resources statement

Prior to Java 7, developers used `finally` blocks to close resources such as file handlers, and database or network connections. Here's a quick example to show how a `FileInputStream` instance was closed prior to Java 7:

```
try {
    FileInputStream fis = /* instantiate */
    /* other code */
}
finally {
    if (fis != null)
        try {
            fis.close();
        }
    catch (Exception e) {/* */}
}
```

As you can see, closing a resource required a lot of boilerplate code and was error-prone too. What if a developer didn't close a resource in a `finally` block?

Starting with Java 7, you can use a try-with-resources statement to *auto-close* resources defined with the `try` statement.

6.5.1   *How to use a try-with-resources statement*

The try-with-resources statement is a type of `try` statement that can declare one or more resources. A *resource* is an object such as file handlers and database or network connections, which *should* be closed after it's no longer required. If you declare a resource by using a try-with-resources statement, it automatically *closes* the resource by calling its `close` method, *just* before the end of the `try` block. A resource must implement the `java.lang.AutoCloseable` interface or any of its subinterfaces to be eligible to be declared in a try-with-resources statement. Let's start with an example.

AN EXAMPLE

In the following example, a try-with-resources statement declares and initializes an object (`fin`) of type `FileInputStream`. Because the try-with-resources statement is supposed to automatically call method `close()` on `fin`, the following code doesn't explicitly make this call:

```
class AutoClose {
    void readFileContents(String fileName) {
        File file = new File(fileName);
        try (FileInputStream fin = new FileInputStream(file)){    ◁─┐
            //.. some code                              ◁─┐
        }
```

Code to open
FileInputStream;
can throw FileNot-
FoundException

Some code

```
        catch (FileNotFoundException e) {          ◁─┐  Catch FileNotFoundException
            System.out.println(e.toString());            that might be thrown by code
        }                                                 to initialize fin.
    }
}
```

But wait! This code doesn't compile and gives the following compilation error:

```
AutoClose.java:7: error: unreported exception IOException;
must be caught or declared to be thrown
            try (FileInputStream fin = new FileInputStream(file)){
                                    ^
  exception thrown from implicit call to close() on resource variable 'fin'
1 error
```

So what went wrong? The try-with-resources statement calls method close() *just* before the completion of the try block. Note that if method close() throws any exception, it should be taken care of by *your* method; it must either catch it or declare it to be thrown. Code that handles both FileNotFoundException and IOException is correct:

```
class AutoClose {                                              Code to initialize fin
    void readFileContents(String fileName) {                   can throw FileNot-
        File file = new File(fileName);                        FoundException;
        try (FileInputStream fin = new FileInputStream(file)){ ◁─ calling close on fin can
            //.. some code                                     throw IOException.
        }
        catch (IOException e) {
            System.out.println(e.toString());      ◁─┐ Catch IOException
        }                                              (IOException is superclass
    }                                                  of FileNotFoundException).
}
```

Details of this code not required points to the `//.. some code` / catch block region.

The following code declares IOException to be thrown, and so it's also correct:

```
                                                          Declares
                                                          IOException
class AutoClose {                                         to be thrown.
    void readFileContents(String fileName) throws IOException {  ◁─┘
        File file = new File(fileName);
        try (FileInputStream fin = new FileInputStream(file)){   ◁─┐
            //.. some code                                         │
        }                                          Initialization of fin may throw
    }                                         FileNotFoundException; calling close on
}                                                   fin may throw IOException.
```

Did you notice that the try block defined in the preceding code wasn't followed by either a catch or a finally block? This is unlike a regular try block, which must be followed by either a catch or a finally block.

NOTE FileInputStream implements java.io.Closeable, which, starting with Java 7, extends java.lang.AutoCloseable. So FileInputStream is a valid resource to be used by the try statement.

6.5.2   *Suppressed exceptions*

In a try-with-resources statement, if both the code in the try block and close() throw an exception, the exception thrown by close() is *suppressed* by the exception thrown by the try block.

The resources initialized by the try-with-resources statement are automatically closed, just before the end of execution of the try block. This happens regardless of whether any exceptions are thrown. Let's understand the flow of code by using class RiverRaft, which implements the AutoCloseable interface:

```java
class RiverRaft implements AutoCloseable {
    public RiverRaft() throws Exception {
        System.out.println("Start raft");
    }
    public void crossRapid() throws Exception {
        System.out.println("Cross rapid");
        throw new Exception("Cross Rapid exception");
    }
    public void close() throws Exception {
        System.out.println("Reach river bank");
    }
}
```

The class SuppressedExceptions initializes an instance of RiverRaft by using a try-with-resources statement:

```java
public class SuppressedExceptions {
    public static void main(String[] args) throws Exception {
        try ( RiverRaft raft = new RiverRaft(); ) {
            raft.crossRapid();

        }
        catch (Exception e) {
            System.out.println("Exception caught:" + e);
        }
    }
}
```

1 Instantiate RiverRaft; no exceptions thrown.

2 Method crossRapid() throws Exception.

3 close() called on raft, before control is transferred to exception handler

 EXAM TIP   Though not required, I've deliberately used a semicolon (;) after declaring and initializing raft in the preceding code. Watch out for questions on the exam that include or exclude a semicolon at the end of the resource defined by a try-with-resources statement. A try-with-resources statement can declare multiple resources, which are separated by a semicolon. After the last resource declaration, a semicolon is optional.

For the code at **1**, the try-with-resources statement creates a RiverRaft instance. For the code at **2**, method crossRapid() throws an exception, but the try-with-resources

statement executes `close()` ❸ before passing the control to the exception handler. Here's the output of the preceding code:

```
Start raft
Cross rapid
Reach river bank
Exception caught:java.lang.Exception: Cross Rapid exception
```

Now what happens if `close()` in `RiverRaft` also throws an exception? Which exception will be propagated to the exception handler? Will it be the exception from `close()` or from `crossRapid()`? Here's the modified code:

```java
public class SuppressedExceptions {
    public static void main(String[] args) throws Exception {
        try ( RiverRaft raft = new RiverRaft(); ) {
            raft.crossRapid();
        }
        catch (Exception e) {
            System.out.println("Exception caught:" + e);
        }
    }
}
class RiverRaft implements AutoCloseable {
    public RiverRaft() throws Exception {
        System.out.println("Start raft");
    }
    public void crossRapid() throws Exception {
        System.out.println("Cross rapid");
        throw new Exception("Cross Rapid exception");      ⟵⎯  Method crossRapid()
    }                                                            throws Exception.
    public void close() throws Exception {
        System.out.println("Reach river bank");
        throw new Exception("Close exception");            ⟵⎯  Method close() also
    }                                                            throws Exception.
}
```

The exception from method `crossRapid()` made it the exception handler. Here's the output of the preceding code:

```
Start raft
Cross rapid
Reach river bank
Exception caught:java.lang.Exception: Cross Rapid exception
```

Because the output of the previous code snippets looks identical, what do you think happened to the exception thrown by method `close()`? This exception was *suppressed* by the exception thrown by `crossRapid()`. This is a new automatic resource management feature in Java 7. In a `try`-with-resources statement, when the code enclosed within the `try` body (try block minus its initialization code) throws an exception, followed by an exception thrown by the `try`-with-resources statement (which implicitly calls method `close()`), then the latter is suppressed.

Even though the exception thrown by `close()` is suppressed in the preceding code, it's associated with the exception thrown by `crossRapid()`. You can retrieve the suppressed exceptions by calling getSuppressed() on the exception that has suppressed the other exceptions. The getSuppressed() method returns an array containing all of the exceptions that were suppressed in order to deliver the exception thrown by crossRapid(). The following modified code shows how you can trace the exception thrown by method close(). Because only one exception was suppressed, the code accessed the first element of the array returned by getSuppressed():

```
public class SuppressedExceptions {
    public static void main(String[] args) throws Exception {
        try ( RiverRaft raft = new RiverRaft(); ) {
            raft.crossRapid();
        }
        catch (Exception e) {
            System.out.println("Exception caught:" + e);
            Throwable[] exs = e.getSuppressed();          ◁──┐ Retrieves and prints
            if (exs.length>0)                                 │ first suppressed
                System.out.println(exs[0]);              ◁──┘ exception.
        }
    }
}
class RiverRaft implements AutoCloseable {
    public RiverRaft() throws Exception {
        System.out.println("Start raft");
    }
    public void crossRapid() throws Exception {
        System.out.println("Cross rapid");
        throw new Exception("Cross Rapid exception");
    }
    public void close() throws Exception {
        System.out.println("Reach river bank");
        throw new Exception("Close exception");
    }
}
```

 EXAM TIP In a try-with-resources statement, when the code enclosed within the try body (try minus its initialization code) throws an exception, followed by an exception thrown by the try-with-resources statement (which implicitly calls method close()), then the latter exception is suppressed. getSuppressed() never returns null. If there aren't any suppressed expressions, the length of the returned array is 0.

Now, let's take a quick look at the nuts and bolts of using a try-with-resources statement, which you should know for this exam.

6.5.3   *The right ingredients*

Working with a try-with-resources statement can be tricky because it involves several points to be taken care of. Let's start with the declaration of multiple resources in a try-with-resources statement.

DECLARING AND INITIALIZING RESOURCES

The variables used to refer to resources are implicitly final variables. You must *declare* and *initialize* resources in the try-with-resources statement. You can't define un-initialized resources:

```
void copyFileContents(String inFile, String outFile) throws IOException{
    try (FileInputStream fin;
         FileOutputStream fout;){          Won't compile; resources
         //..rest of the code             must be initialized.
    }
}
```

It's acceptable to the Java compiler to initialize the resources in a try-with-resources statement to null, only as long as they aren't being reassigned a value in the try block (as they are implicitly final):

```
void copyFileContents(String inFile, String outFile) throws IOException{
    try (FileInputStream fin = null;
         FileOutputStream fout = null;){       Will compile successfully,
         //..rest of the code                  if initialized with null, only
    }                                          as long as it isn't used.
}
```

But it doesn't make much sense to initialize a final variable with null. Once initialized to null, a resource can't be reassigned a value in a try-with-resources statement. If you try to do so, the code won't compile:

```
void copyFileContents(String inFile, String outFile) throws IOException{
    try (FileInputStream fin = null;
         FileOutputStream fout = null;){        Assigned null
                                                to resources.
         fin = new FileInputStream(inFile);  ◄─
         //..rest of the code                   Won't compile; you
    }                                           can't reassign another
}                                               value to fin.
```

 EXAM TIP The variables defined in a try-with-resources statement are implicitly final.

SCOPE OF THE RESOURCE DECLARED BY TRY-WITH-RESOURCES IS LIMITED TO IT

The resource declared by try-with-resources is closed just before the completion of the try block. Also, its scope is limited to the try block. So if you try to access it outside the try block, it won't compile. Following is an example of a simple method that tries to copy contents of one file to another:

```
class AutoClose {
    void copyFileContents(String inFile, String outFile)
                                        throws IOException{         Scope
                                                                   of fout
        try (FileInputStream fin = new FileInputStream(inFile);    limited to
             FileOutputStream fout = new FileOutputStream(outFile)){  ◄─  try block
```

```
            byte [] buffer = new byte[1024];
            int i = 0;
            while ((i = fin.read(buffer)) != -1)
                fout.write(buffer,0,i);
        }                                                   Won't compile; code
        finally {                                           outside try block can't
            fout = new FileOutputStream(inFile);  ◄──┘      access variable fout.
        }

    }
}
```

A SEMICOLON MIGHT NOT FOLLOW THE LAST RESOURCE DECLARED BY TRY STATEMENT

You can initialize multiple resources in a try-with-resources statement, separated by a semicolon (;). It isn't obligatory for a semicolon to follow the declaration of the last resource, as shown in figure 6.9.

RESOURCES MUST IMPLEMENT JAVA.IO.AUTOCLOSEABLE OR ITS SUBINTERFACES (DIRECTLY OR INDIRECTLY)

In the previous examples, I used objects of classes FileInputStream and FileOutput-Stream in a try-with-resources statement. These classes implement the java.io .Closeable interface. Starting with Java 7, java.io.Closeable was modified to extend the java.lang.AutoCloseable interface, so that classes implementing it could be used with a try-with-resources statement.

```
class AutoClose {
    void copyFileContents(String inFile, String outFile)
                                                    throws IOException{

        try (FileInputStream fin = new FileInputStream(inFile);
              FileOutputStream fout = new FileOutputStream(outFile)){
            //..code
        }
    }
}
```

                                                   Okay to
                                                   include or exclude
                                                   the semicolon

```
class AutoClose {
    void copyFileContents(String inFile, String outFile)
                                                    throws IOException{

        try (FileInputStream fin = new FileInputStream(inFile);
              FileOutputStream fout = new FileOutputStream(outFile);){
            //..code
        }
    }
}
```

Figure 6.9 The last resource defined in a try-with-resources statement might not be followed by a semicolon (;).

To use instances of your own class with a try-with-resources statement, you can implement the java.lang.AutoCloseable interface:

```
class MyAutoCloseableRes implements AutoCloseable{          ◄──    MyAutoCloseableRes
    MyAutoCloseableRes() {                                         implements AutoCloseable,
        System.out.println("Constructor called");                 so it can be used in
    }                                                              try-with-resources.
    public void close() {                              ◄──
        System.out.println("Close called");
    }                                                   MyAutoCloseableRes implements
}                                                       the only method, close(), defined
class AutoClose2 {                                      by AutoCloseable.
    void useCustomResources() {                                             An object
                                                                            of MyAuto-
        try (MyAutoCloseableRes res = new MyAutoCloseableRes();){  ◄──      CloseableRes
            System.out.println("within try-with-resources");               can be used
        }                                                                   in try-with-
        finally {                                  ◄──                      resources.
            System.out.println("finally");
        }                                             Try block doesn't
    }                                                 catch any exception,
}                                                     because no method of
class Test {                                          MyAutoCloseableRes
    public static void main(String args[]) {          throws exception
        new AutoClose2().useCustomResources();
    }
}
```

The output of the preceding class Test is as follows:

```
Constructor called
within try-with-resources
Close called
finally
```

DEFINITION OF INTERFACES JAVA.LANG.AUTOCLOSEABLE AND JAVA.IO.CLOSEABLE

On the exam, you might get to answer explicit questions on the exceptions that are thrown by method close() defined in the AutoCloseable and Closeable interfaces. Following is the definition of the AutoCloseable interface from the Java source code (minus the comments):

```
package java.lang;
public interface AutoCloseable {          Method close() of AutoCloseable
    void close() throws Exception;    ◄── throws Exception.
}
```

Here's the definition of the Closeable interface from the Java source code (minus the comments):

```
package java.io;
public interface Closeable extends AutoCloseable {    Method close() of interface
    public void close() throws IOException;       ◄── Closeable throws IOException.
}
```

Method `close()` in the `Closeable` interface overrides method `close()` from the `AutoCloseable` base interface. Method `close()`, which implements the `Closeable` interface, won't be able to throw exceptions that are broader than `IOException`. If you implement an interface, you must have valid implementations for each method defined in the interface.

THE RESOURCES DECLARED WITH TRY-WITH-RESOURCES ARE CLOSED IN THE REVERSE ORDER OF THEIR DECLARATION

Class `MyResource` implements the `AutoCloseable` interface. Its constructor accepts a name for its instance, which is printed when the constructor and method `close()` are called:

```
class MyResource implements AutoCloseable{          ◁──    MyResource implements
    String name;                                            AutoCloseable so it can be
    MyResource(String name) {                               used with try-with-resources.
        this.name = name;
        System.out.println("Created:"+name);
    }
    public void close() {                                   Creates MyResource
        System.out.println("Closed:"+name);                 instance and assigns
    }                                                       it to res1.
}
class TestAutoCloseOrder {
    public static void main(String args[]) {                Creates another
        try (MyResource res1 = new MyResource("1");  ◁──    MyResource instance
             MyResource res2 = new MyResource("2")){  ◁──   and assigns it to res2.

            System.out.println("within try-with-resources"); ◁──
        }
        finally {                                           Method close() is
            System.out.println("finally");                  called first on res2
        }                                                   and then on res1,
    }                                                       after execution of
}                                                           code on this line.
```

Here's the output of the preceding code:

```
Created:1
Created:2
within try-with-resources
Closed:2
Closed:1
finally
```

 EXAM TIP   The resources declared with the `try-with-resources` are closed in the reverse order of their declaration. In this and previous sections, we covered exceptions and worked with how the exception handlers enable you to *recover* from exceptional conditions during the execution of your program. In the next section, you'll see how the assertions enable you to *test* and *debug* your *assumptions* and flow control *during* the development of your code.

6.6 *Using assertions*

While testing your code, have you ever come across a situation that made you think that a variable in your code could be assigned more values than you assumed, or that your code wasn't executing as planned for a combination of values?

Assertions help you test your assumptions about the execution of code. For example, you could test your assumption by using a combination of control-flow and logging statements to print the message Error: pages should NOT be < 200, if the value of pages is greater than 200, as follows:

```java
void printReport() {
    int pages = 100;
    while (/*some condition*/) {
        if (/*some condition*/) {
            pages++;
        }
    }
    if (pages<200)
        System.out.println("Error: pages should NOT be < 200");    ⟵── 
}
```

When assumption is not met, print an error message should not exceed 200

Because it's an assumption, it needs to be tested and fixed during the development phase. So you can use an assert statement to verify the preceding assumption:

```java
void printReport() {
    int pages = 100;
    while (/*some condition*/) {
        if (/*some condition*/) {
            pages++;
        }
    }
    assert (pages<200): " Error: pages should NOT be < 200";    ⟵── 
}
```

Assertion to verify and test assumptions

In the preceding example, the programmer's assumption is coded as an assertion.

An *assertion* offers a way of indicating what should always be true. An assertion is implemented using an assert statement that enables you to test your assumptions about the values assigned to variables and the flow of control in your code. An assert statement uses a boolean expression, which you believe to be true. If this boolean expression evaluates to false, your code will halt its execution by throwing an AssertionError.

Assertions are used for testing and debugging your code. They aren't for error checking, which is why they're off by default. Assertions are disabled by default so they don't become a performance liability in deployed applications.

This exam will query you on testing invariants by using assertions, the short and long form of assertions, and their appropriate and inappropriate use. Assertions were

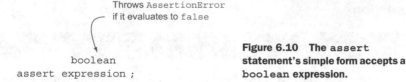

```
            Throws AssertionError
          ⌐ if it evaluates to false

             ↓
        boolean
assert expression ;
```

Figure 6.10   The assert statement's simple form accepts a boolean expression.

introduced in version 1.4, and though powerful, are one of the underused features of Java. Let's start with the forms of assertions.

6.6.1   *Exploring the forms of assertions*

An assertion is defined by using an assert statement that can take two forms. The simpler form uses only a boolean expression, as shown in figure 6.10.

If the boolean expression used in an assert statement (as shown in figure 6.10) evaluates to false, the JRE will throw an AssertionError. Assuming that assertions have been enabled, the following code

```
public class ThrowAssertionError {
    public static void main(String args[]) {        Throws AssertionError
        assert false;                          ◁──  because boolean value
    }                                               following assert is false.
}
```

will throw the following error at runtime:

```
Exception in thread "main" java.lang.AssertionError
    at ThrowAssertionError.main(ThrowAssertionError.java:3)
```

 EXAM TIP   If the boolean expression used in an assert statement evaluates to false, an AssertionError is thrown (if assertions are enabled at runtime).

As you can see, the preceding output doesn't include any custom error message. To include custom details with an AssertionError, you can use the longer form of an assert statement, as shown in figure 6.11.

The *expression* used in the longer form of an assert statement is another way to pass arguments to an AssertionError. If the boolean expression used in the longer form of the assert statement (as shown in figure 6.11) evaluates to false, the JRE

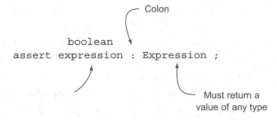

```
                    ⌐ Colon
        boolean     ↓
assert expression : Expression ;
          ↗           ↓
              Must return a
              value of any type
```

Figure 6.11   An assert statement's longer form accepts a boolean expression and an expression.

creates an object of AssertionError by passing the *expression* to its constructor. Assuming that assertions have been enabled, the following code uses the longer form of the assert statement:

```
public class ThrowDetailedAssertionError {
    public static void main(String args[]) {
        assert false : "Testing Assertions";        Throws AssertionError
    }                                                with message "Testing
}                                                    Assertions"
```

The preceding code throws an AssertionError with the message Testing Assertions at runtime:

```
Exception in thread "main" java.lang.AssertionError: Testing Assertions
    at ThrowDetailedAssertionError.main(ThrowDetailedAssertionError.java:3)
```

The exam also will test you on the valid expressions used for the assert statement. The shorter form of the assert statement uses one expression, which *must* evaluate to a boolean value. The longer form of the assert statement uses two expressions: the first one *must* evaluate to a boolean value, but the second can evaluate to any type of primitive value or object. Look out for incorrect use of methods for the second expression, whose return type is void. What do you think is the output of the class ThrowAssertionError?

```
class Person {
    void getNothing() {}                                  Line won't compile
}                                                         because getNothing
public class ThrowAssertionError {                        doesn't return a value.
    public static void main(String args[]) {
        assert false : new Person().getNothing();         Line won't compile
        assert true : new ArrayList<String>().clear();    because clear doesn't
    }                                                      return a value.
}
```

Because the methods getNothing() (class Person) and clear() (class ArrayList) don't return any value, the class ThrowAssertionError won't compile. You might find similar occurrences on the exam.

Class AssertionError uses the String representation of the value passed to its constructor for its detailed message. A String representation of an object is retrieved by calling its method toString(). Let's look at a tricky use of the assert statement. Class TrickAssert defines an assert statement and uses a boolean assignment for its first expression and an object for its second expression. Assuming that assertions are enabled, what do you think is the output of the following code?

```
class Person {
    public String toString() {
        return "Pirates of the Caribbean";
    }
}
```

```
public class TrickAssert {
    public static void main(String args[]) {
        boolean b = false;
        assert (b = true) : new Person();
    }
}
```

A lot of programmers have answered that the preceding code throws an `AssertionError`:

```
Exception in thread "main" java.lang.AssertionError: Pirates of the Caribbean
```

But it doesn't, because the expression `(b = true)` returns `true`. Revisit the example: this expression is assigning the `boolean` literal value `true` to variable b; it isn't comparing b with `true`. Also, the second expression returns an object of class `Person`. `AssertionError` executes `toString()` to retrieve a `String` representation of an object of class `Person`.

 EXAM TIP   The longer form of the `assert` statement uses two expressions: the first one *must* evaluate to a `boolean` value, but the second can evaluate to any type of primitive value or object.

If you use an object of class `Throwable` for the second expression in an `assert` statement, it becomes the *cause* of the thrown `AssertionError`. Here's an example:

```
public class DefineCauseOfAssertionError {
    public static void main(String args[]) {
        assert (false) : new FileNotFoundException("java.txt missing");
    }
}
```

Assuming that assertions are enabled, the preceding example gives the following output:

```
Exception in thread "main" java.lang.AssertionError:
java.io.FileNotFoundException: java.txt missing
    at DefineCauseOfAssertionError.main(DefineCauseOfAssertionError.java:4)
Caused by: java.io.FileNotFoundException: java.txt missing
```

It's time for our next "Twist in the Tale" exercise. Let me check whether you've been able to retain a few concepts discussed in previous chapters.

Twist in the Tale 6.4

Let's modify some of the code used in the previous examples. Which answer correctly shows the output of class `AssertionTwist`?

```
public class AssertionTwist {
    public static void main(String args[]) {
        evenOdd(-11);
    }
    static void evenOdd(int num) {
        if (num%2 == 0)
            System.out.println("Even");
```

```
        else if (num%2 == 1)
            System.out.println("Odd");
        else {
            System.out.println("This should never be printed");
            assert false : new Person();
        }
    }
}
class Person {
    private String toString () {
        return "Pirates of the Caribbean";
    }
}
```

  a Odd

  b This should never be printed:

   `AssertionError: Pirates of the Caribbean`

  c This should never be printed:

   `AssertionError: Person@6b97fd0Odd`

  d Compilation error

  e A runtime exception

Do you think class `AssertionTwist` will give the same output for executing even-Odd(-10)?

In this section, you examined the nitty-gritty of the syntax for the `assert` statement. In the next section, you'll look at how to test invariants in your code.

6.6.2 *Testing invariants in your code*

The exam objective specifically states, test invariants by using assertions. You can use assertions to test your assumptions about multiple types of invariants:

- Internal invariants
- Control-flow invariants
- Class invariants

Let's start with internal invariants.

INTERNAL INVARIANTS

When you implement the business logic for a method, you can make multiple assumptions about the values assigned to your variables. Here's an example, which assumes that a variable of type `State` can be assigned only the value `ON` or `OFF`:

```
enum State {ON, OFF};
public class InternalAssumption {
    private void machineState(State state) {
        switch (state) {
```

```
                    case ON: System.out.println("state is ON");
                                    break;
                    case OFF: System.out.println("state is OFF");
                                    break;
            }
        }
}
```

Let's modify the code to include this assumption using an `assert` statement:

```
enum State {ON, OFF};
public class InternalAssumptionWithAssert {
    private void machineState(State state) {
        switch (state) {
            case ON: System.out.println("state is ON");
                            break;
            case OFF: System.out.println("state is OFF");
                            break;
            default: assert false;
        }
    }
}
```

If value other than ON or OFF is assigned to state, AssertionError is thrown

If the control of flow reaches line `assert false;`, the assumption of the programmer is invalidated and the code throws an error (`AssertionError`). One of my colleagues argued that there is no need for an `assert` statement here because a variable of type `State` can't be assigned values other than `ON` or `OFF`. If you agree, what happens if more values are added to enum `State` during enhancement or maintenance of the project? In this case, the original assumptions won't hold true.

Let's take a look at another example, in which a programmer assumes that the `protocol` variable within `transmitFile()` can exist only with values `FTP`, `HTTP`, and `HTTPS`:

```
public class InternalAssumption {
    void transmitFile(String protocol, String fileName) {
        if (protocol.equals("FTP")) {
            //..code to transmit file using FTP
        }
        else if (protocol.equals("HTTP")) {
            //..code to transmit file using HTTP
        }
        else if (protocol.equals("HTTPS")) {
            //..code to transmit file using HTTPS
        }
        else {
            System.out.println("Control shouldn't reach here");
            System.out.println("Only FTP, HTTP, HTTPS supported");
        }
    }
}
```

Assumption that protocol can take only values FTP, HTTP, HTTPS

Programmers often document their assumptions (within the code), as shown in the previous example. A better alternative is to use assertions, so relevant action can be taken when these assumptions fail. Following is the modified code:

```
public class InternalAssumption {
        void transmitFile(String protocol, String fileName) {
        if (protocol.equals("FTP")) {
            //..code to transmit file using FTP
        }
        else if (protocol.equals("HTTP")) {
            //..code to transmit file using HTTP
        }
        else if (protocol.equals("HTTPS")) {
            //..code to transmit file using HTTPS
        }
        else {
            assert false:"Only FTP, HTTP, HTTPS supported";    ⟵
        }
    }
}
```

Code throws AssertionError (if assertions are enabled and) if protocol takes value other than FTP, HTTP, or HTTPS

Note that there is an important difference between *unreachable code* as defined by the Java specification and *code that shouldn't be reached*, as used in the previous example. Unreachable code won't compile. For example, in class UnreachableCode, the statement placed after the return statement is unreachable and won't compile:

```
class UnreachableCode {
    void unreachableStatement() {
        return;
        System.out.println("code CANNOT reach here");    ⟵
    }
}
```

Code won't compile: unreachable code.

On the other hand, *code that shouldn't be reached* is code that shouldn't execute in a method if all goes as per a programmer's assumption. Though it compiles successfully, its execution represents a flaw in the implementation of programming logic. Here's an example:

```
class CodeThatShouldNotReach {
    void unreachableStatement() {
        int a = (int)(Math.random() * 4) + 1;
        if (a>=2)
            return;
        else if (a <2)
            return;
        System.out.println("code SHOULD NOT reach here");    ⟵
    }
}
```

Code compiles successfully, but its execution means flaw in implementation logic

EXAM TIP   *Unreachable code* isn't the same as a programmer's assumption of *code that shouldn't be reached.* Unreachable code won't compile as per Java's rules. On the other hand, code that shouldn't be reached compiles successfully. But execution of this code means a flaw in the implementation of application logic.

Apart from internal invariants, you may make assumptions about the flow of control in your code, as discussed in the next section.

CONTROL-FLOW INVARIANTS

You can use assertions at locations that you assume control should never be reached. In method processImage(), a programmer assumes that an image (for an application) can be stored only at a server or on a local disk. The programmer uses a comment to state this assumption:

```java
public class ControlFlowAssumption {
    void processImage(String fileName) {
        if (/* image stored on server*/) {
            // get image from server
            return;
        }
        else if (/* image stored on local disk*/){
            // get image from local system
            return;
        }
        // control should never reach here!       Assumption that code
        // because an image can be stored          control will never
        // either on server or on local system     reach this line
    }
}
```

Replace the preceding comments in bold with an assert statement as follows:

```java
public class ControlFlowAssumption {
    void getImage(String fileName) {
        if (/* image stored on server*/) {
            // get image from server
            return;
        }
        else if (/* image stored on local disk*/){
            // get image from local system
            return;
        }
        assert false;          Use of assert statement for
    }                          control-flow invariants if
}                              control reaches here
```

CLASS INVARIANTS

Class invariants are methods that you use to validate the state of an object. The state of an object can change due to explicit assignment or reassignment of its fields, or due to any processing of field values. After each modification, class invariants can be used to check whether all fields have valid data.

Assume that you create a class to define and operate a data structure that stores a sorted list of students in a class, sorted on their overall performance in an academic year. Its methods to add new students or retrieve a student at a particular position might assume that the existing student list is already sorted. A class invariant might be that this list is sorted. You can place code to check this assumption in your methods. For example

```java
import java.util.*;
class Student {}
class SortedStudents {
    List<Student> students = null;
    private boolean sorted() {                      // Class invariant
        // returns true if list students is sorted
        // false otherwise
    }
    public void addStudent(Student newStudent) {
        assert sorted();                            // Using class
        // code to add new student to list          // invariant to validate
    }                                               // object state
    public Student getStudent(String studentID) {
        assert sorted();
        // code to search list and retrieve matching Student object
    }
}
```

It's easy to confuse the appropriate and inappropriate use of assertions, and you're sure to see questions on it on the exam. In the next section, let's cover some rules that will help you answer these questions.

6.6.3 *Understanding appropriate and inappropriate uses of assertions*

The simple fact that assertions can be turned on or off, and are turned off by default, makes them inappropriate for all your assumptions. Let's work with some examples in detail.

DON'T USE ASSERTIONS TO CHECK METHOD PARAMETERS OF PUBLIC METHODS

You can't control the values of the arguments that are passed to your public methods; these values can be called by classes written by other programmers. To validate the parameters to public methods, you must use code that is guaranteed to execute. Because assertions can be turned off, you can't guarantee whether your assertion code will execute.

In the example that follows, the public method result() in class DemoAssertion1 validates the arguments passed to it and throws an IllegalArgumentException for invalid values. It doesn't use an assertion to do so:

```java
public class DemoAssertion1 {
    public double result(int score, int maxVal) {
        double resultVal = 0;
        if (score > 0 && maxVal > 0) {
            resultVal = /* some calculation */
        }
```

```
        else {
            throw new IllegalArgumentException();
        }
        return resultVal;
    }
}
```

Doesn't uses assertion to validate method parameters of a public method.

USE ASSERTIONS TO CHECK METHOD PARAMETERS OF PRIVATE METHODS

A private method can be called by the methods of the class in which it's defined. When a nonprivate method calls a private method, it usually passes validated parameter values to it. You can assert this assumption by using an assert statement. In the following example, method calcResult() uses the assert statement to check that both values passed to it are greater than zero. If the assertion fails, it will throw an AssertionError (if assertions are enabled), or else return the calculated value:

```
class DemoAssertion2 {
    private double calcResult(int score, int maxVal){
        assert(score > 0 && maxVal > 0);
        return (score / maxVal * 100);
    }
}
```

Use assert to validate method parameters of a private method. Don't use Assertions to modify variable values or state of an object.

Examine the following code:

```
public class DemoAssertion3 {
    int number = 10;
    private void inappropriateAssertCondition(State state) {
        assert (++number > 5);
        // some other code;
    }
}
```

❶ Increments variable value to evaluate assert expression.

The code in bold at ❶ increments the value of the number variable, and then determines whether its value is greater than 5. This line of code will *silently increment* the value of the instance variable number whenever method inappropriateAssertCondition() executes on any instance of class DemoAssertion3. Depending on whether assertions are enabled on the host system, the same code might output different values, which might not be expected.

Similarly, you shouldn't modify the state of an object in an assert statement:

```
public class DemoAssertion4 {
    int number = 10;
    MyClass myClass = new MyClass();
    private void inappropriateAssertCondition(State state) {
        assert (++number > 5): myClass.modifyDescription
                              ("assertion error");
        // some other code;
    }
}
```

Modifies state of object myClass.

```
class MyClass {
    String description = "No error";
    public String modifyDescription(String val) {
        description = val;
        return description;
    }
}
```

In the preceding example, *expression2* (myClass.modifyDescription(..)) passed to the assert statement modifies the state of object myClass, which it shouldn't.

DON'T DEPEND ON ASSERTIONS TO MAKE YOUR CODE FUNCTION CORRECTLY

As mentioned previously, assertions can be turned on or off by the host machine on which a piece of Java code is supposed to execute. Also, assertions are turned off by default. So it's never advisable to define code, using assertions, which you must execute for correct functioning of your code.

USE ASSERTIONS FOR SITUATIONS THAT CAN NEVER OCCUR (EVEN IN PUBLIC METHODS)

Use assertions for situations that can never occur, even in public methods. Use assertions to test invariants—internal invariants, control-flow invariants, or class invariants—in your code (discussed in detail in section 6.6.2).

By default, assertions are disabled, because they're meant to test and verify your code during the development and testing phases. But they can be easily enabled when the program starts. You, as a programmer, can test your code during the development and testing phase and execute the same code without the assertions enabled (and the related extra overhead) on the production server. Of course, if the code on the production server behaves unexpectedly, you can enable assertions to determine whether any of your logic is flawed, which is negating your assumptions.

 EXAM TIP Assertions can be turned on or off for specific classes or packages.

You can enable assertions for a class, say, DemoAssertion, by using either of the following commands:

```
java -ea  DemoAssertion
java -enableassertions DemoAssertion
```

All your assert statements are equivalent to blank statements, if assertions are disabled. For example, if assertions are disabled, the following method

```
private static double calcResult(int score, int maxVal) {
    assert (score > 0 && maxVal > 0);
    return (score/maxVal*100);
}
```

will execute as if no assert statement were defined in it, as follows:

```
private static double calcResult(int score, int maxVal) {
    return (score/maxVal*100);
}
```

Similarly, you can use the command options -da and -disableassertions to disable assertions.

6.7   *Summary*

Exception handling is a mechanism for handling errors and exceptional conditions that arise during the course of a program. It also helps you define exception-handling code separate from the main application logic. This chapter specifically covers the throw statement and the throws clause, the try statement with multi-catch and finally clauses, the try-with-resources statement, and custom exceptions and assertions.

I started this chapter by covering the throw statement and the throws clause. The throws clause is added to a method declaration to specify that a method can throw any of the listed exceptions (or its subclasses) during its execution. When an exceptional condition is encountered, a method might handle the exception itself, or *throw* it to the calling method, by using the throw statement within a method.

You can create custom exceptions by extending class java.lang.Exception or any of its derived classes. The name of an exception can convey a lot of information to other developers or users, and this is one of the main reasons for defining a custom exception. Custom exceptions also help you restrict the escalation of implementation-specific exceptions to higher layers. For example, you can wrap a data connection exception in your own custom exception and rethrow the exception. You can create custom checked exceptions by subclassing java.lang.Exception and a custom runtime exception by subclassing java.lang.RuntimeException. You can throw and handle custom exceptions like regular exceptions.

Starting with Java 7, you can handle multiple exceptions in the same handler by using a try statement with multi-catch. This prevents a programmer from duplicating the code required to handle multiple exceptions or to *catch* a much generalized exception. You need to follow the rules to catch multiple exceptions in a single block:

- Exception names are separated by a vertical bar in the catch block.
- The variable that accepts the exception object in the catch handler is implicitly final.
- Exceptions can't share an inheritance relationship.
- You can use multi-catch and single-catch blocks for the same try block.

Prior to Java 7, developers used finally blocks to close resources such as file handlers, databases, or network connections. With the new language feature of the try-with-resources statement, you can declare resources and automatically close them. The scope of the resources declared with a try-with-resources statement is limited to it. Resources (classes) that implement the java.lang.AutoCloseable interface or any of its subinterfaces can be used with the try-with-resources statement. If multiple resources are declared by a try-with-resources statement, they're closed in the *reverse* order of their declaration.

Assertions enable you to test your assumptions about the execution of your code. Assertions are coded by using the `assert` statement. They're used for testing and debugging your code, and so are turned off by default. This also ensures that `assert` statements don't become a performance liability when an application is deployed. An `assert` statement takes two forms: the simpler form uses just a `boolean` expression, and the second form uses a `boolean` expression with an expression, which results in any value. If the `boolean` expression in an `assert` statement evaluates to `false`, an `AssertionError` is thrown. If an `assert` statement uses its second form, its expression is passed to the constructor of `AssertionError`, so that its details are displayed in the call stack when this error is thrown. You can use assertions to test internal invariants, control-flow invariants, and class invariants. Internal invariants are used to assert values in a loop, conditional statements, or a `switch-case`. Control-flow invariants are used to *assert* the business logic implemented in code, to *assert* that a particular line of code won't execute for a set of values. Class assertions are used to *assert* the state of all objects of a class, before or after a method executes on its object. You can also use assertions to validate parameter values to a private method. You must not use assertions to verify method parameters passed to public methods or to define code that must execute for correct functioning of your code. Because assertions can be enabled and disabled, and are usually disabled by default, you can't be sure about execution of your assertions code.

REVIEW NOTES

This section lists the main points covered in this chapter.

Using the throw statement and the throws clause

- The `throws` clause is part of a method declaration and lists exceptions that can be thrown by a method.
- The `throws` clause is used with a method declaration to specify that the method won't handle the mentioned exception (or subclasses) and might throw it to the calling method. The calling method should handle this thrown exception appropriately or declare it to be rethrown.
- The `throw` statement is used to throw an exception from a method, constructor, or an initialization block. When an exceptional condition occurs in a method, that method can handle it (by using a `try` statement), or throw the exception to the calling method by using the `throw` statement.
- A method indicates that it throws a checked exception by including its name in the `throws` clause, in its method declaration.
- When you use a method that throws a checked exception, you must either enclose the code within a `try` block or declare it to be rethrown in the calling method's declaration. This is also known as the handle-or-declare rule.
- A method can throw a runtime exception or error irrespective of whether its name is included in the `throws` clause.

- A method can throw a subclass of the exception mentioned in its `throws` clause but not a superclass.
- A method can handle the exception and still declare it to be thrown.
- A method can declare to throw any type of exception, checked or unchecked, even if it doesn't. But a `try` block can't define a `catch` block for a checked exception (other than `Exception`) if the `try` block doesn't throw that checked exception or use a method that declares to throw that checked exception.

Custom exceptions

- You can create a custom exception by extending class `java.lang.Exception` or any of its subclasses.
- You can subclass `java.lang.Exception` or its subclasses (which don't subclass `RuntimeException`) to create custom checked exceptions.
- You can subclass `java.lang.RuntimeException` or its subclasses to create custom runtime exceptions.
- You can add variables and methods to a custom exception class, like a regular class.
- The name of an exception can convey a lot of information to other developers or users, which is one of the main reasons for defining a custom exception. A custom exception can also be used to communicate a more descriptive message.
- Custom exceptions help you restrict the escalation of implementation-specific exceptions to higher layers. For example, `SQLException` thrown by data access code can be wrapped within a custom exception and rethrown.
- You can throw and catch custom exceptions like the other exception classes.

Overriding methods that throw exceptions

- With overriding and overridden methods, it's all about which checked exceptions an overridden method and an overriding method declare, not about the checked exceptions both actually throw.
- If a method in the base class doesn't declare to throw any checked exception, the overriding method in the derived class can't throw any checked exception.
- If a method in a base class declares to throw a checked exception, the overriding method in the derived class can choose not to declare to throw any checked exception.
- If a method in a base class declares to throw a checked exception, the overriding method in the derived class can declare to throw the same exception or a subclass of the exception thrown by the method in the base class. An overriding method in the derived class can't override a method in the base class, if it declares to throw a more generic checked exception.
- Method overriding rules apply only to checked exceptions. They don't apply to runtime (unchecked) exceptions or errors.

try statement with multi-catch and finally clauses

- A multi-catch handler can be used to handle more than one unrelated exception.
- To *catch* multiple exceptions in a single handler, separate the exceptions in a list by using a vertical bar (|).
- A finally block can follow a multi-catch block, like a regular catch block.
- The exceptions that you catch in a multi-catch block can't share an inheritance relationship. If you try to do so, your code won't compile.
- You can combine multi-catch and single-catch blocks.
- The same rules apply when combining multi-catch and single-catch blocks—that is, more specific exceptions at the top and more general ones at the bottom.
- You must define a single exception variable in the multi-catch block.
- In a multi-catch block, the variable that accepts the exception object is implicitly final.
- In a multi-catch block, the type of variable that accepts the exception object is the most specific, common super-type of all featured exception classes. Most of the time it's likely to be Exception, but it could be more specific (for example, IOException for classes FileNotFoundException and EOFException). If the exception classes implement a common interface, then the variable is of an intersection type, with the exception class and interface as its bounds.
- Multi-catch blocks save you from duplicating code, if you need to execute the same code for handling multiple exceptions.

Auto-close resources with try-with-resources statement

- You can use a try-with-resources statement to define resources with a try statement that will be automatically closed after the try block completes its execution.
- The try-with-resources is a type of try statement that can declare one or more resources.
- A resource is an object such as file handlers, databases, or network connections, which *should* be closed after it's no longer required.
- A resource must implement the java.lang.AutoCloseable interface or any of its subinterfaces (directly or indirectly) to be eligible to be declared by a try-with-resources statement.
- The java.lang.AutoCloseable interface defines method close().
- If declared within the try-with-resources statement, a resource is automatically closed by calling its close() method at the end of the try block.
- If method close() throws any exception, it should be taken care of by the method that defines the try block; the method must either catch it or declare it to be thrown.
- A try-with-resources block might not be followed by a catch or a finally block. This is unlike a regular try block, which must be followed by either a catch or a finally block.

- The resource declared by try-with-resources is closed immediately after the completion of the try block. Its scope is limited to the try block, and if you try to access it outside the try block, your code won't compile.
- The variables used to refer to resources are implicitly final variables. You must *declare* and *initialize* resources in the try-with-resources statement.
- It's acceptable to the Java compiler to initialize the resources in a try-with-resources statement to null, only as long as they aren't being assigned a value in the try block.
- You can initialize multiple resources in a try-with-resources statement, separated by a semicolon (;). The semicolon after the last resource is optional.
- Multiple classes like FileInputStream and FileOutputStream from file I/O implement the java.io.Closeable interface, which extends the java.lang .AutoCloseable interface.

Assertions

- An *assertion* offers a way of asserting what should always be true.
- An assertion is implemented by using an assert statement that enables you to test your assumptions about the values assigned to variables and the flow of control in your code.
- An assert statement uses a boolean expression, which you believe to be true. If this boolean expression evaluates to false, an AssertionError is thrown (if assertions are enabled).
- Assertions are used for testing and debugging your code. They're off by default.
- Assertions are disabled by default so they don't become a performance liability in deployed applications.
- An assertion is defined using an assert statement that can take two forms. The simpler form uses only a boolean expression: assert <boolean expression>;.
- The longer form of an assert statement includes an expression with the boolean expression: assert <boolean expression>:<expression>;. The second expression used here must return a value (of any type).
- In the longer form of an assert statement, when the boolean expression evaluates to false, the JRE creates an object of AssertionError by passing the value of the second expression to AssertionError's constructor.
- In the longer form of an assert statement, if you use a method with no return value (void) for the second expression, your code won't compile.
- In the longer form of an assert statement, you can create an object for the second expression. Note that a constructor creates and returns an object, and so it satisfies the requirement that the second expression must return a value.
- You can test multiple types of invariants in your code by using assertions: internal invariants, control-flow invariants, and class invariants.
- An assertion is used to verify that code that shouldn't execute, never executes.

- Assertions can't be used to verify unreachable code, because unreachable code doesn't compile.
- You can use assertions at locations that you assume control should never be reached.
- You must not use assertions to check method parameters for public methods.
- You can use assertions to check method parameters for private methods.
- You must not use assertions to modify variable values or the state of an object.
- Assertions can be enabled or disabled at the launch of a program.
- Because assertions can be enabled or disabled, don't use them to define code that must execute in all cases.
- Use the command-line option –ea or –enableassertions to enable assertions.
- Use the command-line option –da or –disableassertions to disable assertions.
- All `assert` statements are equivalent to blank statements, if the assertions are disabled.
- A generalized –da switch (no assertions enabled) corresponds to the default JRE behavior.

SAMPLE EXAM QUESTIONS

Q 6-1. Consider the following code and then select the correct options. (Choose all that apply.)

```
class ThrowException {
    public void readFile(String file) throws IOException {        // line1
        System.out.println("readFile");                           // line2
    }
    void useReadFile(String name) throws IOException{             // line3
        try {
            readFile(name);
        }
        catch (IOException e) {
            System.out.println("catch-IOException");
        }
    }
    public static void main(String args[]) throws Throwable{      // line4
        new ThrowException().useReadFile("foo");                  // line5
    }
}
```

a Code on both line 1 and line 2 causes compilation failure.

b Code on either line 1 or line 2 causes compilation failure.

c If code on line 1 is changed to the following, the code will compile successfully:

```
public void readFile(String file) {d}
```

d A change in code on line 3 can prevent compilation failure:

```
void useReadFile(String name) {
```

e Code on either line 4 or line 5 causes compilation failure. If line 4 is changed to the following, a ThrowException will compile:

```
public static void main(String args[]) throws Exception {
```

Q 6-2. Given the following line of code

```
String s = "assert";
```

which of the following code options will compile successfully? (Choose all that apply.)

```
a  assert(s == null : s = new String());
b  assert s == null : s = new String();
c  assert(s == null) : s = new String();
d  assert(s.equals("assert"));
e  assert s.equals("assert");
f  assert s == "assert" ; s.replace('a', 'z');
g  assert s = new String("Assert") : s.toString();
h  assert s == new String("Assert") : System.out.println(s);
i  assert(s = new String("Assert") : System.out.println(s));
```

Q 6-3. What's the output of the following code?

```
class Box implements AutoCloseable {
    Box() {
        throw new RuntimeException();
    }
    public void close() throws Exception {
        System.out.println("close");
        throw new Exception();
    }
}
class EJavaFactory{
    public static void main(String args[]) {
        try (Box box = new Box()) {
            box.close();
        }
        catch (Exception e) {
            System.out.println("catch:"+e);
        }
        finally {
            System.out.println("finally");
        }
    }
}
```

```
a  catch:java.lang.RuntimeException
   close
   finally

b  catch:java.lang.RuntimeException
   finally
```

c `catch:java.lang.RuntimeException`
`close`

d `close`
`finally`

e Compilation exception

Q 6-4. Paul has to modify a method that throws a `SQLException` when the method can't find matching data in a database. Instead of throwing a `SQLException`, the method must throw a custom exception, `DataException`. Assuming the modified method is defined as follows, which option presents the most appropriate definition of `DataException`?

```
void accessData(String parameters) {
    try {
        //..code that might throw SQLException
    }
    catch (SQLException e) {
        throw new DataException("Error with Data access");
    }
}
```

a `class DataException extends Exception {`
`    DataException() {super();}`
`    DataException(String msg) { super(msg); }`
`}`

b `class DataException extends RuntimeException {`
`    DataException() {}`
`    DataException(String msg) {}`
`}`

c `class DataException {`
`    DataException() {super();}`
`    DataException(String msg) { super(msg); }`
`}`

d `class DataException extends Throwable {`
`    DataException() {super();}`
`    DataException(String msg) { super(msg); }`
`}`

Q 6-5. Which of the following options show appropriate usage of assertions? (Choose all that apply.)

```
// INSERT CODE HERE
    assert (b != 0)  : "Can't divide with zero";
    return (a/b);
}
```

a `public float divide(int a, int b) {`

b `public static float divide(int a, int b) {`

c `private static float divide(int a, int b) {`

d `private float divide(int a, int b) {`

Q 6-6. Which options can be inserted at //INSERT CODE HERE so the code compiles successfully? (Choose all that apply.)

```
class BreathingException extends Exception {}
class DivingException extends Exception {}

class Swimmer {
    public void swim() throws BreathingException {}
    public void dive() throws DivingException {}
}

class Swimming{
    public static void main(String args[])throws
                                BreathingException, DivingException {
        try {
            Swimmer paul = new Swimmer();
            paul.swim();
            paul.dive();
        }
        //INSERT CODE HERE
    }
}
```

a ```
catch(DivingException | BreathingException e){
    throw e;
}
```

b  ```
catch(Exception e){
    throw e;
}
```

c ```
catch(DivingException | BreathingException e){
    throw new DivingException();
}
```

d  ```
catch(Exception e){
    throw new Exception();
}
```

e ```
catch(Exception e){
    throw new RuntimeException();
}
```

**Q 6-7.** Selvan defines two custom exception classes:

```
class BaseException extends IOException {}
class DerivedException extends FileNotFoundException {}
```

When Paul tries to use these exception classes in his own interfaces, the code doesn't compile:

```
interface Base {
    void read() throws BaseException;
}
interface Derived extends Base {
    void read() throws DerivedException;
}
```
```

Which definition of read() in the Derived interface compiles successfully?

a `void read() throws FileNotFoundException;`

b `void read() throws IOException;`

c `void read();`

d `void read() throws Exception;`

e `void read() throws BaseException;`

f `void read() throws RuntimeException;`

g `void read() throws Throwable;`

Q 6-8. Given the following code, select the correct options:

```
class AssertTest {
    static int foo = 10;
    static boolean calc() {
        ++foo;
        return false;
    }
    public static void main(String args[]) {
        assert (calc());
        System.out.println(foo);
    }
}
```

a If `AssertTest` is executed using the following command, it will print 11:

   `java -enable AssertTest`

b If `AssertTest` is executed using the following command, it will print 10:

   `java -ea AssertTest`

c If `AssertTest` is executed using the following command, it will print 10:

   `java -da AssertTest`

d If `AssertTest` is executed using the following command, it will throw an AssertionError and print 11:

   `java -enableAssertions AssertTest`

e None of the above

Q 6-9. What's the output of the following code?

```
class Box implements AutoCloseable {
    public void emptyContents() {
        System.out.println("emptyContents");
    }
    public void close() {
        System.out.println("close");
    }
}
```

```
class EJavaFactory{
    public static void main(String args[]) {
        try (Box box = new Box()) {
            box.close();
            box.emptyContents();
        }
    }
}
```

   a close
      emptyContents
      java.lang.RuntimeException

   b close
      java.lang.RuntimeException

   c close
      emptyContents
      close

   d close
      java.lang.NullPointerException

Q 6-10. Which of the following statements are correct? (Choose all that apply.)

   a You must initialize the resources in the try-with-resources statement.

   b try-with-resources can be followed only by the finally block.

   c Method close() on the resource is called irrespective of whether an exception is thrown during its initialization.

   d If the close method is called on a resource within a try block, the implicit call on close() will throw an exception.

   e The resources declared with try-with-resources are accessible within the catch and finally blocks, if an exception is thrown during implicit closing of the resources.

Q 6-11. What's the output of the following code?

```
class Box implements AutoCloseable {
    public void open() throws Exception {
        throw new Exception();
    }
    public void close() throws Exception {
        System.out.println("close");
        throw new Exception();
    }
}
class EJavaFactory{
    public static void main(String args[]) {
        try (Box box = new Box()) {
            box.open();
        }
```

```
        catch (Exception e) {
            System.out.println("catch:"+e);
        }
        finally {
            System.out.println("finally");
        }
    }
}
```

   a catch:java.lang.Exception
      finally

   b catch:java.lang.Exception

   c close
      finally

   d close
      catch:java.lang.Exception
      finally

   e close
      catch:java.lang.Exception
      catch:java.lang.Exception
      finally

Q 6-12. Select the correct statements. (Choose all that apply.)

```
class Assert {
    public void construction(double load){
        double maxLoad = 1322976;
        // calculations to re-assign a value to maxLoad
        try {
            if (maxLoad > 18753) assert false;    // line1
        }
        catch (AssertionError e) {
            // log error
            // recalculate load
        }
    }
}
```

   a When assertions fail, you should avoid recalculating variable values in the error handler.

   b Code on line1 can throw an AssertionException.

   c Class Assert shows inappropriate use of assertions.

   d Class Assert won't compile.

   e Class Assert will throw a runtime error.

Q 6-13. What's the output of the following code?

```
class Box implements AutoCloseable {
    public void close() throws Exception {
        System.out.println("close");
```

```
            throw new Exception();
        }
    }
class EJavaFactory{
    public static void main(String args[]) {
        try (Box box = new Box()) {
            box.close();
            box.close();
        }
        catch (Exception e) {
            System.out.println("catch:"+e);
        }
        finally {
            System.out.println("finally");
        }
    }
}
```

   a `catch:java.lang.Exception`

   b `close`
       `catch:java.lang.Exception`
       `finally`

   c `close`
       `close`
       `catch:java.lang.Exception`
       `finally`

   d `close`
       `close`
       `catch:java.lang.Exception`
       `catch:java.lang.Exception`
       `finally`

   e `close`
       `close`
       `java.lang.CloseException`
       `finally`

   f `close`
       `java.lang.RuntimeException`
       `finally`

Q 6-14. Examine the classes defined as follows and select the correct options. (Choose all that apply.)

```
class Jumpable extends RuntimeException {}
class Closeable extends java.lang.Closeable{}
class Thunder extends Throwable {}
class Storm extends java.io.FileNotFoundException{}
```

   a The classes `Jumpable` and `Closeable` are unchecked exceptions.

   b It isn't mandatory to include the name of exception `Jumpable` in the `throws` clause of a method.

c You shouldn't define a custom exception class the way class `Thunder` has been defined.

d Class `Storm` is a checked exception.

e All these classes will not compile successfully.

Q 6-15. Assuming that assertions are enabled, what's the output of the following code?

```
class MyAssertClass {
    public static void main(String... args) {
        String name = new String("Shreya");
        boolean fail = false;
        if (name == "Shreya") {
            System.out.println(name);
        }
        else {
            // I explicitly set the name to Shreya
            // code cannot reach here
            assert false;
        }
    }
}
```

a No output

b `java.lang.AssertionError`

c `java.lang.Exception`

d `java.lang.RuntimeException`

e `java.lang.AssertionException`

f None of the above

Q 6-16. What's the output of the following code?

```
class Admission implements AutoCloseable{
    String id;
    Admission(String id) {
        this.id = id;
    }
    public void close() {
        System.out.println("close:"+id);
    }
}
class CloseableResources {
    public static void main(String... args) {
        try (Admission admn1 = new Admission("2765");
            Admission admn2 = new Admission("8582");){}
    }
}
```

a `close:8582`
`close:2765`

b `close:2765`
`close:8582`

   c Compilation error

   d Runtime exception

Q 6-17. Which of the options, when inserted at `//INSERT CODE HERE`, will print `close`? (Choose all that apply.)

```
//INSERT CODE HERE
    public void close() {
        System.out.println("close");
    }
}
class EJavaFactory2 {
    public static void main(String... args) {
        try (Carton  arton = new Carton()) {}
    }
}
```

   a `class Carton implements AutoCloseable{`

   b `class Carton implements java.lang.Closeable{`

   c `class Carton implements java.lang.AutoCloseable{`

   d `class Carton implements ImplicitCloseable{`

   e `class Carton implements java.io.Closeable{`

ANSWERS TO SAMPLE EXAM QUESTIONS

A 6-1. f

[6.1] Use throw and throws statements

Explanation: The code as is (without any changes) compiles successfully. Options (a) and (b) are incorrect because a method (`readFile()`) can declare a checked exception (`IOException`) to be thrown in its `throws` clause, even if the method doesn't throw it.

    Option (c) is incorrect. If line 1 is changed so that method `readFile()` doesn't declare to throw an `IOException`, method `useReadFile()` won't compile. The `catch` block in method `useReadFile()` tries to handle `IOException`, which isn't thrown by its `try` block. This causes compilation error.

    Option (d) is incorrect. Code on line 3 will compile as it is. It's okay for `useRead-File()` to handle the exception thrown by `readFile()` using `try-catch` and still declare it to be rethrown using the `throws` clause.

    Option (e) is incorrect. The code compiles successfully.

    Option (f) is correct. Even though `useReadFile()` handles `IOException` and doesn't actually throw it, it declares it to be rethrown in its `throws` clause. So, the method that uses `useReadFile()` must either handle the checked exception—`IOException` (or one of its superclasses)—or declare it to be rethrown. Because `Exception` is a superclass of

IOException, replacing throws Throwable with throws Exception in the declaration of method main() enables the code to compile.

A 6-2. b, c, d, e, f

[6.5] Test invariants by using assertions

Explanation: Option (a) is incorrect. For the longer form of the assert statement that uses two expressions, you can't enclose both expressions within a single parentheses.

Options (b) and (c) are correct. It's optional to include the individual expressions used in the longer form within a single parentheses.

Options (d) and (e) are correct. The shorter form of the assert statement uses only one expression, which might or might not be included within parentheses.

Option (f) is correct. The semicolon placed after the condition s == "assert" delimits the assert statement, and the statement following the semicolon is treated as a separate statement. It's equivalent to an assert statement using its shorter form followed by another statement, as follows:

```
assert s == "assert" ;
s.replace('a', 'z');
```

Option (g) is incorrect because the first expression in an assert statement must return a boolean value. In this code, the first expression returns an object of class String.

Option (h) is incorrect because the second expression in an assert statement must return a value of any type. In this code, the return type of method println() is void.

Option (i) is incorrect. It incorrectly encloses both expressions of the assert statement within a single pair of parentheses. If parentheses were removed, it's also an illegal usage of the long form because it uses an expression that doesn't return a boolean value for its first expression and its second expression doesn't return any value.

A 6-3. b

[6.3] Auto-close resources with a try-with-resources statement

Explanation: The constructor of class Box throws a RuntimeException, and so the box variable isn't initialized in the try-with-resources statement. Method close() of class Box isn't called implicitly because execution didn't proceed inside the try block.

When try-with-resources throws an exception, the control is transferred to the catch block. In this case, the exception handler prints catch:java.lang.Runtime-Exception. The finally block always executes, thereafter printing finally.

A 6-4. b

[6.4] Create custom exceptions

Explanation: Option (a) is incorrect because it defines custom exception `DataException` as a checked exception. To use checked `DataException`, `accessData()` must specify it to be thrown in its `throws` clause.

Option (b) is correct because it defines custom exception `DataException` as an unchecked or runtime exception. Even though method `accessData()` throws a `Data-Exception`, a runtime exception, it need not declare its name in its `throws` clause.

Option (c) is incorrect. Class `DataException` extends class `Object` and not `Exception`. Also, this code won't compile because class `Object` doesn't define a constructor that matches `Object(String)`.

Option (d) is incorrect. If `DataException` extends `Throwable`, `accessData()` won't compile because it's also a checked exception and therefore must be handled or declared.

A 6-5. c, d

[6.5] Test invariants by using assertions

Explanation: Options (a) and (b) are incorrect because assertions must not be used to check method arguments for nonprivate methods. Nonprivate methods can be called by objects of other classes, and you can't validate their method arguments by using assertions. Assertions can be disabled at runtime, so they aren't the right option to validate method arguments to public methods. You should throw exceptions in this case. For example, when you come across invalid values that are passed to a nonprivate method, you can throw an `IllegalArgumentException`.

A 6-6. a, b, c, e

[6.1] Use throw and throws statements
[6.2] Use the try statement with multi-catch and finally clauses

Explanation: Method `swim()` throws a `BreathingException`, and method `dive()` throws a `DivingException`, both checked exceptions. Method `main()` is declared to throw both a `BreathingException` or `DivingException`.

The code that is inserted at `//INSERT CODE HERE` must do the following:

- The option must use the correct syntax of `try` with single-`catch` or multi-`catch`.
- Because method `main()` throws both a `BreathingException` and `Diving-Exception`, the `try` statement might not handle it.
- It must not throw a checked exception more generic than the ones declared by method `main()` itself—that is, `BreathingException` and `DivingException`.

Option (a) is correct. It defines the correct syntax to use `try` with multi-catch, and rethrows the caught instance of `BreathingException` or `DivingException`.

Option (b) is correct. Though the type of the exception caught in the exception handler is `Exception`, the superclass of the exceptions thrown by `main()`, the compiler knows that the `try` block can throw only two checked exceptions, `Breathing-Exception` or `DivingException`. So this thrown exception is caught and rethrown with more inclusive type checking.

Option (c) is correct. The multi-catch statement is correct syntactically. Also, the `throw` statement throws a checked `DivingException`, which is declared by method `main()`'s throws clause.

Option (d) is incorrect. The `catch` block throws an instance of checked exception `Exception`, the superclass of the exceptions declared to be thrown by `main()`, which isn't acceptable.

Option (e) is correct. It isn't obligatory to include the names of the runtime exceptions thrown by a method in its `throws` clause.

A 6-7. c, e, f

[6.1] Use throw and throws statements
[6.4] Create custom exceptions

Explanation: Though the question seems to be testing you on the hierarchy of exception classes `IOException` and `FileNotFoundException`, it's not. This question is about creating custom exception classes with overridden methods that throw exceptions.

To understand the explanation, note the following class hierarchies:

- Exception `FileNotFoundException` extends `IOException`.
- Exception `BaseException` extends `IOException`.
- Exception `DerivedException` extends `FileNotFoundException`.
- Exception `DerivedException` doesn't extend `BaseException`.

This class hierarchy implies the following:

- `BaseException` isn't a type of `DerivedException`.
- `BaseException` and `FileNotFoundException` are unrelated exceptions.

To override `read()` in the `Base` interface, `read()` in the `Derived` interface must either declare to throw a `BaseException`, any derived classes of `BaseException`, any runtime exception or errors, or no exception.

Option (a) is incorrect because `FileNotFoundException` is unrelated to `Base-Exception`.

Options (b), (d), and (g) are incorrect because `IOException`, `Exception`, and `Throwable` are all superclasses of `BaseException` (and not subclasses) and therefore invalid when overriding method `read()`.

A 6-8. c

[6.5] Test invariants by using assertions

Explanation: Options (a) and (d) are incorrect. -enable and -enableAssertions are invalid switch options. The correct switch options to enable assertions are -ea and -enableassertions. If you use an invalid argument (like -enable) the program will not run, but will exit immediately with an "Unrecognized option" error. Option (b) is incorrect. With assertions enabled, assert(calc()) will evaluate to assert(false) and throw an AssertionError, exiting the application, before printing any values.

Option (c) is correct. With assertions disabled, the assert (calc()) statement is equivalent to an empty statement or a nonexistent line of code. So method calc() isn't executed, and the value of the static variable foo (10) is printed.

A 6-9. c

[6.3] Auto-close resources with a try-with-resources statement

Explanation: An implicit or explicit call to method close() doesn't set a resource to null, and you can call methods on it. So the try block results in the following:

- Explicit call to method close()
- Explicit call to method emptyContents()
- Implicit call to method close()

No exceptions are thrown, and the code prints the output as shown in option (c).

A 6-10. a, b

[6.2] Use the try statement with multi-catch and finally clauses
[6.3] Auto-close resources with a try-with-resources statement

Explanation: Option (c) is incorrect. If a resource couldn't be initialized because of an exception, it doesn't exist. There's no point in auto-closing such a resource.

Option (d) is incorrect. Subsequent calls to close() don't throw an exception.

Option (e) is incorrect. The resources declared within a try-with-resources statement are accessible only within the try block.

A 6-11. d

[6.3] Auto-close resources with a try-with-resources statement

Explanation: The code box.open() within the try block throws an Exception. Before the control is transferred to the exception handler, the resource box is implicitly closed by calling its close() method, which also throws an Exception.

If an exception is thrown from the try block and one or more exceptions are thrown from the try-with-resources statement, then those exceptions thrown from the try-with-resources statement are suppressed. So the exception thrown by the implicit call to box.close() is suppressed. A suppressed exception forms the cause of the exception that suppresses it. It can be retrieved by using method getSuppressed() on the exception handler, as follows:

```
catch (Exception e) {
    System.out.println("catch:"+e);
    for (Throwable th : e.getSuppressed())
        System.out.println(th);
}
```

It prints the following:

```
catch:java.lang.Exception
java.lang.Exception
```

A 6-12. c

[6.5] Test invariants by using assertions

Explanation: Option (a) is incorrect, and (c) is correct. Though verifying the value of variable maxLoad using the assert statement is valid and appropriate usage of an assertion, handling an AssertionError isn't. You should never handle an AssertionError. Assertions enable you to test your assumptions while you're developing your applications. You must not try to recover from an AssertionError. If an assumption fails, you must correct the code or logic accordingly. If you foresee exceptional conditions in the production version of your application, use exceptions instead of assertions.

Option (b) is incorrect because the code on line 1 can throw an AssertionError and not an AssertionException.

Options (d) and (e) are incorrect. Class Assert will compile successfully. Note that assert (small *a*) is a keyword, and not Assert (capital *A*). When executed with assertions enabled, the assert statement might throw an AssertionError, which will be handled by the catch block. So class Assert won't throw a runtime exception and might throw an AssertionError.

A 6-13. c

[6.3] Auto-close resources with a try-with-resources statement

Explanation: This question tries to trick you with explicit calls of method close() placed in the try block. Though close() is implicitly called to close a resource, it's possible to call it explicitly in the try block. But the explicit call to close() is independent of the implicit call to close() for each resource defined in the try-with-resources statement.

The first call to method close() prints close. Because this method call throws an exception, the control is ready to be transferred to the catch block and thus the second explicit call to method close() doesn't execute. But before the control is moved to the `catch` block, the implicit call to method `close()` is made, which again prints `close` and throws an exception. The exception thrown by the implicit call of method `close()` is suppressed by the exception thrown by the explicit call of method `close()`, placed before the end of the `try` block.

The control is then transferred to the `catch` block and, last, to the `finally` block.

A 6-14. b, c, d, e

[6.4] Create custom exceptions

Explanation: Option (a) is incorrect because `java.lang.Closeable` is undefined. So class `Jumpable` won't compile.

Option (e) is a correct option because class `Jumpable` won't compile.

A 6-15. b

[6.5] Test invariants by using assertions

Explanation: When the assertion fails, an instance of `AssertionError` is thrown. The condition (`name == "Shreya"`) evaluates to `false` because it compares the object references and not the `String` values.

A 6-16. a

[6.3] Auto-close resources with a try-with-resources statement

Explanation: The code compiles successfully, and no runtime exceptions are thrown during its execution. The resources initialized in a try-with-resources statement are closed in the reverse order.

A 6-17. a, c, e

[6.3] Auto-close resources with a try-with-resources statement

Explanation: The code will print `close`, if class `Carton` implements the `java.lang.AutoCloseable` interface or any of its subinterfaces. Options (a) and (c) are correct, because `Carton` implements the interface `java.lang.AutoCloseable` itself.

Option (b) is incorrect. The `Closeable` interface that extends the `java.lang.AutoCloseable` interface is defined in the `java.io` package.

Option (d) is incorrect. The Java API doesn't define any interface with the name `ImplicitCloseable` in the `java.lang` package.

Option (e) is correct because `java.io.Closeable` is a subinterface of `java.lang.AutoCloseable`.

Java I/O fundamentals 7

Exam objectives covered in this chapter	What you need to know
[7.1] Read and write data from the console	How to access the unique console related to a JVM How to read from and write data to the console
[7.2] Use streams to read from and write to files by using classes in the `java.io package` including `BufferedReader, BufferedWriter, File, FileReader, FileWriter, DataInputStream, DataOutputStream, ObjectOutputStream, ObjectInputStream,` and `PrintWriter`	The definitions of byte I/O streams and character streams, and their similarities and differences How to read and write raw bytes, primitive data, strings, and objects to files by using one class or a combination of classes

The Java I/O API is powerful and flexible. It enables you to read and write multiple types of data: raw bytes, characters, and even objects. You can read data from multiple and diverse data sources such as files, network sockets, and memory arrays, and write them to multiple data destinations. Java I/O also provides the flexibility of reading or writing buffered and unbuffered data. You can also chain multiple input and output sources. You can use the same methods to read from an input resource such as a file, a console, or a network connection.

The Java I/O API is huge and could be a textbook on its own. Coverage in this chapter is limited to the Java I/O exam topics for the OCP Java SE 7 Programmer II exam. This chapter assumes no prior knowledge of Java I/O.

NOTE   Introduction to I/O concepts is covered in warm-up section 7.1. If you're good with the basics of I/O, please skip this section and move to section 7.2.

This chapter doesn't cover the new file I/O (NIO.2). NIO.2 is covered in the next chapter. This chapter covers

- Introduction to Java I/O
- Types of streams: byte streams and character streams
- Buffering data for faster reading and writing
- Reading and writing bytes, primitives, and objects using data streams and object streams
- Chaining I/O streams
- Writing formatted data to character streams
- Reading data from and writing it to the console

Let's start with the basics of Java I/O in the next section.

7.1   *Introducing Java I/O: WARM-UP*

Java I/O lets you read your files, data, photos, and videos from multiple sources and write them to several destinations. You can use it to prepare a formatted report that you can send to a printer. You can copy your files, create directory structures, delete them, and do much more.

Java I/O includes a lot of classes and can be intimidating to work with. You must get the hang of its basics, so you can categorize and work with a group of classes and methods. Java abstracts all its data sources and data destinations as *streams*.

7.1.1   *Understanding streams*

A question that I'm asked quite often is: What is a stream—the data, data source, or data destination? And it's a fair question. A stream is a sequence of data. The Java I/O stream is an abstraction of a data source *or* a data destination. It represents an object that can produce data or receive data. An input stream is used to read data from a data source. An output stream is used to write data to a data destination.

Just as a stream of water represents a continuous flow of water, a Java stream produces or consumes a continuous flow of data. I/O streams are used to move data from a data source to a Java program, and from a Java program to a data destination.

- An *input stream* enables you to *read* data from a data source *to* a Java application.
- An *output stream* enables you to *write* data from a Java application to a data destination.

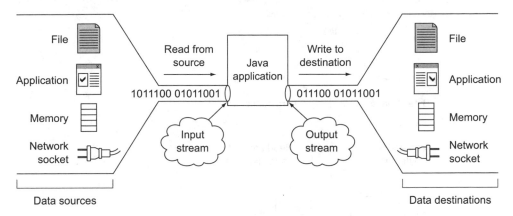

Figure 7.1 Flavors of I/O streams: input streams and output streams. An input stream enables a Java program to read data from a data source. An output stream enables a Java program to write data to a data destination.

A Java program can read from multiple data sources and destinations, like a file on your storage device, another application, an array in memory, a network connection, and others. Figure 7.1 shows the flavors of I/O streams—input streams and output streams—and how they're connected to data sources and destinations.

 NOTE The exam limits the use of streams to reading from and writing to files. So the rest of the chapter covers reading and writing of data in multiple formats from and to only *files*.

The exam covers multiple classes that can read and write bytes, characters, and objects. Before we dive into the details of working with these classes, the next section includes a quick overview of the main types of I/O streams: byte streams and character streams.

7.1.2 Understanding multiple flavors of data

Java I/O uses separate classes to read and write different types of data. The data is broadly divided into byte data and character data. The *byte streams* read and write byte data. To read and write characters and text data, Java I/O uses *readers* and *writers*, referred to as *character streams*. Byte streams can be used to read and write practically all kinds of data including zip files, image or video files, text or PDF files, and others. Character streams are used to read and write character data. Figure 7.2 shows these streams.

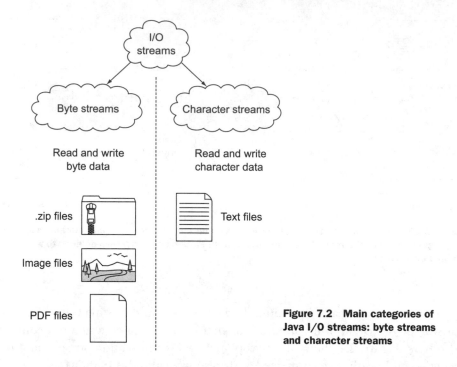

Figure 7.2   Main categories of Java I/O streams: byte streams and character streams

Creating files and reading or writing byte data from them or to them

Though you can read and write practically all byte data by using byte streams, you might need the assistance of specific classes to interpret the read data or written data in a particular format. For example, to create a PDF file, interpret its data, and write data to it, you might need to use an API by Adobe or a third party.

Going back to the basics, a computer system reads and writes all data as binary data (0s and 1s, referred to as *bits*) from all sources and to all destinations. A byte stream reads and write *bytes* (8 bits) to and from data sources. All the other I/O classes build on the byte streams, adding more functionality. For example, character streams take into account Unicode characters and the user's charset. Instead of reading or writing 8-bit data from or to a file, character streams define methods to read or write 16-bit data. But behind the scenes they use byte streams to get their work done. Figure 7.3 shows the input and output streams for reading and writing byte and character data. As mentioned earlier, the exam covers writing data to and reading data from only files. A Java application uses `FileOutputStream` to write bytes to a file and `FileInput-Stream` to read bytes from a file. Similarly, it uses `FileReader` to read Unicode text from a file and `FileWriter` to write Unicode text to a file.

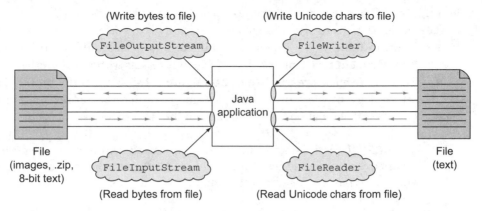

Figure 7.3 A Java application uses `FileInputStream` and `FileOutputStream` to read and write byte data from and to files, respectively. It uses `FileReader` and `FileWriter` to read and write Unicode text from and to files.

Invoking the I/O methods to read and write (very small) basic units of data (byte or character) isn't efficient. *Buffered streams* add functionality to other streams by buffering data. Buffered streams read from a *buffer* (also referred to as memory or an internal array), and the native API is called when it's empty. Similarly, they write data to a buffer and flush it to the underlying output stream when it's full. A buffered stream buffers input/output from another input/output stream. Figure 7.4 shows

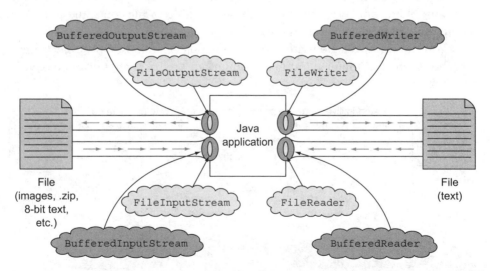

Figure 7.4 A `BufferedInputStream` reads and buffers data from an `InputStream` like `FileInputStream`. `BufferedOutputStream` buffers data before writing it to an `OutputStream` like `FileOutputStream`. Similarly, a `BufferedReader` buffers input from a `Reader` like `FileReader`. A `BufferedWriter` buffers data before sending it off to a `Writer` like `FileWriter`.

how `BufferedInputStream`, `BufferedOutputStream`, `BufferedReader`, and `Buffered-Writer` buffer data from byte and character streams.

As shown in figure 7.4, a Java application communicates with an object of a buffered stream (like `BufferedInputStream`), which interacts with the underlying `Input-Stream` (like `FileInputStream`). Notice how figure 7.4 shows that the buffered stream encloses within it an object of another stream. This pictorial representation will be handy when you instantiate buffered streams in the next sections.

 EXAM TIP   To instantiate a `BufferedInputStream`, you need to pass it an instance of another `InputStream`, like `FileInputStream`. Constructor wrapping (passing instances to instantiate instances) can become complex in Java I/O.

All these buffered classes are specialized *filter* classes for the underlying stream. They modify the way their underlying streams behave, by buffering data. The filter classes such as `BufferedInputStream` and `BufferedOutputStream` are *decorator* classes. They add functionality to the existing base classes.

Other `InputStream` and `OutputStream` subclasses you need to know for the exam are classes `DataInputStream` and `DataOutputStream`. These classes define methods for reading and writing primitive values and strings. For example, a method to read `int` values, say, `readInt`, will read 4 bytes from an input stream and return an `int` value. Similarly, a method to write an `int` value, say `writeInt()`, will write 4 bytes of data. Figure 7.5 shows how you can read and write primitive values and strings from a file by using `DataInputStream` and `DataOutputStream`. As I mentioned previously, because the exam covers reading from and writing to files only, the images show the data source and destination as files.

You can also read and write objects using object streams. Only objects that support serialization (must implement marker interface `Serializable`) can be read from and

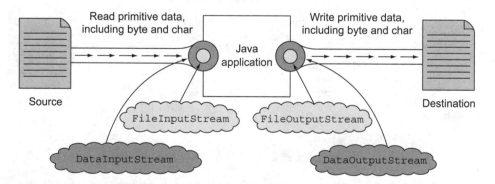

Figure 7.5 A `DataInputStream` can read primitive values (including `byte` and `char`) and strings from a file by using `FileInputStream`. A `DataOutputStream` can write primitive values and strings to a file using `FileOutputStream`.

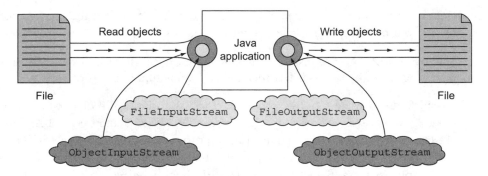

Figure 7.6 An `ObjectInputStream` reads an object from a file by using a
`FileInputStream`. An `ObjectOutputStream` writes an object to a file by using a
`FileOutputStream`.

written to a data source. The object stream classes are `ObjectInputStream` and `Object-`
`OutputStream`. Figure 7.6 shows this arrangement.

To read and write data to a physical file, you need instances of `java.io.File`. All
classes that read from or write to a file either accept an instance of `File` or instantiate
one themselves using a path and filename. Before using streams to read data from and
write data to files, let's work with `File` in the next section.

 NOTE Java version 7 has introduced a new interface that offers the existing functionality of class `File`, addresses its existing issues, and offers
additional functionality: `java.nio.file.Path`. Because `File` is on the
exam, we'll continue to use class `File` for all examples in this chapter.
`Path` is covered in chapter 8.

7.2 *Working with class java.io.File*

 [7.2] Use streams to read from and write to files by using classes in the
java.io package including BufferedReader, BufferedWriter, File,
FileReader, FileWriter, DataInputStream, DataOutputStream,
ObjectOutputStream, ObjectInputStream, and PrintWriter

To read from and write to files by using `java.io` classes, you'll need to work with
class `File`.

`File` is an abstract representation of a path to a file or a directory. It can be *absolute*
or *relative*. An absolute path can be resolved without any further information. A relative path is interpreted from another path. The name of the class `File` is rather mis-
leading because it might *not* be associated with an actual file (or directory) on a system.
You can create objects of class `File` to store information about the files or directories
on your system. You can use an object of class `File` to create a new file or directory,

delete it, or inquire about or modify its attributes. You can read the contents of a file or write to it by using byte and character I/O classes.

 EXAM TIP A `File` instance can refer to either a file or a directory. But it might not be necessarily associated with an actual file or directory.

To read from or write to a file, you'll need to instantiate `File` objects, which can be used by I/O classes such as `FileInputStream`, `FileOutputStream`, `FileReader`, and `FileWriter`. Because a `File` instance can refer to either a file or a directory, you might want to verify that you aren't writing your valuable data to a directory. Let's work with an example to instantiate `File` objects and check whether they represent files or directories. The first step is to examine the `File` constructors:

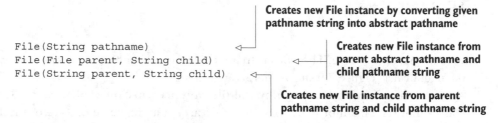

The next section includes an example to instantiate `File` objects (using the preceding `File` constructors) and check whether they're files or directories.

7.2.1 Instantiating and querying File instances

Say you're given the directory in the following listing (C:\\temp, with its child files and directories). Let's count its (first-level) subdirectories and files. As shown in the following listing, the code should print one directory and two files.

Listing 7.1 Working with `File` instances

```java
import java.io.*;
public class CountDirFiles {
    public static void main(String... args) {
        countDirFiles(new File("c:\\temp"));
    }
    public static void countDirFiles(File dir) {       ← If a directory, proceed
        if (dir.isDirectory()) {
            int fileCount = 0;
            int dirCount = 0;
            String[] list = dir.list();                ← Retrieves files and subdirectories
            File item = null;
            for (String listItem : list) {
                item = new File(dir, listItem);        ← Iterates files and subdirectories
                if (item.isFile())
                    ++fileCount;
                else if (item.isDirectory())
                    ++dirCount;                        ← Increments dirCount, for directories
            }
```

Creates File object → `item = new File(dir, listItem);`

Increments fileCount, for files → `++fileCount;`

```
            System.out.println ("File(s):"+ fileCount);
            System.out.println ("Dir(s):"+ dirCount);
        }
        else {
            throw new IllegalArgumentException("Not a directory");   <--
        }
    }
}
```

Throws exception if method argument isn't directory

The output of this code is as follows:

```
File(s):2
Dir(s):1
```

In this example, I created an object of class `File` and passed it to method `count-DirFiles()`. This method checks whether the `File` object represents a directory, using `dir.isDirectory()`. If `dir.isDirectory()` returns `true`, the method retrieves a list of the names of its child files and directories, using method `list()`. Note that the method returns a list of the names as an array of `String`. To determine whether an individual array item is a file or directory, we need to first create a `File` instance using directory `dir` and the item itself. This is accomplished by using the following line of code:

```
item = new File(dir, listItem);
```

You can query a `File` instance to determine whether it represents a file or a directory, and increment the variables used to store the respective count, as follows:

```
if (item.isFile())
    ++fileCount;
else if (item.isDirectory())
++dirCount;
```

 EXAM TIP You can create a `File` instance that represents a nonexistant file on your file system. And you can even invoke methods like `isFile()` without getting an exception.

Revisit the following line of code from listing 7.1:

```
item = new File(dir, listItem)
```

This constructor creates a new file instance from a parent abstract pathname and a child pathname string, using the following constructor defined in class `File`:

```
File(File parent, String child)
```

What happens when you replace `new File(dir, listItem)` from listing 7.1 with this constructor: `new File(listItem)`? The code now prints 0 for both the file and directory count.

Why? If you create a `File` object, *without* specifying its *complete path*, it assumes that the file that you're referring to exists in the current directory (the one that contains your .class file). The variable listItem contains just the filename, *without* its complete path. In the absence of the complete path name, the variable item refers to a *nonexisting file on your system* (because it's looking in the wrong directory). Because the item variable *doesn't* represent a file or directory on your system, methods isFile() and isDirectory() return false, and neither of the variable values, dirCount or file-Count, is modified.

 EXAM TIP   The objects of class File are immutable; the pathname represented by a File object can't be changed.

7.2.2 *Creating new files and directories on your physical device*

Creating an object of class File *won't* create a real file or directory on your system. To create a new file on your system, use method createNewFile(), and to create new directories, use methods mkdir() or mkdirs(), as listed in table 7.1.

Table 7.1   Methods used to create new physical files and directories

File method	Exception thrown	Description (from Java API documentation)
boolean createNewFile()	IOException	Atomically creates a new, empty file named by this abstract pathname if and only if a file with this name doesn't yet exist.
boolean mkdir()	SecurityException	Creates the directory named by this abstract pathname.
boolean mkdirs()	SecurityException	Creates the directory named by this abstract pathname, including any necessary but nonexistent parent directories. Note that if this operation fails, it may have succeeded in creating some of the necessary parent directories.

Here's an example that creates new files and directories:

```
import java.io.*;
public class CreateFileAndDirs {
    public static void main(String... args) throws IOException {
        File dirs = new File("\\usr\\code\\java");
        System.out.println(dirs.mkdirs());          Creates multiple
        File file = new File(dirs, "MyText.txt");    directories in root
        if (!file.exists())                          directory
            System.out.println(file.createNewFile());
    }                                                If file doesn't
}                                                    exist
```

Try to create file

This code creates a directory tree usr\code\java and a file (MyText.txt) on our system:

But the results might vary on your system (you might not have the access permission to create files or directories). Be careful when you create objects of class `File` on your system. Even though the following code creates an object of class `File`, with a weird name, it compiles successfully:

```
File f = new File ("*&^%$.yu");
```

The preceding code doesn't throw any exception because it *won't* create a file on the physical storage on your system. It creates only an object of class `File`, which as mentioned before, might not necessarily represent a file or directory. Because creation of files and directories are system-specific operations, creation of a file with the name *&^%$.yu might succeed on one system, but fail on another. For example, on a system running Windows, calling method `createNewFile()` on this object will throw the following exception at runtime:

```
Exception in thread "main" java.io.IOException: The filename, directory
name, or volume label syntax is incorrect
    at java.io.WinNTFileSystem.createFileExclusively(Native Method)
    at java.io.File.createNewFile(File.java:883)
```

With the basic knowledge of using a `File` object, let's deep-dive into how to read and write the contents of a file by using byte streams.

7.3 Using byte stream I/O

 [7.2]   Use streams to read from and write to files by using classes in the java.io package including BufferedReader, BufferedWriter, File, FileReader, FileWriter, DataInputStream, DataOutputStream, ObjectOutputStream, ObjectInputStream, and PrintWriter

Byte streams work with reading and writing byte data. They're broadly categorized as input streams and output streams. All input streams extend the base abstract class `java.io.InputStream`, and all output streams extend the base abstract class `java.io.OutputStream`. Let's start with input streams.

7.3.1 Input streams

Class `java.io.InputStream` is an abstract base class for all the input streams in Java. It's extended by all the classes that need to read bytes (for example, image data) from multiple data sources. Let's start with the most important method of this class, `read()`, used to read data from a source. The class `InputStream` defines multiple overloaded versions of method `read()`, which can be used to read a single `byte` of data as `int`, or multiple bytes into a byte array:

```
int abstract read()              ◁──┐   Reads the next,
int read(byte[] b)                       single byte of data
int read(byte[] b, int off, int len)     Reads multiple bytes of
                                          data into a byte array
```

But you wouldn't use these methods yourself. You'd use method `read()` by more-specific classes that extend the abstract class `InputStream`. For example, class `File-InputStream` extends `InputStream` and overrides its `read()` method for you to use.

 EXAM TIP Watch out for the use of method `read()` from class `Input-Stream`. It returns the next byte of data, or `-1` if the end of the stream is reached. It doesn't throw an `EOFException`.

Method `close()` is another important method of class `InputStream`. Calling `close()` on a stream releases the system resources associated with it.

Because `InputStream` is an *abstract* class, you *can't* create an instance to read from a data source or destination. You need one of its subclasses to do the work for you. So why do you need to bother with so much theory about it?

> **Why do you need to bother with so much theory on InputStream?**
> On the exam, you'll be tested on whether you can call a particular method on an object. For example, you might be tested on whether you can call the method `read()` or `close()` on an object of, say, `FileInputStream`, a subclass of `InputStream`. Because methods `read()` and `close()` are defined in class `InputStream`, they can be called on objects of any derived classes of `InputStream`.
>
> These might not be straightforward questions. You need to get the hang of the basics to answer them correctly.

Table 7.2 contains a list of the main methods in class `java.io.InputStream` (from the Java API documentation). Don't worry about the details; we'll cover the relevant details in the subsequent sections.

Table 7.2 List of methods in class `java.io.InputStream`

Method name	Return type	Description
`close()`	`void`	Closes this input stream and releases any system resources associated with the stream.
`abstract read()`	`int`	Reads the next byte of data from the input stream.
`read(byte[] b)`	`int`	Reads a number of bytes from the input stream and stores them into the buffer array `b`.
`read(byte[] b, int off, int len)`	`int`	Reads up to `len` bytes of data from the input stream into an array of bytes.

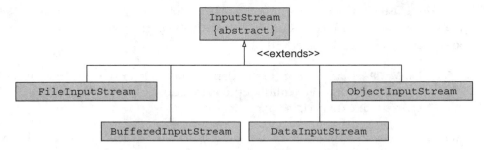

Figure 7.7 Abstract class `InputStream` and its subclasses (the ones that are on the exam)

Figure 7.7 shows the classes that extend the abstract class java.io.InputStream. In the next sections, you'll see how to use all these classes. Don't panic: because they share a *lot* of similarity, they'll be simple to work with.

 EXAM TIP   All the classes that include InputStream in their name— File-InputStream, ObjectInputStream, BufferedInputStream, and DataInput-Stream—extend abstract class InputStream, directly or indirectly.

Apart from image files, you can also read character data by using byte streams. But you aren't encouraged to do so because the Java API defines well-defined classes for character I/O. On the exam, you'll see questions on valid I/O code and recommended I/O code. Though using a byte stream to read (and write) characters is valid code, it's not a recommended practice.

Let's move on to this class's counterpart for writing byte data to sources: class java.io.OutputStream.

7.3.2 *Output streams*

Class java.io.OutputStream is also an abstract class. It's the base class for all the *output* streams in Java. It's extended by all the classes that need to write bytes (for example, image data) to multiple data destinations. The most important method of this class is write(), which can be used to write a single byte of data or multiple bytes from a byte array to a data destination:

```
abstract void write(int b)                    Writes single byte
void write(byte[] b)                          Writes multiple bytes
void write(byte[] b, int off, int len)        from a byte array
```

Methods close() and flush() are other important methods of class OutputStream. Often data isn't written directly to the output stream but buffered for an efficient management of resources. If you want to write data to the output stream right away without waiting for the buffer to be full, call flush(). Method close() is used to release system resources being used by this stream.

You'd usually work with method `write()` defined by more specific classes that extend `OutputStream`. For example, class `FileOutputStream` extends `OutputStream` and overrides its `write()` method.

 EXAM TIP Class `OutputStream` defines methods `write()`, `flush()`, and `close()`. So these are valid methods that can be called on any objects of classes that extend class `OutputStream`.

Table 7.3 contains a list of the methods in class `java.io.OutputStream`. I'll cover the important methods in the subsequent sections.

Table 7.3   Methods in class `java.io.OutputStream`

Method name	Return type	Description
`close()`	void	Closes this output stream and releases any system resources associated with this stream.
`flush()`	void	Flushes this output stream and forces any buffered output bytes to be written out.
`write(byte[] b)`	void	Writes `b.length` bytes from the specified byte array to this output stream.
`write(byte[] b, int off, int len)`	void	Writes `len` bytes from the specified byte array, starting at offset `off` to this output stream.
`abstract write(int b)`	void	Writes the specified byte to this output stream.

Figure 7.8 shows abstract class `java.io.OutputStream` and its subclasses.

 EXAM TIP All the classes that include `OutputStream` in their name—`FileOutputStream`, `ObjectOutputStream`, `BufferedOutputStream`, and `DataOutputStream`—extend abstract class `OutputStream`, directly or indirectly. Let's start reading from and writing to files with byte streams.

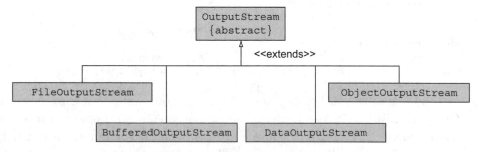

Figure 7.8   Abstract class `OutputStream` and its subclasses covered by this exam

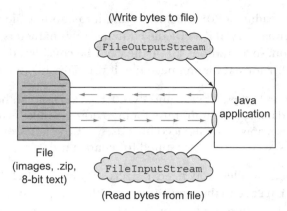

(Write bytes to file)

FileOutputStream

Java
application

File
(images, .zip,
8-bit text)

FileInputStream

(Read bytes from file)

Figure 7.9   A Java application uses `FileInputStream` and `FileOutputStream` to read and write byte data from and to files.

7.3.3   *File I/O with byte streams*

Bytes can represent *any* type of data, *including* character data. Data in any file type—Portable Document Format (PDF), zip, Microsoft Word, and others—can be read and written as byte data. To read and write raw bytes from and to a file, use `FileInput-Stream` and `FileOutputStream`, as shown in figure 7.9.

Before you work with an example of reading from and writing to files, take note of the constructors of `FileInputStream` and `FileOutputStream`. You can instantiate `FileInputStream` by passing it the name of a file as a `File` instance or as a string value. The constructor opens a connection to a file and might throw a `FileNotFound-Exception`, if the specified file can't be found:

```
FileInputStream(File file) throws FileNotFoundException {}
FileInputStream(String name) throws FileNotFoundException {}
```

 EXAM TIP   `FileInputStream` is instantiated by passing it a `File` or `String` instance. It can't be instantiated by passing it another `InputStream`. The above-mentioned constructors of class `FileInputStream` throw a checked exception, `FileNotFoundException`, which must be handled accordingly.

Instantiation of `FileOutputStream` creates a stream to write to a file specified either as a `File` instance or a string value. You can also pass a `boolean` value specifying whether to append to the existing file contents. Here are the overloaded constructors of class `FileOutputStream`:

```
FileOutputStream(File file) throws FileNotFoundException
FileOutputStream(File file, boolean append) throws FileNotFoundException
FileOutputStream(String name) throws FileNotFoundException
FileOutputStream(String nm, boolean append) throws FileNotFoundException
```

 EXAM TIP   The above-mentioned constructors of `FileOutputStream` throw a `FileNotFoundException`, a checked exception. Also, during its instantiation, you can specify whether to append data to an underlying file or override its contents.

Let's work with an example of reading a PDF file and writing it to another file. A PDF file *never* contains *just* character data. Even if a PDF file contains only characters, it also contains formatting information, so as a whole, a PDF file can't be considered character data. You can also use the PDF format for an image file, if you have any doubts.

 EXAM TIP Even though `FileInputStream` and `FileOutputStream` can be used to write character data, you shouldn't use them to do so. Unlike byte I/O streams, character streams take into account a user's *charset* and work with Unicode characters, which are better suited for character data.

To read and write to separate PDF files, you need objects of `java.io.FileInput-Stream` and `java.io.FileOutputStream` that can connect to these input and output PDF files. You need to call at least one method on `FileInputStream` to read data, and one method on `FileOutputStream` to write data. Previously, I mentioned that `InputStream` and `OutputStream` define methods `read()` and `write()` to read and write a single byte of data, respectively. Let's work with these methods in the following listing.

Listing 7.2   Using FileInputStream and FileOutputStream to read and write bytes

```java
import java.io.*;
public class ReadWriteBytesUsingFiles {
    public static void main(String[] args) throws IOException {
        try (
            FileInputStream in = new FileInputStream("Sample.pdf");         // ❶ Instantiates FileInput-Stream
            FileOutputStream out = new FileOutputStream("Sample2.pdf");
        )                                                                   // ❷ Instantiates FileOutputStream
        {
            int data;                          // ❸ Declares variable to store a single byte of data

            while ((data = in.read()) != -1) {     // ❹ Loops until end of stream is reached (no more bytes can be read)

                out.write(data);               // ❺ Writes byte data to destination file
            }
        }
    }
}
```

 EXAM TIP Are you wondering why you need to create a variable of type int to read byte data from a file in the preceding code? When a stream exhausts itself and no data can be read from it, method `read()` returns -1, which can't be stored by a variable of type `byte`.

The code at ❶ and ❷ instantiates `FileInputStream` and `FileOutputStream`. The constructors used in this code accept the filenames as `String` objects. You can also pass the constructors' instances of class `File` or `String`. At ❸, you declare a variable of type `int` to store the byte data you read from the file. At ❹, you call `in.read()`, which reads and returns a single byte from the underlying file Sample.pdf. When no more data can be read from the input file, method `read()` returns -1, and this is when the `while` loop ends its execution. At ❺, you write a single byte of data to another file by using `out`, an instance of `FileOutputStream`.

 NOTE Copying a file's content might not copy its attributes. To copy a file, it's advisable to use methods such as `copy` from class `java.nio .file.Files`.

I/O operations that require reading and writing of a single byte from and to a file are a costly affair. To optimize these operations, you can use a byte array:

```java
import java.io.*;public class ReadWriteBytesUsingFiles2 {
    public static void main(String[] args) throws IOException {
        try (
            FileInputStream in = new FileInputStream(
                                        new File("Sample.pdf"));
            FileOutputStream out = new FileOutputStream("Sample2.pdf");
        )
        {
            int data;
            byte[] byteArr = new byte[1024];          ⟵─┐ Creates byte
                                                         │ array of size 1024
            while ((data = in.read(byteArr)) != -1) {  ⟵─┘ read(byteArr) reads
                                                           data into array byteArr
                out.write(byteArr, 0, data);    ⟵─┐ Writes only
            }                                      │ read bytes to
        }                                          │ output stream
    }
}
```

Programmers are often confused about the correct use of method `read()` that accepts a byte array. Unlike `read()`, `read(byte[])` *doesn't* return the read bytes. It returns the *count of bytes* read, or `-1` if no more data can be read. The actual data is read in the byte array that is passed to it as a method parameter.

So do you think it makes a difference whether I write the complete byte array to the output stream or write the count of the bytes that were read from the input device? Let me test you on this concept in the next "Twist in the Tale" exercise.

Twist in the Tale 7.1

Let's modify some of the code used in the previous example. Select the correct options for the following code.

```java
import java.io.*;

class Twist {
    public static void main(String[] args) throws IOException {
        try (
            FileInputStream in = new FileInputStream("Twist.java");
            FileOutputStream out = new FileOutputStream("Copy.java");
        )
```

```
        {
            int data;
            byte[] byteArr = new byte[2048];
            while ((data = in.read(byteArr)) != -1) {
                out.write(byteArr);
            }
        }
    }
}
```

a Class `Twist` executes successfully and creates its own copy with the name `Copy.java`.

b Class `Twist` executes successfully, doesn't throw any exceptions, but fails to create its own identical copy.

c Class `Copy.java` fails to compile.

d Class `Twist` doesn't compile.

Watch out! Class `FileOutputStream` defines method `write()` that accepts an `int` parameter. But when you use this method to write an `int` value, it writes only 1 byte to the output stream. An `int` data type uses 4 bytes, or 32 bits. `write(int)` writes the 8 low-order bits of the argument passed to it. The 24 high-order bits are ignored. Here's an example that uses binary literals with underscores:

```
class FileStreamsAlwaysReadWriteBytes {
    public static void main(String args[]) throws Exception {
        try (
            OutputStream os = new FileOutputStream("temp.txt");    Writes 1 byte
            InputStream is = new FileInputStream("temp.txt");      (8 lower bits) to
        ) {                                                        underlying file;
            int i999 = 0b00000000_00000000_00000011_11100111;     999 is written
            int i20  = 0b00000000_00000000_00000000_00010100;     as 231
            os.write(i999);
            os.write(i20);
            System.out.println(i999 + ":" + is.read());      ◁
            System.out.println(i20 + ":" + is.read());    ◁
        }
    }
}
```

Writes 20 because 20 can be coded in 8 lower bits.

Prints 20:20   **Prints 999:231**

 EXAM TIP Method `write(int)` in class `OutputStream` writes a byte to the underlying output stream. If you write an `int` value by using this method, only the 8 low-order bits are written to the output stream; the rest are ignored.

In the next section, you'll see how buffering data reads and writes speeds up the I/O processes.

7.3.4   *Buffered I/O with byte streams*

Imagine you need to transfer a couple of boxes from one room of your home to another. Would you need less time if you transferred one box at a time, or if you loaded a couple of them in a container and moved the container? Of course, the latter would need less time. Similarly, buffering stores data in memory before sending a read or write request to the underlying I/O devices. Buffering *drastically* reduces the time required for performing reading and writing I/O operations.

To buffer data with byte streams, you need classes `BufferedInputStream` and `BufferedOutputStream`. You can instantiate a `BufferedInputStream` by passing it an `InputStream` instance. A `BufferedOutputStream` can be instantiated by passing it an `OutputStream` instance. You can also specify a buffer size or use the default size. Here are their constructors:

```
public BufferedInputStream(InputStream in)
public BufferedInputStream(InputStream in, int size)
public BufferedOutputStream(OutputStream out)
public BufferedOutputStream(OutputStream out, int size)
```

 EXAM TIP   The exam might test you on how to instantiate buffered streams correctly. To instantiate `BufferedInputStream`, you must pass it an object of `InputStream`. To instantiate `BufferedOutputStream`, you must pass it an object of `OutputStream`.

Let's compare reading and writing a PDF file of considerable size with and without using buffered streams. To start, let's read and write the PDF file for the Java 7 Language specification (jls7.pdf):

```
import java.io.*;
import java.util.Date;
public class NonBufferedBytesReadWrite {
    public static void main(String[] args) throws IOException {
        try (
            FileInputStream in = new FileInputStream("jls7.pdf");
            FileOutputStream out = new FileOutputStream("jls7-copy.pdf");
        )
        {
            long start = System.currentTimeMillis();

            int data;
            while ((data = in.read()) != -1) {
                out.write(data);
            }

            long end = System.currentTimeMillis();
            System.out.println("MilliSeconds elapsed : " + (end-start));
        }
    }
}
```

Size of jls7.pdf is 2.96 MB

Reads, writes 1 byte at a time

Outputs milliseconds used to copy jls7.pdf to jls-copy.pdf.

Let's see how the same I/O process performs using buffered streams:

```
import java.io.*;                                    Creates BufferedInputStream,
import java.util.Date;                          passing it object of FileInputStream.
public class BufferedReadWriteBytes{
    public static void main(String[] args) throws IOException {
        try (
            FileInputStream in = new FileInputStream("jls7.pdf");
            FileOutputStream out = new FileOutputStream("jls7-copy.pdf");
            BufferedInputStream bis = new BufferedInputStream(in);
            BufferedOutputStream bos = new BufferedOutputStream(out);
        )
        {                                                        Creates
            long start = System.currentTimeMillis();     BufferedOutputStream,
                                                          passing it object of
            int data;                                       FileOutputStream.
            while ((data = bis.read()) != -1) {
                bos.write(data);
            }
            long end = System.currentTimeMillis();
            System.out.println("MilliSeconds elapsed : " + (end-start));
        }                                            Outputs milliseconds used to
    }                                                copy jls7.pdf to jls-copy.pdf.
}
```

Reads and buffers data

Buffers and writes data

As exhibited by the preceding examples, buffered I/O operations are way faster than nonbuffered I/O operations.

You can use FileInputStream and FileOutputStream to read and write *only* byte data from and to an underlying file. These classes (FileInputStream and FileOutputStream) don't define methods to work with any other specific primitive data types or objects, which is what you might need most of the time. In the next section, you'll see how to read and write primitive values and strings by using DataInputStream and DataOutputStream.

7.3.5 *Primitive values and strings I/O with byte streams*

Data input and output streams let you read and write primitive values and strings from and to an underlying I/O stream in a machine-independent way. Data written with DataOutputStream can be read by DataInputStream. You can instantiate a DataInputStream by passing it an InputStream instance. A DataOutputStream can be constructed by passing it an OutputStream instance. Here are their constructors:

```
DataInputStream(InputStream in)
DataOutputStream(OutputStream out)
```

Here's an example of reading and writing char, int, double, and boolean primitive values and strings using data input and output streams.

```
import java.io.*;
public class ReadWritePrimitiveData {
```

```
public static void main(String... args) throws IOException {
    try (
        FileOutputStream fos = new FileOutputStream(
                                new File("myData.data"));
        DataOutputStream dos = new DataOutputStream(fos);

        FileInputStream fis = new FileInputStream("myData.data");
        DataInputStream dis = new DataInputStream(fis);
    ) {
        dos.writeChars("OS");
        dos.writeInt(999);
        dos.writeDouble(45.8);
        dos.writeBoolean(true);
        dos.writeUTF("Will score 100%");

        System.out.println(dis.readChar());
        System.out.println(dis.readChar());
        System.out.println(dis.readInt());
        System.out.println(dis.readDouble());
        System.out.println(dis.readBoolean());
        System.out.println(dis.readUTF());

        //System.out.println(dis.readBoolean());
    }
    }
}
```

Instantiates DataOutputStream by passing instance of FileOutputStream

Instantiates DataInputStream by passing instance of FileInputStream

Reads second char

Writes primitive data and Unicode String to output stream

Reads first char

Reads int value

Reads double value

Reads Boolean value

Reads Unicode string value

If uncommented, this line throws EOFException at runtime.

The contents of file myData.data are shown as a screenshot in figure 7.10. As you can see, this file doesn't store its data in human-readable form. It can be reconstructed using DataInputStream.

Any read operation by DataInput-Stream past the end of the file will throw an EOFException. The data should be read

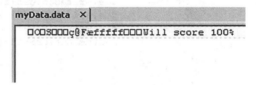

Figure 7.10   Snapshot of contents of file myData.data

in the same order as written by DataOutputStream. DataOutputStream writes the byte data for the corresponding primitive data. Each data type might be interpreted in a different manner and occupy a different number of bytes (for example, int uses 4 bytes, and double uses 8 bytes). If the data being read doesn't match the data that was written, you'll get unexpected values. For example, if you write a double value and read two int values instead, you'll get unexpected values:

```
import java.io.*;
public class ReadWritePrimitiveData1 {
    public static void main(String... args) throws IOException {
        try (
            FileOutputStream fos = new FileOutputStream(
                                    new File("myData.data"));
            DataOutputStream dos = new DataOutputStream(fos);
```

```
            FileInputStream fis = new FileInputStream("myData.data");
            DataInputStream dis = new DataInputStream(fis);
    ) {
        dos.writeDouble(45.8);                          ◁——|  Writes double
        System.out.println(dis.readInt());              ◁——┐      value
        System.out.println(dis.readInt());              ◁——┤  Reads int value
    }
                                                           |  Reads another
  }                                                        |  int value
}
```

The output of the preceding code is:

```
1078388326
1717986918
```

In the preceding code, bytes from a double value could be interpreted as int values, though incorrectly. What happens if you try to read bytes from a char value as int values?

```
import java.io.*;
public class ReadWritePrimitiveData1 {
    public static void main(String... args) throws IOException {
        try (
            FileOutputStream fos = new FileOutputStream(
                                        new File("myData.data"));
            DataOutputStream dos = new DataOutputStream(fos);

            FileInputStream fis = new FileInputStream("myData.data");
            DataInputStream dis = new DataInputStream(fis);          ) {
            dos.writeBoolean(true);
            dos.writeChar('A');                                 ◁——     Writes 2 bytes
            dos.writeInt(99);                                   ◁——┐        of data
            System.out.println(dis.readInt());                 ◁——┤     (char = 2 bytes)
        }
    }                        Reads 4 bytes of data; prints        |  Writes 4 bytes of
}                             16793856; interprets first          |  data (int = 4 bytes)
                              4 bytes as int value.
```

Writes 1 byte of data (Boolean = 1 byte of data) → [pointing to dos.writeBoolean(true);]

EXAM TIP If a mismatch occurs in the type of data written by Data-OutputStream and the type of data read by DataInputStream, you might not get a runtime exception. Because data streams read and write bytes, the read operation constructs the requested data from the available bytes, though incorrectly.

In the next section, you'll read and write the state of your objects to a file.

7.3.6 *Object I/O with byte streams: reading and writing objects*

To read and write objects, you can use *object streams*. An ObjectOutputStream can write primitive values and objects to an OutputStream, which can be read by an Object-InputStream. To write objects to a file, use a file for the stream. Objects of a class that implements the java.io.Serializable interface can be written to a stream. Serialization is making a deep copy of the object so the whole object graph is written—

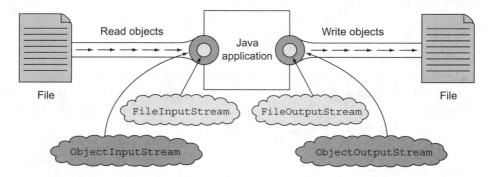

Figure 7.11 `ObjectOutputStream` **writes an object to a file by using** `FileOutput-`
`Stream`. `ObjectInputStream` **can reconstruct saved objects back from a file by using**
`FileInputStream.`

that is, all instance variables, and if some instance variables refer to some other objects, all the instance variables of the referred objects will be too (only if they implement `Serializable`), and so on. The default serialization process doesn't write the values of `static` or `transient` variables of an object. The reading process, or de-serialization, builds the complete object, including the dependencies.

You can use classes `ObjectInputStream` and `ObjectOutputStream` to read and write objects *and* primitive values. Figure 7.11 shows this arrangement.

You can instantiate these classes by passing them objects of `InputStream` or `Output-`
`Stream`. Here are their constructors that read from or write to a specified `InputStream` or `OutputStream`:

```
public ObjectInputStream(InputStream in)
public ObjectOutputStream(OutputStream out)
```

 EXAM TIP You can use `ObjectOutputStream` and `ObjectInputStream` to read and write all serializable objects *and* primitive values.

IMPLEMENT SERIALIZABLE TO READ AND WRITE OBJECTS FROM AND TO A FILE
Let's start by writing an object of class `Car` to a file. The following code declares a bare-bones class `Car` and writes its object to a file, object.data, by using `ObjectOutput-`
`Stream` and `FileOutputStream`:

```
import java.io.*;
class Car {}
class WriteObject{
    public static void main(String args[]) throws IOException{
        try (
            FileOutputStream out = new FileOutputStream("object.data");
            ObjectOutputStream oos = new ObjectOutputStream(out);
        ) {
            Car c = new Car();
            oos.writeObject(c);
```

```
            oos.flush();
        }
    }
}
```

Though the preceding code compiles successfully, it throws a `java.io.NotSerializable-Exception` at runtime. What went wrong? Class `Car` should implement the `Serializable` interface so that it can be written to and read from a file. Here's the modified code:

```
import java.io.*;
class Car implements Serializable {}                    ◄─┐ Car implements
class ReadWriteObject{                                      Serializable interface.
    public static void main(String args[]) throws Exception{
        try (
            FileOutputStream out = new FileOutputStream("object.data");
            ObjectOutputStream oos = new ObjectOutputStream(out);
            FileInputStream in = new FileInputStream("object.data");
            ObjectInputStream ois = new ObjectInputStream(in);
        ) {
            Car c = new Car();                          ┌ Writes object
            oos.writeObject(c);                      ◄─┘ c to file
            oos.flush();
            Car c2 = (Car)ois.readObject();          ◄─┐ readObject() returns
            System.out.println(c2);                      Object, so needs explicit
        }                                                cast to Car class.
    }
}
```

Apart from declaring to throw an `IOException`, method `readObject()` might also throw a `ClassNotFoundException`, if the JRE fails to retrieve the class information corresponding to the retrieved object.

 EXAM TIP   To write objects to a file, their classes should implement `java.io.Serializable`, or the code will throw a `java.io.NotSerializable-Exception`.

READ AND WRITE OBJECTS WITH NONSERIALIZABLE PARENT CLASSES

What happens if class `Car` extends another class, say `Vehicle`, which doesn't implement the `Serializable` interface? Would you be able to write `Car` objects to a file? In this case, the variables of the `Vehicle` class are serialized to a file. For example

```
import java.io.*;
class Vehicle {                              ◄─┐ Base class doesn't
    String name = "Vehicle";                     implement Serializable.
}
class Car extends Vehicle implements Serializable {   ◄─┐ Derived class
    String model = "Luxury";                              implements
}                                                         Serializable.
class ParentNotSerializable{
    public static void main(String args[]) throws Exception{
```

```
        try (
            FileOutputStream out = new FileOutputStream("object.data");
            ObjectOutputStream oos = new ObjectOutputStream(out);
            FileInputStream in = new FileInputStream("object.data");
            ObjectInputStream ois = new ObjectInputStream(in);
        ) {
            Car c = new Car();
            oos.writeObject(c);
            oos.flush();
            Car c2 = (Car)ois.readObject();
            System.out.println(c2.name + ":" + c2.model);     ⟵    Prints
        }                                                           Vehicle:Luxury
    }
}
```

READ AND WRITE OBJECTS WITH NONSERIALIZABLE DATA MEMBERS

Would you be able to write objects to Car to a file, if any of its object fields doesn't implement the Serializable interface? In this case, the code will throw a java .io.NotSerializableException when you attempt to *write* a Car object to a file. For example

```
import java.io.*;
class Engine {                            ⟵    Engine doesn't
    String make = "198768";                    implement Serializable.
}
class Car implements Serializable {       ⟵    Car
    String model = "Luxury";                    implements
    Engine engine = new Engine();               Serializable.
}
class DataMemberNotSerializable{
    public static void main(String args[]) throws Exception{
        try (
            FileOutputStream out = new FileOutputStream("object.data");
            ObjectOutputStream oos = new ObjectOutputStream(out);
        ) {
            Car c = new Car();
            oos.writeObject(c);               ⟵    Throws
            oos.flush();                            NotSerializableException.
        }
    }
}
```

 EXAM TIP A class whose object fields don't implement the Serializable interface can't be serialized even though the class itself implements the Serializable interface. An attempt to serialize such object fields will throw a runtime exception.

READ AND WRITE OBJECTS ALONG WITH PRIMITIVE VALUES FROM AND TO A FILE

You can use ObjectInputStream and ObjectOutputStream to read and write both objects and primitive values from and to a file. The data should be retrieved in the order that it was written. In the following example, class WritePrimAndObjects writes a boolean value and then a `Car` instance. These values should be retrieved in this order. An attempt to read mismatching data types will result in throwing runtime exception `OptionalDataException`:

Checked exceptions that readObject can throw: IOException, ClassNot-Found-Exception.

```
class ReadPrimAndObjects{
    public static void main(String args[]) throws IOException,
                                        ClassNotFoundException{
        try (
            FileInputStream in = new FileInputStream("object.data");
            ObjectInputStream ois = new ObjectInputStream(in);
        ) {
            System.out.println(ois.readBoolean());
            Car c = (Car)ois.readObject();
            System.out.println(c.name);
        }
    }
}
class Car implements Serializable{
    String name;
    Car(String value) {
        name = value;
    }
}
```

readObject returns instance of Object and can throw Optional-DataException ❶

 EXAM TIP   Retrieve the data (primitive and objects) in the order it was written using object streams, or it might throw a runtime exception.

The code at ❶ reads an object from the underlying stream. Method `readObject()` returns `Object`, which is explicitly casted to class `Car`. For the exam, you should know that this method can throw multiple exceptions:

- `ClassNotFoundException`—Class of a serialized object cannot be found
- `OptionalDataException`—Primitive data was found in the stream instead of objects.
- `IOException`—Any of the usual input-/output-related exceptions

THE TRANSIENT AND STATIC VARIABLES AREN'T WRITTEN TO A FILE

When you write objects to a file using `ObjectOutputStream`, its `transient` or `static` variables aren't written to the file. For example

```
import java.io.*;
class Car implements Serializable{
    String name;
    transient String model;        transient
    transient int days;            variables
    static int carCount;
    Car(String value) {
        name = value;
        model = "some value";      Assign value to
        days = 98;                 transient variables
        ++carCount;
    }
}
```

static variable

```
class ReadWriteCarObjects{
    public static void main(String args[]) throws Exception {
        try (
            FileOutputStream out = new FileOutputStream("object.data");
            ObjectOutputStream oos = new ObjectOutputStream(out);
            FileInputStream in = new FileInputStream("object.data");
            ObjectInputStream ois = new ObjectInputStream(in);
        ) {
            Car c = new Car("AAA");
            oos.writeObject(c);
            oos.flush();

            new Car("BBB");

            Car c2 = (Car)ois.readObject();
            System.out.println(c2.name);
            System.out.println(c2.model + ":" + c2.days);           Prints
                                                                    null:0
            System.out.println(c2.carCount);
        }                                                Prints 2
    }
}
```

In the preceding code, because the value of `transient` variables `model` and `days` wasn't written to the file, the deserialization process assigns default values to these variables: `null` for objects and 0 for `int` type.

 NOTE You can also change the serialization process using methods `defaultReadObject()` and `defaultWriteObject()`. But this is beyond the scope of this exam.

METHODS OF OBJECTINPUTSTREAM AND OBJECTOUTPUTSTREAM

Figure 7.12 shows the methods to read and write byte data, primitive data, objects, and a few miscellaneous methods of classes `ObjectInputStream` and `ObjectOutputStream`.

In this section, we covered how to read and write primitive data, strings, and objects to an underlying file by using *byte* I/O classes. Let's move forward with covering character I/O with readers and writers.

7.4   *Using character I/O with readers and writers*

 [7.2]   Use streams to read from and write to files by using classes in the java.io package including BufferedReader, BufferedWriter, File, FileReader, FileWriter, DataInputStream, DataOutputStream, ObjectOutputStream, ObjectInputStream, and PrintWriter

`Reader` and `Writer` are abstract base classes for reading and writing Unicode-compliant character data. They don't replace the byte-oriented I/O classes, but supplement them.

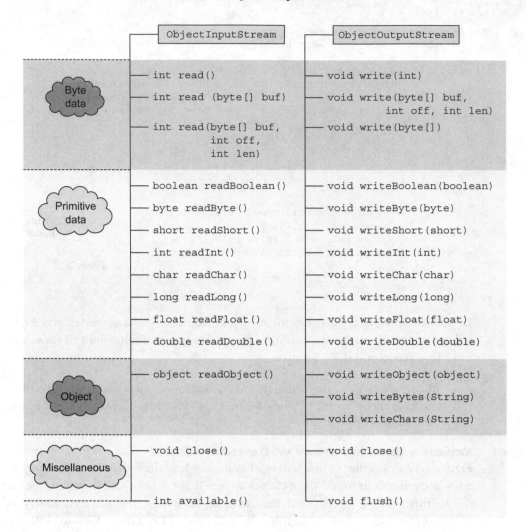

Figure 7.12 Methods of class `ObjectInputStream` **and** `ObjectOutputStream` **to read and write byte data, primitive data, and objects**

Classes `Reader` and `Writer` handle 16-bit Unicode well, which isn't supported by the byte-oriented `InputStream` and `OutputStream` classes. Also note that Java's primitive data type `char` stores 16-bit Unicode values. Even though you can use `InputStream` and `OutputStream` to read and write characters, you should use the character-oriented `Reader` and `Writer` classes to read and write character data. Internationalization is possible only by using 16-bit Unicode values. Also `Reader` and `Writer` classes offer faster I/O operations.

7.4.1 Abstract class java.io.Reader

Class `Reader` defines overloaded `read()` methods to read character data from an underlying data stream:

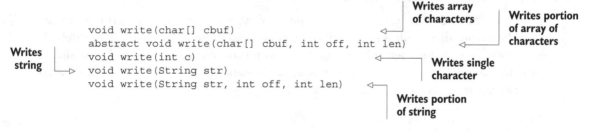

```
int read()
int read(char[] cbuf)
abstract int read(char[] cbuf, int off, int len)
```

Reads single character ←
Reads characters into array ←
Reads characters into portion of array ←

Class `Reader` implements `Closeable` (and its parent interface `AutoCloseable`). So `Reader` objects can be declared as resources with a try-with-resources statement.

 EXAM TIP Compare the overloaded `read()` methods of class `Input-Stream` with the `read()` methods of class `Reader`. The `read()` methods of `InputStream` accept an array of `byte` as their method parameter, and the `read()` methods of `Reader` accept an array of `char` as their method parameter.

Because class `Reader` is an abstract class, you won't use it to read data. Instead you'll use one of its concrete subclasses to do the reading for you. Figure 7.13 shows abstract class `Reader` and its subclasses (`BufferedReader` and `FileReader`) that are on the exam.

7.4.2 Abstract class java.io.Writer

The abstract class `Writer` defines overloaded `write()` methods to write character data to an underlying data source:

```
void write(char[] cbuf)
abstract void write(char[] cbuf, int off, int len)
void write(int c)
void write(String str)
void write(String str, int off, int len)
```

Writes array of characters ←
Writes portion of array of characters ←
Writes single character ←
Writes string →
Writes portion of string ←

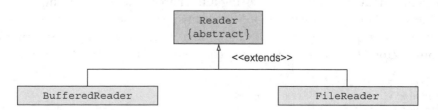

Figure 7.13 Abstract class `Reader` and its subclasses that are on the exam

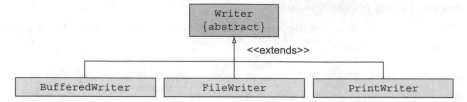

Figure 7.14   Abstract class `Writer` and its subclasses that are on the exam

Class `Writer` implements `Closeable` (and its parent interface `AutoCloseable`). So you can instantiate and use its objects with a try-with-resources statement, which results in an implicit call to `Writer`'s method `close()`. Reader's method `close()` is used to close the resources associated with the stream. Method `flush()` is used to write any saved values from a previous write, from a buffer, to the intended destination.

 EXAM TIP   With the overloaded `write()` methods of class `Writer`, you can write a single character or multiple characters, stored in `char` arrays or `String`, to a data source.

Because class `Writer` is an abstract class, you won't use it to write data. Instead you'll use one of its concrete subclasses to do the writing for you. Figure 7.14 shows abstract class `Writer` and its subclasses (`BufferedWriter`, `FileWriter`, and `PrintWriter`) that are on the exam.

Let's read and write files by using classes `FileReader` and `FileWriter`.

7.4.3   *File I/O with character streams*

`FileReader` and `FileWriter` are convenience classes for reading and writing character data from files. Unless specified, the instances of these classes assume the default character set of the operating system. You can instantiate a `FileReader` by passing it the name of a file as a string value or as a `File` instance. Following are the overloaded constructors of class `FileReader`:

```
FileReader(File file)
FileReader(String fileName)
```

You can instantiate `FileWriter` by passing it the name of a file as a string value or as a `File` instance. You also have the option of specifying whether you want to override the existing content of a file or append new content to it, by passing a `boolean` value to the constructor. Here are the overloaded constructors of class `FileWriter`:

```
FileWriter(File file)
FileWriter(File file, boolean append)
FileWriter(String fileName)
FileWriter(String fileName, boolean append)
```

The following listing shows an example of reading and writing characters from a file by using FileReader and FileWriter.

Listing 7.3 Reading and writing characters from files

```java
import java.io.*;

public class ReadChars{
    public static void main(String[] args) throws IOException {
        try (
            FileReader input = new FileReader("ReadChars.java");
            FileWriter output = new FileWriter("CopyReadChars.java");
        )
        {
            int data;

            while ((data = input.read()) != -1) {      ⟵┐  Read from
                output.write(data);      ⟵┐                 ReadChars.java until no
            }                             │                 more characters found
        }                                 │
    }                                Write character to
}                                    CopyReadChars.java
```

The preceding code is similar to the code shown in listing 7.2, which uses FileInput-Stream and FileOutputStream to read and write bytes from files. But it uses File-Reader to read characters from a source and FileWriter to write it to a destination.

Data buffering helps produce efficient and faster I/O operations. Buffered I/O with character streams is covered in the next section.

7.4.4 *Buffered I/O with character streams*

In the real world, nonbuffered data read and write operations are rare, because reading characters one at a time from a file is a costly affair. Whenever you call method read() on FileReader, it makes a read request to the underlying character stream. This slows the performance of your application.

To buffer data with character streams, you need classes BufferedReader and BufferedWriter. You can instantiate a BufferedReader by passing it a Reader instance. A BufferedWriter can be instantiated by passing it a Writer instance. You can also specify a buffer size or use the default size. Here are their constructors:

```java
public BufferedReader(Reader in)
public BufferedReader(Reader in, int sz)
public BufferedWriter(Writer out)
public BufferedWriter(Writer out, int sz)
```

 EXAM TIP The exam might test you on how to instantiate buffered character streams correctly. To instantiate BufferedReader, you must pass it an object of Reader. To instantiate BufferedWriter, you must pass it an object of Writer.

Class `BufferedReaderWriter` copies characters from `BufferedReaderWriter.java` to `Copy.java` using `BufferedReader` and `BufferedWriter`:

```java
import java.io.*;
public class BufferedReaderWriter{
    public static void main(String... args){
        try (
            FileReader fr = new FileReader("BufferedReaderWriter.java");
            BufferedReader br = new BufferedReader(fr);
            FileWriter fw = new FileWriter("Copy.java");
            BufferedWriter bw = new BufferedWriter(fw);
        ){
            String line = null;
            while ((line = br.readLine())!= null) {      Reads
                bw.write(line);                           single line
                bw.newLine();           Write characters to
            }                           BufferedWriter
        }
        catch (IOException ioe) {       readLine() and close() can
            System.out.println (ioe);   throw IOException; Reader and
        }                               Writer instantiation can throw
    }                                   FileNotFoundException
}
```

The preceding code instantiates `BufferedReader` by using a `FileReader` instance and `BufferedWriter` by using a `FileWriter` instance. Instead of using method `read()`, it uses method `readLine()` to read a single line from the character stream. Method `readLine()` doesn't include line-feed (`\n`) and carriage-return (`\r`) characters. So you use `bw.newLine()` to insert a new line in the output file.

Class `BufferedReader` also defines methods `read()` and `read(char[])` to read single characters of data from `Reader`. But these methods are implemented differently than the same methods of class `FileReader`. Class `BufferedReader` buffers data on the first read, and the subsequent request to the `read()` methods returns data from the buffer. But this isn't the case with class `FileReader`.

In the next section, you'll work with `PrintWriter`, which can be used to write all primitive values and strings to an underlying `File`, `OutputStream`, or `Writer` object.

7.4.5 *Data streams with character streams: using PrintWriter to write to a file*

Class `PrintWriter` can be used to print (write) formatted representations of objects to a file. This class implements all the `print` methods found in class `PrintStream`. This essentially means that you can use all the overloaded `print` methods that you've been using (via the class variable `System.out`) to write data to a file, a `PrintWriter` instance. Here's an example:

```java
public class WriteToFileUsingPrintWriter{
    public static void main(String... args){
```

```
try {
    FileWriter fw = new FileWriter("file1.txt", true);        Instantiates
    PrintWriter pw = new PrintWriter(fw);              ◄       PrintWriter

    pw.write(97);                                ◄       Overloaded write()
    pw.write("String");                                  methods
    pw.write("PartialString", 0, 4);
    pw.write(new char[]{'c','h','a','r'});
    pw.write(new char[]{'c','h','a','r'}, 1, 1);

    pw.print(true);                              ◄       Overloaded print()
    pw.print('a');                                       methods
    pw.print(12.45f);
    pw.print(41.87);
    pw.print(39865L);
    pw.print(pw);
    pw.print(new Integer(10));

    pw.println(true);                            ◄       Overloaded println()
    pw.println('a');                                     methods
    pw.println(12.45f);
    pw.println(41.87);
    pw.println(39865L);
    pw.println(pw);
    pw.println(new Integer(10));

    pw.close();                                  ◄       Flush and
}                                                        close stream
catch (IOException ioe) {
    System.out.println(ioe);
}
    }
}
```

The preceding example creates a `PrintWriter` instance by using a `FileWriter` instance. It then uses the overloaded version of methods `write()`, `print()`, and `println()` to write to the underlying file. The overloaded versions of methods `print()` and `println()` are convenient methods to print (or write) data of primitive types and objects. A `PrintWriter` instance can be created by passing it the name of a file as a string value or as a `File` instance with or without specifying an explicit character set to use. These are created without automatic line flushing. You can also instantiate `PrintWriter` by passing it a `Writer` instance and a `boolean` value specifying auto-flushing. Here's the list of its constructors:

```
PrintWriter(File file)
PrintWriter(File file, String charset)
PrintWriter(String fileName)
PrintWriter(String fileName, String charset)
PrintWriter(Writer out, boolean autoFlush)
```

Table 7.4 shows the commonly used methods for class `PrintWriter` and the valid method arguments.

Table 7.4 Commonly used methods with their valid arguments

Method	Valid method arguments
write	int/ char[]/ String
print	boolean/ int/ char[]/ char/ long/ float/ double/ Object/ String
println	boolean/ int/ char[]/ char/ long/ float/ double/ Object/ String
format	(Locale locale, String format, Object... args)
format	(String format, Object... args)
printf	(Locale locale, String format, Object... args)
printf	(String format, Object... args)

 NOTE Methods format() and printf(), listed in table 7.4, accept a format string and arguments. These methods are covered in detail in chapters 5 and 12.

It's easy to confuse how the constructors of the I/O classes can be chained. The next section will help you understand the concept.

7.4.6 *Constructor chaining with I/O classes*

Most programmers get cold feet when they think about constructor chaining in I/O classes. It's quite intimidating. Do you think the following line of code instantiates a BufferedReader using FileReader and File instances correctly?

```
BufferedReader br = new BufferedReader(new FileReader(new File("ab.txt")));
```

Let's evaluate the preceding line of code. The only way to construct an object of class BufferedReader is by passing to it an object of class Reader. Because class FileReader passes the IS-A Reader test, FileReader is a valid argument to the constructor of class BufferedReader. Now, class FileReader can accept an argument of either String or File, and class File accepts an argument of type String. So the preceding line of code is valid.

Figure 7.15 shows the inheritance tree of the I/O classes you need to know for the exam, together with their constructors. It should help answer all questions related to chaining of constructors in file I/O.

With a firm understanding of working with byte and character streams to read and write all types of data to a file, let's move on to reading and writing data from a console.

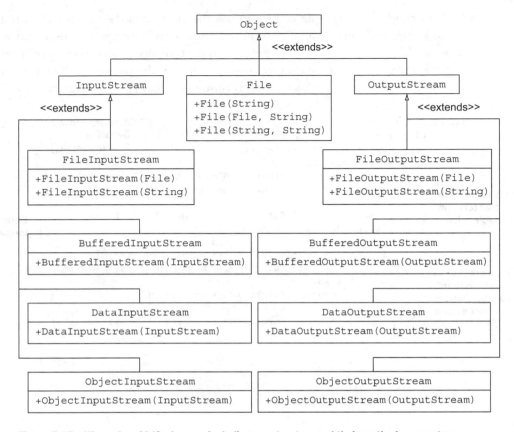

Figure 7.15 Hierarchy of I/O classes, including constructors and their method parameters

7.5 *Working with the console*

 [7.1] Read and write data from the console

Class `java.io.Console` defines methods to access the character-based console device, associated with the current Java virtual machine. It's interesting to note that you *may* or *may not* be able to access the console associated with a JVM, depending on the underlying platform and how the JVM was started. If you invoke a JVM from the command line without redirecting the standard input and output streams, you'll be able to access its console, which will typically be connected to the keyboard and display from which the virtual machine was launched. You may *not* be able to access the console associated with a JVM, if it started automatically as a result of execution of some other program.

> **NOTE** You'll not get access to the console when using IDEs like Eclipse. To execute code that needs to access the console, work with a text editor and command prompt.

Let's work with an example of how to use the class `Console` to interact with a user. Code in the following example outputs a formatted message to a user and accepts input and a password. The `Console` object supports secure password entry by its method `readPassword()`. This method suppresses echoing of the password when a user enters it. Also the return type of this method is (mutable) `char[]` and not `String`:

```java
public class InteractWithUserUsingConsole{
    public static void main(String... args){
        Console console = System.console();
        if (console != null) {
            String file = console.readLine("Enter File to delete:");
            console.format("About to delete %s %n", file);

            console.printf("Sure to delete %s(Y/N)?", file);
            String delete = console.readLine();

            if (delete.toUpperCase().trim().equals("Y")) {
                char[] pwd = console.readPassword("Enter Password:");
                if (pwd.length>0)
                    console.format("Deleted %s", file);
                else
                    console.format("No password. Cancelling deletion");
            }
            else
                console.format("Operation cancelled... %nNow exiting.");
        }
        else
            System.out.println("No console");
    }
}
```

❶ Accesses console by calling System.console().

❷ Prompts user to enter filename to delete.

❸ Uses format() to display text and variable values.

❹ Outputs formatted data.

❺ Prompts user to enter password; password values aren't echoed

The code at ❶ accesses an object of class `Console` by calling `System.console()`. This method returns `null` if no console is associated with the current JVM. You can't create an object of this class yourself. Class `Console` doesn't define a public constructor.

The code at ❷ uses `readLine()` to prompt a user to enter the name of the file to delete. The answer is read by the same method. The code at ❸ and ❹ uses methods `format()` and `printf()` to print formatted data to the user and accept whether the code proceeds with deleting the file. If the user enters Y or y, the code at ❺ prompts the user to enter the password and reads it using `readPassword()`. If a password is entered, an appropriate message is displayed to the user.

 EXAM TIP If no console device is available, `System.console()` returns `null`. A `null` value signals that either the program was launched in a non-interactive environment or perhaps the underlying operating system doesn't support the console operations.

Table 7.5 lists important methods of class `Console`.

Coverage of class `Console` brings us to the end of this chapter on the basics of file I/O.

Table 7.5 Important methods of class `Console` from the Java API documentation

Constructor	Description
`Console format(String fmt, Object... args)`	Writes a formatted string to the console's output stream by using the specified format string and arguments.
`Console printf(String format, Object... args)`	A convenience method to write a formatted string to the console's output stream by using the specified format string and arguments
`String readLine()`	Reads a single line of text from the console.
`String readLine(String fmt, Object... args)`	Provides a formatted prompt, and then reads a single line of text from the console.
`char[] readPassword()`	Reads a password or passphrase from the console with echoing disabled.
`char[] readPassword(String fmt, Object... args)`	Provides a formatted prompt, and then reads a password or passphrase from the console with echoing disabled.

7.6 *Summary*

This chapter covers the fundamentals of Java I/O. It starts with an introduction to the streams. The Java I/O stream is an abstraction of a data source or a data destination. An input stream is used to read data from a data source. An output stream is used to write data to a data destination.

To read from and write to files, you'll need to work with class `File`. `File` is an abstract representation of a path to a file or a directory. You can use an object of class `File` to create a new file or directory, delete it, or inquire about or modify its attributes. You can read the contents of a file or write to it by using byte and character I/O classes.

Byte streams work with reading and writing byte data. They're broadly categorized as input streams and output streams. All input streams extend the base abstract class `java.io.InputStream`, and all output streams extend the base abstract class `java.io.OutputStream`.

Class `java.io.InputStream` is an abstract base class for all the input streams in Java. It's extended by all the classes that need to read bytes (for example, image data) from multiple data sources. Class `java.io.OutputStream` is also an abstract class. It's the base class for all the output streams in Java. It's extended by all the classes that need to write bytes (for example, image data) to multiple data destinations.

To read and write any byte data from and to files, you can use `FileInputStream` and `FileOutputStream`. To buffer data with byte streams, use classes `BufferedInput-Stream` and `BufferedOutputStream`.

Data input and output streams let you read and write primitive values and strings from and to an underlying I/O stream in a machine-independent way. `DataInput-Stream` and `DataOutputStream` are decorator classes that define methods for reading and writing primitive values and strings. Data written with `DataOutputStream` can be read by `DataInputStream`.

To read and write objects, you can use object streams. An `ObjectOutputStream` can write primitive values and objects to an `OutputStream`, which can be read by an `ObjectInputStream`. The objects to be written to a file must implement the `java.io.Serializable` interface.

`Reader` and `Writer` are abstract base classes for reading and writing Unicode-compliant character data. `FileReader` and `FileWriter` are convenience classes for reading and writing character data from files. To buffer data with character streams, use `BufferedReader` and `BufferedWriter` classes.

Class `PrintWriter` can be used to print (write) formatted representations of objects to a file. Class `java.io.Console` defines methods to access the character-based console device associated with the current JVM.

REVIEW NOTES

This section lists the main points covered in this chapter.

Working with class java.io.File

- `File` is an abstract representation of a path to a file or a directory.
- You can use an object of class `File` to create a new file or directory, delete it, or inquire about or modify its attributes.
- A `File` instance might not be necessarily associated with an actual file or directory.
- `File`'s method `isDirectory()` returns `true` if the path it refers to is a directory.
- `File`'s method `isFile()` returns `true` if the path it refers to is a file.
- For a directory, `File`'s method `list()` returns an array of subdirectories and files.
- You can create a `File` instance that represents a nonexisting file on your file system. And you can even invoke methods like `isFile()` without getting an exception.
- The objects of class `File` are immutable; the pathname represented by a `File` object can't be changed.
- Methods `createNewFile()`, `mkdir()`, and `mkdirs()` can be used to create new files or directories.

Using byte stream I/O

- Class `java.io.InputStream` is an abstract base class for all the input streams.
- Class `InputStream` defines multiple overloaded versions of method `read()`, which can be used to read a single byte of data as `int`, or multiple bytes into a byte array.
- Method `read()` returns the next byte of data, or `-1` if the end of the stream is reached. It doesn't throw an `EOFException`.

- Method `close()` is another important method of class `InputStream`. Calling `close()` on a stream releases the system resources associated with it.

- Class `java.io.OutputStream` is an abstract class. It's the base class for all the output streams in Java.

- The most important method of `OutputStream` class is `write()`, which can be used to write a single byte of data or multiple bytes from a byte array to a data destination.

- Class `OutputStream` also defines methods `write()`, `flush()`, and `close()`. So these are valid methods that can be called on any objects of classes that extend class `OutputStream`.

- All the classes that include `OutputStream` in their name—`FileOutputStream`, `ObjectOutputStream`, `BufferedOutputStream`, and `DataOutputStream`—extend abstract class `OutputStream`, directly or indirectly.

- To read and write raw bytes from and to a file, use `FileInputStream` and `FileOutputStream`.

- `FileInputStream` is instantiated by passing it a `File` instance or string value. It can't be instantiated by passing it another `InputStream`.

- Instantiation of `FileOutputStream` creates a stream to write to a file specified either as a `File` instance or a string value. You can also pass a `boolean` value specifying whether to append to the existing file contents.

- Copying a file's content might not copy its attributes. To copy a file, it's advisable to use methods such as `copy()` from class `java.nio.file.Files`.

- I/O operations that require reading and writing of a single byte from and to a file are a costly affair. To optimize the operation, you can use a byte array.

- Unlike `read()`, `read(byte[])` doesn't return the read bytes. It returns the count of bytes read, or `-1` if no more data can be read. The actual data is read in the byte array that's passed to it as a method parameter.

- Method `write(int)` in class `OutputStream` writes a byte to the underlying output stream. If you write an `int` value by using this method, only the 8 low-order bits are written to the output stream; the rest are ignored.

- To buffer data with byte streams, you need classes `BufferedInputStream` and `BufferedOutputStream`.

- You can instantiate a `BufferedInputStream` by passing it an `InputStream` instance.

- A `BufferedOutputStream` can be instantiated by passing it an `OutputStream` instance.

- You can specify a buffer size or use the default size for both `BufferedInputStream` and `BufferedOutputStream`.

- To instantiate `BufferedInputStream`, you must pass it an object of `InputStream`. To instantiate `BufferedOutputStream`, you must pass it an object of `OutputStream`.

- You can use `FileInputStream` and `FileOutputStream` to read and write only byte data from and to an underlying file. These classes (`FileInputStream` and `FileOutputStream`) don't define methods to work with any other specific primitive data types or objects.

- Data input and output streams let you read and write primitive values and strings from and to an underlying I/O stream in a machine-independent way. Data written with `DataOutputStream` can be read by `DataInputStream`.

- If a mismatch occurs in the type of data written by `DataOutputStream` and the type of data read by `DataInputStream`, you might not get a runtime exception. Because data streams read and write bytes, the read operation constructs the requested data from the available bytes, though incorrectly.

- An `ObjectOutputStream` can write primitive values and objects to an `OutputStream`, which can be read by an `ObjectInputStream`.

- To write objects to a file, their classes should implement `java.io.Serializable`, or the code will throw a `java.io.NotSerializableException`.

- If a class implements the `Serializable` interface, but its base class doesn't, the class's instance can be serialized.

- A class whose object fields don't implement the `Serializable` interface can't be serialized even though the class itself implements the `Serializable` interface. An attempt to serialize such object fields will throw a runtime exception.

- Retrieve the data (primitive and objects) in the order it was written using object streams, or it might throw a runtime exception.

- When you write objects to a file using `ObjectOutputStream`, its `transient` or `static` variables aren't written to the file.

Using character I/O with readers and writers

- `Reader` and `Writer` are abstract base classes for reading and writing Unicode-compliant character data.

- Classes `Reader` and `Writer` handle 16-bit Unicode well, which isn't supported by the byte-oriented `InputStream` and `OutputStream` classes.

- Abstract class `Reader` defines overloaded `read()` methods to read character data from an underlying data stream.

- Class `Reader` implements `Closeable` (and its parent interface `AutoCloseable`). So `Reader` objects can be declared as resources with a try-with-resources statement.

- Compare the overloaded `read()` methods of class `InputStream` with the `read()` methods of class `Reader`. The `read()` methods of `InputStream` accept an array of `byte` as their method parameter, and the `read()` methods of `Reader` accept an array of `char` as their method parameter.

- Abstract class `Writer` defines overloaded `write()` methods to write character data to an underlying data source.

- With the overloaded write() methods of class Writer, you can write a single character or multiple characters stored in char arrays or string to a data source.
- FileReader and FileWriter are convenience classes for reading and writing character data from files.
- You can instantiate a FileReader by passing it the name of a file as a string value or as a File instance.
- You can instantiate a FileWriter by passing it the name of a file as a string value or as a File instance. You also have the option of specifying whether you want to override the existing content of a file or append new content to it by passing a boolean value to the constructor.
- To buffer data with character streams, you need classes BufferedReader and BufferedWriter.
- You can instantiate a BufferedReader by passing it a Reader instance.
- You can instantiate a BufferedWriter by passing it a Writer instance.
- You can also specify a buffer size or use the default size for both Buffered-Reader and BufferedWriter.
- Class PrintWriter can be used to print (write) formatted representations of objects to a file. This class implements all the print() methods found in class PrintStream.
- This essentially means that you can use all the overloaded print() methods that you've been using (via the class variable System.out) to write data to a file, a PrintWriter instance.

Working with the console

- Class java.io.Console defines methods to access the character-based console device associated with the current JVM.
- You may or may not be able to access the console associated with a JVM, depending on the underlying platform and how the JVM was started.
- If you invoke a JVM from the command line without redirecting the standard input and output streams, you'll be able to access its console, which will typically be connected to the keyboard and display from which the virtual machine was launched.
- You may not be able to access the console associated with a JVM if it started automatically as a result of the execution of some other program.
- You will not get access to the console when using IDEs like Eclipse.
- You can access an object of class Console by calling System.console().
- If no console device is available, System.console() returns null. A null value signals that either the program was launched in a noninteractive environment or perhaps the underlying operating system doesn't support the console operations.
- You can't create an object of Console yourself. Class Console doesn't define a public constructor.

SAMPLE EXAM QUESTIONS

Q 7-1. What's the output of the following code?

```java
import java.io.*;
class Q1 {
    public static void main(String args[]) throws IOException {
        DataOutputStream dos = new DataOutputStream(
                                new FileOutputStream("contacts.txt"));
        dos.writeDouble(999.999);
        DataInputStream dis = new DataInputStream(
                                new FileInputStream("contacts.txt"));
        System.out.println(dis.read());
        System.out.println(dis.read());
        dis.close();
        dos.close();
    }
}
```

    a   999.999
        -1

    b   999
        999

    c   999.999
        EOFException

    d None of the above

Q 7-2. Which options are true for the following code?

```java
import java.io.*;
class ReadFromConsole {
    public static void main(String args[]) throws IOException {
        Console console = System.console();
        String name = "";
        while (name.trim().equals("")) {
            name = console.readLine("What is your name?\n");
            console.printf(name);
        }
    }
}
```

    a Class `ReadFromConsole` can be used to repeatedly prompt a user to enter a name, until the user doesn't enter a value.

    b `console.readLine` prints the prompt `What is your name?` and waits for the user to enter a value.

    c `console.printf(name)` prints the value, entered by the user, back to the console.

    d Class `ReadFromConsole` can never throw a `NullPointerException`.

Q 7-3. Select the incorrect statements.

a PrintWriter can be used to write a String to the text file data.txt.

b PrintWriter can be used to write to FileOutputStream.

c PrintWriter's format and println methods can write a formatted string by using the specified format string and arguments.

d None of the methods or constructors of class PrintWriter throw I/O exceptions.

Q 7-4. Assuming that a user enters the values *eJava* and *Guru*, when prompted to enter username and password values, what values would be sent to file login-credentials.txt when using the following code?

```
class FromConsoleToFile {
    public static void main(String args[]) throws Exception {
        try (PrintWriter pw = new PrintWriter(
                          new File("login-credentials.txt"));) {
            Console console = System.console();
            String username = console.readLine("Username:");
            String pwd = console.readPassword("Password:");

            pw.println(username);
            pw.println(pwd);
            pw.flush();
        }
    }
}
```

a eJava
   Guru

b eJava
   ****

c eJava
   \<BLANK LINE>

d eJava
   String@b6546

e Compilation error

f Runtime exception

Q 7-5. Assuming that the variable file refers to a valid File object, which of the following options can be used to instantiate a BufferedInputStream?

a BufferedInputStream bis = new BufferedInputStream(file);

b BufferedInputStream bis = new DataInputStream(new FileInputStream (file));

c BufferedInputStream bis = new BufferedInputStream(new DataInput-Stream(new FileInputStream(file)));

d BufferedInputStream bis = new BufferedInputStream(new FileInput-Stream(new DataInputStream(file)));

Q 7-6. Which option(s) will make the `Console` object accessible?

- **a** `Console console = new Console(System.in, System.out);`
- **b** `Console console = System.console();`
- **c** `Console console = System.getConsole();`
- **d** `Console console = System.accessConsole();`
- **e** `Console console = new Console();`
- **f** `Console console = System.createConsole();`
- **g** None of the above

Q 7-7. Given the following code to read and write instances of `Phone`, which definition of class `Phone` will persist only its variable model?

```
class ReadWriteObjects {
    public void write(Phone ph, String fileName) throws Exception {
        ObjectOutputStream oos = new ObjectOutputStream(
                                    new FileOutputStream(fileName));
        oos.writeObject(ph);
        oos.flush();
        oos.close();
    }
    public Phone read(String fileName) throws Exception {
        ObjectInputStream ois = new ObjectInputStream(
                                    new FileInputStream(fileName));
        Phone ph = (Phone)ois.readObject();
        ois.close();
        return ph;
    }
}
```

- **a**
  ```
  class Phone implements Serializable {
      int sessionId;
      String model = "EJava";
  }
  ```

- **b**
  ```
  class Phone {
      transient int sessionId;
      String model = "EJava";
  }
  ```

- **c**
  ```
  class Phone implements Persistable {
      transient int sessionId;
      String model = "EJava";
  }
  ```

- **d**
  ```
  class Phone implements Serializable {
      transient int sessionId;
      String model = "EJava";
  }
  ```

Q 7-8. Which lines of code, when inserted at //INSERT CODE HERE, will enable class Copy to copy contents from file ejava.txt to ejava-copy.txt?

```
class Copy {
    public static void main(String args[]) {
        try {
            InputStream fis = new DataInputStream(new FileInputStream(
                                    new File("eJava.txt")));
            OutputStream fos = new DataOutputStream(new FileOutputStream(
                                    new File("eJava-copy.txt")));
            int data = 0;
            while ((data = fis.read()) != -1) {
                fos.write(data);
            }
        }
        //catch (/* INSERT CODE HERE */) {
        }
        finally {
            try {
                if (fos != null) fos.close();
                if (fis != null) fis.close();
            }
            catch (IOException e) {}
        }
    }
}
```

a catch (IOException e) {

b catch (FileNotFoundException e) {

c catch (FileNotFoundException | IOException e) {

d catch (IOException | FileNotFoundException e) {

Q 7-9. Which option, when inserted at //INSERT CODE HERE, will enable method read() in class ReadFile to read and output its own source file?

```
class ReadFile{
    public void read() throws IOException{
        File f = new File("ReadFile.java");
        FileReader fr = new FileReader(f);
        BufferedReader br = new BufferedReader(fr);
        String line = null;
        //INSERT CODE HERE
            System.out.println(line);
        br.close();
        fr.close();
    }
}
```

a while ((line = br.readLine()) != null)

b while ((line = fr.readLine()) != null)

```
c  while ((line = f.readLine()) != null)

d  while ((line = br.readLine()) != -1)

e  while ((line = fr.readLine()) != -1)

f  while ((line = f.readLine()) != -1)
```

Q 7-10. Given the following XML, which code options, when inserted at `//INSERT CODE HERE`, will write this XML (in exactly the same format) to a text file?

```
<emp>
<id>8743</id>
<name>Harry</name>
</emp>
class WriteXML{
    public void writeEmpData() throws IOException{
        File f = new File("empdata.txt");
        PrintWriter pw = null;
    //INSERT CODE HERE
        pw.close();
    }
}
```

```
a  pw = new PrintWriter(f);
   pw.println("<emp>");
   pw.write("<id>");
   pw.writeInt(8743);
   pw.println("</id>");
   pw.print("<name>Harry</name>");
   pw.print("</emp>");
   pw.flush();

b  pw = new PrintWriter(new FileOutputStream(f));
   pw.write("<emp>");
   pw.write("<id>8743</id>");
   pw.write("<name>Harry</name>");
   pw.write("</emp>");
   pw.flush();

c  pw = new PrintWriter(f);
   pw.println("<emp>");
   pw.println("<id>8743</id>");
   pw.println("<name>Harry</name>");
   pw.println("</emp>");
   pw.flush();

d  pw = new PrintWriter(new FileOutputStream(f));
   pw.println("<emp>");
   pw.println("<id>8743</id>");
   pw.println("<name>Harry</name>");
   pw.println("</emp>");
   pw.flush();
```

ANSWERS TO SAMPLE EXAM QUESTIONS

A 7-1. d

[7.2] Use streams to read from and write to files by using classes in the java.io package including BufferedReader, BufferedWriter, File, FileReader, FileWriter, DataInput-Stream, DataOutputStream, ObjectOutputStream, ObjectInputStream, and PrintWriter

Explanation: `dos.writeDouble(999.999)` writes 8 bytes of data to the underlying stream, and `dis.read()` reads a single byte of data from the underlying stream, interprets it as an integer value, and outputs it. So the code neither prints `999.999` nor throws an `EOFException`.

A 7-2. a, b, c

[7.1] Read and write data from the console

Explanation: Option (d) is incorrect because `System.console()` might return `null`, depending on how the JVM is invoked. A console isn't available to a JVM if it's started using another program or a background process, or if the underlying OS doesn't support it. In such cases, `console.readLine` throws a `NullPointerException`.

A 7-3. d

[7.2] Use streams to read from and write to files by using classes in the java.io package including BufferedReader, BufferedWriter, File, FileReader, FileWriter, DataInput-Stream, DataOutputStream, ObjectOutputStream, ObjectInputStream, and PrintWriter

Explanation: Options (a) and (b) are correct statements. A `PrintWriter` can be used to write to a file, an `OutputStream`, and a `Writer`.

Option (c) is also a correct statement because the `PrintWriter`'s methods `format()` and `printf()` can write a formatted string by using the specified format string and arguments.

Option (d) is an incorrect statement. Some of the constructors of `PrintWriter` may throw I/O exceptions (for example, when a file couldn't be found). But none of the methods of `PrintWriter` throw an exception. You can use `checkError()` to verify if an error has occurred (for example, format conversion has failed).

A 7-4. e

[7.2] Use streams to read from and write to files by using classes in the java.io package including BufferedReader, BufferedWriter, File, FileReader, FileWriter, DataInput-Stream, DataOutputStream, ObjectOutputStream, ObjectInputStream, and PrintWriter

[7.1] Read and write data from the console

Explanation: The code fails to compile because the return type of method read-Password() is char[] and not String. If the type of the variable pwd is changed from

String to char[], the contents of the file login-credentials.txt will match as shown in option (a). The overloaded println() method in class PrintWriter accepts a char[] parameter and prints its individual characters to the underlying file, OutputStream, or Writer.

A 7-5. c

[7.2] Use streams to read from and write to files by using classes in the java.io package including BufferedReader, BufferedWriter, File, FileReader, FileWriter, DataInput-Stream, DataOutputStream, ObjectOutputStream, ObjectInputStream, and PrintWriter

Explanation: Options (a), (b), and (d) won't compile. Option (a) is incorrect. To instantiate BufferedReader, you must pass to its constructor an instance of Input-Stream. In option (b), you can't instantiate BufferedInputStream by invoking a constructor of DataInputStream. In option (d), you can't instantiate FileInputStream by passing it an instance of InputStream. It needs an instance of a File or String.

A 7-6. b

[7.1] Read and write data from the console

Explanation: Options (a), (c), (d), and (f) are invalid code options. Option (e) is incorrect because Console's constructor is defined as private. They won't compile.

A 7-7. d

[7.2] Use streams to read from and write to files by using classes in the java.io package including BufferedReader, BufferedWriter, File, FileReader, FileWriter, DataInput-Stream, DataOutputStream, ObjectOutputStream, ObjectInputStream, and PrintWriter

Explanation: To persist instances of a class, the class must implement the Serializable interface. Serializable is a marker interface; it doesn't define any methods. Also, to prevent a field from persisting, define it as a transient variable.

   Option (a) doesn't mark the field sessionId as transient.
   Option (b) doesn't implement either Serializable or Externalizable.
   Option (c) implements the Persistable interface, which doesn't exist.

A 7-8. a

[7.2] Use streams to read from and write to files by using classes in the java.io package including BufferedReader, BufferedWriter, File, FileReader, FileWriter, DataInput-Stream, DataOutputStream, ObjectOutputStream, ObjectInputStream, and PrintWriter

Explanation: Code in class Copy can throw two checked exceptions: FileNotFound-Exception and IOException. Instantiation of FileInputStream and FileOutput-Stream can throw a FileNotFoundException. Calling methods read() and write()

can throw an IOException. Because IOException is the base class of FileNotFound-Exception, the exception handler for IOException will handle FileNotFound-Exception also.

Option (b) won't handle the IOException thrown by methods read() and write().

Options (c) and (d) are incorrect because alternatives in a multi-catch statement must not pass the IS-A test. The alternatives used in these options pass the IS-A test; FileNotFoundException extends IOException.

A 7-9. a

[7.2] Use streams to read from and write to files by using classes in the java.io package including BufferedReader, BufferedWriter, File, FileReader, FileWriter, DataInput-Stream, DataOutputStream, ObjectOutputStream, ObjectInputStream, and PrintWriter

Explanation: Method readLine() isn't defined in classes File and FileReader. It's defined only in class BufferedReader. Also, readLine() returns null if the end of the stream has been reached.

A 7-10. c, d

[7.2] Use streams to read from and write to files by using classes in the java.io package including BufferedReader, BufferedWriter, File, FileReader, FileWriter, DataInput-Stream, DataOutputStream, ObjectOutputStream, ObjectInputStream, and PrintWriter

Explanation: Option (a) won't compile. Class PrintWriter doesn't define method writeInt(). It defines overloaded write() methods with accepted method parameters of type char[], int, or String.

Option (b) is incorrect because it writes all the given XML in a single line, without inserting line breaks.

Option (c) is correct. The overloaded println() method in PrintWriter writes data to the underlying stream and then terminates the line.

Option (d) is correct. A PrintWriter can be used to write to a byte stream (OutputStream) and a character stream (Writer).

Java file I/O (NIO.2)

8

Exam objectives covered in this chapter	What you need to know
[8.1] Operate on file and directory paths with the `Path` class	How to create and manipulate real, absolute, and symbolic paths to files and directories.
[8.2] Check, delete, copy, or move a file or directory with the `Files` class	How to work with class `Files` and `Path` objects to create files and directories, check for their existence, and delete, copy, and move them.
[8.3] Read and change file and directory attributes, focusing on the `BasicFileAttributes`, `DosFileAttributes`, and `PosixFileAttributes` interfaces	How to use class `Files` to access and modify the individual and group of file and directory attributes—namely, `basic`, `dos`, and `posix`. How to access or modify attributes that aren't supported by the underlying operating system.
[8.4] Recursively access a directory tree using the `DirectoryStream` and `FileVisitor` interfaces	How to use `DirectoryStream`, `FileVisitor`, and `SimpleFileVisitor` to walk a directory tree. How to define code that should execute when a file is visited, before and after a directory is visited.
[8.5] Find a file with the `PathMatcher` interface	How to use `PathMatcher` to find directory names and filenames that match a regex or glob pattern.
[8.6] Watch a directory for changes by using the `WatchService` interface	How to set a watch on a directory for creation, modification, and deletion of elements from it. How to listen to these events and define code that should execute when an event occurs.

Think of any real-world application—almost all of them need to communicate with the file system to store, access, or manipulate their data or configuration values. Prior to Java 7, file system access and management has always been full of challenges. Often developers used native code to work with simple or advanced operations like copying or moving files atomically, querying their attributes, monitoring changes in a folder, or traversing a directory structure. But Java applications with native code lose platform independence.

Released with Java 7, NIO.2 (New Input/Output version 2) extensively improved the existing I/O capabilities and added new ones. Though NIO was introduced with Java 1.4, Java 7 further extended the NIO API, which resulted in a name change, now called NIO.2. NIO.2 adds new file access and management functionality, such as defining new classes and interfaces to access files and file systems, accessing their metadata, the ability to traverse file trees, networking with the socket API, Asynchronous Channel API, WatchService API, the ability to support a new file system, and more.

Though Java NIO.2 defines a lot of functionality, the good news is that the exam doesn't include all of it. This chapter covers the NIO.2 topics that are relevant to the exam:

- Using the `Path` interface
- Using class `Files`
- Working with file and directory attributes
- Walking a directory tree using the `DirectoryStream` and `FileVisitor` interfaces
- Using the `PathMatcher` interface
- Using the WatchService API

The topics covered in this chapter include coverage of a lot of classes from the Java NIO.2 that deal with working with paths, files, and their attributes, and walking and watching directory structures and more. This boils down to using a *lot* of Java API classes and their methods, which can become boring. So let's make it interesting and fun. Let's work with building a sample application, Exam FlashCards, to help you apply most of the exam topics covered in this chapter.

In this application, you'll read and write your favorite exam tips and notes from and to text files on your system. The notes will be organized according to the main objective and subobjective numbers. Each main exam objective will map to a directory and the tips or notes for a main exam objective will be stored in a text file, on separate lines. Figure 8.1 shows the file and directory hierarchy for text files 8-1.txt, 8-2.txt, and 8-3.txt.

In this application, let's start with storing exam notes in a file. This application uses Swing components to create a simple UI for accepting the exam objective number, the subobjective, and notes to the file. Play around with creating directories and files using the application, and add notes and check your physical files. Figure 8.2 shows a screenshot of the application.

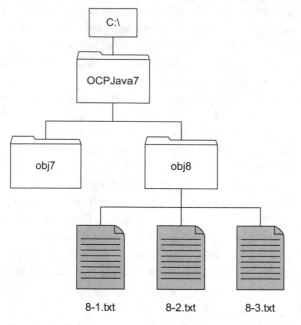

Figure 8.1   File and hierarchy directory for text files 8-1.txt, 8-2.txt, and 8-3.txt

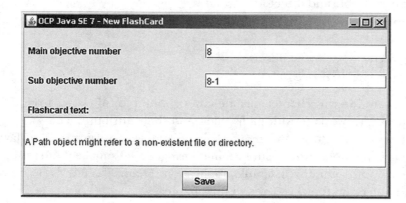

Figure 8.2   Sample application to add a new flash card

Listing 8.1 shows the code for figure 8.1. Don't worry if you can't follow all the code—it uses Swing components, which aren't on the exam. I've annotated the code so that it's easier to follow.

Listing 8.1   Building sample application's UI

```
import java.io.*;
import java.nio.file.*;
import javax.swing.*;
import java.awt.*;
import java.awt.event.*;
```

```
          public class NewFlashCard implements ActionListener {
               JFrame f = new JFrame("OCP Java SE 7 - New FlashCard");
               JTextField tfMainObj = null;
               JTextField tfSubObj = null;          Textfields to accept input for
               JTextField tfNote = null;            main and subobjective numbers
                                                    and flash card text
               JButton btnSave = null;
               JButton btnClear = null;
               JButton btnExit = null;

               private void buildUI() {
                    tfMainObj = new JTextField();         Initialize
                    tfSubObj = new JTextField();          text fields
                    tfNote = new JTextField();
                    btnSave = new JButton("Save");        Initialize button and
                    btnSave.addActionListener(this);      add ActionListener to it

                    JPanel topPanel = new JPanel();
                    topPanel.setLayout(new GridLayout(6,2));
                    topPanel.add(new JLabel(""));
                    topPanel.add(new JLabel(""));

                    topPanel.add(new JLabel("  Main objective number"));
                    topPanel.add(tfMainObj);
                    topPanel.add(new JLabel(""));
                    topPanel.add(new JLabel(""));
                    topPanel.add(new JLabel("  Sub objective number"));
                    topPanel.add(tfSubObj);
                    topPanel.add(new JLabel(""));
                    topPanel.add(new JLabel(""));
                    topPanel.add(new JLabel("  Flashcard text:"));
                    topPanel.add(new JLabel(""));

                    JPanel middlePanel = new JPanel();                    Build UI
                    middlePanel.setLayout(new BorderLayout());
                    middlePanel.add(tfNote);

                    JPanel bottomPanel = new JPanel();
                    bottomPanel.add(btnSave);

                    JPanel mainPanel = new JPanel();
                    mainPanel.setLayout(new BorderLayout());
                    mainPanel.add(BorderLayout.NORTH, topPanel);
                    mainPanel.add(BorderLayout.CENTER, middlePanel);
                    mainPanel.add(BorderLayout.SOUTH, bottomPanel);

                    f.getContentPane().setLayout(new BorderLayout());
                    f.setSize(500, 250);
                    f.getContentPane().add(mainPanel);
                    f.setVisible(true);
               }
                                                            Code in action-
               public void actionPerformed(ActionEvent e) {  Performed will
                    // Code to execute when Save button is activated  execute when user
               }                                                      activates Save button
```

Button to initiate saving of text to file

```
    public static void main(String[] args) {
        NewFlashCard nfc = new NewFlashCard();
        nfc.buildUI();
    }
}
```
Create NewFlashCard instance and build the UI

In this application, the main objective number corresponds to a directory and the sub-objective number corresponds to a text file, to which flash card text is written. You need to follow these steps to write an exam note to a file:

1 Get a Path referring to file /8/8-1.txt.
2 Create a corresponding file or directories if they don't already exist.
3 Open the file in append mode and copy the flash card text to the file.

Before you can move forward with the first step of creating a Path object, let's discuss Path objects in detail.

8.1   *Path objects*

 [8.1]   Operate on file and directory paths with the Path class

Objects of the java.nio.file.Path interface are used to *represent* the *path* of files or directories in a file system. The interface represents a hierarchal path containing directory names and filenames separated by platform-specific delimiters. A path can contain multiple directories, a single filename, or both.

> **NOTE**   Prior to Java 7, class java.io.File was used to represent the path of a file or directory in a file system. But it had several drawbacks. Its methods didn't throw exceptions when they failed, which was essential to determine the cause of failure. Most of the methods of class File didn't scale. For example, a request to a large directory listing could make a system hang. It didn't support much access to the metadata. These reasons and more were responsible for the introduction of Path in Java 7.

Figure 8.3 shows a sample directory tree in both a Windows and a Unix OS, with a root node, directories, and files.

In figure 8.3 (Windows OS), the path to file Hello.txt can be represented using the Path interface both as c:\users\harry\Hello.txt (absolute path) and as Hello.txt (relative path). An absolute path includes the complete path from the root directory to the file or directory. Because a path is system-specific, the paths that a Path object represent are platform-dependent. It's interesting to note that an object of Path might not be tied to a real file or directory on a system. The Path interface defines methods to work with and to manipulate Path objects, resolving one path to another. But it doesn't contain methods to work with the actual physical directories and files that a Path object refers to. To work with the actual files and directories, you

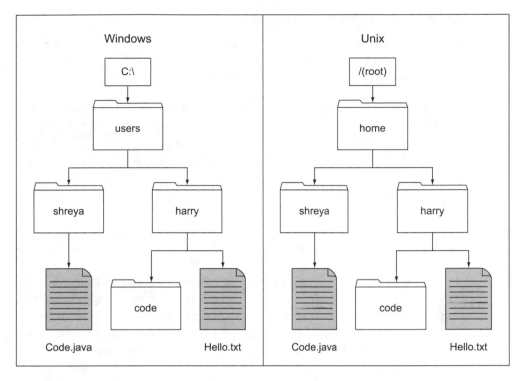

Figure 8.3   Sample directory tree structure on Windows and Unix

can use `java.nio.file.Files`. We'll use the directory structure shown in figure 8.1 to show you how to work with `Path` objects.

 EXAM TIP   Because a `Path` object might not be tied to a real file or directory on a system, it can refer to a nonexistent file or directory.

Apart from referring to a file and a directory, a `Path` object can also refer to a *symbolic link*. A symbolic link is a special file that refers to another file. The file referred to by a symbolic link is called its *target*. All operations with a symbolic link are channeled to the symbolic link's target. When you read data from or write data to a symbolic link, you write to its underlying target file. But if you delete a symbolic link, the target file isn't deleted. Apart from working with paths that refer to files and directories, NIO can work with symbolic links also. It includes multiple methods where you can specify whether you want the symbolic links to be followed or not. NIO can also determine circular references in symbolic links where a target refers back to the symbolic link.

A `Path` object is system-dependent. A `Path` can never be equal to a `Path` associated with another file system, even if they include exactly the same values. For example, a `Path` object to file 'Hello.txt' on Windows isn't equal to a `Path` object to file 'Hello.txt' on Solaris. Let's get started with creating some `Path` objects.

8.1.1   *Multiple ways to create Path objects*

You can create `Path` objects by using methods from multiple classes: `java.nio` `.file.Paths`, `java.nio.file.FileSystem`, and `java.io.File`. Table 8.1 shows a list of these classes, together with the relevant methods.

Table 8.1   List of classes and their respective methods that can be used to create objects of `Path`

Class name	Method declaration
`java.nio.file.Paths`	`public static Path get(String first, String... more)`
`java.nio.file.FileSystem`	`public abstract Path getPath(String first, String... more)`
`java.io.File`	`public Path toPath()`

`Paths` (notice an extra "s" at the end) is a *factory* class that defines static methods to create `Path` objects. Method `get(String first, String... more)` converts a string representation of a file or directory to a `Path` object. You can use a single string or sequence of string objects to create a `Path` object. You can use a forward slash (`/`) as a file and directory separator. Here are multiple ways of specifying a path to file 8-1.txt, using `Paths.get()`:

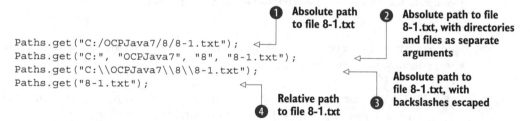

```
Paths.get("C:/OCPJava7/8/8-1.txt");
Paths.get("C:", "OCPJava7", "8", "8-1.txt");
Paths.get("C:\\OCPJava7\\8\\8-1.txt");
Paths.get("8-1.txt");
```

❶ **Absolute path to file 8-1.txt**

❷ **Absolute path to file 8-1.txt, with directories and files as separate arguments**

❸ **Absolute path to file 8-1.txt, with backslashes escaped**

❹ **Relative path to file 8-1.txt**

The code at ❶, ❷, and ❸ defines an absolute path to file 8-1.txt. The code at ❹ defines a relative path. For a relative path, the target file or directory is assumed to exist in your current directory. Note how the code at ❸ uses a backward slash (`\`) as a file separator. You *must* escape a backslash in a Java string value:

```
Path path = Paths.get("c:\users\harry\Hello.txt");
Path path2 = Paths.get("c:\\users\\harry\\Hello.txt");
```

Won't compile; need to escape \ used as a separator, by using another \.

Okay

When the path is provided as one string, where individual subpaths are separated by a path separator, only the last method argument is considered as a filename. All the others are assumed to be directory names.

CREATING PATH OBJECTS BY USING FILESYSTEM CLASS

You can also create `Path` objects by using method `getPath()` in class `FileSystem`. Because class `FileSystem` is an abstract class, you can get a reference to the current class `FileSystem` object by calling `getDefault()` on class `FileSystems`. Assuming that this application executes on a Unix or Linux machine, here's how you can create objects of `Path` to refer to file 8-1.txt:

```
FileSystems.getDefault().getPath("/home/OCPJava7/8/8-1.txt");
FileSystems.getDefault().getPath("/home", "OCPJava7", "8", "8-1.txt");
FileSystems.getDefault().getPath("\\home\\OCPJava7\\8\\8-1.txt");
FileSystems.getDefault().getPath("8-1.txt");
```

> **Absolute path to file 8-1.txt**

> **Relative path to file 8-1.txt**

A `Path` object can refer to a nonexistent file or directory. Watch out for this point on the exam. Even though you didn't create the file 8-1.txt until this point, a `Path` object that refers to it is valid.

 EXAM TIP   A `Path` object can refer to a nonexistent file or directory.

CREATING PATH OBJECTS BY USING FILE CLASS

As discussed in chapter 7, prior to Java 7, objects of class `java.io.File` were used to represent the file and directory paths. Starting with Java 7, a new method, `toPath()`, was added to class `File` to bridge the gap between the existing I/O classes and NIO classes. You can create a `Path` object by using a `File` instance:

```
File file = new File("Hello.txt");
Path path = file.toPath();
```

> **Object of java.io.File**

What happens if you create a `Path` object as follows?

```
Path path = Paths.get("");
```

> **Path created using one element that's empty.**

Created using a zero-length string value, the preceding `path` variable refers to the current directory. Though `path.toString()` returns a zero-length string value, `path.get-AbsolutePath()` would return its absolute path.

 NOTE   Behind the scenes, both `Paths.get()` and `File.toPath()` call `FileSystems.getDefault().getPath()`.

Let's refer back to the sample application Exam FlashCards and add functionality to it—that is, code that executes when a user activates the Save button. Let's create `Path` objects by adding code to method `actionPerformed()` as shown in the following listing.

Listing 8.2   Adding functionality to the sample application

```
public void actionPerformed(ActionEvent e) {
    String baseDir = "E:\\OCPJava7\\";
    String subDir = tfMainObj.getText();
    String fileName = tfSubObj.getText() + ".txt";
    Path path = Paths.get(baseDir, subDir, fileName);

    JOptionPane.showMessageDialog(f, path.toString());
}
```

Base dir ← (points to `String baseDir = "E:\\OCPJava7\\";`)

Directory for objectives ← (points to `String subDir = tfMainObj.getText();`)

Create Path object ⇨ (points to `Path path = Paths.get(baseDir, subDir, fileName);`)

File name—one file per subobjective ← (points to `String fileName = tfSubObj.getText() + ".txt";`)

Show Path in a message box ← (points to `JOptionPane.showMessageDialog(f, path.toString());`)

Until this point, you're only creating `Path` objects. They aren't tied to a real file or directory. Before you can move on with creating real files and directories that can be tied to this `Path` interface, you need to familiarize yourself with the `Path` objects and how they can be manipulated.

INTERFACE JAVA.NIO.FILE.PATH VERSUS CLASS JAVA.NIO.FILE.PATHS

Due to the similarity in their names, it's easy to confuse `Paths` with `Path`. But they are different—`Path` is an *interface* and `Paths` is a *class*. The class `Paths` is a utility class, with static methods to create objects that can be referred to by variables of the `Path` interface. The `Path` interface is used to represent the path of files or directories on a system. Figure 8.4 shows a UML representation of the `Path` interface and class `Paths`.

The `Path` interface extends interfaces `Comparable`, `Iterable`, and `Watchable`. This essentially means that the `Path` objects can be compared (with each other), iterated

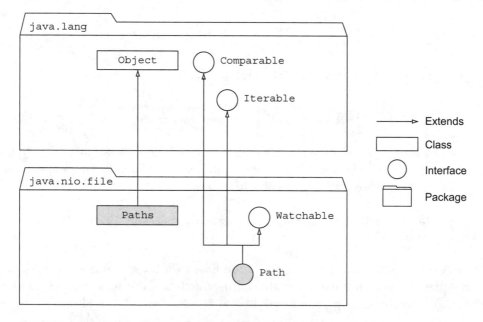

Figure 8.4   Comparing class `Paths` and interface `Path`

(over their directories and file components), and watched for changes. We'll cover these in the later sections of this chapter.

 EXAM TIP Most of the `Path` methods perform syntactic operations. They manipulate the paths to a file or directory without accessing the file systems. They're logical operations on paths in memory.

Let's get started with working with `Path` methods that access its components.

8.1.2 *Methods to access Path components*

`Path` objects are used to work with the files and directories in a file system, and so the paths are system-dependent. On the exam, you'll be asked to use `Path` objects to retrieve information about a path like its subpath and root or parent directories. Let's work with a quick example:

```
class ManipulatePaths {
    public static void main(String args[]) {
        Path path = FileSystems.getDefault().getPath
                                ("c:\\users\\obj8\\8-1.txt");
        System.out.println("toString()-> " + path.toString());
        System.out.println("getRoot()-> " + path.getRoot());
        System.out.println("getName(0)-> " + path.getName(0));
        System.out.println("getName(1)-> " + path.getName(1));
        System.out.println("getFileName()-> " + path.getFileName());
        System.out.println("getNameCount()-> " + path.getNameCount());
        System.out.println("getParent()-> " + path.getParent());
        System.out.println("subpath(0,2)-> " + path.subpath(0,2));

    }
}
```

Here's the output of the preceding code:

```
toString()-> c:\users\obj8\8-1.txt
getRoot()-> c:\
getName(0)-> users
getName(1)-> obj8
getFileName()-> 8-1.txt
getNameCount()-> 3
getParent()-> c:\users\obj8
subpath(0,2)-> users\obj8
```

Figure 8.5 shows a pictorial representation of the preceding code that makes it easy to retain this information. Note how the root of a path is not used in all the `Path` methods. Though it's used by a method like `getRoot()`, it's ignored by other methods like `subpath()` and `getName()`.

 EXAM TIP Methods `getName()`, `getNameCount()`, and `subpath()` don't use the root directory of a path. Method `getRoot()` returns the root of an absolute path and `null` for relative paths. Play around with these methods—you might see them on the exam.

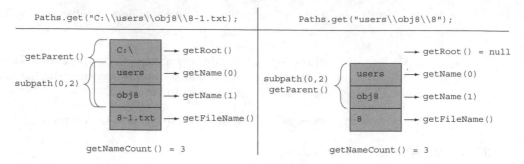

Figure 8.5   Representation of calling various `Path` methods

The `Path` methods that accept positions throw an `IllegalArgumentException` at runtime for invalid positions. For example, `getName()` and `subpath()` throw an `Illegal-ArgumentException` if you pass invalid path positions to them:

```
Path path = FileSystems.getDefault().getPath("c:\\users\\obj8\\8-1.txt");
System.out.println("subpath(0,4)-> " + path.subpath(0,4));    ⟵─┐ Throws
                                                                  IllegalArgument-
                                                                  Exception
```

The code `path.subpath(0,4)` will throw an `IllegalArgumentException` because it refers to an invalid position in the value referred by `path`.

8.1.3   *Comparing paths*

You can compare paths lexicographically using the method `compareTo(Path)`. To check whether a path starts or ends with another path, you can use `startsWith(String)`, `startsWith(Path)`, `endsWith(String)`, and `endsWith(Path)`:

```
class ComparePaths {
    public static void main(String args[]) {
        Path path1 = FileSystems.getDefault().
                        getPath("c:\\users\\obj8\\8-1.txt");        Returns a negative
        Path path2 = Paths.get("d:\\users\\obj8\\8-1.txt");        number—path1 is
                                                                    lexicographically
Returns    System.out.println(path1.compareTo(path2));    ⟵───┘  smaller than path2.
false  └─▷ System.out.println(path2.startsWith("\\"));

Returns ┌─▷ System.out.println(path1.endsWith("-1.txt"));
false   │   System.out.println(path1.endsWith(Paths.get("8-1.txt\\")));    ⟵──┐
        }
    }                                              Returns true—trailing separators
                                                      aren't taken into account.
```

Methods `startsWith(String)` and `endsWith(String)` convert the method argument to a `Path` object before comparing it with the first or last element of the `Path` object. Although you're using `String`, a string comparison isn't executed. It's comparing paths, and path `"1.txt"` isn't the same as `"8-1.txt"` (two different files or directories). This explains why `path1.endsWith("-1.txt")` returns `false`.

 EXAM TIP Methods `startsWith()` and `endsWith()` are overloaded: `startsWith(String)`, `startsWith(Path)`, `endsWith(String)`, and `endsWith(Path)`. So if you pass `null` to these methods, you'll get a compiler error.

8.1.4 *Converting relative paths to absolute paths*

The code in listing 8.2 uses a hard-coded value for the base directory. Let's see how you use your current directory and parent directories to create `Path` objects. Let's assume that your current working directory is E:/OCPJavaSE7/FileNIO. Now assume you enter the value of the subobjective as `8-1`. The following will create an absolute path to 8-1.txt in your current working directory, that is, E:\OCPJavaSE7\FileNIO\8-1.txt:

```
Path file = Paths.get("8-1.txt");
Path path = file.toAbsolutePath();
```

Imagine that you want to create a text file 8-1.txt in the parent directory of your current working directory. Knowing that you can use `..` to denote your parent directory, do you think the following will help?

```
Path file = Paths.get("..\\8-1.txt");
Path path = file.toAbsolutePath();
```

Yes, it will. Though the preceding code will insert `..` in the `Path` object, if you use it to create the corresponding file, it will be created in the parent directory of the current working directory.

 EXAM TIP Note that the method name to retrieve the absolute path from a `Path` object is `toAbsolutePath()` and not `getAbsolutePath()`. These method names are similar and might be used on the exam.

In the preceding code, path will refer to E:\OCPJavaSE7\FileNIO\.\8-1.txt. As you can see, inclusion of directories FileNIO and .. is redundant in the preceding path. You can remove these redundant values by calling method `normalize()` on `Path`:

```
Path file = Paths.get("..\\8-1.txt");
Path path = file.toAbsolutePath();          Prints
path = path.normalize();                ◄──  E:\OCPJavaSE7\8-1.txt
System.out.println(path);
```

 EXAM TIP `Path` is immutable and calling `normalize()` on a `Path` object doesn't change its value.

Though implicit, it's common to use a period (.) to denote the current directory. For example, if you refer to file 8-1.txt, you refer to this path in the current directory. But it's common for programmers to refer to this path as ./8-1.txt. Again, when you include a period in a Path object, you're including redundant information, which can be removed too using method normalize(). The following code assumes your current working directory is E:/OCPJavaSE7/FileNIO:

```
Path file = Paths.get(".\\8-1.txt");
Path path = file.toAbsolutePath();
path = path.normalize();
System.out.println(path);
```

Prints
E:\OCPJavaSE7\FileNIO\8-1.txt

 EXAM TIP   Method normalize() doesn't check the actual file system to verify if the file (or directory) the resulting path is referring to actually exists.

Do you think, when a Path object includes redundancies like . or .., that calling information retrieval methods like subpath() or getName() will also include these redundancies in the returned values? Let's see whether you can answer this question in the first "Twist in the Tale" exercise for this chapter.

Twist in the Tale 8.1

Examine the following code and select the correct answers.

```
import java.nio.file.*;
class Twist8_1{
    public static void main(String args[]) {
        Path path = Paths.get("c:\\OCPJavaSE7\\..\\obj8\\.\\8-1.txt");

        System.out.println(path.toString());        //line1
        System.out.println(path.getName(1));         //line2
        System.out.println(path.getParent());        //line3
        System.out.println(path.subpath(2,4));        //line4
    }
}
```

a Code on line 1 outputs c:\OCPJavaSE7\..\obj8\.\8-1.txt

b Code on line 1 outputs c:\obj8\8-1.txt

c Code on line 2 outputs OCPJavaSE7

d Code on line 2 outputs c:\

e Code on line 2 outputs ..

f Code on line 3 outputs c:\OCPJavaSE7\..\obj8\

g Code on line 3 outputs c:\obj8\

h Code on line 4 throws an IllegalArgumentException

8.1.5 *Resolving paths using methods resolve and resolveSibling*

The overloaded methods resolve(String) and resolve(Path) are used to join a relative path to another path. If you pass an absolute path as a parameter, this method returns the absolute path:

```
Path path = Paths.get("/mydir/code");
System.out.println(path.resolve(Paths.get("world/Hello.java")));
System.out.println(path.resolve ("/world/Hello.java"));

Path absolutePath = Paths.get("E:/OCPJavaSE7/");
System.out.println(absolutePath.resolve(path));
System.out.println(path.resolve(absolutePath));
```

The output of the preceding code is:

```
\mydir\code\world\Hello.java
\world\Hello.java
E:\mydir\code
E:\OCPJavaSE7
```

Imagine you need to retrieve the path to a file in the same directory, say, to create its copy or to rename it. To do so, you can use the overloaded methods resolve-Sibling(String) and resolveSibling(Path). These resolve a given path against a path's parent. If the given path is an absolute path, this method returns the absolute path. If you pass it an empty path, it returns the parent of the path:

```
Path path = Paths.get("/mydir/eWorld.java");
Path renamePath = path.resolveSibling(Paths.get("newWorld.java"));
Path copyPath = path.resolveSibling("backup/eWorld.java");
Path absolutePath = Paths.get("E:/OCPJavaSE7/");

System.out.println(renamePath);
System.out.println(copyPath);
System.out.println(path.resolveSibling(""));

System.out.println(absolutePath.resolveSibling(path));
System.out.println(path.resolveSibling(absolutePath));
```

The output of the preceding code is as follows:

```
\mydir\newWorld.java
\mydir\backup\eWorld.java
\mydir

E:\mydir\eWorld.java
E:\OCPJavaSE7
```

 EXAM TIP Methods resolve() and resolveSibling() don't check the actual file system to verify if the file (or directory) the resulting path is referring to actually exists.

8.1.6   *Method relativize()*

Imagine you need a path to construct a path between two Path objects. To do so, you can use method relativize(). It can be used to construct a path between two relative or absolute Path objects:

```
Path dir = Paths.get("code");
Path file = Paths.get("code/java/IO.java");
System.out.println(file.relativize(dir));
System.out.println(dir.relativize(file));

dir = Paths.get("/code");
file = Paths.get("/java/IO.java");
System.out.println(file.relativize(dir));
System.out.println(dir.relativize(file));
```

Relative paths

Absolute paths

The output of the preceding code is:

```
..\..
java\IO.java
..\..\code
..\java\IO.java
```

What happens when you try to use relativize() to construct a path between a relative path and an absolute path or two absolute paths having different roots (say, C:\ and D:\)? Invocation of method relativize() in the following code would throw a runtime exception:

```
Path dir = Paths.get("/code");
Path dirC = Paths.get("C:/code/MyClass.java");
Path dirD = Paths.get("D:/notes/summary.txt");

System.out.println(dir.relativize(dirD));
System.out.println(dirC.relativize(dirD));
```

Would throw runtime exception

 EXAM TIP   You can't create a path from a relative path to an absolute path and vice versa using method relativize(). If you do so, you'll get a runtime exception (IllegalArgumentException). Also, method relativize() doesn't check the actual file system to verify if the file (or directory) the resulting path is referring to actually exists.

Unlike method toRealPath(), most of the Path methods perform syntactic operations—that is, logical operations on paths in memory. Let's see whether you remember this important point while determining the output of the Path methods in the next "Twist in the Tale" exercise.

Twist in the Tale 8.2

Assuming that the byte code for class Twist8_2 (Twist8_2.class) is located in directory /home, what is the output of the following code?

```
class Twist8_2{
    public static void main(String args[]) {
        Path dir = Paths.get("code");
```

```
        Path file = Paths.get("code/java/IO.java");
        Path relative = file.resolve(file.relativize(dir));
        Path absolute = relative.toAbsolutePath();
        System.out.println(absolute);
    }
}
```

   a /home/code/

   b /home/code/../..

   c /home/java/IO.java/../..

   d /home/code/java/IO.java/../..

In this section you learned how to create `Path` objects and manipulate them in memory without connecting them to the real files or directories on your file system. In the next section, you'll see how class `Files` uses these `Path` objects to create, move, copy, delete, walk, and query files and directories on a system.

8.2 Class Files

[8.2] Check, delete, copy, or move a file or directory with the Files class

Class `java.nio.file.Files` consists entirely of static methods for manipulating files and directories. Because the creation and deletion of files and directories are dependent on the underlying platform, most of the methods of class `Files` delegate these tasks to the associated system provider.

Let's get started with the creation of files and directories.

8.2.1 Create files and directories

Class `Files` defines multiple methods to create files and directories:

```
public static Path createFile(Path path, FileAttribute<?>... attrs)
                                            throws IOException
public static Path createDirectory(Path dir, FileAttribute<?>... attrs)
                                            throws IOException
public static Path createDirectories(Path dir, FileAttribute<?>... attrs)
                                            throws IOException
```

Method `createFile()` *atomically* checks for the existence of the file specified by the method parameter `path` and creates it if it doesn't exist. The (checking and creation) operation is atomic with respect to all the file system operations that might affect the directory. Method `createFile()` fails and throws an exception if the file already exists, if a directory with the same name exists, if its parent directory doesn't exist due to an I/O error, or if the specified file attributes can't be set.

Method `createDirectory()` creates the specified directory (not the parent directories) on the file system. This method also atomically checks for the existence of the specified directory and creates it if it doesn't exist. Method createDirectory() throws an exception if a file or directory exists with the same name, if its parent directory doesn't exist, if an I/O error occurs, or if the specified directory attributes can't be set.

Method createDirectories() creates a directory, creating all nonexistent parent directories. If the target directory already exists, createDirectories() doesn't throw any runtime exceptions. It throws an exception if the specified dir exists but isn't a directory, if an I/O occurs, or if the specified directory attributes can't be set.

 EXAM TIP   Specifying file or directory attributes is optional with methods createFile(), createDirectory(), and createDirectories(). All these methods declare to throw an IOException, which is a checked exception.

Let's use these methods and add some action to the sample application Exam Flash-Cards. Let's create directories corresponding to the objective number entered by a user and text file corresponding to the subobjective number. Directory and file creation will happen when a user activates the Save button. When a user activates the Save button, code defined in method actionPerformed will execute (the remaining code listing remains the same as shown in listing 8.1). Here's the code for method actionPerformed():

```
public void actionPerformed(ActionEvent e) {          ❶ Base
    String baseDir = "E:\\OCPJava7\\";                      directory to    ❷ Retrieve main
    String subDir = tfMainObj.getText();                    store data         objective value
    String fileName = tfSubObj.getText() + ".txt";                             entered by user

    Path filePath = Paths.get(baseDir, subDir, fileName);   ❹ Create Path object by
                                                               converting base directory
    try {                                                      to absolute path
        Files.createDirectories(filePath.getParent());
        Files.createFile(filePath);                         ❻ Create file on
                                                               file system
        PrintWriter pw = new PrintWriter(
                new FileWriter(filePath.toFile(), true));   ❼ Open a PrintWriter
        pw.println(tfNote.getText());                          to file and write
        pw.flush();                                            text from text-field
    }                                                          note to it
    catch (IOException ioe) {
        JOptionPane.showMessageDialog(f, ioe.toString());   ❽ Handle IOException
    }                                                          from creation of
}                                                              directories, file, and
                                                               writing to file
```

❸ Retrieve subobjective value entered by user

❺ Create complete directory tree on file system

The code at ❶ defines a base directory to store your flash card data: E:\OCPJava7\. The code at ❷ and ❸ retrieves the value of the main objective and subobjective entered by a user. Because you're writing the flash cards text to a text file, the extension .txt is appended to it. The code at ❹ creates an absolute path corresponding to the .txt file. The code at ❺ executes createDirectories() from class Files, creating all nonexistent parent directories on your system. The code at ❻ calls createFile() from class Files to create the target file on your system. If it can't create a file because the file already exists, it throws a `FileAlreadyExistsException`. The code at **❼** creates a `PrintWriter` and writes the flash card tip to the text file. Because it's a Swing application, I've defined a message box to show you the name of the thrown exception **❽**.

 EXAM TIP In class `Files`, method `createDirectories()` can create both the target directory and multiple nonexistent parent directories. If the directory already exists and it can't create a directory, no exceptions are thrown. Methods `createDirectory()` and `createFile()` create a single directory and file respectively. They throw a `FileAlreadyExists-Exception` if a directory or file with the same name already exists.

In the sample application, click the Save button twice; the code that creates the text file will throw a `FileAlreadyExistsException`. In the next section, let's see how you can check for the existence of files or directories before you issue a command to create them.

8.2.2 *Check for the existence of files and directories*

You can check for the existence of a file or directory referred by a `Path` object using methods `exists()` and `notExists()` in class `Files`:

```
public static boolean exists(Path path, LinkOption... options)
public static boolean notExists(Path path, LinkOption... options)
```

Method `exists()` checks whether a file or directory referred by a `Path` exists or not; it returns `true` if the file or directory exists and `false` if the target doesn't exist or its existence can't be determined.

Method `notExists()` is *not* a complement of method `exists()`. It returns `true` if a target doesn't exist. If these methods can't determine the existence of a file, both of them will return `false`. By default, these methods follow a symbolic link. To override this behavior, you can pass `LinkOption.NOFOLLOW_LINKS` to these methods (`java.nio.file.LinkOption` is an enum). What happens if you check for the existence of a target path and before you can create a new file or directory another application creates it? In this case, you must handle the exception accordingly.

Let's add checks to verify the existence of your target directory and file in the sample application:

```
public void actionPerformed(ActionEvent e) {
    String baseDir = "E:\\OCPJava7\\";
    String subDir = tfMainObj.getText();
    String fileName = tfSubObj.getText() + ".txt";

    Path filePath = Paths.get(baseDir, subDir, fileName);

    try {
        if (Files.notExists(filePath.getParent()))
            Files.createDirectory(filePath.getParent());
        if (!Files.exists(filePath))
            Files.createFile(filePath);
```

```
        PrintWriter pw = new PrintWriter(
                new FileWriter(filePath.toFile(), true));
        pw.println(tfNote.getText());
        pw.flush();
    }
    catch (IOException ioe) {
        JOptionPane.showMessageDialog(f, ioe.toString());
    }
}
```

 EXAM TIP   Watch out for questions that state that exists() and not-Exists() will never return the same boolean value for the same Path object. Both methods exists() and notExists() would return false if they can't determine the existence of the target file or directory.

8.2.3   *Copy files*

Imagine you create a study group to prepare for this exam. To get going, the members plan to share their individual flash card notes that they created using this application. To do so, they email the text files with flash card notes to everyone in the group. How would you use the notes from these files in your application? You might

- Copy the file to the directory that's used by your application
- Copy the contents of the received file to a file that's used by your application

Class Files's overloaded copy() method enables you to read from InputStream and write to a Path object, read from a Path object and write to OutputStream, and read from and write to Path objects:

```
public static long copy(InputStream in, Path target, CopyOption... options)
public static long copy(Path source, OutputStream out)
public static Path copy(Path source, Path target, CopyOption... options)
```

 EXAM TIP   Files.copy() can copy only files, not directories. If the source is a directory, then in the target an empty directory is created (without copying the entries in the directory). This method returns a long or Path value, not a boolean value. Watch out for its invalid use in exam questions that use copy() to copy directories, use it in try-with-resources statements, or use its return value to test whether a file was copied or not.

Method copy() accepts objects of the CopyOption interface. You can use objects of enum StandardCopyOption (shown in table 8.2), which implements this interface.

Table 8.2   Enum constants of StandardCopyOption can be passed to methods that accept CopyOption. StandardCopyOption implements the CopyOption interface.

Enum constant	Description
StandardCopyOption.ATOMIC_MOVE	Hasn't been implemented yet
StandardCopyOption.COPY_ATTRIBUTES	Copy attributes
StandardCopyOption.REPLACE_EXISTING	Replace existing entity with the same name

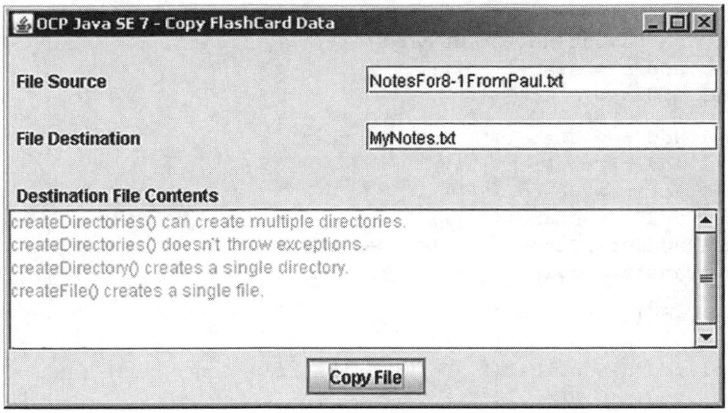

Figure 8.6 Swing application used to copy a source file to a destination

For the example, let's copy the flash card notes received in a .txt file to a folder that's used by your application. Figure 8.6 shows the screenshot of this application after the Copy File button is activated.

Here's the code of this Swing application, which accepts the path to the source and destination files from a user and copies the source file to the destination. It might seem unnecessary to you to define an elaborate example to copy files. Reading or browsing through the Java API, particularly the Java File I/O API, can be very boring. Try out the following code with different combinations of source and target files. It displays the error messages in a popup box and the contents on the copied file. Try it with different combinations of the source and target files, using relative or absolute paths.

```java
import java.io.*;
import java.nio.file.*;
import java.nio.charset.*;
import javax.swing.*;
import java.awt.*;
import java.awt.event.*;
public class CopyFlashCardData implements ActionListener {
    JFrame f = new JFrame("OCP Java SE 7 - Copy FlashCard Data");
    JTextField tfCopyFrom = null;
    JTextField tfCopyTo = null;
    JTextArea taFileContents = null;
    JButton btnCopyFile = null;

    private void buildUI() {
        tfCopyFrom = new JTextField();
        tfCopyTo = new JTextField();
        taFileContents = new JTextArea("Click 'Copy file' to " +
                                        "view contents");
        taFileContents.disable();
        btnCopyFile = new JButton("Copy File");
        btnCopyFile.addActionListener(this);
```

Text field to accept file source

Text field to accept file destination

Button to initiate file copy

Text area to display copied file

Build application's UI

```
                    JPanel topPanel = new JPanel();
                    topPanel.setLayout(new GridLayout(6,2));
                    topPanel.add(new JLabel(""));
                    topPanel.add(new JLabel(""));

                    topPanel.add(new JLabel("  File Source"));
                    topPanel.add(tfCopyFrom);
                    topPanel.add(new JLabel(""));
                    topPanel.add(new JLabel(""));
                    topPanel.add(new JLabel("  File Destination"));
                    topPanel.add(tfCopyTo);

                    topPanel.add(new JLabel(""));
                    topPanel.add(new JLabel(""));
                    topPanel.add(new JLabel("  Destination File Contents"));
                    topPanel.add(new JLabel(""));                                    Build
                                                                                    application's
                    JPanel middlePanel = new JPanel();                              UI
                    middlePanel.setLayout(new BorderLayout());
                    middlePanel.add(taFileContents);

                    JPanel bottomPanel = new JPanel();
                    bottomPanel.add(btnCopyFile);

                    JPanel mainPanel = new JPanel();
                    mainPanel.setLayout(new BorderLayout());
                    mainPanel.add(BorderLayout.NORTH, topPanel);
                    mainPanel.add(BorderLayout.CENTER, middlePanel);
                    mainPanel.add(BorderLayout.SOUTH, bottomPanel);
                    f.getContentPane().setLayout(new BorderLayout());
                    f.setSize(500, 550);
                    f.getContentPane().add(mainPanel);
                    f.setVisible(true);

                    tfCopyFrom.setText("E:/OCPJava7/downloads/8-1.txt");   Define default values for
                    tfCopyTo.setText("E:/OCPJava7/8/8-1.txt");             source and target fields.
                }
                public void actionPerformed(ActionEvent e) {              Create Path object
                    try {                                                 from source value
                        Path source = Paths.get(tfCopyFrom.getText());    entered by user
                        Path target = Paths.get(tfCopyTo.getText());

                        Files.copy(source, target,                        Create Path
                                   StandardCopyOption.REPLACE_EXISTING);  object from
                                                                          target value
                        byte[] bytes = Files.readAllBytes(target);        entered by
                        taFileContents.setText(new String(                user
                                          bytes, Charset.defaultCharset()));
                    }
                    catch (IOException ioe) {                             Shows message for
                        JOptionPane.showMessageDialog(f, ioe.toString()); exception caught
                    }                                                     in a dialog box
                }
                public static void main(String[] args) {
                    CopyFlashCardData fc = new CopyFlashCardData();
                    fc.buildUI();
                }
            }
```

Call Files.copy to copy file to destination; StandardCopyOption.REPLACE_EXISTING replaces existing file

Reads target file and displays its contents in a text area.

You can use absolute links and relative links to copy files. When you use a relative link to a target file, where do you think the target file is created? Is it created relative to your Java code (.class) and not relative to your source file?

 EXAM TIP If you use a relative path to the target file, the file is created relative to your Java class (.class file) and not relative to the source file (passed as a parameter to method `Files.copy()`).

The preceding code shows you how to copy a file to another location. Method `copy()` in class `Files` doesn't allow you to append data to an existing file. If you want to add the notes sent to you by your study group to your own text files, you need to open the target file in append mode and use I/O streams or readers/writers to do so. If you're not sure how to do this, refer to chapter 7.

 EXAM TIP Method `copy()` in class `Files` doesn't allow you to append data to an existing file; rather, it creates a new file or replaces an existing one.

The overloaded version of method `copy()` that reads from `InputStream` and writes to a `Path` object can also be used to read from your system's standard input stream using `System.in` and write it to a file as follows:

```
try (InputStream in = System.in){
    Path target = Paths.get("myNotesFromConsole.txt");
    Files.copy(in, target, StandardCopyOption.REPLACE_EXISTING);
}
catch (IOException ioe) {
    System.out.println(ioe);
}
```

You can also read from a `Path` object and write its contents to `OutputStream`:

```
import java.io.*;
import java.nio.file.*;
public class WriteDataFromPathToStream{
    public static void main(String[] args) {
        try (OutputStream out = new FileOutputStream("Copy.txt")){
            Path source = Paths.get("WriteDataFromPathToStream.java");
            Files.copy(source, out);          ←┐
        }                                        Copy Path
        catch (IOException ioe) {                object to
            System.out.println(ioe);            OutputStream
        }
    }
}
```

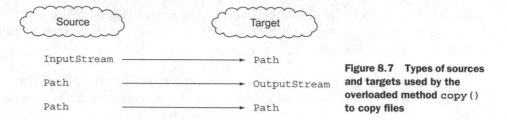

Figure 8.7   Types of sources
and targets used by the
overloaded method `copy()`
to copy files

Figure 8.7 shows the types of sources and targets that can be used with the overloaded method `copy()` in class `Files`.

8.2.4 Move files and directories

Moving files and directories is a common requirement. To move files or directories programmatically, you can use `Files.move()`, which moves or renames a file to a target file:

```
public static Path move(Path source, Path target, CopyOption... options)
```

To rename a file notes.txt to copy-notes.txt, keeping the file in the same directory, you can use the following:

```
Path source = Paths.get("notes.txt");
Files.move(source, source.resolveSibling("copy-notes.txt"));
```

To move a file to a new directory, retaining the same filename and replacing any existing file of that name in the new directory, you can use the following:

```
Path source = Paths.get("notes.txt");
Path target = Paths.get("/home/myNotes/");
Files.move(source, target.resolve(source.getFileName()),
                          StandardCopyOption.REPLACE_EXISTING);
```

 EXAM TIP You can only move empty directories using method `Files`
`.move()`. You can rename a nonempty directory by using `Files.move()`.
But you can't move a file or directory to a nonexisting directory.

8.2.5 Delete files and directories

To delete a directory or a file referred to by a `Path` object, you can use the following methods from class `Files`:

```
public static void delete(Path path)
public static boolean deleteIfExists(Path path)
```
← **Deletes a file**

← **Deletes a file
if it exists**

Both the preceding methods can delete a file or directory (if it's empty). If you try to delete a directory that isn't empty, these methods will throw a `DirectoryNotEmpty-Exception`. If you try to delete a nonexistent file or directory using method `delete()`, it will throw a `NoSuchFileException`. But method `deleteIfExists()` won't throw an

exception if the file or directory at the specified path doesn't exist—it will return
`false`. The deletion operation might also fail if the target file is in use, because some
operating systems don't allow deletions of files or directories if they're in use by an
active program.

 EXAM TIP Methods `delete()` and `deleteIfExists()` can be used to
delete files and (nonempty) directories.

8.2.6 Commonly thrown exceptions

File creation, copying, renaming, moving, and deletion throw a couple of common
checked and unchecked exceptions:

- `IOException` (checked exception)—The I/O devices are beyond the immediate
  control of JVM, so operations involving the I/O devices can fail at any time,
  throwing an `IOException`.
- `NoSuchFileException` (runtime exception)—This exception is thrown when
  you try to delete, move, or copy a nonexistent file or directory.

When you operate on files and directories, you might want to query their existing
attributes. Let's see how you can do that in the next section.

8.3 Files and directory attributes

 [8.3] Read and change file and directory attributes, focusing on the
BasicFileAttributes, DosFileAttributes, and PosixFileAttributes
interfaces

Imagine you want to set the last modification time stamp for a file or directory or add
a new user-defined attribute to it. You can do so by adding, accessing, or modifying the
attributes of a file or directory. The file or directory attributes refer to their metadata,
or data about data. You use files or directories to store your data. The OS stores additional data about your data that helps it to determine when it was created, modified,
accessed, and so on. You can access individual attributes or a group of attributes for
files and directories.

Prior to version 7, Java supported limited access to the attributes of files and directories. To access non-supported attributes, developers often worked with native code.
With its `java.nio.file.attribute` package, NIO.2 supports access to and (if allowed)
modification of a larger set of file and directory attributes.

8.3.1 Individual attributes

Class `Files` defines static methods to access individual attributes of a file or directory
referred by a `Path`, such as its size, when was it last modified, whether it's readable or

writable, and whether it's a directory or a file. Following is an example to access some of the attributes of a java source file:

```
import java.nio.file.*;
public class AccessAttributes{
    public static void main(String[] args) throws Exception {
        Path path = Paths.get("MyAttributes.java");

        System.out.println("size:" + Files.size(path));
        System.out.println("isDirectory:" + Files.isDirectory(path));
        System.out.println("isExecutable:" + Files.isExecutable(path));
        System.out.println("isHidden:" + Files.isHidden(path));
        System.out.println("isReadable:" + Files.isReadable(path));
        System.out.println("isSameFile:" + Files.isSameFile(path, path));
        System.out.println("isDirectory:" + Files.isDirectory(path));
        System.out.println("isSymbolicLink:" + Files.isSymbolicLink(path));
        System.out.println("isWritable:" + Files.isWritable(path));
        System.out.println("getLastModifiedTime:" +
                                        Files.getLastModifiedTime(path));
        System.out.println("getOwner:" + Files.getOwner(path));
    }
}
```

Here's the output of the preceding code (the value of some of these attributes might vary depending on your system):

```
size:958
isDirectory:false
isExecutable:true
isHidden:false
isReadable:true
isSameFile:true
isDirectory:false
isSymbolicLink:false
isWritable:true
getLastModifiedTime:2014-12-09T08:03:54.609375Z
getOwner:AD-3B5C889B134A\Administrator (User)
```

You can also access the individual attributes of a file or directory by using method `Files.getAttribute()`, passing to it the name of the attribute as a string value. To modify the attributes of an existing file or directory, you can use `Files.setAttribute()`. Table 8.3 shows the relevant methods of class `Files` that can be used to update existing attributes.

Table 8.3   Methods to modify individual attributes of files or directories

Method	Description
`public static Path setAttribute(Path path, String attribute, Object value, LinkOption... options)`	Sets the value of a file attribute
`public static Path setLastModifiedTime(Path path, FileTime time)`	Updates a file's last modified time attribute
`public static Path setOwner(Path path, UserPrincipal owner)`	Updates the file owner

The following code displays the existing creation time of a Java source file using method `Files.getAttribute()` and then modifies it using method `Files.setAttribute()`:

```
import java.nio.file.*;
import java.nio.file.attribute.*;
public class ModifyAttributes{
    public static void main(String[] args) {

        Path path = Paths.get("ModifyAttributes.java");
        System.out.println("creationTime:" +
        Files.getAttribute(path, "creationTime"));

        FileTime newTime = FileTime.fromMillis(System.currentTimeMillis());
        Files.setAttribute(path, "creationTime", newTime);

        System.out.println("creationTime:" +
                            Files.getAttribute(path, "creationTime"));
    }
}
```

Retrieves value of attribute creationTime.

Updates value of attribute creationTime.

 EXAM TIP   Methods `Files.setAttribute()` and `Files.getAttribute()` can be used to access a file or directory attribute and modify it (if allowed). The attribute name is passed to these methods as a string value.

Rather than accessing individual attributes, you can also access a group of attributes, as discussed in the next section.

8.3.2   *Group of attributes*

Querying the file system multiple times to access all file or directory attributes can affect your application's performance. To get around this, you can access a group of file attributes by calling `Files.getFileAttributeView()` or `Files.readAttributes()`.

INTERFACES TO READ AND MODIFY ATTRIBUTE SETS

Different file systems might support different attribute sets. Java groups related attributes that correspond to a specific file system implementation like DOS or POSIX, or to a common functionality like file owner attributes. You can use multiple interfaces to access file and directory attributes and modify them. These groups are defined as interfaces, and the ones on the exam are as follows:

- `BasicFileAttributes` and `BasicFileAttributeView`—The `BasicFileAttributes` interface defines methods to access the basic attributes that should be supported by all the file systems. The `BasicFileAttributeView` interface can be used to modify the basic attributes.

- `DosFileAttributes` and `DosFileAttributeView`—The `DosFileAttributes` interface extends `BasicFileAttributes` and defines methods to access attributes specific to Windows files and directories. The `DosFileAttributeView` interface defines methods to modify the DOS file attributes.

- `PosixFileAttributes` and `PosixFileAttributeView`—The `PosixFileAttributes` interface also extends `BasicFileAttributes` and defines methods to access attributes related to the POSIX family of standards, like Linux or UNIX. The `PosixFileAttributeView` interface defines methods to modify attributes related to the POSIX family.

- `AclFileAttributeView`—Available only for Windows OS, this interface supports access and updates of a file's access control list (ACL).
- `FileOwnerAttributeView`—This interface supports access and updates to the owner of a file or directory. It's supported by all systems that support the concept of file owners.
- `UserDefinedFileAttributeView`—This interface supports the addition, modification, and deletion of user-defined metadata.

 NOTE For the preceding list of interfaces, the ones that end with the term "View" are collectively referred to as the *view interfaces*, and they're used to update file and directory attributes.

Figure 8.8 shows `BasicFileAttributes`, `DosFileAttributes`, and `PosixFileAttributes` interfaces with their methods to help you get a better understanding of the methods that they define.

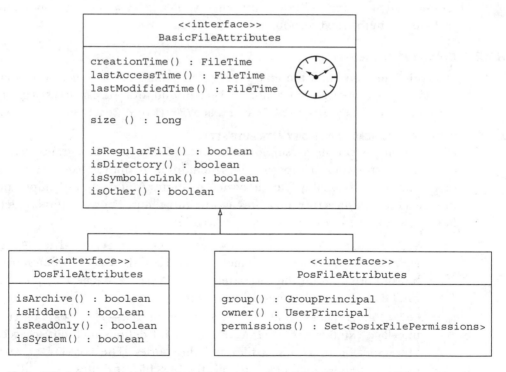

Figure 8.8   Interface `BasicFileAttributes` **is extended by interfaces** `DosFileAttributes` **and** `PosixFileAttributes`

EXAM TIP The `BasicFileAttributes`, `DosFileAttributes`, and `Posix-FileAttributes` interfaces define methods to access attributes. They don't define methods to modify (or set) the attributes. Use class `Files` or view interfaces (covered in this section) to modify the attributes.

Figure 8.9 shows the view interfaces, which can be used to modify file or directory attributes.

To access and update a group of attributes for a directory or file, you can access an attribute view by using method `File.getFileAttributeView()`. To only access (not update) an attribute group, you can use method `File.readAttributes()`. You can also call method `readAttributes()` on an attribute view to get its corresponding attribute set. Following is an example that uses these methods:

```
Path path = Paths.get("pathToaFile");
PosixFileAttributeView view = Files.getFileAttributeView(path,
                                      PosixFileAttributeView.class);
PosixFileAttributes attr = view.readAttributes();
PosixFileAttributes attr2 = Files.readAttributes(path,
                                      PosixFileAttributes.class);
```

 EXAM TIP If a file system doesn't support an attribute view, `Files.get-FileAttributeView()` returns null. If a file system doesn't support an attribute set, `File.readAttributes()` will throw a runtime exception.

Let's get started with accessing basic attributes and modifying them.

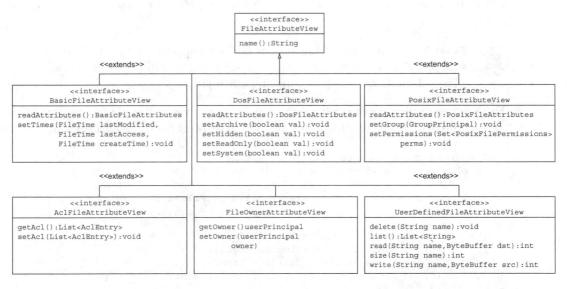

Figure 8.9 Interfaces `BasicFileAttributeView`, `DosFileAttributeView`, `PosixFileAttribute-View`, `AclFileAttributeView`, `FileOwnerAttributeView`, and `UserDefinedFileAttributeView` can be used to update attribute values using Files.readAttributes() and Files.getFileAttributeView().

8.3.3   *Basic attributes*

Imagine you need to delete all files in a directory, whose creation time is older than one day, using your Java code. If you can access the creation time of a file, you can determine if the file needs to be deleted or not. Here's an example:

```
import java.io.*;
import java.nio.file.*;
import java.nio.file.attribute.*;
class DeleteOldFiles {
    public static void delDayOldFile(String fileName) throws IOException {
        Path file = Paths.get(fileName);

        BasicFileAttributes attr = Files.readAttributes(file,
                                        BasicFileAttributes.class);
        FileTime fileCreationTime = attr.creationTime();

        long currentTime = System.currentTimeMillis();
        FileTime dayOldFileTime = FileTime.fromMillis(
                            currentTime - (24*60*60*1000));

        if (fileCreationTime.compareTo(dayOldFileTime) < 0)
            Files.delete(file);
    }
}
```

Create a path to filename

Get basic file attributes of file

Get file's creation timestamp

Get current time's milliseconds

Compute FileTime for a day old

Check if file creation-timestamp is older than one day

Delete file

You can access an object of a class that implements the `BasicFileAttributes` interface by calling `Files.readAttributes()` and passing it `BasicFileAttributes.class`. You don't need to be bothered about the exact type of the object that's returned to you.

 EXAM TIP If an underlying system doesn't support all the basic time-stamps—that is, `creationTime`, `lastAccessTime`, and `lastModified-Time`—it might return system-specific information.

The next example uses `BasicFileAttributeView` to modify the file creation, modification, and access time of a file to 60, 50, and 30 seconds from the current time:

```
public class ModAttributes{
    public static void modifyDateAttr(String fileName) throws IOException {
        Path file = Paths.get(fileName);
        BasicFileAttributeView view = Files.getFileAttributeView(file,
                                        BasicFileAttributeView.class);

        long now = System.currentTimeMillis();
        FileTime creation = FileTime.fromMillis(now - 60000);
        FileTime lastModified = FileTime.fromMillis(now - 50000);
        FileTime lastAccess = FileTime.fromMillis(now - 30000);

        view.setTimes(lastModified, lastAccess, creation);
    }
}
```

Another method that you can use to read the file attributes is:

```
static Map<String,Object> readAttributes(Path path,
                                         String attributes,
                                         LinkOption... options)
                                  throws IOException
```

The parameter attributes take the form [view name:]attribute-list. The square brackets mean that the view name is optional—it can take values basic, dos, and posix. If this value is absent, it defaults to basic. The attributes are specified as a comma-separated list of the attributes to be read (without any spaces). You can specify * to read all the attributes for a group. Here's an example for accessing all the attributes of a file, printing them (attribute names and their values), and changing the last-ModifiedTime of the file:

```
Path file = Paths.get(fileName);
Map<String,Object> values = Files.readAttributes(file, "*");

for (String attribute:values.keySet()) {
    System.out.println(attribute + " : " + values.get(attribute));
}

FileTime newTime = FileTime.fromMillis(System.currentTimeMillis());
Files.setAttribute(file, "lastModifiedTime", newTime);
```

You can also use a comma-delimited list of values:

```
Map<String,Object> values = Files.readAttributes(file,
                                 "lastModifiedTime,isDirectory");
```

To modify an attribute, you can call an XxxFileAttributeView interface, call Files.setAttribute(), or call a specific method from class Files, if it exists. For example, you can modify the last modified time of a Path object by calling Files.setLastModifiedTime(). The following line of code updates the last modified time for the file referred to by the variable file:

```
Files.setLastModifiedTime(file, dayOldFileTime);
```

 EXAM TIP Methods Files.setAttribute() and Files.getAttribute() throw an IllegalArgumentException or UnsupportedOperationException if you pass them an invalid or unsupported attribute.

8.3.4 *DOS attributes*

As shown in figure 8.9, the DosFileAttributes interface makes the following attributes available:

- archive
- hidden
- readonly
- system

EXAM TIP   The DOS attributes are available on a Windows system only. Trying to access them on other systems will throw a runtime exception.

The following example uses the DosFileAttribute and DosFileAttributeView interfaces to access DOS attributes of a file, updating them if a file is read only:

```
Path file = Paths.get("name-of-a-file");
DosFileAttributeView dosView = Files.getFileAttributeView(file,
                                        DosFileAttributeView.class);
DosFileAttributes dosAttrs = dosView.readAttributes();
if (dosAttrs.isReadOnly()) {
    dosView.setHidden(true);
    dosView.setArchive(false);
    dosView.setReadOnly(false);
    dosView.setSystem(true);
}
else
    System.out.println("Don't modify the attributes");
```

Use DosFileAttributeView to update file attributes.

Use DosFileAttributes to access file attributes.

You can also access file or directory attributes by using class Files. The following code reads DOS attributes:

```
Map<String,Object> values = Files.readAttributes(file,
                                    "dos:archive,hidden");
Map<String,Object> values2 = Files.readAttributes(file, "dos:*");
DosFileAttributes attr = Files.readAttributes(file,
                                    DosFileAttributes.class);
DosFileAttr
```

Read listed DOS attributes

Read all DOS attributes

 EXAM TIP   When you read *all* DOS attributes using method Files.readAttributes(), you also read the basic attributes.

To modify a DOS attribute, you must prefix the attribute name with dos: because an attribute is implicitly prefixed with basic: (which can result in an invalid attribute). Imagine that you wish to prevent listing a specific file in a files explorer on a Windows system. You can use Files.setAttribute() to modify its hidden property and set it to true:

```
Files.setAttribute(file, "dos:hidden", true);
```

 EXAM TIP   When you read or write an invalid value to a file attribute, the code throws the runtime exception ClassCastException.

8.3.5   *POSIX attributes*

The POSIX attributes are as follows:

- group
- owner
- permissions

EXAM TIP   The POSIX attributes are available on the POSIX family of standards, like UNIX, LINUX, etc. Trying to access them on other systems will throw a runtime exception.

The following example updates the permissions of a file depending on whether it's owned by admin or not. It uses the `PosixFileAttributeView` and `PosixFileAttributes` interfaces:

```
PosixFileAttributeView posixView = Files.getFileAttributeView(file,
                                        PosixFileAttributeView.class);
PosixFileAttributes posixAttrs = posixView.readAttributes();
if (posixAttrs.owner().getName().equals("admin"))
    posixView.setPermissions(PosixFilePermissions.fromString("rwxrwxrwx"));
else
    posixView.setPermissions(PosixFilePermissions.fromString("rwxr-x---"));
```

You can also use class `Files` to read all POSIX file attributes:

```
Map<String,Object> values = Files.readAttributes(file, "posix:*");
PosixFileAttributes attr = Files.readAttributes(file,
                                        PosixFileAttributes.class);
```

8.3.6   *AclFileAttributeView interface*

The `AclFileAttributeView` interface supports reading and updating a file's ACL or file owner attributes. It defines methods `getAcl()` and `setAcl()`. This view is available only for Windows systems.

8.3.7   *FileOwnerAttributeView interface*

The `FileOwnerAttributeView` interface is supported by all file systems with a file owner concept, and this view includes methods to access and update the owner of a file or directory. If defines methods `getOwner()` and `setOwner(UserPrincipal)`.

 EXAM TIP   To read or update the owner of a file or directory you can use the `AclFileAttributeView`, `FileOwnerAttributeView`, and `PosixFile-Attribute` interfaces.

8.3.8   *UserDefinedAttributeView interface*

The `UserDefinedAttributeView` interface can be used to add, delete, access, and modify additional user-defined attributes to a file or directory. It defines methods `delete(String)`, `list()`, `read(String, ByteBuffer)`, `size(String)`, and `write (String, ByteBuffer)` to, respectively, delete, list, read, get the attribute's size, and write attribute values.

Imagine you're developing a file management application that enables multiple users to delete files. But the files chosen for deletion are only marked for deletion and the actual deletion is executed separately. To accomplish this, you can add a user-defined attribute `delete` to a file with a value of, say, `true`. This attribute can be queried before actually deleting a file. The following sample code shows how you can do it. It defines code to write and read the user-defined attribute delete in method main(). But in a real application, this would usually be defined in separate classes or methods.

```
import java.io.*;
import java.nio.file.*;
import java.nio.*;
import java.nio.file.attribute.*;
import java.nio.charset.*;
public class UserAttrs{
    public static void main(String args[]) throws IOException {
        Path file = Paths.get("eJava.txt");

        UserDefinedFileAttributeView view= Files.getFileAttributeView(file,
                                  UserDefinedFileAttributeView.class);

        writeAttr(view,"delete",true);
        if (readAttr(view, "delete"))
            Files.delete(file);
    }
    static void writeAttr( UserDefinedFileAttributeView view,
                           String attr,
                           boolean value) throws IOException {
        if (value)
            view.write(attr,Charset.defaultCharset().encode("true"));
        else
            view.write(attr,Charset.defaultCharset().encode("false"));
    }
    static boolean readAttr( UserDefinedFileAttributeView view,
                             String attr) throws IOException {
        ByteBuffer buf = ByteBuffer.allocate(view.size(attr));
        view.read(attr, buf);
        buf.flip();
        String value = Charset.defaultCharset().decode(buf).toString();
        return (value.equalsIgnoreCase("true"));
    }
}
```

Use write(String, ByteBuffer) to write a user-defined attribute.

Use read(String, ByteBuffer) to read a user-defined attribute.

Use size() to get the size of attribute value delete.

The preceding code would delete the file referred by the variable file from your system. The possibilities are endless for how you can use a user-defined attribute that you add to a file or directory. In this section, you learned how to access and update the attributes of a single file or directory. If you combine it with recursive access of a directory tree, it can open a lot of possibilities. For example, you can create, read, identify, update, or delete files with a particular attribute or a group of attributes. Recursive access of a directory tree is a breeze with the supporting classes in NIO.2. Let's examine it in detail in the next section.

8.4   *Recursively access a directory tree*

> [8.4]   Recursively access a directory tree using the DirectoryStream and
> FileVisitor interfaces

Imagine you're ready to write your exam and want to view all the notes that you created using the sample application Exam FlashCards. Because you've been storing the text files corresponding to all the exam objectives in separate subdirectories, you can recursively access the directory, which includes all these subdirectories, thereby accessing all the text files.

Before we move further, let me briefly cover the difference between a recursive and nonrecursive access of a directory for directory OCP, as shown in figure 8.10.

A nonrecursive access of directory OCP will only access its immediate subdirectories: obj2 and obj8. On the other hand, a recursive access of the directory OCP will access all its subdirectories and files.

There are multiple ways to access a directory. Common and popular access algorithms are *breadth-first* and *depth-first.* In a breadth-first search algorithm, all the directories and files on the first level are accessed before moving on to the members on the next level, and so on until no more are remaining. In a depth-first algorithm, a direct subdirectory of the main directory is accessed recursively before moving forward with searching the next subdirectory. Further, there are multiple ways in which a directory and its members can be accessed in a depth-first search: *preorder, in-order,* and *postorder.*

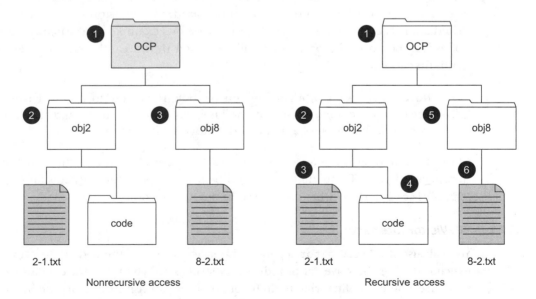

Figure 8.10   Sample directory structure to show recursive and nonrecursive access of directory OCP.

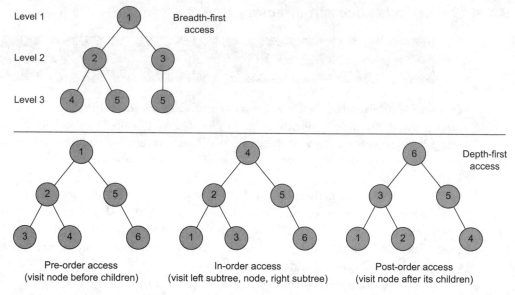

Figure 8.11   Breadth-first and depth-first directory tree access

You can compare the directory and its subdirectories and files with a *tree data structure*. A tree data structure has a root node, with multiple children. The preorder access will visit a node prior to accessing its children. The in-order access will access its left subtree, the node itself, and then its right subtree. The in-order access applies to binary tree structures, which have no more than two subtrees. In postorder access, a node is visited after its children are visited. Figure 8.11 shows example tree structures and the nodes numbered in the order they will be visited in a breadth-first access and in a depth-first access.

 NOTE   The exam won't query you on details of how to access a tree, breadth-first or depth-first. But it will help you to understand (and remember) how the access of a tree or a directory structure works.

Class `Files` defines overloaded method `walkFileTree()` to walk recursively through the specified path. To define the traversal behavior, this method accepts an object of `FileVisitor` interface, which is covered in the next section.

8.4.1   *FileVisitor interface*

You can use the `FileVisitor`, a generic interface to define the code that you want to execute during the traversal of a directory structure. When you traverse a directory structure, you can define what to do before or after you visit a directory, when you visit a file, or when access to a file is denied. The methods of the `FileVisitor` interface are listed in table 8.4.

Table 8.4 Methods of interface `FileVisitor<T>`

Method	Method signature
`FileVisitResult postVisitDirectory(T dir, IOException exc)`	Invoked for a directory after entries in the directory, and all of their descendants, have been visited.
`FileVisitResult preVisitDirectory(T dir, BasicFileAttributes attrs)`	Invoked for a directory before entries in the directory are visited.
`FileVisitResult visitFile(T file, BasicFileAttributes attrs)`	Invoked for a file in a directory.
`FileVisitResult visitFileFailed(T file, IOException exc)`	Invoked for a file that couldn't be visited.

Let's assume that you stored your exam tips in text files 2-1.txt and 8-2.txt using the directory structure shown in figure 8.12.

Let's create a class, say `MyFileVisitor`, which implements the `FileVisitor` interface and traverses this directory structure, storing the exam objective numbers (2-1 and 8-2) and their corresponding tips as a `List<String>` in a `HashMap<String, List<String>>`. The code is shown in listing 8.3.

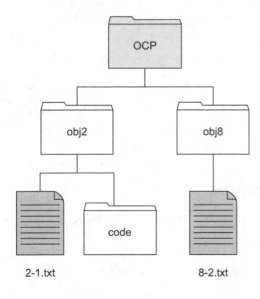

Figure 8.12 Example of directory structure used to store exam tips in text files 2-1.txt and 8-2.txt

Listing 8.3   Using `FileVisitor` to recursively access exam tips from files

① **MyFileVisitor implements FileVisitor<Path>.**

② **Hash map to store objective number and its corresponding exam tips as List<String>**

```
class MyFileVisitor implements FileVisitor<Path> {

    Map<String, java.util.List<String>> flashcards = new HashMap<>();

    public FileVisitResult preVisitDirectory(Path dir,
                                    BasicFileAttributes attrs) {
        String dirName = dir.getFileName().toString();
        if (dirName.startsWith("code"))
            return FileVisitResult.SKIP_SUBTREE;
        else
            return FileVisitResult.CONTINUE;

    }
    public FileVisitResult postVisitDirectory(Path dir,
                                    IOException exc) {
        return FileVisitResult.CONTINUE;
    }
    public FileVisitResult visitFile(Path file,
                                    BasicFileAttributes attrs) {

        String fileName = file.getFileName().toString();

        if (fileName.endsWith(".txt")) {
            java.util.List<String> tips = new ArrayList<>();

            try (
                BufferedReader reader = new BufferedReader(
                                new FileReader(file.toFile()));
            ){
                String line = null;
                while((line = reader.readLine()) != null)
                    tips.add(line);
            }
            catch (Exception e) {
                System.out.println(e);
            }

            flashcards.put(fileName.substring(
                                0, fileName.length()-4),tips);
        }
        return FileVisitResult.CONTINUE;
    }
    public FileVisitResult visitFileFailed(Path file, IOException exc) {
        System.out.println(exc);
        return FileVisitResult.SKIP_SUBTREE;
    }
    public Map<String, java.util.List<String>> getFlashCardsMap() {
        return flashcards;
    }
}
```

③ Called prior to visiting subdirectories and files of a directory.

④ Called after visiting subdirectories and files of a directory.

⑤ Called when a file (not a directory) is visited.

⑥ Reads text files with exam tips using BufferedReader and adds them to List<String>.

⑦ Add objective number and its list of tips to a hash map

⑧ Called when a file can't be accessed.

NOTE In listing 8.3, I've deliberately excluded multiple checks to keep the example simple.

In listing 8.3, notice how all the methods of the `FileVisitor` interface return a constant of enum `FileVisitResult` to signal whether to continue with the traversal of a directory or to skip it (table 8.5 lists all the constant values for `FileVisitResult`).

The code at **❶** for class `MyFileVisitor` implements the `FileVisitor<Path>` interface. The code at **❷** defines a hash map to store the exam objectives as its keys and the corresponding exam tips as values. The code at **❸** for method `preVisit-Directory()` skips traversing the subtree for directories with the name "code" by returning `FileVisitResult.SKIP_SUBTREE`. The code at **❹** defines `postVisitDirectory()`, which is called after all the children of a directory are visited. Because the example didn't require any action in the method, it simply returns `FileVisitResult.CONTINUE`. The code at **❺** defines `visitFile()`, which is called when code accesses a file (not a directory). At **❻**, method `visitFile()` includes a simple check of reading a file that ends with .txt; for this simple example, assume that all text files will define the exam objectives. It reads the file contents using a `BufferedReader` and adds each line to a `List<String>`. At **❼**, the exam objective and the list of exam tips are added to the hash map. Method `visitFile()` is passed file attributes. If the file can't be visited for some reason—for example, reading the attributes failed due to an `IOException`—method `visitFileFailed()` is called, defined at **❽**.

 EXAM TIP Methods `preVisitDirectory()` and `visitFile()` are passed `BasicFileAttributes` of the path that they operate on. You can use these methods to query file or directory attributes.

Table 8.5 Enum `FileVisitResult` constants and their descriptions

Enum constant	Description
CONTINUE	Continue
SKIP_SIBLINGS	Continue without visiting the siblings of this file or directory
SKIP_SUBTREE	Continue without visiting the entries in this directory
TERMINATE	Terminate

You can also work with `SimpleFileVisitor` from the Java API, a class that implements the `FileVisitor` interface and all its methods. It saves you from implementing methods that you might not need.

8.4.2 *Class SimpleFileVisitor*

Class `SimpleFileVisitor` is a simple visitor of files with default behavior to visit all files and to rethrow I/O errors. It implements the `FileVisitor` interface (methods of

FileVisitor interface are listed in table 8.5). You can extend this class to implement methods for only the required behavior.

Imagine you need to recursively traverse a directory structure and print only the names of all the files. In this case, you can extend the SimpleFileVisitor class and override only the visitFile() method. Following is the code that accomplishes it:

```java
import java.nio.file.*;
import java.nio.file.attribute.*;
class ListFileNames extends SimpleFileVisitor<Path> {
    public FileVisitResult visitFile(Path file,
                                     BasicFileAttributes attributes) {
        System.out.println("File name :" + file.getFileName());
        return FileVisitResult.CONTINUE;
    }
}
public class TestListFiles2 {
    public static void main(String[] args) throws Exception {
        Path path = Paths.get("E:/OCPJavaSE7");
        ListFileNames listFileNames = new ListFileNames();
        Files.walkFileTree(path, listFileNames);
    }
}
```

❶ Class ListFileNames extends SimpleFileVisitor

❷ Initiate directory tree traversal

In the preceding code, at ❶, class ListFileNames declares to extend SimpleFile-Visitor class. Because this example code doesn't need to define other directory traversal behavior, like pre- and post-directory visits or file visit failure, ListFileNames overrides only one method, visitFile(). The code at ❷ initiates the traversal of the directory structure (discussed in detail in the next section) referred by variable path in method main(). You can assign path to any valid directory on your system.

8.4.3   *Initiate traversal for FileVisitor and SimpleFileVisitor*

You can initiate traversal of a directory by calling the overloaded method walkFile-Tree() from class Files:

```java
public static Path walkFileTree(Path start,
                                FileVisitor<? super Path> visitor)
                throws IOException

public static Path walkFileTree(Path start,
                    Set<FileVisitOption> options,
                                int maxDepth,
                                FileVisitor<? super Path> visitor)
                throws IOException
```

This method traverses through a directory structure, the root of which is specified by a Path object. The directory tree is traversed depth-first. The traversal is considered complete when either all the members of a tree are visited, any of method File-Visitor returns FileVisitResult.TERMINATE, or if an exception is thrown during the traversal.

Figure 8.13 Sample
application displaying
exam objective and
exam tip

EXAM TIP A directory tree is traversed depth-first. But the order in which the subdirectories are traversed is unpredictable.

Let's see how you can initiate traversal of a directory and display the flash cards in the sample application. Figure 8.13 shows a screenshot of the sample application, displaying the exam tips from the text files as shown in the directory structure in figure 8.12.

Here's the code to display the exam tips (as shown in figure 8.13), persisted in the text files, as shown in figure 8.12.

Listing 8.4 Reading and displaying exam tips from files

```java
import java.io.*;
import java.nio.file.*;
import java.nio.charset.*;
import javax.swing.*;
import java.awt.*;
import java.awt.event.*;
import java.util.*;
import java.nio.file.attribute.*;

public class DisplayFlashCards implements ActionListener{
    JFrame f = new JFrame("OCP Java SE 7 - Display FlashCard Data");
    JLabel lblObjectiveNo = null;
    JLabel lblFlashcard = null;
    JButton btnNext = null;

    private void buildUI() {
        lblObjectiveNo = new JLabel();
        lblFlashcard = new JLabel();
        lblObjectiveNo.setBorder(
                BorderFactory.createLineBorder(Color.BLACK));
        lblFlashcard.setBorder(
                BorderFactory.createLineBorder(Color.BLACK));
        btnNext = new JButton(" > ");
```

❶ **Build UI of application**

```
        btnNext.addActionListener(this);

        JPanel topPanel = new JPanel();
        topPanel.setLayout(new GridLayout(6,1));
        topPanel.add(new JLabel(""));
        topPanel.add(new JLabel("  Exam Objective"));
        topPanel.add(lblObjectiveNo);
        topPanel.add(new JLabel(""));
        topPanel.add(new JLabel(""));
        topPanel.add(new JLabel("  Exam Tip"));

        JPanel middlePanel = new JPanel();
        middlePanel.setLayout(new BorderLayout());
        middlePanel.add(lblFlashcard);

        JPanel bottomPanel = new JPanel();
        bottomPanel.add(btnNext);

        JPanel mainPanel = new JPanel();
        mainPanel.setLayout(new BorderLayout());
        mainPanel.add(BorderLayout.NORTH, topPanel);
        mainPanel.add(BorderLayout.CENTER, middlePanel);
        mainPanel.add(BorderLayout.SOUTH, bottomPanel);

        f.getContentPane().setLayout(new BorderLayout());
        f.setSize(500, 550);
        f.getContentPane().add(mainPanel);
        f.setVisible(true);
    }

    MyFileVisitor fileVisitor = new MyFileVisitor();

    Map<String, java.util.List<String>> flashcards = null;
    Iterator<String> examObjIterator = null;
    ListIterator<String> tipsIterator = null;

    public void accessAllExamTips() throws IOException {
        Files.walkFileTree(Paths.get("E:\\OCP"), fileVisitor);
        flashcards = fileVisitor.getFlashCardsMap();
    }

    public void initExamTips() {
        examObjIterator = flashcards.keySet().iterator();
        showNextTip();
    }

    private void showNextTip() {
        if(tipsIterator != null && tipsIterator.hasNext()) {
            lblFlashcard.setText("<html>" +
                            tipsIterator.next() + "</html>");
        }
        else {
            if(examObjIterator.hasNext()) {
                String currentExamObj = examObjIterator.next();
                lblObjectiveNo.setText(currentExamObj);

                tipsIterator = flashcards.get(currentExamObj)
                                        .listIterator();
                if(tipsIterator != null && tipsIterator.hasNext()) {
```

❶ Build UI of application

❷ Instantiate MyFileVisitor, used by Files.walkFileTree().

❸ Variables to store flashcards as a hash map and iterators to its keyset and values.

❹ Files.walkFileTree() is called to walk the file tree rooted at E:\\OCPJava7; accepts instance of FileVisitor.

❺ Obtain iterator to all exam objectives, stored as keys in hash map flashcards; displays first exam tip.

❻ Shows the next tip

```
                lblFlashcard.setText("<html>" +
                        tipsIterator.next() + "</html>");
            }
        }
    }
}
    public void actionPerformed(ActionEvent e) {
        try {
            showNextTip();
        }
        catch (Exception ioe) {
            JOptionPane.showMessageDialog(f, ioe.toString());
        }
    }

    public static void main(String[] args) throws Exception {
        DisplayFlashCards fc = new DisplayFlashCards();
        fc.buildUI();
        fc.accessAllExamTips();
        fc.initExamTips();
    }
}
```

6 Shows the next tip

7 Called when Next button is clicked

The preceding code creates a class, DisplayFlashCards, which reads text files stored in the directory structure as shown in figure 8.12, and displays the exam tips in a swing application. You can display the next exam tip by activating the Next button. The example shows how you can use File.walkFileTree() to walk a directory structure, read the exam tips from the text files, and store them in a hash map.

The code at **1** builds the UI of the swing application. Don't worry if you can't follow all of it—swing components aren't on the exam. The code at **2** instantiates MyFileVisitor, a class that implements the FileVisitor interface. Complete code for class MyFileVisitor is shown in listing 8.3. The code at **3** defines variables to store the exam tips in a hash map, with iterators to its keyset (exam objectives) and values (List<String>). At **4**, Files.walkFileTree() initiates the traversal of the file tree rooted at E:\OCP using the FileVisitor instance. The code at **5** obtains an iterator to all the exam objectives, stored as keys in the hash map flashcards. And also the first exam tip is displayed. Method showNextTip() displays the next available exam tip in the swing application **6**. The code at **7** is called when the Next button is activated by a user. Method main() calls methods to build the UI of the swing application, traverses the mentioned path retrieving all exam tips from the file system, and displays the first tip.

 NOTE This sample application doesn't include the Previous button, to keep the example code simple. If you want, you can add this functionality yourself to hone your skills with the collection classes.

8.4.4 *DirectoryStream interface*

The DirectoryStream interface can be used to iterate over all the files and directories in a directory. You can use an Iterator or for-each construct to iterate over a directory.

The order in which the directory contents are iterated is unpredictable. Following is an example that uses DirectoryStream with a for-each construct:

```java
import java.io.*;
import java.nio.file.*;
public class DirStream{
    public static void main(String args[]) throws IOException {
        Path dir = Paths.get("E:/OCPJavaSE7");
        try (DirectoryStream<Path> stream=Files.newDirectoryStream(dir)) {
            for (Path value : stream) {
                System.out.println(value + ":" + Files.isDirectory(value));
            }
        }
    }
}
```

The preceding code outputs a list of all the files and directories in the directory referred by the variable dir. The code uses Files.newDirectoryStream(Path) to get a DirectoryStream object, the values of which are iterated over by using a for-each construct. What happens if you try to iterate a file (and not a directory) using Directory-Stream? In this case you'll get a runtime exception (NotDirectoryException).

 EXAM TIP   If you pass Path to a file (and not a directory) to Files.new-DirectoryStream(), it will throw a runtime exception. The order of iteration of files and directories in a specified directory using Directory-Stream is unpredictable.

The next example uses an Iterator to iterate over the files and directories of a directory using method Files.DirectoryStream(Path dir, String glob) (glob is covered in the next section):

```java
import java.io.*;
import java.nio.file.*;
import java.util.*;
public class DirStream{
    public static void main(String args[]) throws IOException {
        Path dir = Paths.get("E:/OCPJavaSE7/FileNIO");
        try (DirectoryStream<Path> stream = Files.newDirectoryStream(
                                        dir, "*.{txt,java}")) {
            Iterator iterator = stream.iterator();
            while (iterator.hasNext()) {
                System.out.println(iterator.next());
            }
        }
    }
}
```

The preceding code iterates over the files and directories of the directory referred to by the variable dir. The glob value *.{txt,java} passed to the overloaded method new-DirectoryStream() limits the values that are iterated to the ones that end with "txt" or "java." Method `iterator()` returns an `Iterator` associated with the `DirectoryStream` object. `Iterator`'s method `hasNext()` checks whether more elements are available or not and method `next()` retrieves the next object.

Other common examples that can be used to demonstrate walking a directory structure include copying, deleting, querying, or modifying the attributes of files and directories in a directory structure.

Another common requirement while traversing a directory structure is to search for files or directories with a pattern of, say, *.txt. Next we'll cover the use of `Path-Matcher` to find a file.

8.5 Using PathMatcher

  [8.5]   Find a file with the PathMatcher interface

Imagine you want to count all the text files in a directory, or count only the .pdf files whose names start with "report", or perhaps delete all files whose names include "system". To do so, you can create a pattern using special characters and then match your file or directory names against those patterns. You can define these patterns using regex, glob, or other syntax.

Regex syntax is covered in detail in chapter 5 of this book. A glob pattern supports a simpler form of pattern matching than the regex. It supports fewer special constructs. The asterisk (`*`) matches anything or nothing. The question mark (`?`) matches any single character and the characters classes (like `[0-9]` or `[a-zA-Z]`). A glob doesn't support substring matches, which are supported by regex.

 EXAM TIP   In glob * matches zero or more characters. In regex .* matches zero or more characters.

To match a `Path` object with a pattern, you should create an object of `java.nio` `.file.PathMatcher`. `PathMatcher` is an interface with just one method: `matches()`. It returns `true` if a given path matches this matcher's pattern:

```
boolean matches(Path path)
```

You can create a `PathMatcher` by calling `FileSystem.getPathMatcher()` and passing it the pattern to be matched:

```
public abstract PathMatcher getPathMatcher(String syntaxAndPattern)
```

The method parameter accepts a string of the form `syntax:pattern`. `FileSystem` supports glob and regex syntax. It can also support other syntax (which are beyond the scope of this book). Before moving on with an example of how to use the `PathMatcher` interface, let's browse through some of the patterns that you can use to match `Path` objects, as described in table 8.6.

Table 8.6 A few examples of patterns that you can pass to `FileSystem.getPathMatcher` to match `Path` objects

Pattern to match	Description of pattern
`glob:*.{java,class}`	Match path names that end with extension .java or .class
`glob:*{java,class}`	Match path names that end with java or class. They might not include a dot just before (note the missing dot just before {).
`glob:*java,class`	Match path names that end with java,class; for example, Hellojava,class, and Hello.java,class (java,class doesn't evaluate to either java or class).
`glob:???.class`	Match path names that include exactly three characters followed by .class. For example, it will match abc.class, ab,.class, and a!b.class. It won't match abcd.class or abcde.class.
`glob:My[notes,tips,ans].doc`	Match an exact match of 'My' followed by any one character included within [], followed by .doc. For example, it matches Mys.doc and My,.doc. It doesn't match notes.doc, Mytips.doc, or Myans.doc.
`regex:MyPics[0-9].png`	Match MyPics followed by any digit, followed by .png. For example, MyPics0.png, MyPics1.png, and MyPics9.png.
`glob:/home/*/*`	Matches a path like home/shreys/code on UNIX platforms.
`glob:/home/**`	Matches a path like home/shreys/code and home/shreys on UNIX platforms.

In the sample application, recall that you stored all the exam tips in a text file with a name that reflects its exam objective number—for example, 2-1.txt, 8-2.txt, and 12-4.txt. The following code snippet uses class `PathMatcher` to determine whether a path matches the target regex pattern:

```
import java.nio.file.*;
class MyMatcher {
    public static void main(String args[]) {
        PathMatcher matcher = FileSystems.getDefault().getPathMatcher
                             ("regex:[1-9]*[0-9]?-[1-9]?.txt");

        Path file = Paths.get("12-1.txt");
        if (matcher.matches(file)) {
            System.out.println(file);
        }
    }
}
```

Get default FileSystem. Create PathMatcher object, passing it regex pattern. ❶

❷ Create Path object to match against the pattern.

Prints path

❸ file is matched against matcher's pattern.

The code at ❶ defines a regex pattern that will match files and directories of the pattern `[1-9]*[0-9]?-[1-9]?.txt` against the `Path` object defined by the code at ❷. At ❸, file is matched against the `matcher`'s pattern, using `matcher.matches()`.

8.6 *Watch a directory for changes*

[8.6] Watch a directory for changes by using the WatchService interface

Imagine your application displays arrival and departure times of flights, which it reads from a file. What happens if this data is updated while it's being displayed by the application? In this case, you might want to update the displayed times also. To do so, your application should be able to detect when the file, which stores its data, is modified. The *WatchService API* can help you. It enables you to *watch* a directory for changes like addition, modification, or deletion of contents of a directory. A thread-safe option for watching directories for changes, WatchService API is one of the interesting additions to Java 7.

To see how you can work with the WatchService API, let's work with a simplified example of a command-line application (say, `WatchDirectories`) that watches changes to a directory and one of its directories and outputs the name of the affected file. The following sections will cover partial code of the application WatchDirectories to understand how to use the WatchService API. The application's complete code is included at the end.

8.6.1 *Create WatchService object*

The first step to watch a directory for changes is to create a `WatchService` object. A file system operates independently of a JVM. To create a `WatchService` object, you can use the `FileSystem` class, which provides an interface to a file system and is the factory for objects to access files and other objects in the file system. It defines method `new-WatchService()` to create a `WatchService` object:

```
WatchService watchService = FileSystems.getDefault().newWatchService();
```

The next step is to register directories with the `WatchService` object.

8.6.2 *Register with WatchService object*

The directories that need to be watched for additions, modifications, or deletions must be registered with a `WatchService` object. A `WatchService` object watches a directory for the following events:

- `StandardWatchEventKinds.ENTRY_CREATE`—This event occurs when a new file or directory is created, moved, or renamed in the directory being watched.
- `StandardWatchEventKinds.ENTRY_DELETE`—This event occurs when an existing file or directory is deleted, moved, or renamed in the directory being watched.
- `StandardWatchEventKinds.ENTRY_MODIFY`—This event is platform-dependent. It usually occurs when contents of an existing file are modified. It can also occur if the attributes of a file or directory (in the directory being watched) are modified.
- `StandardWatchEventKinds.OVERFLOW`—This indicates that an event has been lost.

You can register multiple directories to be watched with the same `WatchService` object, by using method `register()` of `Path`. Multiple events can be registered in the same method call. Each registration process returns a `WatchKey` (discussed in the next section). The following example registers two directories (to be watched for multiple events) with the same `WatchService` object:

```
WatchService watchService = FileSystems.getDefault().newWatchService();
Path dir1 = Paths.get("E:/OCPJavaSE7");
Path dir2 = Paths.get("E:/OCPJavaSE7/8");

WatchKey regWatchKey = dir1.register(watchService,
                            StandardWatchEventKinds.ENTRY_MODIFY,
                            StandardWatchEventKinds.ENTRY_DELETE,
                            StandardWatchEventKinds.ENTRY_CREATE);
dir2.register(watchService,
                            StandardWatchEventKinds.ENTRY_MODIFY,
                            StandardWatchEventKinds.ENTRY_DELETE,
                            StandardWatchEventKinds.ENTRY_CREATE);
```

 EXAM TIP   You can watch a directory for changes. If you try to register a file for changes, you'll get a runtime exception (`NotDirectoryException`). Registering a directory for any event (create, modify, or delete) doesn't implicitly register its subdirectories.

In the next section, you'll see how the WatchService API stores the registered `Watchable` events, using the `WatchKey` objects.

8.6.3   *Access watched events using WatchKey interface*

The `WatchKey` object is a token that represents the registration of a `Watchable` object with a `WatchService`. As seen in the code in the previous section, a `WatchKey` object is created when you register your directory to be watched for create, modify, or delete events with a `WatchService`. A `WatchKey` can be in multiple states:

- *Ready*—A `WatchKey` is initially created with a ready state.
- *Signaled*—When an event is detected, the `WatchKey` is signaled and queued. It can be retrieved using `WatchService`'s methods `poll()` or `take()`.
- *Cancelled*—Calling method `cancel()` on a `WatchKey` or closing the `WatchService` cancels a `WatchKey`.
- *Valid*—A `WatchKey` in a ready or signaled state is in a valid state.

In the next section, you'll see how the detected events are processed using `Watch-Service`.

8.6.4   *Processing events*

A `WatchService` queues the registered events when they occur. The registered consumers can retrieve the queued `WatchKeys` and process the corresponding events. The `WatchService` interface defines method `take()` and overloaded method `poll()` to retrieve the queued WatchKeys. Once a key is processed, the consumer invokes the key's method reset() so that it can be signaled and requeued for further events.

To wait for registered events to occur, you need an infinite loop. Method take() of the WatchService interface retrieves and removes the next WatchKey, waiting if none are yet present. On the other hand, its poll() method retrieves and removes the next WatchKey, or returns null if none is present (no waiting). You can also use its over-loaded method poll(long timeout, TimeUnit unit) to specify the waiting time if none is present.

When the registered events occur, methods WatchService's poll() or take() return to retrieve the queued WatchKeys. For each retrieved WatchKey, call the Watch-Key's method pollEvents() to retrieve and remove all pending events for the key. Method pollEvents() returns a list of the events (WatchEvent) that were retrieved. Because you can register multiple paths and events with the same WatchService object, you can query the WatchEvent to determine the source of the event and its type, and process the event as required.

The following example watches two directories for create, modify, and delete events. Execute this code and, while it's running, use another system utility, like a file explorer, to modify, create, or delete files in the directories that this code is watching. The code will display the name of the newly created, modified, or deleted file or directory:

```
import java.io.*;
import java.nio.file.*;
import static java.nio.file.StandardWatchEventKinds.*;    ← ❶ Static import

public class WatchDirectories {

    public static void main(String args[]) {
        WatchService watchService = null;
                                                            ❷ Create
        try {                                                 Watch-
            watchService = FileSystems.getDefault().newWatchService();   ← Service
            Path dir1 = Paths.get("E:/OCPJavaSE7/");
            Path dir2 = Paths.get("E:/OCPJavaSE7/8");

            dir1.register(watchService,                       ❸ Register multiple
                        ENTRY_MODIFY, ENTRY_DELETE, ENTRY_CREATE);    directories and
            dir2.register(watchService, ENTRY_DELETE);        events with
                                                              watchService

            WatchKey watchKey = null;
                                                            ❹ Wait for a
            while(true) {                                      registered
                watchKey = watchService.take();    ←           event to occur
                for (WatchEvent<?> watchEvent: watchKey.pollEvents()) {    ❺ For a WatchKey,
                                                                           get a list of
                    WatchEvent.Kind<?> kind = watchEvent.kind();          events
                    Path path = ((WatchEvent<Path>)watchEvent).context();

                    if (kind == OVERFLOW) {        ← ❽ If event lost, skip
                        continue;                       remaining for loop
                    }
```

❻ Get type of event

❼ Retrieve event source

```
Process event      ┌─▷    else if (kind == ENTRY_CREATE) {
ENTRY_CREATE  ⑨                 System.out.format("\nCreate - %s", path);
                           }
Process event      ┌─▷    else if (kind == ENTRY_MODIFY) {
ENTRY_MODIFY  ⑩                 System.out.format("\nModify - %s", path );
                           }
Process event      ┌─▷    else if (kind == ENTRY_DELETE) {
ENTRY_DELETE  ⑪                 System.out.format("\nDelete - %s", path );
                           }
                     }
                     if(!watchKey.reset()) { break; }      ◁──┐   Reset WatchKey
                 }                                              so that it can be
             }                                            ⑫   queued again
             catch (IOException ioe) {
                 System.out.println(ioe.toString());
             }
             catch (InterruptedException ioe) {
                 System.out.println(ioe.toString());
             }
             finally {
                 try {
                     watchService.close();          ◁──┐   Close
                 } catch (IOException e) {           ⑬   watchService
                     System.out.println(e);
                 }
             }
         }
     }
}
```

In the preceding code, the static import at ❶ enables the code to use constants `ENTRY_CREATE`, `ENTRY_MODIFY`, and `OVERFLOW` without prefixing them with `Standard-WatchEventKinds`. The code at ❷ creates a `WatchService` object by calling method `newWatchService()` on `FileSystem`. The code at ❸ registers two directories, referred by paths `dir1` and `dir2`, with the same `watchService` object. The code uses an infinite loop to retrieve the queued `WatchKeys`. At ❹, `watchService.take()` waits for a registered event to occur and retrieves the corresponding `WatchKey`. For the `WatchKey` retrieved, the code at ❺ retrieves a list of events by calling `watchKey.pollEvents()`. At ❻ and ❼, the code retrieves the type and source of the event that has occurred. A file system might generate a lot of events, such that an event might be lost. The type of event reported is `OVERFLOW` ❽ if an event is lost. At ❾, ❿, and ⓫, the code processes events for creation (`ENTRY_CREATE`), modification (`ENTRY_MODIFY`), or deletion (`ENTRY_DELETE`) of a file or directory within the registered directories. At ⓬, the code resets the `watchKey` by calling `watchKey.reset()` so that it can be queued and signaled again. At the end, the code at ⓭ closes the `WatchService` object by calling `close()`.

The possibilities are immense in how you process the events, detected using `WatchService`, and are limited only by your needs or your imagination.

8.7 *Summary*

We started this chapter with an introduction to NIO.2 and the sample application. We covered the `Path` interface and worked with examples on how `Path` objects are created. You learned how to use `Path` methods to access path components, compare paths, convert relative paths to absolute paths, and resolve paths. Class `Files` is used to manipulate files and directories. It can be used to automatically check and create single or multiple files and directories, check for their existence, and copy, move, or delete them.

You learned how to access and update attributes of files and directories by using attribute views or class `Files`. NIO.2 defines a rich set of classes and interfaces that enable you to access and update basic, dos, Posix, Acl, and user-defined attributes of files or directories.

You can use the `FileVisitor` interface and classes `SimpleFileVisitor` and `DirectoryStream` to traverse and access a directory stream. You can find a file with a matching regex or glob pattern using the `PathMatcher` interface.

One of the most interesting features of NIO.2, the WatchService API enables you to watch a directory for creation, modification, and deletion of new or existing files and directories. When the registered events are triggered, they can be processed as required.

REVIEW NOTES

This section lists the main points covered in this chapter.

Path objects

- Objects of the `Path` interface are used to represent the path of files or directories in a file system.
- Because a `Path` object might not be tied to a real file or directory on a system, it can refer to a nonexistent file or directory.
- Apart from referring to a file or a directory, a `Path` object can also refer to a symbolic link. A symbolic link is a special file that refers to another file.
- When you read data from or write data to a symbolic link, you read from or write to its underlying target file. But if you delete a symbolic link, the target file isn't deleted.
- A `Path` can never be equal to a `Path` associated with another file system, even if they include exactly the same values.
- You can create `Path` objects by using `Paths.get()` or `FileSystems.get-Default().getPath()`.
- You can convert a `File` instance to a `Path` object by calling `toPath()` on the `File` instance.
- Behind the scenes, both `Paths.get()` and `File.toPath()` call `FileSystems.getDefault().getPath()`.

- Most of the `Path` methods perform syntactic operations. They manipulate the paths to a file or directory without accessing the file systems. They're logical operations on paths in memory.

- Methods `getName()`, `getNameCount()`, and `subpath()` don't use the root directory of a path. Method `getRoot()` returns the root of an absolute path and `null` for relative paths.

- The `Path` methods that accept positions throw an `IllegalArgumentException` at runtime for invalid positions. For example, `getName()` and `subpath()` throw an `IllegalArgumentException` if you pass invalid path positions to them.

- You can compare paths lexicographically using method `compareTo(Path)`.

- To check whether a path starts or ends with another path, you can use `startsWith(String)`, `startsWith(Path)`, `endsWith(String)`, and `endsWith(Path)`.

- Methods `startsWith()` and `endsWith()` are overloaded—`startsWith(String)`, `startsWith(Path)`, `endsWith(String)`, and `endsWith(Path)`. So if you pass `null` to these methods, you'll get a compiler error.

- The method name to retrieve the absolute path from a `Path` object is `toAbsolutePath()` and not `getAbsolutePath()`.

- You can remove redundant path values by calling method `normalize()` on `Path`.

- `Path` is immutable and calling `normalize()` on a `Path` object doesn't change its value.

- Method `normalize()` doesn't check the actual file system to verify if the file (or directory) the resulting path is referring to actually exists.

- If a `Path` object includes redundancies like `.` or `..`, calling information retrieval methods like `subpath()` or `getName()` will include these redundancies in the returned values.

- The overloaded methods `resolve(String)` and `resolve(Path)` are used to join a relative path to another path. If you pass an absolute path as a parameter, this method returns the absolute path.

- To retrieve the path to a file in the same directory, say, to create its copy or to rename it, you can use the overloaded methods `resolveSibling(String)` and `resolveSibling(Path)`.

- Method `resolveSibling()` resolves a given path against a path's parent. If the given path is an absolute path, this method returns the absolute path. If you pass it an empty path, it returns the parent of the path.

- Methods `resolve()` and `resolveSibling()` don't check the actual file system to verify if the file (or directory) the resulting path is referring to actually exists.

- To construct a path between two `Path` objects, use method `relativize()`. It can be used to construct a path between two relative or absolute `Path` objects.

- You can't create a path from a relative path to an absolute path and vice versa using method `relativize()`. If you do so, you'll get a runtime exception (`IllegalArgumentException`).

- Method `relativize()` doesn't check the actual file system to verify if the file (or directory) the resulting path is referring to actually exists.

Class Files

- Class `java.nio.file.Files` defines static methods for manipulating files and directories.
- Method `createFile()` atomically checks for the existence of the file specified by the method parameter path and creates it if it doesn't exist.
- Method `createFile()` fails and throws an exception if the file already exists, a directory with the same name exists, its parent directory doesn't exist due to an I/O error, or the specified file attributes can't be set.
- Method `createDirectory()` creates the specified directory (not the parent directory) on the file system. It also atomically checks for the existence of the specified directory and creates it if it doesn't exist.
- Method `createDirectory()` throws an exception if a file or directory exists with the same name, its parent directory doesn't exist due to an I/O error, or the specified directory attributes can't be set.
- Method `createDirectories()` creates a directory, creating all nonexistent parent directories.
- If the target directory already exists, `createDirectories()` doesn't throw any runtime exception. It throws an exception if the specified `dir` exists but isn't a directory, an I/O occurs, or the specified directory attributes can't be set.
- Specifying file or directory attributes is optional with methods `createFile()`, `createDirectory()`, and `createDirectories()`. All these methods declare to throw an `IOException`, which is a checked exception.
- You can check for the existence of a file or directory referred by a `Path` object using methods `exists()` and `notExists()`.
- Method `notExists()` isn't a complement of method `exists()`. It returns `true` if a target doesn't exist or `false` if its existence can't be determined. If these methods can't determine the existence of a file, both of them will return `false`.
- Class `Files`'s overloaded method `copy()` enables you to read from `InputStream` and write to a `Path` object, read from a `Path` object and write to `OutputStream`, and read from and write to `Path` objects.
- `Files.copy()` can copy only files, not directories. If the source is a directory, then in the target an empty directory is created (without copying the entries in the directory). This method returns a `long` or `Path` value, not a `boolean` value.
- If you use a relative path to the target file, the file is created relative to your Java class file (.class) and not relative to the source file (passed as a parameter to method `Files.copy()`).
- To move files or directories programmatically, you can use `Files.move()`, which moves or renames a file to a target file.

- You can only move empty directories using method `Files.move()`. You can rename a nonempty directory by using `Files.move()`. But you can't move a file or directory to a nonexisting directory.

- To delete a directory or a file referred to by a `Path` object, you can use methods `delete(Path)` or `deleteIfExists(Path)`.

- If you try to delete a directory that isn't empty, methods `delete(Path)` and `deleteIfExists(Path)` will throw a `DirectoryNotEmptyException`.

- If you try to delete a nonexistent file or directory using method `delete()`, it will throw a `NoSuchFileException`. But method `deleteIfExists()` won't throw an exception if the file or directory at the specified path doesn't exist—rather, it will return `false`.

- Methods `delete()` and `deleteIfExists()` can be used to delete files and (nonempty) directories.

Files and directory attributes

- Class `Files` defines static methods to access individual attributes of a file or directory referred by a `Path`.

- You can access the individual attributes of a file or directory by using method `Files.getAttribute()`, passing to it the name of the attribute as a string value. To modify the attributes of an existing file or directory, you can use `Files.set-Attribute()`.

- You can access a group of file attributes by calling `Files.getFileAttribute-View()` or `Files.readAttributes()`.

- The `BasicFileAttributes` interface defines methods to access the basic attributes that should be supported by all the file systems.

- The `BasicFileAttributeView` interface can be used to modify the basic attributes.

- The `DosFileAttributes` interface extends `BasicFileAttributes` and defines methods to access attributes specific to Windows files and directories.

- The `DosFileAttributeView` interface defines methods to modify the DOS file attributes.

- The `PosixFileAttributes` interface also extends `BasicFileAttributes` and defines methods to access attributes related to the POSIX family of standards, like Linux or UNIX.

- The `PosixFileAttributeView` interface defines methods to modify attributes related to the POSIX family.

- Available only for Windows OS, the `AclFileAttributeView` interface supports access and updates of a file's ACL.

- The `FileOwnerAttributeView` interface supports access and updates to the owner of a file or directory. It is supported by all systems that support the concept of file owners.

- The `UserDefinedFileAttributeView` interface supports the addition, modification, and deletion of user-defined metadata.
- The `BasicFileAttributes`, `DosFileAttributes`, and `PosixFileAttributes` interfaces define methods to access attributes. They don't define methods to modify (or set) the attributes.
- The `BasicFileAttributeView`, `DosFileAttributeView`, `PosixFileAttributeView`, `AclFileAttributeView`, `FileOwnerAttributeView`, and `UserDefinedFileAttributeView` interfaces can be used to update attribute values.
- If a file system doesn't support an attribute view, `Files.getFileAttributeView()` returns null. If a file system doesn't support an attribute set, `File.readAttributes()` will throw a runtime exception.
- If an underlying system doesn't support all the basic timestamps—that is, `creationTime`, `lastAccessTime`, and `lastModifiedTime`—it might return system-specific information.
- Methods `Files.setAttribute()` and `Files.getAttribute()` throw an `IllegalArgumentException` or `UnsupportedOperationException` if you pass them an invalid or unsupported attribute.
- The `DosFileAttributes` interface makes the following attributes available:
  - `archive`
  - `hidden`
  - `readonly`
  - `system`
- The DOS attributes are available on a Windows system only. Trying to access them on other systems will throw a runtime exception.
- When you read all DOS attributes using method `Files.readAttributes()`, you also read the basic attributes.
- The POSIX attributes are as follows:
  - `group`
  - `owner`
  - `permissions`
- The POSIX attributes are available on the POSIX family of standards, such as UNIX and LINUX. Trying to access them on other systems will throw a runtime exception.
- To read or update the owner of a file or directory you can use the `AclFileAttributeView`, `FileOwnerAttributeView`, and `PosixFileAttributeView` interfaces.
- The `UserDefinedAttributeView` interface can be used to add, delete, access, and modify additional user-defined attributes to or from a file or directory. It defines methods `delete(String)`, `list()`, `read(String, ByteBuffer)`, `size(String)`, and `write(String, ByteBuffer)` to, respectively, delete, list, read, get an attribute's size, and write attribute values.

Recursively access a directory tree

- Class `Files` defines overloaded method `walkFileTree()` to walk recursively through the specified path. To define the traversal behavior, this method accepts an object of the `FileVisitor` interface.

- You can use the `FileVisitor`, a generic interface, to define the code that you want to execute during the traversal of a directory structure. When you traverse a directory structure, you can define what to do before or after you visit a directory, when you visit a file, or when access to a file is denied.

- Method `postVisitDirectory()` is invoked for a directory after entries in the directory and all of their descendants have been visited.

- Method `preVisitDirectory()` is invoked for a directory before entries in the directory are visited.

- Method `visitFile()` is invoked for a file in a directory.

- Method `visitFileFailed()` is invoked for a file that couldn't be visited.

- Methods `preVisitDirectory()` and `visitFile()` are passed `BasicFile-Attributes` of the path that they operate on. You can use these methods to query file or directory attributes.

- Class `SimpleFileVisitor` is a simple visitor of files with default behavior to visit all files and to rethrow I/O errors. It implements the `FileVisitor` interface.

- You can initiate traversal of a directory by calling the overloaded method `walk-FileTree()` from class `Files`.

- The `DirectoryStream` interface can be used to iterate over all the files and directories in a directory. You can use an `Iterator` or for-each construct to iterate over a directory. The order in which the directory contents are iterated is unpredictable.

- If you pass `Path` to a file (and not a directory) to `Files.newDirectoryStream()`, it will throw a runtime exception. The order of iteration of files and directories in a specified directory using `DirectoryStream` is unpredictable.

Using PathMatcher

- You can match your file or directory names against a regex or glob pattern by using `PathMatcher`.

- A glob pattern supports a simpler form of pattern matching than the regex. It supports fewer special constructs.

- In glob, `*` matches zero or more characters. In regex, `.*` matches zero or more characters.

- To match a `Path` object with a pattern, you should create an object of `java .nio.file.PathMatcher`. `PathMatcher` is an interface with just one method: `matches()`. It returns `true` if a given path matches this matcher's pattern.

- You can create a `PathMatcher` by calling `FileSystem.getPathMatcher()` and passing it the pattern to be matched.

Watch a directory for changes

- `WatchService` enables you to watch a directory for changes like addition, modification, or deletion of contents of a directory.
- The first step to watch a directory for changes is to create a `WatchService` object.
- A `WatchService` object watches a directory for the following events:
  - `StandardWatchEventKinds.ENTRY_CREATE`—This event occurs when a new file or directory is created, moved, or renamed in the directory being watched.
  - `StandardWatchEventKinds.ENTRY_DELETE`—This event occurs when an existing file or directory is deleted, moved, or renamed in the directory being watched.
  - `StandardWatchEventKinds.ENTRY_MODIFY`—This event is platform-dependent. It usually occurs when contents of an existing file are modified. It can also occur if the attributes of a file or directory (in the directory being watched) are modified.
  - `StandardWatchEventKinds.OVERFLOW`—This indicates that an event has been lost.
- You can register multiple directories to be watched with the same `WatchService` object by using method `register()` of `Path`.
- You can watch a directory for changes. If you try to register a file for changes, you'll get a runtime exception (`NotDirectoryException`). Registering a directory for any event (create, modify, or delete) doesn't implicitly register its subdirectories.
- The `WatchKey` object is a token that represents the registration of a `Watchable` object with a `WatchService`. A `WatchKey` object is created when you register your directory to be watched for create, modify, or delete events with a `WatchService`.
- A `WatchKey` can be in multiple states:
  - *Ready*—A `WatchKey` is initially created with a ready state.
  - *Signaled*—When an event is detected, the `WatchKey` is signaled and queued. It can be retrieved using method `WatchService`'s `poll()` or `take()`.
  - *Cancelled*—Calling method `cancel()` on a `WatchKey` or closing the `WatchService` cancels a `WatchKey`.
  - *Valid*—A `WatchKey` in a ready or signaled state is in a valid state.
- A `WatchService` queues the registered events when they occur. The registered consumers can retrieve the queued `WatchKey`s and process the corresponding events.
- The `WatchService` interface defines method `take()` and overloaded method `poll()` to retrieve the queued `WatchKey`s. Once a key is processed, the consumer invokes the key's method `reset()` so that it can be signaled and requeued for further events.

- Method `take()` of the `WatchService` interface retrieves and removes the next `WatchKey`, waiting if none is yet present.
- Method `poll()` of the `WatchService` interface retrieves and removes the next `WatchKey`, or null if none is present (no waiting). You can also use its overloaded method `poll(long timeout, TimeUnit unit)` to specify the waiting time if none is present.
- For each retrieved `WatchKey`, you can call the `WatchKey`'s method `pollEvents()` to retrieve and remove all pending events for the key.
- Method `pollEvents()` returns a list of the events (`WatchEvent`) that were retrieved.

Because you can register multiple paths and events with the same `WatchService` object, you can query the `WatchEvent` to determine the source of the event and its type, and process the event as required.

SAMPLE EXAM QUESTIONS

Q 8-1. Given the following directory structure

```
root dir
|- MyDir
   |- 8_1.java
   |- 8_1.class
   |- Hello.txt
```

which options when inserted at /* INSERT CODE HERE */will delete the file represented by the `Path` object path?

```
import java.nio.file.*;
class Q8_1 {
    public static void main(String... args) throws Exception {
        Path path = Paths.get("Hello.txt");
        Files.delete(/* INSERT CODE HERE */);
    }
}
```

   a `path.toAbsolutePath()`

   b `path.resolveSibling("Q8_1.class")`

   c `path.toRealPath()`

   d `path.resolve()`

Q 8-2. What is the output of the following code?

```
class Q8_2 {
    public static void main(String... args) {
        Path path1 = FileSystems.getDefault().getPath("/main/sub/notes/
    file.txt");
        Path path2 = Paths.get("code/Hello.java");
        System.out.println(path1.getRoot()+ ":" + path2.getRoot());
```

```
            System.out.println(path1.getName(0) + ":" + path2.getName(0));
            System.out.println(path1.subpath(1, 3) + ":" + path2.subpath(0,1));
    }
}
```

a `\main:null`
  `file.txt:Hello.java`
  `sub\notes\file.txt:code\Hello.java`

b `\:null`
  `file.txt:Hello.java`
  `sub\notes:code`

c `main:code`
  `file.txt:Hello.java`
  `sub\notes:code`

d `\:null`
  `main:code`
  `sub\notes:code`

e None of the above

f Compilation fails

Q 8-3. Which definition of class `MyFileVisitor` will enable the following code to delete recursively all files that are smaller than 100 bytes in size?

```
Path path = Paths.get("/myHomeDir");
Files.walkFileTree(path, new MyFileVisitor());
```

a
```
class MyFileVisitor implements FileVisitor<Path> {
    public FileVisitResult visitFile(Path file, BasicFileAttributes
attrs) throws IOException{
        if (attrs.size() <= 100) {
            Files.delete(file);
        }
        return FileVisitResult.CONTINUE;
    }
}
```

b
```
class MyFileVisitor extends SimpleFileVisitor<Path> {
    public FileVisitResult visitFile(Path file, BasicFileAttributes
attrs) throws IOException{
        if (attrs.size() <= 100) {
            Files.delete(file);
        }
        return FileVisitResult.CONTINUE;
    }
}
```

c
```
class MyFileVisitor implements FileVisitor<Path> {
    public FileVisitResult visitFile(Path file,
                        BasicFileAttributes attrs) throws IOException{
        if (attrs.size() <= 100) {
            Files.delete(file);
        }
```

```
                return FileVisitResult.CONTINUE;
            }
            public FileVisitResult preVisitDirectory(Path dir,
                                    BasicFileAttributes attrs) {}
            public FileVisitResult postVisitDirectory(Path dir,
                                    IOException exc) {}
            public FileVisitResult visitFileFailed(Path file,
                                    IOException exc) {}
        }
 d  class MyFileVisitor extends SimpleFileVisitor {
        public FileVisitResult visitFile(Path file, BasicFileAttributes
    attrs) throws IOException{
            if (attrs.getSize() <= 100) {
                Files.deleteFile(file);
            }
            return FileVisitResult.CONTINUE;
        }
    }
```

e   Compilation error

f   Runtime exception

Q 8-4. What is the output of the following code?

```
Path path1 = Paths.get("MyDir/hello.java");
Path path2 = Paths.get("FriendDir/code");
Path path3 = path1.relativize(path2);
for (Path path : path3)
    System.out.println(path);
```

a   ..
    ..
    FriendDir
    code

b   ..
    ..
    MyDir
    hello.java

c   FriendDir
    code

d   MyDir
    hello.java

e   ..
    MyDir

f   Compilation error

g   Runtime exception

Sample exam questions 571

Q 8-5. Select the correct statements:

   a `Paths.get()` can throw a `FileNotFoundException`.

   b `getParent()` in `Path` returns an empty path if a path doesn't have a parent.

   c `getNameCount()` in `Path` excludes the root of a path.

   d For absolute paths, `toAbsolutePath()` in `Path` returns `null`.

Q 8-6. Which code options when inserted at `/* INSERT CODE HERE */` will copy the specified file from the specified source to the destination?

```
public static void copyFile (String src, String dest) throws IOException{
    /* INSERT CODE HERE */
    java.nio.file.Files.copy(source, destination);
}
```

   a
```
Path source = Paths.get(src);
Path destination = Paths.get(dest);
```

   b
```
FileInputStream source = new FileInputStream(new File(src));
Path destination = Paths.get(dest);
```

   c
```
Path source = Paths.get(src);
BufferedOutputStream destination = new BufferedOutputStream(
                                    new FileOutputStream(dest));
```

   d
```
FileInputStream source = new FileInputStream(new File(src));
FileOutputStream destination = new FileOutputStream(new File(dest));
```

Q 8-7. Which options are true for the following code?

```
public static void check(Path path) throws Exception {
    if (!Files.exists(path)) {
        System.out.println("Not exists");
        Files.createDirectories(path.getParent());
        Files.createFile(path);
    }
    else if (!Files.notExists(path)) {
        System.out.println("exists");
        Files.delete(path);
    }
    else {
        System.out.println("can never reach here");
    }
}
```

   a `check()` will output "Not exists" and try to create a new file, if it doesn't exist.

   b `check()` will output "exists" and try to delete the file if it exists. It won't delete a directory.

   c `check()` can never output "can never reach here".

   d `check()` can throw an `IOException`, `NoSuchFileException`.

Q 8-8. Select the incorrect statements for the following code:

```
public static void toggleFile(Path file) throws Exception {
    DosFileAttributes attr = Files.readAttributes(file,
                                        DosFileAttributes.class);
    if (attr.isHidden()) {                                    //line1
        Files.setAttribute(file, "dos:hidden", Boolean.FALSE);    //line2
    }
    else
        Files.setAttribute(file, "dos:hidden", Boolean.TRUE);    //line3
}
```

a   toggleFile() changes the attribute of a file or directory to hidden if it isn't, and vice versa (when executed on a Windows system).

b   If "dos:hidden" is changed to "hidden" on lines 2 and 3, toggleFile() can change the "hidden" attributes of files or directories on all OSs.

c   Replacing attr.isHidden() with attr.hidden() will not modify the code results.

d   toggleFile can throw an UnsupportedOperationException.

Q 8-9. What is the output of the following code?

```
Path path1 = Paths.get("/pin/./bin/tub/../code/../Hello.java");
System.out.println(path1.normalize());
```

a   \pin\bin\tub\Hello.java

b   \pin\bin\tub\code\Hello.java

c   \bin\tub\code\Hello.java

d   \bin\Hello.java

e   \pin\bin\Hello.java

Q 8-10. For which string values will the method match return true?

```
public static boolean match(String filename) throws Exception {
    Path path = Paths.get(filename);
    PathMatcher matcher = FileSystems.getDefault().getPathMatcher("glob:/
     mydir/*/*");
    return (matcher.matches(path));
}
```

a   /mydir/notes/java/String

b   /mydir/notes/java

c   /mydir/notes

d   mydir/notes/java/String

e   mydir/notes/java

Q 8-11. Given the following code, which code options can be inserted at /*INSERT CODE HERE*/ without any compilation errors?

```
Path file = Paths.get("/mydir");
PosixFileAttributes attr = Files.readAttributes(file,
    PosixFileAttributes.class);
System.out.println(/*INSERT CODE HERE*/);
```

   a attr.group()

   b attr.owner()

   c attr.size()

   d attr.permissions()

   e attr.creationTime()

   f attr.isReadOnly()

   g attr.isRegularFile()

ANSWERS TO SAMPLE EXAM QUESTIONS

A 8-1. a, c

[8.1] Operate on file and directory paths with the Path class

Explanation: Option (b) is incorrect. The call path.resolveSibling("Q8_1.class") will resolve the path from file Q8_1.class against the parent directory of file Hello.txt. Because these files exist in the same directory, a (valid) path to file Q8_1.class is returned. So Files.delete() will not delete file Hello.txt, but Q8_1.class instead.

Option (d) will fail compilation. Method resolve() accepts either a Path or a String, resolving it against the path on which it's called.

A 8-2. d

[8.1] Operate on file and directory paths with the Path class

Explanation: The getRoot method returns the root of a path for an absolute path and null for a relative path. Because "/main/sub/notes/file.txt" starts with a /, it's considered an absolute path and getRoot will return / or \ depending on your underlying OS (\ for Windows and / for UNIX).

Method getName() excludes the root of a path and returns the element of this path, specified by the index parameter to this method. The element closest to the root in the directory hierarchy has an index of 0 and the element farthest from the root has an index of count-1 (where count is the total number of Path elements).

Method subpath() (small p) returns the subsequence of the name elements of a Path, starting at the method parameter startIndex (inclusive) up to the name element at endIndex (exclusive).

A 8-3. b

[8.4] Recursively access a directory tree using the DirectoryStream and FileVisitor interfaces

Explanation: Option (a) is incorrect because it won't compile. The `FileVisitor` interface defines four methods: `preVisitDirectory()`, `postVisitDirectory()`, `visitFile()`, and `visitFileFailed()`. Class `MyFileVisitor` in this option implements only one method.

Option (c) is incorrect. Though class `MyFileVisitor` implements all the methods of the `FileVisitor` interface, methods `preVisitDirectory()`, `postVisitDirectory()`, and `visitFileFailed()` don't return a value. All these methods must return a value of type `FileVisitResult`.

Option (d) is incorrect because the correct method name to get the file size from `BasicFileAttributes` is `size`. The correct method name to delete a file using class `Files` is `delete`.

A 8-4. a

[8.1] Operate on file and directory paths with the Path class

Explanation: `path1.relativize(path2)` creates a relative path from `path1` to `path2`. To navigate from relative `path1` (MyDir/hello.java) to relative `path2` (FriendDir/code), you need to do the following steps:

1 (apply ..)—Navigate to the parent directory of MyDir/hello.java—that is, MyDir.
2 (apply ..)—Navigate to the parent directory of MyDir.
3 (apply /FriendDir)—Navigate to /FriendDir.
4 (apply /code)—Navigate to code.

The `Path` interface extends the `Iterable` interface. A `Path` object can iterate over its name elements using the `for`-each loop.

A 8-5. c

[8.1] Operate on file and directory paths with the Path class

Explanation: Option (a) is incorrect. A `Path` object might refer to a nonexistent file or directory. It can throw an `InvalidPathException` if the path string cannot be converted to a `Path` object.

Option (b) is incorrect because `getParent()` returns `null` if a `Path` object doesn't have a parent.

Option (d) in incorrect. For absolute paths, `toAbsolutePath()` returns the path itself. For a relative path, the absolute path is resolved in an implementation-dependent manner.

A 8-6. a, b, c

[8.2] Check, delete, copy, or move a file or directory with the Files class

Explanation: The overloaded `copy()` method in class `Files` can copy a source to a destination in the following formats:

- From `InputStream` to `Path`
- From `Path` to `OutputStream`
- From `Path` to `Path`

Therefore, options (a), (b), and (c) are correct. `FileInputStream` extends `InputStream`, `FileOutputStream` extends `OutputStream`, and `BufferedOutputStream` extends `OutputStream`. So their objects can be passed to `Files.copy()`.

Option (d) is incorrect because method `copy()` in class `Files` doesn't copy `InputStream` to `OutputStream`.

A 8-7. a, d

[8.2] Check, delete, copy, or move a file or directory with the Files class

Explanation: Option (b) is incorrect because `Files.delete()` can be used to delete files and empty directories. If you try to delete a nonempty directory, `Files.delete()` will throw a `DirectoryNotEmptyException`.

Option (c) is incorrect because both `exists()` and `notExists()` can return `false` if the underlying system can't determine the existence of a file.

A 8-8. b, c

[8.3] Read and change file and directory attributes, focusing on the `BasicFileAttributes`, `DosFileAttributes`, and `PosixFileAttributes` interfaces

Explanation: Option (a) is a correct statement because method `toggleFile()` changes the attribute "hidden" of a file to `true` if it's `false` and vice versa.

Option (b) is an incorrect statement. If "dos:hidden" is changed to "hidden", the code will throw a runtime exception. "hidden" is a DOS file attribute. DOS and POSIX attributes must be prefixed with `dos:` or `posix:` in method `Files.setAttribute`. You don't need to prefix the basic file attributes with `basic:`. In the absence of any prefix, `basic:` is added automatically.

Option (c) is an incorrect statement because the correct method name to access the attribute "hidden" from `DosFileAttributes` is `isHidden`.

Option (d) is a correct statement because if you execute this code on an OS that doesn't support `DosFileAttributes`, `Files.readAttributes()` will throw an `UnsupportedOperationException`.

A8-9. e

[8.1] Operate on file and directory paths with the Path class

Explanation: Method `normalize()` removes the redundancies like "." (current directory) and ".." (parent directory) from a path. Because "." denotes the current directory, it's simply removed by `normalize()`. ".." is only removed if it is preceded by a non-".." name. In the following example, no redundancies are removed:

```
System.out.println(Paths.get("../../OCPJava7/8.1.txt").normalize());
```

A8-10. b

[8.5] Find a file with the `PathMatcher` interface

Explanation: The `glob` pattern `/mydir/*/*` evaluates to root (`/`), followed by dir `mydir`, followed by any two subdirectories. Only option (b) matches this pattern.

A8-11. a, b, c, d, e, g

[8.3] Read and change file and directory attributes, focusing on the `BasicFile-Attributes`, `DosFileAttributes`, and `PosixFileAttributes` interfaces

Explanation: The `PosixFileAttributes` interface extends the `BasicFileAttributes` interface, so a `PosixFileAttributes` object can access methods `creationTime()`, `size()`, and `isRegularFile()` defined in the `BasicFileAttributes` interface. Method `isReadOnly()` is defined in the `DosFileAttributes` interface and it can't be used with an object of `PosixFileAttributes`.

Building database applications with JDBC

Exam objectives covered in this chapter	What you need to know
[9.1] Describe the interfaces that make up the core of the JDBC API (including the `Driver`, `Connection`, `Statement`, and `ResultSet`) and their relationships to provider implementations	Identification of the interfaces that make up the core of the JDBC API How an application creates objects of these interfaces
[9.2] Identify the components required to connect to a database using class `DriverManager` (including the JDBC URL)	The steps and components required to connect to a database using class `DriverManager`, for JDBC API version 3.0 and before and JDBC API version 4.0 and later
[9.3] Submit queries and read results from the database (including creating statements, returning result sets, iterating through the results, and properly closing result sets, statements, and connections)	How to execute SQL statements against a database using the interfaces `Connection`, `Statement`, and `ResultSet` How to combat the `SQLException` thrown by database operations How to use `try-catch-finally` and try-with-resources statements to close database resources
[9.4] Use JDBC transactions (including disabling auto-commit mode, committing and rolling back transactions, and setting and rolling back to savepoints)	How to create transactions, `Savepoint`, commit, and roll back changes Effects of auto-commit mode on a transaction
[9.5] Construct and use `RowSet` objects using class `RowSetProvider` and the `RowSetFactory` interface	How to create `RowSet` objects using class `RowSetProvider` and the interface `RowSetFactory` The specialized types of `RowSet` objects

Exam objectives covered in this chapter	What you need to know
[9.6] Create and use `PreparedStatement` and `CallableStatement` objects	How to use `PreparedStatement` and `CallableStatement` statements to execute static and dynamic SQL statements and stored procedures

Given multiple options, choosing the right technology to connect a Java application to a database is challenging.

At present, there are multiple approaches and technologies to connect a Java application with a database. Examples include the EJB Entity Beans, Java Persistence API (JPA), Java Database Objects (JDO), and others. Hibernate™ is a popular JPA implementation. Hibernate is an Object Relational Mapping (ORM) framework for the Java language. Each of these approaches or implementations has its own set of advantages and disadvantages. For example, you can't use JPA entities or EJB Entity Beans with Java's Standard Edition (JSE). Apart from accessibility, other factors like license fees, ease of use, backward compatibility, and availability of expertise in a particular technology might affect your choice of approach or API to use to connect to a database.

The exam has included a simple industry standard to connect your Java application to any tabular data: Java Database Connectivity (JDBC). JDBC has been around since Java version 1.1.

Before I go further, let me clarify that the exam won't query you on your capabilities to connect tables in a database or write complex SQL queries. The exam will focus on testing your capabilities on how to connect a Java application to a database using the JDBC API. It will query you on the prerequisites for establishing a connection, such as the existence of JDBC drivers, the connection URL, submitting queries, reading results, performing transactions, and using multiple flavors of results (`ResultSet` and `RowSet`) and statements (`Statement`, `CallableStatement`, and `PreparedStatement`).

Let's get started with an introduction to the JDBC API so that you understand what it is and how it connects your Java class to a database, before getting our hands dirty with the actual code.

9.1   Introduction

JDBC is a Java API. It's an industry standard for database-independent connections from Java applications to tabular data stored in relational databases, flat files, or spreadsheets. The JDBC API defines multiple interfaces, which must be implemented by the database vendors or a third party, and is supplied as a driver. As shown in figure 9.1, you can think of the bridge between a Java application and a database to be made of the JDBC API and driver implementation classes. The JDBC API provides your classes with the interfaces and classes to connect to a database and process the results. The actual classes that implement the interfaces in the JDBC API are defined by the driver for a database.

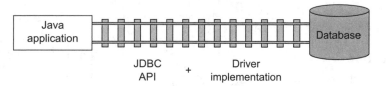

Figure 9.1   JDBC API and driver implementation classes are a bridge between a Java application and a database

Any Java class can use JDBC to connect with a database using a driver. JDBC has been around since 1997, and was added to JSE 1.1 as JDBC 1.0. Since its first version, multiple enhancements have been made to the JDBC API. Java 7 ships with JDBC version 4.1. JDBC classes are defined in Java packages `java.sql` and `javax.sql`.

9.1.1   JDBC API overview

By using the classes and interfaces from the JDBC API, Java classes can connect to a data source, execute SQL (Structured Query Language, the standard language for relational database management systems, RDBMS), and process the results. At the heart of the JDBC API lies the use of SQL to create, modify, and delete database objects like tables, and query and update them, as shown in figure 9.2.

JDBC provides vendor-neutral access to the common database features. So if you don't use proprietary features of a database, you can easily change the database that you connect to. The JDBC API includes an abstraction of a database connection, statements, and result sets.

 NOTE   Though different in meaning, the terms *database* and *database engine* are often used interchangeably by developers. A database refers to the collection of data and the relationships supporting the data. The database software refers to the software like MySQL to access the data. A database engine is a process instance of the software that accesses the database. A database server is the computer on which the database engine runs.

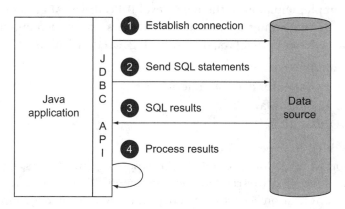

Figure 9.2   JDBC API usage overview

Let's look at the classes and interfaces that make up the core of the JDBC API.

9.1.2   *JDBC architecture*

With the JDBC API, you have a choice of connecting to a local or remote data store either directly or through an application server. The JDBC API supports the use of a two-tier model or *n*-tier (multiple-tier) model to connect to a database or data source. In a two-tier model, your Java application connects directly with a local or remote data source using a JDBC driver. In an *n*-tier model, a Java or non-Java application sends a command to an application server, which connects to a remote or local database using the JDBC API. Figure 9.3 shows an application connecting to a data source using two-tier and *n*-tier architecture.

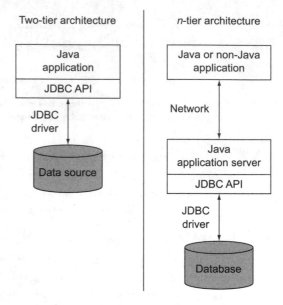

Figure 9.3   JDBC architecture

JDBC drivers provided by the database or a third party work as interpreters to enable the Java applications to "talk" with the databases. These come in multiple flavors, as discussed in the next section.

9.1.3   *JDBC drivers*

The JDBC API includes two major set of interfaces:

- A JDBC API for application developers
- A lower-level JDBC driver API for writing drivers

JDBC drivers are the implementation of the lower-level JDBC driver API as defined in the JDBC specifications. Depending on whether the drivers are implemented using only Java code, native code, or partial Java, they are categorized as follows:

- Type 4—pure Java JDBC driver
- Type 3—pure Java driver for database middleware
- Type 2—native API, partly Java driver
- Type 1—JDBC-ODBC bridge

Figure 9.4 shows the different types of drivers.

For the exam, you won't be questioned on the types of JDBC drivers, how they are implemented, and other driver-related specific details. The exam covers how you'd make your Java application access a given driver, using the correct connection string to establish a connection with the underlying database. Also, for the exam,

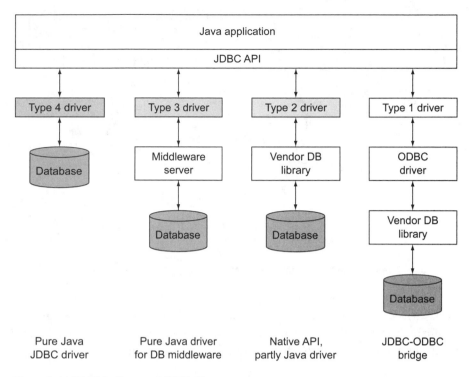

Figure 9.4   **Multiple flavors of JDBC drivers**

you'll only need to connect with the type 4 JDBC driver—that is, the pure Java JDBC driver.

With an overview of the JDBC API, its architecture, and the various drivers that you can use to connect a Java application to a database, let's look next at the main interfaces that make up the core of the JDBC API.

9.2 *Interfaces that make up the JDBC API core*

[9.1]   Describe the interfaces that make up the core of the JDBC API (including the Driver, Connection, Statement, and ResultSet interfaces and their relationship to provider implementations)

The JDBC API defines multiple interfaces, which are implemented by the database vendor or a third party that your Java application is connecting with. The implementation of these interfaces is bundled in a driver and made available to the Java application. JDBC calls from your Java applications are converted to database calls by a driver. Figure 9.5 shows the main interfaces from packages `java.sql` and `javax.sql` that you'll work with in this chapter (and that are covered on the exam).

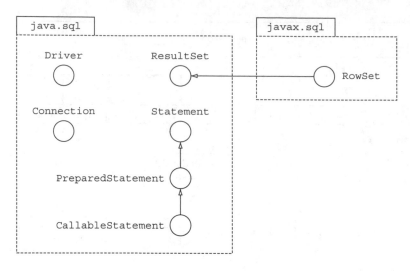

Figure 9.5   Interfaces that make up the core of the JDBC API

Every driver *must* implement a minimum set of interfaces defined in the JDBC API to conform to the JDBC specifications. The interface java.sql.Driver is one that must be implemented by all JDBC drivers, as discussed in the next section.

9.2.1 *Interface java.sql.Driver*

Every driver class must implement the interface java.sql.Driver. A Java system allows for the existence and registration of multiple drivers. When a database vendor or third party develops a JDBC driver, it must implement this interface. When a class implementing this interface is loaded into memory, it must create an instance of itself and register itself with class DriverManager. It does this by defining a static initializer block, which instantiates it and registers itself with class DriverManager. When a Java application requests to establish a connection with a database, class DriverManager searches for an appropriate driver from its list of registered drivers to connect with the target database.

You can manually load and register a driver by calling method forName() from class java.lang.Class. For example, let's assume that the name of the class that implements the interface java.sql.Driver in MySQL's JDBC driver is com.mysql.jdbc .Driver. To load and register this driver, you should execute the following:

```
Class.forName("com.mysql.jdbc.Driver");
```

Manual loading of the drivers was required until JDBC version 3.0. Starting with JDBC 4.0 and later, Java applications can automatically load and register the drivers using the Service Provider Mechanism (SPM), introduced with Java 6 and JDBC 4.0. For SPM, the driver needs to include the configuration file META-INF/services/

java.sql.Driver in the .jar file. This file contains the name of the JDBC driver's implementation of `java.sql.Driver`. An example for MySQL's JDBC driver is `com.mysql.jdbc.Driver`. When `DriverManager` requests a database connection, it loads driver classes.

9.2.2 Interface java.sql.Connection

The interface `java.sql.Connection` represents a connection session with the specified database. It's used to create the SQL statements `Statement`, `PreparedStatement`, and `CallableStatement`, which can be executed against database objects. A `Connection` object can be used to initiate transactions by creating savepoints, and committing or rolling back all changes to specified savepoints.

The `Connection` object can also be used to get a database's metadata—that is, information regarding the data stored in a database. It makes accessible the SQL grammar supported by the database, its stored procedures, and other database-related information.

9.2.3 Interface java.sql.Statement

The interface `java.sql.Statement` is used to create and execute static SQL statements and retrieve their results. These SQL statements can be used to create, modify, and delete database objects like tables, or insert, retrieve, modify, and delete table data. The results from the database are returned as `ResultSet` objects or `int` values indicating the number of affected rows.

The interface `Statement` is extended by interfaces `java.sql.PreparedStatement` and `java.sql.CallableStatement`. Objects of both of these subinterfaces represent precompiled SQL statements, which execute faster than their uncompiled counterparts. They can also be used to execute SQL statements with placeholders, using ?. `CallableStatements` are used to execute database-stored procedures.

9.2.4 Interface java.sql.ResultSet

The interface `java.sql.ResultSet` is retrieved as a result of executing a SQL `SELECT` statement against a database. It represents a table of data. The `ResultSet` object can be read-only, scrollable, or updatable. By default, a `ResultSet` object is only read-only and can be traversed in only one (forward) direction. You can create a scrollable `ResultSet` (that can be traversed forward and backward) and/or an updatable `ResultSet` by passing the relevant parameters during the creation of a `Statement` object.

Let's now dive deep into the first step of connecting to a database using class `java.sql.DriverManager`.

9.3   Connecting to a database

The first step to make a Java class communicate with a database is to establish a connection between them. Class `java.sql.DriverManager` talks with the JDBC driver to return a `Connection` object, which can be used by your Java classes for all further communication with the database.

EXAM TIP   For the exam, it's important to note the difference between a JDBC driver (lowercase d) and a `Driver` class (uppercase D). A JDBC driver is a set of classes provided by the database vendor, or a third party, usually in a .jar or .zip file, to support the JDBC API. A `Driver` class is an implementation of the interface `java.sql.Driver` in a JDBC driver. For example, for MySQL, its platform-independent JDBC driver can be downloaded as mysql-connector-java-5.1.27.zip. The name of the class that implements `java.sql.Driver` in MySQL Connector/J (JDBC driver) is `com.mysql.jdbc.Driver`.

To connect with a database, you need class `DriverManager` only once. When a JDBC client needs to connect with a database, it connects with class `DriverManager`, which finds an appropriate driver, establishes a connection with the database, and returns the `Connection` object to the JDBC client. For further JDBC calls, the JDBC doesn't need class `DriverManager` again. It uses the `Connection` object and other implementations of the JDBC interfaces provided by the JDBC driver to send the SQL queries and get the results. These steps are shown in figure 9.6.

In the next section, let's see how JDBC drivers are loaded in memory and registered with the `DriverManager`.

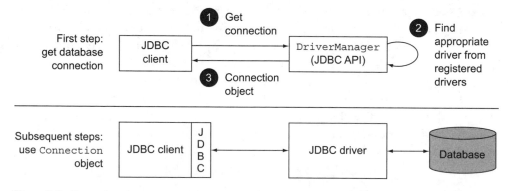

Figure 9.6   **To communicate with a data source, a JDBC client needs the `DriverManager` only once.**

9.3.1 Loading JDBC drivers

For the exam, it's important to understand how JDBC drivers are loaded and registered. There are two approaches to load JDBC drivers:

- Manual (JDBC API version 3.0 and before)
- Automatic (JDBC API version 4.0 and later)

With JDBC 3.0 and its earlier versions, you need to call `Class.forName()`, passing it the name of the class that implements the interface `java.sql.Driver`. An example of loading a JDBC driver for a MySQL database is as follows:

```
Class.forName("com.mysql.jdbc.Driver");
```

 EXAM TIP `Class.forName()` will throw a `ClassNotFoundException` (a checked exception) if the JVM is unable to locate the specified class.

The preceding code will load class `com.mysql.jdbc.Driver` in memory, executing its static initializer block(s). According to the JDBC specification, a driver must register itself with the `DriverManager`. For example, here's the static initializer block defined in MySQL's class `com.mysql.jdbc.Driver` that initializes and registers itself with the `DriverManager`:

```
static {
    try {
        java.sql.DriverManager.registerDriver(new Driver());
    } catch (SQLException E) {
        throw new RuntimeException("Can't register driver!");
    }
}
```

JDBC 4.0 and its later versions support automatic loading and registration of all JDBC drivers accessible via an application's class path. You no longer need to explicitly load the driver in memory using `Class.forName()`. The SPM automates the driver-loading mechanism. Using SPM, every JDBC 4.0 driver implementation must include the configuration file with the name java.sql.Driver within the `META-INF/services` folder in their `.jar` file. The file `java.sql.Driver` contains the full name of the class that the vendor used to implement the interface `jdbc.sql.Driver`. For example, `com.mysql.jdbc.Driver` is the name for the MySQL driver. When `DriverManager` requests a database connection, it loads these driver classes.

The exam might specify the JDBC API version that's being used for an application and then query you on whether you'd need to load the driver explicitly. Figure 9.7 shows the difference in steps in establishing a connection with a database using the JDBC API for versions 3.0 and before and versions 4.0 and later.

JDBC 3.0 and before	Step 1 (Load and register driver)	`Class.forName("----");`
	Step 2 (Establish DB connection)	`DriverManager.getConnection("----");`
JDBC 4.0 and later	Step 1 (Load and register driver and establish DB connection)	`DriverManager.getConnection("----");`

Figure 9.7   Difference in steps to establish a connection with a database using JDBC API version 3.0 (and before) and JDBC API version 4.0 and later

9.3.2   *Use DriverManager to connect to a database*

Class `DriverManager` manages all the instances of JDBC driver implementations registered with a JVM. When loaded into memory, its static initializer attempts to load all JDBC drivers that are referred to in the `jdbc.drivers` system property. `DriverManager` is a starting point to obtain database connections for Java SE.

When you invoke method `getConnection()`, the `DriverManager` finds the appropriate drivers from its set of registered drivers, establishes a connection with a database, and returns a `Connection` object. Here are the overloaded `getConnection()` methods:

```
public static Connection getConnection
            (String url) throws SQLException
public static Connection getConnection
            (String url, Properties info) throws SQLException
public static Connection getConnection
            (String url, String user, String pwd) throws SQLException
```

The JDBC URL determines the appropriate driver for a given URL string. For example

```
jdbc:subprotocol://<host>:<port>/<database_name>
```

Following is an example of a URL string for connecting with a MySQL database on a local host:

```
DriverManager.getConnection
    ("jdbc:mysql://localhost/feedback?"
            + "user=sqluser&password=sqluserpw");
```

The default port for MySQL is 3306. Usually, if the default port is being used by the database server, the `:<port>` value of the JDBC URL can be omitted. Here are a few additional examples of JDBC connection strings for MySQL:

```
jdbc:mysql://data.ejavaguru.com:3305/examDB
jdbc:mysql://localhost:3305/mysql?connectTimeout=0   ⟵   Additional parameter
jdbc:mysql://127.0.0.1:3306/examDB                         connectTimeout
```

In a connection string, apart from specifying the type of driver, host, port, and database to connect to, you can also specify additional parameters like the default connectTimeout, autoConnect, and others. But you don't need to worry about these additional parameters for the exam. Following is an example of using the JDBC API to connect a Java class with a MySQL database:

```java
import java.sql.*;
class CreateConnection {
    public static void main(String[] args) {
        Connection con = null;
        try {
            String url = "jdbc:mysql://localhost/BookLibrary";
            String username = "test";
            String password = "test";

            con = DriverManager.getConnection(url, username, password);
        }
        catch (SQLException e) {
            System.out.println(e);
        }
        System.out.println(con);
    }
}
```

 NOTE To keep it simple, the code in this section doesn't include closing of the Connection object. I'll cover that in the next section.

Alternatively, you can also connect with a database by including the username and password as part of the JDBC connection string (changes in bold):

```java
import java.sql.*;
class CreateConnection {
    public static void main(String[] args) {
        Connection con = null;
        try {
            con = DriverManager.getConnection
                    ("jdbc:mysql://localhost/BookLibrary?"
                    + "user=test&password=test");
        }
        catch (SQLException e) {
            System.out.println(e);
        }
        System.out.println(con);
    }
}
```

It's common to use Properties to specify the login credentials for the JDBC URL:

```java
import java.sql.*;
class CreateConnection {
    public static void main(String[] args) {
        Connection con = null;
        try {
            java.util.Properties prop = new java.util.Properties();
            prop.put("user", "test");
```

```
                prop.put("password", "test");
                con = DriverManager.getConnection
                        ("jdbc:mysql://localhost/BookLibrary", prop);
            }
        catch (SQLException e) {
            System.out.println(e);
        }
        System.out.println(con);
    }
}
```

 EXAM TIP   Make note of the property names for specifying the username and password: the keys are "user" and "password". An attempt to use any other key to specify the username and password to connect to a database will throw a SQLException.

Connecting to a data source

There are two ways to connect to a database: by using class java.sql.Driver-Manager or the interface javax.sql.DataSource. Class DriverManager was included in the JDBC API since its beginning and the interface DataSource was added later in JDBC version 2.0. Class DriverManager is the preferred class to establish database connections with Java SE applications because DataSource works with the Java Naming and Directory Interface (JNDI). JNDI is usually supported by Java applications with a container that supports JNDI like Java Enterprise Edition Server. For the exam, you must only know how to establish a connection using a DriverManager. The use of DataSource isn't on the exam.

9.3.3   *Exceptions thrown by database connections*

Let's see what happens if your application can't load a JDBC driver. For example, I didn't add the JDBC driver to the application's class-path environment variable on purpose. Here's the exception message that I got when I tried to run this code:

```
java.sql.SQLException: No suitable driver found for jdbc:mysql://localhost/
    BookLibrary?user=test&password=test
```

If the class is unable to connect to a database due to invalid login credentials, you'll get a SQLException:

```
java.sql.SQLException: Access denied for user 'test'@'test' (using password:
    YES)
```

The individual SQL exception message will differ across various databases and their versions. After you connect to a database successfully, the next step is to execute SQL statements that can create database objects, and query, update, and delete them.

9.4 CRUD (create, retrieve, update, and delete) operations

[9.3] Submit queries and read results from the database (including creating statements, returning result sets, iterating through the results, and properly closing result sets, statements, and connections)

Since its release as JDBC API version 1.0 with JDK 1.1 in 1997, to JDBC 4.1 with JDK 7, one of the goals of the JDBC API has been to maintain its focus on SQL. The focus of this API has always been to access relational data from the Java classes. This is the core on which this JDBC API is built. For the purpose of the exam, you should be able to identify the SQL statements related to

- How to create a table, including reading a definition of a given table
- How to insert rows in a table
- How to retrieve rows in a table, specifying the columns to be selected and search criteria
- How to update rows in a table
- How to delete rows in a table

Figure 9.8 shows an outline of basic steps for executing a SQL statement against a database. A `ResultSet` is returned for SQL `SELECT` statements. SQL `INSERT`, `UPDATE`, `DELETE`, and other statements will return `int` values specifying successful execution or the number of rows affected.

Let's get started with the execution of a SQL statement to create a table.

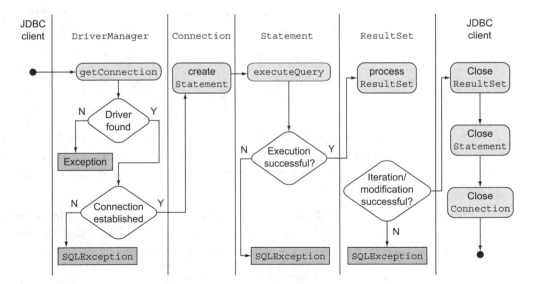

Figure 9.8 Basic steps for executing a SQL `SELECT` statement against a database

9.4.1   *Read table definition and create table*

To create a database table, you need a `Connection` object; use the `Connection` object to create a `Statement` object and call method `executeUpdate()` on the `Statement` object, passing it the SQL statement. For example

```java
import java.sql.*;
class CreateTable {
    public static void main(String[] args) {
        Connection con = null;
        Statement statement = null;
        try {
            String url = "jdbc:mysql://localhost/BookLibrary";
            String username = "test";
            String password = "test";

            con = DriverManager.getConnection(url, username, password);
            statement = con.createStatement();

            int result = statement.executeUpdate("CREATE TABLE book " +
                                " (id INT PRIMARY KEY, " +
                                " title VARCHAR(1000), " +
                                " author CHAR(255), " +
                                " publication_year INT, " +
                                " unit_price REAL)");
            System.out.println(result);
        }
        catch (SQLException e) {
            System.out.println(e);
        }
        finally {
            try {
                if (statement != null) statement.close();
                if (con != null) con.close();
            }
            catch (SQLException e) {}
        }
        System.out.println(con);
    }
}
```

Establish a connection with database

Create Statement

Call executeUpdate on Statement to create new table

createConnection, createStatement, and executeUpdate can throw SQLException

Connection and Statement objects must be closed.

 NOTE   In the book, you'll see the use of uppercase for keywords in all SQL statements. Though the case of SQL is ignored by the underlying database, the use of uppercase for keywords is recommended and practiced for better readability.

Note that you need to call method `executeUpdate()` on `Statement` and not `execute-Query()` to execute a Data Definition Language (DDL) request. What happens if you try to execute the preceding SQL statement using method `executeQuery()`?

```java
statement.executeQuery("CREATE TABLE book " +
                    " (id INT PRIMARY KEY, " +
                    " title VARCHAR(1000), " +
```

```
" author CHAR(255), " +
" publication_year INT, " +
" unit_price REAL)");
```

The use of `executeQuery()` will throw a `SQLException` at runtime (the exact exception message might vary across systems):

```
java.sql.SQLException: Can not issue data manipulation statements with
    executeQuery().
```

EXAM TIP   Method `executeUpdate()` is used to execute SQL queries to insert new rows in a table, and update and delete existing rows. It's also used to execute DDL queries, such as the creation, modification, and deletion of database objects like tables. If you use method `executeQuery()` for any of these operations, you'll get a `SQLException` at runtime.

The SQL statements that you include in your code are defined as string values. This essentially means that even if any of the SQL statements are invalid, the code compiles successfully. The Java application passes the SQL statements to the database, which determines whether the SQL is formed correctly or not. When a database receives an incorrect SQL statement, it notifies the Java application with an appropriate exception and message at runtime.

9.4.2   Mapping SQL data types to Java data types

For the exam, you might be given a table definition and shown related code to insert data into the table, update its values, or delete the values. To do so, you must know how to read a table definition and how SQL types map to Java types. For example, note the following definition of table `Book`:

```
Table Book
id, INTEGER: PK,
title, VARCHAR(100)
author, CHAR(255),
publication_year, INTEGER
unit_price, REAL
```

What data type can you use to insert values into column `title`, which has a SQL type of `VARCHAR`? You can use table 9.1 to answer this question, which shows the different types of data that can be used in a table and their equivalent Java data types.

EXAM TIP   The term `PK` in table 9.1 refers to the table's *primary key*. A primary key is a column, which doesn't accept duplicate values. It's used to uniquely identify a row in a table. In the preceding example, each book can be assigned and identified using a unique `id` (identification) number. On the exam, you might see this term in a table definition, but you won't be asked questions about it.

Table 9.1   Data types in a database and their equivalent Java data types

SQL data type	Java data type	Description
CHAR	java.lang.String	Character data of fixed length
VARCHAR	java.lang.String	Character data of variable length
VARCHAR2	java.lang.String	Character data of variable length
INT	int	Integer values
INTEGER	int	Integer values
INTEGER(4)	int	Integer values
REAL/DOUBLE	double	Decimal numbers
REAL(4,2)/DOUBLE(4,2)	double	Decimal numbers
DATE	java.sql.Date	Date

You don't need to memorize these SQL data types and their corresponding Java data types. But remember the simple data conversion rules. For example, if you try to insert a Date object into a column with the SQL data type INT, you might get a SQL-Exception.

In the next section, let's work with an example to read a table definition and insert data into it.

9.4.3   *Insert rows in a table*

On the exam, you might be given the definition of a table and questioned on the code to insert rows in it. Here's a sample of the definition of table Book from the preceding section (a table definition in SQL may refer to a "table" as an "item"):

```
Item Book
id, INTEGER: PK,
title, VARCHAR(100)
author, CHAR(255),
publication_year, INTEGER
unit_price, REAL
```

It's usual for the exam to include the description of the book as Item Book. Let's work with the code to insert rows in this table using the try-with-resources construct that auto-closes resources Statement and Connection:

```
class InsertIntoTable {
    public static void main(String[] args) {
        try (Connection con = getConnection();          ← Step 1: Establish a connection with database
            Statement statement = con.createStatement()){  ← Step 2: Create Statement object
```

Step 3: Call executeUpdate on statement to insert new row in table; returns number of rows affected

```
            int ret = statement.executeUpdate
                ("INSERT INTO book VALUES (" +
                    "1, 'Expert In Java', 'Mantheakis', 2009, 59.9)");

            System.out.println(ret);          ⟵  Prints "1"
        }
        catch (SQLException e) {
            System.out.println(e);
        }
    }
    static Connection getConnection() throws SQLException{
        String url = "jdbc:mysql://localhost/BookLibrary";
        java.util.Properties prop = new java.util.Properties();
        prop.put("user", "test");
        prop.put("password", "test");
        return DriverManager.getConnection(url, prop);
    }
}
```

 EXAM TIP Because the interfaces `Connection`, `Statement`, and `Result-Set` extend the interface `AutoCloseable`, you can create their instances in a try-with-resources statement.

In the preceding code, the SQL statement used to insert a row in table `Book` didn't specify the column names. You might also see SQL statements on the exam that specify the name of the columns:

Column names included in SQL query

```
int ret = statement.executeUpdate
    ("INSERT INTO book (id, title, author, publication_year, unit_price)"+    ⟵
    " VALUES (1, 'Expert In Java', 'Mantheakis', 2009, 59.9)");
```

 EXAM TIP You'll not be tested on how to write SQL statements on this exam. But you should know how to read basic SQL statements to insert, retrieve, update, and delete table data. Including and excluding column names while inserting new rows in a table are two ways to insert data in a table.

It's easy to get confused with the method name used to insert data into a table. The preceding example used method `executeUpdate()` (and not `execute()`). Method `executeUpdate()` is also used to execute SQL UPDATE and DELETE statements. Here are the overloaded versions of this method, as mentioned in the Java API documentation:

Executes given SQL statement, which may be an INSERT, UPDATE, or DELETE statement or SQL statement that returns nothing, such as a SQL DDL statement

Executes given SQL statement and signals driver with given flag whether auto-generated keys produced by Statement object should be made available for retrieval

```
int executeUpdate(String sql)                         ⟵
int executeUpdate(String sql, int autoGeneratedKeys)  ⟵
```

```
int executeUpdate(String sql, int[] columnIndexes)
int executeUpdate(String sql, String[] columnNames)
```

**Executes given SQL statement and signals driver that auto-generated
keys indicated in given array should be made available for retrieval**

9.4.4   Update data in a table

To update the data in a table, use method `executeUpdate()` from the interface
`Statement`. You can use a single SQL query to update single or multiple rows. To
update data, the database must find and mark the rows that need to be updated, specified using the `WHERE` clause of a SQL statement. Let's update the `unit_price` of book
Expert in Java to `99.9`:

```
class UpdateTable {
    public static void main(String[] args) {
        try (Connection con = getConnection();
             Statement statement = con.createStatement()){
            int ret = statement.executeUpdate
                            ("UPDATE book " +
                             "SET unit_price = 99.9 " +
                             "WHERE title = 'Expert In Java'");

            System.out.println(ret);
        }
        catch (SQLException e) {
            System.out.println(e);
        }
    }
    static Connection getConnection() throws SQLException{
        String url = "jdbc:mysql://localhost/BookLibrary";
        String username = "test";
        String password = "test";
        return DriverManager.getConnection(url, username, password);
    }
}
```

Step 1: Establish a connection with database

Step 2: Create Statement object

Step 3: Call executeUpdate() on statement to update an existing row for title "Expert In Java"

Prints "1"

The following SQL query would update all the existing rows in a table:

```
statement.executeUpdate
            ("UPDATE book " +
             "SET unit_price = 99.9");
```

If no WHERE condition, UPDATE SQL statement will update all rows

You can also update multiple columns and define multiple conditions using `AND`, `OR`,
and comparison operators to find and update matching rows. The following SQL
query would update columns `unit_price` and `author` for all books of author Mantheakis and having a unit price greater than 39.9:

```
int ret = statement.executeUpdate
                ("UPDATE book " +
                 "SET unit_price = 99.9, " +
                 "author = 'Harry Mantheakis' " +
```

```
"WHERE author = 'Mantheakis' " +
"AND unit_price > 39.9");
```

 EXAM TIP   For all SQL operations on a database, the preferred program-ming approach is to close the `Connection` and `Statement` objects. You must either close them explicitly by calling `close()` on them or use them with a `try-with-resources` statement, which auto-closes them. You're very likely to see a question that asks you about closing these resources and in their correct order—first `Statement` and then `Connection` object.

9.4.5   *Delete data in a table*

Deletion of data works in a manner that's similar to updating data in a database, as dis-cussed in the preceding section. Use method `executeUpdate()` to execute a SQL query to delete rows from a table. The following code will delete all rows from table `Book`, if their year of publication is before 1900:

```
class DeleteTableData {
    public static void main(String[] args) {
        try (Connection con = getConnection();        ⟵  Step 1: Establish   Step 2:
                                                          a connection with   Create
            Statement statement = con.createStatement()){  database         Statement
            int ret = statement.executeUpdate                          ⟵      object
                        ("DELETE FROM book " +
                         "WHERE publication_year < 1900");
            System.out.println("ret="+ret);           ⟵  Prints number of
        }                                                 rows deleted
        catch (SQLException e) {
            System.out.println(e);
        }
    }
    static Connection getConnection() throws SQLException{
        String url = "jdbc:mysql://localhost/BookLibrary";
        String username = "test";
        String password = "test";
        return DriverManager.getConnection(url, username, password);
    }
}
```

Step 3: Call executeUpdate on Statement to delete all rows with publication_year < 1900.

9.4.6   *Querying database*

Imagine you need to check your library for the existence of all books with a unit price greater than 47.7. Figure 9.9 shows all existing rows in table `Book`.

```
mysql> select * from Book;
+----+----------------+-----------------+------------------+------------+
| id | title          | author          | publication_year | unit_price |
+----+----------------+-----------------+------------------+------------+
|  1 | Expert in Java | Harry Mantheakis |            2009 |       99.9 |
|  2 | All Objects    | Rosenthal       |            2010 |       49.9 |
|  3 | Oracle DBA     | Selvan Rajan    |            2013 |       45.9 |
|  4 | Quilling Expert| Shreya Gupta    |            2012 |      199.9 |
+----+----------------+-----------------+------------------+------------+
4 rows in set (0.00 sec)
```

Figure 9.9   MySQL client showing results of selecting all rows from table `Book`

To select the required information, you can issue an appropriate SQL SELECT query and the database would return to you a set of information as table rows as a ResultSet object. For example

```
class QueryTableData {
    public static void main(String[] args) {
        try (Connection con = getConnection();
            Statement statement = con.createStatement()){
        ResultSet rs = statement.executeQuery
                            ("SELECT * FROM book " +
                            "WHERE unit_price > 47.7");){
            while (rs.next()) {
                System.out.print(rs.getInt("id") + "-");
                System.out.print(rs.getString("title") + "-");
                System.out.print(rs.getString("author") + "-");
                System.out.print(rs.getInt("publication_year") + "-");
                System.out.println(rs.getDouble("unit_price"));
            }
        }
        catch (SQLException e) {
            System.out.println(e);
        }
    }
    static Connection getConnection() throws SQLException{
        String url = "jdbc:mysql://localhost/BookLibrary";
        String username = "test";
        String password = "test";
        return DriverManager.getConnection(url, username, password);
    }
}
```

Call executeQuery() to execute SQL SELECT statement

next() moves current cursor in ResultSet object to next available row

 EXAM TIP   Method executeQuery() is used for SQL SELECT statements.

As you can see in figure 9.9, table Book has three matching rows for a unit_price greater than 47.7. The output of the preceding code is as follows:

```
1-Expert in Java-Harry Mantheakis-2009-99.9
2-All Objects-Rosenthal-2010-49.9
4-Quilling Expert-Shreya Gupta-2012-199.9
```

Let's take a closer look at the structure of the ResultSet object, returned by method executeQuery(), as shown in figure 9.10.

At the beginning, the cursor position is *before* the first row. Method next() returns a boolean value indicating whether more rows are available in the ResultSet *and* moves the cursor position to the next row, if it's available. The code iterates through all the rows of the ResultSet object and prints the column values by calling Result-Set's methods getString(), getInt(), and getDouble().

For the exam, you must understand multiple concepts when you access a Result-Set using a SQL SELECT query. The preceding example used * to specify that the resulting set must include all the columns for the selected row. You can restrict the

Cursor position before row 1 →	id	title	author	publication_year	unit_price
Row 1 →	1	Expert in Java	Harry Mantheakis	2009	99.9
Row 2 →	2	All Objects	Rosenthal	2010	49.9
Row 3 →	4	Quilling Expert	Shreya Gupta	2012	199.9

Figure 9.10 When you issue a SQL SELECT statement, executeQuery() returns a ResultSet. A ResultSet is a link to a database cursor with selected results—an object that maintains a cursor (or a pointer) to the current row. At the beginning, the cursor is placed before the beginning of the first row.

column data that's returned to you by specifying the column names. The following query will select three columns—id, title, and publication_year—from table Book where the value for the author is 'Harry Mantheakis':

```
ResultSet rs = statement.executeQuery
                    ("SELECT id, title, publication_year FROM book " +
                     "WHERE author='Harry Mantheakis'");
```

Take note of method getString() and its method arguments (column names) used to retrieve the value for a column in a row. The overloaded method getString() in the interface ResultSet accepts either the column position or column label and returns the table value as a string. It takes the following forms:

```
String getString(int columnLabel)
String getString(int columnIndex)
```

 EXAM TIP Although everything in Java is 0-based, column indexes in a ResultSet are 1-based.

The interface ResultSet also defines overloaded methods to retrieve the values from the ResultSet as specific data types, accepting column positions and column labels. Table 9.2 lists these methods.

Table 9.2 Overloaded methods in interface ResultSet to retrieve individual data value as a particular data type

Method return type	Method name
int	getInt(String columnLabel)
int	getInt(int columnIndex)
long	getLong(String columnLabel)
long	getLong(int columnIndex)
float	getFloat(String columnLabel)
float	getFloat(int columnIndex)

Table 9.2   Overloaded methods in interface `ResultSet` to retrieve individual data value as a particular data type *(continued)*

Method return type	Method name
double	getDouble(String columnLabel)
double	getDouble(int columnIndex)
java.lang.String	getString(String columnLabel)
java.lang.String	getString(int columnIndex)
java.sql.Date	getDate(String columnLabel)
java.sql.Date	getDate(int columnIndex)

What happens if the target table doesn't find any matching rows in the table for your `SELECT` query? In this case, the `ResultSet` object isn't set to `null`. It's initialized, but it doesn't contain any rows. For example

```
class QueryTableDataNoData {
    public static void main(String[] args) {
        try (Connection con = getConnection();
            Statement statement = con.createStatement();
            ResultSet rs = statement.executeQuery
                            ("SELECT id, title, author FROM book " +
                             "WHERE unit_price=155.99");) {

            System.out.println(rs);

            ResultSetMetaData rsmd = rs.getMetaData();

            System.out.println(rsmd.getColumnLabel(1));
            System.out.println(rsmd.getColumnLabel(2));
            System.out.println(rsmd.getColumnLabel(3));
        }
        catch (SQLException e) {
            System.out.println(e);
        }
    }
    static Connection getConnection() throws SQLException{
        //code to establish and return connection
    }
}
```

No matching rows for unit_price 155.99.

Won't print null.

Get MetaData for this result set.

Retrieve and print column names for positions 1, 2, and 3.

 EXAM TIP   If your SQL statement doesn't return any rows, the `ResultSet` object doesn't point to a `null` value. In this case, you'll get a `ResultSet` object that won't include any rows.

Even though the SQL statement in the preceding code didn't return any rows, the resultant `ResultSet` doesn't refer to a `null` value. This is verified by calling methods on the `ResultSet` object `rs`. The preceding example retrieves the metadata (data about data) from the `ResultSet` by calling method `getMetaData()`.

In this section, you worked with modification of data in a database as independent operations. However, in the real world, most often, a simple function like updating the last name of an employee might include execution of multiple database statements. In the next section, we'll cover how database transactions logically group multiple database operations, which can be committed or rolled back.

9.5 JDBC transactions

 [9.4] Use JDBC transactions (including disabling auto-commit mode, committing and rolling back transactions, and setting and rolling back to savepoints)

Imagine that a programmer, Selvan, needs to transfer $55 from his bank account to Paul's account. This simple transfer would require multiple steps like a withdrawal of $55 from Selvan's account, depositing the same amount to Paul's bank account, and modification of the total available balances of both these bank accounts.

A typical fund transfer like this might involve multiple changes to the relevant database records. For such cases, you wouldn't like partial completion of steps. For example, what happens if Selvan's bank debits the $55 amount from his bank account but doesn't credit it to Paul's account? Similarly, if the bank credits the amount to Paul's account without debiting it from Selvan's account, its own data would be invalid or inconsistent. For this process to be marked *complete* and *valid*, all individual database changes should complete successfully. If either of them fails, none should be reflected in the database.

By default, the JDBC API initiates all database changes as soon as you execute SQL queries. To ensure that all or none of a set of database modifications happen, you can define them as a single JDBC transaction. The multiple database changes in a JDBC transaction execute as a single unit so that all or none of them execute. Actually, all the changes within a transaction are executed in the database, but they're persisted when they're committed. This is an important conceptual difference.

In the next section, you'll see the typical database changes that might be required to complete a simple funds transfer.

9.5.1 A transaction example

When you establish a connection with a database, by default it's in the *auto-commit* mode—that is, all changes performed by SQL statements are immediately committed to the database. Let's modify this behavior and execute a set of SQL statements to transfer funds ($55) from a bank account (ID: 5555) to another bank account (ID: 7777). Let's assume that the database defines tables `bank_acct` and `transaction` to store the details of each bank account and their related transactions, as shown in figure 9.11. To complete the process of transferring funds, the class must modify the account balances in table `bank_acct` and insert rows in table `transaction`.

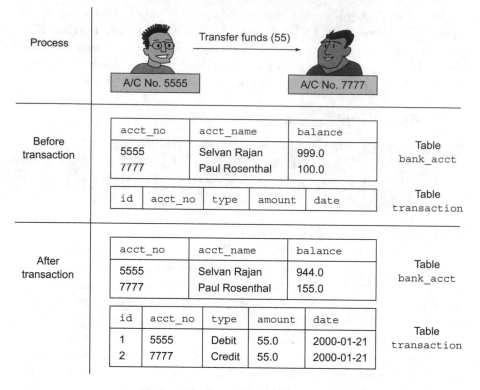

Figure 9.11   **A simple process of a funds transfer can include multiple data modifications in the database.**

Here's the complete code:

```
class TransactionTranferFunds {
    public static void main(String[] args) {
        Connection con = null;
        Statement statement = null;
        try {
            con = getConnection();
            con.setAutoCommit(false);
            statement = con.createStatement();

            int result = statement.executeUpdate
                    ("INSERT INTO transaction VALUES " +
                     " (1, '5555', 'db', 55.0, '2000-01-21')");

            result = statement.executeUpdate
                    ("INSERT INTO transaction VALUES " +
                     " (2, '7777', 'cr', 55.0, '2000-01-21')");

            result = statement.executeUpdate
                    ("UPDATE bank_account " +
                     "SET balance = 944.0 " +
                     "WHERE acct_no='5555'");
```

1 Start transaction by calling setAuto-Commit(false) on Connection object

2 Insert row 1 in table transaction.

3 Insert row 2 in table transaction.

4 Update balance for acct_no 5555 in table bank_account.

```
            result = statement.executeUpdate
                          ("UPDATE bank_account " +
                          "SET balance = 155.0 " +
                          "WHERE acct_no='7777'");

        con.commit();
    }
    catch (SQLException e) {
        System.out.println(e);
        try {
            con.rollback();
        }
        catch(SQLException ex) {
            System.out.println(ex);
        }
    }
}
static Connection getConnection() throws SQLException{
    // code to create and return Connection object
}
}
```

❺ Update balance for acct_no 7777 in table bank_account.

← ❻ Commit all changes to database

← ❼ If any exception is thrown, call rollback() on Connection object

To start a transaction that includes multiple SQL statements, the code calls setAuto-Commit(false) on the Connection object ❶. The code at ❷ and ❸ inserts rows in table transaction. The code at ❹ and ❺ modifies the balance of account numbers 5555 and 7777 in table bank_account. At the end of the execution of all the SQL statements, the code at ❻ calls commit() on the Connection object. If any SQLException is thrown during the execution of any of the SQL statements, the exception handler calls rollback() on the Connection object ❼ so that a partial set of statements isn't persisted in the database.

As mentioned earlier, all statements are sent to the database and all requested changes are performed by the database system. Methods commit() and rollback() only decide whether these changes are persisted (that is, confirmed) in the database or not.

 EXAM TIP   Method executeUpdate() returns a count of the rows that are or would be affected in the database for row insertions, modifications, and deletion. The value is returned even if the statement isn't committed. This method returns 0 for SQL DDL statements, which create database objects and modify their structure or delete them.

Rolling back or losing all the transactions might be undesirable in most situations. In the next section, you'll see how you define *savepoints* in your transactions, so that if any exceptions occur during the course of the transaction, you might consider rolling back to particular savepoints.

9.5.2 *Create savepoints and roll back partial transactions*

By using a savepoint, you can exercise finer control over the work done by a set of SQL statements in a transaction. Within a transaction, you can create and set a savepoint, and later roll back the work done because you set the savepoint. You can create multiple savepoints in a transaction and release them or roll them back.

The following example defines multiple SQL statements to credit the salary of three account holders with IDs 5555, 7777, and 9999. For each account holder, a row is added to table transaction and then its balance is updated in table bank_account. After executing the SQL statements for these account holders, the bank realizes that it used an incorrect transaction amount. Notice how the following application uses savepoints in a transaction to roll back the transaction:

```
class TransactionSavepoint {
    public static void main(String[] args) {
        Connection con = null;
        Statement statement = null;
        try {                                          ❶ To start a transaction,
            con = getConnection();                        set Connection's auto-
            con.setAutoCommit(false);                     commit mode to false.
            statement = con.createStatement();

            int result = statement.executeUpdate
                    ("INSERT INTO transaction values " +
                    " (101, '5555', 'db', 2099.0, '2020-10-01')");
❷           result = statement.executeUpdate
SQL statements        ("UPDATE bank_account " +
to credit salary      "SET balance = balance + 2099.0 " +     ❸ Set unnamed
for acct_no 5555      "WHERE acct_no='5555'");                   Savepoint
                                                                 sp5555.
            Savepoint sp5555 = con.setSavepoint();

            result = statement.executeUpdate
                    ("INSERT INTO transaction values " +
                    " (102, '7777', 'db', 12099.0, '2020-10-01')");
❹           result = statement.executeUpdate
SQL statements        ("UPDATE bank_account " +
to credit salary      "SET balance = balance + 12099.0 " +      ❺ Set named
for acct_no 7777      "WHERE acct_no='7777'");                     Savepoint
                                                                   sp7777 to
            Savepoint sp7777 = con.setSavepoint("CrSalaryFor7777");  CrSalaryFor7777.

            result = statement.executeUpdate
                    ("INSERT INTO transaction values " +
                    " (103, '9999', 'db', 5099.0, '2020-10-01')");
❻           result = statement.executeUpdate
SQL statements        ("UPDATE bank_account " +
to credit salary      "SET balance = balance + 5099.0 " +
for acct_no 9999      "WHERE acct_no='9999'");
Set named
Savepoint   Savepoint savepoint = con.setSavepoint("CrSalaryFor9999");
sp9999 to
CrSalary-   con.rollback(sp7777);          ❽ Roll back all transactions
For9999.    con.commit();                     to point sp7777.
❼       }
        catch (SQLException e) {           ❾ Commit the rest of
            System.out.println(e);            the transactions.
            try {
                con.rollback();            ❿ If SQLException, roll back
            }                                 all database changes.
```

```
            catch(SQLException ex) {
                System.out.println(ex);
            }
        }
    }
    static Connection getConnection() throws SQLException{
        // code to create and return Connection object
    }
}
```

In the preceding code, ❶ sets the auto-commit mode of a `Connection` object to `false`. This is important. The default auto-commit mode is `true`, which if not changed will make the `commit` and `rollback` methods throw a `SQLException`. The code at ❷ executes a SQL statement to credit the salary of the account holder with ID 5555 by inserting a row in table `transaction` and updating the balance in table `bank_account`. The code at ❸ sets the first savepoint. The code at ❹ defines a SQL statement to credit the salary for the account holder with ID 7777, and the code at ❺ creates a named savepoint, `CrSalaryFor7777`. The code at ❻ defines a SQL statement to credit the salary for the account holder with ID 9999, and the code at ❼ creates another named savepoint, `CrSalaryFor9999`. The code at ❽ rolls back the transaction, discarding all executed statements, going backward, to the point where savepoint `CrSalaryFor7777` is created. The code at ❾ commits all the database changes that were executed before the creation of savepoint `CrSalaryFor7777`. In case the code encounters a `SQLException`, the code at ❿ rolls ba.ck the complete transaction.

9.5.3 *Commit modes and JDBC transactions*

A JDBC connection can have two automatic `commit` (auto-commit) modes:

- `true` (default)
- `false`

To work with a transaction, you must set the auto-commit mode to `false` or methods `rollback()` and `commit()` will throw a `SQLException`.

If the commit mode of a connection is set to `false` and you try to set it to `true` during the course of a transaction, the code will throw a `SQLException` when you call any transaction-related method like `commit()` or `rollback()`.

9.6 *RowSet objects*

[9.5] Construct and use RowSet objects using the RowSetProvider class
       and the RowSetFactory interface

Imagine that you need to show a graph in your application depicting the performance of your organization. The data for the graph needs to be retrieved from a database. This task doesn't seem to be difficult. You can connect to the database using the JDBC

API, send a SQL query to the database, get a ResultSet, extract the values from it, and display the graph accordingly. Now imagine that you need to update the graph whenever any change is made to the underlying data in the database, using any application. A RowSet can help here.

You can configure a RowSet object by setting its properties, connecting to a JDBC data source, executing a SQL statement, and getting the results.

You can register listeners with a RowSet object so that when an event occurs on a RowSet object (like any modification to its value), the registered listeners can be notified.

RowSet objects can be *connected* or *disconnected*. A connected RowSet object, like JdbcRowSet, maintains a connection with its data source throughout its life. On the other hand, a disconnected RowSet object, like CachedRowSet, establishes a connection with the data source, gets the values, and then disconnects itself. It can still update its values and later update them in the data source by reconnecting to it. Figure 9.12 shows the relationship among the interface ResultSet and the interface RowSet and its subinterfaces.

In the next section, let's work with the classes and interfaces that can be used to create RowSet objects.

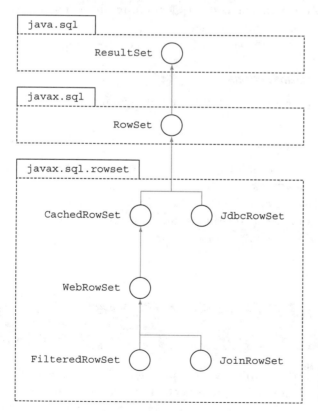

**Figure 9.12	Relationship among interfaces** ResultSet **and** RowSet **and the subinterfaces of** Rowset

9.6.1 Interface RowSetFactory

The interface `javax.sql.rowset.RowSetFactory` defines the implementation of a factory that can be used to obtain different types of `RowSet` implementations. Table 9.3 lists its methods.

Table 9.3 Methods of interface `RowSetFactory`

Method	Description
`CachedRowSet createCachedRowSet()`	Creates a new instance of a `CachedRowSet`
`FilteredRowSet createFilteredRowSet()`	Creates a new instance of a `FilteredRowSet`
`JdbcRowSet createJdbcRowSet()`	Creates a new instance of a `JdbcRowSet`
`JoinRowSet createJoinRowSet()`	Creates a new instance of a `JoinRowSet`
`WebRowSet createWebRowSet()`	Creates a new instance of a `WebRowSet`

To get access to an object of `RowSetFactory`, you can use class `RowSetProvider`, discussed in the next section.

9.6.2 Class RowSetProvider

Class `javax.sql.rowset.RowSetProvider` defines factory methods to get a `RowSet-Factory` implementation. The `RowSetFactory` can then be used to create objects of different types of `RowSet` implementations. Here's how you can create an instance of this default implementation and a `JdbcRowSet` using it:

```
RowSetFactory rowsetFactory = RowSetProvider.newFactory();
JdbcRowSet crs = rowsetFactory.createJdbcRowSet();
```

You can also specify a custom factory implementation by specifying its name. For example

```
RowSetFactory rowsetFactory = RowSetProvider.newFactory(
                  "com.ejava.sql.rowset.CustomRowSetFactory", null);
```

This interface defines the following methods to create objects of `RowSetFactory` implementations:

> **Creates new instance of default RowSetFactory implementation**

```
static RowSetFactory newFactory()
static RowSetFactory newFactory(String factoryClassName, ClassLoader cl)
```

> **Creates new instance of RowSetFactory from specified factory class name**

9.6.3 An example of working with JdbcRowSet

Let's create and use a `JdbcRowSet` by using `RowSetFactory` and `RowSetProvider`. For this example, we'll use the default factory implementation provided by Oracle. The

custom implementation is out of the scope of this exam, so it isn't discussed here. A
JdbcRowSet object accomplishes the following:

- It establishes a connection with a database (so you don't need a separate
  Connection object).
- It creates a PreparedStatement object for the query to execute (so you don't
  need a separate Statement object).
- It executes the SQL statement to create a ResultSet object.

 EXAM TIP   If the execute method isn't successful, you can only call
execute and close methods on it. The rest of the methods will throw an
exception.

Here's an example:

```
class RowSetExample {
    public static void main(String[] args) {
        JdbcRowSet jdbcRS = null;
        try {

            RowSetFactory rowSetFactory = RowSetProvider.newFactory();
            jdbcRS = rowSetFactory.createJdbcRowSet();

            jdbcRS.setUrl("jdbc:mysql://localhost/BookLibrary");
            jdbcRS.setUsername("test");
            jdbcRS.setPassword("test");
            jdbcRS.setCommand("SELECT * FROM book");
            jdbcRS.execute();

            while (jdbcRS.next()) {

                System.out.print(jdbcRS.getString("id") + "-");
                System.out.print(jdbcRS.getString("title") +"-");
                System.out.print(jdbcRS.getString("unit_price"));
                System.out.println();
            }
        }
        catch (SQLException e) {
            System.out.println(e);
        }
        finally {
            try {
                jdbcRS.close();
            }
            catch (SQLException e) {}
        }
    }
}
```

**Use RowSetProvider to get
default implementation of
RowSetFactory** ❶

**Use RowSet-
Factory to
create object
of JdbcRowSet** ❷

**Call setURL
to define
connection URL** ❸

**Call setCommand
to define SQL
statement** ❺

**Call execute to
execute SQL
statement** ❻

**Call setUsername
and setPassword to set
username and password** ❹

**Call next to
determine
whether
more rows
are available
and to move
cursor to
next row** ❼

**Call getString to
extract column
value in a row** ❽

**Call close() on
JdbcRowSet object** ❾

In the preceding code, note how the JdbcRowSet object manages all the database
operations without any separate Connection, Statement, or ResultSet objects. The

code at ❶ and ❷ uses the `RowSetProvider` and `RowSetFactory` to get an object of `JdbcRowSet`. The code at ❸ defines the database connection string using method `setURL()`, and at ❹ it defines the database username and password values. The code at ❺ defines the SQL statement by using `RowSet`'s method `setCommand`. The code at ❻ executes the SQL statement using method `execute()`. It receives the result of the SQL statement and then can check for the existence of more rows by calling the next method ❼. The `JdbcRowSet` object accesses the columns by calling method `getString()` and passing the relevant column names ❽. With database objects, it's important to call `close` on the `JdbcRowSet` object ❾.

9.7 Precompiled statements

 [9.6]   Create and use PreparedStatement and CallableStatement objects

Unlike the objects of the interface `Statement`, the objects of interfaces `Prepared-Statement` and `CallableStatement` represent precompiled SQL statements. Precompiled SQL statements are compiled in the database system. The precompiled statements execute faster than their noncompiled counterparts. Another major advantage offered by `PreparedStatement` and `CallableStatement` is their ability to include placeholders in SQL statements using a ?. You can assign values to these placeholders by calling one of the appropriate `setDataType(parameterIndex, value)` on these objects. And the most critical advantage of using parameters with `Prepared-Statement` and `CallableStatement` is that they prevent SQL injection attacks. Let's get started with using the `PreparedStatement`.

9.7.1 Prepared statements

The interface `java.sql.PreparedStatement` extends the interface `java.sql.Statement`. Its objects represent precompiled SQL statements. The first difference that you'd notice when you compare `PreparedStatement` with `Statement` is in its creation. Unlike `Statement`, you must specify the relevant SQL statement when you create an object of `PreparedStatement`. The following code replaces `Statement` with a `PreparedStatement` object; the rest of the code remains the same:

```
class QueryPrepStatement {
    public static void main(String[] args) {
        try (Connection con = getConnection();
            PreparedStatement stmt = con.prepareStatement
                                    ("SELECT * FROM book " +
                                     "WHERE unit_price > 47.5");
            ResultSet rs = stmt.executeQuery();) {
            while (rs.next()) {
                System.out.print(rs.getString("id") + "-");
                System.out.print(rs.getString("title") +"-");
                System.out.print(rs.getString("author") + "-");
                System.out.print(rs.getString("publication_year") + "-");
```

SQL query is specified when you create an object of Prepared-Statement

```
                        System.out.print(rs.getString("unit_price"));
                        System.out.println();
                    }
                }
                catch (SQLException e) {
                    System.out.println(e);
                }
            }
            static Connection getConnection() throws SQLException{
                // code to get a valid connection
            }
        }
```

 EXAM TIP Unlike the interface Statement, where you specify the SQL query with the issue of method executeQuery() or executeUpdate(), you must specify the SQL query when you create objects of Prepared-Statement.

As shown in the preceding example, you can use the PreparedStatement objects for SQL statements that don't include placeholders. The fact that you can include parameters makes PreparedStatement objects even more useful. Imagine that you need to update the unit price of all books in table book by reading the new prices (column unit_price) from table new_book_price. Here's an example:

```
class UpdateBookPricePrepStatement {
    public static void main(String[] args) throws Exception {
        try {
            Connection con = getConnection();
            PreparedStatement bookUpdStmt = con.prepareStatement
                        ("UPDATE book SET " +
                         "unit_price = ? WHERE id = ?");
            PreparedStatement bookNewPrStmt = con.prepareStatement
                ("SELECT id, unit_price FROM new_book_price");

            ResultSet bookNewPrRs = bookNewPrStmt.executeQuery();

            while (bookNewPrRs.next()) {
                bookUpdStmt.setDouble
                        (1, bookNewPrRs.getDouble("unit_price"));
                bookUpdStmt.setString(2, bookNewPrRs.getString("id"));
                bookUpdStmt.executeUpdate();
            }
        }
        catch (SQLException e) {
            System.out.println(e);
        }
    }
    static Connection getConnection() throws SQLException{
        // code to get a valid connection
    }
}
```

PreparedStatement for input parameters for price and id

Prepared-Statement without any parameters

Call execute-Query to execute SQL SELECT statement

For all data retrieved from table new_book_price

Call execute-Update to execute SQL UPDATE statement

Read id and unit_price from new_book_price and set their values as parameter values for bookUpdStmt.

In the preceding code, note how values are assigned to the parameters in a Prepared-Statement. The interface PreparedStatement defines methods to assign values to its parameters by using its setDataType (parameterIndex, value) methods. Because column unit_price is SQL type REAL, you use the setDouble(int parameterIndex, double value) method to assign the unit price. Because column id is SQL type CHAR, you use the setString(int parameterIndex, String value) method to assign the ID. Table 9.4 lists important methods of the interface PreparedStatement.

Table 9.4 Important methods of interface `PreparedStatement`

Method name	Method description
void clearParameters()	Clears the current parameter values immediately.
boolean execute()	Executes the SQL statement in this PreparedStatement object, which may be any kind of SQL statement.
ResultSet executeQuery()	Executes the SQL query in this PreparedStatement object and returns the ResultSet object generated by the query.
int executeUpdate()	Executes the SQL statement in this PreparedStatement object, which must be a SQL DML statement, such as INSERT, UPDATE, or DELETE, or a SQL statement that returns nothing, such as a DDL statement.
void setByte(int parameterIndex, byte x)	Sets the designated parameter to the given Java byte value.
void setDate(int parameterIndex, Date x)	Sets the designated parameter to the given java.sql.Date value using the default time zone of the virtual machine that's running the application.
void setDouble(int parameterIndex, double x)	Sets the designated parameter to the given Java double value.
void setFloat(int parameterIndex, float x)	Sets the designated parameter to the given Java float value.
void setInt(int parameterIndex, int x)	Sets the designated parameter to the given Java int value.
void setLong(int parameterIndex, long x)	Sets the designated parameter to the given Java long value.

 EXAM TIP PreparedStatement defines three methods to execute its SQL statement: execute(), executeQuery(), and executeUpdate(). Method execute() can execute any type of SQL statement and returns a boolean value—true when a query executes successfully, false when an error occurs. Method executeQuery() executes a SQL SELECT statement and returns a ResultSet. Method executeUpdate() executes a DDL query, like CREATE TABLE, and INSERT, UPDATE, and DELETE SQL statements. It returns 0 for DDL statements and the number of rows affected for SQL INSERT, UPDATE, and DELETE statements.

In the next section, let's see how you can use existing database-stored procedures using java.sql.CallableStatement.

9.7.2 *Interface CallableStatement*

Compare a stored procedure with a method in Java. The same way you can define multiple statements in a method to form a logical unit, a stored procedure defines multiple SQL statements to form a logical unit. For example, a database procedure could update the price of all the books in a table by reading the new values from another table. For database operations, using stored procedures would improve your Java application's performance. On creation, the stored procedures are compiled and stored in the database. It's much more efficient to execute multiple, precompiled SQL statements together in a procedure, rather than sending individual, noncompiled SQL statements from your application.

You can execute the database-stored procedures from your Java applications by using CallableStatement in the JDBC API. Let's begin with creating a simple database-stored procedure using a JDBC call. The creation process is simple. You can use objects of Statement or PreparedStatement to send this logical group of SQL statements to the database. Here's an example using MySQL of the creation of a database procedure that joins tables book and new_book_price and lists id and author columns from table book and the unit_price column from table new_book_price. Don't worry about the fine SQL details to join the tables. What's important is to note that this procedure doesn't accept any parameters and can be created using a JDBC call:

```
class CreateDatabaseProcedure{
    public static void main(String[] args) {
        try {
            Connection con = getConnection();
            PreparedStatement statement = con.prepareStatement
                    ("CREATE PROCEDURE book_details_new_prices() "+
                    "BEGIN "+                                          Create a
                        "SELECT A.id, A.author, B.unit_price " +       stored
                        "FROM book A, new_book_price B " +             procedure
                        "WHERE A.id = B.id; "+
                    "END;");
            int result = statement.executeUpdate();
            System.out.println(result);
        }
        catch (SQLException e) {
            System.out.println(e);
        }
    }
    static Connection getConnection() throws SQLException{
        // code to get a valid Connection object
    }
}
```

NOTE Most of the popular databases support stored procedures but they might have variations with the creation and use of stored procedures. Don't worry; the exam won't query you with these fine details. The exam expects you to know how to create objects of the interface `CallableStatement` and use it to call stored procedures from your Java applications.

Execution of the preceding code will create a procedure called `book_details_ new_prices` in the database. It's important to note database objects are rarely created via the JDBC API, but this is shown in the preceding example code for demonstration purposes.

Let's see how you can call this procedure from your Java application:

```
class CallProcedure{
    public static void main(String[] args) {
        try {
            Connection con = getConnection();
            CallableStatement cs = con.prepareCall
                          ("{call book_details_new_prices()}");

            ResultSet rs = cs.executeQuery();

            while(rs.next()) {
                System.out.println(rs.getString("id") + "--" +
                                   rs.getString("author") + "--" +
                                   rs.getDouble("unit_price"));
            }
        }
        catch (SQLException e) {
            System.out.println(e);
        }
    }
    static Connection getConnection() throws SQLException{
        // code to get a valid connection
    }
}
```

Call prepareCall to create object of CallableStatement, passing it name of stored procedure

Because stored procedure book_details_new _prices executes SQL SELECT statement, it will return ResultSet

Note the similarity in creating objects of `PreparedStatement` and `CallableStatement`. Unlike the `Statement` object, where you specify the SQL statement while calling methods `executeQuery()` or `executeUpdate()`, you must specify the SQL statement when you create objects of `PreparedStatement` and `CallableStatement`. Also note the SQL statement used to call a procedure:

```
call book_details_new_prices()
```

Because the database-stored procedure `book_details_new_prices` doesn't accept any parameters, it's acceptable to drop the `()` following the procedure name:

```
CallableStatement cs = con.prepareCall
        ("{call book_details_new_prices}");
```

9.7.3   *Database-stored procedures with parameters*

The way it's quite usual for you to define method parameters for your Java methods, it's also usual to define parameters for a database-stored procedure. Let's work with an example of a stored procedure that accepts a parameter. The following code creates the relevant database procedure:

```
class DatabaseCreateProcedure{
    public static void main(String[] args) {
        try {
            Connection con = getConnection();
            PreparedStatement statement = con.prepareStatement
                ("CREATE PROCEDURE proc_book_count (OUT count INT) "+
                "BEGIN "+
                    "SELECT COUNT(*) INTO count FROM book; "+
                "END;");
            int result = statement.executeUpdate();
            System.out.println(result);
        }
        catch (SQLException e) {
            System.out.println(e);
        }
    }
    static Connection getConnection() throws SQLException{
        // code to get a valid Connection
    }
}
```

> Code to create a stored procedure with a parameter

Unlike the stored procedure shown in the preceding example, the procedure in the following example accepts multiple parameters: an IN (input) parameter to send values to the procedure, and an OUT (output) parameter to return values from the procedure. The database procedure proc_author_row_count accepts the author name as a CHAR value, and it selects the total book count from table book for author names that match its input parameter. It stores the book count in its OUT parameter:

```
class CreateProcedureRowCount{
    public static void main(String[] args) {
        try {
            Connection con = getConnection();
            PreparedStatement statement = con.prepareStatement
                ("CREATE PROCEDURE proc_author_row_count " +
                    "(IN author_name CHAR(50), OUT count INT) "+
                "BEGIN "+
                    "SELECT COUNT(*) INTO count FROM book " +
                    "WHERE author = author_name; " +
                "END;");
            int result = statement.executeUpdate();
            System.out.println(result);
        }
        catch (SQLException e) {
            System.out.println(e);
        }
    }
```

> Database-stored procedure with IN and OUT parameters

```
      static Connection getConnection() throws SQLException{
          // get a valid Connection object
      }
  }
```

You can define parameters of type IN, OUT, and INOUT with a database-stored procedure. The parameters of type IN can be used to pass values to a procedure, the parameters of type OUT can be used to return values from a procedure, and the parameters of type INOUT can be used to do both—pass values to a procedure and return values from it.

Let's see how you can set the variables for method parameters while calling the database-stored procedure:

```
class CallStoredProcedureWithParameters{                         Use ? for
    public static void main(String[] args) {                     procedure
        try {                                                     parameters
            Connection con = getConnection();
            CallableStatement cs = con.prepareCall
                            ("{call proc_author_row_count(?, ?)}");

            int rowCount = 10;
            String authorName = "Shreya";                Register OUT
                                                          parameter
            cs.setString(1, authorName);
            cs.registerOutParameter(2, Types.NUMERIC);
            cs.setInt(2, rowCount);

            cs.execute();                 Execute
                                          CallableStatement

            System.out.println("rowCount = " + rowCount);  Print value returned
        }                                                  in OUT paramater
        catch (SQLException e) {
            System.out.println(e);
        }
    }
    static Connection getConnection() throws SQLException{
        // code to get a valid Connection object
    }
}
```

Set first procedure parameter using parameter index position and value

Assign second parameter

9.8   Summary

This chapter introduces the JDBC API, and its overview, architecture, and JDBC drivers. The JDBC API is an industry standard for connecting Java to tabular data, typically stored in database systems and also in flat files or Excel spreadsheets. It's a mature and simple technology that has been around since Java Standard Edition version 1.1.

To connect a JDBC client to a database, the JDBC client should have access to a JDBC driver. JDBC drivers implement the interfaces defined in the JDBC API. JDBC drivers are provided by the database vendor or a third party and come in multiple flavors (like type 1 and type 2). The JDBC API is a call-level API. At its core, it works with sending SQL statements to a data source and retrieving the results. It can also modify the return values and update the underlying database.

We worked with the interfaces that make up the core of the JDBC API: `java.sql.Driver`, `java.sql.Connection`, `java.sql.Statement`, `javax.sql.RowSet`, and `java.sql.ResultSet`. Class `DriverManager` manages the registration and loading of JDBC drivers and establishes a connection with a database.

We used `Statement` objects to send SQL statements to the database to create tables, query them, and update and modify their values. `ResultSet` objects store the results returned by the database. The values in a `ResultSet` can be modified and committed to the database. Most of the database operations throw a `SQLException`; therefore almost all the methods of these core interfaces throw a `SQLException`.

We worked with the commit modes of a database connection: auto-commit and manual commit. To start a transaction, you must set the auto-commit mode of the database connection to `false`. You witnessed how to exercise finer control over a subset of the SQL statements in a transaction by creating savepoints and rolling back partial transactions, in the case where an exception is thrown.

The interface `RowSet` extends the interface `ResultSet`. It can be used as a Java-Bean component and it defines multiple properties, which can be set to connect to a database, execute SQL statements, retrieve results, and update them back to the database. `RowSet` is extended by multiple interfaces, such as `JdbcRowSet`, `CachedRowSet`, and others, offering specialized functionalities.

At the end of the chapter, we worked with `PreparedStatement` and `CallableStatement`. Objects of these interfaces represent precompiled statements. `PreparedStatement` can be used to execute SQL statements with or without placeholders. `CallableStatement` can be used to execute stored database procedures with method parameters passed as parameters.

REVIEW NOTES

This section lists the main points covered in this chapter.

Introduction

- JDBC is part of the core Java API; you don't need to download it separately to use it in your Java applications.
- By using the standard classes and interfaces from the JDBC API, Java classes can connect to a database, execute SQL, and process the results.
- JDBC is a standard specification—any Java class can use JDBC to connect with a database using a JDBC driver.
- Contrary to the JDBC API, JDBC drivers are external class bundles not included in the JDK.
- JDBC has been around since 1997 and was added to JSE 1.1 as JDBC 1.0. Since its first version, multiple enhancements have been made to JDBC. Java 7 ships with JDBC 4.1.

- JDBC classes are defined in Java packages `java.sql` and `javax.sql`.
- You can access tabular data stored on relational databases, flat files, and Excel spreadsheets using the JDBC API.
- JDBC provides vendor-neutral access to the common database features. So if you don't use proprietary features of a database, you can easily change the database that you connect to. The JDBC API includes an abstraction of a database connection, statements, and result sets.
- With the JDBC API, you have a choice of connecting to a local or remote data store either directly or through an application server.
- JDBC drivers are the implementation of the lower-level JDBC driver API as defined in the JDBC specifications.
- Depending on whether the drivers are implemented using only Java code, native code, or partial Java, they're categorized as type 4, pure Java JDBC driver; type 3, pure Java driver for database middleware; type 2, native API, partial Java driver; and type 1, JDBC–ODBC bridge.

Interfaces that make up the JDBC API core

- The interfaces that make up the core of the JDBC API are `java.sql.Driver`, `java.sql.Connection`, `java.sql.Statememt`, `java.sql.ResultSet`, and `javax.sql.RowSet`.
- Every JDBC driver implementation *must* implement the interface `Driver`.
- Every driver must implement a minimum set of interfaces defined in the JDBC API to conform to the JDBC specifications.
- `Connection` represents a connection session with the specified database. It's used to create SQL statements, execute them against the database, start and commit transactions, and retrieve other details.
- The interface `Statement` is used to create and execute static SQL statements and retrieve their results.
- Interfaces `PreparedStatement` and `CallableStatement` extend the `Statement` interface. They represent precompiled statements.
- `PreparedStatement` can be used to execute static or dynamic SQL statements.
- `CallableStatement` is used to execute stored database procedures.
- A `ResultSet` is retrieved as a result of executing a SQL `SELECT` statement against a database. It represents a table of data.

Connecting to a database

- The first step to make a Java class communicate with a database is to establish a connection between them.
- Class `java.sql.DriverManager` talks with the JDBC driver to return a `Connection` object, which can be used by your Java classes for all further communication with the database.

- For the exam, it's important to note the difference between a JDBC driver (lowercase d) and a `Driver` (uppercase D). A JDBC driver is a set of classes provided by the database vendor or a third party, usually in a .jar or .zip file, to support the JDBC API. A `Driver` class is an implementation of the interface `java.sql.Driver`.
- To connect with a data source, you need class `DriverManager` only once.
- Manual loading of drivers is required for JDBC API version 3.0 and before.
- JDBC drivers should be manually loaded by calling `Class.forName()`, passing it the name of the `Driver` class.
- If `Class.forName()` can't load the JDBC driver, it throws a `ClassNotFound-Exception` (a checked exception).
- For JDBC API 4.0 and later, JDBC drivers can be automatically loaded and registered by class `DriverManager`.
- When a class is loaded in memory, its static initializer block executes. According to the JDBC specifications, a driver must register itself with the `DriverManager`.
- The JVM loads class `DriverManager` when you call any of its methods.
- Class `DriverManager` manages all the instances of JDBC driver implementations registered with a system.
- When you invoke method `getConnection()`, class `DriverManager` finds the appropriate drivers from its set of registered drivers, establishes a connection with a database, and returns the `Connection` object.
- There are three overloaded versions of method `getConnection()`.
- You can connect to a database by including the username and password as part of the JDBC connect URL string.
- It's common to use `Properties` to specify the login credentials for the JDBC URL in method `getConnection()`.
- The property names for specifying the username and password to establish a connection are `"user"` and `"password"`. An attempt to use any other key to specify and use username and password will throw a `SQLException`.
- If your application can't load a JDBC driver or connect to a database due to invalid login credentials, it will throw an exception.

CRUD (create, retrieve, update, and delete) operations

- To create a `Statement` object, call method `createStatement()` on a `Connection` object.
- To define and execute a static SQL statement for a `Statement` object, call `executeQuery()` or `executeUpdate()` on `Statement`.
- Method `executeQuery()` returns `ResultSet`.
- Method `executeUpdate()` returns an `int` value specifying the number of affected rows.
- Method `executeUpdate()` is used to execute SQL queries to insert new rows in a table, and update and delete existing rows. It's also used to execute DDL queries

like the creation, modification, and deletion of database objects like tables. If you use method `executeQuery()` for any of these operations, you'll get a `SQLException` at runtime.

- The SQL statements that you include in your code are defined as string values. This essentially means that if any of the SQL statement is invalid, no compilation errors are thrown.

- If a SQL `SELECT` returns no rows, `ResultSet` doesn't refer to a `null` value. It refers to an initialized `ResultSet` object with zero rows.

- `Connection`, `Statement`, and `ResultSet` objects should be closed by calling their method `close()` either implicitly or explicitly.

- If you create `Connection`, `Statement`, and `ResultSet` objects using a try-with-resources statement, it will auto-close them.

JDBC transactions

- A transaction is a logical set of SQL statements. Either all or none of the statements must execute from a transaction.

- To initiate a transaction, set the default database auto-commit mode to `false`.

- If the auto-commit mode of a connection is set to `true`, calling any of the transaction methods like `commit()` or `rollback()` will throw a `SQLException`.

- Method `executeUpdate()` returns a count of the rows that are or would be affected in the database for row insertions, modifications, and deletion. The value is returned even if the statement isn't committed to a database.

- By using a savepoint, you can exercise finer control over the work done by a set of SQL statements in a transaction.

RowSet objects

- You can use `RowSet` objects as JavaBeans components, which can be created and configured at design time.

- You can configure a `RowSet` object by setting its properties, connecting to a JDBC data source, executing a SQL statement, and getting the results.

- The interface `javax.sql.RowSet` extends the interface `java.sql.ResultSet`.

- You can register listeners with a `RowSet` object so that when an event occurs on a `RowSet` object (like any modification to its value), the registered listeners can be notified.

- `RowSet` objects can be *connected* or *disconnected*. A connected `RowSet` object, like `JdbcRowSet`, maintains a connection with its data source throughout its life. On the other hand, a disconnected `RowSet` object, like `CachedRowSet`, establishes a connection with the data source, gets the values, and then disconnects itself.

- The interface `javax.sql.rowset.RowSetFactory` defines the implementation of a factory that can be used to obtain different types of `RowSet` implementations.

- Class `javax.sql.rowset.RowSetProvider` defines factory methods to get a `RowSetFactory` implementation. The `RowSetFactory` can then be used to create objects of different types of `RowSet` implementations. The Java API defines a default implementation of `RowSetFactory`.
- If the execute method isn't successful on a `RowSet` object, you can only call execute and close methods on it. The rest of the methods will throw an exception.

Precompiled statements

- Interfaces `java.sql.PreparedStatement` and `java.sql.CallableStatement` extend the `java.sql.Statement` interface.
- The objects of interfaces `PreparedStatement` and `CallableStatement` represent precompiled SQL statements.
- Precompiled statements execute faster than their noncompiled counterparts.
- Another major advantage offered by `PreparedStatement` and `CallableStatement` is their ability to include placeholders in SQL statements using ?. You can assign values to these placeholders by calling one of the appropriate `setDataType(parameterIndex, value)` on these objects.
- Unlike `Statement`, you must specify the relevant SQL statement when you create an object of `PreparedStatement`.
- `PreparedStatement` defines three methods to execute its SQL statement: `execute()`, `executeQuery()`, and `executeUpdate()`. Method `execute()` can execute any type of SQL statement and returns a `boolean` value. Method `executeQuery()` executes a SQL `SELECT` statement and returns a `ResultSet`. Method `executeUpdate()` executes DDL statements and table `INSERT`, `UPDATE`, and `DELETE` SQL statements. It returns 0 for DDL statements and the number of rows affected for SQL `INSERT`, `UPDATE`, and `DELETE` statements.
- You can execute the database-stored procedures from your Java applications by using `CallableStatement` in the JDBC API.
- If a database-stored procedure doesn't accept any parameter, it's acceptable to drop the () following the procedure name in a call to execute it using `CallableStatement`.
- A database stored procedure can accept multiple parameters: an `IN` (input) parameter to send values to the procedure, and an `OUT` (output) parameter to return values from the procedure.
- You can define parameters of type `IN`, `OUT`, and `INOUT` with a database-stored procedure using `CallableStatement`.

SAMPLE EXAM QUESTIONS

Q 9-1. Given that method `getConnection()` returns a valid `Connection` object, the query variable defines a valid SQL statement, and class `PrepStatement` prints 0, select the options for the following code that can be correct individually:

```
class PrepStatement {
    public static void main(String[] args) {
        try {
            String query = ".....";                      //line1
            Connection con = getConnection();
            PreparedStatement statement =
                        con.prepareStatement(query);
            System.out.println(
                statement.executeUpdate());
        }
        catch (SQLException e) {
            System.out.println(e);
        }
    }
}
```

    a Line 1 defines a SQL `SELECT` statement that returned zero rows.

    b Line 1 defines a SQL `UPDATE` statement that affected zero rows.

    c Line 1 defines a SQL `DELETE` statement that affected zero rows.

    d Line 1 defines a SQL `CREATE TABLE` statement, which would always return zero rows.

Q 9-2. Which SQL standard is JDBC 4.1 (Java 7) consistent with?

    a SQL99

    b SQL:2003

    c SQL:2010

    d SQL7

Q 9-3. Given the following table

```
Item tree
id INT PRIMARY KEY,
average_age REAL,
name CHAR(100)
```

which statements are true about the following code if con is a valid `Connection` object?

```
try (Connection con = getConnection();
    Statement statement = con.createStatement();
    ResultSet rs = statement.executeQuery("SELECT * FROM tree");) {
    if (rs.next()) rs.getString(2);        //line1
}
```

```
catch (SQLException e) {
   System.out.println(e);
}
```

   a If table `tree` has one or more rows, the code throws a runtime exception at line 1.

   b The code prints the `average_age` for all rows in table `tree`.

   c The code prints the `name` for all rows in table `tree`.

   d If there are no rows in table `tree`, the code won't throw an exception.

   e If table `tree` has five rows, the code prints the value for the `average_age` for the first row.

   f If table `tree` has five rows, the code prints the value for `name` for the first row.

Q 9-4. A programmer is unable to connect her Java application to a database using JDBC. Assuming that she is using Java 7 on her system and trying to connect with a remote MySQL database, what are the possible solutions that can help her?

   a Add the driver .jar file—that is, mysql-connector-java-5.1.26-bin.jar—to the Java application's class path.

   b Add the driver .jar file—that is, mysql-connector-java-5.1.26-bin.jar—to the system's class path.

   c Add the driver .jar file—that is, mysql-connector-java-5.1.26-bin.jar—to the remote system's class path hosting the MySQL database.

   d Call method `Class.forName()` passing it the string value `mysql-connector-java-5.1.26-bin.jar`.

   e Call method `DriverManager.loadDriver()` to load the MySQL driver in memory.

   f Create a new `Driver` instance by calling `new` and pass it to `DriverManager`'s method `connect()`.

   g Call `DriverManager`'s method `getConnection()`, passing it the database URL, username, and password.

   h Call `DriverManager`'s method `connect()`, passing it the database URL, username, and password.

Q 9-5. Which of the following code options would create objects of `RowSet`?

   a
```
RowSetFactory aFactory = RowSetProvider.newFactory();
CachedRowSet rowset = aFactory.createCachedRowSet();
```

   b
```
RowSetFactory aFactory = RowSetProvider.newFactory();
JDBCRowSet rowset = aFactory.createJDBCRowSet();
```

   c
```
RowSetFactory aFactory = RowSetProvider.createFactory();
CachedRowSet rowset = aFactory.cachedRowSet();
```

   d
```
RowSetFactory aFactory = RowSetProvider.newFactory();
ComparableRowSet rowset = aFactory.createComparableRowSet();
```

Q 9-6. Which of the following options will populate `ResultRet` rs with all rows from table `Contact`, assuming `getConnection()` returns a valid `Connection` object?

a
```
public static void main(String[] args) throws Exception{
    Connection con = getConnection();
    Statement statement = con.createStatement();
    ResultSet rs = statement.executeQuery("SELECT * FROM contact");
}
```

b
```
public static void main(String[] args) {
    Connection con = getConnection();
    Statement statement = con.createStatement();
    ResultSet rs = statement.executeQuery("SELECT * FROM contact");
}
```

c
```
public static void main(String[] args) throws SQLException{
    Connection con = getConnection();
    Statement statement = con.prepareStatement();
    ResultSet rs = statement.executeQuery("SELECT * FROM contact");
}
```

d
```
public static void main(String[] args) throws Throwable{
    Connection con = getConnection();
    Statement statement = con.callableStatement("SELECT * FROM contact");
    ResultSet rs = statement.executeUpdate();
}
```

Q 9-7. Select the correct option to be inserted at `//INSERT CODE HERE` that calls the database-stored procedure `hello_world`.

```
class Procedure{
    public static void main(String[] args) {
        try {
            Connection con = getConnection();
            //INSERT CODE HERE
            cs.setString(1, "eJavaGuru");
            cs.registerOutParameter(2, Types.NUMERIC);
            cs.setInt(2, 10);
            System.out.println(cs.executeUpdate());
        }
        catch (SQLException e) {}
    }
}
```

a `CallableStatement cs = con.prepareCall("{hello_world(?, ?)}");`

b `CallableStatement cs = con.prepareCall("{call procedure_hello_world (?, ?)}");`

c `CallableStatement cs = con.prepareCall("{call hello_world}");`

d `CallableStatement cs = con.prepareCall("{call hello_world(?, ?)}");`

e `CallableStatement cs = con.prepareCall("hello_world(?, ?)");`

Q 9-8. Given the following table

```
Item Book
id INT PRIMARY KEY,
title CHAR(100),
publisher CHAR(100),
unit_price REAL,
```

what is the result of the following code?

```
class Transact1 {
    public static void main(String[] args) throws SQLException{
        Connection con = null;
        try {
            con = getConnection();      //assume this get a valid connection
            con.setAutoCommit(false);
            Savepoint sv1 = con.setSavepoint();                  // line 1
            Statement statement = con.createStatement();
            statement.executeUpdate("UPDATE book " +
                                    "SET unit_price = 10.0");
            Savepoint sv2 = con.setSavepoint("sv2");             // line 2
            statement.executeUpdate("UPDATE book " +
                                    "SET unit_price = 20.0");
            con.rollback();
            con.commit();                                        // line 3
        }
        catch (SQLException e) {
            con.rollback();                                      // line 4
        }
    }
}
```

a   The code updates the unit_price of all rows in table book to 10.0.

b   The code updates the unit_price of all rows in table book to 20.0.

c   There is no change in the value of unit_price in table book.

d   The code fails to compile on either line 1, line 2, or line 4.

e   If the code on line 3 throws a runtime exception other than SQLException, the code will update the unit_price of all rows in table book to 20.0.

Q 9-9. Which of the following options demonstrates the correct use and closing of database resources?

```
a   public static void main(String[] args) throws Exception {
        Connection con = getConnection();
        Statement statement = con.createStatement();
        ResultSet rs = statement.executeQuery("SELECT name, email FROM
    doctor");
    }
```

```
b   public static void main(String[] args) throws Exception {
        try (Connection con = getConnection();
        Statement statement = con.createStatement();
        ResultSet rs = statement.executeQuery("SELECT name, email FROM
    doctor");) {}
    }

c   public static void main(String[] args) throws Exception {
        try {
            Connection con = getConnection();
            Statement statement = con.createStatement();
            ResultSet rs = statement.executeQuery("SELECT name, email FROM
    doctor");
        }
        catch (SQLException e) {
            rs.close();
            statement.close();
            con.close();
        }
    }

d   public static void main(String[] args) throws Exception {
        try {
            Connection con = getConnection();
            Statement statement = con.createStatement();
            ResultSet rs = statement.executeQuery("SELECT name, email FROM
    doctor");
        }
        catch (SQLException e) {
            con.close();
            statement.close();
            rs.close();
        }
    }

e   public static void main(String[] args) throws Exception {
        try {
            Connection con = getConnection();
            Statement statement = con.createStatement();
            ResultSet rs = statement.executeQuery("SELECT name, email FROM
    doctor");
        }
        catch (SQLException e) {
            try {
                con.close();
                statement.close();
                rs.close();
            }
            catch (Exception e) {}
        }
    }
```

ANSWERS TO SAMPLE EXAM QUESTIONS

A 9-1. b, c, d

[9.6] Create and use PreparedStatement and CallableStatement objects

Explanation: You can't use method `executeUpdate()` to execute a SQL SELECT query. If you do, you'll get a `SQLException` with a similar message:

```
java.sql.SQLException: Can not issue executeUpdate() for SELECTs
```

Similarly, you can't execute data deletion and modification queries with method `executeQuery()`. If you do so, you'll get a `SQLException`:

```
java.sql.SQLException: Can not issue data manipulation statements with
     executeQuery().
```

A 9-2. b

[9.1] Describe the interfaces that make up the core of the JDBC API (including the Driver, Connection, Statement, and ResultSet interfaces and their relationship to provider implementations)

Explanation: One of the goals of JDBC 4.1, which is shipped with Java 7, is to be consistent with SQL:2003. JDBC 3.0 supported SQL99 features that were widely supported by the industry. JDBC 4.1 is supporting major components of SQL:2003.

A 9-3. d, e

[9.3] Submit queries and read results from the database (including creating statements, returning result sets, iterating through the results, and properly closing result sets, statements, and connections)

Explanation: This question makes you take note of multiple points:

- What happens if the database data type doesn't match with Java's `getXXX()` methods used to retrieve the database column value? You can use method `get-String()` to retrieve all types of database values. But if you use other `getXXX()` methods like `getDouble()` to retrieve a database column value, the method will throw a `SQLException` if the column value can't be implicitly converted to Java data type `double`.
- The index of the column values in a `ResultSet` start with position 1 and not 0. `rs.getString()` will return the value of the second database column—that is, `average_age`.
- Like any `if` statement, if `rs.next()` returns `true`, the code in its block will execute once.

A 9-4. a, b, g

[9.2] Identify the components required to connect to a database using the Driver-Manager class (including the JDBC URL)

Option (c) is incorrect. To connect a Java application to a database using JDBC, the driver class should be added to the class path of the application or system executing the Java class. Its addition to the class path of the system on which the database is hosted doesn't matter.

Option (d) is incorrect. Starting with Java 6 (JDBC 4.0) you don't need to call `Class.forName()` to explicitly load the JDBC driver. Starting with JDBC 4.0, SPM automates the driver loading and registration process. The drivers must include a configuration file with the name `java.sql.Driver` (containing the name of the actual class file implementing the `java.sql.Driver` interface) within the META-INF folder in their .jar file. `DriverManager` class searches for drivers on the classpath and registers them automatically.

Option (e) is incorrect because method `loadDriver()` doesn't exist.

Option (f) is incorrect because you aren't supposed to create new `Driver` instances yourself.

Option (h) is incorrect because the correct method name is `getConnection()`.

A 9-5. a

[9.5] Construct and use RowSet objects using the RowSetProvider class and the RowSetFactory interface

Option (b) is incorrect because the correct class name is `JdbcRowSet`. Also, the method invoked on `aFactory` is invalid.

Option (c) is incorrect because the correct factory method name is `newFactory()` and not `createFactory()`. Also, the method invoked on `aFactory` is invalid.

Option (d) is incorrect because the Java API doesn't define the interface `ComparableRowSet`.

A 9-6. a

[9.3] Submit queries and read results from the database (including creating statements, returning result sets, iterating through the results, and properly closing result sets, statements, and connections)

Explanation: The code in option (b) won't compile. This code neither handles the checked `SQLException` thrown by the JDBC API statements, nor declares the `main` method to throw it.

Option (c) is incorrect because you must pass the SQL query when you create an object of `PreparedStatement` using `Connection`'s method `prepareStatement()`.

Option (d) is incorrect because class `Connection` doesn't define method `callable-Statement()`. The correct method to create an object of `CallableStatement` is `prepareCall()` (from class `Connection`).

A 9-7. d

[9.6] Create and use PreparedStatement and CallableStatement objects

Explanation: To call a stored procedure using Java's `CallableStatement`, you must prefix the procedure name with the word `call`. Stored procedures that accept method parameters must be followed by parentheses. The question marks used in the code in this question are placeholders to insert variable values.

A 9-8. c

[9.4] Use JDBC transactions (including disabling auto-commit mode, committing and rolling back transactions, and setting and rolling back to savepoints)

Explanation: The code sets multiple savepoints. The first, `Savepoint-sv1`, isn't tagged with a name. When `rollback()` is called on a `Connection` object without the savepoint name, it's rolled back to the unnamed savepoint.

A 9-9. b

[9.3] Submit queries and read results from the database (including creating statements, returning result sets, iterating through the results, and properly closing result sets, statements, and connections)

Option (a) is incorrect because it doesn't care to call `close` on the database objects `con`, `resultset`, and `statement`.

Option (b) is correct because the `try-with-resources` statement declares the database resources and closes all of them in reverse order of their creation. The main method declares to throw the exception `Exception` so the `try-with-resources` statement doesn't need to be followed by a catch handler to take care of the exceptions thrown during the creation and auto-closing of the resources.

Options (c) and (d) won't compile. The reference variables are created in the try-block, so they are out of scope (and thus unknown) in the `catch`-block.

Option (e) is incorrect. The code doesn't compile. The reference variables are created in the `try`-block, so they are out of scope (and thus unknown) in the `catch`-block. The `catch` handler around the `close()` method invocations has exactly the same name (e) as its surrounding `catch` handler. Also, in the `catch` handler, the `close()` methods are invoked in the order `Connection`, `Statement` and `ResultSet`. On the other hand, the automatic resource closing will call `close()` in the order `ResultSet`, `Statement`, and `Connection`.

Threads

Exam objectives covered in this chapter	What you need to know
[10.1] Create and use the `Thread` class and the `Runnable` interface	How to use class `Thread` and the `Runnable` interface to create classes that can execute as a separate thread of execution.
[10.2] Manage and control thread lifecycle	What states a thread of execution can be in, and how it transitions from one state to another including the methods involved. What is or can't be guaranteed by each method. How the execution of a method depends on the thread scheduling by the underlying operating system.
[10.3] Synchronize thread access to shared data	How sharing of objects between threads can lead to inconsistent memory and invalid object state. How to make your classes thread safe.
[10.4] Identify code that may not execute correctly in a multithreaded environment	How to identify classes, methods, and variables that might not work as expected in a multithreaded environment. How to fix them.

Have you ever watched a movie with a group of friends, laughing, shouting, and sharing popcorn, nachos, or fries—all at the *same* time? If yes, you've already practiced *multithreading* and *concurrency*. You can compare these separate tasks—watching a movie, laughing, shouting, and so on—with multiple threads (multithreading), which you execute *concurrently* (at the same time). Can you imagine watching a movie with your friends, pausing it so that you can (only) laugh, followed by (only) shouting, and so on? It sounds bizarre. Similarly, apart from executing multiple applications concurrently, multithreading facilitates optimal use of a computer's processing capabilities. Modeled around human behavior, multithreading is the need of the hour.

Multithreading is implemented by the underlying OS by dividing and allotting processor time to the running applications using multiple algorithms (round-robin, high priority first, preemptive, and so on). Applications can execute as single or multiple *processes*, which might run multiple *threads*. Java supports multithreading by enabling you to define and create separate threads of execution in your applications. Most Java Virtual Machine (JVM) implementations run as a single *process*. A process is a self-contained execution environment complete with its own private set of basic runtime resources, including memory. A process can create multiple threads, also known as *lightweight* processes. Creation of a thread requires fewer resources. Multiple threads share the resources of the process in which they're created, like memory and files. They also have their own exclusive working space, like stacks and PC registers.

"Every problem has a solution, and every solution has a problem"—this statement holds true for threads. Threads were created so that they could make the best use of a processor's time. An application can create multiple threads. When threads share objects among themselves, it can result in interleaving operations (*thread interference*) and reading inconsistent object values (*memory inconsistency*). You can protect shared data by synchronizing its access. But this can lead to other issues like thread contention through *deadlock*, *starvation*, and *livelock*.

 NOTE Even if you don't create a multithreaded Java application, you can't ignore these concepts. Java technologies like swing in Core Java and Servlets in web applications and many popular Java frameworks implicitly multithread and call your code from multiple threads. Developing safe code that works and behaves well in a multithreaded environment demands knowledge about multithreading and synchronization.

Multithreading is a *big* topic and its coverage in this chapter is limited to the topics covered on the exam. This chapter also includes an introduction to a few threading concepts that you must know to understand the chapter contents. These introductory sections can be identified by the use of the term *warm-up* in section headings. You can skip these if you're familiar with these concepts.

For the exam, you must be able to clearly identify what is guaranteed and what isn't by threads. For example, a thread is guaranteed to execute its own code in the sequence in which it's defined. But you can't guarantee when a thread *exactly* starts, pauses, or resumes its execution. Make note of these points.

 EXAM TIP For the exam, it's important to understand what threads guarantee and what they don't. Expect multiple questions on *expected*, *probable*, and *assured* thread behavior.

This chapter covers

- How to create threads using class `Thread` and the `Runnable` interface
- How to define and use `Thread` instances to create separate threads of execution
- How to manage and control the thread lifecycle
- How to protect data from concurrent access by threads
- How to identify code that might not execute correctly in a multithreaded environment

Let's get started with creating and using threads.

10.1 Create and use threads

 [10.1] Create and use the Thread class and the Runnable interface

All nontrivial Java applications are multithreaded. A JVM supports multiple thread execution. Multiple threads can be supported by an underlying system by using multiple hardware processors, by time-slicing a single processor, or by time-slicing multiple processors. Java language supports multithreading. Class `Thread` and the `Runnable` interface can be used to define and start your own threads. In the next chapter on concurrency, we'll explore the `java.util.concurrent` package to execute your threads.

You'll often hear about thread objects and threads of execution in a multithreaded or concurrent application. Though related, a `Thread` instance and a *thread of execution* aren't the same. A `Thread` instance is a Java object. The implementation of Java threads is JVM-specific. A JVM implementation might even choose not to map Java threads to native threads at all! Creation of a thread of execution is passed to the OS by a JVM implementation. A thread of execution has its own set of program counter (PC) registers to store the next set of instructions to execute. It also has its own *stack* that stores *method frames* to store the state of a method invocation. The state of a method invocation includes the value of local variables, method parameters, method return values, exception handler parameters, and intermediate values. A process like JVM's can create multiple threads of execution to execute multiple tasks simultaneously. A `Thread` instance and a thread of execution are depicted in figure 10.1.

Have you ever wondered how many threads your Java application has? At least one—the *main* thread. A JVM starts execution of a Java application using a thread of execution: main. This thread executes code defined in method `main()` and can create other threads of execution.

 NOTE The main thread is named 'main' by the JVM. Don't confuse it with the method `main()`.

In this section, you'll see how to define and start your own threads using Java classes that either extend class `Thread` or implement the `Runnable` interface. Let's get started with an example.

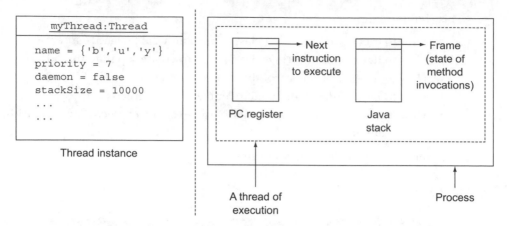

Figure 10.1   A `Thread` instance and a thread of execution

Have you tried dancing and singing simultaneously? Let's create a small program that emulates this behavior by creating and starting multiple threads simultaneously. Let's get started with extending class `Thread`.

10.1.1 *Extending class Thread*

Class `Thread` can be used to create and start a new thread of execution. To create your own thread objects using class `Thread`, you *must*

- Extend class `Thread`
- Override its method `run()`

To create and start a new thread of execution, you *must*

- Call `start()` on your `Thread` instance

When a new thread of execution starts, it will execute the code defined in the thread instance's method `run()`. Method `start()` will trigger creation of a new thread of execution, allocating resources to it. We'll cover the methods of class `Thread` as we move forward in the chapter.

The following listing shows the code for the sample application that creates a new thread `Sing` by extending class `Thread`, and instantiates this thread in method `main()`.

Listing 10.1   Using class `Thread` to create a thread

```
class Sing extends Thread{
    public void run() {
        System.out.println("Singing.......");
    }
}
```

◁┐ **run() begins execution when
you call start() on a thread.**

```
class SingAndDance {
    public static void main(String args[]) {
        Thread sing = new Sing();              <── Instantiate Thread
        sing.start();
        System.out.println("Dancing");          <── Start thread
    }                                               sing
}
```

When you execute the code in listing 10.1, method `main()` might complete its execution before *or* after the thread `sing` starts its execution. The same code might generate different output when you execute it on the same or different systems, at different times. The exact time of thread execution is determined by how the underlying thread scheduler schedules the execution of threads. Because thread scheduling is specific to a specific JVM and depends on a lot of parameters, the same system might change the order of processing of your threads. The probable outputs of the code in listing 10.1 are shown in figure 10.2.

C:\WINDOWS\system32\cmd.exe	C:\WINDOWS\system32\cmd.exe
E:\code>java SingAndDance Dancing Singing.......	E:\code>java SingAndDance Singing....... Dancing

Figure 10.2   Probable outputs of class `SingAndDance`

 EXAM TIP   The exam might question you on the probable output of a multithreaded application. Because you can't be sure of the order of execution of threads by an underlying OS, such questions can have multiple correct code outputs.

In listing 10.1, note that calling `start()` on a `Thread` instance creates a new thread of execution. The default implementation of method `start()` in class `Thread` checks if you're starting it for the first time; if yes, it calls a native method to start a new thread of execution, calling its method `run()`. What happens if you override method `start()` without calling the superclass's default implementation?

```
class Sing extends Thread{
    public void run() {
        System.out.println("Singing.......");
    }                                                  Sing overrides
    public void start() {                       <──    start
        System.out.println("Starting...");
    }
}
class SingAndDance {
    public static void main(String args[]) {           Overridden start() doesn't start
        Thread sing = new Sing();                       the thread; it won't create new
        sing.start();                           <──     thread of execution
        System.out.println("Dancing");
    }
}
```

The preceding code is guaranteed to output the following because it isn't starting another thread:

```
Starting...
Dancing
```

 EXAM TIP   Watch out for code that overrides method `start()` in a class that extends `Thread`. If it doesn't call method `start()` from its superclass `Thread`, it won't start a new thread of execution.

When you create a thread class by extending class `Thread`, you lose the flexibility of inheriting any other class. To get around this, instead of extending class `Thread`, you can implement the `Runnable` interface, as discussed next.

10.1.2 *Implement interface Runnable*

If a class implements the `Runnable` interface, its instances can define code that can be executed by threads of execution. The `Runnable` interface defines just one method, `run()`:

```
public interface Runnable {
    public abstract void run();
}
```

Steps for a class to use the `Runnable` interface

- Implement the `Runnable` interface
- Implement its method `run()`

Let's modify class `Sing` defined in listing 10.1 so that it implements the `Runnable` interface instead of extending class `Thread` (modifications are in bold):

Listing 10.2   Using the `Runnable` interface to create a thread

```
class Sing implements Runnable{                              Sing implements
    @Override                                                Runnable
    public void run() {
        System.out.println("Singing.......");                run begins execution when
    }                                                        you call start on a thread.
}
class SingAndDance2 {
    public static void main(String args[]) {                 Instantiate thread by passing
        Thread sing = new Thread(new Sing());                instance of Runnable to
        sing.start();                                        Thread's constructor
        System.out.println("Dancing");
    }                                                        Start
}                                                            thread sing.
```

 NOTE   While implementing or overriding methods, I won't use the annotation `@Override` in all code examples in the rest of the chapters because the code examples on the exam might not use it.

The preceding code will generate the same output as shown in figure 10.1. Apart from the most obvious difference that class Sing implements the Runnable interface, compare the difference in how sing is instantiated:

```
Thread sing = new Thread(new Sing());
```

If your class implements the Runnable interface, then you should pass its instance to the constructor of class Thread. If your class extends class Thread, then you can create a new thread by using the new operator and invoking its constructor.

Class Thread defines multiple overloaded constructors. The following constructors allocate a new Thread object:

```
Thread()
Thread(String name)
Thread(Runnable target)
Thread(Runnable target, String name)
```

A Thread constructor that accepts a string value enables you to create a thread with a name. But if you don't assign an explicit name to a thread, Java automatically generates and assigns a name to it. Make note of the Thread constructor that accepts a Runnable object. A Thread instance stores a reference to a Runnable object and uses it when you *start* its execution (by calling start()). Here's the partial code of class Thread:

```
public class Thread implements Runnable {
    /* What will be run. */
    private Runnable target;
    /*.. rest of the code.. */
}
```

Because class Thread implements the Runnable interface, you can instantiate a thread by passing it another Thread instance. So what happens when you create a thread, say, A, using another Thread instance, say, B? Does Java create multiple threads of execution in this case? When you execute A.start(), will it execute A.run() or B.run()? Let's answer all these questions using the next "Twist in the Tale" exercise.

Twist in the Tale 10.1

Class SingAndDance instantiates a thread by passing it an instance of the class that extends the thread itself. Will the following class execute method start() or run() twice? What do you think is the output of the following code?

```
class SingAndDance3 {
    public static void main(String args[]) {
        Thread sing = new Sing();
        Thread newThread = new Thread(sing);
        newThread.start();
    }
}
class Sing extends Thread{
    public void run() {
        System.out.println("Singing");
```

```
        }
    }
```

   a The code fails to compile.

   b The code prints `Singing`.

   c The code prints `Singing` twice.

   d Class `SingAndDance3` starts one new thread of execution in `main`.

   e Class `SingAndDance3` starts two new threads of execution in `main`.

   f There is no output.

Each thread is created with a *priority*. Its range varies from 1 to 10, with 1 being the lowest priority and 10 the highest priority. By default, a thread creates another thread with the same priority as its own. It can also be explicitly set for a `Thread` instance, using `Thread`'s method `setPriority(int)`. A thread scheduler *might* choose to execute threads with higher priorities over threads with lower priorities, though you can't guarantee it.

 EXAM TIP You can't guarantee that a thread with a higher priority will always execute before a thread with a lower priority.

When you call `start()` on a `Thread` instance, it creates a new thread of execution. A thread of execution has a lifecycle: a thread is created, it *might* be paused, and eventually it completes its execution. The next section explores the different states in which a thread can exist, the methods that you can call on a thread, and how these methods affect the states of a thread.

10.2   *Thread lifecycle*

    [10.2] Manage and control thread lifecycle

A thread's lifecycle consists of multiple states. You can control the transition of a thread from one state to another by calling its methods. The methods signal the JVM regarding the change in status of a thread. The *exact time* of state transition is controlled by a thread scheduler, which is bound to vary across platforms.

10.2.1   *Lifecycle of a thread*

A thread can exist in multiple states: NEW, RUNNABLE, WAIT, TIMED_WAITING, BLOCKED, or TERMINATED. A thread doesn't begin its execution with its instantiation. Figure 10.3 shows the various phases of a thread, including the methods that can be called on a thread object in each state, which makes it transition from one state to another. For the exam, you must know how a thread transitions from one state to another and what methods you can call on a thread when it's in different phases.

   A Java thread can officially exist in the states as defined by a thread's inner enum, `State`. Table 10.1 lists the values of enum `Thread.State`.

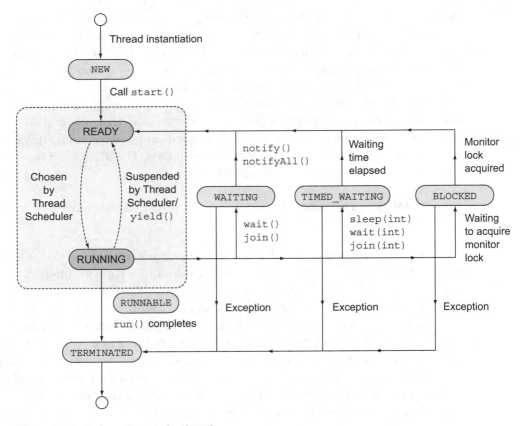

Figure 10.3   Various phases of a thread

Table 10.1   States of a thread as defined by enum `Thread.State`

Thread state	Description
NEW	A thread that has been created but hasn't yet started is in this state.
RUNNABLE	Thread state for a runnable thread. A thread in this state is executing in the JVM but it may be waiting for other resources from the OS, such as a processor.
BLOCKED	A thread that's blocked waiting for a monitor lock is in this state.
WAITING	A thread that's waiting indefinitely for another thread to perform a particular action is in this state.
TIMED_WAITING	A thread that's waiting for another thread to perform an action for up to a specified waiting time is in this state.
TERMINATED	A thread whose `run()` method has finished is in this state (still a thread object but not a thread of execution).

Calling `start()` on a new thread instance implicitly calls its `run()`, which transitions its state from `NEW` to `RUNNABLE`. A thread in the `RUNNABLE` state is all set to be executed. It's just waiting to be chosen by the thread scheduler so that it gets the processor time. Thread scheduling is specific to the underlying OS on every system. As a programmer, you can't control or determine when a particular thread transitions from the READY state to the RUNNING state, and when it actually gets to execute. A thread scheduler follows various scheduling mechanisms to utilize a processor efficiently, and also to give a fair share of processor time to each thread. It might suspend a running thread to give way to other READY threads and it might execute it later. The READY and the RUNNING states are together referred to as the `RUNNABLE` state.

 EXAM TIP   The states READY and RUNNING are together referred to as the `RUNNABLE` state.

A running thread enters the `TIMED_WAITING` state, when it might need to wait for a specified interval of time, before it can resume its execution. It happens when `sleep(int)`, `join(int)`, or `wait(int)` is called on a running thread. On completion of the elapsed interval, a thread enters the queue eligible to be scheduled by the thread scheduler. When `join()` or `wait()` is called on a running thread, it transitions to the `WAITING` state. It can change back to the `RUNNABLE` state when `notify()` or `notifyAll()` is called (the details of all these methods are discussed later). A `RUNNABLE` thread might enter the `BLOCKED` state when it's waiting for other system resources like network connections or to acquire an object lock to execute a synchronized method or code block. Depending on whether the thread is able to acquire the monitor lock or resources, it returns back to the `RUNNABLE` state.

With the successful completion of `run()`, a thread enters the `TERMINATED` state. A thread might transition from any state to the `TERMINATED` state due to an exception. You can execute the following quick code to get a list of all the threads that are active on your system and the state they're in:

```
Set<Thread> threadSet = Thread.getAllStackTraces().keySet();
for(Thread t : threadSet)
    System.out.println(t + " --- " + t.getState());
```

Here's probable output of this code (which might vary on each individual's system):

```
Thread[Reference Handler,10,system] --- WAITING
Thread[Finalizer,8,system] --- WAITING
Thread[Attach Listener,5,system] --- RUNNABLE
Thread[Signal Dispatcher,9,system] --- RUNNABLE
Thread[Thread-1,5,main] --- TIMED_WAITING
```

It's very likely for the exam to question you on what happens if you call a method (and how many times) that you weren't supposed to in a particular thread state. For example, can you call `join()` on a thread in its `NEW` state, or, say, can you call `start()`

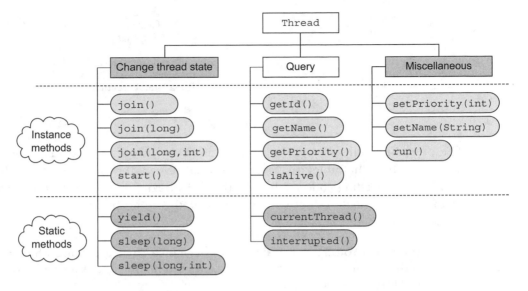

Figure 10.4 Main methods of class `Thread`

on a thread twice? To answer these questions, you'll need to know the thread methods, covered next.

10.2.2 Methods of class Thread

Before we can move forward with the methods that can be called in a particular thread state, let's categorize the methods of class `Thread` as instance or static methods, and if these methods can be used to change a thread's state or to query it. The thread methods are shown in figure 10.4.

>
> **NOTE** Class `Thread` includes deprecated methods, like `resume()`, `stop()`, and `suspend()`. Because their use isn't encouraged, they aren't discussed in this chapter. You won't find the deprecated methods on the exam either.

The next section dives into the methods that you can call to transition a thread in the NEW state to a thread in the RUNNABLE state.

10.2.3 Start thread execution

Calling `start()` on a `Thread` instance creates a new thread of execution, which executes `run()`. You can call `start()` on a thread that's in the NEW state. Calling `start()` from any other thread state will throw an `IllegalThreadStateException`:

```
class CantCallStartOnSameThreadMoreThanOnce {
    public static void main(String args[]) {
        Thread sing = new Sing();
```
**State of thread
sing is NEW**

```
            sing.start();
            sing.start();
        }
    }
class Sing extends Thread{
    public void run() {
        System.out.println("Singing");
    }
}
```

Calls start()—state of thread sing changes to RUNNABLE.

Can't call start() on a thread state other than NEW; throws java.lang.Illegal-ThreadStateException.

The preceding code might print `Singing` and then throw an `IllegalThreadState-Exception`. It might throw an `IllegalThreadStateException` without printing `Singing`. How? The preceding code might start the thread `sing`, but *before* it prints `Singing`, method `main()` might call `start()` on the `sing` thread again, throwing an `Illegal-ThreadStateException`.

EXAM TIP   You can call `start()` only once on a `Thread` instance when it's in the NEW state. Calling `start()` on a thread in any other state will throw an `IllegalThreadStateException`.

What happens if you replace `sing.start()` with `sing.run()`?

```
class CanCallRunMultipleTimes {
    public static void main(String args[]) {
        Thread sing = new Sing();
        sing.run();
        sing.run();
    }
}
class Sing extends Thread{
    public void run() {
        System.out.println("Singing");
    }
}
```

State of thread sing—NEW

Calls run()—State of thread remains NEW.

The output of the preceding code is as follows:

```
Singing
Singing
```

In the preceding code, `run()` neither starts a new thread of execution in `main`, nor modifies the state of thread `sing` ❶. The `main` calls `run` like any other method—waiting for `run` to complete execution, before executing the code at ❷. The code at ❷ again executes `run()` and prints `Singing`.

EXAM TIP   Calling `run()` on a `Thread` instance doesn't start a *new* thread of execution. The `run()` continues to execute in the *same* thread. Watch out for trick questions on using `start()` versus `run()` in the exam.

Because `start()` starts a new thread of execution, you might find it interesting how the exceptions are handled in multithreaded applications. For example, if both the calling thread and the called thread throw unhandled exceptions at runtime, do you think the code will encounter only one or both? Let's find out using the next "Twist in the Tale" exercise.

Twist in the Tale 10.2

What do you think is the output of the following code?

```
class Twist10_2 {
    public static void main(String args[]) {
        Thread sing = new Sing();
        sing.start();
        throw new RuntimeException("main");
    }
}
class Sing extends Thread{
    public void run() {
        System.out.println("Singing");
        throw new RuntimeException("run");
    }
}
```

a java.lang.RuntimeException: main
   Singing
   java.lang.RuntimeException: run

b Singing
   java.lang.RuntimeException: run
   java.lang.RuntimeException: main

c java.lang.RuntimeException: main

d Singing
   java.lang.RuntimeException: run

e Singing
   java.lang.RuntimeException: main
   java.lang.RuntimeException: run

Once a thread begins its execution, multiple factors might pause its execution. Let's examine them in detail in the next section.

10.2.4 *Pause thread execution*

A thread might pause its execution due to the calling of an explicit method or when its time slice with the processor expires.

THREAD SCHEDULING

A processor's time is usually time-sliced to allow multiple threads to run, with each thread using one or more time slices. A thread scheduler might suspend a running thread and move it to the ready state, executing another thread from the ready queue. Thread scheduling is specific to JVM implementation and beyond the control of an

application programmer. The scheduler moves a thread from the READY state to RUN-
NING and vice versa, to support concurrent processing of threads.

 EXAM TIP   As a Java programmer, you can't control or determine when
the thread scheduler moves a thread from the RUNNING state to READY and
vice versa. It's specific to an OS.

METHOD THREAD.YIELD()

Imagine while debugging or testing your code, you need to reproduce a bug due to
race conditions (that is, when multiple threads compete). You can insert a call to
Thread.yield() in one of the threads. The static method yield() makes the currently executing thread pause its execution and give up its current use of the processor. But it only acts as a hint to the scheduler. The scheduler might also ignore it. The
static method yield() can be placed literally anywhere in your code—not only in
method run():

```
class YieldProcessorTime {
    public static void main(String args[]) {
        Thread sing = new Sing();
        sing.start();
        Thread.yield();                      Might cause thread main
    }                                        to yield its processor time.
}
class Sing extends Thread{
    public void run() {                      When executed, might
        yield();                             cause thread sing to
        System.out.println("Singing");       yield its processor time.
    }
}
```

As shown in figure 10.5, when called from two threads, thread 1 and thread 2,
yield() might or might not *yield* its execution.

So what's guaranteed from this method call? To be precise, nothing. It might not
make the currently executing thread give up its processor time. If it does, it doesn't
guarantee when it will happen and when the thread will resume its execution.

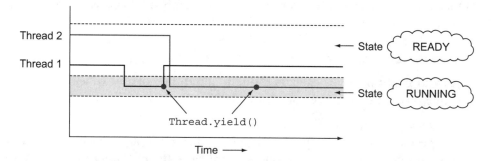

Figure 10.5   **Calling** yield() **might yield the current thread's execution slot as soon as it's
called or after a delay, or it might be ignored.**

EXAM TIP   Method `yield()` is static. It can be called from any method, and it doesn't throw any exceptions.

METHOD THREAD.SLEEP()

The static method `Thread.sleep()` is *guaranteed* to cause the currently executing thread to temporarily give up its execution for *at least* the specified number of milliseconds (and nanoseconds) and move to the READY state. You use `sleep()` to *slow down* the execution of your thread. Imagine you're using a thread to animate a ball across a visible frame. Execute the following class and you'll see that a black ball zooms across the screen:

```java
import javax.swing.*;
import java.awt.*;
class MyFrame {
    public static void main(String args[]) {
        JFrame frame = new JFrame();                        // Create a frame.
        frame.setSize(400, 300);
        frame.setVisible(true);
        MovingBall ball = new MovingBall(60, frame);         // Create and start
        ball.start();                                        // MovingBall thread.
    }
}
class MovingBall extends Thread{
    int radius;
    Graphics g;
    int xPos, yPos;                                          // x and y positions
                                                             // to draw an oval
    JFrame frame;
    MovingBall(int radius, JFrame frame) {
        this.radius = radius;
        this.g = frame.getGraphics();
        this.frame = frame;
    }
    public void run() {                                      // Execute it
        while (true) {                                       // forever.
            g.setColor(Color.WHITE);                                    // Paint whole
            g.fillRect(0, 0, frame.getWidth(), frame.getHeight());      // screen white
            ++xPos; ++yPos;              // Modify x and y position of moving ball
            g.setColor(Color.BLACK);                                    // Draw ball at new
            g.fillOval(xPos, yPos, radius, radius);                     // x and y position
        }
    }
}
```

In the preceding code, method `run()` tries to animate a ball by first painting the complete visible frame area with white and then drawing a black oval at the specified x and y positions. Each loop repeats these steps with modified x and y coordinates that make the ball move across the frame. You can slow down the moving ball by making `MovingBall` sleep for the specified milliseconds (modifications are in bold):

```java
class MovingBall extends Thread{
    int radius;
    Graphics g;
```

```
        int xPos, yPos;
        JFrame frame;
        MovingBall(int radius, JFrame frame) {
            this.radius = radius;
            this.g = frame.getGraphics();
            this.frame = frame;
        }
        public void run() {
            while (true) {
                try {
                    Thread.sleep(10);
                }
                catch (InterruptedException e) {
                    System.out.println(e);
                }
                xPos = xPos + 2; yPos = yPos + 2;
                g.setColor(Color.WHITE);
                g.fillRect(0, 0, frame.getWidth(), frame.getHeight());
                g.setColor(Color.BLACK);
                g.fillOval(xPos, yPos, radius, radius);
            }
        }
    }
```

← **Guarantees to sleep for at least 10 milliseconds (if not interrupted).**

← **If interrupted, sleeping thread might throw InterruptedException**

Class Thread defines the overloaded versions of sleep() as follows:

```
public static native void sleep(long milli) throws InterruptedException;
public static void sleep(long milli, int nanos) throws InterruptedException
```

Whether a thread will sleep for the precise duration specified in nanoseconds will depend on an underlying system. Unless interrupted, the currently executing thread will sleep at least for the specified duration. On the exam, watch out for questions that state a thread will become runnable *exactly* after the expiration of the sleep duration. Unless interrupted, a thread is guaranteed to sleep for *at least* the specified duration. The exact time to resume execution depends on the thread scheduler.

 EXAM TIP   A thread that's suspended due to a call to sleep doesn't lose ownership of any monitors.

You can also expect questions on where to place a call to method sleep(). The answer depends on who is executing a call to sleep(). Like yield(), sleep() is Thread's static method. It makes the currently executing thread give up its execution and sleep. It can be called from any piece of code—all code is executed by some thread. If it's placed in Runnable's run(), it will cause the thread to sleep. Placed otherwise, it will make the calling thread sleep. What happens if you place sleep() in MovingBall's constructor (showing only relevant code)?

```
class MovingBall extends Thread{
    //..code not shown deliberately
    MovingBall(int radius, JFrame frame) {
```

```
            try {
                Thread.sleep(1000);
            }
            catch (InterruptedException e) {
                System.out.println(e);
            }
            //..code not shown deliberately
        }
        public void run() {
            //..code not shown deliberately
        }
    }
```

A thread that instantiates `MovingBall` will execute `sleep()`, and then sleep for the specified duration before it can complete `MovingBall`'s instantiation.

METHOD JOIN()

A thread might need to pause its *own* execution when it's waiting for another thread to complete its task. If thread A calls `join()` on a `Thread` instance B, A will wait for B to complete its execution before A can proceed to its own completion. Imagine multiple teams—design, development, and testing—are working on a software project. The project can't be sent to a customer until all of these teams complete their tasks. Ideally, the delivery process will wait for design development and testing teams to complete their tasks before the delivery process can move ahead with its own task of handing over the project to a customer. Let's code a subset of this example. The design team must complete the design of a screen before a developer can start coding it:

```
class ScreenDesign extends Thread {
    public void run() {
        for (int i = 0; i < 5; i++) System.out.println(i);   ◁──┐  run() simply
    }                                                             prints a couple
}                                                                 of numbers.
class Developer {
    ScreenDesign design;
    Developer(ScreenDesign design) {          ┐  Developer stores a
        this.design = design;                 ◁──┘  reference to Design.
    }
    public void code() {
        try {
            System.out.println("Waiting for design to complete");
            design.join();
            System.out.println("Coding phase start");
        }
        catch(InterruptedException e) {          ┐  join() throws checked
            System.out.println(e);               │  InterruptedException.
        }
    }
}
class Project {                                                          ┐  Start
    public static void main(String[] args) {                             │  thread
        ScreenDesign design = new ScreenDesign(); design.start();   ◁──┘  design.
```

**code() calls
design.join().** (├─▷)

```
        Developer dev = new Developer(design);
        dev.code();
    }
}
```

→ **dev.code(), which
runs in thread main,
calls design.join.**

Figure 10.6 shows probable outputs of the preceding code. Because class `Developer` isn't a `Runnable` instance, it doesn't execute it in its own thread of execution; rather, it executes in the thread `main`. When `Developer` calls `design.join()`, the thread `main` waits for `design` to complete its execution before executing the rest of its code.

0	0	
Waiting for design to complete	1	Waiting for design to complete
1	2	0
2	3	1
3	Waiting for design to complete	2
4	4	3
Coding phase start	Coding phase start	4
		Coding phase start

Figure 10.6   Probable outputs of calling `join()` on a thread

 EXAM TIP   Method `join()` guarantees that the calling thread won't execute its remaining code until the thread on which it calls `join()` completes.

Class `Thread` defines overloaded `join()` methods as follows:

```
public final synchronized void join(long milli) throws InterruptedException
public final synchronized void join(long millis, int nanos)
                                                throws InterruptedException
public final void join() throws InterruptedException
```

The variations of `join()` that accept milliseconds and nanoseconds wait for at least the specified duration (if they're not interrupted!). Behind the scenes, `join()` is implemented using methods `wait()`, `isAlive()`, and `notifyAll()`.

METHODS WAIT(), NOTIFY(), AND NOTIFYALL()

Imagine a server accepts and queues multiple requests from users that are processed by a thread. This thread might need to wait and pause its own execution if there are no new requests in the queue. A thread can pause its execution and wait on an object, a queue in this case, by calling `wait()`, until another thread calls `notify()` or `notify-All()` on the same object.

Methods `wait()`, `notify()`, and `notifyAll()` can be called on all Java objects, because they're defined in class `Object` and not class `Thread`. Because these methods can be invoked by synchronized methods and blocks and by threads that own the object monitors, we'll cover these methods in detail in the next section after covering object monitors and synchronized methods and blocks.

10.2.5 *End thread execution*

A thread completes its execution when its method `run()` completes. You must not call the deprecated method `stop()` to stop execution of a thread. A thread might perform a task for a finite number of times or it might loop for an indefinite number of times. In the later case, the thread should define an exit condition to indicate its completion:

```
class Sing extends Thread{
    boolean singStatus = true;
    public void run() {                          run() executes until
        while (singStatus)          ◄───┐        singStatus is false.
            System.out.println("Singing");
    }
    public void setSingStatus(boolean value) {
        singStatus = value;
    }
}
```

In the preceding code, the instance of thread `Sing` will execute until its instance variable `singStatus` is assigned a value of `false`. An application can modify the value of `singStatus` using `setSingStatus(boolean)`. Once `run()` completes its execution, the status of a thread changes to `TERMINATED`.

You create threads to speed up execution of a process so that unrelated tasks don't need to be executed in sequence and can execute concurrently. But these multiple threads might share data among themselves. Next, let's see how sharing data among multiple threads can result in incorrect data, and how to protect shared data among threads.

10.3 *Protect shared data*

 [10.3] Synchronize thread access to shared data

Threads are lightweight processes that share certain areas of the memory, unlike regular processes. This makes threads very efficient, but it also introduces additional complexities regarding memory management. You can protect your shared data by making it accessible (for reading and writing) to only one thread at a point of time. Other techniques include defining *immutable* classes (the states of which can't be modified) and defining volatile variables. In this section, you'll identify the data that's shared across threads and needs to be protected, and the related techniques.

Let's get started with the identification of what data can be shared among multiple threads.

10.3.1 *Identifying shared data: WARM-UP*

A JVM instance hosts only one Java application. A Java application can create and execute multiple threads. When a new thread is created, it's allotted its exclusive share in the memory. The JVM also allows partial runtime data to be shared between

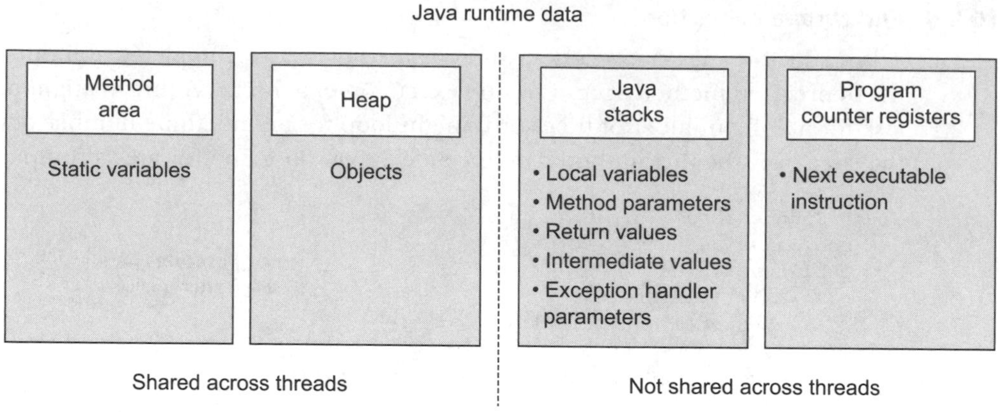

Java runtime data

Figure 10.7   Identifying parts of runtime data that can be shared across threads

threads. A JVM's runtime data set includes the method area, the heap, Java stacks, and PC registers (it also includes native method stacks, which aren't covered by the exam, so they aren't discussed here). The method area includes class information that includes a note on all its variables and methods. This data set includes the static variables, which are accessible and shared by all the threads in a JVM. The static variables are shared by one class loader—that is, each class loader has its own set of static variables. The heap includes objects that are created during the lifetime of an application, again shared by multiple threads and processes. PC registers and Java stacks aren't shared across the threads. On instantiation, each thread gets a PC register, which defines the next set of instructions to execute. Each thread is also assigned a Java stack. When a thread begins execution of a method, a method frame is created and inserted into the java stack, which is used to store the local variables, method parameters, return values, and intermediate values that might be used in a method. Of all this data, the method area and heap are shared across threads. Figure 10.7 shows this arrangement.

In the next section, you'll see how multiple threads can interfere with each other's working.

10.3.2 *Thread interference*

Interleaving of multiple threads that manipulate shared data using multiple steps leads to thread interference. You can't assume that a single statement of Java code executes atomically as a single step by the processor. For example, a simple statement like incrementing a variable value might involve multiple steps like loading of the variable value from memory to registers (working space), incrementing the value, and reloading the new value in the memory. When multiple threads execute this seemingly atomic statement, they might interleave, resulting in incorrect variable values.

NOTE Operations that use arithmetic and assignment operators like ++, --, +=, -=, *=, and /= aren't atomic. Multiple threads that manipulate variable values using these operators can interleave.

Let's work with an example of a class Book, which defines an instance variable copies-Sold that can be manipulated using its methods newSale() or returnBook():

```java
class Book{
    String title;
    int copiesSold = 0;
    Book(String title) {
        this.title = title;
    }
    public void newSale() {
        ++copiesSold;
    }
    public void returnBook() {
        --copiesSold;
    }
}
```

Nonatomic statements include loading variable values from memory to registers, manipulating values, and loading them back to memory.

The threads OnlineBuy and OnlineReturn manipulate the value of class Book's instance variable copiesSold in their run() using methods newSale() and returnBook():

```java
class OnlineBuy extends Thread{
    private Book book;
    public OnlineBuy(Book book) {
        this.book = book;
    }
    @Override
    public void run() {
        book.newSale();
    }
}
```

When started, OnlineBuy calls newSale() on its Book instance.

```java
class OnlineReturn extends Thread{
    private Book book;
    public OnlineReturn(Book book) {
        this.book = book;
    }
    @Override
    public void run() {
        book.returnBook();
    }
}
```

When started, OnlineReturn calls returnBook() on its Book instance.

Let's see what happens when another class, say, ShoppingCart, instantiates a Book and passes it to the threads OnlineBuy and OnlineReturn:

Instantiate Book instance book.

```java
class ShoppingCart {
    public static void main(String args[]) throws Exception {
        Book book = new Book("Java");
        Thread task1 = new OnlineBuy(book); task1.start();
```

Instantiate OnlineBuy using book and start thread task1.

```
        Thread task2 = new OnlineBuy(book); task2.start();
        Thread task3 = new OnlineReturn(book); task3.start();
    }
}
```

Instantiate OnlineReturn instance using book and start thread task3.

Instantiate another OnlineBuy instance using book and start thread task2.

In the preceding code method `main()` starts three threads—`task1`, `task2`, and `task3`. These threads manipulate and share the same `Book` instance, `book`. The threads `task1` and `task2` execute `book.newSale()`, and `task3` executes `book.returnBook()`. As mentioned previously, `++copiesSold` and `--copiesSold` aren't atomic operations. Also, as a programmer you can't determine or command the exact time when these threads will start with their execution (it depends on how they're scheduled to execute by the OS). Let's assume that `task2` starts with its execution and reads `book.copiesSold`. Before it can modify this shared value, it's also read by threads `task3` and `task2`, which are unaware that this value is being modified by another thread. All these threads modify the value of `book.copiesSold` and update it back in order. The last thread to update the value `book.copiesSold` overrides updates of the other two threads. Figure 10.8 shows one of the possible ways in which the threads `task1`, `task2`, and `task3` can interleave.

So, how can you assure that when multiple threads update shared values it doesn't lead to incorrect results? How can you communicate between threads? Let's discuss this in the next section.

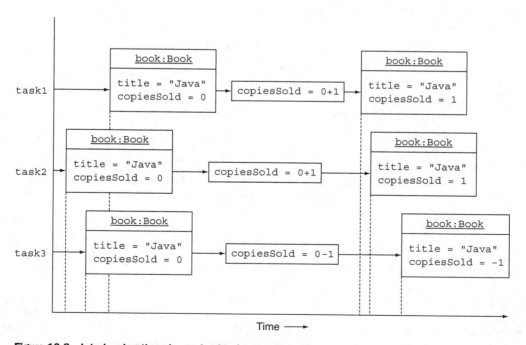

Figure 10.8   Interleaving threads can lead to incorrect results.

10.3.3 *Thread-safe access to shared data*

Imagine if you could lock a shared object while it was being accessed by a thread; you'd be able to prevent other threads from modifying it. This is exactly what Java does to make its data *thread safe*. Making your applications thread safe means securing your shared data so that it stores correct data, even when it's accessed by multiple threads. Thread safety isn't about *safe threads*—it's about safeguarding your shared data that might be accessible to multiple threads. A thread-safe class stores correct data without requiring calling classes to guard it.

You can lock objects by defining *synchronized methods* and *synchronized statements*. Java implements synchronization by using monitors, covered in the next quick warm-up section.

OBJECT LOCKS AND MONITORS: WARM-UP

Every Java object is associated with a *monitor,* which can be *locked* or *unlocked* by a thread. At a time, only one thread can hold lock on a monitor and is referred to as the *monitor owner.* Owning the monitor is also referred to as *acquiring the monitor.* If another thread wants to acquire the monitor of that object, it must wait for it to be released.

When the keyword synchronized is added to a method, only one thread can execute it at a time. To execute a synchronized method, a thread *must* acquire the monitor of the object on which the method is called. When the monitor of an object is locked, no other thread can execute any synchronized method on that object. When acquired, a thread can release the lock on the monitor if

- It has completed its execution.
- It needs to wait for another operation to complete.

For the first case, it releases the lock and exits. For the latter case, it enters a *waiting set* of threads that are waiting to acquire the monitor again. Threads enter the waiting set due to an execution of yield or wait. They can reacquire the monitor when notify-All() or notify() is called.

Figure 10.9 shows how a thread might have to wait to hold a lock on a monitor. Only one thread can own the monitor of an object, and a thread might release the monitor and enter a waiting state.

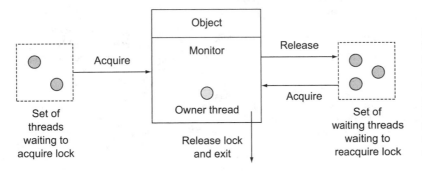

Figure 10.9 A thread must own a monitor before it can execute synchronized code. Only the monitor owner can execute the synchronized code.

With an understanding of how objects and their monitors, threads, and execution of synchronized code work together, let's modify the code used in section 10.3.2 so that threads working with shared data don't interleave.

SYNCHRONIZED METHODS

Synchronized methods are defined by prefixing the definition of a method with the keyword `synchronized`. You can define both instance and static methods as synchronized methods. The methods, which modify the state of instance or static variables, should be defined as synchronized methods. This prevents multiple threads from modifying the shared data in a manner that leads to incorrect values.

When a thread invokes a synchronized method, it automatically locks the monitor. If the method is an instance method, the thread locks the monitor associated with the instance on which it's invoked (referred to as `this` within the method). For static methods, the thread locks the monitor associated with the `Class` object, thereby representing the class in which the method is defined. These locks are released once execution of the synchronized method completes, with or without an exception.

 EXAM TIP　For nonstatic instance synchronized methods, a thread locks the monitor of the object on which the synchronized method is called. To execute static synchronized methods, a thread locks the monitor associated with the `Class` object of its class.

In the following listing, let's modify the definition of class `Book` by defining its methods `newSale()` and `returnBook()` as synchronized methods. The methods that belong to the data being protected are defined as synchronized.

Listing 10.3　Working with synchronized methods

```
class Book{
    String title;
    int copiesSold = 0;
    Book(String title) {
        this.title = title;
    }
    synchronized public void newSale() {          newSale() is now a
        ++copiesSold;                             synchronized method.
    }
    synchronized public void returnBook() {       returnBook() is now a
        --copiesSold;                             synchronized method.
    }
}
class OnlineBuy extends Thread{
    private Book book;
    public OnlineBuy(Book book) {
        this.book = book;
    }
```

```
        @Override
        public void run() {
            book.newSale();
        }
    }
class OnlineReturn extends Thread{
        private Book book;
        public OnlineReturn(Book book) {
            this.book = book;
        }
        @Override
        public void run() {
            book.returnBook();
        }
    }
class ShoppingCart {
        public static void main(String args[]) throws Exception {
            Book book = new Book("Java");
            Thread task1 = new OnlineBuy(book); task1.start();
            Thread task2 = new OnlineBuy(book); task2.start();
            Thread task3 = new OnlineReturn(book); task3.start();
        }
    }
```

Figure 10.10 shows how threads task2, task1, and task3 might acquire a lock on the monitor of object book defined in the main method of class ShoppingCart. As you see, a thread can't execute synchronized methods newSale() and returnBook() on book without acquiring a lock on its monitor. So each thread has exclusive access to book to modify its state, resulting in a *correct* book state at the completion of main.

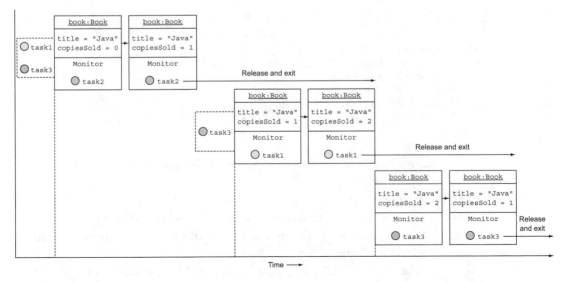

Figure 10.10 Threads acquire a lock on the monitor of object book before executing its synchronized methods newSale() and returnBook(). So threads task1, task2, and task3 don't interleave.

EXAM TIP   A thread releases the lock on an object monitor after it exits a synchronized method, whether due to successful completion or due to an exception.

What happens if, instead of defining methods `newSale()` and `returnBook()` as synchronized methods (see listing 10.3), you define the `run()` methods in the threads `OnlineBuy` and `OnlineReturn` as synchronized methods? Will this modification protect the data of shared object `book` in `ShoppingCart`? Let's answer this question in the next "Twist in the Tale" exercise. Take a closer look; apart from the mentioned modification, I've also modified some other bits of code.

Twist in the Tale 10.3

What do you think is the output of the following code?

```
class Book{
    int copiesSold = 0;
    public void newSale() { ++copiesSold; }
    public void returnBook() { --copiesSold; }
}
class OnlineBuy extends Thread{
    private Book book;
    public OnlineBuy(Book book) { this.book = book; }
    synchronized public void run() {                    //1
        book.newSale();
    }
}
class OnlineReturn extends Thread{
    private Book book;
    public OnlineReturn(Book book) { this.book = book; }
    synchronized public void run() {                    //2
        book.returnBook();
    }
}
class ShoppingCart {
    public static void main(String args[]) throws Exception {
        Book book = new Book();                         //3
        Thread task1 = new OnlineBuy(book); task1.start();      //4
        Thread task2 = new OnlineBuy(book); task2.start();      //5
        Thread task3 = new OnlineReturn(book); task3.start();   //6
    }
}
```

a The code on lines 1 and 2 fails to compile. It can't override `run` by adding the keyword `synchronized`.

b The code compiles, but calling `start()` on lines 4, 5, and 6 doesn't call `run` defined on lines 1 and 2. It calls the default `run()` method defined in class `Thread`.

c Lines 4, 5, and 6 call `run()` defined at lines 1 and 2, but fail to protect data of object `book` defined at line 3.

d Lines 4, 5, and 6 call `run()` defined at lines 1 and 2, and succeed in protecting data of object `book` defined at line 3.

As stated before, when a thread acquires a lock on the object monitor, no other thread can execute any other synchronized method on the object until the lock is released. This could become inefficient if your class defined synchronized methods that manipulate different sets of unrelated data. To do so, you might mark a block of statements with the keyword `synchronized`, as covered in the next section.

SYNCHRONIZED STATEMENTS

To execute synchronized statements, a thread must acquire a lock on an object monitor. For an instance method, it might not acquire a lock on the instance itself. You can specify *any* object on which a thread *must* acquire the monitor lock before it can execute the synchronized statements.

In the previous example for class `Book`, let's remove the keyword `synchronized` from the definition of method `newSale()` and define synchronized statements in it:

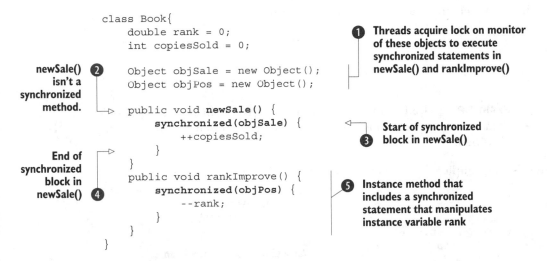

The code at ❶ defines objects `objSale` and `objPos` that are used to execute synchronized statements defined in methods `newSale()` and `rankImprove()`. The code at ❷ shows `newSale()` is no longer a synchronized method. At ❸, a thread that executes `newSale()` must acquire a lock on the object `objSale` before it can execute the synchronized statements that start from the code at ❸ and end at ❹. Method `newSale()` manipulates variable `copiesSold`. The code at ❺ defines an instance method that includes a synchronized statement that manipulates the instance variable `rank`.

While a thread is executing method `newSale()` on a `Book` instance, another thread can execute method `rankImprove()` on the *same* `Book` instance because `newSale()` and `rankImprove()` acquire locks on monitors of separate objects—that is, `objSale` and `objPos`.

 EXAM TIP Multiple threads *can* concurrently execute methods with synchronized statements if they acquire locks on monitors of separate objects.

A thread releases the lock on the object monitor once it exits the synchronized statement block due to successful completion or an exception. If you're trying to modify your shared data using synchronized statements, ensure that the data items are mutually exclusive. As shown in the preceding example, the object references objSale and objPos refer to different objects.

10.3.4 *Immutable objects are thread safe*

Immutable objects like an instance of class String and all the wrapper classes (like Boolean, Long, Integer, etc.) are thread safe because their contents can't be modified. So no matter how and when you access them, it doesn't result in a *dirty read* or *dirty write*. The exam might ask you to identify a class whose instances are safe from concurrent access and modification, without thread synchronization. The simple answer is the use of immutable objects. In the following example, once title is initialized, no matter how it's accessed by multiple threads, it never leads to inconsistent memory or race conditions:

```
class Book{
    private String title;
}
```

 EXAM TIP   Shared immutable objects can't result in inconsistent object data or an incorrect object state because, once initialized, they can't be modified.

Here's an example of how to create an immutable class:

```
import java.util.Date;                             ❶ final class that
final class BirthDate {                              can't be extended
    private final Date birth;
    public BirthDate(Date dob) {            Value to instance variables can be
        birth = dob;                        assigned only during their instantiation.
    }
    public Date getBirthDate() {
        return (Date)birth.clone();
    }
    public boolean isOlder(Date other) {
        // calculate 'other' with 'birth'      ❹ No methods allow
        // return true is 'birth' < 'other'       modifications to private
        return true;                              instance variables of
    }                                             BirthDate.
}
```

private instance variables ❷

Returns ❸ a clone of birth.

The code at ❶ defines class BirthDate as a final class to ensure that no class can extend the immutable class, and to define additional methods to modify the value of its instance variables. The variable birth is defined as a final and private member at ❷. A private variable can't be manipulated outside the class. Declaring a variable as final prevents it from being reassigned a value. But it doesn't prevent its existing value from being modified (remember you can't reassign a value to a final reference variable, but you can modify its value if its methods allow you to). At ❸, getBirthDate() returns a clone of birth, so that any modifications to the returned value don't change the value of instance variable birth. At ❹, you notice that none of the methods of class BirthDate allow modification of its instance value birth.

In the next "Twist in the Tale" exercise, let's change the positions of a few keywords in class BirthDate, defined in the preceding example code, and see whether it will still survive concurrent access by multiple threads and store and report correct data.

Twist in the Tale 10.4

Examine the following class, assuming that java.util.Date is an immutable class. Do you think it will be safe to use it in a multithreaded environment, without any external synchronization of methods that call this class's methods?

```
import java.util.Date;
final class BirthDate {
    private final Date birth;
    public BirthDate(Date dob) {
        birth = dob;
    }
    final public Date getBirthDate() {
        return birth;
    }
    final public boolean isOlder(Date other) {
        // code to compare dates
        return true;
    }
}
```

   a Yes

   b No

Threads might read and write shared values in their own cache memory. Let's see how you can prevent threads from doing so.

10.3.5 *Volatile variables*

Apart from using synchronized methods and code blocks, you can use volatile variables to synchronize access to data. Though simpler to use than synchronized code, volatile variables offer only a subset of the features offered by the synchronized code. A synchronized code block can be executed by only one thread, as an atomic operation. Also before a thread gives up the monitor lock on an object, the changes it made to the data become visible to the next thread that acquires the object's monitor lock. The volatile variables don't support the atomicity feature.

A read or write operation on a volatile variable creates a *happens-before* relationship with operations on the same object by other threads. As a result, the compiler can't include optimizations that might enable threads to read the values of volatile variables from their own local cache. When a thread reads from or writes to a variable (both primitive and reference variables) marked with the keyword volatile, it accesses it from the main memory as opposed to storing its copy in the thread's cache memory. This prevents multiple threads from storing a local copy of shared values that might not be consistent across threads.

So if they don't offer features as good as synchronized code, why do we need them? Because they offer simplicity and better performance when defining thread-safe data within certain limits. The modified value of the volatile variables shouldn't be dependent on their current value (like a counter). Also they shouldn't be dependent on other variables for their values. Here's an example of code that defines and uses the volatile variable closeAcct:

```
class BankAccount {
    volatile boolean closeAcct = false;          ⟵──┐   volatile variable
    public void markClosure() {                       │   closeAcct
        closeAcct = true;                      ⟵──────┘
    }                                               New value of closeAcct
    public void closeAccount() {                    isn't dependent on its
        if (closeAcct) {                            existing value
            //..procceed with account closure
        }
    }
}
```

Another example of using volatile variables is for initializing objects. But if the object is expected to change after initialization, you might need to use additional synchronization to ensure thread-safe data:

```
class StockData{}
class StockExchange{
    static volatile StockData data = null;
    static void loadStockData() {
        // load and initialize reference variable 'data'
        // the variable 'data' is written to only once
    }
}
class BuyStocks {
    public void buy() {
        if (StockExchange.data != null) {
            // analyze data
            // buy stocks
        }
    }
}
```

In this example, if the reference variable data isn't defined as a volatile variable, other classes might access it before it's completely initialized.

Every problem has a solution and every solution has a problem. Though creating multiple threads results in better use of the underlying processor, it can lead to other issues like inconsistent memory, thread deadlock, and more. Let's cover these in detail in the next section.

10.4　*Identify and fix code in a multithreaded environment*

 [10.4]　Identify code that may not execute correctly in a multithreaded environment

Threading issues arise when multiple threads work with shared data and when they're dependent on other threads. This section identifies the data that you need to be careful with when working with multiple threads, the operations (or methods) that can lead to threading issues, the order of operations, and how to get around all of these issues.

Let's get started with identifying the data that the threads can share among themselves. Only when you know *what* data can be shared, will you be able to identify *how* it can be fixed.

10.4.1　*Variables you should care about*

Threads can share the heap that includes class variables and instance variables. Each thread gets its own share of stack memory, which includes local variables, method parameters, and exception handler parameters. So a multithreaded application should safeguard the static and instance variables or attributes of its shared objects. Figure 10.11 shows the type of variables that are always safe in a multithreaded application. So it's always the not-so-safe instance and static variables that you need to care about.

 NOTE　The terms *static variables* and *static attributes*, and *instance variables* and *instance attributes*, are the same and are often used interchangeably.

But what kind of operations should you care about? Should you only be concerned with the methods that change the value of a shared variable? Or, should you also synchronize the read operations? Let's answer these questions in the next section.

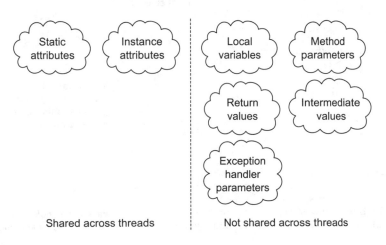

Figure 10.11　Local variables, method parameters, and exception handler parameters are always safe in a multithreaded application.

10.4.2 *Operations you should care about*

To safeguard your data, you might think you only need to worry about methods that modify the value of a variable. Think again. Methods that *only* read shared variable values can also return incorrect or inconsistent data.

Imagine that agents Shreya and Harry (two threads) manage renting an exhibition ground, say, Axiom (shared resource). Harry has agreed to rent it to a customer and is in the process of signing the legal papers (one thread is updating the shared resource). Shreya has no clue about this development. Just before Harry completes signing the rental agreement, Shreya receives an enquiry about the availability of Axiom and she confirms that it's available (another thread reads data while the shared resource is being modified). In this case, Shreya accessed *inconsistent data*.

Similarly, threads that access shared objects can report *inconsistent memory*. Referring back to the previous example of class Book (with an instance variable copiesSold), imagine two threads are accessing the same Book instance. One thread updates the count of copiesSold and the other thread retrieves the value of copiesSold. If the second thread retrieves the value of copiesSold just before the first thread completes the modification, the second thread returns a *dirty value* that is inconsistent. For instance

```
class Book{
    private int copiesSold = 0;
    public void newSale() {
        ++copiesSold;
    }
    public int getCopiesSold() {
        return copiesSold;
    }
}
class OnlineBuy extends Thread{
    private Book book;
    public OnlineBuy(Book book) {
        this.book = book;
    }
    public void run() {
        book.newSale();
    }
}
class OnlineEnquiry extends Thread{
    private Book book;
    public OnlineEnquiry(Book book) {
        this.book = book;
    }
    public void run() {
        System.out.println(book.getCopiesSold());
    }
}
class InconsistentMemory {
    public static void main(String args[]) throws Exception {
        Book eBook = new Book();
        Thread buy = new OnlineBuy(eBook);
        Thread enquire = new OnlineEnquiry(eBook);
```

When started, OnlineBuy executes newSale() on its instance book.

When started, OnlineEnquiry executes getCopiesSold() on its instance book.

Pass same Book instance book to threads buy and enquire.

```
            buy.start();
            enquire.start();
        }
    }
```

> Thread enquire might execute
> ebook.getCopiesSold before thread buy
> completes execution of eBook.newSale.

In the preceding example, the thread enquire might read inconsistent data if it happens to execute eBook .getCopiesSold() before the thread buy executes eBook.newSale(). Depending on how the threads are scheduled, you might see either of the outputs shown in figure 10.12.

1	0

Figure 10.12 Probable outputs of class `InconsistentMemory`

  Imagine a thread that produces data and another thread that consumes it. What happens if the producer thread lags behind, leaving the consumer thread without any data to process? Let's work with this situation in the next section.

10.4.3 *Waiting for notification of events: using wait, notify, and notifyAll*

If interdependent threads share data that's processed alternately by them, the threads should be able to communicate with each other to notify when there's a completion of events, or else the threads might not work correctly.

  Imagine you're waiting for your friend to go river rafting at a camp. You check whether she has arrived by peeping out of your tent every minute. This can become quite inconvenient. How about asking her to notify you when she arrives? Let's implement this in code using the wait and notify methods from class Object. Because these methods are defined in class Object, they can be called on *any* Java object. Methods wait(), notify(), and notifyAll() enable threads sharing the same data to communicate with each other.

 EXAM TIP Methods wait(), notify(), and notifyAll() are defined in class Object and not in class Thread.

To call wait() or notify() a thread must own the object's monitor lock. So calls to these methods should be placed within synchronized methods or blocks. Here's an implementation of the previous example in code:

```
class GoRafting extends Thread {
    Friend friend;
    GoRafting(Friend friend) {
        this.friend = friend;
    }
    public void run() {
        System.out.println("Friend reached:" + friend.reached);
        synchronized(friend) {
            try {
                friend.wait();
            }
        }
```

> ❶ Waits for object friend to call either
> notify() or notifyAll(); call to wait()
> enclosed within a synchronized block.

```
            catch (InterruptedException e) {
                System.out.println(e);
            }
        }
        System.out.println("Reached:" + friend.reached + ",going rafting");
    }
}
class Friend extends Thread {
    boolean reached = false;

    public void run() {
        while (!reached) {
            try {
                Thread.sleep(2000);
            }
            catch (InterruptedException e) {
                System.out.println(e);
            }
            confirmReached();
        }
    }
    public synchronized void confirmReached() {
        reached = true;
        notify();
    }
}
class Camping {
    public static void main(String args[]) {
        Friend paul = new Friend();
        GoRafting rafting = new GoRafting(paul);
        rafting.start();
        paul.start();
    }
}
```

For this example code, thread sleeps for two seconds.

Calls confirmedReached, which calls notify.

❷ Call to notify placed in a synchronized method

❸ Start thread rafting

❹ Start thread friend

The code at ❸ starts the thread rafting. At ❶, when thread rafting calls friend.wait(), it's placed in the waiting set of threads for the object friend, gives up friend's monitor lock, and waits until

- Another thread invokes notify() or notifyAll() on the same object, friend
- Some other thread interrupts GoRafting

At ❹, the thread of execution paul starts its execution. To execute notify at ❷, it must acquire a lock on the monitor for object paul. Once it acquires the lock, it executes notify(), notifying and waking up one of the threads waiting on friend. Because in this example only one thread is waiting on object friend, notify() wakes up the thread rafting. But waking up the thread rafting doesn't guarantee that it will resume its execution immediately. It will enter the RUNNABLE (or execution) state and be ready for when the thread scheduler chooses it for execution.

If multiple threads are waiting on an object's monitor, notify() wakes up one of these threads. Which thread will be chosen isn't defined and is specific to the JVM implementation. Method notifyAll() wakes up all the threads that are waiting on an object's monitor. These threads compete in the usual manner to acquire a lock on the object's monitor and resume their execution.

When `rafting` resumes its execution, it will send its remaining code to execution.

 EXAM TIP Methods `wait()`, `notify()`, and `notifyAll()` *must* be called from a synchronized method or code blocks or else an `IllegalMonitor-StateException` will be thrown by the JVM.

The overloaded `wait()` methods enable you to specify a wait timeout:

```
public final void wait(long timeout) throws InterruptedException
public final void wait(long timeout, int nanos) throws InterruptedException
```

When a thread calls the method `wait()` on an object specifying a timeout duration, it waits until another thread calls `notify()` or `notifyAll` on the same object, it's interrupted by another thread, or the waiting timeout elapses. Even though the overloaded version `wait(long, int)` accepts a timeout duration in nanoseconds, supporting such time precision is JVM- and OS-specific.

 EXAM TIP All overloaded versions of `wait()` throw a checked `InterruptedException`. Methods `notify()` and `notifyAll()` don't throw an `InterruptedException`.

Unlike the `Thread`'s method `join()`, which waits for another thread to complete its execution, methods `wait()` and `notify()` don't require a thread to complete their execution. The thread that calls `wait()`, waits for another thread to notify it using method `notify()` or `notifyAll()`. Some other examples from daily life of using `wait()` and `notify()` are teachers and students waiting to be notified for a next workshop on life skills (which can happen multiple times), an operator who answers a phone whenever she's notified of an incoming call, or customers waiting for notification of new offers on a range of televisions.

The exam is sure to question you on the status of a thread when it executes methods from class `Thread` (`sleep()`, `join()`, `yield()`) and methods from class `Object` (`wait()`, `notify()` and `notifyAll()`), and whether they release or retain the object's monitor locks (if they have acquired one). Figure 10.13 summarizes this information.

Method name	Releases lock?	Change in status of executing thread
`sleep()`	✘	RUNNABLE ⟶ TIMED_WAITING
`yield()`	✘	RUNNABLE ⟶ No change
`join()`	✘	RUNNABLE ⟶ WAITING or TIMED_WAITING
`notify()`/`notifyAll()`	✘	RUNNABLE ⟶ No change
`wait()`	✓	RUNNABLE ⟶ WAITING or TIMED_WAITING

Figure 10.13 Change in thread's status when methods are executed from class `Thread` (`sleep()`, `join()`, `yield()`) and class `Object` (`wait()`, `notify()`, `notifyAll()`)

Multiple threads might deadlock when they have acquired a lock on objects and are waiting to acquire locks on additional objects that are owned by other waiting threads. Let's discuss this threading issue in detail next.

10.4.4 Deadlock

Imagine a tester and a developer are working on two applications, an Android application and an iPhone application. The Android application is in its testing phase; it should be tested and the reported bugs should be fixed by the developer. The iPhone application needs to be developed from scratch; it should be coded by the developer and then tested for bugs. Imagine the tester starts testing the Android application and the developer starts working with the iPhone application. The Android application completes the testing phase and requests for the developer to fix the bugs. At the same time, the iPhone application completes its development phase and requests the tester to test it. The managers working with both the Android and iPhone applications refuse to release their resources (developer or tester) before their project completes. So both projects are waiting for the other project to complete—that is, waiting for the same set of resources. This causes a deadlock—these threads might wait forever. Here's how this looks in code:

```
class Developer {
    synchronized void fixBugs() {
        System.out.println("fixing..");
    }
    synchronized void code() {
        System.out.println("coding..");
    }
}
class Tester {
    synchronized void testAppln() {
        System.out.println("testing..");
    }
}
class AndroidApp extends Thread {
    Developer dev;
    Tester tester;
    AndroidApp(Developer dev, Tester t) {
        this.dev = dev;
        this.tester = t;
    }
    public void run() {
        synchronized(tester) {
            tester.testAppln();
            dev.fixBugs();
        }
    }
}
class iPhoneApp extends Thread {
    Developer dev;
    Tester tester;
```

❶ Synchronized methods

❷ Acquire lock on tester, reentrant lock on tester, lock on dev

```
        iPhoneApp(Developer dev, Tester t) {
            this.dev = dev;
            this.tester = t;
        }
        public void run() {
            synchronized(dev) {                     ❸ Acquire lock on
                dev.code();                           dev, reentrant
                tester.testAppln();                   lock on dev, lock
            }                                         on tester
        }
    }
}
class DeadLock {
    public static void main(String args[]) {      ❹ Same developer
        Tester paul = new Tester();                  and tester work
        Developer selvan = new Developer();          with Android
                                                     and iPhone
        AndroidApp androidApp = new AndroidApp(selvan, paul);  applications
        iPhoneApp iPhoneApp = new iPhoneApp(selvan, paul);

        androidApp.start();
        iPhoneApp.start();
    }
}
```

The code at ❶ defines synchronized code in classes `Tester` and `Developer`. A thread must acquire a lock on an object's monitor before it can execute its synchronized methods. At ❹, code passes the same `Developer` and `Tester` instances—that is, `paul` and `selvan`—to `AndroidApp` and `iPhoneApp` threads. At ❷, the thread `AndroidApp` first acquires a lock on its instance member `tester`, then reacquires the lock to execute its `testAppln`. It then tries to acquire a lock on its instance member `dev` so that it can call its method `fixBugs()`. But by this time, the code at ❸ has begun its execution, where the thread `iPhoneApp` has already acquired a lock on a shared object `dev` and is waiting to acquire a lock on `tester` so that it can execute `testAppln`. At this point, both the threads `AndroidApp` and `iPhoneApp` deadlock. On the exam, you should be able to recognize the conditions that might lead to thread deadlocking.

10.4.5 *Starvation*

Imagine you're invited to dine with the president or your favorite sports star, or say a natural calamity strikes. Will it change your existing engagements for the evening? There's a very high probability that it would. Similarly, all application and OS threads that execute on a system are assigned a priority (default or explicit). Usually threads with a higher priority are preferred to execute by the thread scheduler. But this preference might leave threads with a lower priority *starved* to be scheduled.

A thread can also starve to be scheduled when it's waiting to acquire a lock on an object monitor that has been acquired by another thread that usually takes long to execute and is invoked frequently.

Thread scheduling is dependent on an underlying OS. Usually all OSs support prioritized scheduling of high-priority threads, but this behavior isn't guaranteed across different platforms.

10.4.6   Livelock

Imagine you're talking with your friend on your mobile phone and the call drops. You try to reconnect with her, but her phone is busy (because she's trying to call you!). You wait for a few moments and try to reconnect, only to discover that her phone is still busy, because she waited for exactly the same duration before trying to reconnect again. If you compare yourself and your friend with threads, you both are in a livelock. You and your friend aren't blocked—both of you are responding but aren't being able to do what you both intend to (talk with each other).

 EXAM TIP   Threads in a livelock aren't blocked; they're responding to each other, but they aren't able to move to completion.

Because a livelock depends on the exact time of execution of threads, the same set of threads might not always livelock.

10.4.7   *Happens-before relationship*

With threads, there's little that can be guaranteed. You can't determine exactly when a particular method will start, pause, or resume its execution. You can't guarantee the sequence in which multiple threads might execute. On the exam, you'll be questioned on the correct, incorrect, or probable outcome of code that defines or works with threads. The Java language uses a *happens-before* relationship, which is when one task is guaranteed to happen before another in a multithreading environment. Figure 10.14 shows this relationship.

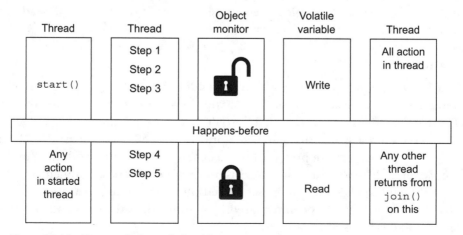

Figure 10.14   Happens-before relationship

The *happens-before* relationship, as included in Java's language specification, will enable you to answer a lot of questions on threading on the exam. For example

- The execution of start() *happens-before* any action in a thread is started.
- When code is defined in a sequence, step 1 *happens-before* step 2.
- Unlocking of an object monitor *happens-before* any other thread acquires a lock on it.
- A write to a volatile field *happens-before* every subsequent read of that field.
- All actions in a thread *happens-before* any other thread returns from a join on that thread.

As you attempt the sample exam questions at the end of this chapter, mark the answers that could be determined using the happens-before relationship. If you discover other threading behavior that can be added to the happens-before relationship, please notify me too!

10.5 Summary

This chapter covers how threads enable systems to use their single or multiple processors to execute applications concurrently. We worked with class Thread and interface Runnable to define and create threads. Threads can exist in multiple states (NEW, RUNNABLE, WAITING, TIMED_WAITING, BLOCKED and TERMINATED), and we used multiple methods (start(), yield(), join(), sleep(), wait(), notify(), notifyAll()) to transition threads from one state to another. With multithreading you can guarantee very little when it comes to commanding or determining when a thread actually transitions from one state to another. The actual thread scheduling is handled by the underlying OS.

We covered how threads can be independent or dependent. Dependent threads communicate with each other by sharing data, which can lead to thread interference and memory inconsistency issues. Prevention techniques include synchronizing thread access to data by acquiring locks and defining atomic operations. We used synchronized methods and code blocks to synchronize data access. The volatile variables, though not as powerful and effective as synchronized methods, offer a simple solution to safeguard data from multiple concurrent thread access.

Using locks on objects safeguards object data, but it also leads to thread contention. Other threading issues include deadlock, starvations, and livelock.

REVIEW NOTES

This section lists the main points covered in this chapter.

Create and use threads

- All nontrivial Java applications are multithreaded.
- Multiple threads can be supported by an underlying system by using multiple hardware processors, by time-slicing a single processor, or by time-slicing multiple processors.

- Implementation of Java threads is JVM-specific.
- Though related, a `Thread` instance and a thread of execution aren't the same. A `Thread` instance is a Java object.
- The main thread is named `main` by the JVM. Don't confuse it with the method `main()`.
- Class `Thread` and interface `Runnable` can be used to create and start a new thread of execution.
- To create your own thread objects using class `Thread`, you must extend it and override its method `run()`.
- When you call `start()` on a `Thread` instance, it creates a new thread of execution.
- When a new thread of execution starts, it will execute the code defined in the thread instance's method `run()`. Method `start()` will trigger the creation of a new thread of execution, allocating resources to it.
- Because you can't be sure of the order of execution of threads by an underlying OS, multithreaded code might output different results when executed on the same or a different system.
- When you create a thread class by extending class `Thread`, you lose the flexibility of inheriting any other class.
- When you implement the `Runnable` interface, you must implement its method `run()`.
- If your class implements the `Runnable` interface, then you should pass its instance to the constructor of class `Thread`.
- The `Thread` constructor accepts a `Runnable` object. A `Thread` instance stores a reference to a `Runnable` object and uses it when you start its execution (by calling `start()`).
- Because class `Thread` implements the `Runnable` interface, you can instantiate a thread by passing it another `Thread` instance.
- Each thread is created with a priority. Its range varies from 1 to 10, with 1 being the lowest priority and 10 the highest priority. By default, a thread creates another thread with the same priority as its own.
- You can't guarantee that a thread with a higher priority will always execute before a thread with a lower priority.

Thread lifecycle

- You can control the transition of a thread from one state to another by calling its methods.
- The exact time of thread state transition is controlled by a thread scheduler, which is bound to vary across platforms.
- A thread can exist in multiple states: NEW, RUNNABLE, WAIT, TIMED_WAITING, BLOCKED, or TERMINATED.

- A thread that hasn't yet started is in the NEW state.
- Calling start() on a new thread instance implicitly calls its method run(), which transitions its state from NEW to READY.
- A thread in the RUNNABLE state is all set to be executed. It's just waiting to be chosen by the thread scheduler so that it gets the processor time.
- As a programmer, you can't control or determine when a particular thread transitions from the READY state to the RUNNING state, and when it actually gets to execute.
- The states READY and RUNNING are together referred to as the RUNNABLE state.
- A thread in the RUNNABLE state is executing in the JVM, but it may be waiting for other resources from the OS, such as a processor.
- A thread that's blocked waiting for a monitor lock is in the BLOCKED state.
- A thread that's waiting for another thread to perform an action for up to a specified waiting time is in the TIMED_WAITING state.
- A RUNNING thread enters the TIMED_WAITING state when you call sleep(int), join(int), or wait(int) on it.
- A thread that's waiting indefinitely for another thread to perform a particular action is in the WAITING state.
- When you call wait() on a RUNNING thread, it transitions to the WAITING state. It can change back to the READY state when notify() or notifyAll() is called.
- A RUNNING thread might enter the BLOCKED state when it's waiting for other system resources like network connections or to acquire an object lock to execute a synchronized method or code block. Depending on whether the thread is able to acquire the monitor lock or resources, it returns back to the READY state.
- With the successful completion of run(), a thread is in the TERMINATED state.
- A thread might transition from any state to the TERMINATED state due to an exception.

Methods of class Thread

- Calling start() on a Thread instance creates a new thread of execution, which executes run().
- You can call start() on a thread that's in the NEW state. Calling start() from any other thread state will throw an IllegalThreadStateException.
- Calling run() on a Thread instance doesn't start a new thread of execution. The run() continues to execute in the same thread.
- A thread might pause its execution due to the calling of an explicit method or when its time slice with the processor expires.
- Method yield() makes the currently executing thread pause its execution and give up its current use of the processor. But it only acts as a hint to the scheduler. The scheduler might also ignore it.

- Method `yield()` is static. It can be called from any method, and it doesn't throw any exceptions.
- Method `yield()` can be placed literally anywhere in your code—not only in method `run()`.
- Method `sleep()` is guaranteed to cause the currently executing thread to temporarily give up its execution for at least the specified number of milliseconds (and nanoseconds).
- Unless interrupted, the currently executing thread will sleep for at least the specified duration. It might not start its execution immediately after the specified time elapses.
- Method `sleep()` is `Thread`'s static method and it makes the currently executing thread give up its execution. Because all code is executed by some thread, placement of `sleep()` will determine which `Thread` instance will give up its execution.
- A thread that's suspended due to a call to `sleep()` doesn't lose ownership of any monitors.
- If thread A calls `join()` on a `Thread` instance B, A will wait for B to complete its execution before A can proceed to its own completion.
- Method `join()` guarantees that the calling thread won't execute its remaining code until the thread on which it calls `join()` completes.
- A thread can pause its execution and wait on an object, a queue in this case, by calling `wait()`, until another thread calls `notify()` or `notifyAll()` on the same object.
- Methods `wait()`, `notify()`, and `notifyAll()` can be called on all Java objects, because they're defined in class `Object` and not class `Thread`.
- A thread completes its execution when its method `run()` completes.

Protect shared data

- Interleaving of multiple threads that manipulate shared data using multiple steps leads to thread interference.
- A simple statement like incrementing a variable value might involve multiple steps like loading of the variable value from memory to registers (working space), incrementing the value, and reloading the new value in memory.
- When multiple threads execute this seemingly atomic statement, they might interleave, resulting in incorrect variable values.
- Making your applications thread safe means securing your shared data so that it stores correct data, even when it's accessed by multiple threads.
- Thread safety isn't about safe threads—it's about safeguarding your shared data that might be accessible to multiple threads.
- A thread-safe class stores correct data without requiring calling classes to guard it.
- You can lock objects by defining synchronized methods and synchronized statements.

- Synchronized methods are defined by prefixing the definition of a method with the keyword `synchronized`. You can define both instance and static methods as synchronized methods.

- For nonstatic synchronized methods, a thread locks the monitor of the object on which the synchronized method is called. To execute static synchronized methods, a thread locks the monitor associated with the `Class` object of its class.

- A thread releases the lock on an object monitor after it exits a synchronized method, whether due to successful completion or due to an exception.

- To execute synchronized statements, a thread must acquire a lock on an object monitor. For instance methods an implicit lock is acquired on the object on which it's called. For synchronized statements, you can specify an object to acquire a lock on.

- To execute synchronized statements, a lock must be acquired before the execution of the statements.

- Multiple threads can concurrently execute methods with synchronized statements if they acquire a lock on monitors of separate objects.

- A thread releases the lock on the object monitor once it exits the synchronized statement block due to successful completion or an exception.

- Immutable objects like an instance of class `String` and the wrapper classes (like `Boolean`, `Long`, `Integer`, etc.) are thread safe because their contents can't be modified.

- You can define an immutable class by limiting access to its attributes within the class and not defining any methods to modify its state.

- Once initialized, an immutable instance doesn't allow modification to its value.

- You can use volatile variables to synchronize access to data.

- When a thread reads from or writes to a variable (both primitive and reference variables) marked with the keyword `volatile`, it accesses it from the main memory, as opposed to storing its copy in the thread's cache memory. This prevents multiple threads from storing a local copy of shared values that might not be consistent across threads.

Identify and fix code in a multithreaded environment

- Threading issues arise when multiple threads work with shared data and when they're dependent on other threads.

- Local variables, method parameters, and exception handler parameters are always safe in a multithreaded application.

- Class and instance variables might not always be safe in a multithreaded application.

- Methods `wait()`, `notify()`, and `notifyAll()` can be used for interthread notification.

- To call wait() or notify() a thread must own the object's monitor lock. So calls to these methods should be placed within synchronized methods or blocks or else an IllegalMonitorStateException will be thrown by the JVM.

- All overloaded versions of wait() throw a checked InterruptedException. Methods notify() and notifyAll() don't throw an InterruptedException.

- Unlike Thread's method join(), which waits for another thread to complete its execution, methods wait() and notify() don't require a thread to complete their execution.

- Multiple threads might deadlock when they have acquired a lock on objects and are waiting to acquire locks on additional objects that are owned by other waiting threads.

- All threads are assigned a priority, either implicitly or explicitly. Usually threads with a higher priority are preferred to execute by the thread scheduler. But this preference might leave threads with a lower priority starved to be scheduled.

- A thread can also starve to be scheduled when it's waiting to acquire a lock on an object monitor that has been acquired by another thread that usually takes long to execute and is invoked frequently.

- Threads in a livelock aren't blocked; they're responding to each other, but they aren't able to move to completion.

- With threads, there's little that can be guaranteed. The Java language uses a happens-before relationship, which is when one task is guaranteed to happen before another in a multithreading environment.

- The execution of start() happens-before any action in a thread is started.

- When code is defined in a sequence, step 1 happens-before step 2.

- Unlocking of an object monitor happens-before any other thread acquires a lock on it.

- A write to a volatile field happens-before every subsequent read of that field.

- All actions in a thread happens-before any other thread returns from a join on that thread.

SAMPLE EXAM QUESTIONS

Q 10-1. What is the probable output of the following code?

```
enum Seasons{SPRING,SUMMER}
class ETree extends Thread {
    String name;
    public ETree(String name) {this.name = name;}
    public void run() {
        for (Seasons season : Seasons.values())
            System.out.print(name + "-" + season + " ");
    }
    public static void main(String args[]) {
        ETree oak = new ETree("Oak"); oak.start();
```

```
        ETree maple = new ETree("Maple"); maple.start();
    }
}
```

a Oak-SPRING Maple-SPRING Oak-SUMMER Maple-SUMMER

b Oak-SUMMER Oak-SPRING Maple-SPRING Maple-SUMMER

c Oak-SUMMER Maple-SUMMER Oak-SPRING Maple-SPRING

d Oak-SPRING Oak-SUMMER Maple-SPRING Maple-SUMMER

e Maple-SPRING Maple-SUMMER Oak-SPRING Oak-SUMMER

f Maple-SPRING Oak-SPRING Oak-SUMMER Maple-SUMMER

g Compilation error

h Runtime exception

Q 10-2. Examine the following code and select the correct options.

```
public class EThread {
    public static void main(String[] args) {
        Thread bug = new Thread() {
            public void run() {
                System.out.print("check bugs");
            }
        };
        Thread reportQA = new Thread(bug);
        reportQA.run();
    }
}
```

a No code output

b Code prints check bugs once.

c Code prints check bugs twice.

d Code prints check bugs in an infinite loop.

e Replacing reportQA.run() with reportQA.start() will throw a compilation exception.

f Replacing reportQA.run() with reportQA.start() will generate the same output on the system's console.

Q 10-3. What is the output of the following code?

```
1. class EPen implements Runnable {
2.     public void run() {
3.         System.out.println("eJava");
4.         start();
5.     }
6.     public static void main(String... args) {
7.         new Thread(new EPen()).start();
8.     }
9. }
```

a It prints eJava once.

b It prints eJava multiple times.

c Compilation error

d Runtime exception

Q 10-4. The thread paul must start only after the thread shreya has completed its execution. Which of the following code options, when inserted at //INSERT CODE HERE, will ensure this?

```
1. class EJob extends Thread {
2.     public void run() {
3.         System.out.println("executing");
4.     }
5.     public static void main(String[] args) {
6.         Thread paul = new EJob();
7.         Thread shreya = new EJob();
8.         shreya.start();
9.         paul.start();
10.        //INSERT CODE HERE
11.    }
12. }
```

a shreya.join();

b paul.join();

c shreya.sleep(1000);

d shreya.wait();

e paul.notify();

f None of the above

Q 10-5. What is the output of the following code?

```
class ELock{}
class EPaper implements Runnable {
    public void run() {
        synchronized(ELock.class) {
            System.out.println("Hand made paper");
        }
    }
    public static void main(String args[]) throws Exception {
        Thread epaper = new Thread(new EPaper());
        epaper.start();
        synchronized(ELock.class) {
            epaper.join();
        }
    }
}
```

a The threads main and epaper will always deadlock.

b The threads main and epaper might not deadlock.

    c Compilation error

    d Runtime exception

Q 10-6. Selvan is testing a multithreaded application in which thread A downloads data in a hash map. Thread B uses the data from the same hash map and displays it to a user for modification. Thread C is supposed to save the modified data and replace the existing data in the hash map. When a user tries to save the data, the application stops responding. What could be the probable reasons?

    a Thread A and thread C deadlock.

    b Thread B and thread C deadlock.

    c Thread C is discovered to be a high-priority thread that performs complex calculations and doesn't allow other threads to execute.

    d Thread C throws an exception.

Q 10-7. Instances of which of the following classes will always be safe to use in a multithreaded environment?

    a `class ESafe {final int value; /*constructor to initialize value*/}`

    b `class ESafe {final Object value; /*constructor to initialize value*/}`

    c
```
final class ESafe {
    ESafe(Object obj) {value = obj;}
    private final Object value;
    synchronized Object read() {return value;}
    synchronized void modify(Object obj) {}
}
```

    d `class ESafe {final String value; /*constructor to initialize value*/}`

Q 10-8. What is the output of the following code?

```
class EProcess extends Thread {
    public void run() {
        this.yield();                       //line1
        for (int i = 0; i < 1000; i++)
            System.out.print(i);
    }
    public static void main(String... args) {
        Thread myThread = new EProcess();
        myThread.run();                     //line2
    }
}
```

    a On execution, code at line 1 might make the thread `main` give up its execution slot.

    b On execution, code at line 1 makes the thread `myThread` give up its execution slot.

    c Compilation error at line 1

    d Runtime exception at line 2

Q 10-9. Select the correct options for the following code.

```
class EAppln extends Thread {
    String name;
    EAppln(String name) { this.name = name; }
    public void run() throws InterruptedException {      //1
        sleep(1000);                                     //2
        System.out.println("executing-" + name);
    }
}
class EJava {
    public static void main(String args[]) {
        EAppln app1 = new EAppln("Detect");
        EAppln app2 = new EAppln("Analyze");
        app1.start();
        app2.start();
    }
}
```

a The output is

```
executing-Detect
executing-Analyze
```

b The output is

```
executing-Analyze
executing-Detect
```

c The thread app1 sleeps for a maximum of 1000 milliseconds before it's rescheduled to run again.

d The treads app1 and app2 might sleep at the same time.

e Compilation error

f Runtime exception

Q 10-10. On execution, class DeclareResults might not display all of the four string values passed to ProcessData constructors at lines 18 and 19. How can you fix this situation?

```
1.  import java.util.*;
2.  class Admission{
3.      static int id;
4.      static Map<Integer, String> results = new HashMap<>();
5.      static int getNextId() {return ++id; }
6.      static void qualify(Integer i, String s) {results.put(i, s);}
7.  }
8.  class ProcessData extends Thread{
9.      List<String> list;
10.     ProcessData(String[] val) {list = Arrays.asList(val);}
11.     public void run() {
12.         for (String item : list)
13.             Admission.qualify(Admission.getNextId(), item);
14.     }
15. }
16. class DeclareResults {
17.     public static void main(String args[]) throws Exception {
```

```
18.            ProcessData thread1 = new ProcessData(
                                    new String[]{"Paul", "Shreya"});
19.            ProcessData thread2 = new ProcessData(
                                    new String[]{"Shreya", "Harry"});
20.            thread1.start(); thread2.start();
21.            thread1.join(); thread2.join();
22.            for (String name : Admission.results.values())
23.                System.out.println(name);
24.        }
25. }
```

a By declaring only the getNextId method as synchronized at line 5

b By declaring only the qualify method as synchronized at line 6

c By declaring both the getNextId and qualify methods as synchronized at lines 5 and 6

d By passing unique values to the threads thread1 and thread2 at lines 18 and 19

e By changing the type of variable results from Map to List

f None of the above

ANSWERS TO SAMPLE EXAM QUESTIONS

A 10-1. a, d, e, f

[10.1] Create and use the Thread class and the Runnable interface

Explanation: Each thread instance oak and maple, when started, will output the values of enum Seasons—that is, SPRING and SUMMER (always in this order). The order of the elements returned by Seasons.values() isn't random. The enum values are always returned in the order in which they are defined.

You can't guarantee whether thread oak completes or begins its execution before or after thread maple. The thread scheduler can start oak, make it print Oak-SPRING, run maple so that it prints Maple-SPRING, return the control to oak, or run maple to completion. Whatever the sequence, the happens-before contract guarantees that code in a thread executes in the order it's defined. So the thread oak or maple can never print the enum value SUMMER before the enum value SPRING.

A 10-2. b, f

[10.1] Create and use the Thread class and the Runnable interface

Explanation: The following code creates an anonymous class that subclasses class Thread. Its instance is referred by bug, a reference variable of type Thread.

```
Thread bug = new Thread() {
    public void run() {
        System.out.print("check bugs");
    }
};
```

Because class `Thread` implements the `Runnable` interface, you can pass its instance as a target object to instantiate another `Thread` instance, `reportQA`:

```
Thread reportQA = new Thread(bug);
```

The variable `reportQA` refers to an anonymous class instance that overrides its method `run()`. So calling `reportQA.run()` executes the overridden method `run()` and prints check bugs only once.

Option (f) is correct. Even though calling `reportQA.run()` doesn't start a separate thread of execution and `reportQA.start()` does, both will print check bugs once on the system's console.

A 10-3. c

[10.1] Create and use the Thread class and the Runnable interface

Explanation: Class `EPen` implements the `Runnable` interface; it doesn't extend class `Thread`. So it doesn't have access to method `start()`. Calling `start()` at line 4 results in the compilation failure.

A 10-4. f

[10.2] Manage and control thread lifecycle

Explanation: Calling `join` from a thread ensures that the thread on which `join` is called completes before the calling thread completes its execution. If the thread `main` calls `shreya.join()` before starting the thread `paul`, it can ensure that `paul` will start after `shreya` completes its execution. For this to happen, `main` should call `shreya.join()` at line 9 and `paul.start()` at line 10.

Options (a) and (b) are incorrect. Calling `shreya.join()` or `paul.join()` at line 10 will ensure that these threads complete their execution before the thread `main` completes its own execution.

Option (c) is incorrect. The thread `main` executes `shreya.sleep()`. Because `sleep()` is a static method, it will make `main` sleep for at least the specified time in milliseconds (if not interrupted).

Options (d) and (e) are incorrect because they won't serve the purpose. Method `wait()` makes a thread release its object lock and makes it wait until another object that has acquired a lock on it calls `notify()` or `notifyAll()`. Also `wait()`, `notify()`, and `notifyAll()` must be called from a synchronized block of code or else JVM will throw an `IllegalMonitorStateException`.

A 10-5. b

[10.4] Identify code that may not execute correctly in a multi-threaded environment

Explanation: You can't determine the exact time that a scheduler starts the execution of a thread. So the thread `epaper` can acquire the lock on a monitor associated with class ELock, execute the epaper's method run(), and exit *before* method main() gets its turn to acquire a lock on ELock.class and call epaper.join().

A 10-6. a, b, c

[10.3] Synchronize thread access to shared data

Explanation: The application stops responding after a user tries to save data. So the issue is the series of actions that execute when thread C is initiated. All the three threads, A, B, and C, are sharing the same data set. Thread C might try to write data that is being modified by thread A or B. So thread C might deadlock with thread A or B.

Option (c) is correct. Saving the data is supposed to start thread C. An application might appear to stop responding if it doesn't respond to user events. A scheduler chooses from a pool of threads to execute the threads that are ready for execution. Though OS-specific, threads of high priority are usually preferred over threads with lower priority.

Option (d) is incorrect. An unhandled exception should make the application exit.

A 10-7. a, c, d

[10.4] Identify code that may not execute correctly in a multi-threaded environment

Explanation: Option (a) is correct. Once assigned a value, a primitive variable can't be changed. So it's safe from reading and writing inconsistent or dirty values.

Option (b) is incorrect. Even though defining the instance variable value of class ESafe as a final member prevents reassigning a value to it, it doesn't prevent modifications to its state. The reference variable value isn't private, so it's accessible outside class ESafe.

Option (c) is correct. Marked with the keyword private, value isn't accessible outside class ESafe. Also, access to the state of ESafe is synchronized and is safe from concurrent reading or writing by multiple threads.

Option (d) is correct. Once initialized, the state of class ESafe (value of variable value) can't be modified because class String is immutable.

A 10-8. a

[10.2] Manage and control thread lifecycle

Explanation: The code at line 2 doesn't start a new thread of execution. So myThread .run() executes in the main thread and not a separate thread. When main executes this.yield() (yield() is a static method), it might make main give up its execution slot and wait until the scheduler allows it to run again.

A 10-9. e

[10.2] Manage and control thread lifecycle

Explanation: Method run() in class EAppln can't override method run() in class Thread by declaring to throw a checked InterruptedException. The class fails to compile.

A 10-10. c

[10.3] Synchronize thread access to shared data
[10.4] Identify code that may not execute correctly in a multi-threaded environment

Explanation: The variable results, a hash map, stores unique keys. Concurrent access to the unsynchronized getNextId() can return the same ID values if it's accessed concurrently by multiple threads. This can lead to overriding values for the same keys in a hash map. So getNextId() should be declared as a synchronized method at line 5.

Method qualify() must also be declared as a synchronized method to make Map results thread safe; concurrent updates to a Map can result in overriding values. Internally, a hash map uses hash values of its keys to determine in which bucket it should add a value. When a hash map adds multiple values to a bucket, it links them so that it can retrieve all the values for a bucket value. But concurrent modification of a Map object might report an empty bucket to multiple threads and so no linking will happen between the values added to the same bucket. This can lead to untraceable values.

Concurrency 11

Exam objectives covered in this chapter	What you need to know
[11.1] Use collections from the `java.util.concurrent` package with a focus on the advantages over and differences from the traditional `java.util` collections	How collections from the `java.util.concurrent` package resolve common concurrency issues How to replace traditional collections with concurrent collections
[11.2] Use `Lock`, `ReadWriteLock`, and `ReentrantLock` in the `java.util.concurrent.locks` package to support lock-free, thread-safe programming on single variables	How to exercise fine control over locking objects by using `Lock`, `ReadWriteLock`, and `ReentrantLock`
[11.3] Use `Executor`, `ExecutorService`, `Executors`, `Callable`, and `Future` to execute tasks using thread pools	How to separate task and threads using `Executor` How to manage a pool of threads by using `ExecutorService` How to define tasks using `Runnable` and `Callable` How to use `Executors` to access objects of `Executor`, `ExecutorService`, and thread pools
[11.4] Use the parallel fork/join framework	How to work with a fork/join framework using subclasses of `ForkJoinTask` and `ForkJoinPool`

679

With the increasing processing power of devices, your applications must support concurrent execution of tasks for faster outputs. Concurrent applications also make optimal use of the processors. But concurrent applications are difficult to develop, maintain, and debug. To develop thread-safe, high-performance, and scalable applications, Java's low-level threading capabilities are insufficient. This chapter outlines the common issues with the concurrent execution of tasks and how to combat these issues using various approaches, frameworks, classes, and interfaces. Again, the coverage of concurrency issues and their solutions is limited to the topics on the exam.

This chapter covers

- Using collections from the `java.util.concurrent` package
- Applying fine-grained locking using locking classes from the `java.util.concurrent.locks` package
- Using `ExecutorService` and pools of threads to execute and manage tasks
- Using the parallel fork/join framework

Let's get started with effectively resolving common concurrency problems by using collection classes from the `java.util.concurrent` package.

11.1 *Concurrent collection classes*

[11.1] Use collections from the java.util.concurrent package with a focus on the advantages over and differences from the traditional java.util collections

The concurrent collection classes avoid memory inconsistency errors by defining a happens-before relationship between an operation that adds an object to the collection and subsequent operations that access or remove that object. Developers have long been developing thread-safe versions of the collection objects from the `java.util` package. The `java.util.concurrent` package includes a number of additions to the Java Collections Framework. These are most easily categorized by the collection interfaces provided:

- `BlockingQueue` defines a first-in-first-out data structure that blocks or times out when you attempt to add items to a full queue, or retrieve from an empty queue.
- `ConcurrentMap` is a subinterface of `java.util.Map` that defines useful atomic operations. These operations remove or replace a key-value pair only if the key is present, or add a key-value pair only if the key is absent. Making these operations atomic helps avoid synchronization. The standard general-purpose implementation of `ConcurrentMap` is `ConcurrentHashMap`, which is a concurrent analog of `HashMap`.
- `ConcurrentNavigableMap` is a subinterface of `ConcurrentMap` that supports approximate matches. The standard general-purpose implementation of

ConcurrentNavigableMap is ConcurrentSkipListMap, which is a concurrent analog of TreeMap.

Writing concurrent programs is difficult—you need to deal with thread safety and performance. The individual operations of ConcurrentHashMap are safe—that is, multiple threads can put values into the same map object in a safe manner. But these can be misused by the developers if they try to combine multiple safe operations into a single operation.

11.1.1 Interface BlockingQueue

The BlockingQueue interface is a queue that's safe to use when shared between multiple threads. The implementing classes like ArrayBlockingQueue include a constructor to define an initial capacity (which can't be modified) from which items are added and removed. It blocks adding new elements if the queue has reached its capacity. It also blocks removing elements from an empty queue. It works on the *producer–consumer* pattern, which is when a single thread or multiple threads produce elements and add them to a queue to be consumed by other threads.

Imagine multiple clients (producers) that send requests to a server. The server (consumer) responds to all the requests that it receives. To manage the requests that all the clients might send to the server, the server can limit the maximum number of requests that it can accept at a given point in time. The requests can be added to a blocking queue, which will block adding new requests if it reaches its upper limit. Similarly, if no new requests are available in a queue, the server thread will block until requests are made available to it. Here's an implementation of this example in code:

```
class Request {}

class Client implements Runnable {
    private BlockingQueue<Request> queue;
    Client(BlockingQueue<Request> queue) {
        this.queue = queue;
    }
    public void run() {
        try {
            Request req = null;
            while(true) {
                req = new Request();
                queue.put(req);                          ◄── Inserts Request objects
                System.out.println("added request - " + req);    into BlockingQueue,
            }                                            waiting if necessary for
        }                                                space to become available.
        catch (InterruptedException ex) {
            System.out.println(ex);
        }
    }
}

class Server implements Runnable {
    private BlockingQueue<Request> queue;
```

```
        Server(BlockingQueue<Request> queue) {
            this.queue = queue;
        }
        public void run() {
            try {
                while (true) {
                    System.out.println("processing .. " + queue.take());
                }
            }
            catch (InterruptedException ex) {
                System.out.println(ex);
            }
        }
    }
}

class LoadTesting{
    public static void main(String args[]) {
        BlockingQueue<Request> queue = new ArrayBlockingQueue<Request>(3);

        Client client = new Client(queue);
        Server server = new Server(queue);

        new Thread(client).start();
        new Thread(server).start();
    }
}
```

Retrieves and removes the head of BlockingQueue, waiting if necessary until a Request object becomes available.

Pass the same BlockingQueue object to client and server

client adds Request objects to queue and server retrieves them from the queue.

11.1.2 *Interface ConcurrentMap*

The ConcurrentMap interface extends the java.util.Map interface. It defines methods to replace or remove a key-value pair if the key is present, or add a value if the key is absent. Table 11.1 lists methods of ConcurrentMap.

Table 11.1   Methods of interface ConcurrentMap

Method	Description
V putIfAbsent(K key, V value)	If the specified key isn't already associated with a value, this associates it with the given value.
boolean remove(Object key, Object value)	Removes the entry for a key only if it's currently mapped to a given value.
V replace(K key, V value)	Replaces the entry for a key only if it's currently mapped to some value.
boolean replace(K key, V oldValue, V newValue)	Replaces the entry for a key only if it's currently mapped to a given value.

11.1.3 *Class ConcurrentHashMap*

A concrete implementation of the ConcurrentMap interface, class ConcurrentHashMap is a concurrent class analogous to class HashMap. A HashMap is an unsynchronized collection. If you're manipulating a HashMap using multiple threads, you must synchronize its access. But locking the entire HashMap object can create serious performance issues when it's being accessed by multiple threads. If multiple threads are retrieving values, it makes sense to allow concurrent read operations and monitor write operations.

The ConcurrentHashMap class is the answer to improving the responsiveness of HashMap when it needs to be accessed concurrently by multiple threads. Instead of exclusively locking itself to be accessed by one thread, ConcurrentHashMap allows access by multiple threads. It concurrently allows multiple threads to read its values and limited threads to modify its values. Also, the iterators of ConcurrentHashMap don't throw a ConcurrentModificationException, so you don't need to lock the collection while iterating it. So what happens if new elements are added to Concurrent-HashMap *after* you accessed its iterator? The iterator may still traverse only the elements that existed at the time of creation of the iterator. Though not guaranteed on all platforms, the iterators might reflect the new additions.

With the added benefits of offering better performance when accessed by multiple threads concurrently, this collection also offers some drawbacks. Because it doesn't lock the complete collections while modifying their elements, methods like size() might not return the exact accurate size of a ConcurrentHashMap when invoked by multiple threads.

Let's work with an example of class ConcurrentHashMap:

```
class UseConcurrentMap {
    static final ConcurrentMap<Integer, String> map =
                           new ConcurrentHashMap<>();
    static {
        //code to populate map
    }
    static void manipulateMap(Integer key, String value) {
        // complex computations                          Check for existence
        if (!map.containsKey(key))                       of key in map
            map.put(key, value);          Replace existing
    }                                     value for key
}
```

When you work with multiple threads, you need to synchronize access to your shared resources so that concurrent access doesn't leave them in an inconsistent state. In the preceding example, the individual operation containsKey(key) is a read operation and put(key, value) is a write operation. Though individually these methods are thread safe, together (execute method 1, then method 2) they aren't. A race condition can occur when method manipulateMap() is executed by multiple threads. The solution is to replace them with a single atomic method call:

```
static void manipulateMap(Integer key, String value) {
    // complex computations
    map.replace(key, value);          Atomic operation replaces
}                                      value in map if corresponding
                                       key is present
```

Before moving on to the next section, let's revisit the mapping of classes and interfaces from `java.util.concurrent` and its corresponding `java.util` analog, as shown in table 11.2.

Table 11.2   Mapping of classes and interfaces from package `java.util.concurrent` and its corresponding package `java.util` analog

Package `java.util.concurrent`	`java.util` analog
BlockingQueue	Queue
ArrayBlockingQueue	Queue
LinkedBlockingQueue	Queue
ConcurrentMap	Map
ConcurrentHashMap	HashMap
ConcurrentSkipListMap	TreeMap
CopyOnWriteArrayList	ArrayList
LinkedBlockingDeque	Deque

In chapter 10, we worked with synchronized methods and code blocks. Before a thread can execute a synchronized method's code it implicitly acquires a lock on an object's monitor. But these implicit locking techniques are inefficient to develop scalable concurrent applications. In the next section, we'll work with explicit lock objects that offer finer locking control.

11.2 Locks

[11.2]   Use Lock, ReadWriteLock, and ReentrantLock in the java.util.concurrent.locks package to support lock-free, thread-safe programming on single variables

Lock objects offer multiple advantages over implicit locking of an object's monitor. Unlike an implicit lock, a thread can use explicit lock objects to wait to acquire a lock until a time duration elapses. Lock objects also support interruptible lock waits, non-block-structured locks, multiple condition variables, lock polling, and scalability benefits.

 NOTE To execute synchronized code, a thread must acquire either an *implicit* or an *explicit* lock on an object's monitor. Where no explicit `Lock` classes are used, I'll refer to it as an implicit lock.

Table 11.3 shows a list of the methods of the `Lock` interface from the Java API documentation.

Table 11.3 Methods of interface `Lock`

Method	Description
`void lock()`	Acquires the lock. If the lock isn't available then the current thread becomes disabled for thread scheduling purposes and lies dormant until the lock has been acquired.
`void lockInterruptibly()`	Acquires the lock unless the current thread is interrupted.
`Condition newCondition()`	Returns a new `Condition` instance that's bound to this `Lock` instance.
`boolean tryLock()`	Acquires the lock only if it's free at the time of invocation.
`boolean tryLock(long time, TimeUnit unit)`	Acquires the lock if it's free within the given waiting time and the current thread hasn't been interrupted.
`void unlock()`	Releases the lock.

Let's get started with using class `ReentrantLock` that implements the `Lock` interface.

11.2.1 Acquire lock

Method `lock()` acquires a lock on a `Lock` object. If the lock isn't available, it waits until the lock can be acquired. For instance

```
class Rainbow {
    Lock myLock = new ReentrantLock();          ←┐  Lock object
    static List<String> colors = new ArrayList<>();
    public void addColor(String newColor) {
        myLock.lock();                     ←┐  Call lock to acquire lock;
        try {                               │  wait if lock not available
            colors.add(newColor);
        }
        finally {
            myLock.unlock();        ←┐  Call unlock to
        }                            │  release lock
    }
}
```

Method `lock()` is comparable to intrinsic locks because it waits until a lock can be acquired on a `Lock` object.

 EXAM TIP Call method `unlock()` on a `Lock` object to release its lock when you no longer need it.

Let's see how you can poll and check whether method `lock()` is available, without waiting for it, in the next section.

11.2.2 *Acquire lock and return immediately*

Imagine you're waiting for your favorite soccer star to sign an autograph for you. If you've been waiting for too long, it makes sense to quit waiting and leave. But threads waiting to acquire implicit object locks can't quit. Once a thread initiates a request to acquire an implicit lock on an object monitor, it can neither stop itself nor can it be asked to do so by any other thread. With explicit locks, you can request a thread to acquire a lock on an object monitor if it's available and return immediately.

Following is example code in which class Order uses implicit locks on two reference variables *before* it can manipulate them. When method main() starts two instances of class Shipment, passing them Inventory objects in reverse order, they might deadlock, without generating any output:

```
class Inventory {
    int inStock; String name;
    Inventory(String name) { this.name = name; }
    public void stockIn(long qty) { inStock += qty; }
    public void stockOut(long qty) { inStock -= qty; }
}
class Shipment extends Thread {
    Inventory loc1, loc2; int qty;
    Shipment(Inventory loc1, Inventory loc2, int qty) {
        this.loc1 = loc1;
        this.loc2 = loc2;
        this.qty = qty;
    }
    public void run() {                          Acquire lock
        synchronized(loc1) {                     on loc1
            synchronized(loc2) {                 Acquire lock
                loc2.stockOut(qty);              on loc2
                loc1.stockIn(qty);
                                                 
Release                     System.out.println(loc1.inStock + ":" + loc2.inStock);
lock on loc2        }
            }                      Release lock
        }                          on loc1
    }
    public static void main(String args[]) {
        Inventory loc1 = new Inventory("Seattle"); loc1.inStock = 100;
        Inventory loc2 = new Inventory("LA"); loc2.inStock = 200;
        Shipment s1 = new Shipment(loc1, loc2, 1);
        Shipment s2 = new Shipment(loc2, loc1, 10);
        s1.start();
        s2.start();
    }
}
```

Depending on how an underlying scheduler executes the threads s1 and s2, they might or might not deadlock. Let's modify the preceding example and add an explicit lock object to class Inventory on single variables loc1 and loc2, so that threads s1 and s2 *never* deadlock. Now, instead of locking on the Inventory object's monitor, method `run()` in `Shipment` can lock on an explicit lock object, `ReentrantLock` (modifications in bold):

```java
import java.util.concurrent.locks.*;
class Inventory {
    int inStock; String name;
    Lock lock = new ReentrantLock();
    Inventory(String name) { this.name = name; }
    public void stockIn(long qty) { inStock += qty; }
    public void stockOut(long qty) { inStock -= qty; }
}
class Shipment extends Thread {
    Inventory loc1, loc2; int qty;
    Shipment(Inventory loc1, Inventory loc2, int qty) {
        this.loc1 = loc1;
        this.loc2 = loc2;
        this.qty = qty;
    }
    public void run() {
        if (loc1.lock.tryLock()) {
            if (loc2.lock.tryLock()) {
                loc2.stockOut(qty);
                loc1.stockIn(qty);
                System.out.println(loc1.inStock + ":" + loc2.inStock);
                loc2.lock.unlock();
                loc1.lock.unlock();
            }
            else
                System.out.println("Locking false:" + loc2.name);
        }
        else
            System.out.println("Locking false:" + loc1.name);
    }
    public static void main(String args[]) {
        Inventory loc1 = new Inventory("Seattle"); loc1.inStock = 100;
        Inventory loc2 = new Inventory("LA"); loc2.inStock = 200;
        Shipment s1 = new Shipment(loc1, loc2, 1);
        Shipment s2 = new Shipment(loc2, loc1, 10);
        s1.start();
        s2.start();
    }
}
```

❶ Inventory defines a variable of type Lock, assigned an object of ReentrantLock.

❷ loc1.lock.tryLock() tries to acquire a lock on object loc1.lock and returns immediately.

❸ loc2.lock.tryLock() tries to acquire a lock on object loc2.lock and returns immediately.

❹ Manipulate loc1 and loc2.

❺ If lock couldn't be acquired, outputs appropriate messages

At **❶**, the code defines a reference variable of type `Lock`, which is assigned an object of class `ReentrantLock`. When started, the thread `Shipment` must acquire a lock on *both* Inventory objects `loc1` and `loc2` so that it can execute methods `stockOut()` and `stockIn()`, thereby ensuring that no other thread is modifying these objects. With explicit locks, `Shipment` can acquire a lock on object `lock`, which is defined as an instance member of class `Inventory`.

At **❷**, `run()` calls `tryLock()` on `loc1.lock`. Method `tryLock()` tries to acquire a lock on a `Lock` object, and returns immediately returning a boolean value specifying whether it could obtain the lock or not. If `loc1.lock.tryLock()` returns true, loc2.lock.tryLock() at ❸ tries to obtain a lock on loc2.lock before it can manipulate loc1 and loc2 at ❹. The code outputs appropriate messages if it can't lock at ❺.

Method main() starts two new threads, s1 and s2, passing them objects loc1 and loc2. No matter how threads s1 and s2 execute, they will never deadlock. Unlike waiting to acquire an implicit lock on objects loc1 and loc2, they call loc1.lock.tryLock() and loc2.lock.tryLock(), which return immediately.

 EXAM TIP   Watch out for the use of methods acquire(), acquireLock(), release(), and releaseLock() on the exam. None of these is a valid method. Because the terms *acquire* and *release* are used to discuss methods lock(), unlock(), tryLock(), and lockInterruptibly(), these terms might be used on the exam to confuse you.

11.2.3 *Interruptible locks*

Imagine you have an appointment with a doctor and are waiting for her to arrive. Your waiting can be interrupted by a phone call informing you that you need to attend to other tasks. Also, you might set yourself a time limit, after which you might not be able to wait and will resume your other work.

The following methods of Lock enable you to specify a waiting timeout or to try and acquire a lock while being available for interruption:

- lockInterruptibly()
- tryLock(long time, TimeUnit unit)

In listing 11.1, class Bus defines a Lock object. Class Employee extends class Thread. When started, it tries to acquire a lock on the Lock object associated with a Bus instance using lockInterruptibly().

Listing 11.1   Working with interruptible locks

```
import java.util.concurrent.locks.*;
class Bus {
    Lock lock = new ReentrantLock();
    public void boardBus(String name) {
        System.out.println(name + ": boarded");
    }
}
class Employee extends Thread {
    Bus bus;
    String name;
    Employee(String name, Bus bus) {
        this.bus = bus;
        this.name = name;
    }
    public void run() {
        try {
            bus.lock.lockInterruptibly();      ⟵─┐  ❶ Try to acquire lock
            try {                                  │    while being available
                bus.boardBus(name);               │    for interruption
                                                   └─ ❷ If lock acquired, execute
                                                        required code
```

```
            } finally {                    ③  Release acquired
                bus.lock.unlock();            lock in finally block.
            }
        } catch(InterruptedException e) {              Define action
            System.out.println(name + ": Interrupted!!");   if thread is
            Thread.currentThread().interrupt();      ④  interrupted
        }
    }
    public static void main(String args[]) {
        Bus bus = new Bus();              ⑤  Start
        Employee e1 = new Employee("Paul", bus);    thread e1
        e1.start();
        e1.interrupt();                      Interrupt
                                          ⑥  thread e1
        Employee e2 = new Employee("Shreya", bus);
        e2.start();
    }
}
```

In the preceding code, the outer try-catch blocks at ❶ and ❹ acquire the lock and handle the InterruptedException. If the locking attempt is successful, the try block at ❷ executes the required code and its finally block at ❸ releases the lock. The code at ❺ starts a thread and the code at ❻ tries to interrupt the thread. Even though the code at ❻ interrupts the thread e1, do you think it's sure to be interrupted? Not really, depending on how the thread e1 is executed—that is, whether it's waiting to acquire a lock on bus.lock or it has already completed the code in method run(), the code at ❻ might not interrupt e1. Also, because the thread e2 might actually start its execution before the thread e1, figure 11.1 shows the probable outputs of the preceding example.

Shreya: boarded Paul: Interrupted!!	Paul: Interrupted!! Shreya: boarded	Paul: boarded Shreya: boarded	Shreya: boarded Paul: boarded

Figure 11.1 Probable outputs of listing 11.1

It's important to make note of the order in which you acquire a lock using lock-Interruptibly(), handle the InterruptedException that it throws, and unlock it. Let's see whether you can detect this point in the code (you might be tested on it on the exam!) using the next "Twist in the Tale" exercise.

Twist in the Tale 11.1

What is the probable output of the following code?

```
import java.util.concurrent.locks.*;
class Bus {
    Lock lock = new ReentrantLock();
```

```
        public void boardBus(String name) {
            System.out.println(name + ": boarded");
        }
    }
    class Employee extends Thread {
        Bus bus; String name;
        Employee(String name, Bus bus) {
            this.bus = bus;
            this.name = name;
        }
        public void run() {
            try {
                bus.lock.lockInterruptibly();
                bus.boardBus(name);
            }
            catch (InterruptedException e) {
                System.out.println(name + ": Interrupted!!");
                Thread.currentThread().interrupt();
            }
            finally {
                bus.lock.unlock();
            }
        }
        public static void main(String args[]) {
            Employee e1 = new Employee("Paul", new Bus());
            e1.start();
            e1.interrupt();
        }
    }
}
```

a   Paul: boarded

b   Paul: Interrupted!!

c   Paul: Interrupted!! and IllegalThreadStateException is thrown

d   Paul: Interrupted!! and IllegalMonitorStateException is thrown

e   None of the above

In the next section, you'll see how you can retain a lock on Lock objects, across methods.

11.2.4   *Nonblock-structured locking*

With intrinsic locks, you must release the lock on an object's monitor at the end of the synchronized code blocks or methods. Because code blocks can't span across methods, intrinsic locks can't be acquired across methods. Extrinsic locks or a lock on Lock objects can be acquired across methods. Figure 11.2 compares block and nonblock locking with intrinsic and extrinsic locks.

	Intrinsic locks		Extrinsic locks
		Start (method1)	Start (method1)
Aquire lock			
	Start synchronized (method1)	Start synchronized block	—
	—	—	—
	—	—	End (method1)
	—	—	Start (method2)
	—	—	—
	—	—	—
	—	—	—
	—	—	—
	—	—	—
	End synchronized (method1)	End synchronized block	—
Release lock			
		End (method1)	End (method2)

Figure 11.2 Comparing intrinsic and extrinsic locks for block and nonblock locking

Here's some example code to work with extrinsic locks:

```
import java.util.concurrent.locks.*;
class Bus {
    ReentrantLock lock = new ReentrantLock();
    boolean locked = false;
    public void board(String name) {            Acquire lock in
        if (lock.tryLock()) {                    one method.
            locked = true;
            System.out.println(name + ": boarded");
        }
    }
    public void deboard(String name) {
        if (lock.isHeldByCurrentThread() && locked) {
            System.out.println(name + ": deboarded");
            lock.unlock();
            locked = false;                      Release lock in
        }                                        another method.
    }
}
```

 EXAM TIP Lock fairness: a ReentrantLock lock can be a nonfair or a fair lock. It can acquire locks in the order they were requested or acquire locks out of turn.

11.2.5 *Interface ReadWriteLock*

Interface `ReadWriteLock` maintains a pair of associated locks, one for read-only operations and another for write-only operations. The read-only lock may be held simultaneously by multiple reader threads as long as there are no writing processes in progress. The write-only lock is an exclusive lock. It can be acquired by only one thread. As listed in table 11.4, the `ReadWriteLock` interface defines only two methods: `readLock()` and `writeLock()`.

Table 11.4   Methods of interface `ReadWriteLock`

Method name	Description
Lock readLock()	Returns the lock used for reading.
Lock writeLock()	Returns the lock used for writing.

 EXAM TIP   The `ReadWriteLock` interface doesn't extend `Lock` or *any* other interface. It maintains a pair of associated `Lock`s—one for only reading operations and one for writing.

You can use methods `readLock()` and `writeLock()` to get a reference to the read or write `Lock`. Let's work with a concrete implementation of the `ReadWriteLock` interface, class `ReentrantReadWriteLock`, in the next section.

11.2.6 *Class ReentrantReadWriteLock*

A `ReentrantReadWriteLock` has a read and a write lock associated with it. You can access these locks (reference variables of type `Lock`) by calling its methods `readLock()` and `writeLock()`. You can acquire multiple read locks as long as no write lock has been acquired on a `ReadWriteLock` object. The `writeLock` is an exclusive lock; it can be acquired by only one thread when no read thread has been acquired. For example

```
import java.util.*;                                          ReentrantReadWriteLock
import java.util.concurrent.locks.*;
class Rainbow {
    private final ReadWriteLock myLock = new ReentrantReadWriteLock();  ←
    private static int pos;
    static Map<Integer, String> colors = new HashMap<>();

    public void addColor(String newColor) {          myLock.writeLock() returns
        myLock.writeLock().lock();                 ← writeLock and lock acquires
        try {                                        a lock on it.
            colors.put(new Integer(++pos), newColor);
        }
        finally {                                    Release lock
            myLock.writeLock().unlock();          ← on writeLock.
        }
    }
}
```

```
    public void display() {
        myLock.readLock().lock();              ◄────┐   myLock.readLock()
        try {                                        │   returns readLock and
            for (String s : colors.values()) {       │   lock acquires a lock on it.
                System.out.println(s);
            }
        }
        finally {                                       │   Unlock
            myLock.readLock().unlock();        ◄────────┘   readLock.
        }
    }
}
```

11.2.7 *Atomic variables*

The `java.util.concurrent.atomic` package defines multiple classes that support atomic operations of read-compare/modify-write on single variables. At the surface, these operations might seem similar to the operations with volatile variables. Though modifications to a volatile variable are guaranteed to be visible to other threads, volatile variables can't define a sequence of operations (like read-compare/modify-write) as an atomic operation.

Here's an example of class `Book` from chapter 10 to show you how nonatomic operations with primitive variables can lead to thread interference:

```
class Book{
    String title;
    int copiesSold = 0;
    Book(String title) {
        this.title = title;
    }
    public void newSale() {
        ++copiesSold;              ◄──┐  ❶  Nonatomic statements include loading
    }                                 │     of variable values from memory to
    public void returnBook() {        │     registers, manipulating values, and
        --copiesSold;              ◄──┘     loading them back to memory.
    }
}
```

The code defined at ❶ isn't atomic. Incrementing or decrementing primitive values includes multiple steps. When executed by multiple concurrent threads, `newSale()` and `returnBook()` can result in thread interference. To get around this, you can define these methods as synchronized methods, but it will block thread execution. Java defines multiple convenient classes in the `java.util.concurrent.atomic` package that define frequently used operations like read-modify-write as atomic operations. Let's use one of these classes, `AtomicInteger`, in class `Book`, and replace the type of its primitive `int` variable `copiesSold`:

```
class Book{
    String title;
    AtomicInteger copiesSold = new AtomicInteger(0);
```

```
    Book(String title) {
        this.title = title;
    }
    public void newSale() {
        copiesSold.incrementAndGet();
    }
    public void returnBook() {
        copiesSold.decrementAndGet();
    }
}
```

 Atomic operations

Methods `incrementAndGet()` and `decrementAndGet()` defined at ❶ are atomic operations. Concurrent execution of these methods won't result in interfering threads.

Class `AtomicInteger` defines multiple methods `xxxAndGet()` and `getAndXxx()`, where Xxx refers to an operation like increment, decrement, and add. `xxxAndGet()` returns an updated value and `getAndXxx()` returns the previous value.

> **EXAM TIP** Method `incrementAndGet()` returns the updated value but method `AtomicInteger`'s `getAndIncrement()` returns the previous value.

The other commonly used operations with `AtomicInteger` are to add or subtract specified values from it, assign it a value, and compare values before assignment. Table 11.5 lists these methods.

Table 11.5   Methods of class `AtomicInteger`

Method	Description
`int addAndGet(int delta)`	Atomically adds the given value to the current value. Returns the updated value.
`int getAndAdd(int delta)`	Atomically adds the given value to the current value.
`compareAndSet(int expect, int update)`	Atomically sets the value to the given updated value if the current value == the expected value.
`int getAndSet(int newValue)`	Atomically sets to the given value and returns the old value.
`public final void set(int newValue)`	Sets to the given value.
`int getAndDecrement()`	Atomically decrements by one the current value. Returns the previous value.
`int getAndIncrement()`	Atomically increments by one the current value. Returns the previous value.
`int decrementAndGet()`	Atomically decrements by one the current value. Returns the updated value.
`int incrementAndGet()`	Atomically increments by one the current value. Returns the updated value.

EXAM TIP Class `AtomicInteger` defines method `compareAndSet()` but not method `setAndCompare()`.

Other commonly used classes defined in the `java.util.concurrent.atomic` package are `AtomicBoolean`, `AtomicLong`, `AtomicIntegerArray`, `AtomicLongArray`, and `Atomic-Reference<V>`. `AtomicLong` defines the same methods as class `AtomicInteger` (as listed in table 11.5). The difference is the type of method parameters and their return types (`long` instead of `int`).

 EXAM TIP The `java.util.concurrent.atomic` package doesn't define classes by the names `AtomicShort`, `AtomicByte`, `AtomicFloat`, or `Atomic-Double`. These invalid class names might be used on the exam.

In this section, you learned how to exercise finer control over how locks are acquired, managed, and released. In the next section, we'll work with exercising finer control over the tasks done by threads and the threads themselves.

11.3 Executors

 [11.3] Use Executor, ExecutorService, Executors, Callable, and Future to execute tasks using thread pools

In chapter 10, we used class `Thread` and the `Runnable` interface to create multiple threads that execute asynchronously. Class `Thread` and the `Runnable` interface define a close connection with a *task* (that is, a logical unit of work) done by a thread and the thread itself. Though okay for smaller applications, large applications call for a separation of tasks and the threads for thread creation and their management.

The `Executor` framework enables decoupling of task submission with task execution. By using this framework, you can create tasks using interfaces `Runnable` and `Callable`. These tasks are submitted to `Executor` to launch new tasks. `Executor-Service` extends `Executor` and adds methods to manage the lifecycle of tasks and executors. `ScheduledExecutorService` extends `ExecutorService` and supports future or periodic execution of tasks. `Future` represents the state of asynchronous tasks and can be used to query their status or cancel them. Class `Executors` defines utility and factory methods for interfaces `Executor`, `ExecutorService`, and `Scheduled-ExecutorService`.

Figure 11.3 shows the classes and interfaces that we'll work with in this section, how they're related to each other, and where they're placed in the `java.util.concurrent` package.

Let's get started with the `Executor` interface.

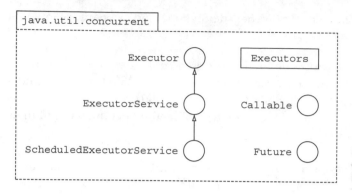

Figure 11.3 Interfaces and classes that we'll work with in this section

11.3.1 *Interface Executor*

With class `Thread` and the `Runnable` interface, the task executed by a thread and the thread itself are closely connected. The `Executor` interface allows you to define classes that know *how* to execute `Runnable` tasks. It allows you to decouple task submission and its execution. By implementing its sole method, `void execute(Runnable)`, you can determine how you want to execute the tasks:

- Which task will execute first
- The order of execution of tasks
- How many tasks can execute concurrently
- How many tasks can be queued

Here's an example of a `Runnable` object, `Order`, which is processed by `Hotel`, an `Executor`:

```
class Order implements Runnable {
    String name;
    Order(String name) {this.name = name;}
    public void run() {
        System.out.println(name);
    }
}
class Hotel implements Executor {
    final Queue<Runnable> custQueue = new ArrayDeque<>();     ❶ Implement
    public void execute(Runnable r) {                             execute.
        synchronized(custQueue) {
            custQueue.offer(r);                    ❷ Add Runnable
        }                                             object to a queue.
        processEarliestOrder();
    }

    private void processEarliestOrder() {
        synchronized(custQueue) {                  ❸ Retrieve Runnable
            Runnable task = custQueue.poll();         object from execute.
            new Thread(task).start();
        }                                ❹ Start new thread for
    }                                      executing submitted task
}
```

In the preceding code, class Hotel controls how it processes the Runnable tasks submitted to it. At ❶, Hotel implements Executor's method execute(). At ❷, it adds the submitted task to a queue. Method execute() calls processEarliestOrder(), which at ❸ retrieves a task from the queue, and at ❹ starts a new thread to execute it.

By decoupling task submission from task execution, it's simple to modify how to execute tasks. In the preceding code, you can modify execute() so that class Hotel works with a pool of worker threads ready to be assigned a task to execute, rather than executing each task using a new thread.

You can code execute() to exercise complete control over how to execute tasks. You might wish to process tasks with high priority earlier than the lower-priority ones, or process the last submitted task as the first task.

In the next "Twist in the Tale" exercise, let's modify just a line of code from the preceding example and see whether you can determine its overall impact on the execution of the tasks submitted to class Hotel.

Twist in the Tale 11.2

What is the output of the following code?

```java
class Order implements Runnable {
    String name;
    Order(String name) {this.name = name;}
    public void run() {
        System.out.println(name);
    }
}
class Hotel implements Executor {
    final Queue<Runnable> custQueue = new ArrayDeque<>();
    public void execute(Runnable r) {
        synchronized(custQueue) {
            custQueue.offer(r);
        }
        processEarliestOrder();
    }

    private void processEarliestOrder() {
        synchronized(custQueue) {
            Runnable task = custQueue.poll();
            task.run();
        }
    }
    public static void main(String args[]) {
        Hotel hotel = new Hotel();
        hotel.execute(new Order("tea"));
        hotel.execute(new Order("coffee"));
        hotel.execute(new Order("burger"));
    }
}
```

a The code will fail to compile.

b The code will throw an exception at runtime.

c The code can output "tea", "coffee", and "burger" in any order.

d The code will output "tea", "coffee", and "burger" in a fixed order for all executions of class Hotel.

The java.util.concurrent package defines an advanced interface, ExecutorService, which enables you to control and manage the submitted tasks better. Apart from accepting Runnable objects, it also accepts Callable objects. Before exploring the ExecutorService interface, let's examine the Callable interface.

11.3.2 *Interface Callable*

Comparing interfaces Runnable and Callable, method run() of the Runnable interface doesn't return a value and can't throw a checked exception. Both of these are taken care of by the Callable interface:

```
public interface Callable<V> {
    /**
     * Computes a result, or throws an exception if unable to do so.
     *
     * @return computed result
     * @throws Exception if unable to compute a result
     */
    V call() throws Exception;
}
```

In the following example, class Order implements the Callable interface. Because it isn't interested in returning a value from call(), it uses Void as its parameterized argument:

```
class Order implements Callable<Void> {
    String name;
    Order(String name) {this.name = name;}
    @Override
    public Void call() throws Exception {
        System.out.println(name);
        if (name.equalsIgnoreCase("berry"))
            throw new Exception("Berry unavailable");
        return null;
    }
}
```

  EXAM TIP   If you don't want your Callable to return a value, you can create it using Callable<Void>.

You can submit Callable and Runnable objects to an ExecutorService. Let's move forward with discussing the ExecutorService interface in the next section.

11.3.3 *Interface ExecutorService*

The `ExecutorService` interface extends the `Executor` interface and defines methods to manage progress and termination of tasks that are submitted to it. It defines methods to

- Submit single `Runnable` and `Callable` objects for execution, returning `Future` objects
- Submit multiple `Runnable` objects for execution, returning `Future` objects
- Shut down the `ExecutorService`, allowing or disallowing submitted tasks to be completed

Table 11.6 shows the methods of the `ScheduledService` interface.

Table 11.6 Methods of interface `ScheduledService`

Method name	Description
`boolean awaitTermination(long timeout, TimeUnit unit)`	Blocks until all tasks have completed execution after a shutdown request, the timeout occurs, or the current thread is interrupted—whichever happens first.
`<T> List<Future<T>> invokeAll(Collection<? extends Callable<T>> tasks)`	Executes the given tasks, returning a list of `Futures` holding their statuses and results when all complete.
`<T> List<Future<T>> invokeAll(Collection<? extends Callable<T>> tasks, long timeout, TimeUnit unit)`	Executes the given tasks, returning a list of `Futures` holding their statuses and results when all complete or the timeout expires—whichever happens first.
`<T> T invokeAny(Collection<? extends Callable<T>> tasks)`	Executes the given tasks, returning the result of one that has completed successfully (that is, without throwing an exception), if any do.
`<T> T invokeAny(Collection<? extends Callable<T>> tasks, long timeout, TimeUnit unit)`	Executes the given tasks, returning the result of one that has completed successfully (that is, without throwing an exception), if any do before the given timeout elapses.
`boolean isShutdown()`	Returns `true` if this executor has been shut down.
`boolean isTerminated()`	Returns `true` if all tasks have completed following shutdown.
`void shutdown()`	Initiates an orderly shutdown in which previously submitted tasks are executed, but no new tasks will be accepted.
`List<Runnable> shutdownNow()`	Attempts to stop all actively executing tasks, halts the processing of waiting tasks, and returns a list of the tasks that were awaiting execution.

Table 11.6 Methods of interface `ScheduledService` (continued)

Method name	Description
`<T> Future<T> submit(Callable<T> task)`	Submits a value-returning task for execution and returns a `Future` representing the pending results of the task.
`Future<?> submit(Runnable task)`	Submits a `Runnable` task for execution and returns a `Future` representing that task.
`<T> Future<T> submit(Runnable task, T result)`	Submits a `Runnable` task for execution and returns a `Future` representing that task.

In the next section, we'll work with thread pools, and you'll learn what they are, why you need them, and how they're implemented using `ExecutorService`.

11.3.4 *Thread pools*

Imagine only one chef is employed in a restaurant to prepare orders from its customers. As the restaurant consistently increases its customer count, it makes sense to employ more chefs to speed up service and reduce waiting time. But an increased count of chefs wouldn't decrease the food preparation time in the same proportion, because they would be waiting to access the same resources—that is, the oven, refrigerator, food-processing equipment, etc. Also, even if they aren't doing anything, they would consume restaurant resources like monetary benefits, physical space in the kitchen, and more. What happens when the kitchen runs out of all its physical space from the constant addition of new chefs? In an application, a similar condition called *exhaustion of physical resources* can lead to a crash.

By limiting the number of concurrent tasks, an application ensures that it doesn't fail or have resource exhaustion or suffer performance issues. The solution is to use pools of threads, which create a predefined number of threads and reuse them to execute tasks. You must optimize the size of the thread pool. The threads shouldn't overwhelm the scheduler and introduce unnecessary thread contention and performance degradation. There should be enough to only keep the processor busy.

A thread pool includes a homogeneous pool of worker threads. These are usually bound to a work queue, holding references to tasks that are waiting to be executed. A worker thread would typically request the next task for execution, execute it, and go back to waiting to execute the next task.

Class `Executors` in the `java.util.concurrent` package defines convenient static methods to retrieve multiple preconfigured thread pools:

- Fixed thread pool, which creates a pool with a fixed number of threads
- Cached thread pool
- Single thread executor
- Scheduled thread pool

Let's work with an example of Callable objects that are submitted to a thread pool:

```
class Order implements Callable<Void> {
    String name;
    Order(String name) {this.name = name;}
    public Void call() throws Exception {
        System.out.println(name);
        if (name.equalsIgnoreCase("berry"))
            throw new Exception("Berry unavailable");
        return null;
    }
}
class Hotel {
    ExecutorService service = Executors.newFixedThreadPool(5);

    public void orderFood(Order order) {
        service.submit(order);
    }
    public void hotelClosedForDay() {
        service.shutdown();
    }
    public void hotelClosedForever() {
        service.shutdown();
        try {
            if (!service.awaitTermination(60, TimeUnit.SECONDS)) {
                service.shutdownNow();

                if (!service.awaitTermination(60, TimeUnit.SECONDS))
                    System.err.println("Pool did not terminate");
            }
        } catch (InterruptedException ie) {
            service.shutdownNow();
            Thread.currentThread().interrupt();
        }
    }
}
```

Annotations:
- call() doesn't return any value; its return type is Void.
- Create ExecutorService object by calling Executors.newFixed-ThreadPool.
- Submit Callable to ExecutorService for execution.
- Disable new tasks from being submitted.
- Wait awhile for existing tasks to terminate.
- Cancel currently executing tasks.
- Wait awhile for tasks to respond to being cancelled.
- (Re-)cancel if current thread also interrupted
- Preserve interrupt status.

In the preceding example, class Hotel uses Executors to retrieve a fixed thread pool of five threads. This thread pool implements the ExecutorService interface. When a task is submitted to ExecutorService using execute(), it uses one of its available worker threads to execute it. If no worker threads are available to execute the task, the submitted task waits for a worker thread to become available. Method shutdown() doesn't accept submission of new tasks and waits for the existing tasks to complete to execution. Method shutdownNow() cancels currently executing tasks, apart from refusing to accept new tasks. Method awaitTermination() blocks until all tasks have completed execution after a shutdown request, the timeout occurs, or the current thread is interrupted—whichever happens first.

11.3.5 Interface ScheduledExecutorService

The ScheduledExecutorService interface supports future or periodic execution of tasks.

Imagine you need to send out reminder emails to all the employees of your organization to submit their daily status reports. This email is sent out every day. Let's see how you can use ScheduledExecutorService in this case:

```
import static java.util.concurrent.TimeUnit.*;
import java.util.concurrent.*;
class Reminder implements Runnable {
    public void run() {
        // send reminder emails to all employees
        System.out.println("All Mails sent");
    }
}
class ReminderMgr {
    ScheduledExecutorService service =
                        Executors.newScheduledThreadPool(1);
    Reminder reminder = new Reminder();

    public void sendReminders() {
        service.scheduleAtFixedRate(reminder, 0, 24, HOURS);
    }
    public static void main(String args[]) {
        ReminderMgr mgr = new ReminderMgr();
        mgr.sendReminders();
    }
}
```

When started, this Runnable object sends out emails to all employees.

Call Executors .newScheduled-ThreadPool to get a Scheduled-ExecutorService object.

Execute task reminder now and every 24 hours.

Table 11.7 lists all the methods of the ScheduledExecutorService interface.

Table 11.7   Methods of interface ScheduledExecutorService

Method name	Description
`<V> ScheduledFuture<V> schedule(Callable<V> callable, long delay, TimeUnit unit)`	Creates a ScheduledFuture that becomes enabled after the given delay.
`ScheduledFuture<?> schedule(Runnable command, long delay, TimeUnit unit)`	Creates and executes a one-shot action that becomes enabled after the given delay.
`ScheduledFuture<?> scheduleAtFixedRate(Runnable command, long initialDelay, long period, TimeUnit unit)`	Creates and executes a periodic action that becomes enabled first after the given initial delay, and subsequently within the given period—that is, executions will commence after initialDelay, then initialDelay + period, then initialDelay + 2 × period, and so on.
`ScheduledFuture<?> scheduleWithFixedDelay(Runnable command, long initialDelay, long delay, TimeUnit unit)`	Creates and executes a periodic action that becomes enabled first after the given initial delay, and subsequently within the given delay between the termination of one execution and the commencement of the next.

The `ScheduledExecutorService` interface greatly simplifies thread handling for developers. It provides methods to manage tracking of progress and termination of asynchronous tasks (threads). In their absence, developers used to write their own classes or work with third-party classes to manage concurrent applications. Starting with version 7, Java has a new addition to the `java.concurrent` package, the fork/join framework. As you'll see in the next section, it makes the best use of multicore processors.

11.4   Parallel fork/join framework

  [11.4] Use the parallel fork/join framework

Today, all computing devices—servers, desktops, tables, and mobile phones—feature multicore processors, so it made a lot of sense to add a feature to the programming language itself to utilize them. Introduced with Java 7, the fork/join framework extends the existing Java concurrency package, supporting hardware parallelism, a key feature of multicore systems. The fork/join framework isn't intended to replace or compete with the existing concurrency classes from the `java.util.concurrent` package. It works by breaking down larger, processing-intensive tasks into smaller, independent tasks recursively, processing each unit of a task and then merging back the results.

 EXAM TIP   The fork/join framework is best suited for tasks that are processor intensive and that can be divided into smaller tasks that can execute independently, in parallel. Tasks that block, work with I/O, or need synchronization aren't good candidates to use with the fork/join framework.

Figure 11.4 shows the logic of the fork/join framework's divide-and-conquer parallel algorithm.

As you can see in figure 11.4, the size of a problem is evaluated *before* it's further divided. If the problem is small enough (smaller than or equal to a threshold limit), it isn't subdivided and is executed sequentially. The bigger problems are subdivided into two or more subproblems, and the fork/join framework recursively invokes itself on the subproblems in parallel, waits for their results, and then combines them. You should select the threshold limit carefully.

 NOTE   The fork/join framework is named so because it initiates execution of a task that *forks* or starts multiple subtasks, and waits for them to *join* back (or complete their execution).

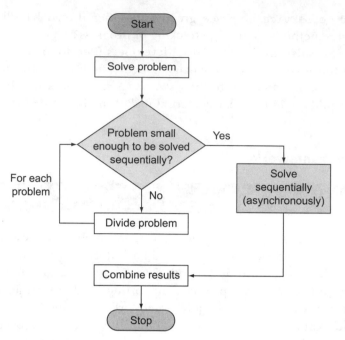

Figure 11.4   Divide-and-conquer algorithm used by fork/join framework

Class `ForkJoinPool` is a concrete implementation of the fork/join framework. It implements the `ExecutorService` interface. Like `ExecutorService`, a fork/join framework maintains a queue of tasks that are used to assigns tasks to its multiple worker threads. But it's different from an `ExecutorService` because a fork/join framework implements

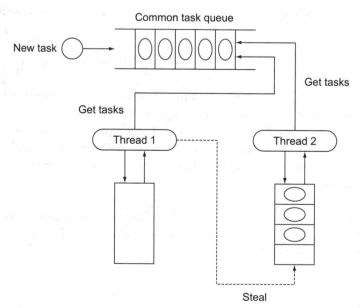

Figure 11.5   Threads in a fork/join framework use work-stealing algorithms. When a thread runs out of tasks in its own deque, it can steal tasks from other threads to avoid blocking waiting threads.

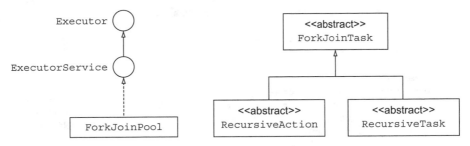

Figure 11.6 Classes implemented in the fork/join framework

a *work-stealing algorithm.* In this algorithm, when worker threads run out of tasks, they steal tasks from other worker threads to avoid blocking waiting threads.

Figure 11.5 shows how a fork/join pool maintains a common task queue but reduces contention by implementing a work-stealing algorithm. Individual threads maintain their own task queue using Deque. When a task forks a new thread, it's pushed to the thread's deque. When threads are waiting for a task to join, they pop one of their tasks, instead of simply waiting. When threads run out of all the tasks in their deque, they steal a task from the tail of another thread's deque.

Class ForkJoinPool provides the entry point for submissions from non-ForkJoinTask clients, as well as management and monitoring operations. Your problem-solving class should be a subclass of ForkJoinTask. ForkJoinTask is an abstract base class for tasks that run within a ForkJoinPool. A ForkJoinTask can be compared to a much lighter-weight version of a thread. A large number of ForkJoinTasks can be executed by a smaller number of actual threads in a ForkJoinPool. Figure 11.6 shows class ForkJoin-Pool and class ForkJoinTask and its two subclasses, RecursiveTask and Recursive-Action. RecursiveAction is used for computations that don't return a result, and RecursiveTask is used for computations that return a result.

Let's apply the fork/join framework to a simple example of calculating the sum of an integer array, by dividing it into smaller tasks of calculating the sum of its subarrays that execute as asynchronous tasks. In this example we'll work with ForkJoinPool and RecursiveTask.

Listing 11.2 Implement fork/join framework using `ForkJoinPool`

```
import java.util.concurrent.*;
public class CalcSum extends RecursiveTask<Integer> {          CalcSum extends
    private int UNIT_SIZE = 15;                                 RecursiveTask-
    private int[] values;                                    ❶ <Integer>.
    private int startPos;
    private int endPos;

    public CalcSum(int[] values) {
        this(values, 0, values.length);
    }
```

```
                public CalcSum(int[] values, int startPos, int endPos) {
                    this.values = values;
                    this.startPos = startPos;
                    this.endPos = endPos;
                }
                @Override
                protected Integer compute() {
                    final int currentSize = endPos - startPos;
                    if (currentSize <= UNIT_SIZE) {
                        return computeSum();
                    }
                    else {
                        int center = currentSize/2;
                        int leftEnd = startPos + center;
                        CalcSum leftSum = new CalcSum(values, startPos, leftEnd);
                        leftSum.fork();

                        int rightStart = startPos + center+1;
                        CalcSum rightSum = new CalcSum(values, rightStart, endPos);
                        return(rightSum.compute() + leftSum.join());
                    }
                }

                private Integer computeSum() {
                    int sum = 0;
                    for (int i = startPos; i < endPos; i++) {
                        sum += values[i];
                    }
                    System.out.println("Sum(" + startPos + "-" + endPos + "):" + sum);
                    return sum;
                }

                public static void main(String[] args) {
                    int[] intArray = new int[100];
                    java.util.Random randomValues = new java.util.Random();

                    for (int i = 0; i < intArray.length; i++) {
                        intArray[i] = randomValues.nextInt(10);
                    }

                    ForkJoinPool pool = new ForkJoinPool();
                    CalcSum calculator = new CalcSum(intArray);

                    System.out.println(pool.invoke(calculator));
                }
            }
```

② For CalcSum, overridden method compute() returns an integer value.

③ Calling fork on leftSum makes it execute asynchronously.

④ leftSum.join waits until it returns a value; compute is main computation performed by task.

⑤ Private helper method

⑥ Instantiates a ForkJoinPool.

⑦ invoke() awaits and obtains result

Depending on how the asynchronous tasks are scheduled on a system, each execution of the preceding code might yield a different output. Here's one of the probable outputs:

```
Sum(89-100) : 56
Sum(76-88)  : 46
Sum(64-75)  : 62
Sum(39-50)  : 48
Sum(51-63)  : 43
```

```
Sum(26-38)  :  32
Sum(13-25)  :  57
Sum(0-12)   :  54
398
```

In the preceding code, ❶ defines class `CalcSum`, which extends `RecursiveTask` `<Integer>`. This parameter, `Integer`, is the type of the value returned by method `compute()`. Method `compute()`, defined at ❷, is called once for the main task when `invoke()` is called on a `ForkJoinPool` instance, passing it an object of `CalcSum`. It also gets called when `fork()` is called on a `RecursiveTask` instance. Method `compute()` calculates the size of an array and compares it with a unit size (15 in this case). If it's less than this unit size, it computes the sum of its array elements using `computeSum()` ❺. If the array size is greater, it creates an instance of `CalcSum`, passing it the left half of the array, and the code at ❸ calls `fork()` on it. Calling `fork` executes a `Recursive-Task` asynchronously. Then method `compute()` creates another instance of `CalcSum`, passing it the right half of the array. At ❹, it calls `compute()` on the right part and `join()` on the left part. Calling `compute()` will recursively create (left and right) `CalcSum` objects, if it still needs to be divided into smaller tasks. Calling `join()` will return the result of the computation when it's done. Method `main()` creates an array `intArray` and initializes it by generating random integer values using class `Random`. The code at ❻ creates a `ForkJoinPool`. The code at ❼ calls `invoke()`, which executes the given task, returning its result on completion.

 NOTE The preceding code example is for demonstration purposes. The fork/join framework recommends 100–10,000 computational steps in the `compute` method so that its work-stealing algorithm and `join()` can work effectively.

The order of execution of calling `compute()` and `join()` is important in the preceding code. Do you think the preceding code results in equally efficient code if you modify this execution order? Take a look in the next "Twist in the Tale" exercise.

Twist in the Tale 11.3

What is the result of replacing method `compute()` with the following modified method `compute()` from listing 11.2?

```
protected Integer compute() {
    final int currentSize = endPos - startPos;
    if (currentSize <= UNIT_SIZE) {
        return computeSum();
    }
    else {
        int center = currentSize/2;
        int leftEnd = startPos + center;
        CalcSum leftSum = new CalcSum(values, startPos, leftEnd);
        leftSum.fork();
```

```
        int rightStart = startPos + center+1;
        CalcSum rightSum = new CalcSum(values, rightStart, endPos);
        return(leftSum.join() + rightSum.compute());
    }
}
```

    a The code might generate an incorrect sum of array elements.

    b The code will always generate the correct sum of array elements.

    c The code won't benefit from the fork/join framework.

    d The code will throw a runtime exception.

This coverage of the fork/join framework brings an end to the concurrency topics that you need to know for the exam.

11.5   *Summary*

To develop thread-safe, high-performance, and scalable applications, Java's low-level threading capabilities are insufficient. In this chapter, we used collections from Java's `java.util.concurrent` package to effectively resolve common concurrency issues. We worked with multiple concurrent classes and interfaces, such as `BlockingQueue`, `ConcurrentMap`, and `ConcurrentSkipListMap`.

By relying on synchronized code blocks to coordinate access between threads, you can't develop scalable applications. You learned about explicit `Lock` objects used to wait to acquire a lock on an object's monitor. `Lock` objects also support interruptible lock waits, nonblock-structured locks, multiple condition variables, lock polling, and scalability benefits.

The `Executor` framework enables decoupling of task submission with task execution. By using this framework, you can create tasks using interfaces `Runnable` and `Callable`. These tasks are submitted to `Executor` to launch new tasks. `Executor-Service` extends `Executor` and adds methods to manage the lifecycle of tasks and executors. `ScheduledExecutorService` extends `ExecutorService` and supports future or periodic execution of tasks. `Future` represents the state of asynchronous tasks and can be used to query their status or cancel them. You use class `Executors` to call utility and factory methods for interfaces `Executor`, `ExecutorService`, and `Scheduled-ExecutorService`.

The fork/join framework extends the existing Java concurrency package, supporting hardware parallelism, a key feature of multicore systems. The fork/join framework isn't indented to replace or compete with the existing concurrency classes from the `java.util.concurrent` package. It works by breaking down a larger task into smaller tasks recursively, processing each unit of the task and then combining back the results.

REVIEW NOTES

Concurrent collection classes

- `BlockingQueue` defines a first-in-first-out data structure that blocks or times out when you attempt to add to a full queue or retrieve from an empty queue.
- `ConcurrentMap` is a subinterface of `java.util.Map` that defines useful atomic operations.
- `ConcurrentMap` operations remove or replace a key-value pair only if the key is present, or add a key-value pair only if the key is absent. Making these operations atomic helps avoid synchronization.
- The standard general-purpose implementation of `ConcurrentMap` is `Concurrent-HashMap`, which is a concurrent analog of `HashMap`.
- `ConcurrentNavigableMap` is a subinterface of `ConcurrentMap` that supports approximate matches.
- The standard general-purpose implementation of `ConcurrentNavigableMap` is `ConcurrentSkipListMap`, which is a concurrent analog of `TreeMap`.
- A concurrent collection helps avoid memory consistency errors by defining a happens-before relationship between an operation that adds an object to the collection and subsequent operations that access or remove that object.

Locks

- `Lock` and `ReadWriteLock` are interfaces.
- `ReentrantLock` and `ReentrantReadWriteLock` are concrete classes.
- `Lock` objects offer multiple advantages over the implicit locking of an object's monitor. Unlike an implicit lock, a thread can use explicit lock objects to wait to acquire a lock until a time duration elapses.
- `Lock` objects also support interruptible lock waits, nonblock-structured locks, lock polling, and scalability benefits.
- Method `lock()` acquires a lock on a `Lock` object. If the lock isn't available, it waits until the lock can be acquired.
- Method `lock()` is comparable to intrinsic locks because it waits until a lock can be acquired on a `Lock` object.
- Call `unlock` on a `Lock` object to release its lock when you no longer need it.
- If you don't call `unlock()` on a `Lock` object after acquiring a lock on it, the code will still compile successfully.
- Method `tryLock()` tries to acquire a lock on a `Lock` object, and returns immediately a `boolean` value specifying whether it could obtain the lock or not.
- Watch out for the use of methods `acquire()`, `acquireLock()`, `release()`, and `releaseLock()` on the exam. None of these is a valid method. Because the terms *acquire* and *release* are used to discuss methods `lock()`, `unlock()`, `try-Lock()`, and `lockInterruptibly()`, these terms might be used on the exam to confuse you.

- Methods `lockInterruptibly()` and `tryLock(long time, TimeUnit unit)` of the `Lock` interface enable you to specify a waiting timeout or to try and acquire a lock while being available for interruption.
- Extrinsic locks or the lock on `Lock` objects can be acquired across methods.
- An interface, `ReadWriteLock` maintains a pair of associated locks, one for read-only operations and another for write-only operations.
- The `ReadWriteLock` interface doesn't extend `Lock` or any other interface.
- The `ReadWriteLock` interface defines only two methods, `readLock()` and `writeLock()`.
- A `ReentrantReadWriteLock` has a read and a write lock associated with it. You can access these locks (reference variables of type `Lock`) by calling its methods `readLock()` and `writeLock()`.
- You can acquire read locks until a write lock has been acquired on a `ReadWriteLock` object.
- `WriteLock` is an exclusive lock; it can be acquired by only one thread when no read thread has been acquired.
- The `java.util.concurrent` package defines multiple classes that support atomic operations of read-compare/modify-write on single variables.
- Other commonly used classes defined in the `java.util.concurrent.atomic` package are `AtomicInteger`, `AtomicBoolean`, `AtomicLong`, `AtomicIntegerArray`, `AtomicLongArray`, and `AtomicReference<V>`.
- The `java.util.concurrent.atomic` package doesn't define classes by the names `AtomicShort`, `AtomicByte`, `AtomicFloat`, or `AtomicDouble`. These invalid class names might be used on the exam.

Executors

- The `Executor` framework enables decoupling of task submission with task execution.
- By using this framework, you can create tasks using interfaces `Runnable` and `Callable`.
- The `Runnable` interface defines method `run()` and the `Callable` interface defines method `call()`.
- `Executor` allows you to decouple task submission and its execution.
- The `Executor` interface defines only one method, `void execute(Runnable)`.
- You can define your own execution policy by implementing `Executor`'s method `execute()`.
- Comparing the `Runnable` and `Callable` interface, method `run()` of `Runnable` doesn't return a value and can't throw a checked exception. But method `call()` of `Callable` can return a value and throw a checked exception.
- If you don't want `Callable` to return a value, you can create it using `Callable<Void>`, defining the return type of `call()` as `Void` and returning `null` from it.

- The `ExecutorService` interface extends the `Executor` interface and defines methods to manage progress and termination of tasks that are submitted to it.
- Implemented using `ExecutorService`, thread pools use a pool of worker threads to execute new tasks. If the pool runs out of worker threads, the submitted task waits for a worker thread to become available.
- Thread pools prevent spawning of new threads to execute each new submitted task, thereby avoiding overwhelming the scheduler.
- Class `Executors` defines utility and factory methods for interfaces `Executor`, `ExecutorService`, and `ScheduledExecutorService`.
- `ScheduledExecutorService` extends `ExecutorService` and supports future or periodic execution of tasks.
- `Future` represents the state of an asynchronous task and can be used to query its status or cancel it.
- `ScheduledExecutorService` can schedule `Callable` or `Runnable` tasks that execute just once, after a given delay.
- `ScheduledExecutorService` can schedule only `Runnable` tasks (not `Callable` tasks) that can execute multiple times, starting its first execution after an initial delay and subsequent execution after the specified period.

Parallel fork/join framework

- The parallel fork/join framework makes the best use of multicore processors.
- The fork/join framework extends the existing Java concurrency package, supporting hardware parallelism, a key feature of multicore systems.
- The fork/join framework isn't intended to replace or compete with the existing concurrency classes from the `java.util.concurrent` package.
- The fork/join framework works by breaking down a larger task into smaller tasks recursively, processing each unit of the task, and then combining back the results.
- You can define a recursive task using either `RecursiveTask` or `RecursiveAction`. `RecursiveAction` is used to define tasks that don't return a value. `RecursiveTask` returns a value.
- You can instantiate a fork/join pool by using `ForkJoinPool` and passing it the number of processors it should use. By default, `ForkJoinPool` uses all the available processors.
- Execution of `RecursiveAction` or `RecursiveTask` starts when you call `invoke` on `ForkJoinPool`, passing it a `RecursiveAction` or `RecursiveTask` object, which calls their `compute()`.
- Method `compute()` determines whether the task is small enough to be executed or if it needs to be divided into multiple tasks. If the task needs to be split, a new `RecursiveAction` or `RecursiveTask` object is created, calling `fork` on it. Calling `join` on these tasks returns their result.

SAMPLE EXAM QUESTIONS

Q 11-1. Which of the following options is a thread-safe variant of `ArrayList`?

- **a** `ConcurrentList`
- **b** `ConcurrentArrayList`
- **c** `CopyOnReadWriteArrayList`
- **d** `CopyOnReadArrayList`
- **e** `CopyOnWriteArrayList`

Q 11-2. Which line of code, when inserted at `//INSERT CODE HERE`, will ensure that on execution, single or multiple `MyColors` instances won't throw a `Concurrent-ModificationException` at runtime?

```
class MyColors extends Thread{
    static private Map<Integer, String> map;
    MyColors() {
    //INSERT CODE HERE
        map.put(1, "red");
        map.put(2, "blue");
        map.put(3, "yellow");
    }
    public void iterate() {
        Iterator iter = map.keySet().iterator();
        while(iter.hasNext()) {
            Integer key = (Integer)iter.next();
            String val = (String)map.get(key);
            System.out.println(key + "-" + val);
            add(4, "green");
        }
    }
    public void add(Integer i, String v){
        map.put(i, v);
    }

    public void run() {
        iterate();
    }
}
```

- **a** `map = new HashMap<Integer, String>();`
- **b** `map = new NoExceptionHashMap<Integer, String>();`
- **c** `map = new ConcurrentMap<Integer, String>();`
- **d** `map = new ConcurrentHashMap<Integer, String>();`
- **e** `map = new CopyOnWriteHashMap<Integer, String>();`
- **f** None of the above

Q 11-3. Which of the following concurrent collection classes can you use to implement the producer–consumer design pattern?

   a `WaitNotifyQueue`

   b `BlockingQueue`

   c `LinkedBlockingQueue`

   d `ArrayBlockingQueue`

   e `ConcurrentBlockingQueue`

   f `ProducerConsumerQueue`

   g `ProducerConsumerList`

Q 11-4. Examine the following code and select the correct options.

```
1. class UseConcurrentHashMap {
2.      static final ConcurrentMap<Integer, String> map =
3.                              new ConcurrentHashMap<>();
4.      static {
5.          //code to populate map
6.      }
7.      static void manipulateMap(Integer key, String value) {
8.          if(!map.containsKey(key))
9.              map.put(key, value);
10.     }
11.}
```

   a Because code at lines 2 and 3 uses `ConcurrentHashMap`, operations in method `manipulateMap()` are thread safe.

   b Operations in `manipulateMap()` will be thread safe if lines 8 and 9 are replaced with `map.putIfAbsent(key, value);`.

   c If line 2 is replaced with the following code, there won't be any concurrency issues with `manipulateMap()`: `static final ConcurrentHashMap<Integer, String> map =`.

   d Removing code at lines 4, 5, and 6 will ensure calling `manipulateMap()` won't override any values.

Q 11-5. Which of the following methods from class `AtomicLong` can be used to atomically compare values and modify them?

   a `compareAndSet`

   b `compareAndModify`

   c `modifyAndCompare`

   d `compareValuesAndSet`

   e `compareAndSetModifySafely`

Q 11-6. Examine the following code and select the correct answer options.

```
class University {
    Lock myLock = new ReentrantLock();                        //1
    static List<String> students = new ArrayList<>();
    public void add(String newStudent) {
        myLock.lock();                                        //2
        try {
            students.add(newStudent);
        }
        finally {
            myLock.unlock();                                  //3
        }
    }
}
```

  a At line 1, if a reference variable lock is assigned an object of `ReentrantRead-WriteLock`, it won't make a difference.

  b The code at line 2 tries to acquire a lock on object `myLock`. If the lock isn't available, it waits until the lock can be acquired.

  c The code at line 2 tries to acquire a lock on object `myLock`. If the lock isn't available, it returns immediately.

  d If the code at line 3 is removed, the code will fail to compile.

Q 11-7. Select the incorrect statements.

  a The `ReadWriteLock` interface maintains a pair of associated locks, one for read-only operations and another for write-only operations.

  b A read-only lock may be held simultaneously by multiple reader threads, irrespective of whether there are any writing processes in progress or not.

  c A write-only lock is an exclusive lock. It can be acquired by only one thread.

  d The `ReadWriteLock` interface defines only two methods, `readLock()` and `writeLock()`.

Q 11-8. Objects of which of the following can be executed by an `Executor`?

  a ```
class Order implements Runnable {
    public void run() {}
}
```

  b  ```
class Order implements Callable {
    public void call() {}
}
```

  c ```
class Order implements Executable {
    public void execute() {}
}
```

  d  ```
class Order implements Schedulable {
    public void schedule() {}
}
```

Q 11-9. Which of the following can be used to execute a `Runnable` or `Callable` object after an initial delay of 10 minutes?

- a `ForkJoinPool`
- b `ScheduledExecutorService`
- c `TimedExecutorService`
- d `SchedulableExecutorService`

Q 11-10. Code in which of the following options can be inserted at `//INSERT CODE HERE`?

```
class MyService {
    public static void main(String args[]) {
        ExecutorService service = Executors.newFixedThreadPool(5);
        service.submit(new Task());
    }
}
//INSERT CODE HERE
```

- a `class Task implements Executor {public void execute() {} }`
- b `class Task implements Executable {public void execute() {} }`
- c `class Task implements Submittable {public void submit() {} }`
- d `class Task implements Callable<Void> {public Void call() {return null;} }`
- e `class Task implements Callable<Integer> {public Integer call() {return 1;} }`
- f `class Task implements Callable {public void call() {} }`

Q 11-11. Which of the following objects can be passed to `ForkJoinPool.invoke()`?

- a `ForkJoin`
- b `ForkJoinThread`
- c `ForkJoinTask`
- d `AbstractForkJoinTask`
- e `RecursiveThread`
- f `RecursiveAction`
- g `RecursiveTask`

Q 11-12. Which of the following problems make a good candidate to be solved using the fork/join framework?

- a Problems that can be divided into independent tasks
- b Problems that work with a lot of external files
- c Problems the subtasks of which rely on synchronization to calculate their results
- d Problems that need to connect with an external server to choose their courses of action

ANSWERS TO SAMPLE EXAM QUESTIONS

A 11-1. e

[11.1] Use collections from the java.util.concurrent package with a focus on the advantages over and differences from the traditional java.util collections

Explanation: Options a, b, c, and d are incorrect because the Java API doesn't define these interfaces or classes.

A 11-2. d

[11.1] Use collections from the java.util.concurrent package with a focus on the advantages over and differences from the traditional java.util collections

Explanation: Option (a) is incorrect because iterators returned by HashMap are fail-fast. If a collection changes (addition, deletion, or modification of elements) after you retrieved an iterator, it will throw a ConcurrentModificationException.

Options (b) and (e) are incorrect because these use invalid class names.

Option (c) is incorrect because ConcurrentMap is an interface; therefore, it can't be instantiated.

Option (d) is correct because iterators returned by ConcurrentHashMap are fail-safe. If a collection changes (elements are added, deleted, or modified) after the iterator is created, they don't throw any runtime exception. These iterators work with a clone of the collection rather than working with the collection itself.

A 11-3. c, d

[11.1] Use collections from the java.util.concurrent package with a focus on the advantages over and differences from the traditional java.util collections

Explanation: Methods put() and take() of the BlockingQueue interface specify in-built locking support to be provided by all the implementing classes to implement the producer–consumer design pattern. LinkedBlockingQueue and ArrayBlockingQueue are concrete implementations of the BlockingQueue interface.

A 11-4. b

[11.1] Use collections from the java.util.concurrent package with a focus on the advantages over and differences from the traditional java.util collections

Explanation: Option (a) is incorrect. The individual operations of classes Concurrent-HashMap, containsKey, and put are atomic and safe to be used concurrently by multiple threads. But when these methods are used together in manipulateMap, it doesn't guarantee thread safety for the time between these two method calls. Multiple calls to atomic operations don't form an atomic operation. You need external locking or synchronization to make such operations thread safe.

Option (b) is correct because method putIfAbsent() in ConcurrentHashMap combines two steps: checking for the existence of a key and replacing its value in a method, and synchronizing the key-value pair access across threads.

Options (c) and (d) are incorrect because these steps will not make a difference in this case.

A 11-5. a

[11.2] Use Lock, ReadWriteLock, and ReentrantLock classes in the java.util.concurrent.locks package to support lock-free, thread-safe programming on single variables

Explanation: Options (b), (c), (d), and (e) are incorrect because they're invalid method names.

A 11-6. b

[11.2] Use Lock, ReadWriteLock, and ReentrantLock classes in the java.util.concurrent.locks package to support lock-free, thread-safe programming on single variables

Explanation: Option (a) is incorrect because, on assigning an object of Reentrant-ReadWriteLock to reference variable myLock, the code won't compile. Class Reentrant-ReadWriteLock and the Lock interface are unrelated. ReentrantReadWriteLock doesn't implement Lock, directly or indirectly.

Option (d) is incorrect because you should unlock an object when you no longer require a lock on it. If you don't, your code will compile anyway.

A 11-7. b

[11.2] Use Lock, ReadWriteLock, and ReentrantLock classes in the java.util.concurrent.locks package to support lock-free, thread-safe programming on single variables

Explanation: Option (b) is incorrect because the read-only lock may be held simultaneously by multiple reader threads, as long as no write lock is acquired.

A 11-8. a

[11.3] Use Executor, ExecutorService, Executors, Callable, and Future to execute tasks using thread pools

Explanation: Option (b) is incorrect because the Executor interface defines just one method, void execute(Runnable). It only accepts objects of Runnable, not Callable.

Options (c) and (d) are incorrect because they use invalid interface names.

A 11-9. b

[11.3] Use Executor, ExecutorService, Executors, Callable, and Future to execute tasks using thread pools

Explanation: Option (a) is incorrect because `ForkJoinPool` doesn't support execution of a scheduled delay of tasks.

Options (c) and (d) are incorrect because they use invalid class names.

A 11-10. d, e

[11.3] Use Executor, ExecutorService, Executors, Callable, and Future to execute tasks using thread pools

Explanation: You can pass either `Runnable` or `Callable` to method `submit()` of `ExecutorService`. Options (d) and (e) correctly implement the `Callable<T>` interface. `Callable`'s method `call()` returns a value. If you don't want it to return a value, implement `Callable<Void>`, define the return type of `call()` to `Void`, and return `null` from it.

A 11-11. c, f, g

[11.4] Use the parallel fork/join framework

Explanation: `ForkJoinPool.invoke()` accepts objects of class `ForkJoinTask`, which is an abstract class. `RecursiveAction` and `RecursiveTask` are abstract subclasses of `ForkJoinTask`.

A 11-12. a

[11.4] Use the parallel fork/join framework

Explanation: A fork/join framework is best suited to be applied to problems that can be divided into independent tasks that can be executed in parallel. Subtasks that need to work a lot with I/O or network connections can't utilize the processors optimally because they might be blocked waiting for an I/O operation. Similarly, when subtasks need to synchronize among themselves, they defeat the whole purpose of executing in parallel to speed up the execution.

Localization

Exam objectives covered in this chapter	What you need to know
[12.1] Read and set the locale by using objects of class Locale	How to access a host's default locale. How to access and assign a Locale for different locale-specific formatting classes and loading resource bundles.
[12.2] Build a resource bundle for each locale	How to define resource-bundle families as Property files or Java classes for each supported Locale.
[12.3] Call a resource bundle from an application	How to load and access a resource bundle for a given Locale in an application. Determine what happens if the specified resource bundle family, resource bundle, or Locale includes invalid values.
[12.4] Format dates, numbers, and currencies for localization with classes NumberFormat and DateFormat (including number format patterns)	The classes that are used to format dates, numbers, and currencies for a given Locale. The factory methods that are defined in classes NumberFormat and DateFormat to retrieve their instances. How to pass Locale information to these classes. The available default and custom patterns to format numbers, currencies, dates, and times.
[12.5] Describe the advantages of localizing an application	The requirements and advantages of localizing an application to multiple locales.
[12.6] Define a locale using language and country codes	How to use Locale constructors, Locale constants, and factory methods to construct and access objects of class Locale, using language and country codes.

719

Imagine you're based in England. You log in to a web application to book movie tickets for 5/1/2020. But when you visit the cinema hall on 5 January 2020, you find out that the tickets were booked for May 1, 2020! What went wrong here? Apparently, the application developer was unaware of the difference in the date formats used by people across the globe and assumed the application to work with the date format used in the United States. The date formats differ in the United States and England. The date formats in the United States are displayed in the format MM-DD-YYYY (month-day-year), whereas in England they're displayed in the format DD-MM-YYYY (day-month-year). The application didn't consider the region you were in, to display the dates appropriately. Will you ever go back and use the same application again? Perhaps not.

The term *user experience* is used to describe a user's experience with an application or an organization and its services or products. Around the world, organizations are striving to improve the experience of their users because happy customers result in profitable businesses.

Apart from improving the user experience, localized applications have become the need of the hour. Creating an internationalized application that can be localized to different users according to their regions, languages, or cultures is an important aspect of application development.

Java includes built-in support for creating internationalized applications that can be easily localized. This chapter covers

- The need and advantages of localizing an application
- Using class `Locale` to create different locales
- Reading and setting locales for an application
- Building a resource bundle for a locale
- Calling a resource bundle from an application
- Formatting dates, numbers, and currencies for localization with classes `Number-Format` and `DateFormat`

Let's get started with an example to help you understand the various aspects of an application that should be localized to improve the user experience.

12.1   *Internationalization and localization*

 [12.5]   Describe the advantages of localizing an application

 [12.6]   Define a locale using language and country codes

Can you spot the difference in the images and the text accompanying them between the left and right panes in figure 12.1? These are screenshots of the same Java application—"Indian Folk Art"—used to register for an art course. The screenshot on the left

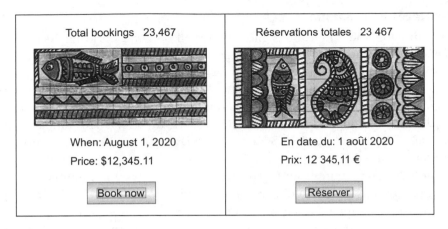

Figure 12.1 **Differences between screenshots of the same Java application for customers in the United States (left) and France (right)**

shows the application screen when used in the United States. The screenshot on the right shows the application screen when used in France.

This is an example of how an internationalized application can be localized to different locations, suiting different users. It's important to adapt applications to location-specific and cultural differences. As you can see in figure 12.1, the screenshots differ in the image used, the text language, and the format of the date, numbers, and currencies. The one on the left uses an image that the designer specifically designed for U.S. users, the text is displayed in English, and the currencies, dates, and numbers are formatted according to how they're used in the United States. The image on the right was specifically created to be displayed for French users. The text is displayed in French, and the currencies, dates, and numbers are formatted according to how they're used in France.

If you want more users from around the world to use your applications, respect their preferences in terms of the languages they use and special formatting (if any) of dates, numbers, and currencies.

Internationalization and localization go hand in hand. *Internationalization* is the process of designing an application in a manner that it can be adapted to various locales. *Localization* is the process of adapting your software for a locale by adding locale-specific components and translating text. The better internationalized an application is, the easier it is to localize it for a particular locale. You can also compare internationalization to making an application generic, and localization to making it specific.

 NOTE Internationalization is also abbreviated as *i18n* because there are 18 letters between i and n. Localization is also abbreviated as *l10n* because there are 10 letters between l and n.

12.1.1 *Advantages of localization*

Different geographical locations and cultures all over the world might use different languages and different formats to display dates, numbers, and currencies. For example, the decimal number 1789.999 is displayed using a different format in the United States (1,789.999), France (1 789,999), and Germany (1.789,999). The date for "the 30th of August 2073" is displayed using a different format in the United States (8/30/73), the United Kingdom (30/08/73), and Germany (30.08.73). Similarly, the currency signs used in the United States ($), the United Kingdom (£), France (€), and Germany (€) are different.

The following phrase from David Brower has been used in multiple contexts like education, business, and building computer applications: "Think globally, act locally." The users of a computer application can span the whole globe. The applications that respect their users by using their language and a regionally and culturally specific display will be more successful than the ones that don't.

BETTER USER EXPERIENCE

User experience includes all aspects of a user's interaction with an application or an organization and its services or products. Localizing an application is a subset of the user's experience. When users get to see data like numbers, currencies, dates, and times in their own languages and formatting styles, it results in a better user experience. In figure 12.1, do you think you'd be happier to use a customized version of this application, for your own country and language?

INTERPRETING INFORMATION IN THE RIGHT MANNER

In the United States, the date October 4, 2020 would be written as 10/04/20 (MM/DD/YY) in short form. On the other hand, the same date in India would be written as 04/10/20 (DD/MM/YY). Users in these countries could misinterpret the dates if they aren't formatted to their own locations.

CULTURALLY SENSITIVE INFORMATION

Different cultures might prefer the use of different colors, or symbols during certain occasions or festivals. An application that can tap this information will not appear indifferent to various cultures and will add to its revenue.

 EXAM TIP   The exam might query you on practical cases of advantages of localizing your application.

In the next section, let's get started with the Java classes that you need to work with to internationalize your application.

12.1.2 *Class java.util.Locale*

Java's API documentation defines a locale as "a specific geographical, political, or cultural region." You can use class `Locale` to capture the information regarding a user's language, country, or region. Figure 12.2 is a world map showing locales that refer to only a language, a region, or both. You can define locales to refer to languages

Figure 12.2   Pictorial representations of multiple locales defined using language, region, or both

like Chinese, English, or Japanese; or regions like Japan, the United Kingdom, and the United States. You can define locales that refer to both language and region. It's interesting to note that the same region or country, like Switzerland, might need to work with multiple languages like German (`Locale("de", "CH")`) and French (`Locale("fr", "CH")`).

Class `Locale` itself doesn't provide any method to format numbers, dates, or currencies. It just encapsulates the data related to the locale of a user, which can be used by other classes such as `NumberFormat` or `DateFormat` to format the data according to a particular locale. Displaying numbers, dates, and currencies according to a user's native language, country, and region are *locale-sensitive* because they need information about the user's locale.

 EXAM TIP   Class `Locale` doesn't itself provide any method to format the numbers, dates, or currencies. You use `Locale` objects to pass locale-specific information to other classes like `NumberFormat` or `DateFormat` to format data.

12.1.3 *Creating and accessing Locale objects*

You can create and access objects of class `Locale` by using

- Constructors of class `Locale`
- `Locale` methods
- `Locale` constants
- Class `Locale.Builder`

Let's get started with using the constructors of class Locale.

CREATE LOCALE OBJECTS USING ITS CONSTRUCTORS

You can create an object of class Locale using one of its following constructors:

```
Locale(String language)
Locale(String language, String country)
Locale(String language, String country, String variant)
```

Here are some examples:

```
Locale french = new Locale("fr");
Locale germany = new Locale("de", "DE");
Locale japan = new Locale("ja", "JP", "MAC");
```

Specify only language ←

Specify language and country ←

Specify language, country, and variant ←

 EXAM TIP　Language is the most important parameter that you pass to a Locale object. All overloaded constructors of Locale accept language as their first parameter. Watch out for exam questions that pass language as the second or third argument to a Locale constructor, which might return an unexpected value.

The preceding constructors accept up to three method parameters. No exceptions are thrown if you pass incorrect or invalid values for these arguments. Because passing correct values for these parameters is important to construct a valid Locale object, let's take a look at the valid values that can be passed to them:

- Language is a *lowercase*, two-letter code. Some of the commonly used values are en (English), fr (French), de (German), it (Italian), ja (Japanese), ko (Korean), and zh (Chinese). You can access the complete list of these language codes at http://www.loc.gov/standards/iso639-2/php/English_list.php.
- Country or region code is an uppercase, two-letter code or three numbers. Table 12.1 shows some commonly used country and region codes. You can access the complete list of these country codes at http://www.chemie.fu-berlin.de/diverse/doc/ISO_3166.html.
- Variant is a vendor- or browser-specific code, such as WIN for Windows and MAC for Macintosh.

Table 12.1　Commonly used country and region codes (ISO-3166)

Description	A-2 code
United States of America	US
United Kingdom	GB
France	FR
Germany	DE

Table 12.1 Commonly used country and region codes (ISO-3166)

Description	A-2 code
Italy	IT
Spain	ES
Japan	JP
Korea	KR
China	CN

 EXAM TIP You don't need to memorize all of the language or country codes that are used to initialize a `Locale`. But the exam expects you to be aware of commonly used values like `en`, `US`, and `fr`.

ACCESS LOCALE OBJECT USING LOCALE'S STATIC METHOD

You can access the current value of a JVM's default locale, by using class `Locale`'s static method `getDefault()`:

```
public static Locale getDefault()
```

 EXAM TIP Watch out for the use of invalid combinations of class and method names to access a JVM's default locale. `Locale.getDefault-Locale()`, `System.getLocale()`, and `System.getDefaultLocale()` are invalid values.

ACCESS LOCALE OBJECTS USING LOCALE CONSTANTS

Class `Locale` defines `Locale` constants for a region, a language, or both. Examples include `Locale.US`, `Locale.UK`, `Locale.ITALY`, `Locale.CHINESE`, `Locale.GERMAN`, and a couple of others for commonly used locales for languages and countries.

 EXAM TIP If you specify only a language constant to define a `Locale`, its region remains undefined. Look out for exam questions that print the region when you don't specify it during the creation of a `Locale`.

CREATE LOCALE OBJECTS USING LOCALE.BUILDER

Starting with Java 7, you can also use `Locale.Builder` to construct a `Locale` object, by calling its constructor and then calling methods `setLanguage()`, `setRegion()`, and `build()`:

```
Locale.Builder builder = new Locale.Builder();
builder.setLanguage("fr");
builder.setRegion("CA");
Locale locale = builder.build();
```

RETRIEVING INFORMATION ABOUT A LOCALE OBJECT

Let's create an object of class `Locale` and use some of its methods:

```
import java.util.*;
public class LocaleMethods {
    public static void main(String[] args) {
        msg("Default Locale:"+Locale.getDefault());
        Locale.setDefault(Locale.ITALY);

        Locale[] all = Locale.getAvailableLocales();

        Locale loc = new Locale("fr", "FR");

        msg("Code Country:"+loc.getCountry());
        msg("Code Language:"+loc.getLanguage());
        msg("Display Country:"+loc.getDisplayCountry());
        msg("Display Language:"+loc.getDisplayLanguage());
        msg("Display Name:"+loc.getDisplayName());
    }
    static void msg(String str) { System.out.println (str); }
}
```

① getDefault() gets default locale

② setDefault() changes default locale

getAvailable-Locales() retrieves all installed and supported Locales.

③ Create a Locale object using Locale's constructor.

getCountry() gets two-letter country code

getLanguage() gets two-letter language code

getDisplay-Name() calls toString on Locale.

getDisplay-Country() gets full country name

getDisplayLanguage() gets full language name

The output of the first line (with added spaces for readability) might differ on your system, depending on your default locale:

```
Default Locale      :en_US
Code Country        :FR
Code Language       :fr
Display Country     :Francia
Display Language    :francese
Display Name        :francese (Francia)
```

The code at **①** retrieves and prints the current default locale associated with the JVM. The code at **②** resets the default locale for the current JVM. It's important to note that only one default locale can be associated with an instance of the JVM. The code at **③** creates an object of `Locale` using the language `fr` (French) and country `FR` (France). It's interesting to note that the invocation of the methods `getDisplayCountry()`, `getDisplayLanguage()`, and `getDisplayName()` display the values in Italian. Assuming your default locale is `Locale.FRANCE`, if you comment out the code at **②**, these methods will print the following values:

```
Diplay Country      :France
Display Language    :français
Display Name        :français (France)
```

But if you create the `Locale` object on line **③** using invalid language and country values (for example, `Locale loc = new Locale ("fren", "FRen")`), the code will not complain and will print out values similar to the following:

```
Display Country     :FREN
Display Language    :fren
Display Name        :fren (FREN)
```

An overloaded version of getDisplayXxx() methods also accepts an object of class Locale to print out the values according to the specified locale.

 EXAM TIP You can use class Locale to retrieve and set the current default locale with a JVM. You can also retrieve an array of all the available and installed locales using Locale.

Now that you know multiple ways to create Locale objects, let's see if you can determine whether Locale objects created using these methods are equivalent or not, in the first "Twist in the Tale" exercise.

Twist in the Tale 12.1

Given the following code:

```
Locale locale1 = Locale.FRENCH;
Locale locale2 = Locale.FRANCE;
Locale locale3 = new Locale.Builder().setLanguage("fr").build();
Locale locale4 = new
     Locale.Builder().setLanguage("fr").setRegion("FR").build();
Locale locale5 = new Locale("fr");
Locale locale6 = new Locale("fr", "FR");
```

what is the output of the following code?

```
System.out.print(locale1.equals(locale3));
System.out.print(locale2.equals(locale6));
System.out.print(locale4.equals(locale5));
```

a truetruefalse

b truefalsefalse

c falsetruefalse

d truetruetrue

12.1.4 Building locale-aware applications

To build locale-aware applications, first you must identify and isolate locale-specific data, like currencies, date-time format, numbers, text messages, labels in a GUI application, sounds, colors, graphics, icons, phone numbers, measurements, personal titles, postal addresses, and so on. Note that this exam covers a subset of building locale-aware applications limited to text, numbers, currencies, dates, and times.

The next step is to identify code that works with locale-specific data. Instead of consuming and displaying this data directly, use locale-specific classes to display and format data according to a selected locale.

Identify the locales that your application must support. The application must ship with locale-specific data for all supported locales in resource bundles. For example, for displaying text in different languages that an application supports, it must be accompanied with the translated text in separate Java classes or properties files (as key-value pairs).

This section outlined the requirements and importance of internationalizing applications so that they can be localized to multiple locales. Java encapsulates the notion of geographical and culturally different locations using class `Locale`. To localize an application to a locale, you must create and pass it appropriate `Locale` objects, so that the application can display locale-specific data, like translated text messages, from appropriate resource bundles.

Let's get started with how to create resource bundles for multiple locales for an application.

12.2   *Resource bundles*

[12.1] Read and set the locale by using the Locale object

[12.2] Build a resource bundle for each locale

[12.3] Call a resource bundle from an application

An abstract class, `java.util.ResourceBundle` represents locale-specific resources. These locale-specific resources, like text messages, the name and location of images and icons, and labels for your GUI application, are stored in a *resource bundle*. Applications supporting multiple locales define locale-specific information in multiple resource bundles, which form part of a *resource-bundle family*. All these resource bundles share a common base name with additional name components specifying the region, language, or variant.

`ResourceBundle` is subclassed by concrete classes `ListResourceBundle` and `PropertyResourceBundle`. You can localize your application by defining your locale-specific resources like text messages, icons, and labels in text files (as .properties files) or as `Object` arrays (two-dimensional) stored in your custom classes that extend `List-ResourceBundle`. In the next section, you'll see how to work with defining locale-specific information stored in .properties files.

 EXAM TIP   An application can include multiple resource bundles to localize to separate locales.

12.2.1   *Implementing resource bundles using .properties files*

Let's start with outlining the resource-bundle family for the sample application shown in figure 12.1, as .properties files. Imagine that you wish to localize the application

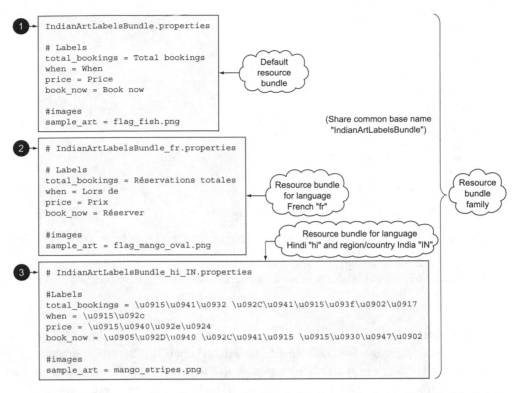

Figure 12.3 Resource-bundle family as .properties files to localize application Indian Folk Art shown in figure 12.1. The resource-bundle family shares a common base name (`IndianArtLabelsBundle`) with additional components to identify their locales.

"Indian Folk Art" for countries and languages United States/English, France/French, and India/Hindi. Figure 12.3 shows the .properties file with key-value pairs. The keys remain constant in all these .properties files and the values vary.

Figure 12.3 shows three .properties files, each referred to as a resource bundle. Together they form part of the resource-bundle family `IndianArtLabelsBundle`:

- IndianArtLabelsBundle.properties (❶ in figure 12.3)
- IndianArtLabelsBundle_fr.properties (❷ in figure 12.3)
- IndianArtLabelsBundle_hi_IN.properties (❸ in figure 12.3)

These three .properties files define the same set of keys. The values for these keys differ in each file. Figure 12.3 shares the bigger picture of the resource bundles. Here's the code of all these individual .properties files (# is used to add comments in a .properties file):

```
# IndianArtLabelsBundle.properties
# Labels
total_bookings = Total bookings
```

```
when = When
price = Price
book_now = Book now
#images
sample_art = flag_fish.png

# IndianArtLabelsBundle_fr.properties
# Labels
total_bookings = Réservations totales
when = Lors de
price = Prix
book_now = Réserver
#images
sample_art = flag_mango_oval.png

# IndianArtLabelsBundle_hi_IN.properties
# Labels
total_bookings = \u0915\u0941\u0932 \u092C\u0941\u0915\u093f\u0902\u0917
when = \u0915\u092c
price = \u0915\u0940\u092e\u0924
book_now = \u0905\u092D\u0940 \u092C\u0941\u0915 \u0915\u0930\u0947\u0902
#images
sample_art = mango_stripes.png
```

Note the use of Unicode values used to display the Devanagri font (characters in Hindi language) for India in file IndianArtLabelsBundle_hi_IN.properties. Because using language in multiple scripts isn't on the exam, I didn't use classes to read text in other scripts; instead, I used Unicode characters in the .properties file.

NOTE   To load and use your resource bundles, correct placement of your class file and resource bundle files is important.

Let's see how you can load these resource bundles in your application to display locale-specific information. Moving ahead with the sample application Indian Folk Art, the following listing (a swing application) can be used to load locale-specific resources.

Listing 12.1   Load and use resource bundles

```java
import java.io.*;
import java.util.*;
import java.text.NumberFormat;
import javax.swing.*;
import java.awt.*;
public class IndianArt {
    JFrame f = new JFrame("BookNow");
    JLabel lTotalBookings = new JLabel();
    JLabel lWhen = new JLabel();
    JLabel lPrice = new JLabel();
    JLabel lImage;
    JButton btnBook = new JButton();
```

 GUI components

```
        private void buildShowUI() {
            f.getContentPane().setLayout(new FlowLayout());
            f.setSize(300, 400);

            f.getContentPane().add(lTotalBookings);
            f.getContentPane().add(lImage);

            JPanel panel1 = new JPanel();
            panel1.setLayout(new GridLayout(4, 1));
            panel1.add(lWhen);
            panel1.add(lPrice);
            panel1.add(new JLabel(""));
            panel1.add(btnBook);

            f.getContentPane().add(panel1);
            f.setVisible(true);
        }
        private void setLocaleSpecificData(Locale locale) {
            ResourceBundle labels = ResourceBundle.getBundle
                        ("resource-bundle.IndianArtLabelsBundle", locale);

            String text = null;
            text = labels.getString("total_bookings");
            lTotalBookings.setText(text);

            text = labels.getString("when");
            lWhen.setText(text);

            text = labels.getString("price");
            lPrice.setText(text);

            text = labels.getString("book_now");
            btnBook.setText(text);

            ImageIcon artImage = new ImageIcon
                            (labels.getString("sample_art"));
            lImage = new JLabel(artImage);
        }
        public static void main(String[] args) {
            IndianArt ia = new IndianArt();
            ia.setLocaleSpecificData(new Locale("hi", "IN"));
            ia.buildShowUI();
        }
    }
```

2 Code to build and show GUI components

3 Load resource-bundle family

4 Get values for keys in individual resource bundles

5 Load different images for different locales.

6 Intantiate IndianArt.

7 Use Locale("hi", "IN") to load resources from IndianArtLabelsBundle _hi_IN.properties.

8 Build and show GUI components.

Let's walk through the code in listing 12.1. The code at **1** and **2** creates and builds a UI using Java's swing components. The code is easy to understand, but don't worry if you don't understand it because swing components aren't on the exam. They're used here to work with a practical example.

The code at **3** loads the locale-specific resource bundle from the resource-bundle family for the specified locale. The static method getBundle() of ResourceBundle accepts the location of the resource-bundle family as the first argument and Locale as the second argument, and loads the single resource bundle, not the complete family.

The resource bundles can also be defined in separate folders (resource-bundle in this example).

The code at ❹ retrieves values for the keys defined in the .properties files, using method getString(), and assigns them to relevant labels. Note how the code at ❺ uses the location of an image file to load locale-specific images. The code at ❻ instantiates class IndianArt. The code at ❼ uses locale Locale("hi", "IN") to load resources from file IndianArtLabelsBundle_hi_IN.properties. The code at ❽ builds and displays the relevant GUI.

You can load a resource bundle for the French language by replacing the line at ❼ with the following:

```
ia.setLocaleSpecificData(Locale.FRANCE);
```

The default resource bundle for family IndianArtLabelsBundle will be loaded if you don't specify an explicit Locale, or if the Locale that you specify doesn't have a corresponding resource bundle for this application. For example

```
ResourceBundle labels = ResourceBundle.getBundle
                ("resource-bundle.IndianArtLabelsBundle");   ◁── No Locale
ia.setLocaleSpecificData(Locale.JAPAN);   ◁──                    argument passed;
                                                                 loads default
                                                                 resource bundle.
```

No Locale argument passed; loads default resource bundle.

Default bundle loaded because application doesn't have corresponding .properties file for Canada.

What happens if the locale that you specify (like Locale.CANADA_FRENCH) or your default locale has French as the language? In this situation, the IndianArtLabelsBundle_fr.properties file will be loaded.

Figure 12.4 shows the output for the sample application when it's loaded with the default resource bundle IndianArtLabelsBundle.properties; the resource bundle for

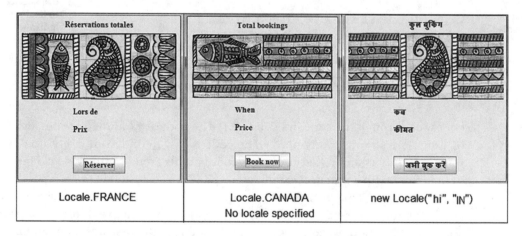

Figure 12.4 Output for the application Indian Folk Art when executed by loading locale-specific data from separate resource bundles

the locale India—language Hindi and region India, IndianArtLabelsBundle_hi_IN .properties; and the resource bundle for the locale France, for the language French, IndianArtLabelsBundle_fr.properties.

As you can see, figure 12.4 doesn't include the formatted numbers. We'll work with them in section 12.3.

 EXAM TIP To implement resource bundles using Property Resource Bundle, create text files with the extension ".properties". Each .properties file is referred to as a *resource bundle*. All the resource bundles are collectively referred to as a *resource-bundle family*.

Because ResourceBundle is an abstract class, when you load the resource bundle using a .properties file, method getBundle() returns an object of class PropertyResource-Bundle (a subclass of ResourceBundle). In the next section, let's see how you can work with ListResourceBundle to define custom classes to manage resource bundles.

12.2.2 *Implementing resource bundles using ListResourceBundle*

You can also define locale-specific data in resource bundles by defining them as subclasses of ListResourceBundle, a subclass of abstract class ResourceBundle. In the previous section, you used .properties files to define resource bundles. The following classes include the same data in a Java class; note the similarity in the naming of the classes, the keys, and their values:

```
import java.util.*;
public class IndianArtLabelsBundle extends ListResourceBundle{
    protected Object[][] getContents() {
        return new Object[][] {
            {"total_bookings", "Total Bookings"},
            {"when", "When"},
            {"price", "Price"},
            {"book_now", "Book Now"},
            {"sample_art", "flag_fish.png"},
        };
    }
}

import java.util.*;
public class IndianArtLabelsBundle_fr extends ListResourceBundle{
    protected Object[][] getContents() {
        return new Object[][] {
            {"total_bookings", "Réservations totales"},
            {"when", "Lors de"},
            {"price", "Prix"},
            {"book_now", "Réserver"},
            {"sample_art", "flag_mango_oval.png"},
        };
    }
}
```

```
import java.util.*;
public class IndianArtLabelsBundle_hi_IN extends ListResourceBundle{
    protected Object[][] getContents() {
        return new Object[][] {
            {"total_bookings", "\u0915\u0941\u0932
\u092C\u0941\u0915\u093f\u0902\u0917"},
            {"when", "\u0915\u092c"},
            {"price", "\u0915\u0940\u092e\u0924"},
            {"book_now", "\u0905\u092D\u0940 \u092C\u0941\u0915
\u0915\u0930\u0947\u0902"},
            {"sample_art", "mango_stripes.png"},
        };
    }
}
```

Given that there's no difference in the name of these resource-bundle files, the code in code listing 12.1 will work without any modifications. But in this case, the code at ❸ from listing 12.1 (ResourceBundle.getBundle) will return an instance of List-ResourceBundle.

Figure 12.5 shows the resource bundles defined as Java classes.

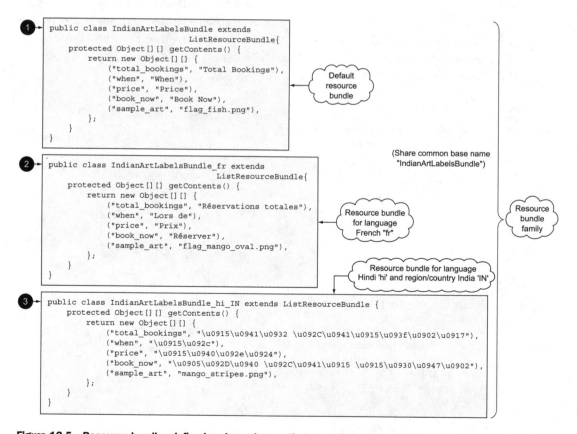

Figure 12.5   Resource bundles defined as Java classes that are subclasses of class `ListResourceBundle`

Because no changes were made to listing 12.1, you'll get the same results when you execute the application.

So far so good. What happens if you can't load a resource-bundle family or a particular resource bundle? Let's examine this situation in detail in the next section.

12.2.3 *Loading resource bundles for invalid values*

On the exam, you're very likely to be asked questions on what happens if you pass invalid resource-bundle names or locales while loading your resource-bundle family.

ISSUE WITH LOADING RESOURCE-BUNDLE FAMILY

When your class can't load the specified resource bundle due to an incorrect name of the resource-bundle family or because it can't locate it, it will throw a runtime exception. For example, imagine that the resource bundle XYBundle doesn't exist or isn't locatable:

```
ResourceBundle bundle = ResourceBundle.getBundle("XYBundle", Locale.JAPAN);
```

This code will throw a runtime exception:

```
Exception in thread "main" java.util.MissingResourceException: Can't find
    bundle for base name XYBundle, locale ja_JP
```

ISSUE WITH LOADING RESOURCE BUNDLE FOR A LOCALE

Now what happens if you specify a Locale for which no matching resource bundle exists? Given a Locale, table 12.2 lists the order in which Java searches for a matching resource bundle.

Table 12.2   Search order for a resource bundle for a Locale

Order	Resource bundle
1	bundleName_localeLanguage_localeCountry_localeVariant
2	bundleName_localeLanguage_localeCountry
3	bundleName_localeLanguage
4	bundleName_defaultLanguage_defaultCountry_defaultVariant
5	bundleName_defaultLanguage_defaultCountry
6	bundleName_defaultLanguage
7	bundleName

Imagine that you've defined the following resource bundles as .properties files for an application. Assuming that the default locale on your system is en_US, which resource bundle will be loaded by the Java Runtime Environment (JRE) for Locale.FRANCE? (For Locale.FRANCE, region is FR and language is French, abbreviated as fr.)

- MyResourceBundle_de_DE.properties
- MyResourceBundle_de.properties

- MyResourceBundle_FR.properties
- MyResourceBundle.properties

Because an exact match isn't found for MyResourceBundle_fr_FR.properties, the JRE looks for MyResourceBundle_fr.properties, which is also missing. No matches are found for the default locale—that is, en_US. So the JRE loads the base resource bundle—that is, MyResourceBundle.properties.

 EXAM TIP   If no matching resource bundles can be found or loaded, the JRE throws the runtime exception MissingResourceException. If no matching resource bundle is found, the JRE tries to load the base resource bundle—that is, one that doesn't include any additional name components, bundleName.

The next "Twist in the Tale" exercise uses modified values for the resource bundles and a given locale. Let's see whether you can determine the correct answer. Good luck.

Twist in the Tale 12.2

The default locale of the host system is Locale.JAPAN and the following list of resource-bundle files is included with the application:

- a MessagesBundle_fr.properties
- b MessagesBundle_fr_FR.properties
- c MessagesBundle_DE.properties
- d MessagesBundle_de.properties
- e MessagesBundle.properties

Which of these resource bundles will be loaded for locale de_DE?

In this section, we created resource bundles to store constant text, like messages and file locations, used by an application to localize to a particular locale. We created the resource bundles as text files (.properties files) and as subclasses of List-ResourceBundle.

In the next section, you'll see how to format dates, numbers, and currencies for different locales in an application.

12.3   Formatting dates, numbers, and currencies for locales

> [12.4]   Format dates, numbers, and currencies for localization with the
> NumberFormat and DateFormat classes (including number format
> patterns)

To parse or format numbers, dates, and currencies for a specific locale, you can use classes from packages `java.util` and `java.text`. Table 12.3 will help you better relate the features with the relevant classes.

Table 12.3   List of features and the relevant classes used to implement them

Feature	Relevant class
Format or parse numbers	`java.text.NumberFormat`, `java.text.DecimalFormat`
Format or parse currencies	`java.text.NumberFormat`
Format or parse dates	`java.text.DateFormat`, `java.util.Date`, `java.util.Calendar`

Classes `java.text.NumberFormat` and `java.text.DateFormat` are abstract classes that define static methods to retrieve an object from these classes. Because abstract classes cannot be instantiated, these static methods return an object of subclasses of these classes. The static method `getInstance()` in class `NumberFormat` returns an object of class `DecimalFormat`. The static method `getInstance()` in class `DateFormat` returns an instance of class `SimpleDateFormat`. So a reference variable of classes `NumberFormat` and `DateFormat` refers to an object of their subclasses—that is, `DecimalFormat` and `SimpleDateFormat`. Figure 12.6 shows a hierarchial relationship between the relevant formatting classes.

 EXAM TIP   Classes `NumberFormat` and `DateFormat` are abstract classes. If an exam question tries to instantiate these classes, be aware that they won't compile.

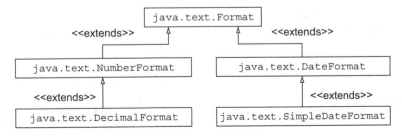

Figure 12.6   Hierarchical relationship between classes used for formatting numbers, currencies, dates, and times

12.3.1 *Format numbers*

Class `NumberFormat` can be used to format and parse numbers according to the default
or a particular locale. To do this, you need an object of this class. Class `NumberFormat`
defines convenient static methods `getInstance()` and `getInstance(Locale)` to retrieve
`NumberFormat` objects for the default locale or a specific locale. Because `NumberFormat`
is an abstract class, these methods return an object of its subclasses. If you need to format or parse numbers according to a specific locale, use the latter method. Once you
have access to an object of class `NumberFormat`, call its methods `format()` and `parse()`
to format a number and parse a string value according to a particular locale.

Let's get started with an example, which formats and parses number and string values for the default and specific locales:

```
import java.util.Locale;
import java.text.NumberFormat;
public class FormatNumbers {
    public static void main(String[] args) {
        double num = 12345.1111;
        defaultLocale(num);
        specificLocale(Locale.GERMANY, num);
        specificLocale(Locale.FRANCE, num);
        specificLocale(Locale.US, num);
    }
    static void defaultLocale(double num) {
        NumberFormat nfDefault = NumberFormat.getInstance();
        msg("\nDefault Locale");
        msg("formatting: " + nfDefault.format(num));
        try {
            msg("parsing    : " + nfDefault.parse("12345.1111"));
        }
        catch (java.text.ParseException e) {
            msg(e.toString());
        }
    }
    static void specificLocale(Locale locale, double num) {
        NumberFormat nfSpecific = NumberFormat.getInstance(locale);
        msg("\n"+locale.getDisplayCountry());
        msg("formatting: " + nfSpecific.format(num));
        try {
            msg("parsing    : " + nfSpecific.parse("12345.1111"));
        }
        catch (java.text.ParseException e) {
            msg(e.toString());
        }
    }
    static void msg(String str) { System.out.println(str); }
}
```

Get `NumberFormat` for the current default locale.

Get `NumberFormat` for the specified locale.

The output of this code is as follows (this might vary on your system):

```
Default Locale
formatting: 12,345.111
parsing    : 12345.1111
```

```
Germany
formatting: 12.345,111
parsing   : 123451111

France
formatting: 12 345,111
parsing   : 12345

United States
formatting: 12,345.111
parsing   : 12345.1111
```

As visible from the output, different locales may use different thousand and decimal separator values. Here's what's happening in the preceding example:

- Method `main()` calls methods `defaultLocale()` and `specificLocale()` with Locale values `Locale.GERMANY`, `Locale.FRANCE`, and `Locale.US`.
- Method `defaultLocale()` retrieves a `NumberFormat` using method `getInstance()` and calls its methods `format()` and `parse()` to format and parse the values according to the JVM's current default locale.
- Method `specificLocale()` performs the same tasks as method `default-Locale()`, but with a locale-specific `NumberFormat`.

This exam requires you to determine the appropriate methods to use if you want to use the default locale or a specific locale. The preceding example shows that you just need to retrieve an appropriate `NumberFormat` that caters to the default locale or a specific locale. When you execute methods `format()` and `parse()`, the instance of class `Number-Format` executes them according to the `Locale` information passed to it. Table 12.4 lists all the factory methods that can be used to access an object of `NumberFormat`.

Table 12.4 Factory methods in `NumberFormat` to create and return its objects

Method name	Method description
`getInstance()`	Returns a general-purpose number format for the current default locale.
`getInstance(Locale inLocale)`	Returns a general-purpose number format for a specified locale.
`getIntegerInstance()`	Returns an integer number format for the current default locale.
`getIntegerInstance(Locale inLocale)`	Returns an integer number format for a specified locale.
`getNumberInstance()`	Returns a general-purpose number format for the current default locale.
`getNumberInstance(Locale inLocale)`	Returns a general-purpose number format for a specified locale.
`getPercentInstance()`	Returns a percentage format for the current default locale.

Table 12.4 Factory methods in `NumberFormat` to create and return its objects *(continued)*

Method name	Method description
`getPercentInstance(Locale inLocale)`	Returns a percentage format for a specified locale.
`getCurrencyInstance()`	Returns a currency format for the current default locale.
`getCurrencyInctance(Locale inLocale)`	Returns a currency format for the specified locale.

The instances retrieved using `getIntegerInstance` would only consider the integer part of a number. The instances retrieved using `getPercentInstance` would display fractions as percentages. For example, it will format 98% for the value `.98`.

12.3.2 Format currencies

You can use class `java.text.NumberFormat` to format the currencies for the default or any specific locale. For example

```
import java.util.Locale;
import java.text.NumberFormat;
public class FormatCurrency {
    public static void main(String[] args) {
        double amt = 12345.1111;
        defaultLocale(amt);
        specificLocale(Locale.UK, amt);
        specificLocale(Locale.GERMANY, amt);
        specificLocale(Locale.FRANCE, amt);
        specificLocale(Locale.US, amt);
        specificLocale(Locale.JAPAN, amt);
    }
    static void defaultLocale(double num) {
        NumberFormat nfDefault = NumberFormat.getCurrencyInstance();      // Default NumberFormat for currency
        msg("\nDefault Locale Currency:"+nfDefault.getCurrency());
        msg("formatted amt: " + nfDefault.format(num));
    }
    static void specificLocale(Locale locale, double num) {
        NumberFormat nfSpec = NumberFormat.getCurrencyInstance(locale);   // Numberformat for currency, a specific locale
        msg("\n"+locale.getDisplayCountry()+
                        " Currency:"+nfSpec.getCurrency());               // Display locale country and currency as three-letter word
        msg("formatted amt: " + nfSpec.format(num));
    }
    static void msg(String str) { System.out.println (str); }
}
```

The output of this code on the Command prompt is as follows (this might vary on your system):

```
Default Locale Currency:USD
formatted amt: $12,345.11

United Kingdom Currency:GBP
formatted amt: £12,345.11
```

```
Germany Currency:EUR
formatted amt: 12.345,11 €

France Currency:EUR
formatted amt: 12 345,11 €

United States Currency:USD
formatted amt: $12,345.11

Japan Currency:JPY
formatted amt: ?12,345
```

Before we discuss why the currency symbols didn't display properly, here's a quick summary of the code:

- Method `main()` calls method `defaultLocale()` without passing any `Locale` arguments and `specificLocale` with `Locale` values like `Locale.GERMANY`, `Locale.FRANCE`, `Locale.US`, and others.
- Method `defaultLocale()` retrieves an object of class `NumberFormat` using method `getCurrencyInstance()` and calls its method `format()` to format the amount according to the JVM's current default locale.
- Method `specificLocale()` performs the same tasks as method `default-Locale()`, but with a locale-specific instance of class `NumberFormat`, retrieved using method `getCurrencyInstance(Locale)`.

Now, going back to the output of the code, did you notice the Yen symbol didn't print properly in the previous output? This can be due to either an issue with the range of values that can be displayed by the Command prompt, or if the `NumberFormat` instance doesn't support the symbol of a particular locale. There's little you can do about the latter reason, so let's experiment with the first one. Here's the code to send the formatted amount to a `JTextArea` (same as before, with just the introduction of a `JFrame` and `JTextArea` to display the output), and the rest of the code remains the same (modifications in bold):

```
import java.util.Locale;
import java.text.NumberFormat;
import javax.swing.*;
public class FormatCurrencyVer2 {
    static JTextArea textArea = new JTextArea();
    public static void main(String[] args) {
        JFrame f = new JFrame("Currency");
        f.getContentPane().add(textArea);
        f.setSize(300, 400);
        double amt = 12345.1111;
        defaultLocale(amt);
        specificLocale(Locale.UK, amt);
        specificLocale(Locale.GERMANY, amt);
        specificLocale(Locale.FRANCE, amt);
        specificLocale(Locale.US, amt);
        specificLocale(Locale.JAPAN, amt);
        f.setVisible(true);
    }
```

```
// methods defaultLocale ..same as defined in previous example
// method specificLocale ..same as defined in previous example
static void msg(String str) {
    textArea.append("\n" + str);
}
```
}

Figure 12.7 shows the output from this modified code—the image of the JFrame that outputs the result.

As visible in Figure 12.7, the currency symbol for Japan is displayed properly. The font used in swing components covers a greater subset of the Unicode chart than the one used in the Windows console.

The examples that we used to format the numbers and currencies are the same, except in retrieving the instance of class NumberFormat. To format currencies, we used the NumberFormat's static methods getCurrencyInstance() and getCurrencyInstance (Locale). To format the numbers, we used NumberFormat's static methods getInstance() and getInstance(Locale) (static method getNumber-Instance() can also be used).

When you execute the format method on an instance of class NumberFormat, it knows whether it's supposed to format it as a currency value or as a number. I deliberately used a version of this code that didn't display the currency sign correctly so you could see the symbols displayed with the modified code. This is just to make you understand that the code that you write to format currencies may be fine, but you still may not get the expected output, due to other issues.

Figure 12.7 Output in a JTextArea that can handle the display of a greater subset of the Unicode character set

 EXAM TIP The exam requires you to determine the appropriate methods to use if you want to use the default locale or a specific locale, given a scenario. To format numbers and currencies, you need an instance of Number-Format. To format numbers and currencies in the default locale, retrieve an instance of NumberFormat using the methods getInstance() or get-NumberInstance() and getCurrencyInstance(), respectively. To format numbers and currencies in a specific locale, retrieve an instance of NumberFormat using the methods getInstance(Locale) or getNumber-Instance(Locale) and getCurrencyInstance(Locale), respectively. Once the NumberFormat instance has the locale information with it, it can format and parse the numbers and currencies accordingly.

12.3.3 *Format dates*

You can use class DateFormat to format and parse dates and times according to the default locale or a particular locale. Class DateFormat defines a lot of overloaded static methods to retrieve an instance of a DateFormat. Because class DateFormat itself is an abstract class, these static methods return an instance of its subclass, SimpleDate-Format. Whenever an *object* of class DateFormat is referred to, you should read it as an object of class SimpleDateFormat. Once you get an object of class DateFormat, you can use its format() and parse() methods to format and parse dates according to the default or a specific locale.

Let's get started with the static overloaded methods to retrieve an object of class DateFormat. Here's a list of these factory methods, defined in class DateFormat:

```
static DateFormat getInstance()
static DateFormat getDateInstance()
static DateFormat getDateInstance(int style)
static DateFormat getDateInstance(int style, Locale aLocale)
static DateFormat getDateTimeInstance()
static DateFormat getDateTimeInstance(int dateStyle, int timeStyle)
static DateFormat getDateTimeInstance(int dateStyle,
                                      int timeStyle, Locale aLocale)
static DateFormat getTimeInstance()
static DateFormat getTimeInstance(int style)
static DateFormat getTimeInstance(int style, Locale aLocale)
```

These factory methods accept zero to three method arguments. Let's take a look at the values that can be passed on these method arguments:

- aLocale—A specific locale for which you need to format your date value
- style, dateStyle, timeStyle—One of the following integer constant values defined in DateFormat
  - DateFormat.SHORT: is completely numeric, such as 31.07.20 or 10:30 pm
  - DateFormat.MEDIUM is longer, such as Jul 31, 2020 or 10:30:17 pm
  - DateFormat.LONG is longer, such as July 31, 2020 or 3:30:32 pm PST
  - DateFormat.FULL is pretty completely specified, such as Saturday, July 31, 2020 AD or 10:30:32 pm PST

For the overloaded method getDateTimeInstance(), if you pass on DateFormat.FULL to the variable argument dateStyle, and DateFormat.SHORT to the argument time-Style, the time will be returned in format DateFormat.FULL. If the value that you pass to the argument dateStyle has a more elaborate style value than the value passed to the variable timeStyle, the argument dateStyle overshadows the argument time-Style. Once you have an object of class DateFormat in place, call its parse and format methods to parse and format a date for the default of a specific locale.

The following listing is an example that formats a given date according to the default locale and a number of predefined Locale values, each with the styles FULL, LONG, MEDIUM, and SHORT:

Listing 12.2   Format date according to different locales

```java
import java.util.*;
import java.text.DateFormat;
public class FormatDates {
    static int[] styles = new int[]{DateFormat.FULL,
                                    DateFormat.LONG,
                                    DateFormat.MEDIUM,
                                    DateFormat.SHORT};
    static String[] desc = new String[]{"FULL","LONG","MEDIUM","SHORT"};
    public static void main(String[] args) {
        Date date = new Date();
        defaultLocale(date);
        specificLocale(Locale.GERMANY, date);
        specificLocale(Locale.FRANCE, date);
        specificLocale(Locale.CHINA, date);
    }
    static void defaultLocale(Date date) {
        msg("\nDefault Locale:");
        for (int style : styles) {
            DateFormat nfDefault = DateFormat.getDateInstance(style);
            msg(desc[style]+"\t:" + nfDefault.format(date));
        }
    }
    static void specificLocale(Locale locale, Date date) {
        msg("\n"+locale.getDisplayCountry());
        for (int style : styles) {
            DateFormat spec = DateFormat.getDateInstance(style, locale);
            msg(desc[style]+"\t:" + spec.format(date));
        }
    }
    static void msg(String str) { System.out.println(str); }
}
```

Valid date and time styles

DateFormat for default locale, with a specific style

DateFormat for a specific locale, with a specific style

Here's the output of this code on the Command prompt (this might vary depending on your system):

```
Default Locale:
FULL        :Sunday, August 1, 2020
LONG        :August 1, 2020
MEDIUM      :Aug 1, 2020
SHORT       :8/1/20

Germany
FULL        :Sonntag, 1. August 2020
LONG        :1. August 2020
MEDIUM      :01.08.2020
SHORT       :01.08.20

France
FULL        :dimanche 1 août 2020
LONG        :1 août 2020
MEDIUM      :1 août 2020
SHORT       :01/08/20
```

```
China
FULL        :2020?8?1? ???
LONG        :2020?8?1?
MEDIUM      :2020-8-1
SHORT       :20-8-1
```

Let's look at what's happening in the preceding code:

- Method `main()` calls methods `defaultLocale()` and `specificLocale()` with `Locale` values `Locale.GERMANY`, `Locale.FRANCE`, and `Locale.CHINA`.
- Method `defaultLocale()` retrieves an object of class `DateFormat` using method `getDateInstance()`, passing to it `style` values. It then calls its method `format()` to format the date according to the JVM's current default locale and a specified style.
- Method `specificLocale()` performs the same tasks as method `default-Locale()`, but with a locale-specific instance of class `DateFormat`, retrieved using method `getDateInstance(style, Locale)`. Method `format()` formats the date according to the specified locale and style.

Again, because the Command prompt might not support the Unicode character set, the Chinese characters aren't displayed as required on the Command prompt. The formatted date value when printed to a `JTextArea` prints it appropriately (the default font used by swing components can handle the Unicode characters). Figure 12.8 shows the screenshot.

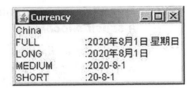

Figure 12.8 Formatted date and time in Chinese

12.3.4 *Formatting and parsing time for a specific locale*

The previous example prints dates formatted for different locales and styles (`FULL`, `LONG`, `MEDIUM`, and `SHORT`). Similarly, you can also format the time for different locales and styles. To do so, you just need to retrieve the `DateFormat` instance using one of the following factory methods:

```
static DateFormat getTimeInstance()
static DateFormat getTimeInstance(int style)
static DateFormat getTimeInstance(int style, Locale aLocale)
```

Let's see this in action. Revisit the previous example and listing 12.2. Replace the following lines of code:

```
DateFormat nfDefault = DateFormat.getDateInstance(style);
DateFormat spec = DateFormat.getDateInstance(style, locale);
```

with these lines of code:

```
DateFormat nfDefault = DateFormat.getTimeInstance(style);
DateFormat spec = DateFormat.getTimeInstance(style, locale);
```

The output of the code after making these changes (using `getTimeInstance()`) is as follows (this might vary on your system):

```
Default Locale:
FULL            :11:05:07 AM IST
LONG            :11:05:07 AM IST
MEDIUM          :11:05:07 AM
SHORT           :11:05 AM

Germany
FULL            :11.05 Uhr IST
LONG            :11:05:07 IST
MEDIUM          :11:05:07
SHORT           :11:05

France
FULL            :11 h 05 IST
LONG            :11:05:07 IST
MEDIUM          :11:05:07
SHORT           :11:05
```

12.3.5 *Formatting and parsing date and time together for a specific locale*

To print the date and time together, use one of the following factory methods to retrieve the `DateFormat` instance:

```
static DateFormat getDateTimeInstance()
static DateFormat getDateTimeInstance(int dateStyle, int timeStyle)
static DateFormat getDateTimeInstance(int dateStyle,
                                      int timeStyle, Locale aLocale)
```

Revisit listing 12.2 and replace the following lines of code:

```
DateFormat nfDefault = DateFormat.getDateInstance(style);
DateFormat nfSpecific = DateFormat.getDateInstance(style, locale);
```

with these lines of code:

```
DateFormat nfDefault = DateFormat.getDateTimeInstance(style, style);
DateFormat nfSpec = DateFormat.getDateTimeInstance(style, style, locale);
```

The output of the modified code includes both the date and time:

```
Default Locale:
FULL            :Sunday, August 1, 2010 11:33:33 AM IST
LONG            :August 1, 2010 11:33:33 AM IST
MEDIUM          :Aug 1, 2010 11:33:33 AM
SHORT           :8/1/10 11:33 AM

Germany
FULL            :Sonntag, 1. August 2010 11.33 Uhr IST
LONG            :1. August 2010 11:33:33 IST
MEDIUM          :01.08.2010 11:33:33
SHORT           :01.08.10 11:33
```

```
France
FULL           :dimanche 1 août 2010 11 h 33 IST
LONG           :1 août 2010 11:33:33 IST
MEDIUM         :1 août 2010 11:33:33
SHORT          :01/08/10 11:33
```

In this example, note that we're passing the same style argument to the dateStyle and timeStyle. If the method argument passed to the dateStyle is more liberal in terms of the method argument passed to timeStyle, the latter will be ignored.

 EXAM TIP   If the method argument passed to the dateStyle is more liberal in terms of the method argument passed to timeStyle, the latter will be ignored.

12.3.6 *Using custom date and time patterns with SimpleDateFormat*

All the previous examples used the predefined formats (FULL, LONG, MEDIUM, and SHORT). Though these styles are sufficient for formatting dates and times for almost every condition, you can create your own style by using class java.text.SimpleDate-Format, using one of the following constructors:

```
SimpleDateFormat()
SimpleDateFormat(String pattern)
SimpleDateFormat(String pattern, Locale locale)
```

You can pass the customized pattern as a string value to format the date and time. For example, if you'd like to format the date as year-month(in digits)-day, you can use class SimpleDateFormat, as follows:

```
Date date = new Date();
SimpleDateFormat defaultFormatter = new SimpleDateFormat("yyyy-MM-dd");
System.out.println(defaultFormatter.format(date));
```

If you run this code on August 2, 2020, its output would be:

```
2020-08-02
```

It's quite interesting to note the change in the formatted date value, if you vary the count of the letter *M* in the preceding pattern from one to four or more, as follows:

```
Date date = new Date();
defaultFormatter = new SimpleDateFormat("yyyy-M-dd");        Prints
System.out.println(defaultFormatter.format(date));      ⟵ "2020-8-02"

defaultFormatter = new SimpleDateFormat("yyyy-MMM-dd");      Prints
System.out.println(defaultFormatter.format(date));      ⟵ "2020-Aug-02"

defaultFormatter = new SimpleDateFormat("yyyy-MMMM-dd");     Prints
System.out.println(defaultFormatter.format(date));      ⟵ "2020-August-02"
```

If you wish to format the preceding date as "Day Sun, 02th Aug 2020", modify the pattern and create an object of class `SimpleDateFormat`, as follows:

```
defaultFormatter = new SimpleDateFormat("'Day' EE", 'dd'th' MMM yyyy");
System.out.println(defaultFormatter.format(date));
```
◁── **Prints "Day Sun, 02th Aug 2020"**

To format according to a specific locale, create an object of `SimpleDateFormat` by passing it a `Locale` instance:

```
Date date = new Date();
SimpleDateFormat spFormatter = new SimpleDateFormat
                         ("yyyy-MMMM-dd HH:mm:ss", Locale.FRANCE);
System.out.println(spFormatter.format(date));
```
◁── **Prints "2020-août-02 18:00:29"**

Table 12.5 includes a list of the pattern letters, what they mean, and an example or range of their values.

Table 12.5   List of the pattern letters that can be used to create a custom pattern for formatting dates and times

Letter	Date/time component	Example/range
G	Era designator	AD
Y	Year	2010; 10
w (small w)	Week in year	30
W	Week in month	2
D	Day in year	232
d (small d)	Day in month	11
E	Day in week	Tuesday; Tue
a (small a)	am/pm marker	pm
H	Hour in day	(0-23)
h (small h)	Hour in am/pm	(1-12)
m (small m)	Minute in hour	29
S (small s)	Second in minute	12
S	Millisecond	869
z (small z)	General time zone	Pacific Standard Time; PST; GMT-08:00
Z	RFC 822 Time Zone	-0800

Be very careful with the case of the letters that you use in a pattern for formatting dates. While working with a project, I used the pattern yyyy-mm-dd to format a date, but the code repeatedly returned the month number as 30! After validating the pattern, I realized that *mm* is used for minutes and not months (I executed my code at 18.30 hrs! ☺). This is a perfect recipe for subtle bugs, which are difficult to trace!

 EXAM TIP Make note of the case of the letters that you use in patterns for formatting dates. The pattern *m* is used for minutes in an hour, not months in a year.

12.3.7 *Creating class Date object using class Calendar*

Method `format()` defined in classes `DateFormat` and `SimpleDateFormat`, which you use to format your date values, accepts objects of class `java.util.Date`. But many of the methods defined in class `Date` have been deprecated and you should only use it to create the current date and time using the default constructor. To create other dates

- Create an object of class `Calendar` with the current date and time.
- Call one of its overloaded `set()` methods to set the year, month, day, hour, minute, and seconds:
  - `set(int year, int month, int date)`
  - `void set(int year, int month, int date, int hourOfDay, int minute)`
  - `void set(int year, int month, int date, int hourOfDay, int minute, int second)`
- Use its method `getTime()` to retrieve the corresponding `Date` object.

For example

```
Calendar cal = Calendar.getInstance();          ◄———  Current date and time
cal.set(1973, Calendar.AUGUST, 30, 14, 10, 40); ◄———  Set date value as Aug 30 1973, 14:10:40
Date date = cal.getTime();                       ◄———  Create Date object from calendar
```

 NOTE In real projects, working with literal values to specify months or days (Sunday, Monday, and so on) is never preferred. Always use constant values for them.

Don't get confused by the name of the method `getTime()`. Class `Calendar`'s method `getTime()` returns a `Date` object. But `Date`'s method `getTime()` returns a `long` value (number of milliseconds since January 1, 1970, 00:00:00 GMT represented by the Date object).

12.4 *Summary*

Users of an application span the whole globe and internationalized applications that can be localized to specific locales have become a *need* rather than a *want*. In this chapter, you learned how you can internationalize your Java applications using `Locales`, resource bundles, and classes for formatting numbers, dates, and currencies, so that they can be localized to multiple locales.

The first step in building locale-aware applications is to identify and isolate locale-specific data, like currencies, dates, times, numbers, text messages, labels in a GUI application, and so on. The next step is to identify code that works with locale-specific data. Instead of consuming and displaying the locale-specific data directly, use locale-specific classes to display and format data according to a selected locale.

Java captures the idea of regions with geographical, language, and cultural differences using a Locale. A Locale object doesn't format or select your locale-aware data. It's used by other classes to load locale-specific resource bundles and locale-specific formatting classes. Locale-specific resources like text messages, name and location of images and icons, and labels for your GUI application (constant data) are stored in a resource bundle. Applications supporting multiple locales define locale-specific information in multiple resource bundles, which form part of a resource-bundle family. All these resource bundles share a common base name with additional name components specifying the region, language, or variant.

Abstract class ResourceBundle is subclassed by concrete classes ListResource-Bundle and PropertyResourceBundle. You can localize your application by defining your locale-specific resources in text files (as .properties files) or as Object arrays stored in your custom classes that extend ListResourceBundle.

Abstract classes java.text.NumberFormat and java.text.DateFormat are used to format locale-specific numbers, currencies, dates, and times.

REVIEW NOTES

This section lists the main points covered in this chapter.

Internationalization and localization

- An internationalized application can be localized to different regions.
- Internationalization is the process of designing an application in a manner that it can be adapted to various locales.
- Localization is the process of adapting your software for a locale by adding locale-specific components and translating text.
- Different locales might use different languages or formats of currency, dates, and numbers.
- Advantages of localization
  - Better user experience
  - Interpreting information in the right manner
  - Adapting according to culturally sensitive information
- Class Locale doesn't itself provide any method to format the numbers, dates, or currencies. You use Locale objects to pass locale-specific information to other classes like NumberFormat or DateFormat to format data.

- You can create and access objects of class `Locale` by using
  - Constructors of class `Locale`
  - `Locale` methods
  - `Locale` constants
  - Class `Locale.Builder`
- Overloaded constructors of `Locale`
  - `Locale(String language)`
  - `Locale(String language, String country)`
  - `Locale(String language, String country, String variant)`
- No exceptions are thrown if you pass incorrect or invalid values to a `Locale` constructor.
- Language is a lowercase, two-letter code. Some of the commonly used values are en (English), fr (French), de (German), it (Italian), ja (Japanese), ko (Korean), and zh (Chinese).
- Country or region code is an uppercase, two-letter code. Some of the commonly used values are US (United States), FR (France), JP (Japan), DE (Germany), and CN (China).
- Variant is a vendor- or browser-specific code, such as WIN for Windows and MAC for Macintosh.
- Language is the most important parameter that you pass to a `Locale` object. All overloaded constructors of `Locale` accept language as their first parameter.
- You don't need to memorize all of the language or country codes that are used to initialize a `Locale`. But the exam expects you to be aware of commonly used values like EN, US, and FR.
- You can access the current value of a JVM's default locale by using class `Locale`'s static method `getDefault()`. The methods `Locale.getDefaultLocale()`, `System.getLocale()`, and `System.getDefaultLocale()` are invalid methods to access a system's default locale.
- Class `Locale` defines `Locale` constants for a region, a language, or both. Examples include `Locale.US`, `Locale.UK`, `Locale.ITALY`, `Locale.CHINESE`, and `Locale.GERMAN` for commonly used locales for languages and countries.
- If you specify only a language constant to define a `Locale`, its region remains undefined. Look out for exam questions that print the region when you don't specify it during the creation of a `Locale`.
- You can also use `Locale.Builder` to construct a `Locale` object by calling its constructor and then calling methods `setLanguage()`, `setRegion()`, and `build()`.
- To build locale-aware applications, first you must identify and isolate locale-specific data, like currencies, date-time format, numbers, text messages, labels in a GUI application, sounds, colors, graphics, icons, phone numbers, measurements, personal titles, postal addresses, and so on.
- Instead of consuming and displaying this data directly, locale-specific classes are used to display or format data according to a selected locale.

Resource bundles

- To implement resource bundles using property files, create text files with the extension .properties. Each .properties file is referred to as a resource bundle. All the resource bundles are collectively referred to as a resource-bundle family.

- An abstract class `ResourceBundle` represents locale-specific resources.

- Locale-specific resources like text messages, the name and location of images and icons, and labels for your GUI application are stored in a resource bundle.

- Applications supporting multiple locales define locale-specific information in multiple resource bundles, which form part of a resource-bundle family.

- All these resource bundles share a common base name with additional name components specifying the region, language, or variant.

- You can implement resource bundles using either .properties files or Java classes.

- To support countries and languages United States/English (US/en) and France/French(FR/fr), an application (myApp) might define the resource-bundle files as:
  - myapp_en.properties, myapp_fr.properties
  - myapp_en_US.properties, myapp_fr_FR.properties

- There's no link between an application name and the resource bundle base name. The following names for resource bundle files are also valid for the previous note:
  - messages_en.properties, messages_fr.properties
  - messages_en_US.properties, messages_fr_FR.properties

- All the .properties files in a bundle contain the same keys, with different values.

- Here's the code to load the locale-specific resource bundle from the resource-bundle family for a locale:

```
ResourceBundle labels = ResourceBundle.getBundle("resource-
bundle.IndianArtLabelsBundle", locale);
```

- The static method `getBundle()` of `ResourceBundle` accepts the location of the resource-bundle family as the first argument and `Locale` as the second argument, and loads the single resource bundle, not the complete family.

- You can call methods `getString()`, `getObject()`, `keySet()`, `getKeys()`, and `getStringArray()` from class `ResourceBundle` to access its keys and values.

- You can also define locale-specific data in resource bundles by defining them as subclasses of `ListResourceBundle`, a subclass of abstract class `Resource-Bundle`.

- When your class can't load the specified resource bundle due to an incorrect name of the resource-bundle family or because it can't locate it, it will throw a runtime exception.

- Given a `Locale`, here's the order in which Java searches for a matching resource bundle.

1 `bundleName_localeLanguage_localeCountry_localeVariant`
2 `bundleName_localeLanguage_localeCountry`
3 `bundleName_localeLanguage`
4 `bundleName_defaultLanguage_defaultCountry_defaultVariant`
5 `bundleName_defaultLanguage_defaultCountry`
6 `bundleName_defaultLanguage`
7 `bundleName`

Formatting dates, numbers, and currencies for locales

- To format or parse
  - Numbers, use `NumberFormat` and `DecimalFormat` classes
  - Currencies, use `NumberFormat` class
  - Dates, use `DateFormat`, `SimpleDateFormat`, `Date` and `Calendar` classes
- `NumberFormat` and `DateFormat` are abstract classes. Class `DecimalFormat` extends class `NumberFormat`. Class `SimpleDateFormat` extends class `DateFormat`.
- The static method `getInstance()` in class `NumberFormat` returns an object of class `DecimalFormat`.
- The static method `getInstance()` in class `DateFormat` returns an instance of class `SimpleDateFormat`.
- To format numbers or parse string values
  - Use `NumberFormat`.
  - Call methods `NumberFormat.getInstance()`, `NumberFormat.getInstance(Locale)`, or `NumberFormat.getNumberInstance(Locale)` to get a `NumberFormat` instance.
  - Call method `NumberFormat`'s `format(num)` or `parse(String)` to format a number or parse a string value.
- To format currency
  - Use `NumberFormat`.
  - Call `NumberFormat.getCurrencyInstance()` or `NumberFormat.getCurrencyInstance(Locale)` to get a `NumberFormat` instance.
  - Call method `NumberFormat`'s `format(num)`.
- To format dates
  - Use `DateFormat`.
  - Call methods `DateFormat.getInstance()`, `DateFormat.getDateInstance()`, `DateFormat.getDateTimeInstance()`, or `DateFormat.getTimeInstance()` to get a `DateFormat` instance.
  - Call method `DateFormat`'s `format(Date)`.

- Predefined date formatting styles
  - `DateFormat.SHORT` is completely numeric, such as 31.07.20 or 10:30 p.m.
  - `DateFormat.MEDIUM` is longer, such as Jul 31, 2020 or 10:30:17 p.m.
  - `DateFormat.LONG` is longer, such as July 31, 2020 or 3:30:32 p.m. PST.
  - `DateFormat.FULL` is longer, such as Friday, July 31, 2020.
- Use class `SimpleDateFormat` for complete control of the formatting style of date and time.
- Create a `SimpleDateFormat` object by calling its constructors, passing it a formatting pattern as a string, together with a `Locale`.
- Call method `SimpleDateFormat`'s `format()`, passing it a `Date` object to format it.
- The case of the letters used in specifying patterns for `SimpleDateFormat` is case-sensitive.
- To use `Date` objects with date formatting classes, you can call `new Date()` to get the current date and time.
- To create `Date` objects with a specific date, use class `Calendar`. Call `Calendar .getInstance()` and then its method `set()`.

SAMPLE EXAM QUESTIONS

Q 12-1. Given the language code for Spanish is `es` and the country code for Spain is `ES`, which of the following code options defines a `Locale` to work with the Spanish language?

```
a   Locale locale = new Locale();
    locale.setLanguage("es");
    locale.setCountry("ES");
b   Locale locale = new Locale("es", "ES");
c   Locale locale = new Locale("ES", "es");
d   Locale locale = new Locale("es");
```

Q 12-2. Assume the following code executes on the following date and time:

Date: 2009 Jan 21

Time: 21:45:12

```
Date today = new Date();
//INSERT CODE HERE
System.out.println(dateFmt.format(today));
System.out.println(timeFmt.format(today));
```

Which of the following lines of code, when inserted at `//INSERT CODE HERE`, will output the date and time that coincides with the UK's `Locale`?

```
21/01/09
21:45:12
```

```
a   Locale.setDefault(Locale.UK);
    DateFormat dateFmt = DateFormat.getDateInstance(DateFormat.SHORT);
    DateFormat timeFmt = DateFormat.getTimeInstance(DateFormat.MEDIUM);
```

```
b  DateFormat dateFmt = new SimpleDateFormat("dd/MM/yy");
   DateFormat timeFmt = new SimpleDateFormat("HH:mm:ss");

c  DateFormat dateFmt = DateFormat.getDateInstance(DateFormat.SHORT);
   DateFormat timeFmt = DateFormat.getTimeInstance(DateFormat.MEDIUM);

d  DateFormat dateFmt = DateFormat.getDateInstance(DateFormat.SHORT,
   Locale.UK);
   DateFormat timeFmt = DateFormat.getTimeInstance(DateFormat.MEDIUM,
   Locale.UK);
```

Q 12-3. Given the following code, which of the options will load resource bundle "foo_en_UK" for Locale.UK and assign it to the variable bundle? The default language for the U.K. region is English (en).

```
ResourceBundle bundle = null;
```

    a `bundle = ResourceBundle.getBundle("foo_en_UK.properties");`

    b `bundle = ResourceBundle.getListBundle("foo_en_UK");`

    c `bundle = ResourceBundle.getBundle("foo_en_UK.properties", Locale.UK);`

    d `bundle = ResourceBundle.getListBundle("foo_en_UK", Locale.UK);`

    e `bundle = ResourceBundle.getPropertyBundle("foo.properties");`

    f `bundle = ResourceBundle.getBundle("foo_en_UK", new Locale("en", "UK"));`

Q 12-4. Which of the following code options accesses the default locale for the host system and creates a new locale with the default locale's language and country?

    a
```
Locale locale = Locale.getDefaultLocale();
Locale newLocale = new Locale(locale.getLanguage(), locale.getCountry());
```

    b
```
Locale locale = Locale.getDefault();
Locale newLocale = new Locale(locale.getLanguage(), locale.getCountry());
```

    c
```
Locale locale = Locale.getDefault();
Locale newLocale = new Locale(locale.getDisplayLanguage(),
locale.getDisplayCountry());
```

    d
```
Locale locale = Locale.getDefaultLocale();
Locale newLocale = new Locale(locale);
```

Q 12-5. What is the output of the following code?

```
NumberFormat fmt = new NumberFormat(Locale.US);
System.out.println(fmt.format(123123.99));
```

    a `123123.99`

    b `123,123.99`

    c `1,23,123.99`

    d `123 123.99`

    e `1 23 123.99`

    f `123,124.00`

    g Compilation error

    h Runtime exception

Q 12-6. Given that an application must support the languages Spanish (es) and German (de), which of the following options includes correct definitions to build resource bundles that support these languages?

a
```
class MyBundle_DE extends ListResourceBundle { /* code */ }
class MyBundle_de extends ListResourceBundle { /* code */ }
class MyBundle_es extends ListResourceBundle { /* code */ }
```

b
```
class MyBundle_DE extends ResourceBundle { /* code */ }
class MyBundle_de extends ResourceBundle { /* code */ }
class MyBundle_es extends ResourceBundle { /* code */ }
class MyBundle_spanish extends ResourceBundle { /* code */ }
```

c
```
class MyBundle_es extends PropertyResourceBundle { /* code */ }
class MyBundle_DE extends PropertyResourceBundle { /* code */ }
class MyBundle_de extends PropertyResourceBundle { /* code */ }
```

d
```
class MyBundle_de extends Bundle { /* code */ }
class MyBundle_DE extends Bundle { /* code */ }
class MyBundle_es extends Bundle { /* code */ }
```

Q 12-7. Select the incorrect statements:

a To localize an application, you don't need to internationalize it.

b A localized application improves user experience by displaying numbers in a region-specific format.

c A localized application can define its location-specific data in a separate .properties file.

d A translator can read locale data as key-value pairs from a .properties file, translate it, and define a new .properties file with the same keys and different values.

e To support additional locales, an application might not need to recompile any of its code.

Q 12-8. An application supports resource bundles for languages French (fr), Spanish (es), and English (en). The following are the listings of the corresponding resource bundles:

```
#GlobalBundle_en.properties
greeting=Hi
```

```
#GlobalBundle_fr.properties
greeting=Salut
```

```
#GlobalBundle_es.properties
greeting=Hola
```

Given that the default locale is Spanish, what's the output of the following code?

```
Locale.setDefault(new Locale("ja", "JP"));
Locale newLocale = Locale.getDefault();
ResourceBundle messages = ResourceBundle
                                  .getBundle("GlobalBundle", newLocale);
System.out.println(messages.getString("greeting"));
```

a   Hi
b   Salut
c   Hola
d   No output
e   Compilation error
f   Runtime exception

Q 12-9. Given that the letters *e* and *r* don't have any special meaning in defining a custom date and time format, what's the output of the following code if it's executed at 21:00 hrs on Jan. 21, 2020?

```
SimpleDateFormat dateFormat = new SimpleDateFormat("YYYY year");
System.out.println(dateFormat.format(new Date()));
```

a   2020 year
b   2020 ya
c   2020; 20 pm
d   2020 ypm
e   Compilation error
f   Runtime exception

Q 12-10. What's the output of the following code?

```
Locale locale = new Locale("fr", "FR");
Locale.setDefault(locale);
Locale locale1 = Locale.FRENCH;
System.out.println(locale1.getDisplayCountry());
```

a   France
b   FR
c   fr
d   No output
e   Runtime exception

Q 12-11. Which of the options when inserted at //INSERT CODE HERE will format the currency for Locale with the language German (de)?

```
double amt = 12345.1111;
//INSERT CODE HERE
System.out.println(format.format(amt));
```

a   `Locale.setDefault(Locale.GERMAN);`
    `NumberFormat format = NumberFormat.getCurrencyInstance();`

b   `CurrencyFormat format = CurrencyFormat.getCurrencyInstance(Locale.GERMAN);`

c   `NumberFormat format = NumberFormat.getInstance("currency", Locale.GERMAN);`

d   `NumberFormat format = NumberFormat.getCurrencyInstance(new Locale("de"));`

Q 12-12. Select the correct statements:

a   `ListResourceBundle` is a subclass of `ResourceBundle`.

b   `PropertiesResourceBundle` is a subclass of `ResourceBundle`.

c   If you change any key or value used with `ListResourceBundle`, you must recompile at least one class file.

d   If you change any key or value defined in .properties files, you might not recompile any class file.

e   You can't define resource bundles defined as `ListResourceBundle` in packages.

ANSWERS TO SAMPLE EXAM QUESTIONS

A 12-1. b, d

[12.6] Define a locale using language and country codes

Explanation: Option (a) is incorrect because it uses an invalid `Locale` constructor and methods. Class `Locale` defines the following constructors:

```
Locale(String language)
Locale(String language, String country)
Locale(String language, String country, String variant)
```

Option (c) is incorrect. To create a `Locale`, language code must be the first argument, and region or country is the second argument. This option passes language as the second argument.

Option (d) is correct because you need to work with Spanish. So it's acceptable to pass only this value and leave the region code.

A 12-2. a, b, d

[12.1] Read and set the locale by using the Locale object
[12.4] Format dates, numbers, and currency values for localization with the Number-Format and DateFormat classes (including number format patterns)

Option (c) is incorrect because this code would format the date and time values according to the host's default locale. The output should be formatted according to `Locale.UK` or by using the exact pattern.

A 12-3. f

[12.3] Call a resource bundle from an application

Explanation: Options (b), (d), and (e) are incorrect because they use the nonexistent factory methods `getListBundle` and `getResourceBundle`. The correct and only factory method to retrieve a resource bundle is to call one of the overloaded methods, `getBundle()`.

Options (a) and (c) are incorrect because the file extension '.properties' must not be included to load a resource bundle.

A 12-4. b

[12.1] Read and set the locale by using the Locale object

Explanation: Options (a) and (d) are incorrect because they use nonexistent method names to access the default locale. The correct factory method name is `Locale.get-Default`.

Option (c) is incorrect because the `Locale`'s constructor should be passed language and country codes and not their display names. The methods `getDisplay-Language` and `getDisplayCountry` retrieve display names for languages and countries. The correct methods to use here are `getLanguage()` and `getCountry()`, which return codes for the language and country.

A 12-5. g

[12.4] Format dates, numbers, and currency values for localization with the Number-Format and DateFormat classes (including number format patterns)

Explanation: Class `NumberFormat` is an abstract class—you can't instantiate it. Class `NumberFormat` defines multiple factory methods to create and return an object of the relevant classes that implement `NumberFormat`, like `getInstance()`, `getInstance (Locale)`, `getNumberInstance()`, and `getNumberInstance(Locale)`.

A 12-6. a

[12.2] Build a resource bundle for each locale

Explanation: Options (b), (c), and (d) are incorrect because they don't extend the right class. To define a resource bundle in a Java class, it must extend class `List-ResourceBundle`.

A 12-7. a

[12.5] Describe the advantages of localizing an application

Explanation: Only option (a) is an incorrect statement because applications that are internationalized can be localized to particular locales.

A 12-8. f

[12.2] Build a resource bundle for each locale
[12.3] Call a resource bundle from an application

Explanation: The application defines resource bundles to support languages French (`fr`), Spanish (`es`), and English (`en`). The following code changes the default locale for the application to `Locale.JAPAN`, with the language as Japanese:

```
Locale.setDefault(new Locale("ja", "JP"));
```

When the code retrieves the default locale for the same application, it returns `Locale`
`.JAPAN` and not the earlier default locale language, Spanish:

```
Locale newLocale = Locale.getDefault();
```

Because no matching resource bundle for the language Japanese and country Japan
can be found, this application throws a `MissingResourceException` at runtime.

A 12-9. f

[12.4] Format dates, numbers, and currency values for localization with the Number-
Format and DateFormat classes (including number format patterns)

Explanation: If you use an illegal character for defining a date and time pattern for
class `SimpleDateFormat`, it will throw an `IllegalArgumentException`, which is a runtime exception.

A 12-10. d

[12.6] Define a locale using language and country codes

Explanation: When you create a locale using only the language component, its region
or country part remains unassigned. Calling `getDisplayCountry` on such a `Locale`
object will return an empty string.

A 12-11. a, d

[12.4] Format dates, numbers, and currency values for localization with the Number-
Format and DateFormat classes (including number format patterns)
[12.6] Define a locale using language and country codes

Explanation: Option (b) is incorrect because it uses a nonexistent class `Currency-`
`Format`. Option (c) is incorrect because it uses a nonexistent `getInstance` method
that accepts a type of the formatter to be returned and a `Locale`.

A 12-12. a, c, d

[12.2] Build a resource bundle for each locale

Explanation: Option (b) is incorrect because the correct name is `PropertyResource-`
`Bundle`. `PropertyResourceBundle` extends `ResourceBundle`.

Option (e) is incorrect because resource bundles defined using `ListResource-`
`Bundle` can be defined in a package like any other class.

appendix
Answers to "Twist in the Tale" exercises

Chapters 1–12 include numerous "Twist in the Tale" exercises. The answers to these exercises are given in this appendix, with comprehensive explanations. The answer to each exercise includes the following elements:

- *Purpose*—The aim of the exercise (the *twist* to which each exercise is trying to draw your attention)
- *Answer*—The correct answer
- *Explanation*—A comprehensive explanation of the answer

Let's get started with the first chapter.

A.1 Chapter 1: Java class design

Chapter 1 includes 4 "Twist in the Tale" exercises.

A.1.1 Twist in the Tale 1.1

Purpose: This exercise demonstrates how decreasing the accessibility of an entity by changing its access modifier might impact the code that uses it.

Answer: On recompilation, the class written by Harry, StoryBook, won't compile.

Explanation: When the accessibility of class Book is changed from public to default, class Book won't be visible and accessible outside its library package. If Book can't be accessed outside its package, class StoryBook in another package, building, won't be able to inherit from it.

A.1.2   Twist in the Tale 1.2

Purpose: This exercise demonstrates that recursive constructor invocation isn't allowed.

Answer: The code fails to compile with the following error message:

```
Employee.java:4: error: recursive constructor invocation
    Employee() {
    ^
1 error
```

Explanation: A constructor can't call itself. If a class defines two overloaded constructors, A and B, A can't call itself. Also, if A calls B, B can't call A because it would again result in a recursive constructor call.

A.1.3   Twist in the Tale 1.3

Purpose: To distinguish between overloaded, overridden, and hidden methods

Answer and explanation: Combination letter (a) compiles successfully. The static method print() in CourseBook hides the static method print() in its base class, Book:

```
class Book {
    static void print() {}
}
class CourseBook extends Book {
    static void print() {}
}
```

Instance methods can override methods from their base class, but static methods don't. When a derived class defines a static method with the same signature as one of the methods in its base class, it hides it. Static methods don't participate in polymorphism.

Combination letter (b) won't compile. The static method print() in the base class Book can't be hidden by the instance method print() in the derived class CourseBook:

```
class Book {
    static void print() {}
}
class CourseBook extends Book {
    void print() {}
}
```

Combination letter (c) won't compile either. The instance method print() in base class Book can't be overridden by the static method print() in derived class CourseBook:

```
class Book{
    void print() {}
}
```

```
class CourseBook extends Book {
    static void print() {}
}
```

Combination (d) compiles successfully. The instance method `print()` in `CourseBook` overrides the instance method `print()` in its base class, `Book`:

```
class Book{
    void print() {}
}
class CourseBook extends Book {
    void print() {}
}
```

A.1.4 Twist in the Tale 1.4

Purpose: To demonstrate appropriate overriding of methods of class `Object`—in particular, `toString()`. Beware: *appropriate* method overriding is not the same as *correct* method overriding.

Answer: `Book1`, `Book3`, and `Book4` exhibit the appropriate overridden method `toString()`.

Explanation: The contract of method `toString()` specifies that it should return a *concise* but informative textual representation of the object that it represents. This is usually accomplished by using the value of the instance variables of an object. The default implementation of this method in class `Object` returns the name of the object's class, followed by an @ sign and its hash-code value.

Class `Book1` overrides method `toString()` to return a textual message followed by the value of its instance variable `title`, so it meets the `toString()` contract. Method `toString()` in class `Book2` returns a product of `copies` and `11`. It isn't appropriately overridden. When used by other developers, the value returned by `toString()` will not make much sense. `Book3` returns title and `Book4` returns title and its class name, which also exhibit the appropriate override of this method and meets the `toString()` contract.

A.2 Chapter 2: Advanced class design

Chapter 2 includes 6 "Twist in the Tale" exercises.

A.2.1 Twist in the Tale 2.1

Purpose: To enable you to draw UML class diagrams, depicting a base-derived class relationship between classes. You'll need to draw similar UML class diagrams (on your rough sheet) in the real exam to quickly answer questions on object casting and IS-A and HAS-A relationships.

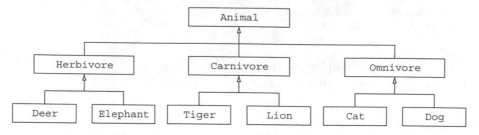

Figure A.1   UML diagram depicting the inheritance relationship between the given classes

Answer: Shown in figure A.1.

A.2.2   *Twist in the Tale 2.2*

Purpose: Unlike constructors and other methods, an initializer block can't reference (access and use) an instance variable before it's defined. Similarly, a static initializer block can't reference a static variable before it is defined. Assessing a variable before it is defined is also known as *forward referencing.* An instance initializer block can refer to a static variable before it is declared, because static variables are made available when a class is loaded in memory, which happens before initialization of objects of its class.

Answer: d

Explanation: The code fails to compile because the first static initializer block defined in class DemoMultipleStaticBlocks can't forward reference the static variable static-Var. The code fails with the following error message:

```
DemoMultipleInstanceBlocks.java:4: error: illegal forward reference
        ++staticVar;
          ^
1 error
```

A.2.3   *Twist in the Tale 2.3*

Purpose: To show that a final variable must be initialized in the class in which it's declared. Its initialization can't be deferred to its derived class.

Answer: The code won't compile.

Explanation: A static or instance final variable must be initialized in the class in which it is declared using any one of these options:

- Initialize the final variable with its declaration.
- Initialize a static final variable in the class's static initializer block.
- Initialize an instance final variable in an instance initializer block or a constructor.

A.2.4 *Twist in the Tale 2.4*

Purpose: To verify that enum constants are created before execution of static blocks

Answer: The code outputs the following:

```
constructor
static init block
BEGINNER
```

Explanation: The definition of an enum starts with its constants, which are created in a static initializer block. Because the static initializer blocks execute in the order of their declaration, any static initializer in an enum will execute *after* the completion of the creation of its own enum constants. So even though it might seem that the static initializer block in enum `Level` will execute after its constructor, it won't.

A.2.5 *Twist in the Tale 2.5*

Purpose: To test multiple facts:

- An enum can define a `main()` method.
- The enum constants are static, so they can be accessed in any static method defined within the enum.
- The overridden method `toString()` in class `Enum` returns the name of the enum constant.

Answer: c

Explanation: There aren't any errors with the code. All enums inherit class `Enum`. The default implementation of `toString()` in `Enum` returns the enum constant's name. So `System.out.println(VANILLA)` outputs `VANILLA`. To use the string values passed to enum constants in enum `IceCreamTwist`, you need to override its method `toString()` as follows:

```
public String toString() {
    return color;
}
```

A.2.6 *Twist in the Tale 2.6*

Purpose: To test multiple points:

- An inner class can define a variable with the same name as its outer class.
- An inner class can define a static variable if it's marked final.
- An inner class can't define a static variable that's not marked final.
- When you initialize an array with some size, the array elements are initialized to `null`. So the default constructor for the array elements isn't invoked.
- Instantiation of an outer class doesn't instantiate its inner class automatically.

Answer: e

Explanation: In inner class `Petal`, the code at line 1 assigns a value to its own instance variable `color`. The inner class `Petal` can access its outer class's (`Flower`) instance variable `color` by using `Flower.this.color`. The only type of static member that an inner class is allowed to define is a final static variable. The code at (#3) initializes an array to hold two `Petal` objects. Both `petal[0]` and `petal[1]` are initialized to `null`. So the default constructor of `Petal` is never invoked and that's why this program outputs nothing.

A.3   *Chapter 3: Object-oriented design principles*

Chapter 3 includes 3 "Twist in the Tale" exercises.

A.3.1   *Twist in the Tale 3.1*

Purpose: To enable you to understand that the choice of implementing either the class inheritance or the interface inheritance is not very obvious. Apart from class design considerations, you also need to pay attention to any conflicting method signatures that lead to overlapping of overloaded and overridden methods in a class that extends another class or implements an interface.

Answer: d

Explanation: To enable an object of class `MyLaptop` to be used in a `try-with-resources` statement, class `MyLaptop` should implement the `AutoCloseable` interface or any of its subinterfaces. But the definition of method `close()`, which is already defined in class `MyLaptop`, conflicts with the definition of the `close()` method defined in the `AutoCloseable` interface. Methods `close()` defined in class `MyLaptop` and the `Auto-Closeable` interface qualify as neither overridden or overloaded methods because they differ only in their return type:

Class: `MyLaptop` - `public int close()`
Interface: `AutoCloseable` — `void close()`

So, class `MyLaptop` will fail to compile if it implements the `AutoCloseable` interface or any of its subinterfaces.

A.3.2   *Twist in the Tale 3.2*

Purpose: To encourage you to draw simple UML class diagrams on your erasable boards (that you receive at the testing center for your rough notes) to represent an inheritance relationship between classes and interfaces to answer questions on IS-A and HAS-A relationships. A quick UML diagram won't take long to draw and will simplify answering exam questions, similar to this one.

Answer: a, c

Explanation: Figure A.2 shows two UML class diagrams. The one on the left takes care of all the UML notations. Though the UML diagram on the right doesn't take care of

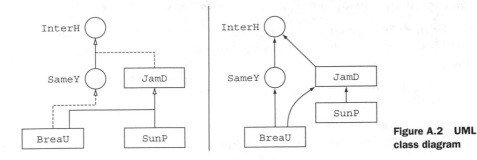

Figure A.2   UML class diagram

all the UML diagram notations (not the one that you can send to your prospective clients), it still makes clear the inheritance relationship between the classes and interfaces so that you can quickly answer similar questions on the exam. To answer whether an entity IS-A another type or not, just walk up the hierarchy tree. Also, TypeA IS-A TypeA is always true.

A.3.3   Twist in the Tale 3.3

Purpose: To bring your attention to simpler concepts. The exam tip in the chapter that's placed just before this exercise mentions eager initialization, synchronizing getInstance(), or using a synchronization block in getInstance(). When you read about advanced concepts, you might overlook the basic and simple concepts.

Answer: No.

Explanation: The constructor of this class must be marked private and variable anInstance and method getInstance() must be marked static.

The singleton pattern restricts the creation of instances of a class to one. The code in this example has multiple issues: its constructor isn't private and variable anInstance and method getInstance() are defined as instance members.

Marking the constructor as private will guarantee no more than one instance of class Singleton can be created. But without the static method getInstance(), this class is useless. Method getInstance() is an instance method, so you need an instance but can't initialize it with a private constructor. Variable anInstance must be marked static as well, because an instance variable can't be accessed in a static method.

A.4   Chapter 4: Generics and collections

Chapter 4 includes 7 "Twist in the Tale" exercises.

A.4.1   Twist in the Tale 4.1

Purpose: To differentiate between the notion <T> and T used in the definition of generic methods in generic and nongeneric classes or interfaces.

Answer: After the modification, the MyMap interface will fail to compile.

Explanation: For a generic interface or class, its type information follows the name of the class or interface. In the following example, the type information <K, V> follows the interface name MyMap:

```
interface MyMap<K, V>{
}
```

The generic methods get() and put() can use the type parameters K and V defined by the MyMap interface in its type declaration <K, V>:

```
interface MyMap<K, V>{
    V get(K key);
}
```

For method get(), when you enclose V in <>, it's no longer considered as its return type—it becomes type information. Because method get() doesn't define a return type anymore, it doesn't compile.

A.4.2   *Twist in the Tale 4.2*

Purpose: To understand how the combination of raw and generic data types work, including compilation errors and warnings that they generate

Answer: b, c

Explanation: The code that uses a combination of raw and generic data types can run into compilation errors and warnings. The following code defines the generic class and interface, and will compile without any errors or warnings:

```
interface MyMap<K, V>{
    void put(K key, V value);
    V get(K key);
}
class CustomMap<K, V> implements MyMap<K, V> {
    K key;
    V value;
    public void put(K key, V value) {
        //.. code
    }
    public V get(K key) {
        return value;
    }
}
```

When you define a reference variable using the class's raw type, it loses the type information and isn't aware about the type of the objects that you'd use to work with it. In the following code, map loses type information and is unaware about the types Integer and String that are passed to the CustomMap instantiation:

```
CustomMap map = new CustomMap<Integer, String>();
map.put(new String("1"), "Selvan");
String strVal = map.get(new Integer(1));
```

In the preceding code, map is a raw type. Method get() will return a value of type Object. Without an explicit cast, you can't assign an Object to a String reference variable. So assignment of map.get(new Integer(1)) to strVal fails compilation.

Option (a) is incorrect. If you modify the code as mentioned, it will result in another compilation error, this time at line 2. The code at line 2 tries to add a String-String key-value pair to map, when it's supposed to accept an Integer-String key-value pair.

A.4.3 *Twist in the Tale 4.3*

Purpose: To remove an object from a collection, the collection checks for its existence. If you modify the value of an object or reassign another object to the reference variable, you might not be able to find the original object that you added to the collection.

The collections that use hashing algorithms use hashCode(), equals(), or both to compare object values. Collections like ArrayList that don't use hashing algorithms use only equals() to compare object values.

Answer: c

Explanation: The following code adds the Integer object with value 20 (referred by variable age1) to list:

```
ArrayList<Integer> list = new ArrayList<>();
Integer age1 = 20;
list.add(age1);
```

Before the code requests the object referred by age1 to be removed from list, it reassigns another object to it:

```
age1 = 30;
list.remove(age1);
```

Because the Integer object with value 30 was never added to list, it can't be removed from it. Let's see what happens for the following code:

```
list.remove(new Integer(20));
```

After execution of the preceding code, the first occurrence of the Integer object with value 20 will be removed from list. This shows

- An ArrayList uses method equals() to compare its elements before removing them.
- Method remove() removes only the first occurrence of a matching element.

Here's another quick question. Do you think the following code will throw a runtime exception?

```
list.remove(20);
```

Yes, it will. ArrayList defines the overloaded remove() methods:

- remove(int index)
- remove(Object obj)

`list.remove(20)` will try to remove an element at array position 20, throwing an `IndexOutOfBoundException`. It won't autobox the `int` value 20 to an `Integer` instance and try to remove it from `list`.

 EXAM TIP   For an `ArrayList` of `Integer` objects, calling `remove(20)` will remove its element at position 20. It won't remove an `Integer` object with value 20 from the `ArrayList`.

A.4.4   Twist in the Tale 4.4

Purpose: A reference variable of an interface can only access the variables and methods defined in the interface (in the absence of an explicit cast).

Answer: d

Explanation: The `List` interface doesn't define methods `offer()` or `push()`. Class `LinkedList` implements both `List` and `Deque`. Methods `offer()` and `push()` are defined in `Deque`. Though a reference variable of type `List` can be used to refer to a `LinkedList` instance, it can't access methods that it doesn't define.

A.4.5   Twist in the Tale 4.5

Purpose: To highlight the role of `equals()` and `hashCode()` in storing and retrieving elements in a `HashSet`, which is a collection that uses a hashing algorithm.

Answer: a, c

Explanation: To understand the code in this exercise and the answer options, you must know how elements are added to a `HashSet`.

When elements are added to class `HashSet`, it queries method `hashCode()` of the element to get the bucket in which the element would be stored. If the bucket doesn't contain any elements, it stores the new element in the bucket. If the bucket already contains elements, `HashSet` checks for matching `hashCode` values, compares object references, or queries method `equals()` to ensure that it stores unique values.

As per answer option (b), `Person` only overrides the `hashCode` method:

```
public int hashCode() {
    return 10;
}
```

In the absence of the overridden method `equals()`, even though all the reference variables p1, p2, p3, and p4 have the same `hashCode()` values, they aren't considered equal. So all objects referred by these variables are added to `HashSet`. Though option (c) doesn't define an appropriately overridden method `equals()`, it returns `true` for any object compared with a `Person` object:

```
public boolean equals(Object o) {
    return true;
}
```

```
public int hashCode() {
    return 10;
}
```

With the preceding code, all the reference variables p1, p2, p3, and p4 have the same hashCode values *and* they return true when compared with each other. Because Hash-Set doesn't allow duplicate elements, it adds the object referred by variable p1 only.

Option (d) overrides equals() only. Because hashCode() isn't overridden, the objects referred by variables p1, p2, p3, and p4 will have different hashCode() values. Even for two Person objects with the same name, their hashCode() will be different. When the hashCode() values are different, the hashing algorithm doesn't call equals().

A.4.6   *Twist in the Tale 4.6*

Purpose: To show how instances of a class are sorted if both Comparable and Comparator are used

Answer: a

Explanation: When class Twist4_6 instantiates TreeSet that can store Person instances, it also defines a Comparator to compare Person instances on their age values. Class Person implements the Comparable interface, which sorts it on name. Comparator takes precedence over Comparable, so Person instances are sorted using Comparator, returning the output in option (a).

A.4.7   *Twist in the Tale 4.7*

Purpose: To implement an interface, a class *must* include the implements clause in its declaration. If a class defines the interface methods, but its declaration doesn't mention that the class implements it, the class isn't considered as implementing the interface.

Answer: e

Explanation: Though class Person defines method compareTo(), its declaration doesn't mention that it implements Comparable. When you call Arrays.sort(<reference-to-anArray>), the array objects must implement the Comparable interface so that they can be sorted on their natural order. If the class doesn't implement Comparable, you can use the overloaded method sort(), which takes an array and a Comparator instance. Because the code in this exercise doesn't comply with either of these rules, the code throws the following runtime exception:

```
Exception in thread "main" java.lang.ClassCastException: Person cannot be
cast to java.lang.Comparable
```

A.5   *Chapter 5: String processing*

Chapter 5 includes 3 "Twist in the Tale" exercises.

A.5.1   *Twist in the Tale 5.1*

Purpose: To identify correct and incorrect regexes (regular expressions) that match a target string. An incorrect regex is not the same as an invalid regex. Code that defines an invalid regex will compile if it's a valid string value. But it will throw a `Pattern-SyntaxException` at runtime.

Answer: d

Explanation: `\b` matches a word boundary and `\B` matches a nonword boundary.

Option (a) is incorrect because regex `\Bthe\B` will match "the" in a target string, which isn't placed at the start or end of a word. For example, "the" in "leather."

Option (b) is incorrect because regex `\bthe\B` will match words that start with "the" but don't end with it. For example, it will match "the" in "their". This pattern won't find words that end with "the".

Option (c) is incorrect because regex `\Bthe\b` will match words that don't start with "the" but end with "the". For example, it will match "the" in "seethe". But this pattern won't find words that start with "the".

Option (d) is correct. The pattern `\bthe` will match a word that starts with "the" and the pattern `the\b` will match a word that ends with "the". Because the regex `\\bthe|the\\b` uses a logical or operator (`|`), it will match a word that either starts with "the" or ends with "the"—for example, "the" in "their" and "the" in "seethe".

A.5.2   *Twist in the Tale 5.2*

Purpose: To remember that the similar sounding string methods—that is, `replace()`, `replaceAll()`, and `replaceFirst()`—offer different functionality. Also make note of the method parameters that can be passed to these overloaded methods.

Answer: a, d

Explanation: The first three options—(a), (b), and (c)—test the strings that a regex pattern will match. The next options—(d), (e), and (f)—test the use of methods `replace()` and `replaceFirst()`, together with different regex patterns.

Option (a) is correct and (b) and (c) are incorrect. The regex `c.p\\b` will match "cup" and not "cupp". This regex will match letter "c" followed by *any* (one) character, followed by "p", followed by a word boundary (end of word). Method `replaceAll()` matches a target string against a regex pattern and returns a new string, with all occurrences of the matched pattern replaced by the specified text.

Option (d) is correct and (e) and (f) are incorrect. Following are the signatures of the methods `replace()`, `replaceAll()`, and `replaceFirst()` defined in class `String`:

```
String replace(char oldChar, char newChar)
String replace(CharSequence target, CharSequence replacement)
String replaceAll(String regex, String replacement)
String replaceFirst(String regex, String replacement)
```

Unlike methods `replaceAll()` and `replaceFirst()`, which match and replace all or the first occurrence of a matching regex pattern, the overloaded `replace()` methods don't match and replace a *regex* pattern. They find and replace *exact* string matches. If you modify the example in this exercise, replacing `replaceAll()` with `replace()`, the method `replace()` won't be able to find an exact match for c.p\b.

A.5.3 Twist in the Tale 5.3

Purpose: To verify what happens when there is a mismatch in the type of the token returned by `Scanner` and the actual method that's used to retrieve it

Answer: c

Explanation: The tokens of `Scanner` can be retrieved using `next()`, which returns an object of type `String`. It also defines multiple `nextXXX()` methods where XXX refers to a primitive data type. Instead of returning a `String` value, these methods return the value as the corresponding primitive type. There can be a mismatch in the type of the token returned and method `nextXXX()` used to retrieve a token.

In class `MyScan` used in this exercise, `Scanner`'s method `nextInt()` returns the next token as an `int` value. But the second token in string 1 a 10 . 100 1000—that is, a—isn't an `int`. The Java Runtime throws an `InputMismatchException` when it detects this mismatch.

The code compiles because the token values can't be determined during the compilation process.

A.6 Chapter 6: Exceptions and assertions

Chapter 6 includes 4 "Twist in the Tale" exercises.

A.6.1 Twist in the Tale 6.1

Purpose: How to use a method that declares throwing a checked exception in its method declaration, even if it handles it itself and will never throw it.

Answer: c

Explanation: Method `useReadFile()` includes a checked exception, `FileNotFound-Exception`, in its `throws` clause, so the calling method, `main()`, must declare to handle the thrown exception. Because `main()` doesn't, the code fails to compile.

You might argue that method useReadFile() would never throw a FileNotFound-Exception because it handles it itself using a catch block. But this doesn't form a strong reason to convince the compiler to relax its rules. In short, if a method declares to throw a checked exception, the calling method must either handle it or declare it in one of the following ways:

- *Handle exception*—Using a try-catch block
- *Declare exception*—Add the exception to the exception list or throws clause

A.6.2   Twist in the Tale 6.2

Purpose: This exercise has two purposes:

- To establish that a method can declare to throw a checked exception, even though it doesn't include any code that might throw it
- How to use such a method

Answer: c

Explanation: This is similar to the previous exercise, though with subtle differences. It establishes that you can declare to throw checked exceptions (by using the throws clause), even if your code doesn't include any code that throws the mentioned checked exception.

It reconfirms that whenever you use a method that declares to throw a checked exception, you must accomplish either of the following or else your code won't compile:

- A handle exception using a try-catch block
- A declare exception by adding the exception to the exception list or throws clause

A.6.3   Twist in the Tale 6.3

Purpose: To show that in a multi-catch block, the type of the reference variable is the base class of all the exception classes. Also, the default implementation of method toString() in class Throwable returns the fully qualified name of the Throwable instance (all Exception and Error classes) together with its exception message.

Answer: c

Will the code compile after commenting code marked with //line1? No.

Explanation: An attempt to retrieve the value of a reference variable itself calls its method toString(). The common base class of classes Exception1 and Exception2 is Exception. Class Exception inherits class Throwable, which overrides method toString(). The default implementation of method toString() in class Throwable returns the fully qualified name of the Throwable instance (all Exception and Error classes) together with its exception message.

Because exception classes used in this example aren't specifically defined in any package (the *default* package doesn't have an explicit name), an attempt to execute

`System.out.println(ex)`, passing it an `Exception1` instance, outputs `Exception1`. The default implementation of `toString()` in class `Object`, the base class of all the Java classes, returns the class name together with the instance's hash-code value.

When you comment on code marked `//line1`, the code won't compile. After the modification, the `catch` block would try to handle the checked exception `Exception2`, which is never thrown by its corresponding `try` block.

A.6.4   *Twist in the Tale 6.4*

Purpose: To remind you that appearances can be deceptive. A code snippet that *seems* to check you on assertions might actually be checking you on another concept.

Answer: d

Explanation: The code won't compile because while overriding `toString()`, class `Person` assigns a weaker access level (`private`) to it. When you override a base class method, you can assign the same or wider access level to it, but you can't make it more restrictive.

A.7   *Chapter 7: Java I/O fundamentals*

Chapter 7 includes 1 "Twist in the Tale" exercise.

A.7.1   *Twist in the Tale 7.1*

Purpose: To show that though the following operations seem to be the same, they're different:

- Read data into a byte array and write all the byte array contents to an output stream.
- Read data into a byte array and write *only* the filled-in byte array to an output stream.

Answer: b, c

Explanation: When you create a local array of a primitive data type, all its members are initialized to their default values. The following line of code in class `Twist` creates a local array of type `byte`, initializing all its members to `0`.

```
byte[] byteArr = new byte[2048];
```

Class `Twist` reads the source file into `byteArr` using `FileInputStream`'s method `read(byte[])`. This method returns the total number of bytes read into the `byteArr`, or `-1` if there is no more data because the end of the file has been reached. When `read()` returns `-1`, data might not be read into all the positions of `byteArr`. So it makes sense to write only the data that has been read. If you write all the `byteArr` data, you have a high probability of writing the default value, `0`, resulting in a copy that's not identical. But if you're very lucky and the file size is a plurality of the array length, you still have an identical copy.

Copy.java fails to compile because it isn't identical to Twist.java and includes additional byte values written to it.

A.8   Chapter 8: Java file I/O (NIO.2)

Chapter 8 includes 2 "Twist in the Tale" exercises.

A.8.1   Twist in the Tale 8.1

Purpose: To show what happens with redundancies in a `Path` object when you retrieve its components

Answer: a, e, f

Explanation: Methods `toString()`, `getName()`, `getParent()`, and `subpath()` don't remove any redundancies from the `Path` object. An example of a method that removes a redundancy from a `Path` object is `normalize()`. Also, the root element of a path isn't its first name element. The element that's closest to the root in the directory hierarchy has index 0.

The output of this exercise's code is as follows:

```
c:\OCPJavaSE7\..\obj8\.\8-1.txt
..
c:\OCPJavaSE7\..\obj8\.
obj8\.
```

`Path` objects are used to represent the path of files or directories in a file system. They represent a hierarchal path, containing directory names and filenames separated by platform-specific delimiters. The `Path` methods used in this example don't eliminate the redundancy before returning their values.

A.8.2   Twist in the Tale 8.2

Purpose: To reiterate that most of the `Path` methods perform syntactic operations— that is, logical operations on paths in memory

Answer: d

Explanation: Method `relativize()` is used to construct a path between two relative or absolute `Path` objects. Method `resolve()` is used to join a relative path to another path. If you pass an absolute path as a parameter, this method returns the absolute path. The operation `file.resolve(file.relativize(dir))` returns 'code/java/IO.java/../..'. Given that file Twist8_2 (Twist8_2.class) is located in the directory '/home', calling `toAbsolutePath()` on 'code/java/IO.java/../..' returns '/home/code/java/IO.java/../..'.

A.9   Chapter 9: Building database applications with JDBC

Chapter 9 includes no "Twist in the Tale" exercises.

A.10 *Chapter 10: Threads*

Chapter 10 includes 4 "Twist in the Tale" exercises.

A.10.1 *Twist in the Tale 10.1*

Purpose: When you instantiate a thread, say, A, passing it another Thread instance, say, B, calling A.start() will start one new thread of execution. Calling A.start() will execute B.run.

Answer: b

Explanation: Class Thread defines an instance variable target of type Runnable, which refers to the *target* object it needs to start. When you instantiate newThread by passing it a Sing instance, sing, newThread.runnable refers to sing. When you call newThread.start(), newThread() checks if its target is null or not. Because it refers to sing, calling newThread.start() starts a new thread of execution, calling target.run().

A.10.2 *Twist in the Tale 10.2*

Purpose: To show that a multithreaded application can throw multiple unhandled exceptions

Answer: a, b, e

Explanation: In multithreaded applications, you can't predetermine the order of execution of threads. When multiple threads in your application throw unhandled exceptions, your application can throw *all* of these exceptions from separate threads. This is unlike single-threaded applications, which throw only one unhandled exception. Class Twist10_2 starts a new thread, sing, which outputs Singing before throwing a RuntimeException. After Twist10_2 starts thread sing, it throws a RuntimeException itself. The order of execution of throwing of RuntimeException by threads main and sing is random. But the output of text Singing is sure to *happen-before* thread sing throws a RuntimeException.

A.10.3 *Twist in the Tale 10.3*

Purpose: To synchronize the right methods to protect your shared data

Answer: c

Explanation: Because the methods newSale() and returnBook() aren't defined as synchronized methods, multiple threads can access these methods concurrently, posing a risk of thread interference that fails to protect the data of object book, defined on line 3. Defining the run() methods as synchronized doesn't help to protect the data of object book. It restricts execution of run to a single thread; it doesn't restrict modification of an instance of Book to a single thread. To protect your shared data, you should add the synchronized keyword to the methods that directly manipulate your shared data.

A.10.4 *Twist in the Tale 10.4*

Purpose: To identify classes that can be used and shared safely in a multithreaded application without external synchronization

Answer: a

Explanation: Class BirthDate is defined as a final class, and its methods are declared final, which will prevent this class from being subclassed and its methods can't be overridden. Make note of the methods that modify the value of the BirthDate instance. The objects of this class are immutable—that is, the methods of BirthDate don't allow modification of its instance variable birth. Also, birth is declared as a private member, so it can never be manipulated by any other class. It's safe to be used in a multithreaded application without external synchronization.

A.11   *Chapter 11: Concurrency*

Chapter 11 includes 3 "Twist in the Tale" exercises.

A.11.1 *Twist in the Tale 11.1*

Purpose: Make note of the order in which you acquire a lock using lockInterruptibly(), handle the InterruptedException that it throws, and unlock it. Unlock the lock only if you can acquire it; otherwise, it will throw an IllegalMonitorStateException.

Answer: a, d

Explanation: If the thread e1 in main manages to complete its execution before e.interrupt() executes, class Employee will output the following:

```
Paul: boarded
```

If e.interrupt() executes before thread e1 in main manages to complete its execution, class Employee will output the following:

```
Paul: Interrupted!!
IllegalMonitorStateException
```

Compare the code in this exercise with the code in listing 11.1. The finally block in this exercise calls bus.lock.unlock() irrespective of whether or not a lock could be obtained on bus.lock. When the finally block executes *after* the code fails to acquire a lock on bus.lock, it will throw an IllegalMonitorStateException.

A.11.2 *Twist in the Tale 11.2*

Purpose: How to code method execute() to exercise complete control over how to execute tasks for an executor. Calling start() on a Thread instance starts a new thread of execution. Calling `run()` on a `Runnable` instance executes the thread in the *same* thread of execution.

Answer: d

Explanation: The execute method adds the submitted task at the end of its `custQueue` and calls `processEarliestOrder()`, which retrieves the first task from this queue. But `processEarliestOrder()` calls `task.run()`, which executes method `run()` on `task` in the same thread as the calling thread, without starting any new thread of execution:

```
public void execute(Runnable r) {
    synchronized(custQueue) {
        custQueue.offer(r);
    }
    processEarliestOrder();
}
private void processEarliestOrder() {
    synchronized(custQueue) {
        Runnable task = custQueue.poll();
        task.run();
    }
}
```

Because each invocation of `task.run()` waits for method `run()` to complete before returning from the method, the code will always execute the submitted tasks in the predefined manner.

A.11.3 Twist in the Tale 11.3

Purpose: The order of execution of calling `join()` and `compute()` on divided subtasks is important in a fork/join framework.

Answer: b, c

Explanation: Though the code will always return correct results, it won't benefit from the fork/join framework. Each task waits for its completion (`join()` is called) before starting execution of a new thread.

A.12   Chapter 12: Localization

Chapter 12 includes 2 "Twist in the Tale" exercises.

A.12.1 Twist in the Tale 12.1

Purpose: To show that you can use different methods to create `Locale` objects, such as `Locale` constants, `Locale` constructors, and `LocaleBuilder`. Depending on how `Locale` objects are created or initialized, some of their fields might be initialized with default or `null` values.

Answer: a

Explanation: `Locale.FRENCH` only assigns its language as French. `Locale` assigns `null` to its region field. `Locale.FRANCE` assigns its region to France and its language as

French. Locale's method equals() compares their field values to determine their equality. You can output the value of a Locale object by calling its method toString(). The following code

```
Locale locale1 = Locale.FRENCH;
Locale locale2 = Locale.FRANCE;
System.out.println(locale1);
System.out.println(locale2);
```

outputs the following:

```
fr
fr_FR
```

Locale's method toString() returns a string representation of this Locale object, consisting of language, country, variant, script, and extensions, as

```
language + "_" + country + "_" + (variant + "_#" | "#") + script + "-" +
    extensions
```

A.12.2 Twist in the Tale 12.2

Purpose: To determine the sequence of the search order for a resource bundle from a given set of resource-bundle files, given the target and default Locale values

Answer: d

Explanation: Here's the list of the resource-bundle files:

- MessagesBundle_fr.properties
- MessagesBundle_fr_FR.properties
- MessagesBundle_DE.properties
- MessagesBundle_de.properties
- MessagesBundle.properties

Given that the default locale of the host system is Locale.JAPAN, and you need to load the resource bundle for locale de_DE, here's the search order for the matching resource bundle:

1 MessagesBundle_de_DE.properties
2 MessagesBundle_de.properties
3 MessagesBundle_ja_JP.properties
4 MessagesBundle_ja.properties
5 MessagesBundle.properties

As evident, MessagesBundle_de.properties matches the target locale de_DE.

index